LIBER AMICORUM IN HONOUR OF LORD SLYNN OF HADLEY

VOLUME 1

LIBER AMICORUM

in Honour of

LORD SLYNN OF HADLEY

JUDICIAL REVIEW IN EUROPEAN UNION LAW

Editor

David O'Keeffe

Professor of European Law, University College London
Counsil on EU Affairs, Hammond Suddards

Associate Editor

Antonio Bavasso

Fellow of the Center for the Law of the European Union,
University College London

Kluwer Law International
The Hague - London - Boston

A C.I.P. Catalogue record for this book is available from the Library of Congress

ISBN 90-411-1372-X (VOLUME 1)
ISBN 90-411-1373-8 (Set)

Published by Kluwer Law International,
P.O. Box 85889, 2508 CN The Hague, The Netherlands.

Sold and distributed in North, Central and South America
by Kluwer Law International,
675 Massachusetts Avenue, Cambridge, MA 02139, U.S.A.

In all other countries, sold and distributed
by Kluwer Law International, Distribution Centre,
P.O. Box 322, 3300 AH Dordrecht, The Netherlands.

Printed on acid-free paper

Printed in the Netherlands.

CONTENTS

PREFACE

The Rt Hon The Lord Templeman

The common law of England permeates the English speaking world. The two basic principles of the common law, namely the freedom of the individual and the independence of the judiciary, have spread outside the English speaking world. These principles are now fundamental to the constitutions of all countries which aspire to democracy and are expressed in the Charter and Conventions of the United Nations.

The laws of England have been permeated by the laws of the European Union and by international Conventions, more particularly by the European Convention on Human Rights. The two basic principles of the European Union, namely free trade and free movement, as developed by the European Court of Justice, have been engrafted on domestic law. The two basic principles of the Convention of Human Rights, namely the freedom of individuals and the equality of individuals, as developed by the European Court of Human Rights, have expanded and modernised the principles of the common law of England.

The adoption, interpretation and dissemination of the principles of the law depend on the activities, powers of persuasion and influence of the practitioners and teachers of the law. In England, where the decisions of the judiciary are reasoned and published, the judge is both practitioner and teacher. In the past quarter of a century, at a time when the reconciliation of the common law, European law and international law in the age of jet flight and instant communication, became imperative, Gordon Slynn has been unique in the experience and pre-eminent in the insight required for the purpose of moulding and harmonising the three sets of laws or branches of the law, namely the common law, European law and international law which are now indissolubly linked in the administration of justice in the democratic world and which are essential to the preservation of civilisation in the world.

Gordon was born in 1930, at the beginning of a decade when forces of evil exalted the State over the rights of the individual in Russia, Japan, Germany, Italy and Spain and stamped out democracies in Austria and Czecho Slovakia before, at the end of the decade, France and the whole of the European continent fell victims to the dictatorships. He was called to the Bar by Gray's Inn in 1956 when written constitutions and independent judges were upholding democracy and human rights in all the countries of Western Europe and when the Treaty of Rome and the European Court of Justice were pointing the way to economic prosperity and social justice.

D. O'Keeffe (ed.), Liber Amicorum Slynn xi-xv (2000)

He practised in commercial and common law before being appointed first as Junior Counsel to the Ministry of Labour and then as Junior Counsel to the Treasury to advise and conduct litigation on behalf of government departments. In the latter role as "Treasury devil" he was in post when the European Communities Act 1972 came into force and Community law became paramount within its sphere. After a spell as Queen's Counsel engaged in civil litigation, and as Recorder coping in a judicial role with crime and punishment, he entered the main stream of English judicial advancement as a High Court Judge sitting in the Queen's Bench Division dealing with all manner of criminal and civil matters, including judicial review, and sitting also as President of the Employment Appeals Tribunal where Community law frequently falls to be applied.

Ready to face the challenge presented by Community Law, he was in 1981, on the recommendation of Lord Hailsham and on the nomination of the then government, appointed Advocate General to the European Court of Justice.

He was already a Vice President of the Union International des Avocats and married to Odile whose name and attractive French accent indicated her country of birth. At Luxembourg the oral and written advice of the Advocate General assigned to each case is rightly afforded great respect and exercises great influence. Gordon, in his own words, "went to the European Court as a technician and not as a missionary for any particular European ideal ... convinced that the United Kingdom and the common law have a significant contribution to make and that we only stand any chance of achieving the sort of Community that we really want if we actively and positively make that contribution not only on the political but also on the cultural and legal level ... Independent national cultures are not in conflict with the Community aim. They are complementary to it and it is only by them that the Community system can be enriched." [1]

In 1988, after seven years as Advocate General, Gordon was appointed a Judge of the European Court of Justice and so acted until in 1992 after a four year term, he returned to the main stream of the English judicial system as a Lord of Appeal in Ordinary and life peer, taking his seat in the House of Lords as Lord Slynn of Hadley. This appointment was a recognition of his success at Luxembourg and also a demonstration of the determination of the United Kingdom to assimilate European Law at the highest judicial level.

During his years with the European Court of Justice Gordon was concerned with every aspect of the growing jurisdiction of that Court and in the interpretation of the Treaty of Rome and of the mass of legislation promulgated by the Commission, Council and European Parliament. The majority of the cases were references to the Court by national courts or involved Member States.

The freedom of movement of workers enjoined by the Treaty of Rome thus compelled a Member State which granted interest free loans to its own worker nationals to extend the same benefit to workers in that state who were nationals

1 *Introducing a European Legal Order* by Gordon Slynn, Hamlyn Trust Lectures, p.4.

of other Member States; Case 65/81 *Reina v. Landeskredit Bank Baden.*[2] The Court claimed and exercised power to grant an interlocutory injunction to prevent France from interfering with the free flow of goods by insisting on analysing all imported wines for quality, rejecting customs documents on technical grounds and generally delaying customs clearance; Case 48/82 *Commission v. France*. These cases were decided at the beginning of Gordon's career with the Court and were followed by others with which he was concerned dealing with the freedom of movement of goods, services, establishments and workers within the Community, the application of the principle of equal pay for equal work, discrimination, the acquired rights directives on the transfer of businesses and the rights of employees, and with regulations affecting the steel industry, and the control of mining agriculture and fishing. In Case 107/83 *Ordre des Avocats de Paris v. Klopp*[3] freedom of establishment applied to the legal profession was held to render unlawful a French regulation which forbade a German national to register for practice in Paris on the grounds that he was also practising in Germany. National trade mark laws were not allowed to frustrate Community law against competition; Case 35/83 *B.A.T. v. Commission.*[4] Sadly, since he departed, the Court in the *Silhouette* Case (2)[5] has invented a new intellectual property monopoly which interferes with the free flow within the Community of goods manufactured outside the Community with the consent of the monopolist.

The 300 or so opinions he gave also include Cases 60, 61/84 *Cinetheque*,[6] the German beer case, Case 120/78,[7] and the French wine case, Case 170/78,[8] dealing with restrictions on the free movement of goods, and *Marshall*, Case 152/84,[9] on the direct effect of directives.

In the House of Lords Appellate Committee, Gordon's wide experience of the law of the European Union has been invaluable to his colleagues. In addition, his breadth of vision has exercised an influence on other branches of the law considered by the Appellate Committee and on other laws considered by the Judicial Committee of the Privy Council. In Luxembourg he rejected some of the speculative excesses urged on the Court and endeavoured to achieve certainty in the law despite the vague drafting of Community legislation. In London, he has helped to widen the narrow pedantic approach of past generations in favour of a purposive construction of statutes viewed in the light of changes of society. In the most recent case of *Fitzpatrick v. Sterling Housing*[10] the expression "family" was held to encompass a same sex relationship, the intention of

2 [1982] ECR 53.
3 [1984] ECR 2971.
4 [1988] ECR 355.
5 [1998] ECR I-4799.
6 [1985] ECR 2605.
7 [1979] ECR 649.
8 [1983] ECR 2265.
9 [1986] ECR 723.
10 [1999] 4 All E.R.705.

Parliament being, as Lord Slynn held, to preserve a shared home for the survivor of a partnership whether legal or *de facto*, provided the characteristics of that partnership were a "degree of mutual interdependence, of the sharing of lives, of caring and love, of commitment and support" (p.214).

The influence of Lord Slynn has not however been confined to his role as a judge. Although the presence of Law Lords in a legislative assembly has been criticised, their advice on legislation and draft legislation has proved useful without impairing their impartiality on the Bench. European legislation is not approved by the United Kingdom government until there has been an opportunity for consideration by both Houses.

In the House of Lords draft directives proposed by the Commission are referred to a Select Committee of the House and by them to a Sub Committee on law which almost invariably has a Law Lord as Chairman. The Sub Committee invites evidence, written and oral, from government departments, the officials of the Commission, industry and other interested parties. In important matters the Sub Committee prepares a Report which is submitted by the Select Committee to the House and debated if the Report deals with matters of controversy. The views expressed in such Reports do not always agree with the government or with the Commission. The Reports are highly regarded at home and abroad and may lead to a modification of the Commission's proposals or to explanations which the recipients find satisfactory. With his knowledge of law and experience in the Community Gordon was an invaluable Chairman. Among the subjects which were reported and debated during his Chairmanship are protection of personal data, the right of establishment for lawyers, hallmarking of precious metals, visas and border control and Europol.

Throughout his career Gordon has been an indefatigable globetrotter, for the purpose of lecturing and learning and for the purpose of encouraging the laws to harmonise and the lawyers to fraternise. I have only known him to miss one engagement and that when he was stationary on the Grand Trunk Road outside New Delhi behind ten miles of stationary bullock carts.

He has devoted much time and effort to associations of lawyers in this country and abroad particularly in the context of European and international law. It is a deserved tribute that The Lord Slynn of Hadley European Law Foundation has been set up on the initiative of George Dobry and the support of Sir Henry Brooke, Sir Brian Neill and David Vaughan QC. Through seminars and fellowships the Foundation promotes European law and common law in the former communist countries in Eastern Europe.

The extent of his travels and the number of his friendships thus acquired may be judged from the variety of contributors to this Volume and the subjects which they address. Appellate judges from Australia, Canada, Finland, France, Germany, Norway, India, Israel, the Netherlands, New Zealand and the United States have joined with savants from the International Court, the Court of Human Rights, the International Trade Organisation, the Foreign Office, and the Universities of Cambridge, London and Oxford, amongst others, to fill these volumes in his honour. Much fruitful work lies ahead, but the existing record of the activities of Gordon Slynn and his reputation with the legal profession and with students throughout the world has already earned him the applause of his contemporaries and a place amongst the legal luminaries of past and present generations.

The Right Hon. Lord Templeman

THE RIGHT HONOURABLE LORD SLYNN OF HADLEY

B.A. (London), M.A. LL.M. (Cantab). Hon. Fellow: St Andrew's College, University of Sydney (Australia); John Moores University Liverpool; Goldsmiths' College, University of London; King's College London.

Hon. LLD: University of Birmingham 1983; University of Buckingham 1983; University of Exeter 1985; University of Technology, Sydney 1991; Bristol Polytechnic (C.N.A.A.) 1992; University of Sussex 1992; Stetson (USA) 1993; Staffordshire 1994; Pace New York 1995; Pondicherry University 1997; Kingston University 1997; Strathclyde University 1999; University of London 1999; Hon. D.C.L. University of Durham 1989; City University 1994; Hon.D.Unv. Universidad del Museo Social Argentino 1994; Hon.Dr Juris; Universität des Saarlandes 1994.

Hon.Decanus Legis: Mercer University (USA) 1986; Hon.Fellow, American College of Trial Lawyers; Cordell Hull Peace Medal (Samford University USA) 1993; Member American Law Institute; Fellow of the Chartered Institute of Arbitrators.

K.St.J.

Grand Cross Order of Merit Luxembourg. Knight's Cross Order of Merit, Poland.

Called to the Bar, Gray's Inn, 1956; Master of the Bench 1970; Vice-Treasurer 1987; Treasurer 1988.

Junior Counsel to the Ministry of Labour 1967-68.
Junior Counsel to the Treasury (Common Law) 1968-74.
Appointed Queen's Counsel 1974.
Leading Counsel to the Treasury 1974-76.
President of the Employment Appeal Tribunal 1978-81.

Recorder of the City of Hereford 1971 then a Recorder and Honorary Recorder of Hereford 1972-76.
Judge of the High Court of Justice (Queen's Bench Division) 1976-1981.

Advocate General at the Court of Justice of the European Communities, Luxembourg, 1981-88; Judge, October 1988-1992.

Lord of Appeal in Ordinary, House of Lords, March 1992-; Privy Counsellor 1992 -

Chairman House of Lords: Sub-Committee E, European Communities Committee 1992/95; Select Committee on the Public Service 1996/97

Sub Lector, Trinity College, Cambridge 1956-61; Lecturer in Air Law, London School of Economics 1958-61; Visiting Professor in Law, University of Durham 1981-88; Cornell, USA, 1983; King's College, London, 1988-91; 1995-; University of Technology, Sydney, Australia, 1990-; Visiting Professor, National Law School of India University 1992-.

Lectures: F.A. Mann 1981; Lord Fletcher 1983; Irvine (Cornell, USA) 1984; Lord Denning (B.A.C.F.I.) 1985; Baron Heydon de Lancey 1987; Leon Ladner (Vancouver) 1987; Hamlyn 1991; Lord Fletcher 1992; Butterworth 1992; Lord Denning (I.S.H.) 1992; Royal Bank of Scotland 1992; Lord Morris of Borth y Gest (University of Wales) 1992; Wolters Kluwer 1993; Tanner (Oxford) 1993; Romanes (Oxford) 1994; Edward Bramley (Sheffield) 1995; Nambyar Lectures (India) 1996.

President Bentham Club (UCL) 1992; Holdsworth Club (Birmingham University) 1993.

Hon.Vice-President, Union Internationale des Avocats 1976 – (Vice-President 1973-76); Vice-Chairman, Executive Committee, International Law Association 1986-88; Chairman 1988-; Hon.Member, Society of Public Teachers of Law; Hon.Fellow, International Students House (Governor 1979-85 and 1992-); Hon.Member, Canadian Bar Association; Georgia Trial Lawyers' Association; Florida Defense Lawyers' Association; Colegio de Abagados of Buenos Aires; Indian Society of International Law; Fellow, International Society of Barristers (USA); Trustee, American-European Community Association Trust (1989-91). Visitor Mansfield College Oxford; University of Essex.

Chief Steward of the City of Hereford 1978-; Freedom of the City of Hereford 1996; Governor, Sadler's Wells Theatre 1988-1995; Chairman of Development Board, Academy of Ancient Music 1988-1992; Chairman of Governors of Mill Hill School 1989-1994; Master, Worshipful Company of Broderers 1994-95; Chevalier du Tastevin; Commandeur, Confrerie de St Cunibert; Commandeur d'Honneur de la Commanderie du Bontemps de Medoc et des Graves and of Confrerie des comtés de Nice et de Provence.

President: United Kingdom Environmental Law Association; United Kingdom Association for European Law; British Academy of Experts; European Maritime Law Association.

Prior of England and the Islands of the Order of St. John since October 1999.

Publications: Contributions to Halsbury's Laws of England and Atkins' Court Forms; various lectures published in legal journals; *Introducing a European Legal Order* (Stevens 1992).

LIST OF CONTRIBUTORS

David Anderson
Queen's Counsel, Brick Court Chambers; Visiting Professor of Law, King's College London

Anthony Arnull
Professor of European Law, University of Birmingham

Antonio F. Bavasso
Fellow of the Center for the Law of the European Union, University College London; Associate, Allen & Overy

Sir Christopher Bellamy
Judge of the Court of First Instance of the European Communities since 1992 to 1999; President, Competition Commission Appeal Tribunals since December 1999

Vlad Constantinesco
Professor, The Robert Schuman University of Strasbourg

Deirdre Curtin
Professor of the Law of International Organisations, University of Utrecht

Alan Dashwood
Professor of European Law, University of Cambridge

Ole Due
Honorary Professor, University of Copenhagen; Chairman of the Board of the Danish Institute of International Affairs; former President and Judge of the Court of Justice of the European Communities.

Jacqueline Dutheil de la Rochère
Professeur à l'Université Paris II, Directeur du Centre de Droit Europèen

David Edward

Judge of the Court of Justice of the European Communities

Piet Eeckhout

Herbert Smith Professor of European Law and Co-Director, Centre of European Law, King's College London

Ulrich Everling

Professor at the University of Bonn; Former Judge of the Court of Justice of the European Communities

James Flynn

Barrister, Brick Court Chambers; Legal Secretary, European Court of Justice 1986-1989

Giorgio Gaja

Professor of International Law at the University of Florence; Member of the International Law Commission

Laurence W. Gormley

Barrister; Professor of European Law & Jean Monnet Professor, Rijksuniversiteit Groningen (Jean Monnet Centre of Excellence); Visiting Professor, University College London & Universität Bremen; *Stiftungsprofessor für Europarecht*, Universität Bonn, Winter Semester 1999-2000

Maragaret Gray

Barrister, Brick Court Chambers

Rosa Greaves

Allen and Overy Professor of European Law, Durham European Law Institute

Bob Hepple QC

Queen's Counsel, Master of Clare College and Professor of Law in the University of Cambridge

Francis G. Jacobs

Advocate General, Court of Justice of the European Communities

Thijmen Koopmans

Goodhart Professor in Legal Science, University of Cambridge; former Judge of the Court of Justice of the European Communities.

Koen Lenaerts
Judge of the Court of First Instance of the European Communities; Professor of European Law, Katholieke Universiteit Leuven

Cynthia Crawford Lichtenstein
Professor of Law, Boston College Law School

Timothy Millett
Head of Division in the Legal Service of the European Parliament; Legal Secretary to Advocate General Sir Gordon Slynn from 1984 to 1988

Jean Mischo
Advocate General, Court of Justice of the European Communities

Peter Oliver
Legal Adviser, European Commission; former Legal Secretary to Sir Gordon Slynn

David O'Keeffe
Professor of European Law, University College London; Counsel on EU Affairs, Hammond Suddards, Solicitors

Richard Plender
Queen's Counsel, LLD, Legal Secretary to Sir Gordon Slynn, 1981-1983

Hjalte Rasmussen
Professor of European Community Law, University of Copenhagen; Member of the Conseil Universitaire for the Jean Monnet Programme

Michael Reynolds
Partner, Allen & Overy

Gil Carlos Rodríguez Iglesias
President of the Court of Justice of the European Communities

Jürgen Schwarze
Professor and Director of the Institute of Public Law, University of Freiburg

Eleanor Sharpston
Queen's Counsel, Fellow in Law, King's College, Cambridge; Senior Research Fellow, Centre for European Legal Studies, University of Cambridge; in practice at 4 Paper Buildings, Temple

Denys Simon

Professor, Robert Schuman University, Strasbourg and College of Europe, Bruges; Director of the Centre d'études internationales et européennes, Strasbourg.

Francis Snyder

Professor of European Community Law, European University Institute, Florence: Co-Director, Academy of European Law, Florence; Professor of Law, College of Europe, Bruges: Honorary Visiting Professor of Law, University College London.

John Temple Lang

Director in the Directorate General for Competition, European Commission; Professor, Trinity College, Dublin; Senior Visiting Research Fellow, University of Oxford

The Rt. Hon. The Lord Templeman

Former Lord of Appeal in Ordinary.

Giuseppe Tesauro

President, Autorità Garante della Concorrenza e del Mercato, former Advocate General of the Court of Justice of the European Communities

Takis Tridimas

Professor of European Law, University of Southampton

Walter Van Gerven

Professor of law at the Universities of Leuven and Maastricht, former Advocate-General at the ECJ and a member of the Committee of Independent Experts instituted by the EP to investigate fraud, mismanagement and nepotism in the EU Commission

David Vaughan

Queen's Counsel, Brick Court Chambers

Pieter Verloren van Themaat

Former Advocate General of the Court of Justice of the European Communities

Stephen Weatherill

Jacques Delors Professor of European Community Law, Sommerville College, Oxford

Joseph H.H. Weiler
Manley Hudson Professor and Jean Monnet Chair, Harvard University

Richard Whish
Professor of Law, King's College London

Derrick Wyatt
Queen's Counsel; Professor, University of Oxford; Fellow of St. Edmund Hall, Oxford

TABLES OF CASES

I Court of Justice of the European Communities

C-1 and 176/90 Aragonesa de Publicidad Exterior SA and others v. Departamento de Sanidad y Seguridad Social de la Generalitat de Cataluña [1991] ECR I-4151 530
C-2/90 Commission v. Belgium [1992] ECR I-4431 487
C-6 and 9/90 Francovich and Bonifaci v. Italy [1991] ECR I-5357 39, 40, 55, 188, 238, 242, 245, 251, 254, 256, 284, 403, 467, 486
C-7/90 Vandervenne and others [1991] ECR I-4371 253, 254
C-45/90 Paletta and others v. Brennet AG [1992] ECR I-3423 40
C-48 and 66/90 The Netherlands and others v. Commission [1992] ECR I-565 65, 111, 259
C-69/90 Nakajima All Precision Co. Ltd. [1991] ECR I-2069 451
C-75/90 Roger Guitard [1991] ECR I-4205 526
C-87-89/90 Verholen and others v. Sociale Verzekeringsbank [1991] ECR I-3757 427
C-159/90 Society for the Protection of the Unborn Child Ltd. v. Grogan and others [1991] ECR I-4685 323
C-177/90 Kühn v. Landwirtschaftskammer Weser-Ems [1992] ECR I-35 449
C-208/90 Emmott v. Minister for Social Welfare [1991] ECR I-4269 238, 250, 264, 476
C-240/90 Germany v. Commission [1992] ECR I-5383 64, 253
C-269/90 Technische Universität München v. Hauptzollamt München-Mitte [1991] ECR 5469 449
C-271, 281 and 289/90 Spain and others v. Commission [1992] ECR I-5833 66
C-283/90P Vidranyi v. Commission [1991] ECR I-4339 100, 101
C-286/90 Poulsen and Diva Navigation [1992] ECR I-6019
C-294/90 British Aerospace plc and Rover v. Commission [1992] ECR I-493 451
C-295/90 European Parliament v. Council [1992] ECR I-4193 195
C-313/90 Comité international de la Rayonne et des fibres synthétiques (CIRFS) and others v. Commission [1993] ECR I-1125 259
C-328/90 Commission v. Greece [1992] ECR I-425 277
C-354/90 Fédératon Nationale du Commerce Exterieur des Produits Alimentaires and others v. France [1991] ECR I-5505 259, 491
C-370/90 R. v. Immigration Appeal Tribunal and Surinder Singh, ex parte Secretary of State for the Home Department [1992] ECR I-4265 321
C-373/90 Criminal proceedings against X [1992] ECR I-131 237
C-31-44/91 Lageder and others v. Amministrazione delle Finanze dello Stato[1993] ECR I-1761 238
C-45/91 Commission v. Greece [1992] ECR I-2509 278
C-48/91 The Netherlands v. Commission [1993] ECR I-5611 254
C-67/91 Dirección General de Defensa de la Competencia v. Asociación Española de Banca Privada (AEB) and others [1992] ECR I-4785 399, 575
C-68/91 P Moritz v. Commission [1992] ECR I-6849 100
C-71 and 178/91 Ponente Carni SpA and others v. Amministrazione delle Finanze dello Stato [1993] ECR I-1915 474

Opinions

Rulings

II COURT OF FIRST INSTANCE OF THE EUROPEAN COMMUNITIES

III EUROPEAN COURT OF HUMAN RIGHTS

PART 1

THE EUROPEAN COURT OF JUSTICE AND THE COURT OF FIRST INSTANCE

1

SOME OPINIONS OF SIR GORDON SLYNN AS ADVOCATE GENERAL

Pieter Verloren van Themaat[*]

INTRODUCTORY REMARKS

Gordon Slynn's time as Advocate General of the Court of Justice of the EC will be recalled by his colleagues in the first place for his cordial and hospitable friendship. My wife and I will never forget our stay at his wonderful 17th-century home at Eggington, the inspiring people he invited for dinner with us, nor our visits to the famous Gray's Inn in London, where he introduced us to dine with other members of this distinguished Inn of Court, and a day later to attend a service in its chapel. We only regretted that his charming wife, a busy woman herself, could only rarely come over to Luxemburg. After my departure from Luxemburg in 1986, however, we continued to meet both of them at a number of conferences of the International Law Association, where, because of our common interest in public international law, both of us were active in different functions, he as vice-chairman and later chairman of the Executive Council and I as one of the rapporteurs of a fascinating ILA committee.

These are some of my personal recollections. Because the Advocates General, with their unique independent function, did not usually discuss with their colleagues the merits of their cases, our regular meetings were mainly used to discuss organisational matters of common interest. They were always followed by a lunch, offered by the First Advocate General of the year in one of Luxembourg's restaurants. One of the problems we discussed during our meetings was the challenge of the growing workload. When I arrived at the Court in the late spring of 1981, the First Advocate General at that time, Gerhard Reischl, told me that the common annual production standard was then 30 opinions. In 1983, the statistics of the registrar convinced us, however, that this standard level had to be increased to 40 opinions per Advocate General, corresponding to an annual production of the Court of at least 200 decisions. Gordon Slynn had almost reached this standard already in 1984, and from 1985 onwards often largely surpassed it. This great productivity, calculated on the whole length of his function as Advocate General from 1981 to his task as a judge in September 1988 resulted in even his average annual standard reaching 40 opinions.

---

* Professor Verloren van Themaat was a colleague of Sir Gordon Slynn as Advocate General from 1981 to 1986.

D. O'Keeffe (ed.), Liber Amicorum Slynn 3-16 (2000)

Not only the quantity of his opinions however, but still more their high and often innovative quality drew the attention of both judges and lawyers beyond the Court. I will therefore try to indicate briefly by a small selection from his 288 opinions why the selected cases still merit our attention today. In order to create some order in my selection, I will start with some cases in which procedural questions prevailed. The main part of my contribution, however, will deal exclusively with a number of substantive-law cases, illustrating the interrelationship between various parts of the internal and external parts of EEC-Common Market law in the strict sense of this term. I will therefore not deal with the more 'interventionist', or 'regulatory' aspects of community law. This, notwithstanding the fact that Gordon Slynn, like all his colleagues, had to deal with every type of substantive-law case. The Court indeed rightly considered that none of its members should be specialised in particular parts of the total workload. Gordon Slynn therefore also dealt, for example, with about 50 civil service cases and 30 agricultural cases, to mention only two broad categories.

SOME CASES ON PROCEDURAL QUESTIONS

The principle of legal confidentiality of correspondence between undertakings and their external advocates

After a (rare) second session of the Court in the famous *AM&S v. Commission* case,[1] Gordon Slynn presented his extremely well documented and carefully motivated opinion on the applicability of a general principle of "legal confidentiality of correspondence" between undertakings and their external advocates (barristers or solicitors) in competition cases. He did so on January 26 1982, in order to take into account new information which the Court ordered AM&S to submit (confidentially), namely, the correspondence under discussion. This order was issued after its first session and the opinion of Slynn's predecessor Jean Pierre Warner of twelve months earlier. At the end of this long procedure, the Court, recognising the aforementioned principle of confidentiality as such, annulled, in its judgment of 18 May 1982 the relevant decision of the Commission, ordering the submission of the documents under discussion. This order applied, however, only to those documents which were deemed to be covered by the principle under discussion. The opinions of Warner and Slynn in this matter, in combination with the judgment itself – which recognised the principle of confidentiality as such, but left contested specific borderline cases open to individual judgments, after careful and confidential examination by the Court of the documents concerned – are still of great practical importance.

1 [1982] ECR 1642.

The Lord Bethell case

The efforts of a well-known member of the European Parliament, Lord Bethell, to obtain satisfaction from the Court in his fight against restrictive price practices or abuse of their dominant positions by airline companies in Case 246/81, *Lord Bethell v. Commission*,[2] failed at that time. Both Gordon Slynn, in his again richly documented opinion, and the Second Chamber of the Court indeed considered his appeal to the Court, based on Articles 173 and 175 EEC inadmissible. Nevertheless, the answer of the Commission of 17 July 1981 to his efforts to bring the Commission to action, quoted in Slynn's opinion, in the light of later developments, later proved to be more satisfactory to Lord Bethell. In fact, various elements of this answer paved the way for the Commission's publication of 23 July 1981 on passenger tariffs in air transport. In the second place, these elements, mentioned in the answer of the Commission to Lord Bethell on 17 July 1981, much later also played a decisive role in the spectacular preliminary reference Case 66/86, *Ahmed Saeed Flugreisen and Silver Line Reiseburo v. Zentrale zur Bekämpfung unlauteren Wettbewerbs*.[3] In this judgment, bilateral or multilateral tariff agreements for regular flights were, *inter alia*, considered as automatically void under Article 85(2) EEC, as far the procedural conditions, indicated in the judgment have been fulfilled. In this way, Lord Bethell finally got what he wanted.

The IBM case of 1981

The preceding case also referred to the more important Case 60/81, *IBM v. Commission*,[4] where Sir Gordon also acted as Advocate General. On the analogy of the common sense principle that a breeding hen should not be disturbed before the egg has been produced, but more importantly, in conformity with the opinion of its Advocate General, again richly documented by references to earlier case-law and other sources, the Court decided in this case that neither the communication by the Commission of the start of a procedure for violation of Article 86 EEC (now Article 82 EC), nor the later communication of its complaints constituted decisions in the sense of the treaty. This because, as necessary purely preparatory acts, they lacked any direct legal effects, affecting the interests of the appellant. The appeal against the Commission's communications was therefore declared inadmissible. As a result, the ability of undertakings to frustrate anti-trust procedures was also clearly excluded for the future, when the effective application of the European rules of competition gradually also became a model for many Member States.

---

2 [1982] ECR 2277.
3 [1989] ECR 803.
4 [1981] ECR 2639.

Insufficient sanctions for violations of Community law by its Member States, even after preceding condemnations by the Court

Case 160/85, *Commission v. Italy*,[5] was the first clear-cut case where Gordon Slynn had to deal with the problem, that even after two preceding condemnations by the Court (here in 1981) for non-implementation of two directives of the Council (of 1974) the Member State concerned had still not duly implemented these directives. The opinion of Sir Gordon could therefore be limited to a single page, and the decisive arguments of the Court for its new condemnation of Italy were not much longer. I mention this case therefore only because it is one of many similar signals of that period, that the time had come for providing the Court with power to apply effective sanctions in such cases. Not very long after the judgment in this case, the Treaty of Maastricht, by adding a second paragraph to Article 171 EEC (now Article 228 EC), did indeed provide the Court of Justice, under the procedural conditions indicated there, with the power to impose a lump sum or a penalty payment on any Member State which had not complied with its earlier judgment.

Some interrelationships between various internal or external aspects of the substantive common market case law

The notion of "common market law"

As was the case for all of his colleagues, the bulk of Sir Gordon Slynn's opinions dealt with practically all of the substantive parts of Community law, its more regulatory parts, such as agricultural and transport regulations, economic, monetary and social measures, the regulations on economic and social cohesion, harmonisation directives for the implementation of the environmental, public health, consumer interests and various VAT directives, and still other parts of substantive Community law. In order to respect the available space, I have decided, however, to limit my contribution to one specific aspect of the internal and external aspects of common market law, in the strict sense of the term in the EEC Treaty itself. The objective of the establishment of "a common market" is indeed the first objective, mentioned in Article 2 EEC, and Article 8 EEC demonstrates the way in which this common market had to be progressively established during the transitional period of 12 years.[6]

---

5 [1986] ECR 3245.

6 With regard to the establishment of the "internal market", this period was extended by the Single European Act in a new Article 7a EEC (now Article 14 EC) to 31 December 1992. However, this only applies to the treaty provisions mentioned therein, which do not cover the rules of competition and the foreign commercial policy, where no serious retardation in the implementation of Article 8 par. 7 EEC had taken place. These areas are not covered by the notion of the "internal market" as defined in the quoted new Article. As

Apart from Part One of the EEC Treaty, the concept of a common market is also an essential and often explicit element for the interpretation of provisions in Titles I and III of Part Two of the Treaty (the four "freedoms"), and Titles I (all its three chapters) and II, chapter 4 of its Part Three (Policy of the Community). Apart from the "four freedoms", provided for in Part Two, Title I of Part Three provides not only for free competition, but also for undistorted competition, in the sense of equal conditions of competition for undertakings within the Common Market, without private restrictive practices, dumping, state subsidies or other forms of aids granted by States, national fiscal policies and disparities in national law. From 1958 to 1967, all of these areas were covered by the Directorate-General for Competition of the European Commission, for which I was then responsible as Director-General. Later, the three chapters of this treaty title were split up between various Directorates General, which did not facilitate the necessary consistency in the implementation of these three chapters, all of which had the common objective of ensuring that "competition in the common market is not distorted", as required by Article 3 (g) EEC. This Article is still regularly referred to in the case law of the Court of Justice. During the years 1958–1967, with such problems of co-ordination of policies also having this objective (but not exclusively), the question of how to implement Article 3 (g) of the Treaty arose *inter alia* also in relation to the agricultural, transport and a common (foreign) commercial policy. While the first two policies at that time had a mainly regulatory character, the common commercial policy also had the task of providing for equal conditions of competition between undertakings of the Community for their imports from or exports to third countries. Article 113, par. 1 EEC (now 133) indeed not only provides for common custom – tariffs fixed by the Community itself (the customs union), where necessary after the conclusion of tariff and trade agreements with third countries – but also for "the achievement of uniformity in measures of liberalisation, export policy and measures to protect trade such as those to be taken in case of dumping or (state) subsidies". The whole common commercial policy shall be based, indeed, on "uniform principles", as Article 113 EEC par. 1 starts to underline, before mentioning its particular quoted objectives. The concept of a common market therefore can be put on a par with the notion of a free and undistorted market economy. The concept of Common Market Law as used in this contribution is therefore not identical with the concept of Community law which also covers the other, more regulatory objectives mentioned in Articles 2, 3, 3A and 3B EEC and since the Treaty of Amsterdam also Article 3C EC (now Article 6 EC).[7]

---

will be set out hereafter, the notion of "internal market" is more restricted indeed than the notion of a "common market".

7 See for a more detailed elaboration of the basic principles and the system of the EEC Treaty my contribution to the third English edition of P.J.G. Kapteyn and P. Verloren van Themaat, *Introduction to the law of the European Communities*, edited and further revised to take account of developments after the publication of its fifth Dutch edition (of 1995) by L.W. Gormley in co-operation with the editors of this Dutch edition (Kluwer

After this first, global selection of the sort of substantive law subjects which Gordon Slynn dealt with in a great number of his opinions, I have narrowed down my selection further by concentrating on examples of interrelationships between various parts of the purely internal aspects of common market law, or between the internal and the external aspects of the Community's common-market law.

The Campus Oil case: the interrelationship between Articles 30, 36, 92 and 90.2 EEC (now 28, 30, 87 and 86 respectively)

The first opinion I will briefly deal with under the heading of this main part of my contribution is Slynn's opinion in the famous Irish preliminary reference Case 72/83, *Campus Oil and others v. Minister for Industry and Energy and others*.[8]

This case, we recall, dealt with an Irish regulation which obliged importers of oil products to buy a certain percentage of their sales in Ireland from an oil refinery in the Irish territory. Neither Sir Gordon nor the Court had difficulty in finding that this regulation constituted a measure having equivalent effect to quantitative restrictions, as prohibited by Article 30 EEC between Member States. Of the interrelations between this prohibition and other parts of common market law, the opinion mainly dealt with the Irish High Court's second question. This question referred to the applicability of the safeguard clauses in Article 36 EEC, in particular its exemption ground of "public security". In his exhaustive and duly motivated analysis of all the arguments for and against this applicability, Slynn finally concluded that, as far and as long as necessary (in comparison with less restrictive measures) for non-economic reasons, application of the relevant exemption clause of Article 36 was indeed justified. The opinion adds, however, the warning that the implied accessory price regulation in favour of the Irish refinery concerned (on which no question had been submitted) might be found to be incompatible with Article 92 EEC.

The Court itself, in connection with an intervention of the Greek government, also examined the relevance of Article 90, paragraph 2 EEC for this case, but considered that this provision did not exempt the Member States, when entrusting an undertaking with the operation of services of general economic interest (here the nationalised Irish refinery), from the applicability of the prohibition of Article 30 to measures protecting its activities against the import from other Member countries. The final ruling of the Court on the second question submitted to it did not take up this interesting consideration, dealing only with an intervention from another Member State. More recent case law of the Court on Arti-

Law International 1998) chapter III, pp. 109 – 174.

8 [1984] ECR 2727.

cle 90, paragraph 2 EEC raises doubt however, whether the Court would now still come to the same conclusion.[9]

The interrelationship between Articles 85/86 (now 81/82) and 30/36 EEC (now 28/30) with regard to the protection of industrial and commercial property rights

While Case 35/83, *BAT Cigarettes/MBH v. Commission*,[10] only deals with the relationship between the above mentioned rules of competition and trademarks, the earlier preliminary reference Case 16/83, *Criminal procedure against Karl Prantl*,[11] only dealt with the relation between Articles 30/36 EEC and industrial and commercial property rights, as regulated by a Member State.

The first case is the only one of Gordon Slynn's that I found, in which the interrelationship between Articles 85 and 36 EEC also played a role with regard to import restrictions, either by restrictive agreements in the sense of Article 85 or by the exercise of their industrial or commercial property rights (here trademarks). After having been threatened by the largest German cigarette-producer, BAT, with an action for violation of its registered trademark "Condorcet", for creating confusion in the public with its trademark "Toltecs Special" (with the latter product also registered for sale in Germany), the small Dutch tobacco–producer Segers, in order to avoid long and excessively costly legal procedures, concluded an agreement with BAT. This agreement restricted Segers' potential sales in Germany and their right to contest BAT's right to use their own trademark, even after expiration of its legal validity. In the opinion of both BAT and the German government, which intervened only partly in its favour, such so-called delimitation-agreements on potentially conflicting trademarks were quite normal in Germany, and held not to be covered in principle by rules of competition, like Article 85 EEC. The German government recognised, however, that such agreements could nevertheless violate Article 85 EEC, if their objective was to restrict competition, e.g. by market sharing. The Commission, Gordon Slynn and the Court itself concluded in this case for similar reasons, that Article 85 EEC was indeed applicable here and that it was moreover obvious that the conditions for an exemption under Article 85 paragraph 3 EEC were not fulfilled. We summarised elsewhere the general interest of this case as follows:

> "The Court recognised that so called delimitation agreements in which the parties delimit in their mutual interest the spheres in which their respective trademarks may not be used,

9 See Case C-393/92, *Gemeente Almelo et al. v. Energiebedrijf Grondmaatschappij*, [1997] ECR I 1477, where the Court regarded a ban on the import of electricity by local distributors as acceptable under Article 90.2 EEC, if it was necessary to enable the regional distribution to perform its task of general economic interest to ensure uninterrupted supply of electricity to all consumers it covered.

10 [1985] ECR 363.

11 [1984] ECR 1299.

> intending thereby to avoid confusion and conflict between them are in principle lawful and useful. However it went on to say that such agreements were not excluded from the application of Article 85, if (as was found in the instant case) they also had the aim of dividing up the market or restricting competition in other ways" .[12]

The opinion of Gordon Slynn in the second mentioned case (*Prantl*) also dealt with industrial and commercial property rights, but here only considered on the basis of Articles 30 and 36 EEC. This was after it had found that the European agricultural provisions, cited by the Commission in its intervention, finally proved to be irrelevant in answering the preliminary questions. German legal measures which prohibited the use of a particular type of bottle, as being characteristic of a specific German wine region, imported from another Member State, were finally considered by the Advocate General (followed by the Court) as measures having equivalent effect to quantitative restrictions on imports, prohibited by Article 30 EEC. This because the imported wine bottled in this way had been brought legitimately on to the market in the country of origin.

The question, whether national regulations like those in the case concerned, because of the indirect indication of the origin of the German wine by the form of the bottle and the label on the bottle, would be justified as protection of industrial and commercial property rights, as mentioned in Article 36, was denied both by the Advocate General and the Court, if a similar form of bottle is traditionally used and admitted as legal in other Member States for the sale of wines which originate in these other Member States.

The interrelationship between Articles 30 and 36 EEC (now 28 and 30) and the protection of the natural environment

The selected case 302/86, *Commission v. Denmark*,[13] is the first one where the opinion of Gordon Slynn became in fact a "dissenting opinion", because it was only partly followed by the Court. The case dealt with an ingenious Danish legal system for the protection of the natural environment. This system, in order to promote the production and the possibility of repeated use of glass or plastic bottles or equivalent packing for beer and some popular non-alcoholic drinks, provided for a number of strict obligations for producers, traders and consumers and also for financial incentives, in particular for consumers. This, with the obvious objective of protecting the quality of the natural environment, and ensuring a prudent and rational utilisation of natural resources (in the most recent terms of the treaty, to promote "sustainable development").[14] The obligations of

12 See *op.cit.* in note 7, p. 886 and for the interrelationship between the applicability of Articles 85 and 30 – 36 EEC pp. 664 – 667 of the same work, prepared by different authors (in this case R. Barents and L.W. Gormley under my own co-responsibility as one of the editors of both the last Dutch and the last English edition of this work.)

13 [1988] ECR 4607.

14 Article 130 r, par. 1 EEC (now 174) and after the Treaty of Amsterdam also from the re-

this ingenious system were applicable without differentiation between Danish bottled drinks and ones imported from other Member States. The "sustainable" character of the produced bottles or other regulated packaging had to be controlled and authorised by the competent environmental authority and a return-obligation was imposed on both traders and consumers. This last obligation was supported by a deposit system as financial incentive. The imposed return and deposit system for used packaging as such was considered both by the Commission, the Advocate General and the Court as justified by the so-called "rule of reason", introduced in Case 120/78, *Cassis de Dijon*,[15] as well as by Directive 85/339 EEC and the further development of this new doctrine in many later cases. With regard to the obligations, imposed equally on foreign producers, Slynn concluded, however, that these would often mean in practice that the foreign producers would be obliged to produce themselves or to buy packaging of an already authorised type, both of which would mean significant extra costs, and therewith an obstacle to importation. This not only by the obligation to get their packaging authorised (which was restricted in practice by the limit of thirty available types of packaging), but also by the quantitative selling-limitations for each producer of relevant drinks packed without authorisation (which might often happen because of a lack of available new types) and by the practical implications of the imposed return and deposit system for foreign producers.[16] Slynn therefore concluded that the Danish system did not fulfil one of the requirements of the new "rule of reason", introduced in the *Cassis de Dijon* case, the requirement that even measures which in principle may be justified have to avoid not only formal differentiated treatment of national and foreign producers, but also practical consequences to the same effect. His opinion therefore concluded that the appeal of the Commission in the same sense should be completely endorsed by the Court. The Court, however, analysing the Danish system mainly with regard to the proportionality of the means of implementation of a justified objective and (surprisingly) not dealing at all with the main point made by Sir Gordon, endorsed only one of the objections of the Commission. This notwithstanding the fact that the point of equal treatment of imported products is also explicitly mentioned in the summary of the relevant case law in consideration 6 of its judgment. The argument of the Danish government, mentioned on p. 4625 of Slynn's opinion, that imported beer only represented 0,01% of total Danish beer consumption, reminded me of a famous answer of a former President of the USA, that he did not understand the many foreign protests against the imposition of import restrictions, because there were no such imports.

formulated Article 2 EC and the new Article 2C (in the renumbered text Article 6) EC.

15 [1979] ECR 649.

16 See pp. 4624 (last paragraph) and 4625 of his opinion.

The interrelationship between the Treaty rules on price agreements between undertakings and minimum prices imposed by public authorities for petrol and books

The opinion of Gordon Slynn in Case 34/84, *Leclerc*,[17] dealt with preliminary questions in a criminal case against the well-known "free rider" Leclerc for violating the minimum price, fixed by the relevant French public authority for the resale of petrol.

Although the first question of the *Tribunal de grande instance de Nanterre* did not explicitly say so, Gordon Slynn concluded correctly that this question on the relevance of Articles 3 sub (g) and 5, second paragraph EEC for the present case implicitly also referred to the relevance of Article 85 EEC for this case, where the public authority had imposed minimum resale prices for petrol. On the basis of earlier case law he had no difficulty in denying this relevance. He also rightly concluded that the second question, posed by the Tribunal on the relevance of Article 36 EEC for this case, inevitably implied the need for an answer to the question of the applicability in this case of Article 30 EEC. In conformity with the preceding similar Case 231/83, *Cullet*,[18] Slynn concluded that Article 30 EEC opposed such price regulation when the fixed minimum prices were exclusively based on the prices and costs of national producers and the price advantage for the resale of cheaper imported products was therefore eliminated. Moreover, the French government had not made clear that on the basis of Article 36 EEC the regulation could be justified.

Case 95/84, *Criminal case against Danzas and Tostani*,[19] is another and similar case with regard to the applicability of Article 30 EEC to national minimum prices, fixed for resale prices, this time for the resale of books, re-imported from other Member States, where the book price regulation obliged the importers to respect the resale price fixed by the publishers. Gordon Slynn concluded, here by reference to the Court's ruling in the preceding similar Case 229/83 (another *Leclerc* case) that such national price regulations with regard to a specific form of interstate trade were incompatible with Article 30 EEC and could only be justified on grounds as indicated explicitly in Article 36 EEC and not by other interests. In the light of the still very controversial question, whether cultural interests or consumer interests could justify such a regulation, it is interesting to note, that the Court itself in its ruling explicitly specified, in a different fashion from Slynn, that such interests could not justify it either.

As a general comment upon both the petrol and the book cases, I submit that preliminary questions in such cases with regard to the relevance of Articles 3, sub (g) (and implicitly Article 85) and 5 (2) gradually were made obsolete by the case law of the Court for the interpretation of Articles 30 and 36 EEC (not in all other cases). In fact, the integration of the interpretation of Article 85 (1) and

17 [1985] ECR 2915.
18 [1985] ECR 315.
19 [1985] ECR 2254.

Article 30 EEC as two parts of the common objective of the establishment of a common market has been ensured by the Court in another way. Since its judgment in Case 56 and 58/64, *Consten-Grundig*, with regard to the interpretation of Article 85, par. 1 EEC and Case 8/74, *Dassonville*, with regard to the interpretation of Article 30 EEC, the Court indeed has constantly taken care to interpret "restrictions or distortions of competition affecting trade between Member States" by restrictions of competition between undertakings (Article 85 (1)) and "quantitative restrictions on imports and all measures having equivalent effect" between Member States (Article 30) in an equivalent way.[20] The same is not true with regard to the exemptions, provided for in Articles 36 and 85 par. 3. Indeed, the exemptions from Article 30 in Article 36 have a non-economic character, while the exemptions of Article 85 (3) can only be applied under the economic conditions, mentioned in Article 85 (3). Therefore Article 3 sub (g) EEC is no longer relevant for the interpretation of Articles 30 and 36 EEC, because the case law has now led to the interpretation of the provisions in Part Two of the Treaty on the free movement of goods and in Part Three on rules of competition, applying to undertakings, in a well harmonised way. Together with the other freedoms in Part Two and the other three chapters of Title I of Part Three of the Treaty, those parts form the core of the internal aspects of the common market to be established as first objective of Article 2 E(E)C or in "a free and undistorted Common Market economy".

The interrelationship between the internal and external aspects of Common Market Law in the case law of the Court.

The four freedoms of Part Two and of Part Three Articles 85-102 EEC, which characterised the internal aspects of the common market until the Treaty of Amsterdam were completed – where necessary by treaties to be concluded with third countries – during the transitional period by measures ensuring that competition within the common market was not distorted in its external relations either. Only after the Treaty of Amsterdam have the original EEC provisions with regard to goods (Articles 110-116 EEC) been extended, although with uncertain procedural and institutional guarantees, to services in a new paragraph 5 of Article 113 EC, while Articles 111, 114 and 116 EEC have been repealed. The selected opinions of Gordon Slynn, however, only dealt with the trade in goods.

Although the common commercial policy also played a dominant role in Slynn's *Bulk Oil* case,[21] lack of space has obliged me to deal with his opinion in only one of the four groups of antidumping cases he dealt with, as an illustration of the interrelations between the external and internal aspects of the prescribed

20 Compare *op.cit.* in note 7, pp. 621 and 626 with regard to the formula used in the *Dassonville* case with pp. 837-838 and the formula used in Case 58/64, *Grundig-Consten*, [1966] ECR 299 summary, point 6.

21 [1986] ECR 559.

establishment of a common market. This opinion deals with the first of the joined cases 260/85 (TEC) and 106/86, dealing, like his other opinions of the same date, with electronic typewriters, imported from Japan.

A general interrelationship between the internal and external aspects of the common market is already expressed in Article 3 sub (b) EEC. This Article, in combination with Article 8 EEC, (renumbered in the Treaty of Maastricht as Article 7 and repealed by the Treaty of Amsterdam), provides indeed for the progressive establishment (before the end of the transitional period of 12 years) of both a common customs tariff and a common commercial policy towards third countries. The end of the transitional period, as confirmed also by Article 113 EEC, marked indeed the real start of a common commercial policy, based on uniform principles as indicated in this Article. Its main subjects also explicitly covered antidumping measures, against dumping practices of undertakings in third countries. Exclusively during the transitional period, antidumping measures between the Member States were based on Article 91 EEC, correctly included in the rules of competition for undertakings, because such dumping practices distorted the conditions of competition within the common market. Dumping practices within the common market, but having their origin in third countries, as viewed by Article 113 EEC, of course may have similar effects.

With regard to dumping, this interrelationship between internal and external aspects of the common market is also expressed by the fact, that on the basis of the GATT Antidumping Codes, the implementation of these codes within the Community for the mentioned cases was provided for in the general Regulation 2176/84 (6.7.1984, L201). In this way, the international GATT rules for its Member States also led to Community law, which, however, in such a case should naturally be interpreted in conformity with the GATT rules.

The present case, *Japanese producer Tokyo Electric Company Ltd. (TEC) and others v. Council of the EEC*[22] dealt with the relevant specific Regulation 2698/85, providing for antidumping levies on electronic typewriters, produced in Japan.

Those levies under the first mentioned general antidumping regulation should in the first place correspond to the margin between the normal value (the sales price of the producer within his country or, if no comparable sales took place within the country, a price for sales in a comparable country or an assumed price, calculated by adding a reasonable profit margin to the calculated production costs) and his export prices for the product concerned. The imposition of levies however also had to respect a second condition (serious harm for the corresponding sector within the Community).

The first two groups of TEC's arguments contested different aspects of the way in which the normal value in the home country was calculated, the third group the way in which the export price was calculated with regard to the selling costs of TEC's European subsidiaries, the other main element for determination

22 [1988] ECR 5655.

of the dumping. Although the thesis defended by TEC in this third group of arguments was the only one found to be justified by Gordon Slynn, these first three groups of arguments are not sufficiently interesting from the point of view of my selected specific problems of interrelationship between the internal and external aspects of the common market law to deal with them in more detail.

For this interrelationship, the fourth group of TEC's arguments, dealing with the determination of damage to the Community's home-production sector (and equally important for the calculation of admissible antidumping levies, as the calculated dumping margin) is more important. Indeed, the level of such levies may not exceed any of these two levels according to Articles 4 and 13 of the above-mentioned first general antidumping regulation, implementing the GATT code.

With regard to the interpretation of Article 4 of the general EEC regulation, Slynn agreed with my point of view, explained in my preceding opinion in Case 53/84, *Allied Corporation*,[23] that a method of calculation of the damage on the basis of price objectives instead of the real market prices of the producers in the country of import violates this Article 4. He even did me the honour of quoting the most relevant passages of my preceding opinion on this point. I observed there with regard to this basis for the calculation of damage, that this was not only required by the text of Article 4, but also by its market–economic background, therefore referring implicitly to my opinion that antidumping measures may only be used for the general objective of the treaty, that distortion of competition with effects within the common market (mentioned in Article 3 (g) EEC) must be eliminated. From my experience with the application of the (now repealed) Article 91 EEC, regarding dumping cases between the EEC Member States during the transitional period (for which I was then responsible as Director General of Competition in the Commission), I knew, moreover, that a comparison between the domestic prices of the exporting producer and the real market prices in the importing country was normally sufficient to determine whether the exporting producer was guilty of applying damaging dumping in the importing Member State. In another passage of my opinion, also quoted by Slynn, I recognised, however, that while dumping prices, applied during a number of years, had in the course of time already led to price reductions of the producers in the relevant import countries, and caused them damage, the real market prices in those importing countries might justify reasonable corrections of this real market price, but of course not in the form of price objectives.

With regard to such corrections, as also suggested by Gordon Slynn in the TEC case, injury–determination on the basis of the former Article 4 (since 1989 Article 3) of the EEC's general dumping regulation should now also keep in mind a relevant passage of a report, presented at the first conference of the International Law Association, where, the recently titled Lord Slynn of Hadley acted as chairman of its Executive Council. This passage reads as follows:

23 [1985] ECR, pages 1621 and 1632.

> "Antidumping rules grant investigating authorities an exclusively wide discretion with regard to "injury" determinations. Thus, according to Article 3 of the 1989 GATT Anti-dumping Code, the investigation authorities shall consider whether...the effect of such imports is...to depress to a significant degree or prevent price increases, which otherwise would have occurred".

As competition always tends to have price-depressing effects, there are hardly any effective constraints on finding "injury".[24] This warning against protectionist abuses of the market economic background of undistorted competition of both the internal and external parts of the common market law seems an appropriate final note in this contribution in honour of Gordon Slynn. Both the case law of the Court and later that of the new Court of First Instance showed however, that GATT Antidumping Codes (both by the various alternative criteria for the determination of the dumping margin, and by the criteria for the determination of "injury") even led the Commission and the Council of the EEC sometimes to antidumping measures which had to be condemned by the Court or the Court of First Instance as incompatible with the market-economic background of GATT's Codes and the legal principles of the EEC itself. Gordon Slynn himself of course never needed such warnings, as documented once more by his *TEC* opinion.

24 See pp.264-269 of the ILA's "*Report of the sixty-fourth conference*" (1990). The passage is taken from a summary of a report prepared by Prof. Petersmann as rapporteur of a sub-committee on trade and technology of the ILA Committee on legal aspects of a new international economic order. He also quotes there a rather devastating economic analysis of antidumping practice, published by the OECD.

2

ADVOCATES GENERAL AND JUDGES IN THE EUROPEAN COURT OF JUSTICE: SOME PERSONAL REFLECTIONS

Francis G. Jacobs

Gordon Slynn, among his many exceptional qualities, is unusual in having been both advocate general (from 1981 to 1988) and judge (from 1988 to 1992) at the European Court of Justice. Such transfers between the two branches of the Community judiciary are unusual.[1]

It may be appropriate therefore to consider in this paper the respective roles of advocate general and judge in the European Court; and also to try to bring out some of the interconnections between those roles.[2]

The European Court of Justice is currently composed of fifteen judges (one from each Member State of the European Union) and eight advocates general. Although the roles of judges and advocates general are different, they have much in common. They are appointed in the same way, and under the Treaties the same qualifications are required. Their functions can in many ways be seen as complementary.

ADVOCATES GENERAL

The main function of the advocate general is to deliver an Opinion on the case after the judges and advocate general have heard argument from the parties, the Community Institutions and (often) from the Member States (since all Member States are entitled to present arguments in all cases before the Court).

The Treaties require the advocate general to act "with complete impartiality and independence". The Opinion usually sets out, in the same way as a full judgment – one might almost say an English-style judgment – would do, the facts, the

1 There had been only two previous transfers in the history of the Court (i.e. between 1952 and 1988), and they had been in the opposite direction, from judge to advocate general. At the time of writing, there have been, in all, six transfers; three in each direction.

2 For recent studies (in English) of the advocate general see Nial Fennelly, "Reflections of an Irish Advocate General", *Irish Journal of European Law* 1996, p. 5, and Takis Tridimas, "The role of the Advocate General in the development of Community law", CML Rev. (1997), p. 1349, as well as the papers cited by those authors.

D. O'Keeffe (ed.), Liber Amicorum Slynn 17-28 (2000)

state of the law, the issues, and the submissions and will develop a line of reasoning leading to a considered conclusion as to how all aspects of the case should be resolved. But, unlike a judgment, the Opinion does not decide the case, even provisionally: its purpose, according to the Treaties, is to assist the Court in the performance of its task. The judgment of the Court (and the advocate general does not take part in the Court's deliberations, which commence after the Opinion has been delivered) is generally very much shorter and often more sparingly reasoned, if only because it has always to be a single collective judgment. The Opinion is published, together with the judgment, in the Court's reports.

The institution of advocate general has no counterpart in most of our legal systems, and although there are analogies in some systems there is perhaps no exact counterpart anywhere. In any case, the institution should be understood in the context of the Community legal system, rather than by analogy with other systems.

A fundamental difference from certain other systems is that in the Community system the advocate general is a member of the Court. That point has become particularly important in the light of the *Vermeulen* judgment of the European Court of Human Rights.[3] There the applicant's right to a fair hearing was held to have been infringed because he did not have the right to reply to the submissions of the *procureur général* in the Belgian *Cour de cassation*. It has been convincingly argued that there is an essential difference between the *procureur général* and the advocate general, in that the *procureur général* derives authority, as the Court of Human Rights noted, from the *ministère public*, a notion entirely absent in the role of the advocate general in the European Court of Justice.[4]

Whatever the position with analogous institutions in national legal systems, the position of the advocate general has to be considered in the context of the European Court and the Community legal system. Although the Treaties provide that the Court shall "consist" of 15 judges and shall be "assisted" by eight advocates general, it is accepted that advocates general are members of the Court. As mentioned already, advocates general and judges in the European Court are appointed in the same way, and under the Treaties the same qualifications are required. Moreover, they sit on the same bench, and wear the same robes. They have the same judicial immunities, and take the same judicial oath. They rank equally in precedence. Their Opinions, although not binding, form part of the Court's jurisprudence.

The Court has stated, in a different context, that, without prejudice to their specific function, the advocates general are "members of the Court in the same way as the judges".[5]

Thus it seems clear that the holding of the European Court of Human Rights in the *Vermeulen* case cannot be transposed to the advocate general in the European Court of Justice.[6]

3 *Vermeulen* v *Belgium*, judgment of 22 January 1996.

4 See Fennelly, *op.cit.*, at pp. 11-13.

5 Report of the Court of Justice on certain aspects of the application of the Treaty on European Union (May 1995), para. 18.

6 See now (since this paper was written) the Order of the Court of Justice in Case C-17/98

What then are the advantages of the institution of advocate general? A first advantage is that the advocate general's Opinion will provide a coherent overview of the case both to the judges hearing the case, and more widely (since it is published in the Court's reports) to all those concerned with following and needing to understand the Court's case-law – a very wide constituency. The Opinion will cover all aspects of the case. It may first deal with any questions of jurisdiction, or preliminary procedural issues, which need to be addressed. It will then turn to the substance of the case. It will deal with the facts – examining any disputed factual issues and ensuring that the facts are set out clearly, accurately and systematically. It will collate and, where necessary, seek to clarify the relevant principles and provisions of national law and of Community law.

Next, the Opinion may need to define the issues which the Court must address – and perhaps discard the issues which the Court should not address. On the issues so defined, it will examine the submissions made to the Court – submissions which may come from a variety of sources. There may be submissions by the parties, by Member States, by Community institutions. The advocate general may need to evaluate these, to comment on them, perhaps to add views of his own; to bring in the results of his own research, to survey the national laws of the Member States, perhaps with the benefit of contributions from the Court's research department; or to take in the contribution of scholarly writing on the topic. Yet all this material should be – and I think generally is – presented within a manageable length: the advocate general will be conscious that the judges have much to read – not to mention the burden on the translation service, since the Opinion will be published in full in the Court's reports in eleven languages.

Finally the advocate general will set out what is, in his view, the solution to the case; on a reference from a national court, that will include formulating the ruling which the Court, in his view, should give.

Although the utility of the Opinion – not least in defining the issues and in marshalling the relevant facts and law, not to mention the analysis provided – may not always be apparent to the outside observer (who may assume that what seems tolerably clear from reading the Opinion was also clear beforehand), it will certainly be found useful in providing, from the perspective of a single mind, an overall view of the case.

Yet that is not the main justification for the institution of advocate general.

The explanation lies essentially in the very nature of the Court's work and of the Community's judicial system.

The Treaties have given the Court tasks of fundamental importance – an importance that has necessarily increased as the range and scope of the Community and the Community's activities have themselves increased.

The Court has in the first place a constitutional function. It has to adjudicate on the lawfulness of the acts of the Community, and on the lawfulness, under Community law, of acts of the Member States. It has to resolve disputes over the scope

Emesa Sugar (4 February 2000).

of the Community's powers, over the division of powers between the Community and the Member States, and over the division of powers between the Community institutions themselves.

In terms of judicial review, the Court has to review the acts of the Member States – legislative, administrative and judicial – and the acts of the Community Institutions, including the European Parliament, the Council, the Commission and the European Central Bank.

In these respects the Court has to act as a European Constitutional Court.

The Court is also a supreme court of general jurisdiction across the whole field of Community law. Its jurisdiction thus extends not only to the core aspects of the European internal market – the free movement of goods, persons, services and capital; agriculture, transport, competition, indirect taxation, etc. – but to many other fields of law – employment law, environmental law, company law, intellectual property law, international trade law, etc.

As is the case with supreme courts in many countries, the Court's jurisdiction is general in character and there are as yet no specialised courts or chambers. The general nature of the Court's jurisdiction is widely regarded as valuable because of the connections between the different branches of the law, the need for a coherent system of law and the need to relate the development of the law in a harmonious fashion to the development of the Community itself.

There has to be a final arbiter on questions of Community law, and it is I think widely accepted that there should, so far as possible, be a single supreme court for the European Community.

That is why all courts and tribunals of the currently fifteen Member States of the European Union have the power under the Treaties to refer any question of Community law to the European Court, while the supreme courts of the Member States are obliged under the Treaties to refer all questions of Community law which arise before them, where they consider that a decision on the question is necessary to enable them to give judgment; and the rulings given by the European Court are binding on all courts and tribunals in all the Member States.

While that system for ensuring the uniform application of Community law may be difficult to maintain in its entirety as the Union develops and expands, informed opinion in legal and political circles generally seems to favour the maintenance of the system so far as possible, and indeed its extension to new areas of Union competence.

Not all cases before the Court are of fundamental importance. But many of them are sufficiently important and difficult to be heard by the plenary Court, and many of the rest are still sufficiently important and difficult to be heard by a large chamber.

Yet our Court is very unusual in that we hear almost all cases as a court of one instance only. The main justification for the institution of advocate general lies precisely in the fact that it introduces a two-stage process in which the advocate general provides an independent judicial appraisal of the case.

Both in preliminary rulings on references from national courts, and in direct actions (that is, cases brought by Member States and by Community Institutions), we have to consider points of often great importance and difficulty without the assistance of a judgment from a lower court deciding the point, and with no appeal from our own decision.

Only in the limited number of cases which come to the Court of Justice on appeal from the Court of First Instance (currently about one-tenth of our cases) do we have the luxury of a judgment to consider; and there we do sometimes dispense with the advocate general's Opinion, since we can decide some appeals by way of an order rather than a judgment. Even here, however, the advocate general provides a safeguard: he will have to give his view on whether the appeal can be dismissed by an order. And he will advise also on the drafting of the order.

Each case before the Court is thus followed closely both by the "judge rapporteur", who is responsible for guiding the Court through all procedural stages and ultimately for drafting the judgment, and by the advocate general.

The two-track approach from which we benefit, with the advocate general and judge rapporteur working independently, does I am sure provide a valuable safeguard against errors and oversights.

In effect, each case is judicially considered twice, first by the advocate general, then by the judges under the guidance of the judge rapporteur. Moreover, there may be matters which it is not in the interest of anyone appearing before the Court to bring to the Court's attention. It is not the duty of counsel in the Community system (as it is in England) to inform the Court of matters which may be to the disadvantage of their clients. The advocate general may be needed to fill that gap.

The advantages of the two-stage process – Opinion and judgment – carry, necessarily, a certain price. If the Opinion is to be fully considered – and translated – then it has to be delivered a certain time after the oral hearing. This means that the judges cannot deliberate immediately after the hearing, and there may be an impression that awaiting the Opinion leads to delay. The first point is incontrovertible, but the impression of delay may be illusory. Experience shows that, even in straightforward cases, the judgment will not be delivered until several months after the Opinion. Moreover it seems self-evident that, if there were no Opinion, then a longer judgment would often be necessary and that such a judgment would take substantially longer to prepare and to agree.

Since we are considering the functions of the advocate general in relation to the functions of the judges, mention must be made of the utility of the Opinion for the judges other than the judge rapporteur. Since they may not have the time to read all the papers in every case for themselves, the Opinion should provide them with a useful check on the work and the proposals of the judge rapporteur. Without it, either they will be submerged by the papers in some at least of the cases, or else perhaps excessively dependent upon the judge rapporteur.

I would mention briefly some other advantages of the institution of advocate general, as I see them. It provides a safeguard also, although less visibly, on all the procedural questions that arise as the case proceeds through the Court.

It introduces some of the advantages of separate or dissenting opinions allowed to judges in some other courts, to counteract the monolithic appearance of a single collective judgment, and similarly may have a useful dialectical role in promoting the future development of the case-law; I will return to this point below.

Where, as is most often the case, the judgment is broadly in line with the Opinion, the Opinion can provide a fuller and more articulated explanation of the case; this is recognised in those judgments which, as is often now the practice, explicitly adopt parts of the reasoning by simply referring to passages in the Opinion.

The Opinion may also make for economy of time and effort since the judgment can be less full, and need not deal with all the issues.

Above all, however, there are special features of the European Court which must be taken into account in any consideration of the need for an advocate general.

Cases of some importance and complexity, as I have mentioned, have to be decided by the Court as a court of one instance only. Moreover, our procedure is, for good reasons, not least because of the language factor, relatively streamlined: especially on references from national courts, where there is a single simultaneous round of written observations, and a relatively brief oral hearing. Nor do we always receive as much assistance from counsel, who may be inexperienced in Community law; issues which may seem important to the Court may not be fully ventilated, or indeed not addressed at all. Certainly the function of the Court cannot be regarded as one of deciding between competing submissions.

For all of these reasons, the Opinion of the advocate general may be useful in ways which may not be obvious from the perspective of other systems.

A final matter to be mentioned in discussing the relationship between Opinions and judgments is that of the influence of Opinions on judgments. It is a question which, of course, advocates general are often asked, but which they are perhaps not best placed to answer.[7] A recent study has suggested that the judgment "follows" the Opinion in well over eighty per cent of the cases before the Court.[8] Such statistics have to be treated with caution, and various kinds of qualification are necessary before they can be taken seriously. Nevertheless the high correlation in outcomes between Opinion and judgment is of interest – especially when it is borne in mind that on any legal question two lawyers will often give three answers.

What the reasons are for the high correlation must remain a matter for speculation, and there has indeed been a range of interesting speculation on the subject. But that is an appropriate place for the present author to turn to his next topic.

JUDGES

The functions of a judge are well understood. Judges hear and decide cases. But the ways in which they do so differ considerably in different courts. There are for ex-

7 See however the comments of Advocate General Fennelly, *op.cit.*, pp. 13-19; and see generally Tridimas, *op.cit.*

8 Tridimas, *op.cit.*, p. 1362.

ample fundamental differences between the role of the judge in the European Court and the role of the judge in the supreme courts of the common-law systems.

The European Court is essentially a collegiate court in which the judges are (for good reasons, which will be considered below) required to reach a collective judgment; and they do so with the assistance of one of their number who takes a leading role as "judge rapporteur" in the case.

That is not the way of the common law systems, where usually even in the highest courts judges sit in an individual capacity; there is often little coordination between them; and there is an expectation, if not that each judge will give a separate opinion – since he may in the event be able to join with one or more of his brethren, or even, exceptionally, sign a single judgment of the entire court – that nevertheless he will start to hear the case as if it were simply his own case.

There are good reasons, in the European Court, for following a different system. There are good practical reasons for the institution of the judge rapporteur. And although the suggestion has occasionally been made that individual opinions should be allowed – a question discussed below – the basic features of the judges' working methods have not, I think, been questioned.

Thus the judge rapporteur guides the Court (with the advice of the advocate general) on matters of procedure as the case works its way through the Court, and guides the Court on the judgment (with the assistance which he and the other judges derive from the Opinion of the advocate general) in the collective deliberations of the judges. Those deliberations, again, reflect the collegiate character of the Court.[9]

As a result, much of the work done by the judge is done in committee. Not only in hearing the case, but in deliberation – whether oral or by exchange of written memoranda. This is due in particular to the system of the single judgment.

The single judgment

From the outset, the Court has followed the practice of delivering a single judgment, which all the judges sign: there are no individual opinions, either concurring or dissenting.

The Court follows, in that respect, the practice of most courts in continental Europe, which differs from the practice in England and the rest of the common-law world. It is interesting to note, though, that individual opinions are now accepted in the constitutional courts of some "civil law" systems (e.g. Germany and Spain) where the single collective judgment is otherwise the rule for all courts. These different practices cannot be treated lightly. They are deep-rooted and reflect deep-seated cultural, social and political traditions.

9 In the words of a judge departing from the Court (Judge Murray): "Its collegiality is not merely a term to describe its functional process, it comprehends a body of persons brought together in a shared intellectual endeavour to fulfil a common duty imposed by the Treaty ...".

Individual opinions are also accepted in some international courts including the International Court of Justice and the European Court of Human Rights. But these courts provide no real analogy, since the European Court of Justice is in many respects closer to municipal than to international courts, even though it operates on a transnational scale and fulfils to some extent, like the European Court of Human Rights, the role of a European constitutional court.

Analogies are again, however, more misleading than helpful, and in my view the need for the single judgment in the European Court of Justice has to be viewed in the very specific context of that Court. I suggest also that the issue has been clouded by reliance on rather unconvincing arguments in support of the single judgment.

One somewhat unconvincing argument is that the collective judgment is necessary to preserve the independence of the judges. The argument is that judges have a term limited to six years and that re-appointment is, under the current system, in practice dependent upon the Member State from which the judge comes. Thus the independence of the judiciary, a cardinal feature of the rule of law, might be prejudiced if dissenting opinions were allowed.

The initial response to that argument might well be that the current system of limited terms and the uncertainty of re-appointment is in any event questionable, and that it might be preferable to change the system to provide for a single, non-renewable term, which in the interest of continuity would necessarily be considerably longer than the existing (renewable) six-year term. That is exactly what was done in Germany, where the six-year, renewable term of appointment to the Federal Constitutional Court was replaced by a non-renewable twelve-year term. A similar reform might well be desirable for the appointment of judges and advocates general in the European Court, on grounds of constitutional principle. It has to be mentioned that from time to time the appointment of a particular judge or advocate general has not been renewed, for apparently arbitrary reasons.

The Court of Justice itself has said, in its report for the Inter-Governmental Conference which led to the Treaty of Amsterdam, that it considers that the procedure for appointment laid down by the Treaties, and the practice generally followed in renewing the term of office of its members, have "satisfactorily ensured its independence and the continuity of its case-law". It has, however, indicated that it would not object to a reform which would involve an extension of the term of office, with a concomitant condition that the appointment be non-renewable. "Such a reform", it has said, "would provide an even firmer basis for the independence of its members and would strengthen the continuity of its case-law".

But while such a reform might be desirable on those grounds, I do not think it has much connection with the debate on the single judgment. Judges at the European Court, if allowed to express individual opinions, would no doubt do so without fear or favour. Moreover there is the example of the advocate general, who does express an individual opinion and whose Opinions are not, I think, affected by the prospect of hostile reactions from the public or from governments.

Nevertheless, although I think the argument for "protecting the judges" is somewhat unconvincing, I also think that constitutional principles in Europe have now developed to the point that the introduction of a longer, non-renewable term is highly desirable in itself. It is vital nowadays not only that judges are not affected by pressures of this kind, but that the impression should not be allowed to arise that they might be so affected.

A second argument advanced in favour of the single judgment is that the practice is necessary to maintain the authority of the Court's judgments. Community law is still a relatively young system; it is dependent, for its efficacy, on the national courts and on the Member States. It cannot count on the support of public opinion. The Community legal system operates in areas of increasing sensitivity, yet is far weaker and more vulnerable than national systems, over which its rules must nevertheless prevail. Against that background, dissenting opinions might, it may be said, seriously weaken the authority of the Court's judgments and undermine the very basis of the Community.

That argument has much force, although there is, perhaps, an argument to the opposite effect. In a modern legal system, as more generally in a society based on liberal and pluralist principles rather than on an authoritarian model, debate between opposing views is healthy and creative; to some extent the case-law of a court which has constitutional functions should itself reflect that debate.

This viewpoint is attractive. One part of the answer to it is that this need for dialectic, for opposing views, is sometimes met by the Opinion of the advocate general. Incidentally a reflection of that dialectic is often found in analysis by commentators on the Court's case-law. This is often based on comparing the Opinion and judgment, and such a comparison often provides a far richer basis for understanding, and sometimes for developing, the case-law.

Ultimately, however, it seems to me that there is a very strong case for maintaining the practice of the single judgment – and the main argument is one which would still be very strong even in the absence of the factors mentioned above.

Community law often requires the national laws to be synthesised into a new structure, inspired by, yet different from, the national laws. Judges come to the Court from a variety of national legal system; even if they have some acquaintance with Community law (and some of them considerable expertise), their background in national law will inevitably condition their approach. It is difficult to see how the complex and delicate process of forging a Community rule would function efficiently if judges were free to adopt an individual perspective – a perspective which would, from the outset, inevitably be coloured by the national legal system. Once again, analogies with other systems (here, the existence of separate opinions in other national or international courts) may not be helpful. It may be a specific advantage in the European Court that a minority view is taken into account in the judgment where, in other systems, it might merely have formed a dissenting opinion with no influence on the outcome.

To those advantages of the single judgment I would add a few practical considerations. Experience of courts with individual opinions suggests that it is sometimes difficult to identify the true principle for which the judgment is authority. Even where there is a concise and cogent majority judgment, it may be necessary to study the other opinions – which, experience shows, may be less concise. And then judges in the European Court were to write separate opinions, there be the need for translation; currently judgments have to be published in eleven languages, with all the attendant delays and expense, and the problem will be exacerbated by the enlargement of the Union and the consequent increase in the number of official languages.

In conclusion, there are convincing arguments for retaining the practice of the single judgment. But again, the single judgment necessarily has its disadvantages. It will rarely be possible to include reasoning as full and as cogent as might be possible with dissenting opinions. Often there will be a need to compromise. Critics of the Court's judgments may not fully appreciate the difficulties, especially in the plenary Court, of arriving at a single text to which all the judges can put their name.

And again, the debate on the single judgment has to be seen in the context of the synergy of the judgment of the Court and the Opinion of the advocate general: the Opinion fulfils some of the functions of individual opinions – indeed it is an individual judicial opinion, but one designed not to decide the case but to assist the other members of the Court. Its individuality and its independence may also help to counter a possible misperception of the Court as a monolithic institution or even as an institution with an agenda. At the same time, the advocate general's Opinion does not detract from the judgment as might be the case with a system of dissenting or individual judgments. Such a system might indeed inhibit the development of a coherent Community jurisprudence.

The advocate general's Opinion, in contrast, may provide a useful and constructive adjunct to the collective judgment of the Court: sometimes developing the argument more fully; sometimes providing some additional infrastructure for what must be a relatively compact judgment; sometimes setting the case in the broader context of the development of the law; sometimes illuminating the judgment even – or perhaps especially – where it differs. The system, as it generally operates, offers a good compromise between very different legal traditions.

Finally, the existence of the advocate general's Opinion makes more acceptable a succinct, compact judgment which need not address all the issues or meet all the arguments raised. As well as simplifying the requirements of the judgment, especially in complex cases, the result may be to make the case-law more readily accessible to the practitioners, courts and authorities of the Member States: such accessibility is an essential requirement of the rule of law, especially in so diverse a range of legal (and language) systems as coexist in the European Union.

THE FUTURE

The main challenge in the future is that of enlargement. Politically the decision of principle has been taken to enlarge the European Union, subject to successful completion of the negotiations on accession, to admit countries from central and eastern Europe, as well as Cyprus and Malta.

A Union thus enlarged will look very different from the present Union. What will the enlarged Court look like? It seems likely that the enlarged Court will continue to have a judge from each Member State. Not only is that likely to be a political necessity; it may also be thought desirable, from a legal and constitutional perspective, that all legal systems should continue to be represented among the judges; the judges are not, of course, representatives of the Member States from which they come, but they are, in a sense, representatives of their national legal cultures.

There is however no corresponding argument in the case of advocates general. It should not, therefore, be assumed that there should automatically be a proportionate increase in the numbers of advocates general. There may indeed be advantages in retaining a smaller corps of advocates general, even at the cost of not providing for an advocate general's Opinion in every case.

It may well be argued that the function of advocate general will be of greater importance in an enlarged Court than it is today; and yet that there will not be a need for an advocate general in every case.

As to the first proposition, on the greater significance of the advocate general: an enlarged Court will not easily be able to sit in plenary session: the current fifteen judges are perhaps about the maximum number in which it is possible to have collective deliberations; and it would be desirable to have a significantly smaller number than fifteen. But if not all the judges can sit, even in important cases, it will be all the more difficult to maintain consistency in the case-law.

The advocates general, in that situation, will inevitably have an even greater responsibility for maintaining the integrity of the case-law (or, occasionally, advocating developments in the case-law).

Moreover the legal systems of the Member States, and the background of the judges in the enlarged Court, will be far more diverse: that too may mean a more significant role for the advocates general in maintaining the coherence of the case-law or indeed developing it where appropriate to achieve a new synthesis.

On the other hand, it is clear that, even in an enlarged Court, an Opinion will be less valuable in some cases than in others. There may already be an established line of case-law. There may be technical cases, in which an answer is required but it is less important what the answer is.

It could of course be said that some such cases should not come before the Court at all; that if a case does not require the fullest consideration, then the Court should not be troubled with it.

However it will remain of the greatest importance, and especially in an enlarged Union where the new Member States have less experience of Community law, that all national courts should remain free to refer questions of Community law to the Court and entitled to receive answers. Inevitably a proportion of cases will prove, on reflection, to require more consideration and others less.

If the solution were to be adopted of not providing for an advocate general in every case, a safeguard could be introduced, as it is in other procedures before the Court: the advocate general's view is required at all stages in the procedure. In accordance with that principle, each case would continue to be assigned to an advocate general, and he would be consulted on whether an Opinion was required; the decision would be taken, in the ordinary way, by the judges and advocates general collectively.

There would be a significant incidental advantage in having a more limited number of advocates general. Currently, of the eight posts of advocate general, the five appointed from the five largest Member States are appointed for a renewable six-year term, while the other three posts rotate among the other ten Member States, their posts being tenable for only one term.

There must, I think, be a question whether the departure of several advocates general after a single term of six years is satisfactory from the perspective of the need for continuity in the Court. Moreover, if, after enlargement, there were an increase in the number of advocates general commensurate with the increase in the number of judges, then since Member States would doubtless insist on sharing out the additional posts there would be a large number of "rotating" posts, tenable for only one six-year term and not renewable. There are of course advantages in having advocates general from many different systems, and the idea has I think worked well.

But it should not go too far; that would be undesirable for many reasons: perhaps above all because it is difficult to reconcile with the function of the advocate general – one which will be of even greater importance in the enlarged Union – of maintaining the long-term coherence of the Court's jurisprudence. There would be other disadvantages also.[10]

One final consideration: if a relatively small number of advocates general were to be appointed in the enlarged Court, the question would still arise from which Member States they should come. One possibility would be that the appointment of advocates general should be detached from the idea of national quotas. Member States would be free to propose candidates, the appointment itself being made by selection from those proposed, possibly with the assistance of a judicial appointments commission. Such a system would introduce an element of transparency into the appointment procedure and, if properly managed, might be conducive to appointments of the highest quality. It might indeed be extended, in a modified form, to the appointment of judges, while still retaining the link of one judge per Member State.

10 It substantially disrupts judicial business every three years; it introduces arbitrary factors into the appointment process; it creates two different categories of members in the Court; and it is administratively costly with new posts having to be filled, new archives having to be assembled, new linguistic requirements for chambers staff and translation resources. And it is incompatible with the desirable goal of introducing a single, longer term for all members of the Court.

3

ON THE JUDGE-MADE LAW OF THE EUROPEAN COMMUNITY'S COURTS

Ulrich Everling

I INTRODUCTORY REMARKS

Lord Slynn of Hadley stated in his Cambridge lecture of 1992, that the Court of Justice of the European Communities has, in spite of its limited power, "*built up a new legal order which is only referred to in outline in the Treaty*". After giving examples, he characterised the Court "*as a constitutional court*" which "*has done much to recognise the democratic role of the European Parliament...*" and "*has been involved in important constitutional decisions*".[1]

The constitutional function which Lord Slynn attributed to the Court[2] corresponds to its central position in the institutional system of the Community,[3] understood as a Community of law.[4] But this role is not undisputed. In all the Member States, some judgments are discussed or criticised by scholars as well as the public media. This is not surprising given the number of judgments – nearly 5000 since 1953. It is also not at all unwelcome, as professional criticism is the only effective control of high courts; I myself have published some critical remarks with the intention of being an *amicus curiae.*[5]

---

1 "What is a European Community Judge?" 52 CLJ (1993) 234.

2 This term shall also include the Court of First Instance in the following if there is no indication to the contrary.

3 In the following the Community shall be dealt with in the first place and not the European Union since the Community is up to now the principal legislator and holder of rights whilst the Union is only beginning to take this role. See Busse, *Die völkerrechtliche Einordnung der Europäischen Union,* (Köln, 1999); Curtin, "The Constitutional Structure of the Union: A Europe of Bits and Pieces", 30 CML Rev. (1993) 17-69; Wichard, "Wer ist Herr im europäischen Haus?", 34 EuR (1999) 170-184.

4 This characteristic has been first formulated by the former President Hallstein, *Die Europäische Gemeinschaft,* 5th ed. (Düsseldorf 1979) at pp. 51-79; see MacCormick, "Democracy, Subsidiarity and citizenship in the 'European Commonwealth'" in ibid. (Ed.), *Constructing Legal Systems* (Kluwer, 1997) 1-26 at 7.

5 Everling, "Will Europe Slip on Bananas? The Bananas Judgement of the Court of Justice and National Courts", 33 CML Rev. (1996) 401-437; ibid., "Einlagensicherung im Europäischen Binnenmarkt", 162 ZHR (1998) 403-426.

D. O'Keeffe (ed.), Liber Amicorum Slynn 29-44 (2000)

But the critics sometimes attack the jurisprudence excessively, questioning its very function.[6] In particular, those judgments are questioned which go beyond strict interpretation of the texts and by developing written rules create Judge-made law – called *richterliche Rechtsfortbildung* and *Richterrecht* in Germany.

It seems an appropriate subject for a paper dedicated to Lord Slynn, that long-standing member of the Court, to take this criticism seriously and to study the conditions, difficulties and limits of the Court's law-making. This will not be done through a theoretical study of the foundation and admissibility of judge-made law in modern states and organisations; innumerable books and essays have been written on this topic, and the different opinions are well known.[7] On the contrary, the subject shall be presented on the basis of practical and personal experiences at the Court. This may be considered as carrying coals to Newcastle, as the former member of the Court knows the problems at least as well as the author, or even better. But perhaps it may be interesting to him and to English readers to become acquainted with the view of a former colleague, based on the German, that is, continental, legal order.

In line with the practical orientation of the study, I shall not try to find the often discussed borderline between extensive interpretation of a provision, taking in account its sense or *effet utile* on the one hand and the judicial updating of law, creating judge-made law, on the other. On the contrary, the term judge-made law shall be applied in what follows to the law created by both methods of the Court, since in practice they are bound to each other and are not distinguished in the public discussion.[8] The essential questions arising from such law, in particular its legitimacy, formation and limits, are to be examined equally, in the main.

---

6 See e.g. Neill, *The European Court of Justice, A Case Study in Judicial Activism*, evidence submitted to the House of Lords' Selected Committee to the European Communities, HL Paper 88, July 18, 1995, pp. 218-252; von Danwitz, *Verwaltungsrechtliches System und Europäische Integration* (Tübingen, 1996) at pp. 132 et seq.; Rasmussen, *The European Court of Justice* (Copenhagen, 1998), all with further citations.

7 See from the abundant literature Achterberg (Ed.), *Rechtsprechungslehre* (Köln, 1986); Allan, *Law, Liberty, and Justice* (Oxford, 1994); Bydlinski, *Juristische Methodenlehre,* 2nd ed. (Wien, 1991); Cappeletti, *Le pouvoir des juges* (Paris, 1990); Esser, *Grundsatz und Norm in der richterlichen Fortbildung des Privatrechts,* 3rd ed. (Tübingen, 1976); J. Ipsen, *Richterrecht und Verfassung* (Berlin, 1976); Jacob (Ed.), *Le juge et le jugement dans les traditions juridiques européennes* (Liège, 1996); Kriele, *Theorie der Rechtsgewinnung*, 2nd ed. (Berlin, 1976); Langenbucher, *Die Entwicklung und Auslegung von Richterrecht* (München, 1996); Lenaerts, *Le juge et la Constitution aux Etats-Unis d'Amerique et dans l'ordre juridique européen* (Bruxelles, 1988); MacCormick (Ed.), *Legal Reasoning and Legal Theory* (Oxford, 1994); Wank, *Die Grenzen richterlicher Rechtsfortbildung* (Berlin, 1978).

8 See already Dicey, *Law & Public Opinion in England,* 2nd ed. (1962), at p. 461; for the Court's practice see Borchardt, "Richterrecht durch den Gerichtshof der Europäischen Gemeinschaften", in *Gedächtnisschrift für Eberhard Grabitz* (München, 1995) 29-43 at 37.

II BASES OF JUDGE-MADE LAW BY THE COURT OF JUSTICE

Judge-made law in this broad sense is a reality in all the Member States. This shall briefly be indicated since nobody can understand Community law who regards it only from the point of view of its own legal order.[9]

Judge-made law has always been part of the European law culture. In England, the Courts gained an independent position in the course of the long conflicts between Crown and Parliament. Dicey identified as characteristics of the system of Common Law that the Courts did not decide like arbiters according to equity but as judges on the base of law and that this law was spoken on the line of binding precedents which were cautiously adjusted to changing facts.[10] But the Common Law may be overruled by statute law, which Parliament issued progressively to encounter the needs of a modern society. Statute law has always been narrowly and textually interpreted, because the judge is traditionally not entitled to correct the sovereign Parliament. But this practice is not applied to the EC Treaty, although it was introduced in English law by an act of the Parliament, namely the Community Act. It is interpreted following the continental manner regarding the sense of its disposition, as Lord Denning stated in his famous dictum.[11] Consequently the narrow interpretation of statute law usually applied by English Courts did not influence the practice of the Court of Justice. On the contrary, if this author's observations are right, the methods of the common law seem to have some importance for the Court, in particular with regard to the orientation on precedents, even if they are not regarded as binding.[12] Continental lawyers are not accustomed to such a practice, and have difficulties in understanding it as legitimating progressive jurisprudence.

In the continental Member States, the codification of law following the age of rationalism was the characteristic development. Under the influence of the principle of separation of powers, the *Code civil* of Napoleon as well as the Prussian *Allgemeine Landrecht* were prohibited from being developed by the

9 The lawyer's view across the national frontiers is one of the most important conditions of the concordant understanding and application of Community Law in the Member States. In most law reviews, for instance, the abundant books and articles written in foreign languages are rarely cited, apparently mainly because of linguistic barriers; but even if other languages are known, the national-centred attitude prevails.

10 See the classic presentation by Dicey (supra note 8) at p. 483; furthermore A. Lester, "English Judges as Law Makers", Public Law (1993) 269-290; G.C.Rowe, "Tensions in the Role of the Common Law Judge", 49 RabelsZ (1985) 607-677. The importance of the rules of procedures may be set aside in this context; see on this aspect P. Stein, "Judgements in the European Legal Tradition", in: Universita degli Studi Ferrara, *La Sentenza in Europa,* (1988), p. 27. See also Zimmermann, "Statuta sunt stricte interpretanda? Statutes and the Common Law: a Continental Perspective", 56 CLJ (1997) 315-328.

11 *Bulmer v. Bollinger* [1974] 2 All E.R. 1226.

12 Arnull, "Owning up to Fallibility: Precedent and the Court of Justice, 36 CML Rev. (1993) 247-266; Plender, *European Courts: Practice and Precedents* (London, 1997).

Courts. Nevertheless, the judge was never, in Europe, *«la bouche de la loi qui prononce les paroles de la loi»*, according to Montesquieu's prescription.[13]

In France, as in other Romanic countries, the judges have steadily developed the *Code civil* corresponding to the economic and social requirements of modern society.[14] The administrative law including its general principles has been broadly created by the *Conseil d'Etat,* which has therefore often been denunciated as being a *gouvernement des juges.* In particular, this part of French law has essentially influenced the law of other Member States, and also the rules and procedures of the Court of Justice. Up to now, the Court has been the origin of particularities in its jurisprudence and practice which are strange to lawyers of other legal orders, and difficult for them to apply, as, for instance, the technique of *moyens* presented by the plaintiffs demonstrates.[15]

The German development was not uniform.[16] As in France, the Prussian *Allgemeine Landrecht* was not able to prohibit judicial development of the law, and in great parts of other German territories a *ius commune* was applied on to the basis of elder Roman and German law. This tradition survived the unification of private law at the end of the 19th century. Today, great parts of the private, labour and administrative law are judge-made, even if the *Bundesverfassungsgericht* limited the room for action of the other jurisdictions.[17] But this Court itself was promoting judge-made law on a great scale with precise impositions on the legislator. In particular, on the base of short articles of the *Grundgesetz,* a complete building of detailed fundamental rights was constructed which penetrates the whole of German law and determines the practice of all institutions including the Courts. It is true that this practice has influenced the European Court, but its jurisprudence remains behind that of German practice.[18] This is one of the reasons why judgments of the Court are often badly received in Germany, and why the arguments of German lawyers in Court are sometimes not understood.

On this historical and national background, it seems clear that, from the beginning, the Court has claimed to be entitled to create judge-made law.[19] Its

---

13 So the *Bundesverfassungsgericht* in BVerfGE 75, 223 at 243.

14 See the survey of Terré, *Introduction générale au droit,* T. I du Précis Dalloz, *Droit civil* (1991) Nr. 228 et seq.; Ferid and Sonnenberger, *Das Französische Zivilrecht,* Vol. 1/1, 2nd ed. (Heidelberg, 1994) pp. 155 et seq..

15 Bleckmann, *Europarecht,* 6th ed. (Köln, 1997) at pp. 300 et seq.

16 See Wieacker *Privatrechtsgeschichte der Neuzeit,* 2nd ed. (Göttingen, 1996).

17 BVerfGE 65, 182; 96, 375.

18 Rengeling, *Grundrechtsschutz in der Europäischen Gemeinschaft* (München, 1992) at pp 233 et seq.; Coppel and O'Neill, "The European Court of Justice: Taking Rights seriously?" 29 CML Rev. (1992) 669-692.

19 See of the rich literature Arnull, "Does the Court of Justice have inherent jurisdiction?" 28 CML Rev. (1991) 683-708; Bleckmann, "Die Rolle der richterlichen Rechtsschöpfung im Europäischen Gemeinschaftsrecht", in *Gedächtnisschrift für Leontin-Jean Constantinesco* (Köln, 1983) 61-81; Burley and Mattli, "Europe before the Court: A Political Theory of Legal Integration", International Integration (1993) 41-76; Colin, *Le gou-*

greatest and most praised creation has been the acknowledgement of fundamental rights and of principles of the rule of law in Community law, which the Member States have now introduced in Article 7 (ex F) TEU.[20] Supremacy and direct effect – the pillars of Community law nowadays – were enforced by the Court from the beginning, as well as the understanding of the basic principles of the Common Market as prohibiting not only discriminatory measures but also restrictions. To give an other example, claims to national Courts against Member States on compensation for damage caused by their Treaty infringements were admitted.[21] The necessity of such jurisprudence will be examined more closely.

III Objects of the Judge-Made Law of the Court

The need for judge-made law in the Community is considerable. The provisions of the Treaty which transferred powers to the Community are fragmentary and incomplete, even after the supplements added by the Maastricht and Amsterdam Treaties. But the Community is not a bundle of single competencies the application of which must in every case be accepted by the Member States. It is created by a foundation act in the form of an independent Organisation with own tasks, own institutions, its own legal order and direct relationship to the citizens. Its basic rules include all the elements of a constitution, if this term is understood in a functional sense and not bound to the existence of a state or a *volonté générale* of the people. However the terminology is used, in the Community system the Court of Justice fulfils among its general mission functions similar to those of national constitutional courts.[22] In this context Alexis de Toqueville may be

---

vernement des Juges dans les Communautés européennes (Paris, 1966); Everling, "Rechtsvereinheitlichung durch Richterrecht in der Europäischen Gemeinschaft", 50 RabelsZ (1984) 193-232; Koopmans, "Sources of Law: The New Pluralism", in *Festskrift til Ole Due* (København, 1994) 189-205; Lecourt, *Europe des Juges* (Bruxelles, 1976); Schwarze, *Die Befugnis zur Abstraktion im europäischen Gemeinschaftsrecht. Eine Untersuchung zur Rechtsprechung des Europäischen Gerichtshofes* (Baden-Baden, 1976); Stein, "Richterrecht wie anderswo auch? Der Gerichtshof der Europäischen Gemeinschaften als Integrationsmotor" in Festschrift der jur. Fakultät der Universität Heidelberg (Heidelberg, 1986), 619-641; Wolf-Niedermeier, *Der Europäische Gerichtshof zwischen Recht und Politik* (Baden-Baden, 1997); Ukrow, *Richterliche Rechtsfortbildung durch den EuGH* (Baden-Baden, 1995).

20 See Rengeling (*supra* note 18).

21 Case 479/93, *Francovich v. Italy* [1995] ECR 101.

22 See Frowein, "Die Verfassung der Europäischen Union aus der Sicht der Mitgliedstaaten", 30 EuR (1995) 315-333; Rinze, "The Role of the European Court of Justice as a Federal Constitutional Court", 5 EPL (1999) 426-443; Rodriguez Iglesias, "Zur 'Verfassung' der Europaischen Gemeinschaft", EuGRZ (1997), 125-131; Schwarze, "Die europäische Dimension des Verfassungsrechts", in *Festschrift für Ulrich Everling* (Baden-Baden, 1995) 1355-1378; Seurin, "Towards a European Constitution? Problems of Political Integration, Public Law (1994) 625-636; Van Gerven, "Towards a Coherent Con-

cited, even if comparisons of the Community to federal States and to the conditions in the 19th century should only be made reluctantly. He said, with regard to the American Supreme Court:

> *"Dans les mains des sept juges fédéraux reposent incessamment la paix, la prospérité, l'existence même de l'Union. Sans eux, la constitution est une oeuvre morte; c'est à eux qu'en appelle le pouvoir exécutif pour résister aux empiétements du corps législatif; la législature, pour se défendre des entreprises du pouvoir exécutif; l'Union, pour se faire obéir des Etats; les Etats, pour repousser les prétentions exagérées de l'Union; l'intérêt public contre l'intérêt privé; l'esprit de conservation contre l'instabilité démocratique."*[23]

If these words are transferred in the present understanding of public power and are completed by the protection of citizens which stands today at the centre of judicial tasks, they perfectly describe the constitutional function of the Court of Justice. Such a function can only be exercised by applying judge-made law.

The constitutional function of the Court is particularly apparent in the application of those provisions of the Treaty which confer competencies on the Community's institutions. The Court had always interpreted them in such a way that they may fulfil their *effet utile,* that is, the purpose to which they are destined.[24] The EC Treaty now comprises numerous competencies with different scopes and different intensities. Taken together they amount to more than a patchwork creation; they form a network of more or less far-reaching rules. The Member States in their function as Treaty parties, rather than the Court, transferred these rights, and their representatives in the Council applied them at least by majority. The Court only controls the application.

This is also true with regard to Article 308 (ex 235) EC, the authorisation to complete the Treaty under certain conditions. This provision is regarded with distrust because it could perhaps be used as base of an inadmissible *competence-competence.*[25] In spite of an often told story to that effect, the Court did not interpret this provision extensively. The Court has never been appealed for decid-

---

stitutional System within the European Union, 2 EPL (1996) 81-101; Walker, "European Constitutionalism and European Integration", 2 EPL (1996) 266-289.

23 De Toqueville, *De la Democratie en Amerique,* 14th ed., (Paris, 1864), Vol. II p. 252

24 See Kutscher, *Methods of Interpretation as Seen by a Judge of the Court of Justice* (Luxemburg, 1976) p. I-44; Anweiler, *Die Auslegungsmethoden des Gerichtshofs der Europäischen Gemeinschaften* (Frankfurt, 1976) at pp. 219 et seq.; Weatherill and Beaumont, *EC Law* (London, 1993) at pp. 151 et seq.

25 For a critical view see BVerfGE 89, 155 at 210. See also Beyer, "Die Ermächtigung der Europäischen Union und ihrer Gemeinschaften", Der Staat 35 (1996) 189-220 at pp. 201 et seq.; Kapteyn and Verloren van Themaat, *Introduction to the Law of the European Communities,* 2nd ed. by Gormley (Deventer, 1990) pp. 113 et seq.; Olmi, "La place de l'article 235 CEE dans le système des attributions de compétence à la Communauté", in *Mélanges Fernand Dehousse* (Bruxelles, 1979), Vol 2, 279-295; Oppermann, *Europarecht,* 2nd ed. (München, 1999) at pp. 201 et seq.; Schwartz, "Artikel 235 EG-Vertrag nach 'Maastricht'", in *Festschrift für Ernst-Joachim Mestmäcker* (Baden-Baden, 1996) 467-482.

ing whether the article was a sufficient legal basis for a given legal act. In some cases it had to judge whether the provision could be applied together with another competence, which it has mostly denied.[26] The Court had the first occasion to express its opinion on the significance of this authorisation in its Opinion 2/94 concerning the accession of the Community to the European Convention of Human Rights.[27] It rightly regarded the provision not as a sufficient legal basis of this – in the author's view desirable – accession, since the latter would change the institutional structure of the Community and would, therefore, demand an amendment of the Treaty.

The legal acts issued by the institutions are also defective and incomplete, and sometimes even more so than the often inadequate national legislation. They are rendered in difficult procedures combining several institutions with the participation of representatives of fifteen Member States so that compromises more often conceal than decide the differences between them. The Court must often adjust them through judge-made law to make them applicable.

The consequences of the described situation are paradoxical: Judge-made law is even more necessary within the Community than in the Member States, but it is less founded on a fully developed and historically grown legal system, which is anchored in the consciousness of citizens.

IV Legitimacy of the Judge-Made Law of the Court of Justice

The Court derives its justification for creating judge-made law from its task laid down in Article 220 (ex 164) EC, to "*ensure that in the interpretation and application of this Treaty the law is observed*". Against the background of the traditional role of the judges in the Member States described above, this duty is to be understood as entitling the Court not only to interpret the Treaty, but also to develop the law to give the Community a firm legal base.[28] As the *Bundesverfassungsgericht* stated in its judgment concerning directives,

26 Case 131/86 *UK v. Council,* [1988] ECR 905; Case 165/87, *Commission v. Council,* [1988] 5545; Case 56/88, *UK v. Council*, [1989] ECR 1618. See Breier, "Der Streit um die richtigen Rechtsgrundlage in der Rechtsprechung des Europäischen Gerichtshofs", 30 EuR (1995) 46-53; Emiliou, "Opening Pandora's Box: The Legal Basis of Community Measures before the Court of Justice", 19 EL Rev. (1994) 488-507.

27 Opinion 2/94 under Article 228 para 6 EC Treaty, [1996] ECR I-1759, para 28 et seq. See Burrows, "Question of Community Accession to the European Determined", 22 EL Rev. [1997] 57-63; Vedder, "Die 'verfassungsrechtliche Dimension' – die bisher unbekannte Grenze für Gemeinschaftshandeln?" 31 EuR (1996) 309-319.

28 See Pernice, Die Dritte Gewalt im europäischen Verfassungsverbund, 31 EuR (1996) 27-43; Ukrow (*supra* note 19) at pp. 90 et seq.; Gibson and Caldeira, "The European Court of Justice: A Question of Legimacy", 14 Z.f.Rechtssoziologie, (1993) 204-222.

> *"...no doubts can exist that the Member States intended to vest the Community with a Court to which all means of law-finding should be open which have been constructed over centuries in a legal tradition and culture common to the whole of Europe".*[29]

Even in the Maastricht judgment it confirmed this statement, but it seems that there, the borderline would be narrowly defined.[30]

In the modern democratic state institutions receive their legitimacy to act in the first instance from the representatives of the people. With regard to courts the chain leading to the people seems normally to be relatively weak, and this is particularly true of the Court of Justice. According to Article 223 (ex 167) EC, its members are appointed by common accord of the Member States.[31] The latter take decisions as – so to speak – "*masters of the Treaty*" represented by their governments without participation of Council or European Parliament. But this nomination seems not to be sufficient alone to legitimate the law-making of the Court. It receives its justification – like almost every court – above all by its standing as a legally established and objectively acting institution.[32]

Consequently, in addition, the Court takes the legitimacy to develop the law in the Community from elements which are common to the traditions of national judiciaries: its mandate confined in the Treaty, its position in the institutional system of the Community, its manner of decision-making in formal and strictly regulated judicial procedures, with the independence, impartiality and professional qualification of its members and its jurisprudence all aiming to realise law and justice. The Court fulfils these requirements even if some amelioration may be desirable.[33]

The Court is, like every judiciary, not a monolith, but consists of individual personalities with a variety of experiences and ideas. They must join, at least as a majority, to find common opinions in concrete cases. But, in contrast to national judges sitting in chambers, they do not act on the base of the same intellectual, cultural and professional backgrounds. They come from different Member States and thus are formed by different historical consciousness, different cultural, religious and moral values and in particular by different legal orders. They introduce the traditions, basic ideas and legal values as well as the proce-

29 BVerfGE 75, 223 at 243 (Translation by the author).

30 BVerfGE 89, 155 at 209 et seq.

31 Kennedy, "Thirteen Russians! The Composition of the European Court of Justice", in *Legal Reasoning and Judicial Interpretation of Law, Essays in Honour of Lord Mackenzie Stuart* (Trenton, 1996) 69-91; Epping, "Die demokratische Legitimation der dritten Gewalt der Europäischen Gemeinschaften", 36 Der Staat (1997) 349-380; Siebert, *Die Auswahl der Richter am Gerichtshof der Europäischen Gemeinschaften* (Frankfurt, 1997).

32 See Weber, *Wirtschaft und Gesellschaft,* Ed. for Studies (Tübingen, 1956) at pp. 159 et seq., who refers to the rational, traditional and charismatic character of the institution concerned.

33 Thus e.g. concerning the period of the Judges' nomination. In order to secure and demonstrate their independence they should be nominated for 12 years instead of 6, and their re-nomination should be excluded. See Siebert (*supra* note 31) at pp. 268 et seq.

dural and material peculiarities of their respective legal order in the common deliberations.[34] The law given by the Court is formed by the merger of the individual contributions of its Members. Thus the Court mirrors the integration which proceeds on a larger scale between the European peoples.

It is true that the legal orders of the Members States have common roots in the traditions of occidental culture and that they are influenced to a greater or lesser extent by Roman law. It is also true that the open frontiers in the Community lead to contacts and exchanges of opinions between the lawyers of the Member States, and that the assimilation of the conditions of life in modern societies demand similar solutions. This may to a certain degree facilitate understanding between the judges. Nevertheless, everyday experience demonstrates that law and consciousness of law still considerably differ between the Member States, and that such differences influence the positions taken by the judges in their deliberations.[35] This situation will only change as a result of a lengthy assimilation of societies.

Under these circumstances it is not surprising that several judgments of the Court and their motivations have been discussed or criticised, but that the Court was able to establish a rich jurisprudence which has finally been accepted by the States and citizens concerned.

V Mode of decision-making in the Court of Justice

When the Court is forming its will, it begins – after establishing the facts – like every court, to examine the texts of the applicable provisions. Texts, however, are never unequivocal; they are mostly unclear, uncertain and full of gaps, and this is in particular true of provisions of Community law as has been explained above. Since normally no records exist to base a decision on a historical interpretation, in the first place the teleological and systematic interpretation is applied, as is well-known.[36] It includes also the interpretation pursuant the *effet utile,* according to which provisions are to be interpreted in such a way that they may fulfil the objective for which they are established.

But what is the "telos" of the Community and the Union in the sense of the ancient Greek term, that is the determination of the objective?[37] The Treaties and the Member States, as well as the institutions of the Union, have left their final

34 Everling, "Der Gerichtshof als Entscheidungsinstanz – Probleme der europäischen Rechtsprechung aus richterlicher Sicht", in Schwarze (Ed.), *Der Europäische Gerichtshof als Verfassungsgericht und Rechtsschutzinstanz* (Baden-Baden, 1983) 137-158; Edwards, "How the Court of Justice works", 20 EL Rev. (1995) 539-558; Koopmans, "Judicial Decision-making", in *Legal Reasoning and Judicial Interpretation of European Law, Essays in Honour of Lord Mackenzie Stuart* (Trenton 1996) 93-104.

35 Legrand, "European Legal Systems are not converging", 45 ICLQ (1996) 1-81.

36 References *supra* note 24.

37 Everling (*supra* note 34) at p. 151.

intentions open and obscure, and the Court is not entitled to answer the question itself based on the personal political opinions of its members, which, of course, may differ. The Court must, therefore, derive its orientations from the Treaties. The most important aim is indicated by the introductory sentence of the preamble of the EEC Treaty, namely the determination of the Member States "to lay down the foundations of an ever closer union among the people of Europe". This phrase has been enforced by the preamble of the Treaty on the European Union and must be read together with the more concrete aims established in the first articles of the Treaty and the special provisions and authorisations included in the different chapters. Furthermore, general principles of law must be taken into consideration, in the light of the general mission of the Court to ensure that the "law" – and not only the rules of the Treaty – is observed.[38] These principles are to derive from the principles of the national constitutional and legal orders in "evaluating comparison".[39]

From these elements the Court gains the "telos" on which it bases the teleological interpretation and also the orientation if it transgresses the frontiers of interpretation in making law by jurisprudence. This method of decision-making is jurisprudence and not "judicial activism", which American courts are told to practise. Such activism does not correspond to the traditional role of the judiciary in the Member States.[40] Judges and in particular those of the Court of Justice decide according criteria of law even if they sometimes have to define for themselves the rules of law which they apply. Their task is not to form the political reality or to change the conditions of life following their own ideas, even if their judgments often have far-reaching political consequences.

That this understanding of jurisprudence is practised by the Court may be shown by the flow over time of its jurisprudence. Leaving aside the first years of the Treaty on Coal and Steel, the starting period can be seen in the early sixties when the grand basic judgments like *Van Gend & Loos* and *Costa/Enel* were rendered.[41] At this time the political impetus bearing the foundation of the EEC was still present. This period ended with the policy of the "empty chair" in 1965, after which the Court decided relatively cautiously. The summit of The Hague in 1969 reanimated the Community and subsequently the Court rendered judgments like *AETR, Dassonville* and *van Duyn.*[42] But the tendencies changed once

38 Compare the text of Article 20 para 3 of the German *Grundgesetz* according to which the judiciary is bound to "legal acts and law". See Pernice and Ukrow *supra* note 28.

39 K. Zweigert, "Der Einfluß des Europäischen Gemeinschaftsrechts auf das Recht der Mitgliedstaaten", 28 RabelsZ (1964) 601-643 at p. 611.

40 Koopmans, "The roots of judicial activism", in *Protecting Human Rights: The European Dimension, Studies in Honour of Gérard Wiarda* (Köln, 1988) 317-327; Rasmussen, "Between Self-Restraint and Activism: A Judicial Policy for the European Court", 13 EL Rev. (1988) 28-38; Tridimas, "The Court of Justice and Judicial Activism", 21 EL Rev. (1996) 199-210.

41 Case 26/62, *Van Gend & Loos v. Netherlands,* ECR [1963] 3; Case 6/64, *Costa v. Enel,* [1964] ECR 1253.

42 Case 22/70, *AETR,* [1971] ECR 263; Case 8/74, *Dassonville v. Procureur du Roi,* [1974]

more. In the time of the monetary and oil crises the Court intended in the first place, as all the European institutions did, to save the *aquis communautaire* and to progress by little steps. This time of prudence was followed by the enacting of the European Single Act at the end of the eighties. The euphoria caused by the idea of the internal market was the basis for a series of far-reaching judgments from *Erasmus* to *Francovich.*[43] Following the difficult discussions and events including referenda and national judgments which accompanied the ratification of the Maastricht Treaty, the pendulum swung back again, so that the Court decided more cautiously in judgments like *Keck* and *Dori.*[44] Now, after the entry into force of the Amsterdam Treaty, the practice of the Court seems to be relatively balanced.

This rough drawing is only determined to show tendencies, without denying that there might be cases falling outside the picture. Nevertheless, it may demonstrate that the flow of jurisprudential law-making reflected the fluctuations of the political arena. This was in no way the consequence of direct or indirect interventions of governments, which never influenced the Court. It seems, rather, that the Court was impressed – probably more intuitively than consciously – by broad indications of the public mood, and tendencies expressed by politicians and public opinion. It is true that the Court was ahead of the more progressive forces, but it is and has never been the unscrupulous motor or outrider of integration, as it is sometimes denounced.

One significance of the Court's decision-making is its progression step by step. The Court is not placed, like high national courts, on top of a hierarchy of lower courts, which prepare and discuss the different controversies and arguments through their judgments. On the contrary, the Court is often confronted by new questions which are rarely examined by courts or scholars. Only its own previous judgments can serve as guidelines if it advances in new areas. Precedents are, even if not binding as in English law,[45] important, and are often the only guidelines if the Court is addressing new matters. If the Court renders new principles on this basis, it often decides in giving a relatively general and narrowly motivated judgment, leaving interested lawyers to grope in the dark. But in this manner it reserves for itself the chance to re-examine, to more clearly define, to limit or even to correct the former judgment after the comments of critics or the intrusion of practical inconveniences.[46]

ECR 837; Case 41/74, *Van Duyn v. UK,* [1974] ECR 1337.

43 Cases 242/87, *Commission v. Council,* [1989] ECR 1425; Case 56/88, *UK v. Council,* [1989] ECR 1615; Cases C-6 and 9/90, *Francovich and Bonifaci v. Italy,* [1991] ECR I-5357.

44 Cases C-267 and 268/91, *Keck and Mithouard,* [1993] ECR I-6097; Case C-91/92, *Dori v. Recreb,* [1994] ECR I-3325.

45 See *supra* note 12.

46 Due, "Pourquoi cette solution? -De certain problèmes concernant la motivation des arrêts de la Cour de justice des Communautés européennes", in *Festschrift für Ulrich Everling* (Baden-Baden, 1995) 273-282 at p. 275; Everling, "Reflections on the Reasoning in the Judgments of the Court of Justice of the European Communities", in *Festskrift til Ole*

Indeed, the Court has often acted in this manner. Only a few examples shall be mentioned here from the long series of such judgments. Thus the Court specified the principles of the judgment *Dassonville* concerning the free movement of goods first in *Cassis de Dijon* and then in *Keck*;[47] it limited the bearing of the judgments *van Duyn* and *Ursula Becker* on direct effect of directives through *Dori*;[48] it restricted the judgment *Paletta I* dealing with documents established in other Member States in *Paletta II*;[49] it explained the judgment *Francovich* founding the obligation of Member States to compensate damages caused by infringements of the Treaty in *Brasserie du Pêcheur* and *Factortame*;[50] it completed the judgment on *bananas* about import barriers in *Port*;[51] and it revised the judgment *Christel Schmidt* concerning rights of employees on occasion of transfers of parts of enterprises in *Süzen*.[52] It may be that occasionally the Court fails to clarify the situation. Thus the enigmas presented by the judgment *Daily Mail* on the transfer of the seats of companies are not solved by *Centros* but replaced by other mysteries.[53] In such cases, only chains of judgments will bring about clarity.

Thus, the Court has reacted sensibly if it is shown that its judgments are rightly criticised or that they cause practical difficulties. If correction seems to be necessary it is therefore not hopeless to appeal once more to the Court and not to call at once, as unfortunately is usual in Germany, for national remedies. Problems must rather be discussed on the Community level advancing convincing arguments, as some national courts have successfully done, by presenting carefully motivated questions to the Court.[54]

Due (København, 1994) 56-74, at p. 69.

47 Case 8/74, *Dassonville v. Procureur du Roi,* [1974] ECR 837; Case 120/78, *Rewe v. Bundesmonopolverwaltung,* [1979] ECR 649; Cases 267 and 268/91, *Keck and Mithouard,* [1993] ECR I-6097.

48 Case 41/74, *Van Duyn v. UK,* [1974] ECR 1337; Case 8/81, *Becker v. Finanzverwaltung,* [1982] ECR 53; Case C-91/92, *Dori v. Recreb* [1994] ECR I-3325.

49 Case C-45/90, *Paletta v. Brennet,* [1992] ECR I-3423; Case C-206/94, *Paletta v. Brennet,* [1996] ECR I-2357.

50 Cases C-6 and 9/90, *Francovich and Bonifaci v. Italy,* [1991] ECR I-5357; Cases C-46 and 48/93, *Brasserie du pêcheur v. Deutschland and UK v. Factortame,* [1996] ECR I-1029.

51 Case C-280/93, *Deutschland v. Council,* [1994] ECR I-4973; Case C-68/95, *Port v. Bundesanstalt für Landwirtschaft und Ernährung,* [1996] ECR I-6065.

52 Case C-392/92, *Christel Schmidt v. Spar- und Leihkasse,* [1994] ECR I-1311; Case C-13/95, *Süzen v. Zehnacker,* [1997] ECR I-1259.

53 Case 81/87, *Daily Mail v. UK,* [1988] ECR 5483; Case C-212/97, *Centros v. Erhvervs- og Selskabsstyrelsen,* [1999] ECR I-1459. Out of the numerous commentaries on the *Centros* Judgment see Behrens, "Das internationale Gesellschaftsreht nach dem Centros-Urteil des EuGH", 19 IPRax (1999) 323.

54 See the judgments *Paletta II* and *Brasserie du pêcheur* (*supra* notes 49 and 50).

VI LIMITS OF THE COURT'S JUDGE-MADE LAW

The limits of the courts' law-making have been discussed for a long time now. They are in particular important to modern democracies, because the rule that all state power is derived from the people demands that law-making must principally belong to the representatives of the people, that is, the Parliaments. German criticisms on the jurisprudence of the *Bundesverfassungsgericht* concern, therefore, in the first place its relationship to the legislator.[55]

This is different with regard to the Court of Justice. It admits to the Community's legislature a large room for manoeuvre, and controls the latter relatively cautiously following the practice of most Member States. This tendency even seems to have increased since the procedure of co-decision with the European Parliament, because the Member States are mostly not accustomed that Parliaments are controlled by courts.[56] Consequently it is not appropriate, as with regard to some national constitutional courts, to plead for self-restraint of the Court of Justice, but rather for a more effective control of the Community's legislation. The problems of law-making of the Court arises in the first instance in its relationship to the Member States.

Every extensive interpretation or judge-made law of the Court limits the room for action of the Member States. It seems, therefore, to be understandable that they mostly criticise progressive judgments of the Court. The *Bundesverfassungsgericht* tried in its *Maastricht* judgment to derive limits of this jurisprudence from a narrow interpretation of the national legal act by which the legislative bodies have agreed to the ratification of the Treaty.[57] But this attempt must fail, because the European Treaty has founded an independent organisation which follows its own inherent rules.

According to the modified dualistic theory dominant in German practice and scholarship, this legal act opens up the national legal order, similar to the English Community Act, in order to incorporate the Treaty as applicable law within the national territory without changing its content and character.[58] This incorporation – or, as it has been called in German theory "*Rechtsanwendungsbefehl*", that is, the order to apply the Treaty in the internal law – includes also the provisions of the Treaty which concern the competencies of the institutions to render legal acts and the application of these acts in the Member States. This has been expressly confirmed by the *Bundesverfassungsgericht* in its famous "*Solange II*"

55 On this problem see Schlaich, *Das Bundesverfassungsgericht,* 4th ed. (München, 1997), at pp. 355 et seq.

56 Everling, "Die Kontrolle des Gemeinschaftsgesetzgebers durch die Europäischen Gerichte", in *Freundesgabe für Jürgen Gündisch* (Köln, 1999) 89-111.

57 BVerfGE 89, 155 at 188.

58 This understanding has been basically influenced by a report of the German Society of International Public Law, presented by Partsch, "*Die Anwendung des Völkerrechts im innerstaatlichen Recht, Überprüfung der Transformationslehre*", *Berichte der Gesellschaft für Völkerrecht,* Heft 6 (Karlsruhe, 1964).

decision.[59] The assenting act of Parliament must, therefore, not be permanently present to approve anew every Community act adopted by the institutions.[60] Consequently, national courts even of the highest level are not entitled to control such acts. They must abstain from intervening in Community actions since their competencies are limited by the Treaty, as are those of all the other national institutions. They may only intervene if the practice of the Community and particularly the Court transgresses lastingly and intensively the limits of their competencies[61] or, to put it in the words of the Danish Supreme Court, that "*the extraordinary situation should arise that with the required certainty*" such a transgression can be established.[62]

This understanding of the national act assenting to the Treaty is crucial for the interpretation of the Treaty's provisions conferring competencies on the Community's institutions. It is common opinion since the beginning that the Community only disposes of the competencies which are attributed to it. This principle has been expressively confirmed by the Maastricht Treaty in Article 5 (ex 3b) EC and is binding also for the Court.[63] But it can only mean that the competencies must not be attributed to the Community in a global and unlimited way because the Community does not have the presumed overall-competence of a State. Given the steadily changing conditions of the modern world, it would be extremely unrealistic to demand that the Treaty which has been concluded forty years ago for an unlimited time should define the competencies so narrowly that their application can be foreseen for the future.[64] The Danish Supreme Court rejected such ideas in its *Maastricht* judgment and stated:

59 BVerfGE 73, 339 at 375.

60 Even this is demanded by the so-called "Bridge-Theory" invented by Judge Kirchhof to support the far-reaching theses of the *Maastricht* Judgment. According to this theory the Community Law is valid in the Member States only on behalf of the assenting act of Parliament, and this act is like a bridge over which the Community law is flowing in the national territory under the control of the *Bundesverfassungsgericht.* See Kirchhof, "Die Gewaltenbalance zwischen staatlichen und europäischen Organen", 49 JZ (1998) 965-974 at 966. Against this, Graf Vitzthum,Gemeinschaftsrecht und Verfassungsrecht – Rechtsvergleichende Aspekte", 49 JZ (1998) 161-170.

61 Corresponding limits were formulated by the so called *"Solange II"* decision from the *Bundesverfassungsgericht* with regard to fundamental rights, BVerfGE 73, 339 at 384.

62 Published in *Ugeskrift for Retsvæsen* (1998) 800; the English citations are taken from a translation arranged by the Danish Ministery of Justice. See Høegh, "The Danish Maastricht Judgement", 24 EL Rev. (1999) 80-92; Thomas, "Das *Maastricht*-Urteil des dänischen Obersten Gerichtshofs vom 6. April 1998", 58 ZaöRV (1998) 879-906.

63 Emiliou (*supra* note 26); Barents, "The Internal Market unlimited: Some Observations on the Legal Basis of Community Legislation", 30 CMLRev. (1993) 85-109; Dashwood, "The Limits of European Community Powers", 21 EL Rev. (1996) 113-128; Kraußer, *Das Prinzip begrenzter Ermächtigung im Gemeinschaftsrecht als Strukturprinzip des EWG-Vertrages* (Berlin, 1991).

64 So the *Bundesverfassungsgericht* in its *Maastricht* Judgment BVerfGE 89, 155 at 188.

> *"The fields of responsibility may be described in broad categories, and there is no requirement for the extent of the delegation of sovereignty to be stated so precisely that there is no room left for discretion or interpretation."*[65]

The Court of Justice has to interpret the provisions of the Treaty in such a way that the Community is able to fulfil the purposes for which the Member States as Treaty parties have founded it. Comparable to national constitutional courts the Court is, therefore, not limited to a narrow understanding of the global formulations of the provisions of the Treaty.

But the powers of the Community and also of the Court cannot be and are not unlimited. The limits of the fields transferred to the Community discussed above are also limits of the judge-made law of the Court. Criteria can only be taken from the rules indicated above as orientation for the formation of judge-made law. The general aims expressed in the preamble to the Treaty are decisive, as are its narrower definitions in the basic articles and special chapters, as well as general principles of law.

Thus the Court completes a precarious balancing-act. It must, in conformity with the principle of subsidiarity, contribute to the adequate distribution of tasks and competencies on the different levels of decision-making in the Community system. In the last instance the acceptance by the ensemble of citizens which are subject to the law is decisive, whether or not judge-made law has succeeded. This demands the acknowledgement that the judgments are emanations of a legitimated and qualified institution, which must be followed. The Court can further this approval by the proceedings which have been explained: Orientation on the aims and basic rules of the Treaty and on the general principles of law, ensuring of fundamental rights and the rule of law, granting of effective judicial protection and application of procedures traditionally used by judiciaries, judgments progressing step by step on the basis of precedents, but flexible to necessary corrections, and finally, alignment to the overall political development of the integration. This demands sensibility from the judges to the manifold political, economical and social conditions of the integration within the Member States.

VII Final Remarks

The problem of judge-made law finally leads to the questions of sense, structure, future and limits of the Community. This integrating compound of States and their peoples was founded after war, genocide and dictatorship, with the political mission to contribute to peace and freedom, internal and external security and economic and social welfare of the participating states and their peoples which were long-time enemies. Now the fact seems to become more and more important that States alone are not able to overcome the political, economic and social

65 See *supra* note 62.

difficulties of the modern world. Union and Community have, therefore, increasingly taken on the function of representing and protecting the common interests of the Member States and their people, even under the conditions of growing internationalisation and globalisation. This will also influence the position of the Court.

One of the most serious scruples, particularly in Germany, attached to the integration of the States in the Community, consists in the fear that their democratic orders, based on liberty, protection of fundamental rights and rule of law established after the war, might erode. But it must be conceded that this danger is not initially caused by the Community, but that it is the consequence of the changing conditions of life and society in an open, modern world. States are nowadays in a much weaker position when it comes to protecting the basic principles and the interests of their citizens in isolation. Consequently, it is understandable that the national courts are not able anymore to fully protect the constitutional orders and its citizens' fundamental rights. There are many reasons to believe that this task must in future more and more be secured on the supranational or even international level; this means by the Court of Justice as well as by special courts established on the basis of international law, such as those already founded for commercial disputes, sea conflicts, crimes and human rights.

It may, therefore, occur that the Court of Justice will in future gain even more importance for the stability of the Community and the Member States than is now recognised. This may in particular be the case if the Community will be enlarged, as envisaged, to up to 27 Member States. Consequently politicians, institutions, courts and lawyers all over Europe should be conscious of the need to give their support to the Court's difficult task of law-making.

4

THE THEORY OF INTERPRETATION AND THE COURT OF JUSTICE

Thijmen Koopmans

I INTRODUCTION

In an oft-quoted passage from his "Spirit of the laws", Montesquieu distinguishes three categories of judges. In a republic, he explains, well-defined laws govern the citizens' behaviour, and all judges have to do is to abide by the standards fixed by these laws. "Dans l'Etat républicain, il est de la nature de la constitution que les juges suivent la lettre de la loi." In the despotic State, however, there are no fixed laws; judges have to decide individual cases according to their personal views: "le juge est lui-même sa règle". There is, says Montesquieu, a third possibility, situated somewhere between these two positions: in monarchies, judges steer a middle course. "Dans les Etats monarchiques, il y a une loi; là où elle est précise le juge la suit; là où elle ne l'est pas, il en cherche l'esprit."[1]

Legal historians take the view, nowadays, that there is no clear link between judicial attitudes on the one hand, and the type of political authority on the other. Nevertheless, the distinction Montesquieu made between the three ways in which judges come to their decisions remains valid: analytically speaking, judges will either strictly follow the standards defined in the applicable laws, or just decide autonomously in accordance with their own feelings of justice, or look for an intermediate position. That intermediate position will imply that, in cases where many but not all imaginable situations are covered by laws, the judge will either merely apply the legal provisions in question, or try to interpret them ("il en cherche l'esprit").[2] In most legal systems which used to be founded on comprehensive codification, such as those on the European continent and in Latin America, this third attitude is probably the most commonly adopted. It also prevails in courts entrusted with judicial review of legislation, such as the federal constitutional court in Germany and the United States Supreme Court. These courts work on the basis of written constitutions, but such legal documents rarely have a high degree of precision. The question of judicial subservience or autonomy has thereby developed into a matter of degree rather than of principle. Debates on the limits of judicial autonomy may nevertheless turn into vehement dispute, as experience in the United States shows.

1 *De l'esprit des lois*, VI-3 (éd. l'Intégrale, Paris 1964, p. 557).

2 See G.J. Wiarda, *Drie typen van rechtsvinding* (4th ed. by T. Koopmans, Deventer, 1999), in particular ch. 1-5 and 13.1.

D. O'Keeffe (ed.), Liber Amicorum Slynn 45-58 (2000)

The situation in the United States is somewhat particular, as the U.S. Supreme Court has tended to give a large scope to rules, principles and values aimed at protecting individual liberties (equal protection, freedom of expression, due process of law, etc.), even if such a broad interpretation had far-reaching social consequences (racial integration, protection of radical campaigners, abortion, etc.).[3] Although this line of case law was initially hailed as an example of judicial creativity, most welcome after a period of relative inertia, criticisms grew stronger in the eighties. Some authors bluntly reproached the Supreme Court for assuming a political role, and upsetting the balance of power established by the Constitution.[4] Courts, the argument runs, should take the Constitution as it is, and as it has been made by its drafters; they should not try to make constitutional provisions better, or more palatable to the present generation. This school of thought often relies on what is called the "original understanding" or the "original intent" of the Constitution. The framers of the Constitution, they argue, knew exactly what they were doing, and there is no reason to improve their work; they were interested in power allocation, not in individual rights.[5] Courts should not use their powers of judicial review for transforming the Constitution rather than for upholding it.

It is not difficult to hold the idea of "original intent" up to gentle mockery. As Justice Jackson once observed, in one of his individual opinions, what the framers of the Constitution had in mind, or would have had in mind had they foreseen modern conditions, "must be divined from materials almost as enigmatic as the dream Joseph was called upon to interpret for Pharaoh".[6] And Professor Tribe recently said that a reconstruction of what the framers had in mind can yield little more than "a faded snapshot of a bygone age".[7] This is, of course, an acceptable way of carrying on a controversy, but it does not help to solve the problem. The problem is as Montesquieu had already defined it by the middle of the 18th century: how subservient, or how autonomous, should a judge be when he is trying to make sense of constitutional provisions? Just how much is he bound by the wording of the provision or the intention of the drafters – and how is he to decide if both the text and the intention are obscure?

From that point of view, the American debate is very characteristic. The original Constitution and its first ten amendments (the Bill of Rights) were devised and drafted by white gentlemen of Anglo-Saxon descent, living in rural and slave-holding communities – more akin to life in biblical times than to that

3 See Bernard Schwartz, *A history of the Supreme Court* (New York-Oxford, 1993), ch. 13 and 15; L. Lusky, *By what right?* (2nd ed., Charlottesville Va., 1978), ch. IX-XIV.

4 See, in particular, Robert H. Bork, *The tempting of America – the political seduction of the law* (New York-London, 1990), ch. 3-5.

5 Robert F. Nagel, *Constitutional cultures* (Berkeley Cal.-London, 1989), p. 64-65; Bork, *op.cit.* (note 4), ch. 7-8.

6 Justice Jackson, concurring, in *Youngstown Sheet and Tube Co.* v. *Sawyer* (steel seizure case), 343 US 579 (1952).

7 Laurence H. Tribe, in: Antonin Scalia, *A matter of interpretation – federal courts and the law* (Princeton N.J. 1997), p. 81.

in present-day America. Equal protection simply can not retain the same meaning after the abolition of slavery and after the massive immigration waves that brought people from all over the world to the United States. As the European Court of Human Rights once explicitly said, in a case on the legal position of illegitimate children, human rights "must be interpreted in the light of present-day conditions", with the result that distinctions once regarded as permissible and normal in many countries must now be considered as discriminatory.[8] That is very much the attitude the American Supreme Court adopted in its case law on equal protection, from the moment it held that the Constitution forbids separate educational facilities for black and white children.[9]

Modern critics of judicial freedom in interpreting constitutional provisions take a slightly different stand. They abandon the idea of "original intent" but they emphasize that the overriding duty of judges is to apply a legal provision, not to change its meaning. This is the attitude for which Justice Scalia has coined the term "textualism".[10] "Congress can enact foolish statutes as well as wise ones, and it is not for the courts to decide which is which and rewrite the former", he says; it would be contrary to democratic theory that unelected judges decide what the law ought to mean, as its meaning should be quite simply founded on the text of the relevant provisions.[11] Scalia recognizes that constitutional interpretation raises a distinctive problem, "not because special principles of interpretation apply, but because the usual principles are being applied to an unusual text." There may be a necessity to give old words and phrases of the Constitution an expansive rather than a narrow meaning, but "not an interpretation that the language will not bear".[12] In Montesquieu's terminology: according to Scalia, the U.S. Supreme Court considers too much that it is "lui-même sa règle" and too little that its main task is to follow "la lettre de la loi".

II METHODS OF INTERPRETATION

In continental Europe, the introduction of comprehensive codes of law seemed to stifle the debate on methods of interpretation in the early 19th century. Most authors assumed that the provisions of the codes were well made and that they governed any legal question which might arise. In the unlikely event that these provisions would not give a direct answer to that question, judges could just consult the history of the relevant parts of the code in order to find the intention of the drafters. Detailed commentaries on the Code Napoléon, by French and

8 ECHR 13 June 1979, *Marckx* v. *Belgium*, Series A vol. 31.
9 *Brown* v. *Board of Education of Topeka*, 347 US 483 (1954).
10 Antonin Scalia, *op.cit.* (note 7), p. 23.
11 *Op.cit.* pp. 20 and 22.
12 *Op.cit.* p. 37. See also Leonard W. Levy, *Constitutional opinions – aspects of the Bill of Rights* (New York-Oxford, 1986), ch. 12.

Belgian authors,[13] concerned text and history of individual provisions; in a way, these books are dealing with grammar and with history rather than with the solution of legal problems. The philosophy of these authors was thus summarized by one of them: "Respect à la loi, fût-elle absurde."[14]

This simplistic attitude could not last when, in the final decades of the 19th century, processes of urbanization and industrialization heralded a new era, characterized by entirely new legal problems, particularly in the fields of contract and tort. The problem was how to apply the old codes to new problems, such as industrial conflict, traffic accidents, protection of new technology, mass production and consumption, etc. Legislative activities did not keep up with changes in society, partially – but not exclusively – because politics in the late 19th century were more interested in completely different issues: for example the consolidation of the Republic in France, including the relationship with the Church and the Dreyfus affair.[15] Moreover, the changes of society were part of a very slow evolution. Whatever the reason, lawyers on the European continent began to turn away from doctrines which had been considered as authoritative for nearly the entire 19th century; they discovered new methods of interpretation.

In France, the spokesman of the new generation of lawyers was Gény. He embodied the reaction of legal theory against the excessive legalism of the post-codification era. His views can be briefly summarized as follows.[16] It is impossible to determine the meaning of a given legal provision without considering its relationship to other legal provisions. What judges should do is not just apply an individual legal provision, but the law, i.e. the legal system in general. The purpose of that system is to regulate, together with religious and moral norms, human conduct in society. When applying a given legal rule, one can not disregard the position of that rule in the global context of the applicable norms, and the impact these norms will have on human conduct in society. The interpretation of the rule should, therefore, not only be guided by textual and historical arguments: elements of system and of purpose will have to come into play. These elements can be found by consulting tradition, case law and literature, and by rethinking the cohesion of the different chapters of the legal system.

When the legal system is gradually changing, because of the introduction of new legal rules, or because of the newness of problems to be solved, such a change will necessarily affect the interpretation of existing legal provisions. Similar arguments govern the interpretation of new legal provisions. Their meaning is not only determined by their wording and by the intention of the legislature, since they don't operate in a vacuum: there is a pre-existing legal

13 For example Demolombe and Laurent.

14 Laurent, in 1882 (*Avant-projet de révision du Code civil*, I p. 183).

15 See Michel Winock, *La fièvre hexagonale – les grandes crises politiques 1871-1968* (Paris, 1986), ch. 2-4.

16 See F. Gény, *Méthode d'interprétation et sources en droit privé positif* (1899); *Science et technique en droit privé positif* (1913).

system in which new provisions will have to find their place, and there is also a social order which will be influenced by the new provisions and by their relationship with the existing rules. In Gény's opinion, lawyers ultimately use their techniques in order to construct their materials in such a way as to correspond to the needs of social life.[17]

The position of Gény in the evolution of legal thinking is extremely interesting. On the one hand, he can be considered as one of the founders of the sociological movement in law, which includes, amongst others, the American realist school and Max Weber's sociology of law.[18] On the other hand, his systematic approach had a profound influence on the theory of interpretation on the European continent. It is the latter aspect which makes his thinking relevant for reflections on problems of interpretation in general. The Swiss Civil code, adopted in 1907, shows his influence in its famous opening article on the task of the judge in applying and interpreting code provisions.[19]

Authors influenced by Gény have elaborated the concept of "legal system". One interesting variation considers the legal system as an "open system". Deciding a case cannot merely consist of subsuming certain facts under a preexisting rule of law, the proponents of this vision argue; the decision itself will add to the interpretation of the rule to be applied, and may thus help to define its meaning. The legal system is never finished, as the reality for which it has been made is in a process of continuous flux. Although the system is the basis for every new decision, the new decision, in its turn, adds something to the system. This implies that the legal system has a dynamic character, even if no new legislation is introduced.[20]

In this view, the legal system can be compared to an unfinished mosaic: every new stone (legislative rule, judicial decision, authoritative opinion) must fit in the existing pattern; but at the same time, it adds to this pattern and develops it. In this image, one has to assume that the existing pattern never entirely controls future developments: a succession of new stones may take an unexpected turn.[21]

Later developments of legal doctrine brought new elements to the debate on interpretation. The most important evolution occurred in the post-war years, es-

---

17 See Wolfgang Friedmann, *Legal theory* (5th ed., New York 1967), p. 328-332.

18 See Alan Hunt, *The sociological movement in law* (London-Basingstoke, 1978), ch. 1-3 and 5.

19 "La loi régit toutes les matières auxquelles se rapportent la lettre ou l'esprit de l'une de ses dispositions. A défaut d'une disposition légale applicable, le juge prononce selon le droit coutumier et, à défaut d'une coutume, selon les règles qu'il établirait s'il avait à faire acte de législateur. Il s'inspire des solutions consacrées par la doctrine et la jurisprudence."

20 Paul Scholten, *Algemeen deel van Asser's Handleiding tot de beoefening van het Nederlands burgerlijk recht* (3rd ed. 1974), §17. Scholten relies in particular on Gény and Horvath.

21 I take this image from a conversation I once had with my late friend and colleague Federico Mancini.

pecially after 1950. A constitutional dimension was added to the debate. This development was particularly due to the introduction of judicial review of legislation on the European continent: first in Germany and Italy, later in Spain, Portugal, Greece, Belgium and, to a certain extent, France. The importance of this evolution has been gradually growing since the early fifties, because of the growing emphasis on human rights and fundamental freedoms, first in legal doctrine, later also in case law, legislation and political debates (in that order). In Germany, the combination of judicial review of legislation, the rediscovery of human rights and the vague nature of important constitutional norms and concepts in the German Basic Law gave a value-oriented impetus to legal thinking and to legal practice. Constitutional concepts such as "Rechtsstaat" (the State governed by the rule of law) were seen as repositories of important constitutional values, for example legal certainty. Over the years, the federal constitutional court slowly elaborated sets of rules it saw embodied in the constitutional values indicated by the individual provisions of the Basic Law.[22] This same attitude was gradually adopted by other German courts, in particular by the civil and criminal courts. As a result, German law as applied by the courts is in many important respects inspired by values rather than by legal provisions.

A similar trend can be discovered in the case law of courts of other States on the European continent. The Constitutional Council of France, which exercises a control of constitutionality of legislation before it is promulgated, also finds much of its inspiration in values embodied in the Constitution. In its famous judgment on the nationalizations of the first Mitterrand years, the Council founded its reasoning in particular on the protection of "la propriété" as one of the "droits naturels et imprescriptibles de l'homme" according to the "Déclaration des droits de l'homme et du citoyen" of 1789, to which the preamble of the Constitution refers. As the Constitution itself recognises the possibility of nationalization, the court considered it should have to strike the balance itself between these two competing ideas.[23]

A further example is the case law of the European Court of Human Rights. The court considers that the requirement of "fair trial", expressed by Article 6 of the European Convention, embodies a certain number of standards to be respected in civil and criminal proceedings. One of these standards is the concept of "equality of arms" between the parties, and also between the prosecution and the suspect; this concept, in its turn, gives rise to detailed rules on problems such as the possibility of hearing anonymous witnesses, for example in drugs cases.[24] Here also, the interpretation of the Convention is highly value-oriented.

Summarizing, one could perhaps say that in continental Europe, two layers of conceptions on interpretation have gradually covered the basis of textualism of earlier years: first a system- and purpose-oriented approach, permitting the

---

22 See, for example, Maunz-Zippelius, *Deutsches Staatsrecht* (29th ed., Munich, 1994), § 23-27.

23 Conseil constitutionnel 16 Jan. 1982, loi de nationalisation, Rec. 18.

24 ECHR 20 November 1989, *Kostovski*, Series A vol. 166.

courts to cope with new problems of society, later also a vision based on values to be upheld by the judiciary.

III THE EUROPEAN LEGAL SYSTEM

The construction of the initial EEC Treaty was rather unusual. The Treaty gave detailed rules on some subjects, like the customs union, competition law, and the way of establishing a common agricultural policy. On other matters of some importance, it had no express provisions: it was, for example, silent on the relationship between Community rules and national law, on sources of Community law and on the protection of fundamental rights. For such matters, a textualist approach was just impracticable. At the same time, the Treaty provisions implied that the Community had its own system of law: by describing the task of the Court of Justice as ensuring that "the law is observed", by specifying grounds for annulment which go beyond mere violation of Treaty rules, and by referring – true, for a more or less technical matter – to "the general principles common to the laws of the Member States".[25]

The Treaty thus recognised that such common principles do exist, and that they can be considered as a source of European Community law. It is that idea which has been generalized in the Court's case law. Already in 1957, in a staff case, the Court adopted such a line. The point in issue was whether an administrative decision which was vitiated by illegality could be revoked retroactively, and the Court said: "This is a problem of administrative law well known in the case law and the literature of all Member States" (the old Six, at the time) "but not covered by any provision of the Treaty" (the old Coal and Steel Treaty). "Since the Court can not commit a denial of justice, it is obliged to resolve the problem by looking for inspiration to the rules recognised by legislation and practice in the Member States."[26] This judgment turned out to be the prelude to a steadily growing case law in which principles of law common to the legal systems of the Member States were discovered and further developed. Legal principles such as the principle of proportionality and the protection of legitimate expectations have thus been elaborated by the Court of Justice.

A closer look at this case law shows that, in the conception of the Court, general principles of law have a double role to play. On the one hand, they contribute to shaping the law of the Community: this law would, in a way, be incomplete without, for example, the principle of proportionality. In many judgments, the Court seems to assume it cannot solve a certain legal problem without relying on a general principle of law, because the Treaty reveals a vacuum.[27] On the other hand, however, the definition of a general principle of law must fit in the system of law as it has been fixed by the treaties and developed by the Court.

25 Art. 164, 173 and 215 of the initial EEC Treaty (now Art. 220, 230 and 288 EC Treaty).
26 Joined Cases 7/56 and 3-7/57, *Algera* [1957-58] ECR 55.
27 An early case is Case 48/59, *Lachmüller* [1960] ECR 474.

A clear example of this trend is the way the Court defined a general principle of confidentiality between lawyer and client.[28] The definition is founded on principles common to the legal systems of the Member States, but its scope is linked to the protection of the rights of the defence ("droits de la défense") recognised as a general principle in the Court's earlier case law. To this systematic argument, the Court adds an element of purpose, by considering that it is the very characteristic of the advocate's work to give independent legal advice to anybody who may be in need of it; the essential justification of the confidentiality is, therefore, that everybody should feel free to turn to an advocate for assistance, without any fear of future consequences.

A similar combination of considerations based on system and on purpose can be found in other chapters of the Court's case law. The Court, for example, also relies on principles underlying the provisions of the Treaty. It takes the detailed rules on the abolition of customs duties and charges of equivalent effect, and of quantitative restrictions and measures of equivalent effect, in intra-Community trade, as expressing the requirement of free movement of goods as stipulated in the definition of tasks and activities of the European Community in the opening articles of the Treaty. On the basis of this concept, it then slowly develops standards to be applied to the legality of obstacles to intra-Community trade. The recognition rule laid down in the famous *Cassis de Dijon* judgment is, for example, directly founded on the concept of free movement of goods.[29] The entire case law on free movement of goods is predominantly purpose-oriented: the standards to be developed should contribute to the realization of the common market the Treaty intends to establish.

One of the interesting characteristics of the EC Treaty (and of its predecessor, the EEC Treaty) is its hierarchy of norms. Technical rules, for example on the right of workers to accept offers of employment in other Member States, are preceded by the definition of the aim to be achieved – in this case: free movement of workers. This aim is defined as one of the conditions for the establishment of the common market, which, in its turn, is considered as a means to further reaching political goals fixed by the preamble and the opening articles of the Treaty. The text of the Treaty itself has thus a purpose-oriented nature, and it facilitates interpretations linked to the objectives of the European enterprise. In its early case law, the Court already linked the solution of technical problems, for example, on social security of migrant workers, to the essential features of the common market.[30] The same approach has continued to characterize the Court's way of reasoning.[31]

A further example can be found in the Court's case law on the relationship between free movement of goods and the protection of rights of intellectual property. After a somewhat insecure start, it slowly developed into a set of well-

28 Case 155/79, *A.M.& S. v. Commission* [1982] ECR 1575.
29 Case 120/78, *Rewe ("Cassis de Dijon")* [1979] ECR 649.
30 Case 75/63, *Unger v. DETAM* [1964] ECR 184.
31 Example: Case C-320/91, *Corbeau* [1993] ECR I-2533.

defined standards founded on the position of these rights in the system of rules applicable to free movement of goods.[32]

IV The Court's methods

One of the points to be clarified is in how far the Court's methods are based on a textualist view. There is little doubt that, as a general rule, the Court's judgments are more purpose- and system-oriented than founded on the exact wording of the legal provisions to be applied. Two comments are, however, in order.

Firstly, for regulations and directives which can more or less be isolated from the establishment and the working of the common market in general, such as the common customs tariff or technical measures on conservation of fish stocks, the Court is usually inclined to stick to the texts without any reference to further reaching aims.[33] This is sometimes forgotten, as this part of the Court's case law is less important for the general orientation of the evolution of European Community law. The same attitude prevails with regard to the interpretation of the Brussels Convention on jurisdiction of courts and enforcement of judgments in civil and commercial matters (the judgments Convention). This Convention is, in a way, completely dissociated from the Community system, and its provisions are not easily comparable to those of the EC Treaty. The Court usually follows the wording of the Convention's provisions without much ado, even if the result is unsatisfactory.[34] Of course, the Brussels Convention is a collection of individual rules rather than a coherent set of provisions based on certain principles.

Secondly, in typical EC cases the Court sometimes recognizes that its purpose-oriented method of interpretation finds its limits in the clear words of Treaty provisions. An example can be found in the evolution of case law on direct effect of provisions of EC directives. In the early days, it looked as if it implied the rule that, once a provision of a directive was clear and unconditional, it established a right for a person (citizen or business corporation) which could be relied on in litigation before his national courts. Later judgments, however, made it clear that individuals and corporations can only invoke directly such provisions in their dealings with public authorities. Directives, said the Court, impose duties on these authorities, not on private persons.[35] The result was that female employees could rely on the equal treatment directive in conflicts with their employer if he happened to be the State, or, more generally, a public body, but not in litigation with a private firm. That result was not very satisfactory, and

---

32 See, for example, Case 19/84, *Pharmon* [1985] ECR 2281; Case C-10/89, *Hag II* [1990] ECR I-3711.

33 Example: Case 5/78, *Milchfutter* [1978] ECR 1597.

34 Example: Case 241/83, *Rösler v. Rottwinkel* [1985] ECR 99.

35 Case 152/84, *Marshall I* [1986] ECR 723.

it has been severely criticized in legal literature.[36] The Court, however, did not abandon its view; when it was asked to reconsider its position, its reply was a circumstantial justification of its earlier case law.[37] Quite interestingly, the grounds mentioned by the Court rely heavily on the text of the Treaty: in defining a directive, the Treaty provides that the directive is "addressed to" a Member State, not to individual persons (then Art. 189, now Art. 249). In the Court's view, the consequence is that the State, and its institutions and organs, can not oppose lack of implementation of the directive to individuals who seek to rely on the directive's provisions; but the directive can not, by itself and without being put into effect by rules of national law, impose obligations on private individuals or corporations.

A further proviso should be added. The obligation to follow the applicable texts seems less compelling to the Court when the simple fact of applying these texts would counteract the protection of a right considered as fundamental. In such a case, even a Treaty text can not always form an obstacle to a judicial strategy aimed at upholding fundamental rights. To that degree, the value-oriented approach prevails. When the Court found that, according to the Treaty text, actions for annulment by the European Parliament were inadmissible even if the Parliament alleged that one of its prerogatives under the Treaty had been violated by the Council in the final decision, the judgment formulated an exception to the Treaty rule for this particular situation.[38] In other words: the importance of access to justice was more compelling than the obedience to a Treaty rule. At the next Treaty revision, however, the text of the Treaty was adapted to the Court's judgment.[39]

A second point of analysis is the concept of purpose. National courts may also develop a purpose-oriented method of interpretation but, for them, purposes to be referred to normally concern objectives to be accomplished by a certain piece of legislation, or by a certain legal arrangement: the purpose of bankruptcy, the end to be attained by a statute amending an earlier statute on income tax, or on consumer protection. The Court of Justice considers wider aims: free movement of persons, goods and capital in the Community, the completion of the common market, sometimes even the objectives of the European integration process. If the Court relies on less ambitious aims, it will often recall that these aims must be viewed in the perspective of wider considerations.[40] This way of interpreting the Treaty may have important legal consequences. The duty of mutual collaboration between the Community institutions and those of the Member States is founded, by the Court, on a Treaty provision which only mentions the duty of Member States to help the Community in realizing the aims of the Treaty (now Art.10). In the light of these aims, the Court held that this provi-

36 Example: Sacha Prechal, *Directives in European Community law* (Oxford, 1995), ch. 11.

37 Case C-91/92, *Faccini Dori* [1994] ECR I-3325.

38 Case C-70/88, *European Parliament v. Council* ("Chernobyl") [1990] ECR I-2041.

39 Art. 173, par.3, EC Teaty as amended by the Maastricht Treaty (now Art. 230).

40 Example: Cases C-92 and 326/92, *Phil Collins* [1993] ECR I-5145.

sion was only an expression of the general idea that Member State governments and Community institutions should mutually help each other and refrain from activities which might hinder the other's efforts.[41]

Two explanations can be given for this difference between the Court's method and that of national courts. The first explanation has a purely legal character: the EC Treaty is not as detailed and complete as the French Civil Code, the German Basic Law or the British Carriage of Goods by Sea Act. The Treaty, although occasionally very precise, leaves many important problems unresolved. The second explanation is more political. The Court of Justice occasionally appears to be worried about the course of events in the Community: will the entire fisheries policy end in disaster because one Member State refuses to collaborate? Will the process of harmonization of national laws ultimately fail because one or two Member States are not able or willing to implement Community directives?[42] Normally, such anxieties are absent in the considerations of national courts. Member States are more sturdily built than the European Union. The French Kingdom had already existed for more than eight hundred years when the Republic was established in the late 18th century. And the English common law started its evolution in what English courts call "time immemorial", specifically located in the late 12th century. There is a cohesion in such States which is based on many political, legal and cultural elements and which, so far, finds no parallel in the European Union.

The third problem to be taken into consideration is the relationship between the legal systems of the Member States and the developing common system of the European Union. In the Court's view, this relationship is essentially based on the idea of mutual permeability, rather than on a sharp antithesis. National legal systems provide the building blocks of Community law, by revealing common solutions to problems not explicitly regulated by Treaty rules, and by having common principles underlying their legislation and case law.[43] A similar attitude prevails in matters of sanctions to be applied to violation of Community rules. In many instances, these sanctions are to be imposed on the basis of national rules of criminal law, procedural law or tort law; but the sanctions are influenced by the fact that they concern Community rules. These rules presuppose, for example, that the sanctions to be applied are effective and can actually serve as a deterrent.[44] Community law and national law are more or less considered as belonging to one system consisting of different (and differing) sub-systems. Therefore, Community rules on substantive law and national procedural rules should have a complementary character, and should be adjusted to each other.

That conception also manifests itself in matters of admissibility. According to the Treaty, actions for annulment of regulations can only be brought by

41 See Case C-2/88-Imm., *Zwartveld* [1990] ECR I-3365 and I-4405.

42 See Case 804/79, *Commission v. United Kingdom* ("conservation measures") [1981] ECR 1045; Cases C-6 and 9/90, *Francovich and Bonifaci* [1991] ECR I-5357.

43 See, respectively, *Algera* and *A.M.&S.* (notes 26 and 28).

44 See Case 14/83, *Von Colson* [1984] ECR 1891.

Member State governments and Community institutions, not by private individuals or business corporations (unless the regulation must in fact be considered as an individual decision). The Court does not consider this rule as an infringement of the individual's right of access to justice, because the right to attack the implementation of the regulation before the national courts can always be exercised, so that the legality of the regulation itself can always be challenged. Most commentators of the Court's case law feel that the Court is more lenient in dumping cases, in particular for foreign producers and exporters, who cannot apply to their national courts for challenging the validity of the regulation.[45] The Court's view appears, therefore, to assume a coherence between national and Community rights of action for individuals and corporations.

A fourth problem which should be mentioned is the position of customary law. In the legal systems based on codification, the debate on a larger degree of autonomy of the judge vis-à-vis code provisions had its origin in these provisions' contradictory position in relation to customary law. As the theory of interpretation was elaborated with reference to problems of private law, custom was regarded as a most important source of law to be recognised in the new legal climate. If texts were unclear, or completely lacking, courts should rely on customary law. The famous Article 1 Swiss Civil Code regards custom as the first source of law to be considered when the provisions of the Code are unclear.[46] From this point of view, there is a very sharp distinction between national methods of interpretation and the methods of the Court of Justice. The Court is indeed extremely careful in referring to customary law and, more generally, reluctant to recognise custom as a source of law. It never accepted the binding force of the so-called Agreement of Luxemburg of 1966, whether or not this agreement on decision-making in the Council had in fact resulted in a decision-making practice in conformity with it. Similarly, the Court interpreted the legal powers of the European Parliament on the basis of the applicable Treaty rules, and not in the light of the political practice of the day.

More often than not, the Court disregards practice. National courts are normally very much inclined to look to practice for inspiration, for example in commercial matters. The issues, however, are not comparable. Contract law is meant to provide the legal framework for the freedom of the parties to organize their mutual relations; the intentions of the parties, their expectations and the customs they usually observe when dealing with each other, are part of their engagement. In the Community, customs normally develop in institutional matters; however, institutional provisions have the very aim of establishing a division of tasks and responsibilities which can not be modified by the institutions themselves. The Court expresses this idea by referring to "the institutional balance" willed by the Treaty and not to be disturbed by one of the Community institutions or by individual Member States. Attempts by the Council to push back the

45 This view is based on a line of case law starting with Joined Cases 239 and 275/82, *Allied Corporation* [1984] ECR 1005.

46 See note 19, *supra*.

role of the European Parliament foundered on this ground.[47] On that point, the Court's attitude is inspired by textualism rather than by practical considerations.

V CONCLUSIONS

So much is clear from the foregoing considerations, that the methods of the Court of Justice and those usually applied by national courts have many things in common. It is erroneous to think that national judges would faithfully follow "the texts" and that the Court of Justice would not care very much about the wording of the applicable provisions.[48] System- and purpose-oriented methods of interpretation characterize national as well as Community law. It is true that the limits within which courts feel free to adopt those methods are not always the same. For national courts, these limits may be very tight in matters of family law or of criminal law; but they will be relatively wide in tort cases where, traditionally, judge-made law leads legal evolution.[49] For the Court of Justice, the boundary between these two areas takes a completely different course. Textualism governs institutional issues, whereas a purpose-oriented approach distinguishes the Court's decisions regarding the rights of individuals under Community law and the free movement of goods and persons.

Other parallels can be found. The value-oriented method of interpretation, so important in German law and in the case law of the European Court of Human Rights, is also characteristic of the judgments of the Court of Justice on matters touching human rights and fundamental freedoms. The Court's case law on access to justice bears witness to that.[50]

Comparisons are, however, complicated by the fact that the Court of Justice is charged with a great many roles, which can not always be performed by national courts. The Court of Justice is an administrative court (for example when dealing with actions for annulment) as well as a constitutional court (for example when it decides that the European Parliament can bring actions for annulment in certain cases); it deals with private law matters when interpreting the Brussels Judgments Convention. Sometimes, it acts typically as an international court: in dumping cases, and when it has to decide in conflicts between Member States.[51]

---

47 Case 138/79, *Roquette* [1980] ECR 3333; case C-300/89, *Commission v. Council* ("titanium dioxide") [1991] ECR I-2867.

48 See T.C. Hartley, *The foundations of European Community law* (4th ed., Oxford, 1998), ch. 2.

49 See Tony Weir, "International tendencies in the law of liability", Aktuelle juristische Praxis 4 (1996); J. Spier (ed.), *The limits of liability* (Deventer, 1996).

50 Case 222/84, *Johnston v. Chief constable of the Royal Ulster Constabulary* [1986] ECR 1651; Case 222/86, *Heylens* [1987] ECR 4097.

51 See Art. 227 EC Treaty (ex 170). One of the rare examples is Case 141/78, *France v. United Kingdom* ("sea fishery") [1979] ECR 2923.

A further complication is that national discussions on methods of interpretation are normally conducted in terms of the respective powers of the legislature and the judiciary. The European Union does not have a "sovereign Parliament" or a "pouvoir législatif" in the true sense of the word. Secondary legislation is submitted to judicial review, and the decision making mechanism is unwieldy and incredibly complicated. National courts may feel, sometimes, that the solution of a given legal problem can better be left to the legislative bodies; the Court of Justice, on the contrary, will be aware that lack of judicial interference may very well mean that nothing will happen at all. There is no regular interplay between executive, legislative and judicial power such as often exists at the national level.

VI Epilogue

I come to the end of my reflections. Two considerations should be added.

First, I picked out the subject of this contribution because I had been involved in academic debates on the theory of interpretation after having been a member of the Court of Justice for a couple of years. I felt that it should be possible to combine these two forms of experience, but I must confess that I may have overestimated my talents. The subject turned out to be considerably more unmanageable than I initially thought. This little essay may help, though, to put the debate on a more realistic footing than it has often enjoyed these last years.

Secondly, when writing this essay I became more and more aware that I view problems of interpretation against a continental-European background. Readers trained in the common law of England may have some difficulty in grasping the true nature of the problems which have been discussed. When compared to their Dutch, French or German colleagues, they are used to a more limited role of statute law and, consequently, to a more important task for the courts in helping to shape legal evolution, in particular in some areas of the law like contract law. However, they are also used to a legislative system in which Parliament has the final say (at least in theory), without any impediment arising out of the Constitution, or the European Convention of Human Rights, or general principles of law. Under the common law of England, judges are, therefore, on the one hand more powerful but, on the other hand, more timid than their colleagues on the European continent. The second distinction is as important as the first, although it is normally not mentioned in manuals on comparative law.[52]

In spite of these difficulties, I preferred to write my little essay as planned. I was comforted in that decision by the certainty that my friend Gordon Slynn, to whom the essay is dedicated, will be able to consider my subject from a common law as well as from a continental-European point of view, and perhaps even from a third point of view which I have not yet discovered myself.

52 Example: Peter de Cruz, *A modern approach to comparative law* (Deventer-Boston, 1993), ch. 4.2.

5

THE CONTRIBUTION OF THE COURT OF JUSTICE TO THE PROTECTION OF THE "FEDERAL BALANCE" IN THE EUROPEAN COMMUNITY

Jean Mischo

INTRODUCTION

The European Union or, within its framework, the European Community is, of course, not a federal State.

The three Communities have nevertheless been organised according to what Professor Pescatore has called "the federal method" in the sense that certain major tasks have been concentrated at a central level.[1]

Since the Court of Justice has been entrusted under Article 220 EC (formerly Article 164) with the mission to ensure that, in the application of the Treaty, the law is observed, it also has to make sure that Member States fully respect the competences of the Community and that the Community does not infringe upon the powers of the Member States.

Admittedly, the Treaty establishing the European Community contains only one provision which expressly entrusts the Court of Justice with the mission to decide on questions of competence. It is Article 230 (formerly Article 173), which provides that actions for annulment can be brought against an act of an institution or of the European Central Bank on grounds of lack of competence.

But Article 226 (formerly Article 169) enables the Commission to bring actions against the Member States for failure to fulfill their obligations, and these may lead the Court to conclude that a Member State has infringed upon the competences of the Community.

Furthermore, within the framework of references for a preliminary ruling pursuant to Article 234 (formerly Article 177) the Court frequently has the opportunity to clarify the respective competences of the Community and the Member States, at the request of a national court or tribunal.

Finally Article 300 (6) (formerly Article 228) provides that the Council, the Commission or a Member State may obtain the opinion of the Court of Justice as to

1 P. Pescatore, "La constitution, son contenu et son utilité", (1992) *Zeitschrift für schweizerisches Recht*, (Helbing & Lichtenhahn) Neue Folge, Band 111, 41.

D. O'Keeffe (ed.), Liber Amicorum Slynn 59-72 (2000)

whether an agreement is compatible with the Treaty. This Article has led to a jurisprudence which is essentially concerned with competence questions.

I shall examine the manner in which the Court has dealt with questions of competence under these different procedures.[2] Lord Slynn of Hadley has certainly had, on many occasions, to deal with the problem of "*ultra vires*", in his former capacities as Advocate General and subsequently as judge at the Court of Justice of the European Communities, as well as in his present capacity of Member of the highest judicial body of the United Kingdom.

I therefore hope that he will find this overview of the case law of the European Court of some interest and I take great pleasure in dedicating it to an esteemed colleague and friend alongside whom I was privileged to work at the Court.

I The Protection of the Federal Balance Within the Framework of the Actions for Annulment of an Act of an Institution (Article 230 EC, Formerly 173)

Annulment may be requested, under Article 230 EC, of an act of the Council, of the Commission or of the Parliament. These three types of cases will be examined in succession. I am, of course, aware that the Court could also, in the framework of a preliminary ruling (Article 234 EC, formerly Article 177) find an act of an institution invalid on the grounds of incompetence of that institution. However, to my knowledge, this has never happened.

A Actions brought against the Council on grounds of lack of competence

Among all the judgments rendered by the Court since the entry into force of the Treaty establishing the European Economic Community, I have found only two concerning actions brought by *Member States* against the Council in the framework of which these States expressly contended that the action undertaken by the Council could not be founded on a competence attributed by the treaty to the Community.

The first of these judgments, issued on 13 July 1995[3] concerned a complaint by Spain (which was supported by Greece), against the Council (supported by France and the Commission). Spain requested the annulment of Regulation (EEC) n° 1768/92 of the Council of 18 June 1992 concerning the creation of a supplementary protection certificate for medicinal products. This regulation had been adopted on the basis of Article 100 A (now Article 95) of the Treaty.

---

2 Lack of space prevents me from dealing with the three cases in which the principle of subsidiarity (Art. 5, formerly Art. 3 b) played a certain role, although a very limited one. Suffice it to say that the Court has not so far defined with any precision the scope of this principle.

3 Case C-350/92, *Spain v. Council,* [1995] ECR I-1985.

This certificate is intended to provide a medicinal product with a protection identical to that given by patents, over and above the legal validity of a patent which it has obtained. It serves the purpose of creating a compensation for the fact that the period which elapses between the submission of the request for a patent for a new medicinal product, and the approval of the introduction of this medicinal product can be relatively long. Thus the duration of the actual protection given by the patent can be reduced to a duration which is insufficient to cover the investment put into the research needed to create the product.

Spain submitted that Article 222 of the EC Treaty (now Article 259), according to which the "Treaty shall in no way prejudice the rules in Member States governing the system of property ownership", and Article 36 (now Article 30), which refers among other things to restrictions of trade justified on grounds of the protection of industrial and commercial property, reserved to the national legislation the right to regulate the substance of patent law and excluded any action by the Community in this field.

The Court of Justice expressly rejected this thesis. It also considered that by instituting the "supplementary certificate of protection", the Council had aimed to prevent a heterogeneous development of national legislations leading to new disparities which could have resulted in the obstruction of the free trade in medicines within the Community and thus directly to impair the establishment and functioning of the internal market. It therefore reached the conclusion that the Council had legitimately adopted the regulation on the basis of Article 100 A, acting by a qualified majority.

The second case in which the lack of competence of the Council was relied upon was case C-268/94,[4] brought by Portugal (supported by Greece), against the Council (supported by Denmark, the United Kingdom and the Commission). The complaint was directed against the Council decision approving the conclusion of the cooperation agreement between the EC and the Republic of India on partnership and development.

This decision had been adopted on the basis of Article 113 (common commercial policy) (now Article 130) and 130 y (development cooperation) in connection with Article 228 (now Article 300) paragraph 2, first sentence and paragraph 3, subparagraph 1 of the Treaty.

Portugal maintained that some of the provisions of the agreement should have been adopted according to the procedure laid down in Article 235 (now Article 308), and that the provisions relating to intellectual property and the fight against drugs concerned areas for which the Member States had retained exclusive jurisdiction. Therefore a "mixed agreement" would have had to be negotiated. But the Court of Justice held that all the provisions of the agreement had validly been adopted on the basis of Article 130 y (now Article 181). It explained that the agreement only determined the areas in which the contracting parties undertook to

4 Case C-268/94, *Portugal v. Council*, [1996] ECR I-6177.

cooperate, without settling the concrete modalities of the cooperation in each of these areas.

Thus, despite the fact that the Court has admitted in Case 166/78[5] that a Member State can even request the annulment of an act in favour of which it had voted in the Council, there are only two cases in which Member States have explicitly challenged the competence of the Council. This, nevertheless, is not astonishing, since the Council consists of representatives of the Member States who are thus well placed to see to it that the Council does not exceed the powers devolved upon the Community.

Besides these two judgments there are, of course, numerous cases brought by Member States (or by the European Parliament) against the Council in which they did not question the competence of the Community as such, but the legal basis on which the Council had relied in adopting a legal instrument.[6]

In nearly all these cases, the legal basis which had been relied upon permitted the adoption of the act by a qualified majority (e.g. Articles 7, 43 or 113 as they then were), while the Member State claimed that the Council should have selected another legal basis such as Article 100 (now Article 94) or Article 235 which provide for unanimity.

One may assume that in these cases the Member States saw no possibility of challenging in principle the competence of the Council, but that they wanted, by being able to use the lever of the right of veto after having obtained the annulment of the act, to initiate new discussions as a result of which certain provisions of the act would be redrafted.[7]

In many of these cases, the Court gave a wide interpretation to the legal basis which attributed a specific competence to the Community and which had been relied upon by the Council, and declared that recourse to Article 100 or 235 was not justified.

Under this heading of actions introduced under Article 173, I would also like to recall, in passing, that in certain cases the Commission asked the Court to annul an act of the Council, not because the Council had acted "ultra vires", but because the Commission felt that the Council had based itself upon too narrow an interpretation of the competence of the Community.

This was the case in the judgment concerning the European agreement concerning the work of crews of vehicles engaged in international road transport (best known by its French acronym *AETR*[8]). Another example of this type was the judg-

---

5 Case 166/78, *Italy v. Council*, [1979] ECR 2575.

6 See, *inter alia*, Case C-84/94, *United Kingdom v. Council*, [1996] ECR I-5755.

7 For a thorough discussion of the problem of the legal basis see Kieran St. C. Bradley, "The European Court and the Legal Basis of Community Legislation" in *European Law Review* (1988), 379, and "Choice of Legislative Procedure" in *European Union Law Reporter*, CCH Editions Limited, (3621-28).

8 Case 22/70, *Commission v. Council*, [1971] ECR 263.

ment on the ERASMUS programme.[9] In both cases, the Court largely, although not totally, accepted the reasoning of the Commission.

However, in a more recent case, the Court entirely rejected the Commission's contention that the Council had relied on an excessively narrow interpretation of the Community's competence. The Commission had asked for the annulment of the "joint action adopted by the Council on 4 March 1996 concerning the transit at airports.[10] The Commission criticized the Council for having adopted this "joint action" on the basis of Article K.3 (now Article 31) of the Treaty on European Union, and thus in the framework of the "third pillar", whereas, according to the Commission, Article 100 C, included under the "first pillar", provided the Council with the necessary powers.

The Court noted that a visa for the transit at airports did not entitle its holder to cross the external border of a Member State, in the sense of Article 100 A, and that the contested legal instrument could not be based upon this provision. There was thus no Community competence.

This case is also interesting in another respect, i.e. the competence which the Court attributes to itself to decide on its own competence. The United Kingdom had contended that the Court was not competent to decide such a case according to Article L of the Treaty on European Union, because the joint action, having been adopted on the basis of Article K.3. did not fall under the category of acts which could be annulled by the Court on the basis of Article 173.

The Court, however, declared with reference to Articles L and M, that it was its responsibility to control whether an act which, according to the Council, fell under Article K.3 (2), was not infringing upon the competences which the Treaty assigned to the Community.

In other words, the Court confirmed that it also had the task of preserving these competences in cases where the delimitation between first and third pillar was at stake.

This constitutes, in my view, an eloquent example of the balanced way in which the Court assumes its function of guardian both of the competences of the Community and of the Member States.

B Actions brought against the Commission on grounds of incompetence

One may distinguish between two categories of cases in which the competence of the Commission has been challenged.

1. First there are cases in which, by way of an action against the Commission for incompetence, it was the incompetence of the Community as such which was alleged.

---

9 Case 242/87, [1989] ECR 1425.

10 Case C-170/96, [1998] ECR I-2763.

The first Court case in which a challenge to the Commission's competence implied a challenge to the competence of the Community itself was its judgment of 9 July 1987 concerning migration policies.[11] Germany, France, the Netherlands and the United Kingdom had brought an action for annulment of the Commission decision of 8 July 1985 setting up a prior communication and consultation procedure on migration policies in relation to non-member countries.

This decision was based on Article 118 of the EC Treaty (now Article 137) under which the Commission, in conformity with the general objectives of the Treaty, had the task of promoting close cooperation between Member States in the social field, particularly in matters relating to:

- employment
- labour law and working conditions
- basic and advanced vocational training, etc.

These Member States argued that "neither Article 118, nor any other provision of the Treaty authorised the Commission to take a compulsory decision in an area which, moreover, fell within their exclusive competence". They thus relied on the existence of a national competence in the area of migration policies.

The Court rejected the argument that migration policies in respect of third countries had no link whatsoever with social matters, for which the Treaty provides for cooperation between the Member States. The Commission could therefore set up a prior communication and consultation procedure on migration policies in relation to non-member countries. But it was not entitled to cover matters which did not fall within the scope of social policy within the meaning of Article 118, such as the cultural integration of migrant workers from third countries. Furthermore the Commission was not allowed either to determine the result to be achieved in the consultation it was entitled to initiate, nor could it prevent the Member States from implementing drafts, agreements and measures which it might consider not to be in conformity with Community policies and actions.

The contested decision was thus declared void in part, in so far as the Commission lacked competence. The approach followed by the Court was thus similar to the one it had adopted in the case concerning the Erasmus programme: giving a relatively broad interpretation of the Community's competence but declaring the act concerned void in so far as it clearly exceeds these competences.

Another interesting case in which Community competence was directly challenged together with the Commission's competence is the action brought against the Commission by Germany in 1990 for annulment of a regulation laying down penalties in the muton and goat-meat sector.[12]

It concerned the question of what sanctions Member States had to take against farmers who had committed irregularities when making an application for the financial aid provided for in the Council regulations.

11 Joined Cases 281/85, 283/85 to 285/85 and 287/85, [1987] ECR 3203.
12 Case C-240/90, [1992] ECR I-5383.

The Commission regulation provided for three categories of penalties, the last one being particularly severe. A farmer making a false declaration, either through gross negligence or deliberately, was made ineligible for the payment in respect of the year following that in which the infringement had been established.

The German government argued that such a measure amounted to a penal sanction which neither the Council nor the Commission had the power to enact.

The Court did not accept that it was a penal sanction and held that the measure fell within the scope of Community competence. As it was the sole responsibility of the Community institutions to determine the measures most appropriate to achieve the aims of the Common Agricultural Policy, it followed that it was also up to them to provide for the necessary measures against infringements. Furthermore, the Court also decided that the Commission was entitled to impose on the Member States an obligation to apply such type of measures.

2. A second category of actions brought against the Commission for incompetence are the cases in which the Commission had taken an initiative in a matter which, according to some of the Member States, fell within the competence of the Council. In such cases, it was not the Community's competence which was challenged but only the Commission's.

The first such case was about the scope of Article 90 (now Article 86) concerning public undertakings and undertakings to which Member States grant special or exclusive rights. This treaty provision confers upon the Commission an exclusive power to "address appropriate directives or decisions to Member States".

France, Italy and the United Kingdom challenged the Commission Directive 80/723/EEC of 25 June 1980 on the transparency of financial relations between Member States and public undertakings, arguing that the Commission had no power to enact directives with a general scope. According to these Member States, the Commission was only empowered to adopt directives aimed at dealing with a specific situation in one or more Member States, because all original law-making power is vested in the Council, whereas the Commission only had powers of surveillance and implementation.

The Commission, supported by Germany and the Netherlands, held the contrary view.

The Court upheld the Commission's competence to enact on the basis of Article 90 directives with a general scope in so far as they were necessary to enable the Commission to perform effectively its duty of surveillance under paragraph 3 of Article 90.[13]

In a subsequent judgment of 12 February 1992,[14] the Court also rejected the contrary view according to which the Commission did not have, under Article 90, the power to determine that a specific measure taken by a Member State was in-

13 Joined Cases 188 to 190/80, [1982] ECR 2545.

14 Joined Cases C-48/90 and C-66/90, *Kingdom of the Netherlands and Koninklijke PTT Nederland NV and PTT Post BV v. Commission*, [1992] ECR I-565.

compatible with provisions of the Treaty. As one can see, Member States sometimes hold diametrically opposed views on the Commission's powers.

The Court has thus upheld the powers granted to the Commission by Article 90. This however, did not prevent it from annulling in part Commission decisions about which it reached the conclusion that they could not validly have been based on Article 90.[15]

Under this heading one should also draw attention to several cases in which the Court annulled an act by the Commission because it had been adopted in violation of a Council competence. Although these cases do not concern the "federal balance" directly, they are indirectly relevant because, within the Council, Member States are better able to give effect to their interpretation of the Community's competences and to their views regarding the opportunity of a Community initiative in a given field.

In a series of 8 judgments dated 15 December 1987,[16] the Court annulled, upon request from the Member States which had fishing interests operating in the North Atlantic, Commission decisions which refused the reimbursement by the EAGGF of expenditure incurred in the context of interventions and export refunds in the fisheries sector in excess of fishing quotas laid down by the Commission.

The establishment of fishing quotas is a Council prerogative. In the years 1981 and 1982 the Council was however unable to set fishing quotas even though the Commission had made proposals to that effect.

The Court held that, in such a case, the conservation measures necessary to protect fish stocks might be agreed upon by means of a process of cooperation between the Member States and the Commission. However, even if it was because of the Member States concerned that such a cooperation process could not be launched, proposals unilaterally made by the Commission in relation to the fish quotas to be allocated to individual Member States could not be considered as Community rules within the meaning of the regulation governing the financing of the Common Agricultural Policy, the disregard of which would have justified the Commission's refusal to charge the fund the intervention payments concerned.

Another particularly remarkable case in this category concerned the annulment of a Commission decision which had been published simply by way of a press release announcing the granting of subsidies for European projects to fight social exclusion.

In the past the Council had adopted different programmes to fight poverty and social exclusion on the basis of Article 235 of the Treaty, which were referred to as Poverty 1, 2 and 3. The Commission had proposed a Poverty 4 programme for 1995. Agreement to this proposal could not be reached in the Council. The Commission nevertheless announced in its press release a programme concerning social exclusion and provided financial support for 86 projects.

15 Case C-202/88, *France v. Commission*, [1991] ECR I-1223, and Joined Cases C-271/90, C-281/90 and C-289/90, *Spain e.a. v. Commission*, [1992] ECR I-5833.

16 [1987] ECR 5041 *et seq.*

Upon an application by the United Kingdom, the Court held that the Commission did not have the power to decide such expenditure and that it had violated Article 4 (1) of the Treaty, which provides that "each institution shall act within the limits of the powers conferred upon it by this Treaty".[17] It is obvious that in so deciding the Court not only safeguarded the Council's prerogatives but also ensured that the Member States' will not to take action was respected. It thus contributed to the maintenance of the "federal balance".

C *Actions brought against the Parliament on grounds of incompetence.*

It is obvious that if the European Parliament violates the rights of the Member States, it also jeopardizes the federal balance. There are indeed three cases in which the Court annulled acts of the Parliament on grounds of incompetence.

The first was initiated by Luxembourg, which sought the annulment of a European Parliament resolution concerning the seat of its secretariat.[18] The second concerned a decision of the Bureau of the Parliament on the reimbursement of expenditure incurred by the political groupings which had been challenged by the party "les Verts".[19] Both these acts were annulled because the Court considered that the competence to deal with the matters concerned belonged to the Member States.

It is interesting to note that the latter case is the only one so far where the Court annulled an act of an institution on the grounds of incompetence in a case brought by a natural or legal person, as opposed to a Member State or an institution.

The third case was an action brought by France (supported by Luxembourg) against the decision of the European Parliament to hold, during the year 1996, fewer than 12 ordinary plenary sessions in Strasbourg. The decision of the Parliament was annulled because it violated a decision taken by the governments of the Member States.[20]

II THE SAFEGUARD OF THE FEDERAL BALANCE IN THE CONTEXT OF THE ASSESSMENT OF THE COMPATIBILITY OF NATIONAL MEASURES WITH COMMUNITY LAW

It is, of course, first and foremost in the context of actions brought by the Commission against a Member State under Article 226 EC (formerly Article 169) for failure to comply with the Treaty that the Court is called upon to ensure that Member States respect the competences of the Community.[21]

---

17 Case C-106/96, *United Kingdom v. Commission*, [1998] ECR I-2729.

18 Case 108/83, *Luxembourg v. Parliament*, [1984] ECR 1945.

19 Case 294/83, *"Les Verts" v. European Parliament*, [1986] ECR 1339.

20 Case C-345/95, [1997] ECR I-5215.

21 For a detailed examination of this aspect of the problem, see: Anita Wolf-Niedermaier, *Der Europäische Gerichtshof zwischen Recht und Politik*, (Nomos Verlagsgesellschaft, 1997); Marion Simm, *Der Gerichtshof der Europäischen Gemeinschaften im föderalen Kompe-*

From the establishment of the ECSC in 1951 up to and including 1998, 1446 actions for failure to fulfill obligations were brought to the Court.[22] Out of this total approximately 109 were dismissed by the Court as unfounded, either wholly or in part.

A good example of an Article 169 case where the distribution of competences between the Community and the Member States was clearly at stake is found in the judgment of 21 June 1988[23] concerning the setting of maximum import prices for sheep, goats and the meat of these animals by Greece. According to the defendant government, these maximum prices would facilitate the work of the authorities administering exchange controls, by preventing illegal outflows of foreign exchange. Moreover these prices incidentally safeguarded healthy competition and prevented artificial price increases.

The Court held that the monetary objective of the challenged measure did not justify it. The fact that Member States retained certain monetary powers did not entitle them to take unilateral measures prohibited by the Treaty.

The Court found that the measures concerned were prohibited by the Treaty because they were incompatible with:

- Article 30 of the Treaty, as they constituted measures of equivalent effect to a quantitative restriction,
- the regulation on the common market organisation for mutton and goatmeat,
- Article 113, since they encroached upon the Community's exclusive competence for the common commercial policy,
- the agreements concluded between the Community and certain third countries.

However, except for some very specific cases like the one quoted above, the Court does not as a rule examine actions for infringement of the Treaty from the point of view of the distribution of competences or the federal balance.

Most of the judgments pursuant to Article 169 aim to define the scope of some fundamental concepts, the principle of which is not in dispute, such as the freedom of establishment, the freedom to provide services, equal treatment of men and women, the prohibition on measures of equivalent effect to a quantitative restriction etc. In other words, these cases are about deciding whether a given national measure falls within the scope of a certain rule, and only very indirectly about whether or not the Member States are still entitled to regulate certain matters or not.

It is however striking to note that this issue has very often been at the heart of cases brought under Article 177, despite the fact that in that context, the Court is only supposed to give rulings concerning the validity and interpretation of acts of

---

tenzkonflikt, (Nomos Verlagsgesellschaft, 1998).

22 Under the "old" Art. 169, 170, 171, 225 of the EC Treaty, Articles 141, 142, 143 of the EAEC Treaty and Art. 88 of the ECSC Treaty.

23 Case 127/87, *Commission v. Greece*, [1988] ECR 3333.

the institution and is not entitled to examine whether a national measure is compatible with Community law.

Thus, preliminary rulings have often been an occasion for the Court to confirm that certain powers had been retained by the Member States, although they could only be exercised in full respect of the fundamental freedom guaranteed by the treaty and the principles of non-discrimination, equal treatment and proportionality.

This has been the case in numerous judgements relating to social security.[24]

Concerning direct taxation, the Court held *inter alia* in *Wielockx*[25] that, on the one hand, direct taxation falls within the competence of the Member States who must, on the other hand, exercise that competence consistently with Community law and therefore avoid any overt or covert discrimination by reason of nationality.

The Court similarly confirmed the Member States' retained competence in the following areas:

- registration of vessels;[26]
- protection and promotion of the national language;[27]
- criminal law and criminal procedure;[28]
- civil procedure;[29]
- regulation of the legal profession as regards debt collection;[30]
- penalties in criminal matters[31] or in customs regulations.[32]

III Consultative Opinions Under Article 228 (now Article 300)

Article 228 of the Treaty (now Article 300) provides for a preventive legality review in the field of external relations, of which there is no other example in Community law.

Under this provision, the Council, the Commission or a Member State may obtain the opinion of the Court of Justice as to whether an envisaged agreement is compatible with the provisions of the Treaty. Where the opinion of the Court is adverse, the agreement may only enter into force after a Treaty revision.

This procedure makes it possible to avoid the Community having obligations under international law with respect to a non-member country, that would flow from an agreement incompatible with Community law and which the Community could therefore not apply.

24 See, for instance Case C-280/94, *Posthuma-van Damme*, [1996] ECR I-179, Case C-120/95, *Decker*, [1998] ECR I-1831 and Case C-158/96, *Kohll*, [1998] ECR I-1931.
25 Case C-80/94, [1995] ECR I-2493.
26 Case C-221/89, *Factortame e.a.*, [1991] ECR I-3905.
27 Case C-379/87, *Groener*, [1989] ECR 3967.
28 Case C-226/97, *Lemmens*, [1998] ECR I-3711.
29 Case C-122/96, *Saldanha and MTS*, [1997] ECR I-5325.
30 Case 3/95, *Reisebüro Broede*, [1996] ECR I-6511.
31 Case 299/86, *Drexl*, [1988] ECR 1213.
32 Case C-36/94, *Siesse*, [1995] ECR I-3573.

It is also worth mentioning that before the Court had first been asked for an opinion under Article 228, it had already had an occasion to adjudicate on the extent of Community competences in the field of external economic relations following an action brought by the Commission against the Council under Article 173.

Reference is made here to the judgment in the aforementioned *ERTA* case,[33] in which the Court held that the Community's powers to conclude international agreements were not derived solely from explicit Treaty provisions, "but may equally flow from other provisions of the Treaty and from measures adopted, within the framework of those provisions, by the Community institutions.

In particular, each time the Community, with a view to implementing a common policy envisaged by the Treaty, adopts provisions laying down common rules, whatever form these may take, the Member States no longer have the right, acting individually or even collectively, to undertake obligations with third countries which affect those rules.

As and when such common rules come into being, the Community alone is in a position to assume and carry out contractual obligations towards third countries affecting the whole sphere of application of the Community legal system".

In its first opinion pursuant to Article 228, Opinion 1/75 concerning an OECD understanding on a Local Cost Standard,[34] the Court specified that where the Community had powers in the field of external economic relations, these powers had to be, as a matter of principle, exclusive powers.

In its Opinion 1/76 concerning a draft Agreement establishing a European laying-up fund for inland waterway vessels[35] the Court made clear, in an addition to its *ERTA* case-law, that the existence of the Community's external competence did not depend on the previous exercise of the corresponding internal competence but was also given when the internal competence was first exercised through measures taken to bring into force the international agreement concerned.

The Court has thus, without doubt, given a broad interpretation of the Community's powers in the field of external relations. Nevertheless, it has simultaneously found balanced and at times very complex solutions in order to maintain an equilibrium between the evolving nature of Community integration and of the legal framework of international economic relations, on the one hand, and the powers retained by the Member States on the other hand.

So in its Opinion 1/78 concerning the International Agreement on Natural Rubber,[36] the Court did indeed find that the Community had the exclusive power to conclude the agreement but it resorted to a finely balanced solution with respect to the financing of the agreement. It pointed out that it had not been definitively clarified whether the financial commitments involved would be borne by the Community budget or directly by the Member States. The Court held that the Member

33 *Op.cit.* note 8.
34 Op. 1/75, [1975] ECR 1355.
35 Op. 1/76, [1977] ECR 741.
36 Op. 1/78, [1979] ECR 2871.

States should continue to participate in the negotiations for as long as this matter was not settled. The Commission had defended the opposite view that the distribution of competences was not linked to the choice of financial arrangements.

Another example of the balanced approach of the Court is to be found in its Opinion 1/94 concerning in particular two parts of the WTO agreement, i.e. the TRIPS agreement and the GATS.[37] The Court decided that, contrary to the view expounded by the Commission, Community powers are exclusive only to the extent necessary, in a strict sense, for the achievement of the aims of the Community, in particular the implementation of the Single Market. It followed that trade in services as well as intellectual property issues remained at least partly within the competence of the Member States.

In this context, attention should also be drawn to Opinion 2/94 concerning the possibility for the Communities to accede to the European Human Rights Convention.[38] The Court held that, indeed, the conformity with Human Rights was a precondition for the validity of Community acts. However, in the present state of Community law, the Community was not competent to accede to the Convention because, on the one hand, no Treaty provision confers on the Community institutions any general power to enact rules on human rights or to conclude international conventions in this field, and, on the other hand, such an accession could not be effected on the basis of Article 235, as it implies changes that would be too fundamental in character. The Commission, the European Parliament and most of the Member States which had submitted observations (Belgium, Denmark, Germany, Greece, Italy, Finland, Sweden and, subsidiarily, Austria), had all defended the contrary view.

One can thus conclude that also in the context of Article 228, the Court has followed a finely balanced approach and has by no means systematically opted for the broadest possible interpretation of the Community's competence.

CONCLUSION

From the above, the first conclusion that can be drawn is that the Court has not developed a general, abstract thesis on a distribution of powers between the Community and the Member States which it would deem appropriate by reference, for instance, to such concepts as federation or confederation.

It has limited itself to interpreting the provisions of the Treaty that confer powers to the Community or to a given institution by reference to their wording and the objectives of the Treaty.

Secondly, it can be noted that the Court has sometimes given certain provisions, on the basis of the principle of "effet utile", an interpretation which some

37 Opinion of the Court of 15 Nov. 1994 on the competence of the Community to conclude the WTO agreement, and in particular the GATS and TRIPS agreements, 1/94, [1994] ECR I-5267.

38 Opinion 2/94, [1996] ECR I-1759.

might perhaps have found too extensive. This, however, was nearly always in cases in which the issue was not the existence of a Community competence as such but merely the extent of the powers to be derived from certain Treaty provisions as opposed to other ones, or the need, or not, to resort to Article 235.

Incidentally, the great variety of cases submitted to the Court and the diverging views held by the Member States tend to indicate that it would be very difficult to establish, once and for all, a catalogue of Community competences that would not leave any margin for interpretation.

Thirdly, if the Court has, in various cases, protected the Commission's competences against attempts to minimize their scope, for instance in the context of Article 90, it has, on the other hand, refused on numerous occasions to follow what it saw as Commission attempts to give too broad an interpretation of Community competences. It accordingly annulled several Commission acts and has not always followed the Commission's views in opinions pursuant to Article 228.

Finally, the Court confirmed that the Member States had retained powers in essential areas, while reminding them that such powers have to be exercised in conformity with the general principles of Community law.

6

THE ECJ AS A LAW-MAKER: *PRAETER AUT CONTRA LEGEM*?

Vlad Constantinesco

When the Editors of this book kindly offered me the honour to join this tribute to Lord Slynn, and asked me for the title of my contribution, I suggested: "*La Cour de justice des Communautés européennes et la révision judiciaire: praeter aut contra legem?*" At the time, I was hoping I could write my contribution in French. As I was informed this was not possible (how I wish it was!), the title of my article has been translated into: "*The ECJ as a Law-Maker*". In fact, that is more than just a simple translation: the substance of the original title had been significantly changed, although the English translator did his job perfectly well and with total good faith...In fact, the English title is neither new nor provocative, whilst the French version sounds rather strange and perhaps a little disrespectful to the ECJ. Let us first explain this contradiction before trying to show what exactly is the subject of this article.

"*Les juges de la nation ne sont (...) que la bouche qui prononce les paroles de la loi; des êtres inanimés qui ne peuvent modérer ni la force ni la rigueur.*" Everybody remembers this well-known quotation from Montesquieu:[1] I wonder if Lord Slynn, as the English judge at the ECJ, would share this opinion? Has he considered himself, during the time of his appointment at the ECJ, only as "*la bouche qui prononce les paroles de la loi*", or "*un être inanimé"?* Montesquieu's pronouncement applies to both Common Law and Civil Law Legal systems.[2] In a Civil Law system, the judge is supposed to apply the Statute Law to the case brought before him: he interprets and defines the legislator's will.[3] In that way, he can be described as *"la bouche qui prononce les paroles de la loi"* . Without the judge's intervention, the legislator's will has no reality and no ef-

1 *De l'esprit des lois* (1748), Livre XI Chapitre VI.

2 This opposition between Common and Civil Law has here been exaggerated: some parts of a Civil Law system, like in the French one, the Administrative Law (Droit administratif) are closer to the Common Law system, as a judge made Law, rather than to a Civil Law system, strictly defined...

3 The "volonté générale", in the Rousseauistic conception, means that the individual wills should be oriented towards "le bien commun", which is not the sum of individual interests.

D. O'Keeffe (ed.), Liber Amicorum Slynn 73-79 (2000)

fect. It becomes an "act of speech", it receives life only through the judge's action: he alone will be able to make real and concrete the legislator's will and words. But Montesquieu's words could also be applied to the judge's task in Common Law Legal systems. In this respect, they could mean that, in resolving a case by applying the rule of precedent, the judge expresses and pronounces the legal solution (*la loi*) by referring to previous cases. Law is in the logic of this type of system, the result of experience rather than the projection of abstract reason. But in both systems, apparently the same word is used: loi / droit.[4]

In reality, Community Law can be described as a good mixture of Common and Civil Law. It includes aspects of Civil Law, in that it rests upon a written supreme text, i.e., the treaties; and aspects of Common Law because, in many important decisions, Community Law has shown itself to be judge made law. But these similarities should not be overemphasised: many scholars agree that Community Law is a specific case, arguing that this is a new system of law, as different from Civil Law as it is from Common Law. Precisely because of this generally agreed upon description, it may be useful to look at the position of the ECJ in the Community Law making process, and the way it combines the two approaches of Common and Civil Law to create something new.

But things are more complicated. The EC Legal system not only exists at the intersection of Common and Civil Law, but the system itself is framed, from the beginning, by the structure of an international and functional Organization, founded by sovereign States through treaties, for a limited purpose: the creation of a Common Market and the co-ordination of some national instruments of economic policies. At the same time, the evolution of the EC shows that this organization has received more and more competences from the Member States, not only in the economic field, but also in areas belonging to sovereignty's hard core, such as Monetary and Economic Union, Common Foreign and Security Policy, European Union citizenship, immigration, asylum etc. Many observers predict that, due to the logic of the integration process, this will inevitably end in a kind of a Federal structure and perhaps even in a Federal State.[5] But the role of intergovernmental action is active enough in the development of the Union for some doubt to be cast over this prediction. That is why one can today share the opinion that Community Law should be located somewhere in between international law and national law, because it possesses characteristics from both structures: it is an international organization (its departure point) but, at the same

---

4 Only, of course, apparently: "common law" is neither "droit commun" nor "loi commune". That is why in general this expression is not translated into an other language than the English one. Some rather byzantine discussions are developed, in the francophone doctrine of Comparative Law, to decide if one should say "la" Common Law or "le" Common Law (*la* or *le* referring to *loi* or to *droit*). Let us prefer *la* Common Law, which has against it its unexact meaning, but is supported by a long tradition.

5 Federalism is a good example of a misunderstanding between Member States political cultures: their different historical experiences explain that there is no common signification of this word in Europe.

time, it also has some of the structural and functional elements of a federal State. But, of course, the judge's position (and his "law-making power") is not the same in these two Legal systems.

The Community Legal system and ECJ are in fact between two dialectical processes, combining both characteristics of Civil and Common Law Legal systems and distinctive features belonging to international and national Law. These four parameters should be kept in mind when exploring the notion of what is understood by the term "law making power", because this very general expression does not have the same significance either in Common[6] and Civil Law Legal systems, or in International or in National Legal systems.

Here again, there are some obvious differences between Common and Civil Law Legal systems, or, more exactly, between a Legal system in which the Fundamental law is a written and rigid constitution, distinct from Statute Laws, and a Legal system in which there is no difference between Constitutional and Statute laws. In the first kind of system, there is often a judge (in a constitutional jurisdiction, such as Continental Europe, this will be a specialized judge; in a Common Law system such as the United States, an ordinary judge, without any specialization in constitutional cases, will sit, as they do in the Federal Courts and, of course, in the United States' ultimate degree of jurisdiction, the Supreme Court). In the second system, there is no need for this kind of jurisdiction (or for this kind of jurisdiction's competence), because there is no hierarchy between Constitutional provisions and ordinary Statutes. Therefore, the possibility of a conflict between norms of different levels does not exist. If there is any contradiction between two statutes, the most recent text will prevail over the older one: "*lex posterior derogat priori*" will be applied.

Is the meaning of the *law making* process the same in each of these two Legal systems? Here again things are more complicated. In a Common Law Legal system, organized as in the United States, with a rigid Constitution, every federal judge is at the same time a Constitutional judge.[7] The Constitution is what the Supreme Court decides it is. Therefore, in interpreting the Constitution, the judge is able (if not entitled) to produce Constitutional Law. This is not far from a Civil Law system with a constitutional judge: in interpreting a written and rigid Constitution, this specialized judge directly produces Constitutional Law.[8]

6 "Judges do not generally admit that they make law; they cherish the 'fairy tale' (as Lord Reid once termed it) that the common law is a miraculous something existing from eternity and not made by anyone" G. Williams: *Learning the Law*, London, Stevens and Sons, 1982 p. 92.

7 The same happens at the level of each component State.

8 It should of course be distinguished among constitutional jurisdictions' competences: some of them, like the German *Bundesverfassungsgericht* are able to decide in an abstract way (*Abstrakten Normenkontrolle)*. But the German Constitutional juridiction has the power, like in other countries, to decide on concrete cases. Here again, the peculiarity of the French *Conseil constitutionnel* is obvious, because it is considered by the doctrine as a non-contentious jurisdiction. See M. Waline, Préface à L. Favoreu: *Les grandes décisions du Conseil constitutionnel*, Paris, Dalloz 1997 (9 ème édition) p. XIV

By contrast, in a Common Law system without a constitutional judge, when a judge gives an interpretation of a Statute or rests upon a precedent to solve a case brought before him, he may also produce Constitutional Law, because there is no separation and no hierarchy (other than a temporal one) between different statutes issued at distinct times: the general concept of Law absorbs the different levels of normativity and the different ways of producing them. Thus, the difference between the two legal systems lies not in the opposition between Civil and Common Law but in the existence (or not) of a written and rigid constitution.

There is no doubt that the Community system belongs to the first category. The ECJ finds its origin in international treaties and was created to guarantee their authority in relation to acts of the institutions. The treaties, as the fundamental norm of the Community Law system, may only be amended by the special procedure foreseen in the new Article 48 TEU, which is different from the ordinary Law making process. In *Parti Ecologiste Les Verts v. European Parliament*,[9] the ECJ described the treaties as "*...the constitutional Charter of a Legal Community*", emphasising its fundamental character and ruling that acts adopted by the European Parliament (EP), having legal effects for third parties, could be challenged before the ECJ, although Article 173 EC Treaty did not mention the EP as a possible defendant. In this case, the ECJ clearly ignored the wordings of the treaty provision: to put it another way, it considered that the silence of the treaty regarding the possibility of the EP being a defendant should be interpreted as not excluding that possibility. It is obvious that another interpretation could have prevailed: if the authors of the treaties did not mention the EP among the defendants in an annulment action before the ECJ, it was precisely the opposite signal that was being given, namely that they wanted to exclude such a possibility. In such a case, when a treaty provision is silent, it is possible to say that the ECJ has filled a *lacuna*. In doing so, the ECJ is in a similar position to a Law-making constitutional Court. The purpose of this article will be to establish if the ECJ, like every constitutional Court, indeed like any court or judge in a Civil Law system,[10] has the competence to fill *lacunae*, the obligation to judge when and where the Law is silent. In answering this question, it will be possible to explore the substance of the law-making power of a jurisdiction, particularly with reference to the ECJ.

To explain the ECJ's position, many authors have used the provocative *formula* of "judicial activism", which contrasts with the attitude of "self-restraint" which can be observed, if not all the time and not everywhere, in true Constitutional Courts. "Judicial activism" means that a judicial body does not exactly apply the Law (with or without a *lacuna*), but gives preference to values other than the legal ones, such as, in the case of the ECJ, the reinforcement of the in-

9 Case 294/83, [1986] ECR1339.

10 It is worthy to remember Article 4 of the French Code civil: "Le juge qui refusera de juger, sous prétexte du silence, de l'obscurité ou de l'insuffisance de la loi, pourra être poursuivi comme coupable de déni de justice". The possibility to pronounce a *non-liquet* seems clearly excluded.

tegration process. This is true, undoubtedly, when considering the practical result of a judgment, but it is an insufficient explanation of the process leading to this result. A departure from the wording of a Treaty has to be justified by technical considerations (i.e. by legal values), not only by political preferences or choices. In the case *Parti écologiste Les Verts v. Parlement européen,* the ECJ underlined the necessity of judicial protection, in a Community ruled by Law, when an institution like the European Parliament issues an act with legal effects for third parties. The ECJ tries to adjust the extent of the superior value of judicial protection to the evolution of the European Parliament's powers: if the treaty allows the possibility of the European Parliament acting in a way that affects third parties, then they must be given judicial protection. The ECJ abolishes the contradiction between judicial protection for every subject of the law, and the treaty's wording which does not positively accept an annulment action against the European Parliament's acts. It is in this finding of a superior legal value, deduced from an interpretation of the whole Community Law system, that the ECJ creates Community Law at a constitutional level. The question to be answered is to compare if such an attitude is compatible with the status and the competences of the ECJ in the Community Law system. Here lies, in fact, the question of *propter* or *contra legem*. If an interpretation of an article of a fundamental norm leads to its compatibility with this norm, it would be an acceptable situation, because the fundamental norm is not overruled by the interpretative authority of the Court's judgment. Preference is, in this case, given to the will of the constitutional Power (*le pouvoir constituant*), and to its explicit (or implicit) logic. But if it is vice versa, if an interpretation leads to an open contradiction between the words of the constitutional rule and the result of the interpretation, if there is a clear incompatibility between the two, one can question the admissibility of such an interpretation. In such a case, one may ask if the Court has not in reality created a new supra-constitutional rule, superior in fact to the written constitutional rule: a sort of judge made supra-constitutional law. Is the judge not, in fact acting as a supra-constitutional Power (*une autorité supra-constitutionnelle*), using powers coming from somewhere outside and above the written constitution? In other words, if a *propter legem* interpretation is acceptable, a *contra legem* interpretation would be questionable, because it would signify that a subordinate authority would be able to exercise powers that do not belong to it: is that not the same thing as an *ultra vires* situation?

Other examples of such an interpretation can be given: every scholar of EC Law is able to remember the *ERTA,* the *Foto-Frost* and the *Chernobyl I* cases, among others. All these cases have in common the fact that the Court ruled against the wording of the treaty, always with good reasons, encapsulated in superior principles of law, such as the coherence between external and internal competences (*ERTA*), the inconvenience of the ability of an inferior national jurisdiction to pronounce the invalidity of a community regulation (*Foto-Frost*) or the necessity of protecting the proper prerogatives of the European Parliament by admitting its possibility to bring an annulment action against an act of the Council ignoring them (*Chernobyl I*)

Let us look, from a technical point of view, at these different cases: many authors share the opinion that in such situations, the ECJ has ruled too far, neglecting the self-restraint it has to respect, and has changed the rules rather than applied them. This is very close to a "gouvernement des juges", or to "political preferences". It is why the "judicial activism" of the ECJ is often spoken of.[11] This expression means that the ECJ has slipped from Law to Politics, ruling not only to fill a *lacuna,* but also *contra legem,* preferring to substitute its will to the treaty authors' one. "Judicial activism" is often explained by non-legal considerations: the ECJ as a judiciary Power is a part of the Community political structure and it has to react to some outside inputs and internal insufficiencies, producing judgements in order to fill a legislative inertia (or a constitutional *lacuna*). The fundamental role of a jurisdiction would be to give a concrete answer to a case when the political institutions, and the expression of the Member State's will (the Treaties), have not defined the elements of an appropriate response. If Law is an instrument to achieve political goals, the "judicial activism" of the ECJ only demonstrates its capacity to adapt to external requirements; but this attitude could be questioned or criticized on the grounds of legitimacy.

Would it not be possible to consider another point of view? Instead of explaining these cases by the move from Law to Politics, that is by a move from one field to another, would it not be possible to find an explanation inside the Legal system itself, or inside the Legal reasoning methods themselves? The explanation mentioned before is in fact an incoherent one, because it tries to locate the origin of a phenomenon outside the sphere of validity of the Legal system: if an internal explanation could be found, it would be a coherent one, because it would not be necessary to go outside the Legal system to find an explanation from one of its developments. In other words it could be interesting to explore the possibility and the relevance of a Legal explanation to these situations of "judicial activism".

Let us consider the arguments from those who defend, in such cases, the Court's position: the interpretative rule of the *effet utile* (*ut res magis valeat quam pereat*) or as in the *ERTA* case, the *effet nécessaire* rule, are often put forwards. These arguments insist on the interpretative methods followed by the Court: this seems to be, at first glance, a convincing legal answer to the question of "judicial activism". But the development, by legal reasoning methods, of all the "virtualities" of a legal text, cannot go so far as ignoring the evident meaning[12] of the text. The development of the virtualities of a text has to stay within

11 This is a wide studied theme. See the fundamental work of H. Rasmussen: *On Law and policy in the European Court of Justice*, Dordrecht/Boston/Lancaster: M. Nijhoff 1986 xxv + 555 p. Consider the analysis of this book by M. Cappelletti, "Is the European Court of Justice 'Running Wild'"?, ELRev. Vol. 12, N° 1, February 1987, p. 3., and H. Rasmussen's "mise au point": Between Self-restraint and activism: A Judicial Policy for the European Court, ELRev. Vol. 13, N° 1, February 1988, p. 28.

12 Everybody knows the ambiguity of the "acte clair" doctrine, and the fact that only a former interpretation gives the possibility to say if a text is "clair". This is not exactly the

it's limits, respecting its coherence and not deconstructing or contradicting it. That is why the explanation by legal interpretation is, in my opinion, not able to give a convincing legal answer to the question of "judicial activism", because it still rests, at the end of the day, upon the logic of the use of Legal tools for political purposes.

That is why it should be examined from another direction: more precisely, one can perhaps explain these cases and solutions by considering that the ECJ has, in fact, not acted as a constitutional Power, but has chosen, among the Treaty provisions and rules, a superior principle in the light of which the case has to be resolved. The ECJ has established a hierarchy between Constitutional norms and values: all the Treaty provisions are not at the same level. Some are rather technical, others have a fundamental importance. If there appears a contradiction between these two levels of constitutional normativity, the most important provision, the principal rule has to be followed. The ECJ's "activism" lies in reality in the establishment of a super-constitutionality (and not of a supra-constitutionality) among the Treaty provisions. These fundamental principles – judicial protection, the generality of the judicial review – express the Member States' choices. When a discrepancy occurs between, for example, the extended powers of the EP and the strict conditions for the admission of an annulment action against Parliament acts, it is the principle of judicial protection, encapsulated in ex Article 164 EC, that will justify the solution. To discover such principles, and to elucidate them, is part of a normal judicial activity, but it is not exactly the same as "judicial activism". In others words, the Judge's mission is to respect the will of the constitutional Powers, but also to bring coherence to the articulations between principles and rules, establishing an order of preference and therefore contributing to the reconstruction of the normative system instead of deconstructing it.

---

question opened by the cases quoted before: they have in common the fact that the ECJ did not follow the consequences opened by the treaty's articles. There is here a contradiction between the text and the solution given by the Court.

7

THE COURT OF FIRST INSTANCE: A DAY IN THE LIFE OF A JUDGE

Sir Christopher Bellamy

I had the very great honour of being sworn in as a judge of the Court of First Instance on the day that Gordon Slynn left the Court of Justice on his appointment to the House of Lords. I would like, in respectful tribute to a very special mentor and friend, to describe a little of the life of "a judge in Luxembourg", not from the point view of high legal theory, but by trying to convey something of the daily work of this particular jurisdiction.[1]

In my own case, the cows come down the village street every morning at twenty past eight, after milking, so it is wise to be out of the house by eight fifteen. The road at the top of the lane is Roman, and nearby still stands the milestone erected in the time of Hadrian, and thus roughly contemporaneous with his more famous Wall. Reflecting inconsequentially on these distant links, I turn out of the lane to find that the cows have got there before me.

No matter. Wherever one lives in Luxembourg, it is difficult to take more than 20 minutes to get to work. I arrive, glance at the Financial Times, sip the obligatory (in the British cabinet) cup of tea, and the working day begins.

Depending on the state of the caseload at any particular time, the work to be done involves any one of the four main aspects of the judicial process in the Court of First Instance: the initial stages of the case; the conference of the Chamber; the oral hearing; and drafting the judgment. But before describing each of these stages in their context, I must first briefly set out the structure of the Court, and its current caseload. I will mention at the end the Court's recent proposals to speed up its procedures.

1 Judge Edward has already done a similar job as regards the Court of Justice: see Edward, *How the Court of Justice Works* E L Rev (1995) p. 539. Quite apart from the differences in jurisdiction and rôle, the differences in daily work between the two Courts arise mainly because the CFI (i) works in small chambers (ii) has no Advocate Generals (iii) deals with cases where factual and procedural issues predominate (iv) places more emphasis on the oral hearing and (v) tends to produce fuller judgments, as benefits a court of first instance from which an appeal lies to the Court of Justice.

D. O'Keeffe (ed.), Liber Amicorum Slynn 81-96 (2000)

I THE STRUCTURE OF THE COURT OF FIRST INSTANCE

1 Jurisdiction

Ever since it was founded 10 years ago "to improve the judicial protection of individual interests in cases involving the examination of complex facts", and "to enable the Court of Justice to concentrate its activities on the fundamental task of ensuring uniform interpretation of Community Law",[2] the jurisdiction of the Court of First Instance has been in a state of perpetual evolution.

At the outset its jurisdiction was limited, in substance, to actions brought against the Commission under Article 173 (now Article 230) of the EC Treaty in competition cases, and the staff cases brought by officials of the Community.[3] In 1993, the Council increased the Court's jurisdiction to include all actions brought against Community institutions by national or legal persons, except dumping cases which were subsequently transferred to the Court of First Instance in March 1994. Also in 1994 the Community Trade Mark Regulation[4] gave the Court of First Instance jurisdiction to hear appeals from decisions on trademark matters from the Office for the Harmonisation of the Internal Market in Alicante.

In the result, the Court of First Instance has a general jurisdiction to hear all actions brought against Community institutions or bodies by natural or legal persons. At the time of writing there is also a proposal to transfer to the Court of First Instance certain cases brought by Member States, mainly where parallel proceedings affecting the same decision are pending before both the Court of Justice and the Court of First Instance,[5] as well as a proposal to establish a specialised chamber of the Court of First Instance to deal with certain fraud cases at Community level.[6] Others ideas are in the pipeline.[7]

---

2 See the recitals of Council Decision of 24 October 1988 establishing the Court of First Instance OJ no. L 319, p. 1, corrigenda in OJ no. L 241. This decision has since been amended four times by decisions of 8 June 1993 (OJ no. L 144, p. 21) 7 March 1994 (OJ no. L 66, p. 29) 1 January 1995 L 1, p. 1) and 26 April 1999 (OJ no. L 114, p. 52).

3 Art 179 (now Art 230) of the EC Treaty.

4 Council Regulation (EC) 40/94 of 20 December 1993 on the Community trade mark OJ No L 11, p. 1. There is a similar regulation in relation to plant breeders rights (Reg. 2100/94 OJ 1994 L227/1). A draft regulation has been published in respect of registered designs, which would also confer jurisdiction on the Court of First Instance: see the amended Commission proposal for a Council Regulation (EC) on Community Design of 21 June 1999 (COM/99/0310 final). At the time of writing intensive discussions are proceeding regarding a future Community framework for patents. For a possible rôle for the Court of First Instance, see the Report of House of Lords Select Committee on the European Communities, HL Paper 115, 9 June 1998, point 91.

5 See generally the Report of the House of Lords Select Committee on the European Communities "Enlarging the jurisdiction of the Court of First Instance" (HL Paper 82, 6 July 1999).

6 See The Second Report of the Committee of Independent Experts on the Reform of the Commission, 10 September 1999, Recommendation 55, volume 1, page 16.

2 *The chambers system*

To cover this wide range of work the Court of First Instance has fifteen judges.[8] The Court is organised on a chambers basis, and hardly ever sits in plenary session. The main work is done in the five "small" chambers of three judges each, while State aid cases, dumping cases and, occasionally, other cases, are dealt with by the five "large" chambers of five judges each. Each judge (except the President)[9] belongs to three chambers, one "small", and two "large".

To this structure there must now be added, since July 1999, the single judge cases whereby the chamber may, after hearing the parties, unanimously authorise one of its members (normally the juge rapporteur) to hear and decide the case sitting alone. This possibility should prove useful in simple cases and in a number of staff cases.[10] The first such judgment (in a staff case) was given in October 1999.[11]

The presidency of each chamber rotates annually so that, during a six year mandate, most judges will twice be president of chamber. The president of chamber is responsible for organising the work of each chamber, fixing the dates of chamber conferences, hearings and judgments, ensuring that internal deadlines are met, and taking various interlocutory decisions, for example regarding time limits for filing pleadings, interventions, legal aid, discontinuance etc.

---

7 In May 1999, the Court of Justice and the Court of First Instance submitted a joint paper to the Council of Ministers on the Future Structure of the Community Courts. The Commission has also invited a Group of "wise men", including Lord Slynn, to study the future judicial architecture of the Community. Their final report is expected shortly.

8 This number increased from 12 to 15 with the accession of Austria, Finland and Sweden in 1995. There are no permanent advocates-general, but a judge may be appointed as advocate general in a particular case: see Arts 17-19 of the Rules of Procedure (OJ 1991 L136/1 and L249/34, as amended. In practice this has not been done since 1992. In 1999 the CFI submitted proposals to the Council of Ministers to increase the number of judges by 6, mainly in order to cope with the expected increase in trademark work.

9 The President of the Court presides one 3-judge and one 5-judge chamber, but does not regularly act as juge rapporteur. He also discharges extensive administrative responsibilities regarding the running of the Court and liaising with the Court of Justice, as well as dealing with applications for interim relief which represent an increasingly heavy caseload (26 applications in 1998).

10 See generally the Report of the House of Lords Select Committee on the European Communities "The Court of First Instance: Single judge", 9 June 1998, HL Paper 114. A similar proposal had already been made in 1996 by the EC Advisory Board of the British Institute of International and Competition Law, chaired by Lord Slynn: see The Role and Future of the European Court of Justice (1996) p. 50. The report of the House of Lords Select Committee on the European Communities "Enforcement of Community Competition Rules", HL Paper 7-I, 7 December 1993, also chaired by Lord Slynn, had already recommended that certain interlocutory decisions in competition cases should be appealable to a single judge of the Court of First Instance (points 69 to 73, 112, 129-130, and 160).

11 See Case T-180/98, *Cotrim v. Commission*, judgment of 28 October 1999, nyr.

3 *The "legal Judge"*

The composition of the chambers is fixed by a decision of the Court of First Instance at the beginning of each judicial year taking into account an impossibly complex balance between different legal traditions, judicial experience, and geographical factors. This decision is published in the Official Journal.

Once a case is lodged at the Registry, the President of the Court assigns the case to a chamber, normally on a rotation basis. Within the chamber, the case is then assigned to a juge rapporteur, again on a rotation basis. The details of these systems of rotation are also published each year in the Official Journal.

In this respect the Court of First Instance follows the German law principle of the "legal judge" ("der gesetzliche Richter" or "juge légal") according to which the identity of the judge who tries the case must be determined in advance on the basis of objective criteria. This makes sense in a multinational jurisdiction, where a litigant could wonder how or why judges of particular nationalities have been selected to try his particular case. The system also means that every judge does every kind of case, there being no presumption that one judge with experience in, say, competition law, will do mainly competition cases. However, currently two chambers only are designated to hear trademark cases, the beginnings, perhaps, of an internal "specialisation" of chambers.

4 *Language*

Cases may be brought before the Court of First Instance in any one of the eleven official languages of the Community. In practice the staff cases (of which there are about 100 pending at any one time) are argued in French, but a recent check of the pending cases other than staff cases showed around 26 % lodged in English, 20 % in German, 15 % in French, and the balance in other languages of which the most important (14.5 %) was Dutch.

However, whatever the official language of the case, the Court of First Instance, like the Court of Justice, normally works internally in French, according to an "hour-glass system". This means that all pleadings which are not already French are translated into French[12] and worked on in French by the juge rapporteur and his cabinet, and later by the chamber. Thus, in a typical case, the juge rapporteur will produce the report for the hearing, a synthesis of the main arguments of the parties, in French. This document is then translated back into the language of the case for use by the parties at the oral hearing. The juge rapporteur will also produce, in French, an internal "preliminary report" which constitutes his own preliminary appraisal of the case, and which serves as the basis for the initial discussion of the case by the chamber. Because the Court of First In-

---

12 It is rarely possible to translate the annexes, except where they have a particular importance for the case. Thus anything that is really vital for the case should be included in the main body of the pleading.

stance has no advocates general, this internal document may itself be relatively long and complex. After this discussion, a date for the oral hearing is fixed. The hearing of the case then takes place in the official language of the case, with simultaneous translation available as required. The Juge rapporteur then prepares a draft judgment in French. This is discussed by the chamber in French, until agreement is reached on the French text, at which point the final judgment is retranslated back into the language of the case for judgment to be delivered in that language.[13]

II THE CASELOAD OF THE COURT OF FIRST INSTANCE

1 *The current stock*

The caseload of the Court of First Instance is currently around 960 cases, but from that figure should be deducted certain "groups" of cases which turn on points common to the cases in the group i.e. some 300 cases brought by customs agents whose businesses were affected by the creation of the single market, certain staff cases known as the "Alexopoulou" group and about 100 milk quota cases.[14] The real "stock" (in October 1999) is probably about 500 cases, of which about 20 % are staff cases. Out of this total stock, each judge might expect to have around 30 to 40 cases for which he is responsible as juge rapporteur. This statistic is, however, relatively meaningless because one case may be a relatively simple staff case concerning, say, an orphan's pension, with pleadings and supporting documents of some 40 pages, while in another case concerning say, state aids, the pleadings may run to several hundred pages with voluminous annexes and multiple intervening parties in a complex and high profile matter. Similarly, from the procedural point of view, some cases can proceed to the oral hearing without complication while others may pose a multitude of interlocutory problems relating, for example, to admissibility, interventions, confidentiality, joinder with other cases, discovery of documents, and so on.

In the calendar year 1998, the most productive so far, 348 matters were finally disposed of,[15] and hearings held in 201 cases. However, the statistical re-

13 The rule, generally respected, is that in cases other than staff cases, the judgment should be available in all Community languages on the day it is delivered, both in hard copy form and on the Court's website. The question whether, or if, the working language régime of the Court will evolve over time is outside the scope of this paper.

14 The milk quota cases represent a relatively unknown aspect of the work of the Court. Following certain judgments of the Court of Justice, from 1993 onwards a total of 636 cases were lodged at the Court of First Instance by farmers claiming that they had wrongly been refused a quota for milk production. As a result of a general settlement offer by the Commission and decisions in a selected number of test cases by the Court of First Instance, the number of outstanding cases has now been reduced to 97, with some further discontinuances expected.

15 151 cases were decided in 129 judgments (the difference between these figures is ac-

sults for the "output" of the Court of First Instance do not adequately reflect either the differing degrees of complexity in different cases, or the procedural decisions that may be necessary to put a case in order for the oral hearing.

The following is a very brief description of the subject matter of the cases before the Court of First Instance

2 *The cartel cases*

The cartel cases arising under Article 81 (ex Article 85) of the Treaty are "heavy", in that the pleadings are long, the documents are voluminous, and each piece of evidence has to be carefully scrutinised to verify that the Commission has proved its case, as befits quasi-criminal proceedings where heavy financial penalties, often millions of euros, have been imposed. Procedural (including human rights) and evidential issues are important, and it may well be necessary to order the further production of documents by the Commission and the hearing of witnesses. In *Cartonboard*,[16] decided in 1998, the hearing lasted 9 days and the 17 judgments (in five languages) run to nearly 1400 pages. In *Steel beams*,[17] where the 5 day hearing took place in 1998, the 11 judgments (in four languages) run to about 1200 pages. In that case, in addition to the lengthy written pleadings, the Commission also produced about 11,000 documents and several witnesses were heard. A number of complex interlocutory orders, as well as informal meetings with the parties, were necessary in order to prepare the cases for hearing.[18] But these cases are dwarfed by *Cement* (42 parties) where the pleadings cover many thousand pages, the hearing took place over 3 weeks in 1998, and extensive production of the Commission's file was ordered. A lengthy judgment, in several languages, is expected in early 2000.[19] Despite the use of an internal "task force" of referendaires used for this work, the cartel cases tend to constitute a "bottleneck" in the Court's work, and distort the average figures for the length of proceedings before the Court .

---

counted for by cases joined for the purposes of the judgment) while 197 cases were disposed of in 150 orders, of which 73 were published.

16 See ECR [1998] II-813 to II-2174.

17 Case T-141/94, *Thyssen Stahl v. Commission*, and ten parallel cases, judgments of 11 March 1999, nyr.

18 See particularly Cases T-134/94 etc., *NMH Stahlwerke e.a. v. Commission* [1997] ECR II-2293.

19 An example of a shorter judgment in connection with cartel cases is that in PVC, Cases T-305/94 etc., *Limburgse Vinyl Maatschappij e.a. v. Commission*, 20 April 1999 nyr, where the 11 cases were joined for the purposes of the judgment which runs to nearly 200 pages.

3 *Other competition cases*

Other competition cases, although not "heavy" in the same way as the cartel cases, deal with a wide range of issues under Articles 81 and 82, as well as with mergers under Regulation (EC) 4064/89 as amended. Recent examples under Articles 81 and 82 include judgments on the arrangements for running trains through the Channel Tunnel, which clarified the nature and extent of the Commission's powers to grant exemptions under Article 81(3),[20] various alleged abuses of dominant position, for example in relation to Belgian telephone directories, the practice of "remail" (where intermediaries collect mail in country A, and then post it back to country A from country B, where postal rates are cheaper) and the sale of sugar on the Irish market. Merger cases decided recently or pending affect markets as diverse as the supply of platinum on the world market, retail distribution in Finland, and television services in Germany.

4 *State aids*

Whereas the cartel cases, for example, involve primary fact finding in the context of well understood legal rules, in the State aid cases the issues are more "economic" and the underlying legal concepts, such as aid which "does not adversely affect trading conditions to an extent contrary to the common interest", are not yet clearly defined. The procedures to be followed, especially as regards the rights of third parties, have not yet been clearly laid down. In addition, the Commission has a certain "margin of appreciation" to decide whether a given aid is compatible with the common market or not. In the result, the Court should limit itself to examining whether the Commission has committed an error of law, a manifest error of appreciation or an error of procedure, this last concept including lack of adequate reasoning in the decision.[21]

However, even within these confines, there is considerable scope for effective judicial review in State aids cases. It was Maitland who said that the origins of substantive law are to be found "in the interstices of procedure". By seeing that proper procedures are followed in State aid cases, in particular from the point of view of third parties,[22] and in seeing that all decisions are properly reasoned, in particular as regards the Commission's response to arguments addressed to it during the administrative procedure,[23] the Court can do much to ensure transparency, fairness and consistency in the application of the State aid rules. In addition, the judicial control of "manifest" error of appreciation involves not simply a cursory examination but a proper judicial review of the fac-

20 Cases T-374/94 etc., *European Night Services v. Commission* [1998] ECR II-3141.

21 See generally, for example, Cases T-371/94 and T-394/94, *British Airways e.a. v. Commission* [ECR] 1998 II-2405.

22 See e.g. Case 11/95, *BP Chemicals v. Commission* [1998] ECR II-3239 (failure to open the procedure under Article 93(2)).

23 See generally *British Airways e.a. v. Commission*, cited above.

tual data used by the Commission and the economic conclusions to be drawn therefrom.[24] It can thus properly be said that the State aids cases, once largely political in character, are being steadily subjected to a coherent system of legal rules. Recent State aid cases have involved: the arrangements for off-course betting in France, the restructuring of the Italian chemical industry, environmental taxes affecting water distribution in the Netherlands, aids granted to various airlines by the Flemish regional government, France, and Ireland, respectively, commercial television in Spain,[25] and various aids in relation to the steel and coal industries.

5 *Dumping cases*

Dumping cases tend to raise procedural issues, questions of proof and technical questions of interpretation under the various basic regulations and GATT rules. Occasionally an argument based on a manifest error of appraisal has been known to succeed.[26] A high proportion of the cases originate in the Far East or Eastern Europe.

6 *Freedom of information*

A growing part of the workload of the Court is represented by the "freedom of information" cases, which arise under the Code of Conduct adopted by the Council and the Commission concerning public access to the documents held by these institutions.[27] These cases concern mainly the various exceptions relied on by the institutions to refuse access to their documents. Quite apart from issues of interpretation, the Court has based a number of decisions on the fact that the institution has not done any "balancing exercise" in deciding whether to refuse access, or has not given adequate reasons for its refusal to disclose the document in question.[28] Once again, the duty to give adequate reasons, required by Article 253 (ex Article 190) of the Treaty, is an important aspect of effective judicial review in this area. Following the adoption of the Treaty of Amsterdam, this field of law is likely to develop further, and it will be necessary to ensure that the procedures of the Court are adequate for this purpose.

---

24 See e.g. Case T-380/94, *AIUFASS v. Commission* [1996] ECR II-2169; Case T-140/95 *Ryanair v. Commission* [1998] ECR II-3327.

25 In Case T-95/96, *Gestevision Telecinco v. Commission* [1998] ECR II-3410, the Court held that the Commission had violated Art. 175 of the Treaty (now Art. 232) by failing to respond to a complaint within a reasonable time.

26 See Case T-166/94, *Koyo Seiko v. Conseil* [1995] ECR II-2129.

27 See OJ 1993 L 340, p. 41. For the decisions of the Council and the Commission implementing this Code, see OJ 1993 L 340/43 and OJ 1994 L 46/58 respectively.

28 See e.g. Case T-194/94, *Carvel v. Council* [1995] ECR II-2765; Case T-105/95, *WWF UK v. Commission* [1997] ECR II-313; Case T-188/97, *Rothmans v. Commission*, judgment of 19 July 1999, nyr.

7 *Trademarks*

Appeals (about 11 to date) in trademark cases are beginning to be lodged against decisions of the Office for the Harmonisation of the Internal Market at Alicante. So far, these appeals mainly concern the question whether there is an "absolute bar" to registration of a trademark, e.g. because the mark is not distinctive, or is descriptive in character. The first such case concerning the registrability of the mark "Baby Dry" for nappies was decided recently.[29] In due course the trademark cases are likely to concern decisions of the Office taken after an "opposition" procedure, whereby third parties may object to the registration of the mark. Such cases, when they arrive, will closely resemble normal civil litigation. For this reason certain changes have been made to the rules of procedure.[30]

On current forecasts, the trademark cases could have a very significant impact on the workload of the Court of First Instance. At present efforts are being made to "streamline" judgments in this area, avoiding where possible the translation of the underlying pleadings.

8 *Other Article 230 cases*

Other cases arising under Article 230 (ex Article 173) of the EC Treaty cover a wide range of subject matter e.g. in the fields of payment of customs duties, the financing of vocational training and various other Community aid programmes, the legality of public health measures, the registration of geographical designations of origin, agricultural matters, contractual disputes to which the Community is a party, the non-contractual liability of the Community (in 1998 this last included the repercussions for customs agents of the establishment of the internal market,[31] and the legality of the international embargo against Iraq)[32] and other miscellaneous issues e.g. the legality of the Council decision to rename the ecu the euro.[33] Many of these cases, and indeed cases in other areas such as State aids, raise the question as to whether the applicant has standing to bring the action, i.e. whether he is "individually and directly concerned" within the meaning of Article 230. As the range and impact of Community legislation and decisions becomes ever wider, this issue becomes ever more important.

---

29 Case T-163/98, *Procter & Gamble v. OHIM*, judgment of 8 July 1999, nyr.

30 See Arts 130 to 136 of the Rules of Procedure.

31 Case T-113/96, *Dubois v. Council and Commission* [1998] ECR II-125, a test case out of 295 cases with the same subject matter.

32 Case T-184/95, *Dorsch Consult v. Council and Commission* [1998] ECR II-667.

33 Case T-207/97, *Berthu v. Council* [1998] ECR II-509.

9 *Staff cases*

The jurisdiction of the Court of First Instance as regards staff cases represents the ultimate guarantee of the independence and integrity of the Community civil service, which is a matter of the highest importance. Although, as in any jurisdiction, some such cases may be regarded as frivolous, many staff cases are properly brought and relate to matters of acute concern to the individual in question, such as the fairness and regularity of procedures for recruitment and promotion, judicial control of disciplinary procedures, and the rights of the officials concerned regarding medical insurance, pension rights, including widow's and orphans' pensions, invalidity benefit, child allowances and so on. These cases may raise extremely important issues, such as the right to two persons of the same sex living together to a "marriage" allowance[34] or the liability of the Community towards officials alleged to have contracted various asbestos related diseases as a result of working in the Berlaymont building.[35]

III How a case progresses through the Court

1 *The initial stages*

To revert to the various stages of a case before the Court of First Instance, the first stage is the written procedure, which requires the exchange of 4 pleadings i.e. the application, the defence, the reply and the rejoinder. The application must, in principle, contain all the main pleas in law relied on.[36] There is no facility to amend. In a medium sized case, and allowing for translation time, it is difficult to complete the written procedure in under a year. This period may be extended considerably if it is necessary to deal with an objection to admissibility or to admit interventions by third parties. On the other hand, if the action is plainly inadmissible or unfounded in law,[37] it may be rejected by order within a shorter time scale.

Once the written procedure is complete, and any necessary translations are available, the juge rapporteur is in a position to prepare, with the aid of one of his two legal secretaries, the two documents already mentioned, the "report for the hearing" and the "preliminary report". This process requires a thorough examination of the case, and should result in the facts and issues being "boiled down" to their essentials. In practice, in this jurisdiction the time spent in actually deciding the case is generally less than the time spent simply reducing the case to manageable proportions.

---

34 Case T-264/97, *D v. Council*, judgment of 28 January 1999, nyr.
35 Case T-165/95, *Luccacioni v. Commission* [1998] ECR-SC II-627.
36 Art. 48(2) of the Rules of Procedure.
37 Art. 111 of the Rules of Procedure.

The report for the hearing, as the name implies, is used as the basis for the discussion at the oral hearing, while at the same time enabling the parties to see the arguments which the Court considers relevant and to draw to the Court's attention anything which seems to have been overlooked. In addition, this document, together with the internal "preliminary report" enables the other members of the chamber to concentrate on the essentials of the case.

2 *The conference of the chamber*

The preliminary report forms the basis for the conference of the chamber where an initial discussion of the case takes place. Other members of the chamber may or may not agree with the juge rapporteur, and the juge rapporteur may himself change his mind. Indeed, at this stage it is essential that the juge rapporteur and the chamber maintain an open mind, otherwise the value of the oral hearing is lost. In fact, the purpose of the preliminary report and the conference of the chamber is, first, to identify the issues; second, to enable the chamber to decide what procedural measures are necessary to put the case in order for the hearing – these frequently include putting written questions to the parties or requesting the production of relevant documents;[38] and, third, to enable the hearing to be properly planned. In complicated cases involving a multitude of parties, this may be itself a complex operation, but even in simple cases it is often useful to indicate to the parties before the hearing the main points on which the Court wishes to hear argument.

3 *The oral hearing*

The oral hearing of the case takes place after the conference of the chamber (where, technically speaking, the decision is taken "to open the oral procedure") and the completion of any necessary procedural measures. By this stage, even with a fair wind, so to speak, 18 months could well have elapsed since the case was lodged.

The oral hearing itself is a structured occasion. It is rare to allow the principal parties more than half an hour each to put their case, with fifteen minutes for the interveners. Experience shows that it is not fruitful to interrupt these initial speeches, which enable the parties to present their main points. After that, it is the Court's turn to put questions, and that may well constitute, for the Court, the most instructive part of the hearing. After the Court's questions, which may last a considerable time, there is then a short final round of replies.

Not all advocates are used to these arrangements which, in effect, constitute a "half-way house" between the "continental" tradition of relatively formal oral proceedings in which questions are rarely, if ever, posed and the "common law"

38 Arts 64 (measures for the organisation of the procedure) and 65 (measures of instruction) of the Rules of Procedure.

tradition of probing from the bench to elicit the strengths and weaknesses of the various arguments. However, most advocates seem able to cope. While the complications of simultaneous translation and differing legal traditions make it difficult to reproduce fully the type of Socratic debate familiar to the Court of Appeal or the House of Lords, my own experience is that oral hearings in the Court of First Instance rarely fail to "add value" to the written procedure.

4 Drafting the judgment

Immediately after the hearing, there is a "tour de table" in the chamber, which may result in a consensus enabling the juge rapporteur to start immediately to draft the judgment. In other cases, however, the process of deliberation may be quite prolonged, especially where there are a number of difficult points to decide and differing views within the chamber. In practice, the rule against dissenting judgments reinforces the collegiate nature of the work of the chamber so that, even where initial views differ, discussion will often lead to a narrowing of the differences, and the development of common ground. If at the end of the day there is no agreement on the result, a vote has to be taken, but this, in my experience, is not very common. Even if, at that stage, the result is that a majority view prevails, in my experience the collegiate tradition often leads to the minority view being nonetheless accommodated as far as possible in the final judgment.

In drafting the judgment, the principal responsibility of the juge rapporteur is to reflect the wishes of the chamber, but he must also ensure that the Court has in fact replied to all the main arguments advanced by the losing party.[39] This obligation is largely responsible for the length of the judgments of the Court of First Instance as compared with those of the Court of Justice.

After final approval by the chamber, checking, and translation into the language of the case and (except in staff cases) into all the other Community languages, the judgment is given in open Court. An appeal lies to the Court of Justice on the grounds that the Court of First Instance lacked jurisdiction, erred in law or made an error of procedure.[40] Around 25 % of cases are appealed. To date, around 80 % of appeals have been withdrawn or dismissed, the remainder being allowed in whole or part.[41]

39 Failure to reply to a plea in law may lead to the judgment being quashed on appeal by the Court of Justice; see Case C-104/97 P, *Atlanta v. Council and Commission*, judgment of 14 October 1999, nyr.

40 See Arts 48 to 55 of the Statute of the Court (EC).

41 Out of about 171 appeals decided between 1991 and 1998, 135 were dismissed or abandoned. As regards the remainder, in a significant proportion of cases the Court of Justice reached the same result on other grounds. Some 13 cases were referred back to the Court of First Instance for the case to be continued.

IV PROCEDURAL REFORM

With the range and complexity of its current caseload, and quite apart from whatever view may be taken of the position of the Court of First Instance in the future judicial architecture of the European Union,[42] the introduction of procedural reforms to speed up the work of the Court remains urgent. At the time of writing, the Court of First Instance has formally submitted proposals to the Court of Justice which are currently being discussed with that Court with a view to onward transmission to the Council of Ministers. These proposals focus on the following points:

1 *Shortening the written procedure, by dispensing with the reply and the rejoinder*

In practice, the second stage of the written procedure, i.e. the submission of the reply and the rejoinder, adds at least six months, often more, to the total length of the case. In addition, these documents, often lengthy, have to be translated. Very often, however, the parties simply repeat arguments already found in the application or the defence, so that the "added value", by comparison with the delay involved, can be rather slight, bearing in mind that, in any event, the parties are not allowed to introduce new pleas in law at the stage of the reply or the rejoinder unless these are based on matters which have come to light in the course of the case.[43] In many cases, therefore, it may be more efficient to dispense with the second stage of the written procedure, while giving the parties more time to develop their arguments at the oral hearing. In some cases, extra time at the hearing could save months of written procedure while allowing the parties to make their arguments just as effectively.

2 *Reducing the time for interventions*

Under the existing rules,[44] third parties e.g. competitors, trade associations, Member States etc. have three months in which to apply to intervene as from the date on which the lodging of case is published in the Official Journal. Since the announcement of the case in the Official Journal has to contain a summary of the case, which has to be prepared by the Registry, and has itself to be translated into all eleven official languages, a certain time may, in practice, elapse before the relevant notice is published in the Official Journal. Once the application to intervene is received, often just before the expiry of the three months allowed, it has then to be sent to the other parties for their observations. Often the intervention is uncontentious, but in many cases the applicant asks that parts of the

42 See Footnote 7, above.
43 See Art. 48 (2) of the Rules of Procedure.
44 See Art. 115 of the Rules of Procedure.

pleadings and annexes remain confidential vis-à-vis the intervener.[45] Dealing with such requests, which are sometimes expressed in very wide terms, involves the adoption of an order, often after a relatively minute examination of the documents concerned. Allowing for translation time, this process may again delay the written procedure for some weeks, or, occasionally, months.[46]

It is only once these matters have been resolved that the intervention is admitted, whereupon the existing pleadings are served on the intervener, who is then given a further period in which to present his substantive observations. Once these observations are lodged, they in turn have to be translated. In some cases, it is also necessary to give the applicant a supplementary opportunity to reply in writing to the observations of the intervener.[47]

It can be seen from the foregoing that the intervention procedure, standing alone, can add many months to the written procedure. It is therefore being proposed that the time limit for requesting to intervene be shortened to one month from the date of the publication of the notice in the Official Journal.[48] At the same time, it should be possible, by way of practice direction,[49] to require applicants requesting confidentiality to submit non confidential versions of their pleadings on the basis of which the intervener may be admitted immediately, any remaining questions of confidentiality being sorted out, if necessary, at a later stage.

At the same time, steps may need to be taken by the Court to remind interveners that, by its nature, the intervener's role is to support one of the principal parties and not to repeat arguments that have already been made. A substantial reduction in the length of interveners' written observations is appropriate in many cases.

3 A "Fast track" procedure

In some cases, the value of any judgment the Court may give is largely lost unless the judgment is rendered relatively quickly; obvious examples are merger cases, and decisions under the freedom of information rules regarding access to documents.[50]

To deal with such cases, which are not adequately provided for under existing rules, it is necessary to have a fast track procedure, where the exchange of

45 See Article 5 of the Instructions to the Registrar, JO 1994 L 78/32.

46 For an exceptionally complicated case, see the 26 page order in case T-102/96, *Gencor v. Commission*, [1997] ECR II-881. The request for confidential treatment, rejected in part, delayed the proceedings for about five months.

47 Art. 115(5) of the Rules of Procedure.

48 An alternative possibility is to provide for an "abridged" intervention procedure whereby an intervener would have the limited right to appear at the hearing and make observations within the confines of the report for the hearing.

49 See below point 5.

50 See above under heading 6.

written pleadings is kept to a minimum, with the arguments being supplemented at the oral hearing.[51] A request for such a fast track procedure would normally be made by the applicant; obviously, for such a procedure to work, both the application and the defence would have to be limited to an essential minimum.

4 *Use of technology*

Modern communications technology presents many opportunities. At present, with the exception of some documents in interim measures proceedings, all pleadings are lodged in their original hard copy having been sent by post or courier. These pleadings are then served by the Court physically on the other parties, usually at an address for service in Luxembourg nominated for that purpose.

Obviously, modern means of communication, notably the fax machine and electronic mail,[52] could be used much more extensively, reducing and in some cases obviating altogether other traditional means of communication, as well as the need for an address for service in Luxembourg. However, certain problems remain. In a multinational jurisdiction, containing many different Bars, the lawyer's signature on the original pleading constitutes the Court's guarantee that the pleading has been submitted by a lawyer who is authorised to practise before it, and who takes responsibility for the contents of the pleading vis-à-vis the Court. Since a signature cannot necessarily be verified electronically, it may not be possible to dispense with the rule that the original pleading, signed by the advocate, is lodged in the Registry. Another problem is the somewhat anachronistic "extension on account of distance" which allows the period for bringing proceedings, two months under Article 230 of the EC Treaty (ex Article 173), to be extended, depending on the parties' domicile, for example an extra 6 days for Germany, 10 days for the United Kingdom, one month for countries outside Europe, and so on. These automatic extensions, perhaps once justified by the vagaries of the post, are scarcely appropriate in modern conditions. It remains to be seen, however, whether radical solutions can be adopted in this regard.

5 *Practice directions*

Although the Court already publishes guides for lawyers regarding both the written procedure and the oral hearing, it is now appropriate for the Court to lay down, more actively, what is the most helpful way in which the parties may present their case; in other words, more direct "case management".

---

51 For an interlocutory judgment that dealt with certain preliminary points of law in an attempt to speed up the proceedings, see Case T-110/98, *RBJ Mining v. Commission*, judgment of 9 September 1999, nyr.

52 In the longer term, video conference techniques could also be useful for informal meetings with the parties and, possibly, even hearings.

This is particularly true as regards the written procedure, where there is a tendency for the written pleadings presented by private parties to become too long, the annexes to be too voluminous and both to be badly organised. From a judicial point of view, long pleadings not only add immeasurably to delays in translation, and to the time needed to process the case; they are actively counter-productive. In a pleading that is too long, one runs the risk that the judge will lose the thread of the argument, or will become progressively less receptive as he battles through many pages, probably in a language that is not his mother tongue.[53] Similarly, nothing is more calculated to raise judicial blood pressure than annexes which cannot easily be found or which are unnecessary, or the relevance of which is not apparent.

In these circumstances, the Court will need powers to adopt clear practice directions on such matters as the form, content and length of the written pleadings, and the presentation of annexes.

V Conclusions

It is to be hoped that these procedural reforms will enable the Court of First Instance to respond to the needs of its second decade. In the meantime, another working day has drawn to a close, the advocates have departed, the cows are safely home, the evening church bells ring, the papers for tomorrow's hearing are gathered into the briefcase. What has been achieved?

In my own view, what one should never cease to try to achieve is not only the correct result in the particular case, but a system of justice at Community level which enables every litigant, right or wrong, to feel that his case has been fairly and properly heard and determined. The European Community is still young, relatively unknown, and widely misunderstood; in the long run it will not succeed unless its Courts are accessible, effective and just.

53 Quintillian said, over a thousand years ago, "We must not burden the judge with all the arguments we have discovered, since by so doing we shall at once bore him and render him less inclined to believe us."

8

THE EUROPEAN COURT OF FIRST INSTANCE: TEN YEARS OF INTERACTION WITH THE COURT OF JUSTICE

Koen Lenaerts[*]

INTRODUCTION

Before the establishment of the CFI, there had never been a two-tier system of judicial protection within the Community. The Court of Justice had always acted, in all procedural settings, as a court of first and last instance. Admittedly, the judicial system provided for cooperation between national courts and the Court of Justice by way of the preliminary rulings procedure under Article 234 EC (ex-Article 177). This procedure opens the way for a certain interaction between national courts and the Court of Justice in respect of points of law.[1] Indeed, in its order for reference to the Court of Justice, a national court will often put forward its own opinion on the questions submitted concerning the interpretation of provisions or principles of Community law or on the validity of acts of Community institutions. However, that kind of interaction has only a limited bearing on the operation of the system of judicial protection. First of all, the national court may refer preliminary questions to the Court of Justice without giving any indication as to the answer that might be given to the questions referred. Secondly, where the national court does itself consider possible answers to the questions put to the Court of Justice, the latter court is not required to take formal account of that opinion as part of the reasoning adopted in its judgment.

The establishment of the CFI in 1989 and the gradual extension of its jurisdiction to cover all direct actions brought by natural and legal persons, in 1993 and 1994, drastically changed the Community system of judicial protection. Indeed, where the Community judicature acts as an administrative court, a double degree of jurisdiction will now always be available to private parties in the form of a right of appeal, albeit on points of law alone. This double degree of jurisdiction gives rise to a new kind of interaction on points of law between the lower and the appellate court which has in turn enhanced the clarity and quality

---

* All opinions expressed are personal to the author. This article has been drafted with the assistance of Ignace Maselis and Marc Pittie, Legal Secretaries at the Court of First Instance of the European Communities.

1 The finding of facts and their assessment is, in preliminary ruling proceedings, a matter for the national court.

D. O'Keeffe (ed.), Liber Amicorum Slynn 97-116 (2000)

of reasoning in the Community judicature's case-law and thereby improved considerably the level of judicial protection.

First of all, a court sitting in first and last instance may have a tendency to state the law without having a strong incentive to provide extensive reasoning to justify its conclusion. By contrast, in a system where there is a double degree of jurisdiction, the higher court either endorses the reasoned judgment of the lower court or explains why it has decided to deviate from it. Thus, whatever the outcome of the case, the double degree of jurisdiction increases clarity and improves the level of reasoning in the procedure as a whole. If in a difficult case, the lower court were to shirk its duty to give sufficient reasons for its decision, the judgment could then be set aside by the higher court on the basis that such a failure to give proper reasons amounted to a procedural flaw in the judgment which adversely affected the interests of the party which had lost the case.[2]

Second, where the interpretation by the Court of Justice of a provision of Community law gives rise to some ambiguity, the CFI, when it is called upon to apply that provision of Community law, must "interpret" the interpretation given by the Court of Justice.

This point is illustrated by the *Codorniu* judgment[3] delivered by the Court of Justice shortly after the CFI had been given jurisdiction over all direct actions brought by private parties. In this case an annulment action brought by a Spanish wine producer against a legislative measure, namely a regulation which reserved the right to use the term "crémant" to French and Luxembourgish wine producers,[4] was declared admissible. The Court based its finding that the applicant was "individually concerned" by the contested regulation on the fact that the applicant had been using the trade mark "Gran Cremant de Codorniu" since 1924 to designate one of its quality sparkling wines, that it had moreover registered that trade mark, and that, as a result of the contested regulation, the applicant could no longer use the word "crémant" to market its product.[5]

Due to the brevity of the judgment, it was unclear whether *Codorniu* reflected a more general readiness on the part of the Court of Justice to lower the threshold for private parties to bring actions for the annulment of legislative measures.[6] Since the CFI had been given jurisdiction over all actions for annulment brought by private parties, it was this court which was called upon to interpret the conditions of Article 230(4) EC in the light of the judgment in *Codorniu*.

---

2 See e.g. Cases cited in footnotes 13 and 16.

3 Case C-309/89, *Codorniu* v. *Council*, [1994] ECR I-1853.

4 Council Regulation (EEC) No 2045/89 of 19 June 1989 amending Regulation (EEC) No 3309/85 laying down general rules for the description and presentation of sparkling wines and aerated sparkling wines (O.J. 1989, L 202/12).

5 Case C-309/89, *Codorniu* v. *Council*, [1994] ECR I-1853, paras. 21-22.

6 See by contrast Joined Cases C-267/91 and C-268/91, *Keck and Mithouard*, [1993] ECR I-6097, where the Court clearly indicated that it changed its case law ["contrary to what has previously been decided" (para 16)].

Subsequent case-law indicates that the CFI does not consider that *Codorniu* set a new standard for the admissibility of annulment actions brought by private parties against legislative measures. It thus continues to adopt a restrictive approach to the question of *locus standi* in respect of private parties wishing to obtain judicial review of measures which are of general application.[7] Only in exceptional circumstances will a private party be regarded as individually concerned by such a measure.[8] Recent case-law of the Court of Justice has indicated that it approves the restrictive approach adopted by the CFI with respect to the admissibility of actions brought by private parties against legislative measures.[9] Even though opinions may differ as to the desirability of this development, the interaction between the Court of Justice and the CFI has certainly led to a greater degree of clarity and legal certainty in this area.

Conversely, the Court of Justice may also have to interpret case-law of the CFI since a possible contradiction between a decision of the CFI which has been appealed against and earlier case-law of that court is a point of law which may be raised before the Court of Justice. Thus in *Kruidvat* v. *Commission*[10] the appellant argued that the judgment of the CFI which declared inadmissible its action for the annulment of the Commission's decision exempting Givenchy's selective distribution system from the application of Article 81(1) EC [ex-Article 85(1)] conflicted with the CFI's earlier judgment in *Métropole Télévision and Others* v. *Commission*.[11] The Court of Justice, however, distinguished the contested judgment from *Métropole Télévision and Others* and therefore rejected the plea of the appellant. This kind of interaction between the Court of Justice and the CFI – which flows directly from the existence of a double degree of jurisdiction – again leads to a greater degree of clarity and legal certainty.

7 See e.g. Case T-398/94, *Kahn Scheepvaart* v. *Commission*, [1996] ECR II-477.

8 See e.g. Case T-480/93, *Antillean Rice Mills* v. *Commission*, [1995] ECR II-2305, confirmed on appeal in Case C-390/95 P, *Antillean Rice Mills* v. *Commission*, [1999] ECR I-769.

9 See e.g. Case T-99/94, *Asocarne* v. *Council*, ([1994] ECR II-871) confirmed on appeal (Case C-10/95 P, *Asocarne* v. *Council*, [1995] ECR I-4149). See also Case T-116/94, *CNPAAP* v. *Council* (Order of 11 January 1995), [1995] ECR II-1, paras. 26-32 confirmed by Case C-87/95 P, *CNPAAP* v. *Council* (Order of the Court of Justice of 24 April 1996), [1996] ECR I-2003, para. 36. It should be noted that in an exceptional case where the CFI had found that an action for annulment brought by private parties against a regulation was admissible, the Court of Justice, on appeal, quashed the judgment of the CFI and declared the action inadmissible (See Case T-70/94, *Comafrica and Dole Fresh Fruit Europe* v. *Commission*, [1996] ECR II-1741 and Case C-73/97 P, *French Republic* v. *Commission*, [1999] ECR I-185).

10 See e.g. Case C-70/97 P, *Kruidvat* v. *Commission*, [1998] ECR I-7183, para. 39.

11 Joined Cases T-528/93, T-542/93, T-543/93 and T-546/93, *Métropole Télévision and Others* v. *Commission*, [1996] ECR II-649.

Procedural law and the interaction between the CFI and the Court of Justice

In contrast to the position where there is a single level of jurisdiction, remedies may be available in a two-tier system against violations of the procedural rules which bind the lower court.

Indeed, by virtue of Article 225 EC [ex-Article 168A] and Article 51 of the EC Statute of the Court of Justice (hereinafter "EC Statute"), where an appeal is brought against a judgment of the CFI, the annulment of the contested judgment may be sought on the ground that the CFI has violated a procedural rule in a manner which adversely affects the interests of the appellant. This provision of the EC Statute covers not only possible violations by the CFI of its own Rules of Procedure but also the infringement of "general principles of Community law [...] applicable to the burden of proof and the taking of evidence".[12] Thus, the appeal procedure has not only ensured the enforcement by the Court of Justice of the CFI Rules of Procedure but is also leading to the development of a body of judge made procedural law at Community level.

The Court of Justice has already set out a number of procedural requirements which the CFI should observe.

1 The duty to state reasons

Under Article 33 of the EC Statute, the judgments of the CFI and the Court of Justice must be reasoned. The question whether the grounds of a judgment of the CFI are adequate or not is a point of law and is, as such, subject to review on appeal.[13] A judgment of the CFI will be deemed to be insufficiently reasoned and set aside on that basis, if it does not contain an answer to one of the pleas of law put forward by the applicant[14] or if the answer given in respect of any plea is insufficient.[15] This does not mean, however, that the CFI is obliged to incorporate in full in its judgment all the submissions put forward by the parties. Where the CFI "merely" fails to consider a certain part of an argument, the appellant has to show that this failure affected the outcome of the proceedings and so adversely affected its interests.[16]

---

12 See e.g. Case C-185/95 P, *Baustahlgewebe* v. *Commission*, [1998] ECR I-8417, para. 19; Case C-19/95 P, *San Marco* v. *Commission* (Order of 17 September 1996), [1996] ECR I-4435, para. 40.

13 Case C-283/90 P, *Vidrányi* v. *Commission*, [1991] ECR I-4339, para. 29; Case C-188/96 P, *Commission* v. *V*, [1997] ECR I-6561, para. 24; Case C-401/96 P, *Somaco* v. *Commission*, [1998] ECR I-2587, para. 53.

14 See e.g. Case C-104/97 P, *Atlanta* v. *Council and Commission* (Judgment of 14 October 1999, nyr).

15 See e.g. Case C-68/91 P, *Moritz* v. *Commission*, [1992] ECR I-6849, paras. 21-25.

16 Case C-221/97 P, *Schröder* v. *Commission*, [1998] ECR I-8255, paras. 24-25.

A contradiction in the reasoning of the CFI is also subject to review on appeal.[17] The appellant can seek the annulment of the contested judgment not only on the basis of a contradiction between different paragraphs of that particular judgment, but – as already indicated – also on the basis of a contradiction between the contested judgment and earlier case-law of the CFI.[18]

The case-law of the Court of Justice with respect to the CFI's obligation to state reasons inevitably improves the quality of the CFI's judgments. Since an inadequate or contradictory statement of reasons will lead to the setting aside on appeal of the decision of the CFI, that court will ensure that it states sufficient and coherent grounds for its rulings, whether it rejects or upholds the particular plea of law. However, at the same time, better reasoned judgments of the CFI are more "vulnerable" since the risk of committing an error of law somewhere in the judgment increases with the length of the reasoning.

2 *The duty to take evidence*

Each party has to bear the burden of proving the facts on which its claim or defence is based. However, the CFI and the Court of Justice may lend a helping hand by ordering measures of organisation of procedure or measures of inquiry. It should be noted that the Community judicature's power to order such measures does not release the parties from their obligation to substantiate their assertions. The evidence offered by the parties in support of their allegations must at least establish a *prima facie* case. It is only if the evidence satisfies those conditions that the Community judicature will decide, in an appropriate case, to investigate the allegations further by means of measures of organisation of procedure or measures of inquiry.[19]

In many cases, one of the parties explicitly requests the CFI to order a particular measure of organisation of procedure or of inquiry. Pursuant to Article 48(1) of the CFI Rules of Procedure such requests should, in principle, be made in the application or defence itself.

Thus, in *Baustahlgewebe*,[20] the CFI had rejected as out of time the applicant's offer to adduce oral evidence which had been made in the reply. On appeal, the appellant contended, however, that the CFI had violated the principles

17 Case C-283/90 P, *Vidrányi* v. *Commission*, [1991] ECR I-4339, para. 29; Case C-188/96 P, *Commission* v. *V*, [1997] ECR I-6561, para 24; Case C-401/96 P, *Somaco* v. *Commission*, [1998] ECR I-2587, para. 53; Case C-49/92 P, *Commission* v. *Anic* (Judgment of 8 July 1999, nyr), para. 202.

18 Strictly speaking, this is, of course, not a matter of contradiction in the reasoning of the CFI in the judgment under appeal. See e.g. Case C-70/97 P, *Kruidvat* v. *Commission*, [1998] ECR I-7183, paras. 39-47, in which Kruidvat's plea was rejected.

19 K. Lenaerts and D. Arts (editor R. Bray), *Procedural Law of the European Union* (London, Sweet & Maxwell, 1999), para. 22-067.

20 Case T-145/89, *Baustahlgewebe* v. *Commission*, [1995] ECR II-987.

applicable to the taking of evidence.[21] The Court of Justice upheld the judgment of the CFI on this point. It ruled that offers by the applicant to adduce evidence in proceedings before the CFI must, under Article 48(1) of the CFI Rules of Procedure, be made in the initial application. It nuanced the analysis in the CFI's judgment, however, by stating that evidence in rebuttal and the amplification of the offers of evidence submitted in response to evidence in rebuttal from the opposite party in its defence are not covered by the time-bar laid down in that provision. Article 48(1) of the CFI Rules of Procedure[22] indeed relates to offers of fresh evidence and must be read in the light of Article 66(2), which expressly provides that evidence may be submitted in rebuttal and that evidence previously submitted may be amplified.[23] In the same judgment, the Court of Justice also made clear that the CFI cannot be required to call witnesses of its own motion.[24]

The interaction between the CFI and the Court of Justice in *Baustahlgewebe*[25] has also led to clarification of the case-law regarding requests for the production of documents. The Court of Justice has held that the general principles of Community law governing the right of access to the Commission's file do not apply directly to proceedings before the CFI. Referring to Article 21 of the EC Statute and 64 of the CFI Rules of Procedure, it decided that a party requesting the production of documents in proceedings before the CFI must identify the documents requested and provide the CFI with a minimum of information to establish the relevance of those documents to the proceedings.[26] However, the *Ufex* case[27] demonstrates that where a party before the CFI provides that information, the CFI's rejection of a request that it order production of certain documents, may result in the setting aside of the CFI's judgment.

In many cases the CFI does order measures of organisation of procedure or measures of inquiry either pursuant to a request made by one of the parties or on its own motion. In some cases, this active role played by the CFI in the proceedings reveals facts which are decisive for the outcome of those proceedings. Thus, in *European Parliament* v. *Gutiérrez de Quijano y Lloréns*,[28] for example, the appellant contended that the CFI had violated Article 48(2) of its own Rules of Procedure, under which no new plea in law may be introduced in the course of the proceedings, by basing its judgment on a matter which came to its attention through replies provided to questions which had been put to the parties as

---

21 Case C-185/95 P, *Baustahlgewebe* v. *Commission*, [1998] ECR I-8417.

22 On the interpretation of Art. 48 of the CFI Rules of Procedure, see also Case C-155/98 P, *Alexopoulou* v. *Commission* (Order of 1 July 1999, nyr), paras. 43-58.

23 Case C-185/95 P, *Baustahlgewebe* v. *Commission*, [1998] ECR I-8417, para. 72.

24 *Ibid.*, para. 77.

25 See footnotes 20 and 21.

26 Case C-185/95 P, *Baustahlgewebe* v. *Commission*, [1998] ECR I-8417, para. 93.

27 Case C-119/97 P, *Ufex* v. *Commission* (Judgment of 4 March 1999, nyr), which set aside the Judgment in Case T-77/95, *SFEI and Others* v. *Commission*, [1997] ECR II-1.

28 Case C-252/96 P, *European Parliament* v. *Gutiérrez de Quijano y Lloréns*, [1998] ECR I-7421.

measures of organisation of procedure. The Court of Justice dismissed the appeal, however. It held that it is clear from the wording of Article 48(2) that it applies only to the parties and not to the CFI itself, acting of its own motion.[29]

3 The duty to deliver judgment within a reasonable time

In *Baustahlgewebe* v. *Commission*,[30] the Court of Justice ruled that the right to due process within a reasonable period is a general principle of Community law which is applicable to the procedure before the CFI.[31] The CFI is thus obliged to decide the cases pending before it within a reasonable period.[32] The reasonableness of such a period must be appraised in the light of the circumstances specific to each case and, in particular, the importance of the case for the person concerned, its complexity and the conduct both of the applicant and of the relevant authorities.[33] The CFI is, however, not obliged to deliver judgment within a particular period after the hearing.[34]

In *Baustahlgewebe*, the proceedings before the CFI had lasted for about 5 years and six months. On appeal, the Court of Justice found that, notwithstanding the relative complexity of the case – it concerned proceedings brought against a Commission decision imposing fines on undertakings for infringement of competition law – the CFI had not observed the requirements concerning completion of the proceedings within a reasonable period.[35] However, in the absence of any indication that the length of the proceedings affected their outcome in any way, the Court of Justice held that the procedural irregularity in question could not result in the contested judgment being set aside in full.[36] Nevertheless, an effective remedy should be available against a violation by the CFI of the principle that procedures must be disposed of within a reasonable period. The Court of Justice therefore ruled that, for reasons of economy of procedure and in order to ensure an immediate and effective remedy regarding a procedural irregularity of that kind, the contested judgment should be set aside in so far as it set the amount of the fine imposed on the appellant at ECU 3 million.[37] Giving final judgment, in accordance with Article 54 of the EC Statute, it considered that a sum of ECU 50 000 constituted reasonable satisfaction for the excessive duration of the proceedings and set the new fine at ECU 2 950 000.[38]

---

29 *Ibid.*, paras. 30-31; see also Case C-259/96 P, *Council* v. *De Nil and Impens*, [1998] ECR I-2915, para. 31.
30 Case C-185/95 P, *Baustahlgewebe* v. *Commission*, [1998] ECR I-8417.
31 *Ibid.*, para. 21.
32 *Ibid.*, para. 42.
33 *Ibid.*, para. 29.
34 *Ibid.*, paras. 51-52.
35 *Ibid.*, para. 47.
36 *Ibid.*, para. 49.
37 *Ibid.*, para. 48.
38 *Ibid.*, paras. 141-142.

4 *The duty to raise pleas of law*

The interaction between the CFI and the Court of Justice has also clarified the principles relating to the power – or, arguably, the duty – of the Community judicature to raise a plea in law of its own motion.

In *Daffix* v. *Commission*, the applicant had sought, before the CFI, the annulment of the Commission decision removing him from his post.[39] One of the pleas, concerning the non compliance by the Commission with the obligation to state reasons, had been raised for the first time only in the reply. It will be recalled that Article 48(2) of the CFI Rules of Procedure provides, however, that no new plea in law may be put forward in the course of the procedure.[40] The CFI, having ruled that the plea concerned a matter of public interest and might therefore be raised by the Community Court of its own motion,[41] annulled the contested Commission decision on the ground that the statement of reasons was inadequate.

On appeal, the Court of Justice agreed that the inadequacy of a statement of reasons, where it hinders the Court in the exercise of its power to review the legality of the Community measure at issue, constitutes a matter of public interest which may and indeed must be raised by the Community Court of its own motion.[42] It nevertheless set aside the CFI's judgment since the CFI had committed an error of law in finding that the contested decision was not adequately reasoned. The reasons stated did indeed make possible the judicial review of the legality of the contested decision.[43]

SUBSTANTIVE LAW AND THE INTERACTION BETWEEN THE CFI AND THE COURT OF JUSTICE

The CFI is relatively often called upon to give a ruling on legal issues which have not yet arisen before the Court of Justice.[44] When an appeal is lodged, in-

---

39 Case T-12/94, *Daffix* v. *Commission*, [1995] ECR II-233.

40 "unless it is based on matters of law or of fact which come to light in the course of the procedure" (CFI Rules of Procedure, Art. 48(2)).

41 *Ibid.*, para. 31.

42 Case C-166/95 P, *Commission* v. *Daffix*, [1997] ECR I-983, para. 24.

43 *Ibid.*, paras. 34-38.

44 See e.g. Case T-115/94, *Opel Austria* v. *Council*, ([1997] ECR II-39) on the compatibility of a regulation with principles of customary international law and Case T-135/96, *UEAPME* v. *Council*, ([1998] ECR II-2335) on the admissibility of an action seeking the annulment of a Council Directive. Other striking examples concern the interpretation of Community legal instruments granting rights to natural and legal persons such as the decisions and codes of conduct regarding public access to documents held by Community institutions: see e.g. Case T-194/94, *Carvel and Guardian Newspaper* v. *Council*, [1995] ECR II-2765; Case T-105/95, *WWF UK* v. *Commission*, [1997] ECR II-313; Case T-124/96, *Interporc* v. *Commission*, [1998] ECR II-231; Case T-174/95, *Svenska Journal-*

teraction will take place directly between the CFI and the Court of Justice on the specific points of law concerned. The Court of Justice will either confirm, nuance, alter or reject the reasoning set out by the CFI.

The interaction between the CFI and the Court of Justice in this respect is not, however, limited to cases in which an appeal is lodged against the decisions of the CFI. In every case, where the CFI is called upon to decide a particular point of law, it will take into account the existing case-law of the Court of Justice and will build further on the principles already developed by the latter court. Although the Court of Justice never refers to the case-law of the CFI, the opinions of the Advocates-General indicate that the previous case-law of the CFI also constitutes a source of inspiration for the Court of Justice.

Numerous judgments of the CFI and the Court of Justice can be cited in order to illustrate these different forms of interaction.

1 Cases where the Court of Justice confirms the judgment of the CFI on appeal

Where the CFI rules on a new question of law, one of the parties to the proceedings before the CFI will often lodge an appeal against the judgment. In cases where the Court of Justice dismisses the appeal, without substituting new grounds in its judgment, the impetus for the development of the case-law lies completely with the CFI.

Thus, in *Tetra Pak* v. *Commission*, for example, the CFI ruled[45] and the Court of Justice confirmed[46] that the conduct of an undertaking which takes place on a market separate from, but related to and connected with, the market dominated by this undertaking can, under certain circumstances, be caught by Article 82 EC (ex-Article 86).[47]

---

istförbundet v. *Council*, [1998] ECR II-2289; Case T-188/97, *Rothmans International* v. *Commission* (Judgment of 19 July 1999, nyr); Case T-14/98, *Hautala* v. *Council* (Judgment of 19 July 1999, nyr). See e.g. also the case-law which will be developed with respect to the interpretation of Council Regulation (EC) No 40/94 of 20 December 1993 on the Community trade mark (O.J. 1994, L 11/1) as modified by Council Regulation (EC) No 3288/94 of 22 December 1994 (O.J. 1994, L 349/83). The CFI was called upon to interpret and apply this Regulation for the first time in Case T-163/98, *The Proctor & Gamble Company* v. *Office for Harmonization in the Internal Market (trade marks and designs)* (Judgment of 8 July 1999, nyr).

45 Case T-83/91, *Tetra Pak* v. *Commission*, [1994] ECR II-755.

46 Case C-333/94 P, *Tetra Pak* v. *Commission*, [1996] ECR I-5951; in his opinion (para. 38), the advocate general drew attention to the fact that it was "the first time that the Community judicature has had to consider [this question]".

47 For another example where the Court of Justice confirmed the judgment of the CFI on a new question of law, see Case C-245/95 P, *Commission* v. *NTN and Koyo Seiko*, [1998] ECR I-401.

2 *Cases where the Court of Justice nuances or alters the judgment of the CFI on appeal*

Sometimes the Court of Justice confirms the decision adopted by the CFI but nevertheless feels the need to add to the CFI's reasoning. That happened in *Guérin Automobiles* v. *Commission*[48] where the CFI held that the letter sent by the Commission to a complainant under Article 6 of Regulation No 99/63[49] must be regarded as a definition of its position within the meaning of the second paragraph of Article 232 EC (ex-Article 175).[50] As regards the applicant's argument that allowing such a letter to terminate a failure to act would enable the Commission to evade judicial review since it could not be the object of an action for annulment, the CFI emphasized that, after submitting comments in response to the letter, the applicant is entitled to obtain a definitive decision from the Commission on the complaint, which may be challenged in an action for annulment before the CFI.[51] The Court of Justice confirmed the judgment of the CFI[52] and added that "the Commission's definitive decision must, in accordance with the principles of good administration, be adopted within a reasonable time after it has received the complainant's observations".[53]

Thus, even when the Court of Justice confirms the reasoning adopted by the CFI in its entirety, its input through the double degree of jurisdiction may lead to a more complete and considered result. In *Guérin Automobiles* v. *Commission* this interaction resulted in more comprehensive protection of the complainant's rights *vis-à-vis* the defendant institution.

Where the Court of Justice dismisses the appeal but alters the grounds on which the judgment of the CFI is based, the development of the case-law stems

48 Case T-186/94, *Guérin Automobiles* v. *Commission*, [1995] ECR II-1753. For another example of a case where the Court of Justice nuances the CFI's position: see Case T-84/94, *Bundesverband der Bilanzbuchhalter* v. *Commission*, [1995] ECR II-101 and Case C-107/95 P, *Bundesverband der Bilanzbuchhalter* v. *Commission*, [1997] ECR I-947. The principles developed by the Court of Justice are applied in Case T-17/96, *TF1* v. *Commission* (Judgment of 3 June 1999, nyr).

49 Regulation No 99/63 has been repealed by Commission Regulation (EC) No 2842/98 of 22 December 1998 on the hearing of parties in certain proceedings under Art. 85 and 86 of the EC Treaty (O.J. 1998, L 354/18). Art. 6 of the latter Regulation is similar to Art. 6 of the repealed Regulation No 99/63.

50 Case T-186/94, *Guérin Automobiles* v. *Commission*, [1995] ECR II-1753, para. 32.

51 *Ibid.*, para. 34.

52 Case C-282/95 P, *Guérin Automobiles* v. *Commission*, [1997] ECR I-1503.

53 *Ibid.*, para. 37. In Case T-127/98, *UPS Europe* v. *Commission* (Judgment of 9 September 1999, nyr), the CFI further complemented the principles developed in the case-law by stating that "in considering whether the period between the lodgment of the applicant's observations following the notification under Art. 6 of Regulation No 99/63 and the sending of the formal request to the Commission [pursuant to Art. 232, second paragraph, EC] is acceptable, it is appropriate to take account of the years already spent on the investigation, the present state of the investigation of the case and the attitudes of the parties considered as a whole" (para. 41).

from a genuine interaction between the views of the CFI and the Court of Justice with respect to the point of law concerned. The weight of each jurisdiction in the final outcome depends on the extent to which the core of the CFI's reasoning is maintained in the judgment of the Court of Justice.

This is illustrated by the *Sytraval and Brink's France* v. *Commission* case in which the CFI was called upon to examine, in the absence of any relevant Treaty provision or Community legislation,[54] the procedural rights of the applicants, which had filed a complaint with the Commission concerning an alleged grant of aid by the French Republic. The applicants sought the annulment of the decision formally addressed to them in which the Commission had held that the measures complained of did not constitute state aid within the meaning of Article 87 EC (ex-Article 92).

The CFI first characterised the contested decision as a decision of the Commission rejecting the complainants' allegations. It then examined the question whether the decision explained in a clear and unequivocal manner the reasoning which had led the Commission to conclude that the measures complained of did not constitute state aid. The CFI considered that the Commission's obligation to state reasons for its decisions may, in certain circumstances, require it to engage in an exchange of views and arguments with the complainant, since, in order to justify, to the requisite legal standard, its assessment of a measure characterised by the complainant as state aid, the Commission needs to ascertain the complainant's view of the information obtained by the Commission in the course of its inquiry.[55] In such circumstances, that obligation is the corollary of the Commission's obligation to deal diligently and impartially with its inquiry into the matter by eliciting all such views as may be necessary. The CFI further stated that where the Commission decides to reject a complaint concerning a measure characterised by the complainant as unnotified state aid, without allowing the complainant to comment, prior to the adoption of the definitive decision, on the information obtained in the context of the Commission's investigation, it is under an automatic obligation to examine the objections which the complainant would certainly have raised if it had been given the opportunity of taking cognisance of that information.[56] The CFI annulled the contested decision on the basis that it contained an insufficient statement of reasons.

On appeal, the Court of Justice ruled that the CFI had erred in law,[57] firstly by finding that the contested decision was addressed to the complainants. It held that decisions adopted by the Commission in the field of state aid are always addressed to the Member State concerned. The error of law committed by the CFI did, however, not invalidate the judgment since the decision in question was,

54 Case T-95/94, *Sytraval and Brink's France* v. *Commission*, [1995] ECR II-2651: this point was underlined in para. 50 of the judgment.

55 *Ibid.*, para. 78.

56 *Ibid.*, paras. 66 and 72.

57 C-367/95 P, *Commission* v. *Sytraval and Brink's France*, [1998] ECR I-1719, paras. 43-49.

nevertheless, of direct and individual concern to the complainants.[58] The Court of Justice further held that in the decision where it found that no state aid existed, the Commission should have provided the complainant with an adequate explanation of the reasons why it considered that the facts and legal arguments put forward in the complaint had failed to demonstrate the existence of state aid.[59] The Court of Justice thus accepted the core of the CFI's reasoning, namely that the contested decision had to be sufficiently reasoned *vis-à-vis* the complainants.

Secondly, the Court of Justice also considered that the CFI had erred in law by holding that the Commission was under an obligation, in certain circumstances, to engage in an exchange of views and arguments with the complainant,[60] but nevertheless accepted that the complainants could benefit from the procedural guarantees afforded by Article 88(2) [ex-Article 93(2)].[61] The Court of Justice also explained that the CFI had erred by stating that the Commission was under an obligation to examine, of its own motion, objections which the complainant would certainly have raised had it been given the opportunity of taking cognisance of the information obtained by the Commission in the course of the investigation,[62] but ruled, in addition, that "this finding does not mean that the Commission is not obliged, where necessary, to extend its investigation of a complaint beyond a mere examination of the facts and points of law brought to its notice by the complainant".[63] According to the Court of Justice, the Commission is indeed "required, in the interest of sound administration of the fundamental rules of the Treaty relating to state aid, to conduct a diligent and impartial examination of the complaint, which may make it necessary for it to examine matters not expressly raised by the complainant".[64]

Having found that the CFI had correctly held that, on a number of issues raised in the complaint, the reasons given in the contested decision were incomplete or wholly inadequate, the Court of Justice dismissed the appeal.[65]

---

58 *Ibid.*, para. 47.
59 *Ibid.*, para. 64.
60 *Ibid.*, paras. 58-59.
61 *Ibid.*, para. 47; see also Case T-11/95, *BP Chemicals Ltd* v. *Commission*, [1998] ECR II-3235, paras. 88-89.
62 *Ibid.*, para. 60.
63 *Ibid.*, para. 62.
64 *Ibid.*, para. 62.
65 The Court of Justice however also held (paras. 67 to 72 of the judgment) that the CFI had erred in law treating some pleas raised by the applicant as pleas alleging an infringement of Art. 253 EC (ex-Art. 190) whereas in reality they concerned the substantive legality of the contested decision.

The judgment of the Court of Justice in *Commission* v. *Sytraval and Brink's France*[66] is probably best seen as a "correction" of the principles developed by the CFI[67] in relation to the rights of complainants in state aid matters.[68] The interaction between the CFI and the Court of Justice led to greater legal certainty as to the procedural rights of such complainants.[69]

3 *Cases where the Court of Justice quashes the judgment of the CFI on appeal*

Even when the judgment of the CFI is completely set aside by the Court of Justice, the interaction between the CFI and the Court of Justice still contributes to greater clarity in the judicial statement of the law which results from the procedure. The judgment of the Court of Justice will indicate the error of law committed by the CFI and will clearly state not only how the law should be interpreted and applied but also why that is so.

Thus, in *AssiDomän Kraft Products and Others* v. *Commission*,[70] the applicants were all addressees of the Woodpulp decision[71] which had been partially annulled by the Court of Justice in *Ahlström Osakeyhtiö and Others* v. *Commission*[72] (hereinafter "Woodpulp judgment"). The applicants in *AssiDomän* had not participated in those proceedings before the Court of Justice but, following the judgment of the Court of Justice, they had requested the Commission to reconsider their legal position in the light of that ruling and to refund the fines which they had paid. The Commission, by decision of 4 October 1995, refused to grant that request. Indeed it considered that the Woodpulp judgment did not affect the status of the decision in respect of those addressees who had not participated in the proceedings before the Court of Justice. Although the CFI rejected the plea

66 Case C-367/95 P, *Commission* v. *Sytraval and Brink's France*, [1998] ECR I-1719.

67 As to the implementation by the Commission of the CFI judgment, see Commission Decision 99/676/EC of 20 July 1999 concerning presumed aid allegedly granted by France to Sécuripost (O.J. 1999, L 274/37-44).

68 The CFI further developed its case law on this point in Case T-95/96, *Gestevision Telecinco* v. *Commission*, [1998] ECR II-3407 and in Case T-17/96, *TF1* v. *Commission* (Judgment of 3 June 1999, nyr). It held that the Commission is under an obligation to act within a reasonable time on a complaint alleging aid to be incompatible with the common market.

69 Art. 20(2) of Council Regulation (EC) No 659/1999 of 22 March 1999 laying down detailed rules for the application of Art. 93 of the EC Treaty now provides explicitly that "(a)ny interested party may inform the Commission of any alleged unlawful aid and any alleged misuse of aid".

70 Case T-227/95, *AssiDomän Kraft Products and Others* v. *Commission*, [1997] ECR II-1185. For another example, see Case C-395/95 P, *Geotronics* v. *Commission*, [1997] ECR I-2271.

71 Commission Decision 85/202/EEC of 19 December 1984 relating to a proceeding under Art. 85 of the EEC Treaty (IV/29.725 – Wood pulp) (O.J. 1985, L 85/1).

72 Joined Cases C-89/85, C-104/85, C-114/85, C-116/85, C-117/85 and C-125/85 to C-129/85, *Ahlström Osakeyhtiö and Others* v. *Commission*, [1993] ECR I-1307.

of the applicants that the Woodpulp judgment had an effect *erga omnes*, it nevertheless annulled the Commission decision.[73] According to the CFI, the Commission was indeed required under Article 233 EC (ex-Article 176) to review, in the light of the Woodpulp judgment, the legality of the Woodpulp decision in so far as it related to addressees who had not brought an action for annulment within the time-limit. The CFI stressed in that regard that the annulment of the relevant part of that decision was based on considerations which applied generally to the Commission's analysis of the woodpulp market and was not founded on any examination of particular conduct or practices of individual addressees of the decision.[74] The findings of the Court therefore potentially raised serious doubts as to the legality of the decision with respect to addressees who had not participated in the proceedings leading to the Woodpulp judgment.

However, on appeal, the Court of Justice set aside the judgment of the CFI.[75] It held that the CFI had erred in law in holding that Article 233 EC (ex-Article 176) placed the Commission under a duty to review the legality of the Woodpulp decision in so far as it concerned parties which had not sought the annulment of that decision before the Community judicature. Indeed, according to the Court of Justice, the Woodpulp judgment cannot have decided anything whatsoever with regard to the situation of persons who were not parties to the proceedings.[76] Thus, although Article 233 EC (ex-Article 176) requires the institution concerned to ensure that any act intended to replace the annulled act is not affected by the same irregularities as those identified in the judgment annulling the original act, that article, contrary to what the CFI held, does not mean that the Commission must, at the request of interested parties, re-examine identical or similar decisions allegedly affected by the same irregularity, which are addressed to persons other than the applicant. The principle of legal certainty indeed precludes such an obligation to carry out such a re-examination.[77]

4 *Interaction between the CFI and the Court of Justice in the absence of an appeal*

As already indicated, the interaction between the CFI and the Court of Justice is not limited to cases in which an appeal is lodged against the judgment of the CFI. Indeed, when deciding on a particular point of law, the CFI will take into account the existing case-law of the Court of Justice and will build further on the principles developed by that latter court. Similarly, the Court of Justice when faced with a particular legal issue, may find guidance in previous case-law of the

---

73 Case T-227/95, *AssiDomän Kraft Products and Others* v. *Commission*, [1997] ECR II-1185, para. 56.

74 *Ibid.*, para. 75.

75 Case C-310/97 P, *Commission* v. *AssiDomän Kraft Products and Others* (Judgment of 14 September 1999, nyr).

76 *Ibid.*, para. 55.

77 *Ibid.*, para. 63.

CFI on the point. This interaction between the two Community courts will be illustrated by means of some *capita selecta*.

Cases concerning the rights of the defence

In almost all cases in which the legality of a Commission decision finding an infringement of Articles 81 and 82 EC (ex-Articles 85 and 86) is challenged, a plea relating to the violation of the right to a fair hearing is raised. One important aspect of this right is the applicant's access to the Commission's file in the course of the administrative procedure.[78]

Thus, in *Akzo* v. *Commission*[79] the applicant sought, before the Court of Justice which still had jurisdiction at that time, the annulment of the Commission decision finding an infringement of Article 82 EC *inter alia* on the ground that he had not been given access to certain documents in the Commission's file. In its judgment of 3 July 1991, the Court of Justice dismissed that plea. It held that "although regard for the rights of defence requires that the undertaking concerned shall have been enabled to make known effectively its point of view on the documents relied upon by the Commission in making the findings on which its decision is based, there are no provisions which require the Commission to divulge the contents of its files to the parties concerned".[80] In other words, according to the Court of Justice in *Akzo*, there is only an obligation for the Commission to divulge the incriminating documents on which the decision is to be based, in the course of the administrative procedure.

Only a few months later, on 17 December 1991, the CFI ruled on a similar plea raised by *Hercules Chemicals* in one of the Polypropylene cases.[81] The CFI noted that the Commission, in its Twelfth Report on Competition Policy, had established a procedure for providing access to the file in competition cases. In doing so, the Commission had imposed upon itself rules exceeding the requirements laid down in the previous case-law of the Court of Justice. According to these self-imposed rules by which it was, nevertheless, bound "the Commission has an obligation to make available to the undertakings involved in Article 85(1) [now Article 81(1) EC] proceedings all documents, whether in their favour or otherwise, which it has obtained during the course of the investigation, save

78 Another example of interaction between the CFI and the Court of Justice relating to the right to a fair hearing concerns the right of a person to be heard in a procedure where the Commission takes a decision which is not addressed to that person but which nevertheless adversely affects his interests. See Case C-66/90, *Netherlands and Others* v. *Commission*, [1992] ECR I-565; Case C-135/92, *Fiskano* v. *Commission*, [1994] ECR I-2885; Case T-450/93, *Lisrestal* v. *Commission*, [1994] ECR II-1177; Case C-32/95 P, *Commission* v. *Lisrestal and Others*, [1996] ECR I-5373; Case T-42/96, *Eyckler & Malt* v. *Commission*, [1998] ECR II-401; Case C-163/98 P, *Commission* v. *Eyckler & Malt*, pending.

79 Case C-62/86, *Akzo* v. *Commission*, [1991] ECR I-3359.

80 *Ibid.*, para. 16.

81 Case T-7/89, *Hercules Chemicals* v. *Commission*, [1991] ECR II-1711.

where the business secrets of other undertakings, the internal documents of the Commission or other confidential information are involved".[82]

Since *Hercules Chemicals*, the case-law with regard to access to the file in competition cases has developed further. Thus, on 18 December 1992, in *Cimenteries CBR and Others* v. *Commission*,[83] the CFI having first stated that access to the file was intended to protect the rights of defence, went on to observe that the observance of the rights of defence in all proceedings in which sanctions may be imposed is a fundamental principle of Community law.[84]

In his opinion in Case C-310/93 P *BPB Industries and British Gypsum* v. *Commission*,[85] Advocate General Léger suggested that the Court of Justice complete the step forward taken by the CFI and confirm as a corollary to the principle of the protection of the rights of the defence, the fundamental principle that an undertaking under investigation is entitled to have access to the whole of the Commission's file, save where the business secrets of other undertakings, the internal documents of the Commission or other confidential information are involved.[86] The Court of Justice implicitly endorsed that view of the Advocate General in its judgment in *BPB Industries and British Gypsum* v. *Commission.*

Whilst, according to the initial case-law of the Court of Justice, the right of access of a party concerned by an investigation under Article 81(1) or 82 EC to the Commission's file was limited to incriminating documents, the interaction between the CFI and the Court of Justice has led to the recognition of a fundamental right of general access to all documents in the Commission's file, incriminating or exculpatory, with the exception of documents containing business secrets or other confidential information and internal documents of the Commission.

In the *Soda Ash* cases,[87] the CFI applied these principles and annulled for the first time a Commission decision on the ground that the parties concerned had not had access to documents of the Commission's file which might have exculpated the applicants. In the same cases, the CFI also developed clear principles to prevent the Commission denying effective access to the file by making unwarranted reference to the rights of other companies to have their business secrets protected. The right to the protection of business secrets must, when documents in the Commission's file contain confidential information, be balanced against safeguarding the rights of the defence.[88]

82 *Ibid.*, para. 54.

83 Joined Cases T-10/92, T-11/92, T-12/92 and T-15/92, *Cimenteries CBR and Others* v. *Commission*, [1992] ECR II-2667.

84 *Ibid.*, para. 39.

85 Case C-310/93 P, *BPB Industries and British Gypsum* v. *Commission*, [1995] ECR I-865.

86 *Ibid.*, para. 116.

87 Case T-30/91, *Solvay* v. *Commission*, [1995] ECR II-1775; Case T-36/91, *ICI* v. *Commission*, [1995] ECR II-1847.

88 *Ibid.*, Case T-30/91, para. 88; *Ibid.*, Case T-36/91, para. 98.

In *PVC*,[89] the CFI further specified that an improper application of the principles governing access to the file in the course of the administrative procedure does not automatically lead to the annulment of the contested decision. If a company is not given access to a particular document in the course of the administrative procedure which the Commission should have made available under the principles set out above, the decision will only be annulled if the applicant demonstrates that the non-disclosure of the document in question might have influenced the course of the procedure and thus the content of the decision is to the applicant's detriment.[90]

Cases concerning the compatibility of Community law with rules of international law

In *Opel Austria* v. *Council*,[91] the CFI had to examine the question whether a regulation of the Council was void on the ground that it violated a provision of public international law. The facts of the case were as follows. On the eve of the entry into force of the Agreement on the European Economic Area ("EEA"), which prohibits, *inter alia*, duties on imports and exports within the EEA, the Council adopted a regulation according to which import duties were levied on gearboxes manufactured by the applicant, a company established in Austria. The applicant contended that the Council had thus violated a principle of public international law, namely the principle of good faith, according to which, pending the entry into force of an international agreement, the signatories thereto may not adopt measures which would defeat its object and purpose.

Having recalled that the principle of good faith is a rule of customary international law,[92] the CFI did not have to answer the more delicate question as to whether such a rule can confer rights on individuals which they may invoke before the Community judicature. It held that the principle of good faith is the corollary in public international law of the principle of protection of legitimate expectations which, according to established case-law, forms part of the Community legal order.[93] Traders may rely on this principle of Community law in order

89 Joined Cases T-305/94 to T-307/94, T-313/94 to T-316/94, T-318/94, T-325/94, T-328/94, T-329/94 and T-335/94, *Limburgse Vinyl Maatschappij and Others* v. *Commission* (Judgment of 20 April 1999, nyr), paras. 1019-1021.

90 Appeals have been lodged against the *PVC* judgment of the CFI (Cases C-247/99 P, C-251/99 P, C-252/99 P and C-254/99 P). Appellants contend that where the access to the file has been irregular in the course of the administrative procedure, the decision which was taken at the end of this procedure necessarily infringes the rights of defence of the parties concerned and should be annulled. The further interaction between the CFI and the Court of Justice will thus clarify the question concerning the sanction which should be reserved to an irregular access to the Commission's file in the course of the administrative procedure.

91 Case T-115/94, *Opel Austria* v. *Council*, [1997] ECR II-39.

92 *Ibid.*, paras. 90-91.

93 *Ibid.*, para. 93.

to challenge the legality of an act of the Communities. More precisely, in a situation where the Communities have ratified an international agreement and the date of entry into force of that agreement is known, traders may rely on the principle of protection of legitimate expectations in order to challenge the adoption by the institutions, during the period preceding the entry into force of that agreement, of any measure contrary to the provisions of that agreement which will have direct effect after it has entered into force.[94]

Having found that the contested regulation violated provisions of the EEA Agreement capable of having direct effect following the entry into force of that agreement, namely the provision prohibiting the imposition of import duties, the CFI annulled the contested regulation.

No appeal was lodged against the CFI's judgment in *Opel Austria*.[95] However, in *Racke*,[96] a case involving a preliminary ruling, the Court of Justice had to address the question whether provisions of public international law could be invoked in order to challenge the legality of a Community act. This case concerned the compatibility of the Council Regulation suspending the trade concessions provided for by the Cooperation Agreement between the Community and Yugoslavia, with provisions of public international law, in particular the universal principle *pacta sunt servanda*; the regulation in question was itself based on another principle of international law, namely the *rebus sic stantibus* principle. Racke, which imported wine from Serbia, had benefited from the tariff preferences on imports of wine from Yugoslavia provided for in the Cooperation Agreement which were suspended when the Council adopted the disputed regulation.

Advocate General Jacobs substantially based his opinion of 4 December 1997[97] on the reasoning which the CFI had followed in *Opel Austria*.[98] He considered that, where the provisions of an agreement concluded by the Community have direct effect, the beneficiaries of such rights may have legitimate expectations as to the correct and proper implementation of the agreement in issue.[99] According to the Advocate General, the individual's entitlement to some measure of protection of its legitimate expectations is further supported by the strength of the principle *pacta sunt servanda*, which is the fundamental tenet of the law of treaties.[100]

However, the Advocate General in *Racke* further complemented the principles set forth in *Opel Austria*. He considered that a Community act may be successfully challenged on the basis of rules of customary international law only if there is a *manifest* violation of such rules. By allowing such limited review, an

94 *Ibid.*, para. 94.
95 See footnote 91.
96 Case C-162/96, *Racke*, [1998] ECR I-3655.
97 [1998] ECR I-3659.
98 See footnote 91.
99 [1998] ECR I-3659, para. 87.
100 *Ibid.*, para. 88.

appropriate balance is struck, according to the Advocate General, between the rights of the individual and the decision-making powers of the Community institutions.[101] The Court of Justice followed this opinion[102] ruling that no factor had been disclosed of such a kind as to affect the validity of the regulation suspending the trade concessions provided for by the Cooperation Agreement between the Community and Yugoslavia.

The *Racke* case[103] thus demonstrates that the interaction between the CFI and the Court of Justice cannot be seen as a one way street. Indeed, the Court of Justice also finds guidance in the case-law of the CFI when it has to decide a particular question of law which has already arisen before the latter.

CONCLUDING REMARKS

The enforcement by the Court of Justice of the CFI Rules of Procedure and of general principles of procedural law improves the level of judicial protection enjoyed by individuals who come to the CFI. The double degree of jurisdiction should also have a beneficial effect on judicial protection before the Court of Justice since it may be expected that the Court of Justice will itself respect the general principles of procedural law which it has laid down for the CFI.[104] However, the Court of Justice being the superior court of the European Union, no remedy will generally be available if there is a violation by this court of its Rules of Procedure or of general principles of procedural law. Nevertheless, where the violation by the Court of Justice of a procedural rule causes loss or damage to a party, it cannot be excluded that this party might bring an action for damages against the Community under Articles 235 and 288, second paragraph, EC (ex-Articles 178 and 215, second paragraph). The admissibility of such an action in which the CFI would be called upon to rule on the legality of the conduct of the Court of Justice is a question which has never yet arisen.[105]

The interaction between the CFI and the Court of Justice also leads to greater clarity and legal certainty in the substantive law. Since both jurisdictions are established in Luxembourg, it may be appropriate, to compare this interaction with the procession which takes places annually in the Luxembourg town of Echternach. In this procession, the participants take two steps forward, followed by one step backwards. Faced with new questions of law, the CFI often takes two steps in a certain direction. Although the Court of Justice may nuance the

101 *Ibid.*, paras. 89-90.

102 Case C-162/96, *Racke*, [1998] ECR I-3655, paras. 51-52.

103 See footnote 96.

104 As well as the ECJ Rules of Procedure in their interpretation that coincides with the interpretation given by the Court of Justice to identically worded provisions of the CFI Rules of Procedure.

105 See e.g. S. Cras, note on *Baustahlgewebe*, Nederlands Tijdschrift voor Europees Recht (April 1999), 82.

CFI's approach, often by taking one step back, the result generally is one prudent and justifiable step forward in the development of Community law.

Finally, it should be recalled that the Advocates General play an important role in the interaction between the CFI and the Court of Justice. As an Advocate General, Sir Gordon Slynn (as he then was) delivered opinions in landmark cases dealing with areas of Community law which are of direct interest to the CFI.[106] It is therefore unsurprising that his opinions are not only frequently referred to by parties to proceedings before the CFI but also constitute a highly esteemed source of inspiration for that court in applying and developing the law.[107] May this modest contribution to the *Essays* written in his honour be a tribute to the major contribution made by Lord Slynn of Hadley to the furtherance of the rule of law in the European Union.

106 *Competition law*: see e.g. opinions in Case 60/81, *IBM* v. *Commission*, [1981] ECR 2639, in Joined Cases 100 to 103/80, *Musique Diffusion française and Others* v. *Commission*, [1983] ECR 1825, in Case 68/82, *Hasselblad* v. *Commission*, [1984] ECR 883, in Joined Cases 228 and 229/82, *Ford* v. *Commission*, [1984] ECR 1129, in Case 123/83, *BNIC* v. *Guy Clair*, [1985] ECR 391, and in Joined Cases 25 and 26/84, *Ford* v. *Commission*, [1985] ECR 2725; *State aid*: see e.g. opinion in Joined Cases 67, 68 and 70/85, *Van der Kooy and Others* v. *Commission*, [1988] ECR 219, and in Case 213/85, *Commission* v. *Netherlands*, [1988] ECR 281; *Anti-dumping*: see e.g. Case 250/85, *Brother Industries* v. *Council*, [1988] ECR 5683, and Joined Cases 294/86 and 77/87, *Technointorg* v. *Commission and Council*, [1988] ECR 6077; *Milk quota*: see opinion in Case 120/86, *Mulder*, [1988] ECR 2321.

107 See Joined Cases T-25, 26, 30 to 32, 34 to 39, 42 to 46, 50 to 56, 68 to 71, 87, 88, 103 and 104/95, *S.A. Cementeries CBR and others v. Commission* (Judgment of 15 March 2000, nyr), paras. 2800-2803, 4193, 4269.

PART 2

FORMS OF JUDICIAL REVIEW BEFORE THE EUROPEAN COURTS

9

REFORM OF ARTICLE 234 PROCEDURE: THE LIMITS OF THE POSSIBLE

David Edward

There has been no shortage of papers telling us what is wrong with the preliminary reference system and what should be done to put it right. Most of the problems are already self-evident. So are many of the proposed solutions but they are often mutually incompatible, or, while improving matters in one direction, would only make things worse in another. Some of them proceed from a national viewpoint that takes little or no account of the attitudes and traditions of other member states. Most of them could not be implemented without the unanimous consent of the member states – a scarce commodity.

What is surprising is not how badly, but how well the system still works. It was, after all, devised for a Community of six member states with broadly similar legal systems. Almost fifty years later, in spite of all the problems, references are made in ever-growing numbers, on an ever-expanding range of subject matter, by judges at all levels of the judicial hierarchy in 15 member states with widely differing legal systems and traditions. Given the workload and the complexity of some cases, most references receive an answer within a reasonable time.[1] In all but a few cases, the Court's judgments are available on the Internet in 11 languages by the evening of the day they are pronounced.

Inevitably, some judgments give rise to criticism, but not, proportionately, more so than the judgments of courts in the member states. In very few cases does the referring court make a new reference because the Court's judgment was unhelpful or unclear.

1 What is a "reasonable time" depends, of course, on one's point of view. By the standards of some member states, the Court's speed of reply is positively electric, and delay is a problem even for the best regulated national courts. In Case C-167/97, *Seymour Smith & Perez* [1999] ECR I-623, the claimants were dismissed by their employers and commenced proceedings in 1991. It was five years later, in December 1996, that the decision to refer was taken by the House of Lords. The reference reached the Registry of the Court in May 1997. The Court gave judgment in February 1999 (21 months from beginning to end). The House of Lords gave judgment in February 2000.

D. O'Keeffe (ed.), Liber Amicorum Slynn 119-142 (2000)

So Doomsday has not yet arrived, though it is clear that reform is necessary if the system is not to break down. Rather than add to the corpus of wish-lists and magic solutions, this paper approaches the problem by identifying the legal and practical constraints within which the Court has to work. These are the rocks past which reformers will have to navigate, and it is important to know where they are before setting out.

This approach will, it is hoped, put the proposals submitted by the Court to the Council on 28 May 1999 in context. Their adoption would provide the necessary breathing space for proper consideration of the long-term options. As regards the longer term, this paper points out some of the issues that need to be faced without necessarily offering a solution. The worst course of all would be to rush into radical changes without adequate assessment of their potential consequences.

The constraints on the working of the preliminary reference system fall into the following broad categories:

(1) procedural and structural constraints imposed by the basic texts (the Treaties, the Brussels and other Conventions, the Statute of the Court and the Rules of Procedure);
(2) linguistic constraints;
(3) constraints resulting from "cultural diversity" – the divergences between the legal systems and the underlying traditions and attitudes of lawyers and judges;
(4) constraints of the workload, caused by
    (i) the volume of references (a quantitative constraint) and
    (ii) the subject-matter (a qualitative constraint), and
(5) practical constraints of time, manpower, budget and technical resources.

I Procedural and Structural Constraints

The basic texts dictate in considerable detail how the preliminary reference procedure is to work. Unlike the Court of Human Rights, the Court of Justice has no autonomous power to alter its own rules of procedure or to derogate from them. Every amendment of the rules requires the unanimous approval of the member states in Council or at an Intergovernmental Conference.

The texts impose constraints, first, on the way in which the reference procedure is initiated and, second, on the procedure to be followed thereafter.

A Initiating the reference

1 The texts

If a national court or tribunal decides that a reference is necessary, the Court must, in principle, accept it and answer the questions posed. All references must, in principle, follow the same procedure and ought, if possible, to be dealt with "in the order in which the preparatory inquiries in them have been completed".[2] The President may "in special circumstances" order that a case be given priority but this power must be exercised sparingly if cases are not to become priority cases as a matter of routine.[3]

As far as the referring court is concerned, Article 20 of the Statute envisages that the referring court shall "suspend its proceedings" in order to make the reference. In some countries, the effect of suspension is that the referring court cannot act further until the Court has dealt with the reference.

The texts envisage only one circumstance in which a reference need not go all the way to judgment. That is where the question referred is "*manifestly identical* to a question on which the Court has already ruled". In that case, the Court can dispose of the case by order, but only after informing the referring court and hearing the parties, the intervening governments, the Commission and, where appropriate, the Council.[4]

This provision was introduced in 1991 in response to a proposal of the Court but the administrative procedures involved in consulting the parties, governments and institutions, and the need to translate both the reference and the observations submitted, make the procedure extremely clumsy to operate. The obligation to consult was insisted upon by the Council, though one might have thought that, if a point is manifest, the Court could be trusted to deal with it. This illustrates the extreme caution with which the member states have approached quite modest proposals for reform.

2 Mitigating the rigour of the texts

The Court has mitigated the rigour of the texts in three ways: (1) by informal contacts between the Court Registry and national courts; (2) by rejecting some references as inadmissible; and (3) through the *CILFIT*[5] judgment.

(1) Informal contacts

A number of references are withdrawn following informal contacts between the Registry and the referring court. The Registry draws the attention of the referring court to previous judgments which seem to provide the answer to the ques-

2 Rules of Procedure ("RP"), Article 55 (1).
3 RP, Article 55 (2).
4 RP, Article 104 (3).
5 Case 283/81, *CILFIT v Ministero della Sanità* [1982] ECR 3415.

tions posed. In most cases, the reference is then withdrawn or the questions are reformulated with a more detailed explanation of the reasons for making the reference. The national court rarely insists that the reference be dealt with as it stands.

This informal approach is not available where suspension of the national proceedings has the effect that the referring court is unable to act.

(2) Inadmissibility

Since *Foglia v Novello,*[6] the Court has rejected references as inadmissible for want of clarity, relevance or basic information. This practice has been criticised as a breach of the principle of judicial cooperation, but it is important to keep the criticisms in proportion. In the past nine years, only 27 references have been rejected as inadmissible – on average, around one per cent per year.

In practice, the Registry of the Court makes great efforts to give national courts the opportunity to supplement inadequate references. But even where there is no formal barrier to their doing so, some national judges seem unable or unwilling to see what is needed. Also, where the terms of the reference have been drafted by the parties, the judge may feel unable to amplify the reference without reopening the procedure and hearing the parties. In these cases, it is quicker in the long run to reject the reference as inadmissible, allowing the national court to make a fresh reference if required.

The most telling objection to dismissal of references as inadmissible is that it gives an impression of discourtesy to the national judge. This seems inconsistent with the idea of judicial cooperation as the cornerstone of the system, even though, in the cases that are so dismissed, cooperation has proved impossible.

To overcome these difficulties, the Court has proposed a new rule of procedure[7] which would enable the Court to make a formal request to the referring court for clarification of the order for reference. This would enhance judicial cooperation and overcome the formal problem for those national judges who feel that, under the existing rules, they cannot act. If a national judge were still to decline to provide the clarification requested, this could be made clear in the order rejecting the reference.

(3) CILFIT

The judgment in *CILFIT* provides a basis for applying the doctrine of *acte clair* where the treaty requires a national court whose decision would otherwise be final to make a reference.[8] The *CILFIT* criteria are criticised as being excessively restrictive and the Court is frequently urged to make them more flexible so as to allow a greater degree of latitude to national supreme courts.

The problem lies, not in *CILFIT*, but in the texts. According to its terms, Article 234 leaves no room for *acte clair,* or for any other limitation of the obli-

6 Case 104/79, *Foglia v Novello* [1980] ECR 745.
7 Adding another paragraph to Article 104 RP.
8 Article 234 EC (ex Article 177), third paragraph.

gation to refer, unless there is, in reality, no "question" on which a decision is necessary to enable the national court to give judgment. It is doubtful how far the Court could go in relaxing the *CILFIT* criteria while remaining faithful to the terms and intention of the Treaty.

The real issue is whether the texts should be amended so as either (a) to restrict or abolish the right of lower courts to make a reference, and/or (b) to remove the obligation of supreme and other final courts to do so.

(4) Abolishing the right of lower courts to refer

Many, if not most, references raise technical points of interpretation on which it is clear from the outset that a decision of the Court of Justice will be required. What matters, especially to the affected citizen, is that the court first seised should know how to interpret the texts, and that other national courts should follow the same interpretation of the same text. The points at issue very rarely merit the attention of a national supreme court or the delay and cost involved in getting the case there. A single reference made at an early stage by a lower court is surely more economical than creating a logjam of cases on the same point making their way up the hierarchy of one or more national systems until a reference can be made by one of them.[9]

Where the issue before the national court is one of *validity*, a more complex legal problem would arise. Could the rule in *Fotofrost,*[10] which requires questions of validity to be determined by the Court of Justice, continue to apply? If so, what would be the position of the affected litigant while the case worked its way up to reach a court competent to make a reference? Could an inferior national court grant interim measures? Could the Court of Justice be called on to do so? If not, judicial protection against an invalid Community act could become illusory.

A less extreme suggestion is that there should be some form of filtering mechanism at national level to ensure that references by lower courts are not made prematurely or in an unsatisfactory way. This would involve treaty amendment since, as the texts stand, a lower court is entitled to refer without reference to any higher court or other authority. Moreover, experience of the time taken to deal with appeals against decisions to refer suggests that an institutionalised filtering mechanism could give rise to unnecessary and unacceptable delays.[11]

In the absence of evidence that lower courts are consistently making premature, unnecessary or unsatisfactory references, the merits of maintaining their freedom to refer seem greatly to outweigh the disadvantages. The Court's proposal to allow formal requests for clarification of references, together with a

---

9 By the time *Seymour Smith* (see footnote 1 above) reached the House of Lords, there were said to be thousands of cases awaiting a decision on the same point.

10 Case 314/85, *Fotofrost v Hauptzollamt Lübeck-Ost* [1987] ECR 4199.

11 In a current case, the reference was made by a lower court in 1996 but it was not until 1999 that the national appeal procedure was exhausted allowing the reference to proceed.

power to deal with straightforward cases by order rather than judgment (see below), would go a long way towards meeting the current problem of caseload.

(5) Abolishing the obligation of final courts to refer

It is argued that the Community legal system has reached a sufficient stage of maturity to make it unnecessary to require supreme and other "final" courts to refer. But how, in that event, would uniform interpretation and application of Community texts be ensured? In particular, how could the internal market be maintained if national courts were free to pursue their own interpretation, not only of treaty provisions, but of a host of technical regulations, directives, customs codes and other texts whose very purpose is to ensure uniform application of the law?[12]

To meet that objection, it has been suggested that there should be some form of appeal to the Court of Justice from decisions of final national courts and/or that the Commission (and/or some other authority) should be able to refer decisions of such courts to the Court of Justice "in the interest of the law" (*pourvoi dans l'intérêt de la loi*).

Throughout the history of the Community, both the Commission and the Court have sought to maintain a relationship of cooperation rather than confrontation with national courts. Although there is no reason in principle why the procedure already available to the Commission under Article 226 (ex Article 169) should not be used to challenge decisions of national courts, the objection to using it has always been that it would require the Commission to assume a prosecutorial role, and the Court an appellate role, vis-à-vis the judiciary of the member states.

A formal right of appeal for litigants from national courts to the Court of Justice would create a hierarchical relationship which would not only have profound constitutional implications but would also change a practical working relationship which, with only transitory exceptions, has been amicable and cooperative. It is questionable whether national supreme courts in particular would find this an acceptable price for being relieved of their obligation to refer.

The suggested *pourvoi dans l'intérêt de la loi* would not raise the same problem so acutely, but the following points merit consideration.

First, does the Commission (or any other authority) have the resources to police the decisions of national supreme courts in the way suggested? And can it be guaranteed that political pressure would not be brought to bear to avoid a challenge to sensitive decisions of national supreme courts?

Second, in order to avoid creating an appellate relationship between the final national court and the Court of Justice, the decision of the national court would

---

12 An apparently trivial question as to the tariff classification of, for example, pyjamas (Case C-395/93 *Neckermann* [1994] ECR I-4027) may have considerable implications for the flow of trade since, if the tariff is set lower in one member state than another because of different interpretations of the same text, the goods in question will be routed into the Community through the cheaper port of entry.

presumably have to become *res judicata* as between the original parties, so that their legal relations would not be affected by the judgment of the Court of Justice in the *pourvoi*. In that event, who would be entitled to appear before the Court of Justice and who, in particular, would appear to contradict the Commission's criticisms of the decision of the national court? The national court whose decision was in issue could hardly be involved, and the government of the member state concerned would not necessarily wish to support the decision of its own court. Yet without a contradictor the Commission's criticisms would go unanswered and the Court would be deprived of the benefit of a balanced debate on an issue which, by definition, would be one of considerable importance.

Further, the scope of a reference is, at present, determined by the order for reference. What would be the factual background against which the Court would be asked to rule in the *pourvoi*: the facts of the case in the national court giving rise to the *pourvoi*, hypothetical facts, or no facts at all? And what would be the permissible scope of the arguments that could be advanced?

On the one hand, it is difficult to see how a decision of a national court could be reviewed without reference to the facts and legal arguments on which it was based. On the other hand, it is equally difficult to see how, in justice to the original parties, there could, in effect, be a rehearing of their case without allowing them to participate, and without any possibility for their position to be reviewed in the light of the Court's judgment.

Finally, while it may be true that the final courts of the existing member states are sufficiently familiar with Community law to be absolved of the obligation to refer, will the same be true after enlargement?

B The procedure before the Court

1 The existing constraints

The obligatory steps in procedure before the Court are essentially the following:

- translation and notification of the reference;
- translation and notification of the written observations;
- preparation of the Judge Rapporteur's preliminary report on the basis of which the Court decides whether the case is to be heard by the full plenary (15 judges), a *petit plenum* (11 judges), or a chamber (five or three judges);
- preparation, translation and notification of the Report for the Hearing;
- the oral hearing;
- preparation, translation and presentation of the Advocate General's opinion,
- deliberation by the judges;
- preparation, translation and delivery of the judgment; and
- publication of the judgment and opinion.

Every reference, unless disposed of by order, must follow this procedure. Simple cases cannot be dealt with simply and urgent cases cannot be dealt with fast. Translation is required at five separate stages of the procedure, and a case cannot formally proceed to the next stage until the necessary translations have been completed.[13] On average, translation consumes about seven months of the total time taken to process a reference – *i.e.* one third of the average total time.

Notwithstanding complaints that the procedure takes too long, critics suggest that the written procedure is fundamentally defective in that the parties have no opportunity to comment in writing on the observations of others or, in due course, on the opinion of the Advocate General. Further, it is said that the oral procedure is limited in scope and usefulness, giving little opportunity for exploring the factual and legal issues through the dialogue between bench and bar which is particularly characteristic of the common law system.

No uniform system of procedure adapted to the needs and traditions of fifteen member states could respond adequately to all these difficulties and criticisms. The existing system at least has the merit that it is known, tried and tested; that it affords basic protection for the rights of defence; and that, for the time being, it still works.

It is important to realise that the parties before the Court (as opposed to governments and institutions) are often represented by advocates (or other people[14]) who have no previous experience of the procedure and may never be involved in it again. It is therefore essential to keep the rules reasonably simple such that they can be understood and applied, not only by experienced lawyers from big cities, but by day-to-day practitioners in all sorts of local courts and tribunals. This will be all the more important after enlargement.

The most urgent requirement at this stage is greater flexibility. In essence, the member states, the institutions and the parties must decide whether they are prepared to trust the Court to deal fairly with their concerns and not require it to work within a procedural straitjacket.

---

13 Depending on the language of the case and the linguistic skills of the Judge Rapporteur, the Advocate General and their respective *cabinets*, some work can proceed in the absence of translations.

14 In references, parties can be represented by anyone who is entitled to plead before the referring court. Since many national courts and tribunals dealing with matters such as labour law or social security have no formal rules of representation, parties may be, and quite often are, represented in Luxembourg by people who are not members of a bar and may have no legal training whatever. They are not necessarily the least persuasive advocates !

2 *The Court's proposals*

(1) Procedural autonomy

The most radical solution proposed by the Court would be to allow the Court to be master of its own rules of procedure, like the Court of Human Rights. Fundamental rules or principles of procedure would be "entrenched" in the treaties or in the Statute of the Court – in particular, in Title III of the Statute – and amendment would continue to require the consent of the member states. Within that framework, the Court would be free to make its own rules *and also to modify them in the light of experience*, adapting them to the needs of particular types of cases This would also, over time, allow room for experiment – new types of procedure could be adopted, and maintained if satisfactory but abandoned or modified if not. Such experiment is practically impossible at the moment.

In the shorter term, the Court has proposed four amendments of the Rules of Procedure which would allow greater flexibility and conduce to greater efficiency.

(2) Greater scope for disposing of cases by order

The first proposed amendment would allow the Court, after hearing the Advocate General, to dispose of a case by order (i) where the question posed is identical (rather than *manifestly* identical) to a question previously ruled upon, (ii) where the answer can clearly be deduced from existing case law or (iii) where the answer leaves no room for reasonable doubt.

Provided it were adopted in its entirety, this proposal would, by itself, substantially alleviate the Court's workload overall. In a significant number of references on technical points the answer leaves no room for reasonable doubt, even if it cannot be said to have been *acte clair* from the point of view of the referring court. Although the answer may not have been obvious from the outset, the written submissions point clearly to what the answer should be. In such cases, it is a waste of over-strained resources to require the case to go through all the subsequent stages of normal procedure, with all the costs and delay involved, especially in translation, in order to reach the same result in the end.

Admittedly, the proposal carries the risk that the Court would too quickly reach an answer which, on more mature reflection, would turn out to be wrong. The safeguard lies in the fact that any proposal by a Judge Rapporteur to dispose of a case by order goes before the whole Court at one of its weekly general meetings. In practice, as any Judge of the Court will bear witness, this is a salutary brake on precipitate enthusiasm to dispose of cases.

Another suggestion, which the Court has not adopted at this stage, is that the referring court should be required, in the order for reference, to provide its own answer to the questions referred. If the Court agreed with the proposed answer, this could be confirmed by order without taking the procedure further.

This idea assumes a degree of sophistication on the part of the referring court which is not always evident from some of the references and could certainly not be counted on in the first years after enlargement. In certain cases it might be difficult for the referring court to propose an answer to the question referred without compromising (or being thought to compromise) its objectivity in subsequent proceedings. It should be remembered that the issue of Community law is not necessarily the only issue in the case before the national court.

It is therefore questionable whether it would be wise to *insist* on inclusion of a proposed answer in every case. But if adopted as "best practice" in the majority of cases, it would certainly enhance the usefulness of the simplified procedure proposed by the Court.

(3) Accelerated procedure

The Court's second proposal would allow for an accelerated procedure, omitting or shortening particular stages of procedure, where a national court requests it and the circumstances show unusual urgency. The availability of such a procedure would be particularly important, and may prove to be essential, in Brussels II and Third Pillar cases.

The problem with any acceleration of existing procedure is to know what to leave out and what to speed up. The reactions to the Court's proposal suggest, as might have been expected, that some would prefer to omit the written procedure altogether and proceed straight to an oral hearing, while others attach fundamental importance to written procedure and would be prepared to forego the oral hearing.

The essential point, at this stage, is to decide whether the system can continue without any provision for accelerated procedure. If it cannot, the Court must be allowed some leeway in adapting the accelerated procedure to the needs of the particular case. The worst solution would be to adopt a rule permitting accelerated procedure but to hedge it about with detailed procedural requirements which could cause unnecessary delay or make the procedure so clumsy as to be virtually useless in practice.

(4) Power for the Judge Rapporteur and Advocate General to seek further information

At present, only the Court as such, acting on a report by the Judge Rapporteur, can ask parties, governments or institutions to provide documents or information. Neither the Rapporteur nor the Advocate General can do so without asking the Court to act. This hampers preparation of the case at two crucial stages: first, in preparation of the Rapporteur's Preliminary Report and Report for the Hearing; and second, in preparation for the oral hearing.

The Court therefore proposes that the Judge Rapporteur and the Advocate General should be empowered to ask for documents or information without needing to refer the request to the whole Court for prior approval. Experience suggests that this would, in particular, enhance the usefulness of the oral hearing.

(5) Power to issue Practice Directions
The fourth proposal is that the Court should have power, as in Strasbourg, to issue Practice Directions.[15] This would make it possible to specify in greater detail what is expected of those who take part, particularly as regards the presentation, content and length of written and oral pleadings. It would be particularly useful in the context of accelerated procedure. (It is important to note that it is not proposed that the Court should issue Practice Directions to national courts.)

C Structural constraints

The most serious structural constraint on the working of the Court results from the treaty requirement of partial renewal of half of its membership every three years.[16] Where a new Judge or Advocate General is appointed to succeed another in the course of his mandate, the new member is appointed only for the unexpired portion of his predecessor's mandate, and must receive a new mandate at the appropriate three-yearly renewal.

The effect is that, every three years, the Court has to go into low gear for nine months in order to be sure that all cases that have reached the stage of oral hearing can be completed by October 6th when the terms of office of half the Judges and Advocates General come to an end. It is frequently not known until a very late stage which of them will be reappointed.

This is manifestly inefficient. In its paper submitted to the IGC preparing the Amsterdam Treaty, the Court proposed that, whatever the length of the mandate, the mandate of newly appointed Judges and Advocates General should run from the date of first appointment. Over time, this would stagger departures and arrivals and would allow the Court to operate like any other Court that has to make allowance for retirements, whether on grounds of age or of expiry of the mandate. So far as is known, this proposal was not even considered worthy of discussion by the member states.

II LINGUISTIC CONSTRAINTS

The Court's language regime is laid down in the Rules of Procedure.[17] All languages are treated as being equal. In particular, Judges and Advocates General are entitled to use any language and to require translation of any document into the language of choice.

Some commentators, particularly English-speakers, suggest that the number of permitted languages should be limited, drawing a parallel with the European

15 It has been suggested that the Court already has power to issue Practice Directions. Whether this is so or not, the Court does not have power to enforce such directions.
16 Article 223 EC (ex Article 167), second paragraph.
17 RP, Articles 29-31.

Court of Human Rights which works in English and French. But there is a crucial difference between Strasbourg and Luxembourg. Proceedings in Strasbourg can begin only when all domestic remedies have been exhausted. The essence of the preliminary reference procedure in Luxembourg is that it forms an integral part of on-going domestic proceedings conducted in national courts in the national language.

The strength of the Community legal system lies in the willingness of national lawyers and judges to cooperate in referring questions and applying the judgments of the Court. That is why the Court strives to ensure that its judgments are available to lawyers and judges throughout the Community in their own language on the day they are pronounced. Why should it be supposed that lawyers and judges with "minority languages" would be prepared to cooperate in the same way in a procedure that required them to frame references, argue cases or apply judgments in a language other than their own? Root-and-branch reform of the language regime is in any event most unlikely for political reasons.

That said, the working of the regime should not be more burdensome than necessary. In that respect, the regime applied by the Court is as economical as it can be, consistently with maintaining the equality of languages. Only the orders for reference which start the procedure, the opinions of the Advocates General and the judgments of the Court are translated into all languages. The Judges and Advocates General do not normally insist on their right to have documents translated into their language of choice, and indeed the system would break down if they did.

Internally, the Court uses a single working language. Largely for historical reasons, this is French, but the cost implications would be the same whichever language were chosen. Use of a single working language avoids extensive cross-translation, the bulk of the translators' work being translation into or out of that language. So long as this arrangement can be maintained, it is possible to predict with some accuracy the cost of adding new languages as a consequence of enlargement. In broad terms, each additional language would involve recruiting about 30 translators, interpreters and secretaries.

The use of a single working language has other, less obvious, consequences. In some respects these are advantageous, in others less so.

Differences between legal systems are reflected in lawyers' use of language. Even if legal vocabulary has a common origin, for example in Roman law, development of the same concept in different countries may lead to the same word (*e.g.* fault[18]) acquiring different meanings or at least different nuances. The problem is all the greater when legal systems start from radically different assumptions, as anyone knows who has tried to explain the English concept of "trust" to a civil lawyer, or the difference between *conclusions, moyens* and *arguments* to an English lawyer.

18 See Joined Cases C-46/93 and 48/93 *Brasserie de Pêcheur and Factortame* [1996] ECR I-1029, point 76.

The Court's use of French should be compared with the use of Latin in universities and scholarly exchanges at least until the eighteenth century (and at the Gregorianum in Rome well into the twentieth). It ensures a reasonably consistent use of vocabulary which acquires its own "Community meaning" and provides the degree of linguistic stability that legal certainty requires and national legal systems acquire as a matter of course.

The downside is that French legal terminology, although commendably precise, does not always lend itself to translation into other languages, particularly when one is not sure how much intellectual baggage is packed in the French portmanteau. How, for example, should one translate *marge d'appréciation* into English? It is neither "discretion" nor "room for manoeuvre", nor even "degree of latitude", although each is partly right. Probably the best solution, as with *acquis communautaire*, is to surrender and adopt the French phrase into the language. But that gives an unfortunate impression of francophone dominance, even in circles where leek and potato soup is relished as *vichyssoise.*

The same problem would exist whichever language or languages were chosen as the working language(s). Legal texts in translation can rarely be quite as clear and precise as the original, and there are relatively few lawyers who can read and write with speed and confidence in a language other than their own.

The language regime is one of the most important constraints on the productivity of the Court and the understanding of its judgments. While it is possible to avoid its more extreme consequences, it is, and will continue to be, a fixed point to be steered round rather than removed.

III CONSTRAINTS OF CULTURAL DIVERSITY

A Differences in legal culture

Differences in legal culture are as important as language as a point of reference for reform. The constraints they impose are more difficult to define but are nonetheless real.

It is often suggested that the Community is divided between the Common Law and Civil Law systems. But the longer one spends in the Court, the more one is aware that there are fifteen different legal systems (or more if you count Scotland and other strange animals in the juridical zoo). Some of them have more in common than others but all of them owe something to particular national attitudes and ways of doing things which are themselves the product of history and culture.

Differences in legal culture and approach become apparent in any discussion of possible reforms of the Court and its procedure. German lawyers attach fundamental importance to the principle of "the legal judge" (*gesetzlicher Richter*), according to which the rules for composition of the tribunal deciding a case must be known and published in advance. English lawyers, on the other hand, regard it as normal to allocate cases, or to change the composition of appeal courts, as judges become available or are prevented from sitting.

German lawyers prize the written procedure; English lawyers the oral.

In practice, it is surprising how little this cultural diversity affects the day-to-day working of the Court. Indeed, the bringing together of lawyers from widely differing backgrounds is part of the richness of the Community system, and there is no country (including the most recent accessions) whose legal culture has not influenced the Court's jurisprudence.

Differences of attitude or approach can nevertheless affect a crucial stage in the procedure which outsiders do not and cannot observe – the process of deliberation.

When members of the US Supreme Court visited Luxembourg, Justice Ginsberg perceptively observed that, although the Court of Justice is not a court of first instance, it is often the "court of first view" or of "first look". The point at issue may never have been the subject of a judgment in any national court at any level. If referred at an early stage, the issues and arguments will not have gone through the winnowing process by which irrelevant issues and bad arguments are discarded before a case reaches the higher courts of a member state.

Quite frequently, the parties to the proceedings before the referring court do not submit written observations or take part in the oral procedure, and the member states which might have most to contribute do not intervene. The Commission no longer has the financial resources or the manpower to provide a comprehensive overview of every case and its consequences, and the Advocates General cannot always do so either.

Consequently, it may only be at the stage of deliberation that the points of view of a number of lawyers with different perspectives are brought to bear in identifying the issues and the possible solutions. Even if, at the end of the day, the judgment appears to "follow" the approach of the Commission or of the Advocate General, this does not mean that the issues have not been extensively debated between the Judges so that a decision could be taken in favour of one approach rather than another.

B The case for and against dissenting judgments

Some commentators suggest that the differences of opinion and differences of approach between judges of different traditions should be brought into the open by allowing dissenting opinions. They say this would speed up the process of decision-taking since a vote could be taken at an early stage, leaving the majority to write the judgment and the minority to write their dissents. The majority judgment would then, so it is said, be less obscure since it would not have to accommodate the views of dissentients.

To anyone bred in the common law tradition, the case for allowing dissenting opinions is seductive. Today's powerful dissent can become tomorrow's orthodoxy. Indeed, the case for dissents does not need to be elaborated here because it has been made so often. The contrary case has not been made in any detail, so it is worth pointing out some of the questions that have not, so far, been asked.[19]

The objection normally put forward against dissenting judgments in the Court of Justice is that this would subject the Judges to unacceptable political pressure. This seems a weak argument, considering that Advocates General have to express their own opinions and that dissenting judgments are permitted in Strasbourg.

A more persuasive variant of the argument is that the right to dissent might lead judges to become identified with a particular approach or tendency – progressive or conservative, strict constructionist or purposive constructionist; federalist or nationalist, etc. Having once dissented, Judges might feel compelled to maintain their declared position even if, on reflection, they recognised that it was wrong or at least not worth insisting on. That has happened to most of us, and the absence of a right to dissent is a powerful incentive to judicial modesty.

Dissenting judgments do not form part of the legal tradition of all the member states – perhaps, indeed, only that of a minority. Where dissenting judgments are permitted, this may only be in the Constitutional Court whose members are appointed by a special parliamentary process different from that applying to the ordinary courts. A comparable procedure applies in Strasbourg. The question of dissents cannot therefore be divorced from the process of appointment and the Court cannot by itself, as some commentators appear to imagine, simply change the practice.

Assuming that dissents were to be possible, it is important to clarify what would be allowed. Would all judges, as in Strasbourg or the US Supreme Court, be entitled to file concurring as well as dissenting opinions, or opinions that concur in part and dissent in part? Or would the dissentient minority be required to file a single document of dissent, as is the practice in the Privy Council? If so, what would be the position of a judge who could not, in conscience, agree either with the majority or with the rest of the minority? That is not a far-fetched question in a context where, in a difficult case, the "formation of judgment" could consist of 15 or, after enlargement, more than 20 judges.[20]

In terms of *total time saved*, would the gain, if any, be more than marginal? It would be difficult to write a dissent without knowing what one is dissenting from. Presumably, therefore, the majority judgment would have to be available, at least in draft, before the dissents were written. Could the majority then claim the right, having read the dissents, to adjust their judgment in order to take account of them? At what point would the judgments and dissents become final so that they could be sent for translation – a question that does not arise in a monolingual system?

19 The arguments against dissenting judgments in the Court when dealing with references do not necessarily apply to all direct actions, especially in the Court of First Instance.

20 The Judicial Committee of the Privy Council normally consists of five judges, so the dissentients cannot be more than two.

In terms of *quality,* it is true that Anglo-American legal literature is full of powerful dissents which, in the long run, have changed the course of legal thinking. But the right to file a dissenting or concurring opinion does not always contribute to legal certainty, as any lawyer who has practised in the common law system must admit.

In the Community context, legal certainty is essential to the working of the internal market and it is important that the judgments of the Court be both comprehensible and workable in all languages and all legal systems. Exclusion of the minority from taking part in the deliberations of the majority could result in a situation where the binding judgment of the majority completely overlooked a problem of language or legal technique for one or more member states.

Again, would a member state feel more or less inclined to respect a Court judgment where the "national judge" dissented, particularly if the dissent were based on the ground that the majority judgment would be unworkable in the national legal system? And would the "powerful dissent" be heard in the same way if the dissentient minority were required to concur in a single document of dissent?

Whatever be the merits of dissenting judgments in national legal systems, the merit for the Community system of deliberation *in camera* with no dissents is not that the judgment is (or appears to be) unanimous, but that the points of view of judges representing different legal traditions and languages are fully taken into account *at all stages* in developing and formulating the judgment. So far as is humanly possible, all the judges taking part should feel comfortable with the judgment as a judgment, even if they disagree with it.

C "One Judge per member state" and the size of the plenary

The legal (as opposed to political) justification for having one Judge of the Court per member state is to ensure that, in cases meriting the attention of the plenary, the legal culture and traditions, and the needs of the legal system and language of every member state are taken into account. The need to maintain a broad spread of languages and traditions is taken into account in the composition of chambers and in the decision whether to assign a particular case to a chamber or retain it before the plenary.

It is suggested that, after enlargement, there should continue to be one Judge per member state but that the plenary should be limited to a fixed proportion of the total number, as in Strasbourg. This overlooks two considerations.

First, the Strasbourg system specifically entrenches the concept of the "national judge" by requiring that the judge from the state concerned in the case, or an *ad hoc* judge nominated by that state, should always sit. The Luxembourg system has always resisted that approach. Is it desirable to adopt it now?

Second, cases in Strasbourg are, by definition, concerned with the treatment of an individual by a particular state, as such. Cases in Luxembourg have a much wider range. Why, in a reference raising a point that affects all member states, should priority be given to the judge from the member state from which the reference happens to come?

If the principle of "one judge per member state" should be maintained in order that the legal culture, traditions and language of every member state are taken into account in the most important and sensitive cases, then logic and common sense require that no judge should be excluded from sitting in cases that merit the attention of the full plenary. Of course, with 20 or more Judges, it would have to be accepted that only a small minority of cases should be so treated. But even at the moment, the number of cases heard by the *Grand Plénum*, as opposed to a *Petit Plénum,* is very small and further limitation of recourse to the full plenary would simply involve a development of well-established existing practice.

If it is felt that a plenary of 20 or more Judges would be *inherently* unmanageable, then the honest course would be to abandon the principle of "one judge per member state" as little more than a political figleaf, and to find a new and acceptable way of appointing a Court consisting of fewer judges than there are member states.

D Legal culture after enlargement

Judges and lawyers in all the existing member states have experienced some degree of culture shock in coming to terms with Community law, and some have still not come to terms with it. The culture shock for judges and lawyers in the new member states will be infinitely greater since many of them will have had little or no experience of legal methods which are second nature to judges and lawyers in the existing member states. Moreover, the resources available to judges and lawyers in some of the candidate countries are still very limited.[21]

Proposals for reform must therefore, more than ever, take account of the need for the resulting structure to be understood – and made to work in a consistent way – by judges and lawyers with very diverse backgrounds and resources.

21 The author was able to measure the scale of the problem during a recent visit to Poland. There is still no set of *European Court Reports* available to students in Wrocław, the third largest university in Poland. A Polish judge asked a Community law enthusiast how he could find the law, and was assured that he would soon be able to find all the law on Internet with his computer. "My computer!", exclaimed the judge; "I don't even have a typewriter".

IV Constraints of workload

A The problem

Currently, the workload imposes constraints on the working of the Court in two respects, quantitative and qualitative.

First, it is obvious that, if the number of incoming cases rises disproportionately to the number of cases decided, delays can only get longer and, ultimately, the system will break down. The same result is likely to follow if the member states refuse to give the Court the minimum degree of flexibility that it considers essential. On the other hand, given greater flexibility, the Court could be significantly more productive and the Doomsday scenario will be avoided in the short and probably the medium term.

Second, however, the character of the workload is changing. The 1992 programme put in place a range of regulations and directives whose provisions are now coming forward for interpretation. Although the pace of Community legislation has slowed down, legislative activity will not come to an end.

Much of the new legislation deals with highly technical questions[22] which, in the member states, would be dealt with by specialist lawyers pleading before specialist courts with specialist judges. Indeed, a large proportion of references now come from such courts. In order properly to interpret the legislative text, the Court must first understand the problem. The problem may be obvious enough to specialist advocates or to the specialist judge making the reference, but not necessarily to the non-specialist.

Consequently, the Court, which is "specialist" only in the sense that it specialises in Community law, must try to identify the true issues, a task which is doubly difficult where it is acting as "court of first view". The Court must, moreover, ensure that its judgment will be capable of being understood and applied in all the national systems, even where only one or two member states have intervened to explain the problem from their point of view.

In times gone by, the Commission was able to provide the detailed analysis and comparative study which, in ideal circumstances, the Court needs. It can no longer do so for reasons both of budget and manpower. Nor is it reasonable to expect that the gap can be completely filled by the Advocates General, so the full technical complexity of the questions raised may once again appear only at the stage of deliberation by the Judges.

By the stage of deliberation, it is normally too late, if judgment is not to be delayed indefinitely, to seek further clarification from the parties, the member states or the Commission. Although there may be no fundamental disagreement between the Judges as to the result, the precise formulation of the judgment may

22 These include VAT and other forms of indirect taxation; the effect of double taxation conventions; intellectual property rights; regulation of financial services; company law and company accounts; detailed aspects of labour law; and social security.

entail a succession of drafts and deliberations which have to be fitted into an already tight schedule of hearings and deliberations.

B The remedy

The increasing technicality of the questions referred is a problem that would be alleviated, to some extent, by the proposal to allow the Judge Rapporteur and Advocate General to ask for additional documents or information while preparing the case.

It is important, too, that referring courts take care (as the Court has asked) to explain the factual and legal background of the questions and the reason why, as Article 234 itself provides, an answer to *those* questions is *necessary* to enable the referring court to give judgment. Experience shows that a well-drafted order for reference promotes written observations that address the real issues and help the Court to find a solution.

The problem would be further alleviated if the Commission's Legal Service were once again given sufficient manpower (and sufficient funds to consult experts where required) in order to provide an overview of the case from a Community perspective.

In that connection, it might be helpful to establish a series of specialist committees (on the lines of the Customs Code Committee) to which technical problems could be referred by the Commission, by national authorities, and possibly also by national courts, for a non-binding opinion. Even if, at the end of the day, it became necessary to refer the question to the Court for a binding ruling, the availability of an opinion from such an expert committee would provide the Court with the "first look" which, at the moment, it often lacks.

In terms of finance and time, this would almost certainly be less costly than the creation of new specialist courts (or specialist chambers of the Court of First Instance).

V CONSTRAINTS OF TIME, MANPOWER, BUDGET AND TECHNICAL RESOURCES

These constraints interact, as indeed do all the others. As the workload increases in volume and complexity, less time can be devoted to cases that are simple or straightforward in order that more time can be given to important or difficult cases. The more time that is spent by the judges in listening to oral argument, the less time they have for reading files and attending to the finer points of judgments. If there are not enough translators, the procedure cannot go faster and will gradually slow down as the backlog increases.[23] The Court cannot take

23 By way of illustration, when the Court started issuing judgments in all languages on the day they are pronounced, the delay between final deliberation and judgment was approximately 3 weeks. This has now extended to 5 weeks because of shortage of transla-

advantage of new technologies unless it has the budget to do so, and access to new technologies is limited by the extent to which the software on offer is adapted to a multilingual environment and can operate with the hardware and software currently in use.

Such constraints are inevitable since the Court is not immune from the constraints of the real world. They will not go away – though they may present themselves in a different form – if the problem is moved elsewhere.

Thus it is suggested that the productive capacity of the Court will be increased if competence to deal with certain classes of references is transferred to the Court of First Instance. That is true – provided that enough additional judges are appointed to the already overloaded Court of First Instance and provided that the two courts do not get bogged down in demarcation disputes (for example, "Is this case a social security case for the CFI or a citizenship case for the ECJ?" – see *Martínez Sala*[24]).

Whichever court has competence, the translation problem will remain the same, as will the other budgetary and technical constraints. The issue therefore comes to be one of priorities, and to some extent of rationality and a sense of proportion.

For example, as regards the budget, should it really be necessary for the Court to apply to *three* other institutions[25] for authority to transfer funds from the telephone account to the computer account? And is it necessary that the Council and Parliament should control the precise number of translators the Court may employ? The administrative budget of the Court amounts to 2.7% of the total administrative budget of the European Union[26] – less than the shared administrative budget of the Economic and Social Committee and the Committee of the Regions.

The general trend in public administration in the member states is towards a greater degree of budgetary autonomy – that is to say, greater power for institutions to allocate their use of resources within a global package, subject to control by the national equivalent of the Court of Auditors. Are the member states and, in this case, the European Parliament prepared to follow this trend, as the Court has asked them to do?

The Court's proposals for greater procedural autonomy and flexibility (discussed above) can be seen in the same light. The present allocation of resources is inefficient because all references are required to jump through the same procedural hoops. So long as the existing procedural and budgetary straitjackets are in place, it will be impossible to achieve significantly better allocation of time, manpower and other limited resources.

Against that background, four issues merit closer examination, though they can be touched on only briefly in this paper:

---

tors and the increasing number *and length* of documents to be translated.

24 Case 85/96, *Martínez Sala v Freistaat Bayern* [1998] ECR I-2691.

25 The Council and Parliament must authorise and the Commission must give its opinion.

26 This amounts to about 0.14% of the total EU budget.

(1) the need for, and the role of, the oral hearing;
(2) the problems of the translation service;
(3) access to new technologies; and
(4) the desirability of moving some of the burden of dealing with preliminary references away from Luxembourg altogether.

(1) The oral hearing
There is a cultural divide between those who value the oral hearing and those who do not. In terms of usefulness, some oral hearings contribute greatly to the judges' understanding of the case and serve to clarify the questions to which an answer is required. Some, however, do not. They amount to little more than a ritual in which the parties (especially, it must be said, governments) read out memoranda repeating, sometimes word for word, what has already been said in their written pleadings and summarised in the Report for the Hearing.

At present, the Judges spend much of Tuesday and Thursday, and sometimes Wednesday too, at oral hearings.[27] Time spent at oral hearings is time not spent in reading files, discussing problems with *référendaires* or other judges, drafting judgments and taking part in deliberations. Even an oral hearing that lasts only from 0930 till 1030 eats substantially into a useful morning's work.

Time spent in unprofitable oral hearings is an unprofitable use of resources which must be balanced against the legitimate concern to preserve the rights of defence. In 1991, the step was taken of allowing the Court to dispense with an oral hearing if no party asked for one.[28] At the moment, the oral hearing is dispensed with in about 10% of references.

The Court has now proposed to take this a step further, but *not* to give the Court exclusive discretion to decide whether there should be an oral hearing or not. All that is proposed is that those who ask for an oral hearing should be required to specify why they want it. Both the Court and the other parties could then come to the hearing with a much clearer idea than at present of the purpose of the hearing and the scope of the arguments. The Court's proposal should therefore be seen, not as an attempt to restrict the rights of defence, but as a way of making oral hearings more useful.

(2) The translation service
For reasons already discussed under linguistic and cultural constraints, the task of a translator (more accurately, a "lawyer-linguist") in the Court of Justice is unique. It involves a familiarity with, and a capacity to convey the nuances of

27 The position of the Judges differs, in this respect, from that of the Advocates General. An Advocate General has to attend hearings only in cases where he is acting as Advocate General. Judges have to attend all hearings in which they are part of the "formation of judgment".

28 RP, Article 44a.

legal language as used, on the one hand, in the Court and, on the other, in 15 member states using 11 languages.

When translating documents coming in to the Court, the translator must not only be familiar with the established conventions for translating legal expressions from one language to another but also be ready to find an adequate translation for an expression that has not been encountered before, often in highly technical fields. When translating an Advocate General's opinion or a judgment of the Court, the translator must be aware of subtle differences in emphasis – for example, between "discrimination", "inequality of treatment" and "difference in treatment". These nuances may shift over time, so it is just as important to know when the conventional translation is not appropriate as to know when it is. There is a constant coming and going between the translators, the members of the Court and their *référendaires* on such points.

Over the past few years, the Court has insistently sought an increase in the number of translators. For the 1999 budget, the Court asked for 40 additional translators. The Council allowed 10 (one less than the number of languages that have to be translated). The Parliament then froze five of those posts, requiring the Court to produce a report with proposals for "stabilising the volume of documents to be translated". The Court produced a report (dated 23 March 1999) demonstrating, not only that the productivity of the Court's translators is already *significantly* higher than that of the other institutions, but also that the volume of documents to be translated is not under the control of the Court and is rising at an alarming rate. In the light of that report, the Court asked for an additional 51 translators. The Council and Parliament have allowed 30 additional posts.

Privatisation, farming-out and greater use of individual freelance translators[29] is no answer to the Court's problem. Close and continuous contact between the translators and *cabinets* would be impossible. But the overriding consideration is the need for confidentiality. The need for confidentiality of draft opinions and judgments is obvious, but many other documents that pass through the Court are of considerable commercial or political sensitivity, and therefore of considerable value if leaked.

In any event, experience shows that it takes a considerable time fully to train a Court translator and that any saving in use of freelances can be more than offset by the additional costs involved in revision of the text by an experienced translator based in the Court.

(3) Access to new technologies

Access to new technologies is subject, like all other aspects of the Court's activities, to budgetary constraints. Considerable progress has, however, been made on this front. The Court now has a Division specially dedicated to com-

29 Approximately 12% of translation is done by freelance translators.

puters and new technologies, and the Translation Division is making imaginative use of computer technology to reduce the burden of routine translation.

The aim is, to the greatest extent possible, to move from paper-based to electronic communication and storage, both within the Court and between the Court and the outside world. Three particular constraints have been encountered which are not insuperable, but for which there is no straightforward solution:

(i) the need to ensure confidentiality;
(ii) the need to authenticate documents in terms both of content and date of lodging; and
(iii) the need for multilingual compatibility.

Taken together, these constraints restrict the extent to which the Court can buy in commercially available software. Consequently, special programs have to be written for the Court which requires manpower, time and money.

Looking towards the longer term (particularly in connection with the replacement of the asbestos-ridden Palais), consideration is being given to the use of video-conferencing as a means of access to the Court and of communication between the Court and parties, governments and institutions. In the context of enlargement, with a catchment area potentially extending from Portugal to Estonia and from Ireland to Cyprus, there would be considerable cost savings overall if parties did not need to come to Luxembourg to plead.

In references, the availability of video links might make it easier for poorer litigants to be represented. At present, particularly in social security cases, the claimant is frequently not represented before the Court and observations are submitted only by governments and institutions. In complex cases (particularly before the Court of First Instance) informal video conferences could be used to clarify the issues and identify the points for discussion at the hearing.

At this stage, video-conferencing seems to present three particular difficulties:

(i) the need for mutual compatibility of systems since the participants would have to be linked not only to the Court, but to one another;
(ii) the need to maintain continuous communication with all participants since, if one link went down, the proceedings would have to be suspended until it was restored; and
(iii) the need to make facilities for video-conferencing conveniently available in all the member states (possibly in local courthouses), with staff trained and available to operate the machinery.

These difficulties are again not insuperable, but setting up and working such a system would require a considerable collaborative effort on the part of the institutions, the member states and the European Bars. Up to now, no-one has attempted to put in place a system of electronic filing or video-conferencing on a continent-wide basis, and certainly not in the context of 11 or more languages and 15 or more legal systems. Imagination is required as well as money.

When the difficulties have been overcome, the use of new technologies will go a long way towards meeting the last point to be discussed here: moving work away from Luxembourg.

4 Moving work away from Luxembourg

Numerous proposals have been made for "renationalising" preliminary references, creating regional courts or, in one way or another, shifting some of the burden away from Luxembourg. It should, however, be recognised that moving work away from Luxembourg would not necessarily make the system more efficient or less costly. The linguistic and cultural constraints are unavoidable components of any Community system. To take only one example, it could be inordinately costly to move interpreters round Europe in order that all national governments could be represented in national or regional courts and plead in their own languages.

Given the constraints, the question must be whether it is not better to concentrate adequate resources in one place (Luxembourg) and develop the new technologies so as to make that place more readily accessible and user-friendly. The long-term aim of any reform must, after all, be to make the system work better. That will not be achieved by applying mid-twentieth century solutions to twenty-first century problems.

Many of the Court's existing problems can be overcome with the political will of the member states and the goodwill of national courts and legal practitioners. The true challenge lies in finding imaginative ways of creating a system that will stand the test of time in the uncertain world of the new Millennium.

10

THE GROWING VARIETY OF PROCEDURES CONCERNING PRELIMINARY RULINGS

Giorgio Gaja

I INTRODUCTION

Procedures that national courts should follow in order to request a preliminary ruling from the Court of Justice have become increasingly complex and varied.

The basic procedure is governed by Article 234 of the EC Treaty, which reads simply enough, but has to be viewed in the light of some landmark decisions by the Court of Justice. Thus, for instance, the rule in Article 234, that "a court or tribunal of a Member State against whose decisions there is no judicial remedy under national law [...] shall bring the matter before the Court of Justice", suffers some exceptions, which are laid out in the *Da Costa*[1] and *CILFIT*[2] judgments with regard to interpretation of Community law and in the *International Chemical Corporation*[3] judgment in respect of questions of validity of acts taken by a Community institution. On the other hand, the discretion that courts other than those of last resort are given under Article 234 for deciding whether to request a preliminary ruling on validity has been significantly curtailed by the Court's judgment in *Foto-Frost*.[4]

Another development has occurred because the Court has also admitted requests for preliminary rulings when a question of interpretation was raised outside the scope of application of Community law: this when a provision of national law extends the effect of provisions of EC law through an unconditional reference.[5] It is

1 Joined Cases 28, 29 and 30/62, *Da Costa en Schaake N.V.* v. *Nederlandse Belastingadministratie*, [1963] ECR 31 at 38.
2 Case 283/81, *Srl CILFIT and Lanificio di Gavardo SpA* v. *Ministry of Health*, [1982] ECR 3415 at 3429-3431, paras. 12-21.
3 Case 66/80, *Spa International Chemical Corporation* v. *Amministrazione delle Finanze dello Stato*, [1981] ECR 1191 at 1215-1216, paras. 11-15.
4 Case 314/85, *Foto-Frost* v. *Hauptzollamt Lubeck-Ost*, [1987] ECR 4199 at 4230-4232, para.s 11-20.
5 An example may be provided by the *Dzodzi* case. A national court raised a question of interpretation of an EEC directive on free movement of persons because under Belgian law some nationals of third States – the spouses of Belgian citizens – were given the same treatment as was granted to EC nationals under the directive. See Joined Cases C-297/88 and C-197/89, *Massam Dzodzi* v. *Belgian State*, [1990] ECR I-3763.

D. O'Keeffe (ed.), Liber Amicorum Slynn 143-152 (2000)

not certain whether courts of last resort are under an obligation to request a ruling in this type of case.

An amendment to the EC Treaty by the Treaty of Amsterdam has added to the complexity. Article 68 of the EC Treaty has brought about the first derogation from Article 234 within the field of Community law. Courts or tribunals against whose decisions there is no judicial remedy are not entitled to request rulings with regard to questions of interpretation and validity concerning the new title IV, "Visas, Asylum, Immigration and Other Policies Related to Free Movement of Persons". Moreover, no court may raise questions "on any measure or decision taken pursuant to Article 62(1) relating to the maintenance of law and order and the safeguarding of internal security".

In addition, a variety of models of procedures for requesting preliminary rulings has been used with regard to the interpretation of conventions that Member States have concluded under Article 293 of the EC Treaty and Article 31 of the TEU in its Maastricht version.

Thus, Article 3 of the 1971 Luxembourg Protocol[6] relating to the 1968 Brussels Convention on Jurisdiction and the Enforcement of Judgments in Civil and Commercial Matters allows only some courts or tribunals to request rulings: the highest courts (which are under an obligation to make a preliminary referral) and the courts which decide on appeals, including those lodged under Article 37 of the Convention against a decision granting enforcement of a judgment. A similar system may be found in Article 3 of the 1989 Luxembourg Agreement Relating to Community Patents[7] for the interpretation of the 1975 Luxembourg Convention for the European Patent and the related Protocol on the Settlement of Litigation Concerning the Infringement and Validity of Community Patents. A few courts, which are listed in Article 3(2)(a), are under an obligation to request rulings on interpretation from the Court of Justice, while courts deciding on appeals "may [...] request the Court to give a ruling thereon"; the other courts are not entitled to make a preliminary referral. The same model has been followed by Articles 2 and 3 of the 1997 Protocol[8] relating to the Convention on the Service in the Member States of Judicial and Extrajudicial Documents in Civil or Commercial Matters, and by Articles 3 and 4 of the 1998 Protocol[9] on the interpretation of the Convention on Jurisdiction and the Recognition and Enforcement of Judgments in Matrimonial Matters. Under the latter Protocol, each Member State may opt to give the right to request preliminary rulings either to the highest courts or to the highest courts and other courts sitting in an appellate capacity.

---

6 The text of the Protocol, as amended by the Convention of 9 October 1978 on the accession of Denmark, Ireland and the United Kingdom, and by the Convention of 25 October 1982 on the accession of Greece, is reproduced in O.J. 1983, C 97/23.

7 O.J. 1989, L 401/1.

8 O.J. 1997, C 261/18.

9 O.J. 1998, C 221/20.

According to Article 2 of the First Protocol[10] to the 1980 Rome Convention on the Law Applicable to Contractual Obligations, only the highest courts and those deciding on appeals are entitled to submit questions of interpretation to the Court of Justice. No obligation to do so is stated in the Protocol.

Some conventions that were concluded under Article K.3 of the TEU use a different model, which Article 35 of the TEU has made applicable to the interpretation of all the conventions to be established under Title VI of the TEU, to "the validity and interpretation of the measures implementing them" and to the "validity and interpretation of framework decisions" to be adopted under the same Title. According to this model, national courts are entitled to request rulings only on the condition that their respective State has made a declaration to this effect "at the time of signature of the Treaty of Amsterdam or at any time thereafter".

Before the entry into force of the Treaty of Amsterdam, this type of provision has been included in the following texts: Article 2 of the 1996 Protocol[11] to the Convention on the Protection of the European Communities' Financial Interests; Article 2 of the 1996 Protocol[12] to the Convention on the Establishment of a European Police Office; Article 2 of the 1997 Protocol[13] to the Convention on the Use of Information Technology for Customs Purposes; Article 12 of the 1997 Convention on the Fight against Corruption Involving Officials of the European Communities or Officials of Member States of the European Union;[14] Article 13 of the Second Protocol[15] to the Convention on the Protection of the European Communities' Financial Interests; Article 26 of the 1997 Convention on Mutual Assistance and Cooperation between Customs Administrations;[16] Article 14 of the 1998 Convention on Driving Disqualifications.[17]

Article 35 of the TEU and the provisions of international instruments listed above give Member States the choice of declaring that a request may be made by any court or tribunal or that only those courts "against whose decisions there is no judicial remedy" are entitled to make a referral. Here again, no obligation to request preliminary rulings is stated for courts of last resort.

Given the fact that only some Member States have yet made declarations under Article 35 of the TEU and the said protocols or conventions, it is likely that only the courts of some States will be entitled to submit requests. This does not necessarily mean that the Court's rulings will not have the same effects throughout the Community.

The great variety of systems for preliminary referrals is likely to create some confusion in their application by national courts. Moreover, doubts could be ex-

10 O.J. 1989, L 48/1.
11 O.J. 1996, C 151/2.
12 O.J. 1996, C 299/2.
13 O.J. 1997, C 151/16.
14 O.J. 1997, C 195/2.
15 O.J. 1997, C 221/12.
16 O.J. 1998, C 24/2.
17 O.J. 1998, C 216/2.

pressed about whether this variety is adequately justified in functional terms. While certain restrictions on the ability of national courts to address questions are understandable in view of the ever increasing workload of the Court of Justice,[18] the logic underlying some choices remains obscure.

All the protocols and conventions referred to above expressly state that the Protocol on the Statute of the Court of Justice and the Court's Rules of Procedure shall apply to the requests for the Court's rulings. This is self-explanatory and arguably superfluous. What is less clear is whether, and to what extent, the Court's case-law relating to Article 234 of the EC Treaty also applies to the other systems for preliminary referrals. The following paragraphs will discuss one main question: whether courts which are entitled to request rulings have an obligation to do so. The discussion will rest on the assumption that the courts regard the question of interpretation or validity as relevant for their decision.

II Referrals under Article 68 of the EC Treaty

Article 68 of the EC Treaty provides an important derogation from Article 234 within the scope of application of Community law. However, the basic Treaty system concerning preliminary rulings appears to be affected only in so far as Article 68 specifically provides for this. This is made clear by the opening words of Article 68: "Article 234 shall apply to this Title under the following circumstances and conditions [...]". Thus, since Article 68 says that, when one of the questions listed in paragraph 1 is raised, a court or tribunal of last resort "shall, if it considers that a decision on the question is necessary to enable it to give judgment, request the Court of Justice to give a ruling thereon", it is reasonable to assume that the provision imposes on the court the same type of obligation that exists under Article 234.[19] Little should be made of the fact that, unlike Article 234, Article 68(1) includes for the courts of last resort the words in between commas that have been quoted above. The same wording is used in Article 234 only with regard to courts other than those of last resort; however, it has been generally understood that the condition concerns all referring courts, including those of last resort. This seems quite logical, as it would make little sense for a court to submit a request if it considered that the referred question was irrelevant for the decision of the case.

18 While the Court of Justice has suggested a variety of remedies in a document issued in May 1999, these may not be sufficient should national courts make fuller use of their power to request preliminary rulings.

19 For this view see Curti Gialdino, "Schengen et le troisième pilier: le contrôle juridictionnel organisé par le traité d'Amsterdam", 8 *Revue du Marché Unique Européen* (1998) 2-89-124 at 105-106 and Girerd, "L'article 68 CE: un renvoi préjudiciel d'interprétation et d'application incertaines", 35 *Revue trimestrielle de Droit européen* (1999) 239-260 at 242-243.

If according to Article 68 an obligation to refer exists under the same conditions as under Article 234, the exceptions stated by the Court in *Da Costa*,[20] *CIL-FIT*[21] and *International Chemical Corporation*[22] are also applicable.

A difficult question is raised by what the Court said in *Foto-Frost*.[23] As is well known, in this judgment the Court asserted that national courts have no power to declare that a Community act is invalid and that, in case of doubt concerning the validity of an act, courts are under an obligation to refer the question of validity to the Court, irrespective of whether they are courts of last resort or not. The Court invoked its exclusive competence to review the validity of Community acts under Article 230 for concluding that "the coherence of the system requires that where the validity of a Community act is challenged before a national court the power to declare the act invalid must also be reserved to the Court of Justice."[24]

Should this restriction be applied to acts of Community institutions that are adopted under Title IV of the EC Treaty, the consequence would be that courts which are not entitled to make referrals would have to consider these acts as valid: this would also apply in those cases in which under Article 68(2) not even courts of last resort may refer questions of validity.[25] This conclusion seems unacceptable for several reasons. First of all, the validity of a Community act would have to be upheld by national courts unconditionally, in spite of the fact that the act may conflict with a higher rule of Community law. Moreover, in the cases covered by Article 68(2) the Court, far from having an exclusive power to assess the validity of Community acts, would have no power at all, because no review by the Court is anyway permissible: thus the very basis of the *Foto-Frost* argument would be shaken. Finally, national courts would be even prevented from protecting through interim measures the party which is negatively affected by an allegedly invalid act. As was stated in *Zuckerfabrik*[26] and *Atlanta*,[27] interim measures may be taken by national courts only if the question of validity has been or is referred to the Court. This option is not available to national courts in our case; on the other hand, if neither the Court nor the national court can rule on the question of validity, any measure to be adopted in order to give protection against the allegedly invalid act could hardly be defined as an interim measure.

It would be equally unacceptable to draw from the principle stated in the *Foto-Frost* judgment the conclusion that a referral should anyway be open and that the restrictions expressed in Article 68 have to suffer an exception. National courts

20 *Supra* note 1.
21 *Supra* note 2.
22 *Supra* note 3.
23 *Supra* note 4.
24 *Ibid.*, para. 17.
25 This view was held by Curti Gialdino, *supra* note 19, at 108 and by Girerd, *supra* note 19, at 246.
26 Joined Cases C-143/88 and C-92/89, *Zuckerfabrik Süderdithmarschen AG* v. *Hauptzollamt Itzehoe*, [1991] ECR I-415 at 540-544, paras. 14-33.
27 Case C-465/93, *Atlanta Fruchthandelsgesellschaft mbH and Others* v. *Bundesamt für Ernährung und Forstwirtschaft*, [1997] ECR I-3761 at 3787-3795, paras. 19-51.

would thus be entitled to refer questions of validity.[28] This conclusion flatly contradicts the rationale of the restrictions to judicial review that Article 68 has introduced. It may suffice to note that, should one accept the idea of an exception, in practice all national courts would be free to refer questions of validity of measures relating to maintenance of law and order and the safeguarding of internal security. Article 68 would be turned on its head.

A more acceptable solution would be to apply the principle that was stated in *Foto-Frost* only when national courts may submit questions of validity to the Court of Justice. When, by contrast, courts are not entitled to make a referral, they should not be regarded as barred from ruling on the validity of Community acts. The existence of an exclusive power of the Court presupposes first of all that a power is granted – which is not the case with regard to the Community acts mentioned in Article 68(2) – and then that national courts can activate the Court.

This view does not conflict with the apparent reason why the Treaty of Amsterdam has put restrictions on the Court's competence with regard to the interpretation on validity of Community acts under Title IV of the EC Treaty. Member States were clearly concerned about the impact that rulings made by the Court on matters covered by Title IV could have on their sovereign prerogatives with regard to immigration and related matters. A judgment by a national court would have much more limited consequences. Moreover, Member States could have assumed that national courts will be hesitant in asserting that a Community act is invalid when no referral to the Court of Justice can be made.

III Requests for Interpretation of Community Rules Outside Their Scope of Application

When national courts submit questions of interpretation of Community rules to which national legislation refers outside the scope of application of Community law, it would be unreasonable to assume that national courts are under a stricter obligation to make referrals than when Community law applies. Therefore, the exceptions to the obligation under Article 234 are clearly invokable. The only problem worth discussing is whether national courts of last resort are under an obligation to make a referral in this type of case.

This question has not yet been addressed by the Court of Justice, although especially in *Dzodzi*[29] the Court has viewed its competence to answer questions in the cases now under consideration as coming within the purview of Article 234. The Court has made it clear in *Dorsch Consult*[30] that the question whether a national

28 This view is tentatively held by Adinolfi, "New Modalities for the Preliminary References Procedure: the Amsterdam Treaty and the Conventions among Member States", to be published in *Collected Courses of the Academy of European Law* (1998).

29 *Supra* note 5, at 3793-3795, paras. 33-42.

30 Case C-54/96, *Dorsch Consult Ingenieurgesellschaft mbH* v. *Bundesbaugesellschaft Berlin mbH*, [1997] ECR I-4961 at 4992-4993, paras. 22-23.

court is entitled to refer a question of Community law is to be resolved under Article 234, irrespective of what may be said on this matter in national legislation.

It is true that national legislation could well refrain from referring to Community law outside its scope of application. However, when there is a reference, questions of interpretation of EC law may arise in the same way as when Community law applies. The Court has noted that there is a Community interest that provisions of EC law are uniformly interpreted, thus avoiding the risk of future divergences of interpretation.[31] This argument is meant to reflect the concern that, should the Court not be given an opportunity to hand down a ruling, provisions of Community law which are referred to by national legislation may be interpreted inaccurately, and that this may pave the way for an equally incorrect interpretation of the same provisions when they are applied by national courts within the domain of EC law.

The rationale for asserting the Court's competence under Article 234 in this type of case also supports the existence of an obligation to make a referral on the part of courts of last resort. Since the admissibility of requests is viewed not as a concession made to national courts, but as an evaluation of a Community interest, it seems reasonable to hold that courts of last resort are not released from their obligation under Article 234.

IV Referral under the 1971 Luxembourg Protocol and similar instruments

When a protocol or convention provides for requests of preliminary rulings in a way that can be defined as a variation on the basic system under Article 234 of the EC Treaty – as for instance in the case of the 1971 Luxembourg Protocol relating to the Brussels Convention – there appears to be no reason why the obligation that courts of last resort have to refer questions of interpretation should not have the same import as the obligation under Article 234. Thus, courts of last resort could invoke the exceptions set out in *Da Costa*[32] and *CILFIT*[33] in order to be released from their obligation when a question is identical or similar[34] to one which the Court of Justice has already resolved, and the national court intends to abide by the Court's interpretation. Likewise, a court of last resort could consider the provision to be interpreted as clear under conditions analogous to those that the judgment in

31 *Supra* note 5, at 3793, para. 37. In Case C-28/95, *A. Leur-Bloem* v. *Inspecteur der Belastingdienst/Ondernemingen Amsterdam 2*, [1997] ECR I-4161 at 4201-4202, para. 32 the Court referred to a "Community interest [...] to forestall future differences of interpretation".

32 *Supra* note 1.

33 *Supra* note 2.

34 A wide interpretation of this part of the *CILFIT* judgment has been recently advocated by Jacobs, "The Role of National Courts and the European Court of Justice in Ensuring the Uniform Application of Community Law: Is a New Approach Needed?", *Divenire sociale e adeguamento del diritto. Studi in onore di Francesco Capotorti* (Milan, 1999) II-175-189 at 187-188.

CILFIT[35] stated with regard to provisions of EC law. While one can certainly apply to conventions among Member States the criterion – which was expressed in this judgment – that the meaning of the text should be "autonomous" with regard to similarly worded provisions of national law, the further requirement that a text, in order to be considered clear, should be interpreted "in the light of the provisions of Community law as a whole" depends on the way in which the links of the convention to EC law are appraised.

It is interesting to note that in *Kleinwort Benson*[36] the Court of Justice has found that a preliminary ruling under the Luxembourg Protocol may also be requested when a provision of national legislation refers to the Brussels Convention. Thus one could raise, again with regard to the Luxembourg Protocol – and arguably to similar instruments – the question whether courts of last resort are under an obligation to refer questions of interpretation of the Brussels Convention which arise when applying national legislation referring to the Convention outside its scope of application. A positive answer is called for. There seems to be no reason for adopting a different solution from the one which was suggested above, in Section III, in respect of Article 234 of the EC Treaty.

V Cases in which the relevant instrument does not expressly state an obligation to refer

Article 2 of the First Protocol to the Rome Convention on the Law Applicable to Contractual Obligations states that the highest courts and those deciding on appeal may request an interpretation of the Convention from the Court of Justice. The wording clearly appears to imply that these courts have no obligation to make a referral.[37]

Under Article 35 of the TEU and the numerous instruments adopting a similar system, it is left to the Member State making a declaration to this effect to state whether all the courts or only the courts of last resort are entitled to request a preliminary ruling on interpretation. Article 35 of the TEU also concerns questions of validity of certain acts and gives Member States the same option thereon.

None of the said provisions states whether courts of last resort, once a declaration has been made by their respective State, are under an obligation to request a preliminary ruling. The wording of the texts now under consideration only says that

35 *Supra* note 2.

36 Case C-346/93, *Kleinwort Benson Ltd* v. *City of Glasgow District Council*, [1995] ECR I-615 at 639-641, paras. 14-25. The Court noted that under the circumstances replies given to the national court would have been "purely advisory and without binding effect. That would be to alter the function of the Court, as envisaged in the Protocol of 3 June 1971 [...]".

37 The report by Tizzano on the Protocols on the interpretation of the Rome Convention states that even courts of last instance "merely have an option of making referrals, not an obligation to do so". O.J. 1990, C 219/1 at 13.

a court "may request the Court of Justice to give a preliminary ruling". This seems to rule out the existence of an obligation to refer. The texts clearly differ from Article 234 of the EC Treaty in this crucial respect, and the change cannot have been unintended.

It has been suggested that courts are nevertheless bound to submit a request if they intend to depart from a ruling given by the Court of Justice in a previous case.[38] However, this course of action, which is mandated under Article 234 of the EC Treaty according to the judgment in *CILFIT*,[39] can hardly be required when courts are under no obligation to refer. It is noteworthy that even under Article 234 courts which have a discretion in making referrals are not considered to be bound to submit a request for a preliminary ruling when they do not intend to comply with a ruling given by the Court in another case. One can only say that in this type of case it would be appropriate for a national court to make use of its discretion in order to request a fresh ruling from the Court.

With regard to the Protocol relating to the Convention on the establishment of a European Police Office, eight Member States declared "to reserve the right to make provision in their national law to the effect that, where a question relating to the interpretation of the Europol Convention is raised in a case pending before a national court or tribunal against whose decision there is no judicial remedy under national law, that court or tribunal will be required to refer the matter to the Court of Justice".[40] A declaration that was adopted by the Amsterdam Conference with regard to Article 35 of the TEU is identical to the text quoted above, with the only difference that it also comprises questions relating to the validity of framework decisions and measures implementing conventions that are to be established under Title VI of the TEU. Also in view of these declarations, no problem of consistency with the respective system for preliminary rulings appears to arise. Anyway, the functioning of the Court of Justice would not be significantly affected. Should the obligation to refer be introduced on the basis of national law, it would have to be understood that it is subject to the exceptions stated in *Da Costa,*[41] *CILFIT*[42] and, in so far as questions of validity are also covered, *International Chemical Corporation*.[43]

A similar obligation could be imposed, on the basis of national law, with regard to other international instruments. One reason for Member States to take such a step would be to subject their courts of last resort to more uniform rules on referrals, although they would stem from different sources.

---

38 See Adinolfi, *supra* note 28.
39 *Supra* note 2.
40 O.J. 1996, C 299/14.
41 *Supra* note 1.
42 *Supra* note 2.
43 *Supra* note 3.

VI Concluding Remarks

Yet another variety would be added to the collection of procedures for referral if Article 234 of the EC Treaty was amended according to one of the main suggestions made in January 2000 by a reflection group appointed by the Commission. On the basis of this proposal, courts of last resort would be required to submit to the Court of Justice only questions that are sufficiently important to EC law and only if a reasonable doubt exists regarding their solution. As the group refers for this last point to the Court's judgment in *CILFIT*,[44] it is not clear which change, if any, is intended in this respect.

The other part of the proposal is incisive, even if, as the group suggests, the principle stated in *Foto-Frost*[45] will be expressly maintained. An amendment along the lines of the proposal would be likely to induce all national courts, whether of last resort or not, to give less weight to the Court's judgments. One of the reasons why national courts are inclined to make referrals to the Court of Justice or to adopt the Court's perspective is because at a higher instance the question of interpretation of EC law which is raised in the case should in principle be settled according to the Court's view. The proposal would make this less certain, as courts of last resort may well prefer to give their own interpretation. The suggested criterion of the question being of sufficient importance to EC law is too vague to provide guidance to national courts. Thus, if introduced in the first pillar, the system of non-compulsory referrals for courts of last resort is likely to have a serious effect on the uniformity of interpretation of EC law.

44 *Supra* note 2.
45 *Supra* note 4.

11

THE EUROPEAN COURT OF JUSTICE AND THE 'AREA OF FREEDOM, SECURITY AND JUSTICE': CHALLENGES AND PROBLEMS

Piet Eeckhout

INTRODUCTION

This contribution examines the main provisions of both the EC and EU Treaties giving jurisdiction to the European Court of Justice (hereafter ECJ) in matters concerning the 'area of freedom, security and justice' which those Treaties, in their version post-Amsterdam, aim to achieve. It is a subject on which much ink has been spilt,[1] but which none the less deserves further study, in the light of the complexity and significance of the issues involved.

This paper does not aim to be exhaustive. It concentrates rather on what I perceive to be some of the most significant problems and challenges posed by the new provisions. The backdrop against which they are addressed is a double concern. The first relates to the level of protection of 'human', or 'fundamental' rights in the European Union as a whole, and in the framework of the wide-ranging policies which will need to be developed for achieving the 'area of freedom, security and justice' in particular. In a recent paper on "An 'Ever Closer Union' in Need of a Human Rights Policy" Alston and Weiler argue that judicial protection at the instance of individuals is an important, even foundational dimension of an effective human rights regime, but that, whilst such protection is necessary, it is not sufficient, and that the European Union needs a real policy on

1 See e.g. S. Peers, "Who's judging the watchmen? The judicial system of the 'Area of Freedom, Security and Justice'", (1998) *Yearbook of European Law* (forthcoming); O. Due, "The Impact of the Amsterdam Treaty upon the Court of Justice", (1999) *Fordham International Law Journal* S48-S71; N. Fennelly, "A View from Kirchberg", paper presented at the London-Leiden Conference 1999 and "Preserving the Legal Coherence within the New Treaty", (1998) MJECL 185-199; R. Plender, "European migration law: the implications for practitioners", paper presented at the London-Leiden Conference 1999; A. Arnull, "Taming the beast? The Treaty of Amsterdam and the Court of Justice", in O'Keeffe and Twomey (eds), *Legal Issues of the Amsterdam Treaty* (Hart Publishing, 1999); P. Girerd, "L'article 68 CE: un renvoi préjudiciel d'interprétation et d'application incertaines", (1999) RTDEur 239-260; A. Albors-Llorens, "Changes in the jurisdiction of the European Court of Justice under the Treaty of Amsterdam", (1998) CMLRev. 1273-1294; K. Hailbronner, "European immigration and asylum law under the Amsterdam Treaty", (1998) CMLRev. 1047-1067; J. Monar, "Justice and Home Affairs in the Treaty of Amsterdam: Reform at the Price of Fragmentation", (1998) ELRev. 320-335.

D. O'Keeffe (ed.), Liber Amicorum Slynn 153-166 (2000)

human rights protection.[2] I subscribe to most if not all the suggestions made in the paper, but would add that, as far as the ECJ's new competences are concerned, even the foundational dimension of judicial protection at the instance of individuals may be in issue, as this contribution will attempt to show. And as to the contents and impact of the new EC/EU policies related to the 'area', it is probably superfluous to remind the reader that those policies are exponentially more sensitive from a human rights perspective than some of the more classic EC policies, such as those concerned with the internal market. Policies on immigration, asylum and criminal co-operation have an inevitable fundamental rights dimension; they are also subject to intense public scrutiny and pressure in contemporary European society, and not always to the benefit of the rights of the individual.

The second concern may appear more mundane, but may none the less prove equally significant. With new competences for the ECJ comes an increasing workload, at a time when the EU's judicial architecture is already exposed to a rising flood of cases. One cannot therefore (and should not) dissociate the issues raised by the Court's new competences from the overall rethink of that judicial architecture, which is under way.

Both concerns are not unrelated. It is clear that an efficiently functioning court system contributes to the protection of individual rights and that, conversely, such rights are in obvious jeopardy where the court system is unable to produce timely rulings of considerable quality and coherence.

The paper is structured according to the various new competences given to the Court. Those competences are to be found in the new Title IV of the EC Treaty, concerning "Visas, Asylum, Immigration and Other Policies Related to the Free Movement of Persons", and in Title VI of the Treaty on European Union, the so-called Third Pillar, concerning "Provisions on Police and Judicial Cooperation in Criminal Matters". The paper first examines the preliminary rulings procedures of Article 68(1) EC and of Article 35 (1-4) TEU. It then looks at the questions for interpretation rulings of Article 68(3) EC, the judicial review procedure of Article 35(6) TEU and the dispute settlement procedure of Article 35(7) TEU. The paper lastly examines the restrictions on the Court's jurisdiction concerning "law and order" issues.

THE PRELIMINARY RULINGS PROCEDURE OF ARTICLE 68(1) EC

Article 68(1) EC provides:

> "Article 234 shall apply to this Title under the following circumstances and conditions: where a question on the interpretation of this Title or on the validity or interpretation of

2 P. Alston and J.H.H. Weiler, "An 'Ever Closer Union' in Need of a Human Rights Policy: The European Union and Human Rights", in P. Alston (ed), *The EU and Human Rights* (Oxford University Press, 1999) at 13.

acts of the institutions of the Community based on this Title is raised in a case pending before a court or tribunal of a Member State against whose decisions there is no judicial remedy under national law, that court or tribunal shall, if it considers that a decision on the question is necessary to enable it to give judgment, request the Court of Justice to give a ruling thereon."

It must be noted at the outset that Title IV does not mention EC Treaty provisions on the jurisdiction of the Court other than Article 234 on preliminary rulings, which can only be taken to mean that all such provisions fully apply to Title IV. Infringement proceedings, actions for annulment, actions for failure to act, actions in damages and requests for an opinion are all available for Title IV matters. That is not the case for Title VI TEU, where the Court's jurisdiction is limited to those forms of action which are expressly mentioned. From the perspective of individuals, the action for annulment is probably the second most significant judicial avenue, after the preliminary rulings procedure. However, as most measures adopted by the Community under Title IV are likely to be of a general legislative character, the restrictions on standing for individuals under Article 230(4) EC will preclude general use.

Article 68(1) EC extends Article 234 EC to Title IV, but limits the scope for references to cases which are before the highest courts ("a court or a tribunal of a Member State against whose decisions there is no judicial remedy under national law"). Such a court shall, if it considers that a decision on the question is necessary to enable it to give judgment, request the Court of Justice to give a ruling. In other words, only the last paragraph of Article 234 EC applies, according to which highest courts are obliged to refer; and the second paragraph of Article 234 EC does not apply, which means that lower courts cannot refer. Article 68(1) EC further specifies, in much the same way as Article 234 EC, that it concerns questions of interpretation of the Treaty (in this case Title IV) and questions on the validity or interpretation of acts of the Community institutions based on Title IV.

The limitation to highest courts is said to be inspired by the concern for the potentially high number of cases at national level involving a point of Community law under Title IV, and the concomitant concern to avoid a flood of cases in Luxembourg. It remains to be seen whether the limitation will be an effective dam. There may be another type of concern which inspired it, which is that for some of the cases coming under the new Title, especially those concerning asylum and immigration, there is an issue of expediency: Member State governments are seeking a swift resolution of such disputes, and references to the ECJ could be used as a delaying tactic.[3]

This second concern is understandable, but if one looks at the development of the law in the medium term, it is not necessarily justified. One could refer to a

3 Cf. the reported words of Mr Straw, Home Secretary, in the *Financial Times* of 6 October 1999 ("Any attempt to give the court wide powers could undermine the Home Office's resolution of 80,000 outstanding asylum applications").

somewhat older piece by Francis Jacobs, where he pointed out that there will be many situations where both time and costs will be saved by an early reference, and that points of the first importance have often arisen in cases where little is at stake between the parties.[4] In his capacity as Advocate General Jacobs has further developed what he considers to be appropriate references.[5]

It is clear that, in matters concerning the new Title IV as well, early references may serve to resolve issues of law which have general relevance and are broadly contentious. Uniform interpretation by the ECJ creates legal certainty, which in turn contributes to the effectiveness of the law and of law enforcement. It may in the medium and longer term reduce litigation.

Questions of Interpretation

The limitation to highest courts does not appear to give rise to dramatic issues where questions of interpretation are involved, as opposed to questions of validity, which are considered below. Most questions of interpretation are likely to concern Community legislation rather than the provisions of Title IV itself: the latter does not as a rule lay down substantive rules, in contrast with other parts of the EC Treaty, such as those on the internal market and the four freedoms. In general, the Court's approach to questions of interpretation of Community legislation is well known,[6] which is not to say of course that national courts can readily dispense with references.

But there is a further set of questions of interpretation with which the Court may be frequently confronted in Title IV cases, namely questions concerning fundamental rights. As is well known, it is established case-law that, within the scope of Community law, fundamental rights as embodied in international law instruments on human rights to which the Member States are parties, and as resulting from the constitutional traditions of the Member States, are to be respected. That case-law is confirmed by Article 6(2) TEU, over which the ECJ now has jurisdiction pursuant to Article 46(d) TEU. Fundamental rights are of particular significance for the validity of Community acts, but they are also a touchstone for the lawfulness of action by Member States which comes within the scope of Community law. The latter is the case where Member States implement Community acts and where they rely on a derogation permitted by the Treaty.[7] It is obvious that the implementation by Member States of Community

---

4 F.G. Jacobs, "When to refer to the European Court", (1974) LQR 492.

5 Case C-338/95 *Wiener* v *Hauptzollamt Emmerich* [1997] ECR I-6495; see also extra-judicially "The Role of National Courts and of the European Court of Justice in Ensuring the Uniform Application of Community Law: Is a New Approach Needed?", in *Studi in Onore di Francesco Capotorti (II)* (Giuffrè editori, 1999) 176-189.

6 See e.g. P. Eeckhout, "The European Court of Justice and the legislature", (1998) *Yearbook of European Law*, forthcoming.

7 See e.g. Case 5/88 *Wachauf* v *Bundesamt für Ernährung und Forstwirtschaft* [1989] 2609, para 19; Case C-260/89 *ERT* [1991] ECR I-2925, paras 42-43; Case C-368/95 *Fa-*

legislation in matters of asylum and immigration may give rise to fundamental rights issues, and that the Court may be asked to rule on whether or not such rights are violated. One sensitive issue here is clearly the scope of the Court's jurisdiction or, to put it differently, the interpretation given to the concept of implementation of Community legislation triggering the application of Community fundamental rights law. With the development of fairly general Community law on issues such as asylum and immigration it will no doubt be argued in many cases that there is a link with implementation of Community legislation. Much will therefore depend on how the Court construes the required nexus between national measures and Community legislation for it to review compliance with fundamental rights.

Questions of validity

In the case of questions on the validity of Community acts adopted on the basis of Title IV there is a particularly grave issue. It has been reported by others,[8] but the discussion on it is certainly not yet exhausted. One could formulate the issue as follows: given that lower courts are unable to refer questions of validity to the ECJ, what is the fate of the Court's ruling in *Foto-Frost*, according to which national courts or tribunals cannot themselves declare Community acts invalid?[9] That ruling was inspired by obvious concern for the uniform application of Community law, yet it seems very difficult to maintain in a system where lower courts are not entitled to refer questions to the ECJ. There are various considerations here.

One could take the view that, for the sake of uniformity, *Foto-Frost* needs to be maintained, and that, where a party challenges the validity of a Community act adopted on the basis of Title IV, the issue will simply need to be litigated up to the highest court, which will then be under a duty to make a reference. In my view, such a system would be wholly inappropriate in a Community based on the rule of law and on respect for fundamental rights. To say that a party is entitled to challenge the validity of an act, but that the challenge can only be made at last instance, is not in accordance with the principle of effective remedies, which is also embodied in Article 13 of the ECHR. Even if there were no actual breach of the ECHR – and when one considers that issue one needs to take into account that the European Court of Human Rights has no jurisdiction over Community acts, and accepts this in the light of the fact that the ECJ protects

miliapress v *Bauer Verlag* [1997] ECR I-3689, para 24.
For a classic analysis see J.H.H. Weiler and N.J.S. Lockhart, "'Taking Rights Seriously' Seriously: The European Court and its Fundamental Rights Jurisprudence", (1995) CMLRev. 51-94 and 579-627.

8 Peers, *op.cit.*; Due, *op.cit.* at S63-S64; Hailbronner, *op.cit.* at 1056; Arnull, *op.cit.*; Girerd, *op.cit.* at 245-246.

9 Case 314/85 *Foto-Frost* [1987] ECR 4199, para 15.

fundamental rights[10] – such a system is none the less unacceptable if the EC is to take its human rights language seriously. That is particularly so because challenges to Community legislation adopted under Title IV will no doubt often be themselves based on fundamental rights. And for individuals there is at the moment no alternative to challenges made before a national court, since a direct action for annulment is not available for legislative measures. That in itself is an important remedy issue, but even if the restrictions on standing under Article 230(4) EC were to be relaxed, the action for annulment would still not be a sufficient alternative. For example, one can hardly require a potential future immigrant to challenge Community legislation within the two months period of Article 230 EC, if the person concerned does not even know yet, at the time when the Community act is adopted, that he or she is going to move to the European Union and may face legal obstacles there.

To say that *Foto-Frost* remains intact and that a party needs to litigate up to the highest court may also give rise to awkward procedural issues under national law. An appeal against a lower court decision would normally have to be formulated as a challenge to the correctness of that decision. But how could a lower court be reproached in law that it has failed to declare a Community act invalid, if it has no authority to do so and if it cannot refer to the ECJ?

What are the alternatives? One is not to apply the *Foto-Frost* principle in Title IV cases, where the issue is before a court which cannot make a reference. Obviously, that may jeopardise the uniform application of Community legislation. But arguably that is a concession which can be made for the purpose of safeguarding the principle of effective remedies. Where a lower court declares a Title IV act invalid, one might expect the defending party to appeal against the ruling, especially where it is a public authority – which at least in asylum and immigration cases it is likely to be. It may even be suggested that the authorities of the Member State in question could be under an obligation to lodge an appeal, in application of the duty of co-operation in Article 10 EC. It seems clear that action to safeguard the uniform application of acts of the Community institutions comes within the scope of that duty. Even where a Member State feels that the invalidity ruling by a lower court is justified, an appeal seems required to ensure that the ECJ may make a decision with effect throughout the Community. On such an appeal, the highest court could then refer the question of validity to the ECJ, which will ensure uniformity. This is obviously very cumbersome, but, again, it may be a concession that needs to be made. In this context one should not lose sight of the fact that the *Foto-Frost* principle is entirely court-made, and has little or no basis in the text of the Treaty. The Court could therefore decide that the principle does not apply in Title IV cases before lower courts.

Peers has suggested an intermediate alternative, which is that lower courts could suspend the operation of a Community act whose validity is challenged,[11] in application of the principles which the ECJ laid down in *Zuckerfabrik Süder-*

10 Cf. ECtHR, *Matthews* v *UK*, No 24833/94, judgment of 18 February 1999, paras 32-33.

11 *Op.cit.*

dithmarschen.[12] I am not, however, convinced that that is a workable alternative, as it rests on only one limb of the *Zuckerfabrik* interim protection principle: the court which suspends cannot refer the issue of validity to the ECJ, and therefore appeals need to be brought up to the point where a reference can be made. If that is the case, it seems better simply to allow lower courts to declare a Community act invalid.

The most drastic solution would be for the Court to accept references by lower courts on validity issues, contrary to the clear text of Article 68(1) EC. Such a decision would clearly be highly contentious, much more so than past cases of judicial activism, because the limits on the Court's jurisdiction embodied in Article 68(1) EC were the subject of an express and recent negotiation between the Member States. The Court is therefore unlikely to take that route.

In any event, the present situation is highly unsatisfactory from the perspective of offering an effective remedy, which is, to recall the words of Alston and Weiler, a foundational dimension of an effective human rights regime. One would hope that the Council will make use of the opportunity of Article 67(2) EC and will adapt the provisions relating to the powers of the ECJ.

THE PRELIMINARY RULINGS PROCEDURE OF ARTICLE 35(1-4) TEU

After Amsterdam there is a limited preliminary rulings procedure for Title VI TEU matters. Some of the issues to which that procedure gives rise are similar to those concerning the interpretation and application of Article 68(1) EC.

The procedure is limited in that the Member States have various options. They can either:

a) not give their courts the opportunity to send references to the ECJ – that is the position at present for Ireland, the United Kingdom, France and Denmark (but those Member States may submit observations in all cases heard by the Court under this procedure, see Article 35(4) TEU); or
b) allow only highest courts to make references – that is the position at present for Spain; or
c) allow any court or tribunal to make a reference – that is the position at present for Austria, Belgium, Finland, Germany, Greece, Italy, Luxembourg, the Netherlands, Portugal and Sweden.[13]

In addition, seven Member States, i.e. Austria, Belgium, Germany, Italy, Luxembourg, the Netherlands and Spain, have reserved the right to make references obligatory for highest courts, a right for which Article 35 TEU does not provide.

12 Joined Cases C-143/88 and C-92/89 *Zuckerfabrik Süderdithmarschen and Zuckerfabrik Soest* [1991] ECR I-415.
13 See OJ 1999 L 114/56 and OJ 1999 C 120/24.

The jurisdiction of the Court under this TEU preliminary rulings procedure does not extend to the provisions of Title VI itself; it is limited to questions on the validity or the interpretation of framework decisions or decisions, on the interpretation of conventions established under the Title, and on the validity and interpretation of the measures implementing them (Article 35(1) TEU). There is, however little doubt that the Court, when ruling on such questions, will be called upon to interpret some of the provisions of Title VI. If one may transpose the Court's approach in Article 234 EC cases, the requirement to give a useful reply in order to assist the referring court to decide the case will in some cases necessitate an interpretation of those provisions. For example, where a national court entertains doubts on the validity of an EU decision on grounds of lack of competence of the EU, it would not be in accordance with the spirit of Article 35(1-4) TEU for the ECJ to reply that it cannot rule on the issue because it lacks jurisdiction to interpret the provisions of Title VI.[14]

It is paradoxical that in some Member States this preliminary rulings procedure is identical in scope to the mother of all preliminary rulings (Article 234 EC), with any court or tribunal being permitted to make a reference and highest courts being obliged to do so, whereas for Title IV EC matters lower courts in those Member States cannot refer. However, for those Member States where lower courts cannot refer under Article 35 TEU, similar issues arise as those discussed in the previous section. And for those Member States where no references are possible at all, the question of validity becomes even more poignant, although it must be noted that framework decisions and decisions adopted under Title VI do not have direct effect (see Article 34(2)(b-c) TEU) and may therefore be less likely to affect the position of individuals. Does this mean that courts in those Member States can themselves rule on validity? Perhaps they will need to resolve this on the basis of national law rather than EU law, because it is not clear whether the *Foto-Frost* principle could be readily transposed to the EU legal order – if indeed one may speak of an EU legal order. If EU law is considered to be simply a form of international law, that would mean that Member State courts cannot invalidate EU legal instruments as such (*pacta sunt servanda*), but they could refuse to give them effect on grounds of violation of national constitutional law (to the extent that they have such power under national law).

Again, validity questions will often be based on human rights arguments. That brings us to the issue whether the European Court of Human Rights would accept jurisdiction for Title VI matters. Peers has argued that it should,[15] and the argument is plausible. Or should the Strasbourg Court distinguish between cases coming from Member States which have accepted the new preliminary rulings procedure – where the ECJ may rule on validity, and recourse to Strasbourg may

14 Compare with Case C-170/96 *Commission* v *Council* (Airport transit visas) [1998] ECR I-2763, paras 12-18.

15 *Op.cit.*

therefore not be necessary – and cases coming from Member States where there is no opportunity to refer validity questions to the ECJ?

THE "QUESTION OF INTERPRETATION" RULING OF ARTICLE 68(3) EC

This is a new form of action, probably intended as a counterweight for the restricted preliminary rulings procedure of Article 68(1) EC. Under Article 68(3) EC the Council, the Commission, or a Member State may request the Court of Justice to give a ruling on a question of interpretation of Title IV or of acts of the institutions based on that title. There is no requirement that the question has arisen in any particular dispute or in any pending cases; it is therefore a form of action "in the interest of the law", but it could of course be used in circumstances where there is divergent case-law before national courts on a particular issue.

It is to be noted that there is no reference to questions of validity, and the reason for that is probably that the action for annulment is available for challenging acts based on Title IV. None the less, this means that the new procedure cannot be used for addressing divergent national case-law on the (in)validity of such acts, in case the *Foto-Frost* principle were abandoned for cases before lower courts (nor can actions for annulment be used to that effect since they have to be brought within two months).

Advocate General Fennelly has observed that the procedure seems comparable to a request for an opinion on an envisaged international agreement brought under Article 300(6) EC.[16] There is one notable difference, which is that Article 300(6) clarifies that opinions are binding, whereas Article 68(3) EC only refers to a "negative" feature of Court rulings: they shall not apply to judgments of courts or tribunals of the Member States which have become *res judicata*. But to continue in Latin, *a contrario* one could argue that the rulings are binding in all other cases. The precise legal effect of such rulings will no doubt be a matter for further academic debate – as is the legal effect of preliminary rulings under Article 234 EC[17] – but in practice it seems highly unlikely that ECJ interpretations would not be followed, for the simple reason that challenging the authority of ECJ decisions exposes Community institutions, national authorities or other parties to the criticism of disrespect for the rule of law.

The *res judicata* clarification is welcome, though one wonders whether the Treaty is the appropriate place for confirming a principle which the courts would no doubt have worked out for themselves, and which would in any event appear to be a general principle of Community law, common as it is to the legal systems of the Member States.

---

16 "A View from Kirchberg", *op.cit.*

17 See e.g. A. Arnull, "Interpretation and Precedent in European Community Law", in A. Andenas and F.G. Jacobs (eds), *European Community Law in the English Courts* (Oxford, Clarendon Press, 1998) 115-136.

Perhaps the most difficult aspect of this new procedure concerns the proper framing of questions of interpretation. In Article 234 EC proceedings the Court has often emphasised that its function is to assist in the administration of justice in the Member States and not to deliver advisory opinions on general or hypothetical questions.[18] The Court may take the same view on its jurisdiction to deliver rulings under Article 68(3) EC, and it may feel uneasy about having to reply to questions of interpretation which are too general and too remote from an actual factual and legal context.

THE JUDICIAL REVIEW PROCEDURE OF ARTICLE 35(6) TEU

Article 35(6) TEU mirrors, as regards framework decisions and decisions adopted under Title VI TEU, the action for annulment under Article 230 EC. The Court has jurisdiction to review the legality of such acts, but only in actions brought by a Member State or the Commission. The grounds and time-limit are the same as under Article 230 EC. The European Parliament and individuals do not have standing. For individuals one must connect this with the questions surrounding the scope for invalidity rulings in the context of the preliminary rulings procedure of Article 35(1-4) TEU. At this stage one can only hope that the democratic deficit, which in terms of European Parliament involvement is rather marked in Title VI matters, will not be aggravated by a judicial deficit.[19]

THE DISPUTE SETTLEMENT PROCEDURE OF ARTICLE 35(7) TEU

Article 35(7) TEU gives the Court jurisdiction to rule on any dispute between Member States regarding the interpretation or application of Title VI acts. The condition for starting such proceedings is that the Council has been unable to settle the dispute at political level within a period of six months of it having been referred to the Council by one of its members. There is a second provision, which broadens the scope of these actions to disputes between Member States and the Commission, but such disputes are limited to the interpretation or application of conventions established under Article 34(2)(d) TEU; in other words the procedure is not available for common positions, framework decisions and decisions. Perhaps there was concern that the Commission could otherwise use this procedure as a form of infringement action, which may have been considered undesirable for those legal instruments.

The wording of Article 35(7) is very broad: any dispute regarding interpretation or application. The nature of such disputes is not specified, nor are the legal claims that can be made or the effects of a decision by the Court.

---

18 See e.g. Case C-83/91 *Meilicke* v *ADV/ORGA* [1992] ECR I-4871, para 25.

19 Cf. D. Waelbroeck and A.-M. Verheyden, "Les conditions de recevabilité des recours en annulation des particuliers contre les actes normatifs communautaires", (1995) CDE 403.

THE "LAW AND ORDER" RESTRICTIONS ON THE COURT'S JURISDICTION

A recurring theme in the Amsterdam changes to the Court's competences are the restrictions on the Court's jurisdiction in matters concerning maintenance of law and order and the safeguarding of internal security. There are three similar, but not identical, provisions:

a) Article 68(2) EC – placed in between the preliminary rulings procedure of Article 68(1) and the request for interpretation procedure of Article 68(3) – provides that:

> "In any event, the Court of Justice shall not have jurisdiction to rule on any measure or decision taken pursuant to Article 62(1) relating to the maintenance of law and order and the safeguarding of internal security".

b) Article 35(5) TEU provides:

> "The Court of Justice shall have no jurisdiction to review the validity or proportionality of operations carried out by the police or other law enforcement services of a Member State or the exercise of the responsibilities incumbent upon Member States with regard to the maintenance of law and order and the safeguarding of internal security".

c) Article 2(1), third subparagraph, of the Protocol integrating the Schengen *acquis* into the framework of the European Union provides:

> "... In any event, the Court of Justice shall have no jurisdiction on measures or decisions relating to the maintenance of law and order and the safeguarding of internal security".

It is a provision which follows those on the determination of the legal basis in the EC and EU Treaties of the Schengen *acquis* and on the confirmation of the ECJ's jurisdiction over the allocated Schengen *acquis* in accordance with the provisions of the respective Treaties.[20] As such, it does not appear to add anything to Articles 68(2) EC and 35(5) TEU.

There is an apparent difference between Article 68(2) EC and Article 35(5) TEU. The former provision refers to measures or decisions taken pursuant to Article 62(1) EC. It thus appears to refer to measures or decisions taken by the Community, and not by the Member States: under Article 62(1) EC the Council shall take measures with a view to ensuring, in compliance with Article 14 EC, the absence of any controls on persons, be they citizens of the Union or nation-

20 The allocation was carried out by Council Decision 1999/436/EC of 20 May 1999 determining, in conformity with the relevant provisions of the Treaty establishing the European Community and the Treaty on European Union, the legal basis for each of the provisions or decisions which constitute the Schengen acquis, OJ 1999 L 176/17.

als of third countries, when crossing internal borders. Article 35(5) TEU, by contrast, refers to action by Member States.

At the London-Leiden conference of June 1999 Advocate General Fennelly expressed his confusion about the reference to Article 62(1) EC, and conjectured that the reference might be erroneous, and that Article 64(1) EC was intended.[21] But officials involved in the Amsterdam negotiations confirmed that the reference was correct, and stated that the intention was to safeguard the application of Article 2(2) of the Schengen Implementing Convention,[22] which provides for a derogation from the free movement across internal Schengen borders:

> "Where public policy or national security so require, however, a Contracting Party may, after consulting the other Contracting Parties, decide that for a limited period national border checks appropriate to the situation will be carried out at internal borders. If public policy or national security require immediate action, the Contracting Party concerned shall take the necessary measures and shall inform the other Contracting Parties thereof at the earliest opportunity".

If that is indeed the intention, then the apparent difference between Article 68(2) EC and Article 35(5) TEU is not a real one. But intentions reported at conferences are not an accepted tool of interpretation of Treaty provisions, and it is difficult to construe the text of Article 68(2) EC as referring to measures or decisions taken by Member States only; at most it can be construed as encompassing such measures or decisions, in addition to those adopted by the Community.

Let us now further consider Article 68(2) EC. The provision is clearly strongly worded: *in any event* the Court shall *not have jurisdiction* to rule on *any measure*. As Hailbronner has observed,[23] this restriction on the Court's jurisdiction is not similar to other public policy exceptions in the Treaty. Those exceptions are worded in terms of permitted action by Member States, whereas Article 68(2) excludes the jurisdiction of the ECJ. It is therefore at least arguable that the Court should not apply its classic canon of interpretation according to which exceptions to fundamental Treaty provisions are to be narrowly construed. However, again it is clear that there may be a fundamental rights dimension to cases concerning maintenance of law and order and safeguarding of internal security. In cases where fundamental rights are in issue, the Court should perhaps return to the above canon; surely Article 68(2) cannot be interpreted as a licence to violate or frustrate human rights.

---

21 *Op.cit.* Article 64(1) provides that "This Title shall not affect the exercise of responsibilities incumbent upon Member States with regard to the maintenance of law and order and the safeguarding of internal security".

22 I.e. the Convention, signed in Schengen on 19 June 1990, implementing the Agreement on the gradual abolition of checks at their common borders, signed in Schengen on 14 June 1985, 30 ILM 84 (1991); R. Plender (ed), *Basic Documents on International Migration Law* (The Hague, Martinus Nijhoff, 1999) 815.

23 *Op.cit.* at 1057.

Insofar as Article 68(2) concerns action by Member States, the Court could try to hide behind the formalities of some of the actions brought before it. For example, in a preliminary ruling the Court never formally rules on national measures; it does not exercise jurisdiction as regards such measures, because its jurisdiction is limited to questions of interpretation or validity of Community law. The same is of course true in the case of direct actions involving Community acts. It is really only in infringement proceedings brought by the Commission pursuant to Article 226 EC that the Court expressly looks at national action. None the less, it might be difficult for the Court to "circumvent" the exclusion of jurisdiction provision of Article 68(2) in, for example, a preliminary ruling on the interpretation of Article 2(2) of the Schengen Implementing Convention in a case concerning border controls carried out by a Member State.

Article 35(5) TEU does not refer only to maintenance of law and order and safeguarding of internal security; it also excludes ECJ jurisdiction for operations carried out by the police or other law enforcement services. As stated above, it concerns only action by the Member States and not by the Community. As to the effect of the restriction on the preliminary rulings procedure of Article 35 (1-4) TEU the above considerations concerning Article 68(2) EC can be transposed. The restriction may further be relevant in dispute settlement cases brought under Article 35(7) TEU.

SOME CONCLUDING OBSERVATIONS

It is obvious that the Treaty provisions on the new competences of the ECJ are complex, and they will no doubt give rise to many issues of interpretation. To some extent that may be unavoidable if one accepts the starting-point of the pillar structure of the European Union and the gradual "communitarisation" of certain policies. It may be the price to be paid for progress, and as long as the cost of legal uncertainty is more or less under control, the bargain may be acceptable.

However, one cannot reason so easily in terms of costs when considering the human rights dimension of the new policies and the Court's new competences. This contribution has attempted to highlight some of the human rights issues which may come up in the course of the functioning of the new forms of action. The key issue concerns the approach to the legality/validity of Community action. It is indispensable to have an effective system of remedies for the individual in a Community/Union governed by the rule of law. If anything, Community involvement in the new policies should serve to strengthen the protection of human rights if the Union is to be the forward-looking organisation for political integration of positive relevance to its citizens which it aspires to be in this multi-dimensional world.

I do not wish to suggest that Community measures adopted within the framework of the new policies are in any way likely to actually violate or frustrate human rights. But given the sensitivity of some of these policies, it seems of paramount importance to ensure, not only that justice is done, but also that it is seen to be done. What needs to be avoided, perhaps at all costs, is the criticism that a fundamental rights claim could not be considered by the courts because of a "procedural provision".

To achieve that, the provisions on the Court's competences will need to be revised sooner rather than later. The limitation of references under Article 68(1) EC to highest courts is an obvious candidate for revision, in particular as concerns references on validity. But there are further improvements to be made. Alston and Weiler have suggested that the Court should revisit its jurisprudence on Article 230 EC with a view to facilitating the standing of individuals and public interest groups alleging the violation of fundamental rights.[24] But perhaps it is not sufficient for the Court to revisit this jurisprudence; it is arguable that the restrictions on standing should be relaxed by way of Treaty revision. In today's European Union, I would consider it necessary to allow, for example, an action for annulment brought by a public interest group against a general piece of Community legislation on asylum.

The Community should also in my view reconsider joining the ECHR. As long as the European Court of Human Rights continues to hold that it has no jurisdiction over Community acts, the gradual transfer of Third Pillar matters to the First Pillar has the effect of reducing review by the Strasbourg Court, which is difficult to defend.

If the jurisdiction of the Luxembourg courts is to be broadened, measures will be necessary to cope with an increasing workload. The debate on the EU's judicial architecture is very much under way, and one should hope that it receives the attention which it deserves during the next Intergovernmental Conference. A fundamental rethink may be necessary, including such issues as a more effectively functioning preliminary rulings system. For example, it should be possible for the ECJ to expedite references in urgent asylum or immigration cases. Perhaps here too, flexibility is the key word for the future: we should have flexible and dynamic European courts capable of ensuring the effective protection of rights and the uniform and predictable application of the law.

---

24 *Op.cit.* See also C. Harlow, "Access to Justice as a Human Right: The European Convention and the European Union", in Alston, *op.cit.*, at 197.

12

PRELIMINARY RULINGS ON THE INTERPRETATION OF MIXED AGREEMENTS

Alan Dashwood

INTRODUCTION

It is trite law that the Court of Justice has jurisdiction under Article 234 (ex Article 177) of the EC Treaty to interpret the provisions of an international agreement which has been concluded on behalf of the Community under the procedure laid down by Article 300 (ex Article 228). The rationale, repeatedly stated by the Court, is that, since conclusion is by way of a decision of the Council, such an agreement falls to be regarded in Community law as an act of one of the institutions. Its provisions thus automatically form part of the internal legal order from the moment of their coming into force, without any need for a formal act of incorporation; and the Court's jurisdiction to interpret them follows from the express terms of subparagraph (b) of the first paragraph of Article 234.[1]

That reasoning, though not entirely satisfactory in principle, is now beyond challenge so far as concerns international agreements concluded by the Community without the participation of the Member States.[2] However, it does not provide an answer to the question revisited in this article: whether the interpretative jurisdiction under Article 234 extends to the whole of a mixed agreement, including the parts of it which have been concluded, not under Community powers, but under those of the Member States.[3] If the Court of Justice does have ju-

1 Case 181/73, *R & V Haegeman* v. *Belgian State* [1974] ECR 449, paras. 4 to 6. See the reformulation of the *Haegeman* principle in Case 12/86, *Meryem Demirel* v. *Stadt Schwäbisch Gmünd* [1987] ECR 3719, para. 7. The *Demirel* formulation was recently reiterated in Case C-321/97, *Ulla-Brith Anderson and Susanne Wåkerås-Andersson* v. *Sweden* judgment of 15 June, 1999 (not yet reported), para. 26.

2 A severe critic of the Court's reasoning is Hartley. See the views expressed at pp. 31 to 34 of *Constitutional Problems of the European Union*, Hart Publishing (1999).

3 The question has been debated over many years. For a range of opinions, see: Bleckmann, "Der Gemischte Vertrag im Europarecht", *Europarecht* (1976), p. 301; Stein, "External Relations of the European Community: Structure and Process", in *Collected Courses of the Academy of European Law* (1990), Vol. I, Book 1, Nijhoff (1991), p. 165; Schermers and Waelbroeck, *Judicial Protection in the European Communities*, (5th ed.), Kluwer (1992), p. 430; Macleod, Hendry and Hyett, *The External Relations of the European Community*, Oxford (1996), pp. 156 *et seq.*; Eeckhout, "The domestic legal status of the WTO Agreement: interconnecting legal systems", 34 CMLRev. (1997), p. 11.

D. O'Keeffe (ed.), Liber Amicorum Slynn 167-175 (2000)

risdiction over those parts of a mixed agreement, the reason for this cannot be that the relevant provisions have, through the act of conclusion, acquired the status of secondary Community law.

The question has gained in significance now it is clear that, in policy areas where the Community and the Member States share external relations competence (where neither, in other words, is exclusively competent), the decision for the Council whether to conclude an international agreement under Community powers, or leave it to the Member States to act under national powers, is a matter of political choice.[4] Mixity is not to be seen as a *pis-aller*, resorted to where the Community wishes to enter into an agreement containing elements that fall outside the scope of application of the Treaty. There may be agreements which have a mixed character (or a larger proportion of mixity than is legally indispensable) because non-exclusive Community powers have been less than fully exercised.[5]

Member State powers are, of course, circumscribed by the *AETR* principle.[6] The political choice between Community and national action is lost, once a matter has been made the subject of internal legislation, and for as long as it remains so. Thus in areas which have been partially harmonised, Member States retain the right to enter into international agreements only in respect of matters other than those covered by the existing Community measures. It follows that the same provision of an agreement may be concluded by the EC under the *AETR* principle, for the purposes of any specific matters already regulated at the Community level, and also by the Member States, in respect of matters not so regulated. On the basis of such an analysis, the Court found in Opinion 1/94 that competence to conclude the GATS and the TRIPs was shared between the Community and the Member States.[7]

In the light of the foregoing, three positions, as to the scope of the Article 234 jurisdiction in relation to mixed agreements, seem, in principle, to be possible:

4 Opinion 1/94, [1994] ECR I-5269. See, in particular, what the Court had to say about competence in the fields of transport (paras. 76 to 80) and of intellectual property (paras. 99 to 105).

5 The better view is that the GATS and the TRIPS are such agreements. It appears from the recitals to Council Dec. 94/800/EC (OJ 1994, L336/1) that the Council's intention was only to conclude the elements in the WTO package of agreements which were covered by exclusive Community competence. However, there is wording in the title, and in Art. 1, of the Decision which might be taken to suggest that matters within the Community's non-exclusive competence are also included.

6 The reference is to the principle first formulated by the Court of Justice in Case 22/70, *Commission* v. *Council* [1971] ECR 263, paras. 17 and 22.

7 See the discussion in Part VIII of Opinion 1/94, in particular what is said about partial and complete harmonisation in paras. 96 and 103.

- a "radical position", that the jurisdiction applies to all the provisions of a mixed agreement, regardless of whether a given provision was concluded under Community or Member State powers;
- an "intermediate position", that the jurisdiction applies to all provisions relating to matters within the competence of the Community, including provisions which, in the particular circumstances, were actually concluded under national powers; and
- a "conservative position", that the jurisdiction applies only to those provisions that were concluded under Community powers.

Which of those positions is the legally correct one? It is the thesis of this article that, while the Court of Justice has not yet made its own position explicitly clear, following the judgment in *Hermès International* v. *FHT Marketing Choice BV*[8] an answer can now been given to the question with a fair measure of confidence.

THE REASONING IN *DEMIREL*

The ancestral authority on the status in Community law of international agreements, *Haegeman*,[9] was about the Athens Agreement of 1961 establishing an association between the Community and Greece: that was a mixed agreement, but the fact seems to have played no part in the challenge to the Court's Article 234 jurisdiction.[10] Mixity was first invoked for the purpose of such a challenge in *Demirel*.[11] In that case, the wife of a Turkish migrant worker relied on provisions of the Association Agreement with Turkey, and of the Additional Protocol thereto of 1970, to resist an order requiring her to leave Germany, the country of her husband's employment. The Governments of Germany and the United Kingdom argued that the legal commitments in issue (those relating to the free movement of workers) had been undertaken towards Turkey not by the Community but through the exercise of Member States' powers; therefore, the Court had no jurisdiction to rule on their interpretation.

That argument was refuted by the Court in a passage of its judgment that is very well known and rather long, but nevertheless worth quoting in full because it is liable to be misunderstood:

> "Since the agreement in question is an association agreement creating special, privileged links with a non-member country which must, at least to a certain extent, take part in the Community system, Article 238 must necessarily empower the Community to guarantee commitments towards non-member countries in all the fields covered by the Treaty. Since freedom of movement for workers is, by virtue of Article 48 *et seq.* of the EEC Treaty, one of the fields covered by that Treaty, it follows that commitments regarding

8 Case C-53/96, [1998] ECR I-3603.

9 *Loc.cit.*, footnote 1, above.

10 Eeckhout, *op.cit.* footnote 3, above, makes the same point, at p. 15.

11 *Loc.cit.*, footnote 1, above.

> freedom of movement fall within the powers conferred on the Community by Article 238. Thus the question whether the Court has jurisdiction to rule on the interpretation of a provision in a mixed agreement containing a commitment which only the Member States could enter into in the sphere of their own powers does not arise.
>
> Furthermore, the jurisdiction of the Court cannot be called in question by virtue of the fact that in the field of freedom of movement for workers, as Community law now stands, it is for the Member States to lay down the rules which are necessary to give effect in their territory to the provisions of the Agreement or the decisions to be adopted by the Association Council.
>
> As the Court held in ... *Kupferberg* ..., in ensuring respect for commitments arising from an agreement concluded by the Community institutions the Member States fulfil, within the Community system, an obligation in relation to the Community, which has assumed responsibility for the due performance of the agreement."[12]

Advocate General Tesauro was of the opinion in *Hermès* that the passage indicates "the Court itself considers that the only matters on which it has no interpretative jurisdiction pursuant to Article 177 are matters within the exclusive competence of the Member States ...";[13] in other words, the Court there opted for what has been designated above the "intermediate position".[14] In the writer's respectful view, such a conclusion is unwarranted.

The Court's reasoning in the first quoted paragraph goes like this. The Community has been authorised by the provision which has become Article 310 to enter into an especially intensive form of relationship with chosen third countries, which entails allowing them to participate in some measure, in its system. For that purpose, the Community may undertake commitments in all of the fields covered by the Treaty, which of course includes the free movement of workers. *Ergo*, the objection to the admissibility of the reference was based on a false premise: the legal commitments that fell to be interpreted were not ones "which only the Member States could enter into in the sphere of their own powers".

The jurisdiction point in *Demirel* was thus decided on the footing that, contrary to the claims of the German and United Kingdom Governments, the Community had been competent to conclude the relevant parts of the Association Agreement with Turkey. It does not appear to have been argued, or to have occurred to the Court as a possibility, that, despite the availability of Community powers, the commitments in issue might nevertheless have been undertaken by the Member States. Once having satisfied itself that competence in the matter of the free movement of workers could be derived from Article 310, the Court took

12 *Ibid.*, paras. 9 to 11 of the judgment.

13 *Loc.cit.* footnote 8, above, at para. 18 of the Advocate General's Opinion.

14 Macleod, Hendry and Hyett, *op.cit.* note 3, above, at pp. 156 to 157, appear to take the same view. So does Eeckhout, *op.cit.* footnote 3, above, at pp. 15 *et seq.*, though his main concern is with the provisions of mixed agreements coming within national competence.

it for granted that the competence had been used, and that the obligations in question were those of the Community.

The second and third paragraphs of the quoted passage tend to confirm that interpretation. It is no bar, the Court says, to the application of the Article 234 procedure that, for the time being, any concrete steps to ensure the free movement of workers under the Association Agreement would have to be taken by the Member States. The *Kupferberg* case,[15] which concerned a free trade agreement with no element of mixity, is cited as authority for the proposition that there is a duty on the Member States to play their part in ensuring the fulfilment of international commitments accepted *by the Community*.

To sum up on *Demirel*. The judgment assumes that the Community exercised its competence under Article 310 to conclude the provisions of the Association Agreement with Turkey relating to the free movement of workers. No lessons can, therefore, be drawn from the judgment as to the applicability of the Article 234 jurisdiction in cases where provisions contained in an international agreement have been concluded under Member State powers (whether or not the option of conclusion by the Community may have been available).

THE REASONING IN *HERMÈS*

Before turning to *Hermès*, brief mention needs to be made of *Sevince,*[16] a case mainly of interest because of what the Court of Justice had to say about the internal effect, within the Community order, of certain Decisions of the Council of Association established under the Agreement with Turkey.[17] The relevance of the judgment in *Sevince* for present purposes lies in the form of words chosen by the Court in reformulating the principle that was first stated in *Haegeman*: "... the Court has jurisdiction to give preliminary rulings on the Agreement *in so far as it is an act adopted by one of the institutions of the Community* ...".[18] If taken literally, the italicised words might be read as limiting the Article 234 jurisdiction to the elements of an international agreement that have been concluded by the Council under the procedure of Article 300 (2) (ex Article 228 (2)); in other words, as an endorsement by the Court of the "conservative position". However, it is submitted, that would not be a legitimate inference to draw, since the scope of the Article 234 jurisdiction *ratione materiae* was not in issue in the proceedings. In fact, the two Decisions the Court was asked to interpret related to the free movement of workers, a matter which, we have seen in *Demirel*, the Court

15 Case 104/81, *HZA Mainz* v. *C.A. Kupferberg & Cie. K G a.A.* [1982] ECR 3641, para. 13. The agreement in question was the Agreement of 1972 between the EEC and Portugal.

16 Case C-192/89, *S.Z. Sevince* v. *Staatssecretaris van Justitie* [1990] ECR I-3461.

17 Decs Nos. 2/76 of 20 December 1976 and 1/80 of 19 September 1980.

18 *Loc.cit.* footnote 15, above, para. 10. Emphasis added.

assumed to be within the exercise of the Community's powers under Article 310 of the Treaty.

The opportunity for the Court of Justice to reconsider the scope of its Article 234 jurisdiction in the light of the more recent jurisprudence on mixed agreements finally came in the *Hermès* case,[19] in which a Dutch court sought a preliminary ruling on the interpretation of Article 50 (6) of the TRIPS. Article 50 is about the judicial remedies that must be available for the protection of intellectual property rights, including provisional measures where appropriate. Paragraph (6) of the Article requires provisional measures to be revoked, on application by the defendant, if proceedings to determine the merits of the case have not been initiated in a reasonable time. Hermès International had been granted interim relief in proceedings for the infringement of its trade mark, and wanted the Dutch court to fix a time limit after which it would not be possible for the defendant to apply for the order against it to be lifted. The issue referred to the Court of Justice was whether the imposition of such a limit would be compatible with a defendant's right to have a provisional measure set aside, as envisaged by Article 50 (6).

The jurisdiction of the Court of Justice to give the requested ruling was put in issue because of the explicit finding in Opinion 1/94 that the machinery for the enforcement of intellectual property rights in the Member States had not yet been the subject of Community harmonisation measures, except in the narrow field of the release into free circulation of counterfeit goods.[20] That made it possible to argue that Article 50 had been concluded under Member State powers, and so could not form part of the Community legal order.

The Court responded to that argument by pointing out two things.

First, "the WTO Agreement was concluded by the Community and ratified by its Member States without any allocation between them of their respective obligations towards the other contracting parties".[21] The Court did not develop the point further, but the implication seems clear: in areas of shared competence, it is impossible to tell from the relevant WTO instruments whether a given set of provisions was concluded by the Community or by the Member States (or, indeed, by both, as regards the matters falling within their respective competences).

Secondly, at the time when the Final Act of the WTO Agreement was signed on 15 April 1994, Council Regulation (EC) No. 40/94 on the Community trade mark had been in force for a month. It follows (though the Court evidently thought it unnecessary to spell this out) that the Community must be understood to have concluded the TRIPS, under the *AETR* principle, to the extent that any of the provisions contained in the Agreement affect any of those in the Regulation. So far as concerns Article 50 (6) of the TRIPS, the Court recalled that Regulation 40/94 has an Article 99, under which "[a]pplication may be made to the

19 *Loc.cit.*, footnote 8, above.
20 Opinion 1/94, para. 104.
21 *Hermès* judgment, para. 24.

courts of a Member State... for such provisional, including protective, measures in respect of a Community trade mark ... as may be available under the law of that State in respect of a national trade mark ...". Where such (national) remedies are involved in the framework of the Regulation, there will be an obligation under Community law for the courts concerned to apply the relevant rules, as far as possible, in the light of the wording and purpose of the TRIPS. In those circumstances, at all events, the Court would have jurisdiction to interpret Article 50.[22]

In *Hermès*, to be sure, the dispute was about a Benelux trade mark, not a Community one. Nevertheless, the Court found two reasons for accepting jurisdiction.

A first, and familiar, if not wholly convincing, reason was that it was the responsibility of the court hearing the dispute to decide whether a preliminary ruling was necessary to enable it to give judgment; "[c]onsequently, where the question referred to it concerns a provision *which it has jurisdiction to interpret*, the Court of Justice is, in principle, bound to give a ruling ...".[23] There is more than a hint of circularity in the italicised phrase, since the issue to be decided was precisely whether the Court had jurisdiction, in the circumstances of *Hermès*, to interpret Article 50 of the TRIPS.

Of much more interest for the purposes of this article was the Court's second reason: that "where a provision can apply both to situations falling within the scope of national law and to situations falling within the scope of Community law, it is clearly in the Community interest that, in order to forestall future differences of interpretation, that provision should be interpreted uniformly, whatever the circumstances in which it is to apply".[24] Since, as the Court had already found, Article 50 of the TRIPS applies to Community trade marks, it followed that there must be jurisdiction to provide an interpretation of the Article for use in relation to a national trade mark.

Though carefully focused on the circumstances of the *Hermès* case, that reasoning is extremely far-reaching. What the Court said about Article 50 of the TRIPS would seem to be equally applicable to any of the provisions of the WTO agreement (as well as of other mixed agreements) that relate to a field of activity where competence is shared between the Community and the Member States. In every such field, there is likely to have been some piece of internal legislation enacted, which would be enough to bring the relevant provisions of the agreement in question "within the scope of Community law". Indeed, it is submitted, the Court's reasoning, designed "to forestall future differences of interpretation", would apply with equal force where Community competence remains, for the time being, purely potential. The Court would still have needed jurisdiction, for the reasons given in *Hermès*, to establish an authoritative interpretation of Article 50 (6), even supposing, at the time when the WTO Agreement was con-

22 *Ibid.*, paras. 24 to 29.
23 *Ibid.*, para. 31. Emphasis added.
24 *Ibid.*, para. 32.

cluded, Regulation 40/94 had been nothing more than a twinkle in the Commission's eye.

CONCLUSION: THE THREE "POSITIONS" POST-*HERMÈS*

If the above analysis of the implications of the *Hermès* judgment is right, the question that *Demirel* left open has received at least a partial answer.

The Court of Justice, it appears, has set its face against the "conservative position" that preliminary rulings can be given pursuant to Article 234 only in respect of provisions in an international agreement that have been concluded by the Council under Community powers. The logic of the reasoning in *Hermès* is that the Court has jurisdiction to interpret all of the provisions of a mixed agreement falling within the exclusive or the non-exclusive competence of the Community, regardless as to whether, where the option existed for the Member States to conclude the agreement under their own powers, they in fact did so.

The Court's position is based on the eminently practical ground of the need to ensure that provisions of international agreements, which fall to be implemented in both the Community and the national legal orders, receive consistent interpretation. It has the further practical advantage of detaching the issue as to the scope of the Article 234 jurisdiction, from the often controversial issue of the exercise of the Community's non-exclusive external relations competence. A major attraction of the mixity technique is that it enables the question, of exactly who is doing what, to be passed over in silence.[25] As a friend of mixed agreements, the writer welcomes an outcome which allows them to go on doing their work of defusing disputes about competence, without endangering the internal functioning of the Community order.

A question not definitively resolved by *Hermès* is whether there is any life left in the "radical position", that the Court has jurisdiction to give preliminary rulings on all the provisions contained in a mixed agreement, including on matters that fall within the exclusive competence of the Member States. The possible disadvantages of having the courts of 15 different national jurisdictions resolving for themselves, without guidance from the Court of Justice, questions as to the interpretation of such provisions (including their internal effect) have been ably canvassed by Eeckhout with particular reference to the WTO Agreement.[26] Under the post-*Hermès* dispensation, however, the problem may be more apparent than real. As regards matters belonging unequivocally to the *domaine réservée* of the Member States, such as (to pluck an example out of the air) "the content of teaching and the organisation of education systems",[27] the theoretical

---

25 See the short piece by the author, "Why continue to have mixed agreements at all?" in Bourgeois, Dewost and Gaiffe (eds.), *La Communauté européenne et les acords mixtes*, Presses Interuniversitaires Européennes (1997).

26 *Op.cit.* footnote 3, above, at pp. 20 to 24.

27 See Art. 149(1) (ex Art. 126) EC.

objections to the application of Article 234 seem to the writer, finally, insuperable.[28] Where, however, there is any room at all for arguing that a matter may lie within the Community's (albeit non-exclusive) competence, the reasoning in *Hermès* militates in favour of the Court's having interpretative jurisdiction.

28 Advocate General Tesauro seems to have been of the same opinion in *Hermès*.

13

THE ACTION FOR ANNULMENT: A CASE OF DOUBLE STANDARDS?

*Anthony Arnull**

I INTRODUCTION

In accordance with the spirit of the age, the EEC Treaty was conceived by élites for implementation by élites. The people were expected to be duly grateful.[1] The Treaty therefore showed little concern for accountability or involving individuals in the project. This conception of the Community was epitomised by the appointed Commission, which was to play a central role in shaping and policing the common market. Although there was to be an Assembly, it would not initially be directly elected and its powers would be purely "advisory and supervisory".[2] Notwithstanding the scope of the legislative powers conferred on the Council, that institution was not required to meet in public or to reveal how its members had voted, even after the anticipated transition to qualified majority voting. Acts adopted by the institutions were only to a limited extent subject to judicial review at the suit of private parties, who were apparently to have no right to challenge regulations or directives, however adverse their effects and however doubtful their legality. By contrast, the Member States, the Council and the Commission would have unlimited standing to challenge Community acts.

It was against that background that the Court of Justice delivered its famous ruling in *Van Gend en Loos* v. *Nederlandse Administratie der Belastingen*.[3] That ruling was apparently subversive, in that it proclaimed that the subjects of the new legal order established by the EEC Treaty comprised "not only Member States but also their nationals." Community law did not merely impose obligations on individuals, but was also intended "to confer upon them rights which become part of their legal heritage."[4] The Court's view of the nature of the Community legal order led it to conclude that a provision of the Treaty conferred on individuals rights which the national courts were required to uphold, a

* Thanks are due to my colleague, Professor Evelyn Ellis, for her comments on a draft of this paper. The usual disclaimer applies.

1 See further Craig, "The nature of the Community: integration, democracy, and legitimacy" in Craig and de Búrca (Eds.), *The Evolution of EU Law* (Oxford, 1999), 1-54, 5-7.

2 See Art. 137 EEC.

3 Case 26/62, [1963] ECR 1.

4 [1963] ECR 1, 12.

D. O'Keeffe (ed.), Liber Amicorum Slynn 177-190 (2000)

conclusion which greatly strengthened the position of traders and ordinary people. Subsequent case law was to make it clear that this quality, known as direct effect, also extended to regulations. Even directives, which had to be implemented by the Member States,[5] were held by the Court to be capable of being enforced directly in the national courts against Member States which failed to give effect to them.

In the years which followed *Van Gend en Loos*, the case law was notable for the broad view taken by the Court of the effect of many of the substantive rules of the Treaty. In *Procureur du Roi* v. *Dassonville*,[6] the Court said that the Treaty prohibition against measures having an effect equivalent to quantitative restrictions on imports extended to "[a]ll trading rules enacted by Member States which are capable of hindering, directly or indirectly, actually or potentially, intra-Community trade ..." The suggestion in the judgment, that whether or not the disputed national rule discriminated against imports was simply irrelevant, was confirmed in later case law, although the Court would in due course seek to limit the scope of the prohibition.[7] In *Reyners* v. *Belgium*,[8] the Court held that attaining freedom of establishment was not dependent on the adoption by the Council of the directives envisaged by the Treaty. Thus, once the transitional period had ended, national courts were required to uphold the prohibition against discrimination on grounds of nationality laid down in Article 52 (now 43). Six months later, in *van Binsbergen* v. *Bedrijfsvereniging Metaalnijverheid*,[9] the Court extended that approach to the Treaty rules on the freedom to provide services. Conversely, the Court made it clear that the Treaty derogations from the rules on freedom of movement were to be interpreted strictly.

II THE ACTION FOR ANNULMENT

It might therefore have been expected that the Court would take an equally progressive approach to the interpretation of Article 173 EEC (now, after amendment, Article 230 EC), which gave it jurisdiction to review the legality of certain Community acts. The article was, after all, replete with ambiguity. What were "acts"? What was a "decision"? What did "direct and individual concern" mean? What was one to make of the absence of any reference to the European Parliament? *Van Gend en Loos* suggested that the Court would seek, on the basis of "the spirit, the general scheme and the wording"[10] of the Treaty, to develop from the framework of Article 173 a robust mechanism for judicial review in which

5 The Treaty even gave the Member States a choice as to the "form and methods": see Art. 189 (now 249).
6 Case 8/74, [1974] ECR 837, para. 5.
7 See Joined Cases C-267/91 and C-268/91, *Keck and Mithouard*, [1993] ECR I-6097.
8 Case 2/74, [1974] ECR 631.
9 Case 33/74, [1974] ECR 1299.
10 [1963] ECR 1, 12.

an important part would be played by individuals, upon whom Community law conferred rights which formed part of their legal heritage. However, the Court was to adopt an apparently inconsistent approach to the interpretation of Article 173 which prevented the article's full capacity for ensuring respect for the rule of law from being realised.

The unevenness which was to characterise the Court's approach to the interpretation of Article 173 started to emerge in *Producteurs de Fruits* v. *Council*,[11] decided less than two months before *Van Gend en Loos*. In *Producteurs de Fruits*, the Court had to decide when a natural or legal person could challenge the validity of a Community act which bore the label 'regulation'. The Treaty entitled such an applicant to challenge a decision "in the form of a regulation" and the Court accepted that it was indeed the substance rather than the form of the contested act which was important. However, it went on to define the characteristics of a true regulation in a way which was to make it extremely difficult for natural or legal persons to show that a measure carrying that title in fact constituted a decision. In *Calpak* v. *Commission*,[12] for example, the Court dismissed as inadmissible a challenge by two Italian companies to a regulation restricting the amount of aid payable to processors of Williams pears preserved in syrup. The contested regulation was, the Court said, "by nature a measure of general application within the meaning of Article 189 [now 249] of the Treaty. In fact the measure applies to objectively determined situations and produces legal effects with regard to categories of persons described in a generalized and abstract manner. The nature of the measure as a regulation is not called in question by the mere fact that it is possible to determine the number or even the identity of the producers to be granted the aid which is limited thereby."[13]

Even more striking was a case decided in July 1963, *Plaumann* v. *Commission*.[14] There the applicant, a limited liability partnership, sought the annulment of a Commission decision addressed to the German Government refusing to permit it to reduce the duty imposed on fresh clementines imported from third countries. The Treaty allowed a natural or legal person to challenge a decision addressed to another person which was of direct and individual concern to the applicant. The Commission argued that a Member State could not constitute 'another person' for these purposes. That argument was thoroughly unconvincing: it was tolerably clear from the text of Article 173 that a natural or legal person was intended to have standing to challenge any decision which, while not addressed to him, was of direct and individual concern to him. That was the conclusion reached by the Court, which declared: "The words and natural meaning of this provision justify the broadest interpretation. Moreover provisions of the Treaty regarding the right of interested parties to bring an action

11 Joined Cases 16 and 17/62, [1962] ECR 471.

12 Joined Cases 789 and 790/79, [1980] ECR 1949.

13 Para. 9.

14 Case 25/62, [1963] ECR 95.

must not be interpreted restrictively."[15] However, on the more difficult question of individual concern that is precisely what the Court did, ruling that the applicant was not individually concerned because it was only affected by the contested decision "as an importer of clementines, that is to say, by reason of a commercial activity which may at any time be practised by any person ..."[16]

The *Producteurs de Fruits* and *Plaumann* decisions became classic authorities on the right of individuals to bring annulment proceedings under Article 173 and for many years had the effect of making it extremely difficult for such applicants to challenge any Community acts other than decisions addressed to them. It is true that the Court in due course accepted that natural and legal persons could in principle challenge the validity of true regulations[17] and that even directives might sometimes be contested by private parties.[18] However, the chances of such a challenge succeeding remained slight because the applicant would need to show individual concern. The Court declined to relax significantly the test for that requirement despite its open-textured quality.[19]

1 The "ERTA" case

By contrast, the Court's approach to the type of act which is susceptible to review in annulment proceedings has been markedly more liberal. Article 173 gave the Court jurisdiction to "review the legality of acts of the Council and the Commission other than recommendations and opinions." Recommendations and opinions were two of the measures whose characteristics were defined in Article 189 (now 249). Did that mean that the term "acts" referred to the other types of measure described in that article, or was it a broader term? That question came before the Court in the "ERTA" case,[20] where the Commission sought the annulment of Council proceedings regarding the negotiation and conclusion by the Member States of an agreement with third countries on the working conditions of the crews of vehicles engaged in international road transport.[21] The Commission's objection was to the negotiating procedure agreed by the Council, which had resolved that the negotiations should be conducted and concluded by the Member States acting in common, with the Member State holding the Presidency of the Council acting as spokesperson. The Commission considered that procedure incompatible with Article 228(1) EEC, according to which agreements provided for by the Treaty between the Community and third countries or

15 Pp. 106-107.
16 P. 107.
17 See Case C-309/89, *Codorniu* v. *Council*, [1994] ECR I-1853.
18 See Case C-298/89, *Gibraltar* v. *Council*, [1993] ECR I-3605; see also Case T-135/96, *UEAPME* v. *Council*, [1998] ECR II-2335.
19 See e.g. Case C-209/94 P, *Buralux and Others* v. *Council*, [1996] ECR I-615; Case C-321/95 P, *Greenpeace Council and Others* v. *Commission*, [1998] ECR I-1651.
20 Case 22/70, [1971] ECR 263.
21 The European Road Transport Agreement (ERTA).

an international organization were to be negotiated by the Commission and concluded by the Council.[22] The Council argued that the disputed proceedings did not amount to any of the types of act referred to in Article 189 and could not therefore be challenged. Even if the notion of an act susceptible to review was not limited to the measures (other than recommendations and opinions) described in Article 189, the disputed proceedings had no legal effect, being of purely political significance.

In order to establish whether the proceedings had any legal effect, the Court said it was necessary to determine whether the power to negotiate and conclude the agreement belonged to the Community or to the Member States. This was not an easy question to answer. The Community had legal personality and express powers to enter into international agreements in certain fields but transport was not one of them, even though the adoption of a common policy in the sphere of transport was one of the objectives of the Community. The Court concluded that, whenever the Community adopted, in order to give effect to a common policy envisaged by the Treaty, provisions laying down common rules, the Member States were no longer entitled to enter into agreements with third countries affecting those rules. Once the common rules had come into being, only the Community could "assume and carry out contractual obligations towards third countries affecting the whole sphere of application of the Community legal system."[23] Since the subject-matter of the agreement fell within the scope of a Council regulation designed to contribute to the implementation of a common transport policy, the Court concluded that the Community had been exclusively competent to negotiate and conclude the agreement in question since that regulation entered into force.

As for the admissibility of the application, the Court ruled that it would be inconsistent with the objective of annulment proceedings to confine them to the categories of measure referred to in Article 189: "An action for annulment must therefore be available in the case of all measures adopted by the institutions, whatever their nature or form, which are intended to have legal effects."[24] The Council's proceedings "were capable of derogating in certain circumstances from the procedure laid down by the Treaty regarding negotiations with third countries and the conclusion of agreements."[25] They therefore "had definite legal effects both on relations between the Community and the Member States and on the relationship between institutions."[26]

---

22 See now Art. 300 EC.

23 Para. 18.

24 Para. 42. See also Case 294/83, *Les Verts* v. *Parliament*, [1986] ECR 1339; Case C-57/95, *France* v. *Commission*, [1997] ECR I-1627.

25 Para. 54.

26 Para. 55. The Commission's application was dismissed as unfounded because the origins of the agreement pre-dated the Council regulation as a result of which competence to negotiate and conclude it was conferred on the Community: "... to have suggested to the third countries concerned that there was now a new distribution of powers within the Community might well have jeopardized the successful outcome of the negotiations ..."

The Court's ruling in the "ERTA" case that the Community might have implied external competence was of immense significance for the prerogatives of the Member States. Its conclusion that measures taken by the institutions which did not take the form of those described in Article 189 could be challenged in annulment proceedings was also adventurous, since the textual argument to the contrary seemed quite strong. The boldness of the judgment stands in stark contrast to the decisions in *Producteurs de Fruits* and *Plaumann*, where the Court appeared to attach much greater weight to the language of the Treaty.

2 The position of the European Parliament

The case law on the status of the European Parliament in proceedings under Article 173 EEC involved a gloss on the language of the Treaty every bit as striking as the judgment in "ERTA". Before the amendments introduced at Maastricht, Article 173 contained no reference to the Parliament[27] and the question whether it could sue (so-called *légitimation active*) or be sued (so-called *légitimation passive*) became the subject of great controversy, particularly after the first set of direct elections in 1979.[28]

The question of the Parliament's *légitimation passive* was addressed by the Court in *Les Verts* v *European Parliament*.[29] The applicant, a political party, sought the annulment of two measures adopted by the Parliament on the reimbursement of expenses incurred by parties taking part in the 1984 elections. In finding the application admissible, the Court made a series of highly significant statements about the nature of the system established by the Treaty and the importance of judicial review. It began by emphasizing that the Community was based on the rule of law and that neither the Member States nor the institutions could avoid review of whether the measures they adopted were compatible with the Treaty, described by the Court as "the basic constitutional charter".[30] The Treaty, it said, "established a complete system of legal remedies and procedures designed to permit the Court of Justice to review the legality of measures adopted by the institutions."[31] Although Article 173 only mentioned acts of the Council and the Commission, the general scheme of the Treaty was to make a direct action available against any measure adopted by the institutions which was intended to have legal effect. The reason the Parliament was not expressly

(para. 86). Cf. Hartley, *The Foundations of European Community Law*, 4th ed. (Oxford, 1998), pp. 101-102.

27 Cf. Art. 38 ECSC, on which the Court relied in Case 230/81, *Luxembourg* v. *European Parliament*, [1981] ECR 255.

28 See Bradley, "The variable evolution of the standing of the European Parliament in proceedings before the Court of Justice", 8 YEL (1988), 27-57; Dehousse, *The European Court of Justice*, (Macmillan, 1998), pp. 97-104.

29 Case 294/83, [1986] ECR 1339.

30 Para. 23.

31 *Ibid.*

mentioned in Article 173 was that, in its original form, the Treaty gave it no power to adopt measures intended to have legal effect *vis-à-vis* third parties.[32] The Court concluded:[33]

> "An interpretation of Article 173 of the Treaty which excluded measures adopted by the European Parliament from those which could be contested would lead to a result contrary both to the spirit of the Treaty as expressed in Article 164 [now 220] and to its system. Measures adopted by the European Parliament in the context of the EEC Treaty could encroach on the powers of the Member States or of the other institutions, or exceed the limits which have been set to the Parliament's powers, without its being possible to refer them for review by the Court. It must therefore be concluded that an action for annulment may lie against measures adopted by the European Parliament intended to have legal effects *vis-à-vis* third parties."

What were the implications of *Les Verts* for the *légitimation active* of the Parliament under Article 173? The Court's departure in that case from the strict wording of the article meant that it could not convincingly be maintained that the Parliament had no right to bring annulment proceedings simply because Article 173 did not refer to it. In the "Comitology" case,[34] the Parliament sought the annulment under Article 173 of a Council decision laying down the procedures for the exercise of implementing powers conferred on the Commission. The Council raised an objection of inadmissibility which the Court decided to deal with without considering the substance of the case. Rejecting the advice of Advocate General Darmon, the Court concluded that "the applicable provisions, as they stand at present, do not enable the Court to recognize the capacity of the European Parliament to bring an action for annulment."[35] The Court said that there was no parallel between the capacity to be a defendant and the capacity to be an applicant in annulment proceedings. It was not necessary for the Parliament to be given the right to bring proceedings under Article 173 in order to ensure that its prerogatives were protected. Disregard of the Parliament's prerogatives constituted an infringement of an essential procedural requirement which could be raised in annulment proceedings instituted by someone else. The Court noted that, under Article 155 (now 211), the Commission had a particular responsibility for defending the Parliament's prerogatives and for bringing proceedings under Article 173 for that purpose where these proved necessary. In addition, an infringement of the Parliament's prerogatives during the procedure leading to the adoption of an act could be raised before the national courts and the matter referred to the Court of Justice for a preliminary ruling.

32 The motion of censure on the activities of the Commission under Art. 201 (ex 144) of the Treaty might have been thought to fall within this category but, as AG Mancini explained, "the political character of that act overshadows its legal character to such a degree that it was inappropriate (or pointless) to provide a right of action against the body competent to adopt it": [1986] ECR 1339, 1351.

33 Para. 25.

34 Case 302/87, *Parliament* v. *Council*, [1988] ECR 5615.

35 Para. 28.

The Parliament was understandably less than reassured by the Court's claim that the defence of its interests could safely be left in the hands of others. It therefore decided to continue with another case, introduced before "Comitology" was decided, in which it was seeking the annulment under Articles 146 EAEC and 173 EEC, the terms of which were then identical, of a Council regulation adopted under the EAEC Treaty following the accident in 1986 at the Chernobyl nuclear power station in the Soviet Union.[36] The contested regulation was based on a provision of the EAEC Treaty which empowered the Council to act by qualified majority after consulting the Parliament. The Parliament had asked the Commission to change the legal basis to a provision of the EEC Treaty requiring recourse to the co-operation procedure,[37] but the Commission failed to comply with the Parliament's request. The Council again raised an objection of inadmissibility, claiming that the "Comitology" decision established that the Parliament had no power to bring annulment proceedings under Article 173 EEC or, by implication, under Article 146 EAEC. The Parliament pointed out, however, that in this case it could not rely on the Commission to defend its prerogatives because the two institutions disagreed over the correct legal basis of the disputed regulation. It added that the possibility that proceedings might be brought by private parties on the basis that the Parliament's prerogatives had been infringed was entirely hypothetical.

The Court began by explaining that the admissibility of the action was to be considered under the EAEC Treaty, but that since Article 146 EAEC was the same as Article 173 EEC, this made no practical difference. The "Comitology" case established that the Parliament could not bring annulment proceedings under either provision. The Court was forced to acknowledge, however, that the alternative means of protecting the Parliament's prerogatives mentioned in that case might sometimes be ineffective. The Parliament could not rely on the hypothetical possibility that proceedings would be started in the national courts or that a Member State or a private party might seek the annulment of a measure which the Parliament considered to have been adopted in breach of its prerogatives. Although the Commission had a duty to ensure respect for those prerogatives, it could not be expected to bring annulment proceedings which it believed to be unfounded.

The existence of those remedies did not therefore provide an absolute guarantee of the Parliament's prerogatives. Those prerogatives constituted one of the elements of the institutional balance created by the Treaties, which obliged the institutions to respect each other's jurisdiction. Any breach of that obligation had to be susceptible to judicial review. Since the Court was responsible under the Treaties for ensuring respect for the law, it had to be able to guarantee respect for the institutional balance and the prerogatives of the Parliament. Although the Court could not include the Parliament among the institutions which had an automatic right to bring annulment proceedings under Articles 173 EEC

36 Case C-70/88, *Parliament* v. *Council*, [1990] ECR I-2041.
37 That procedure is now set out in Art. 252 EC.

and 146 EAEC, it had a duty to ensure that the Treaty provisions regulating the relationship between the institutions were fully respected and that the Parliament, like the other institutions, had an effective legal remedy against threats to its prerogatives. The fact that the Treaties contained no provisions conferring on the Parliament the right to bring annulment proceedings might constitute "a procedural gap",[38] but this could not be allowed to outweigh the fundamental need to ensure respect for the institutional balance created by the Treaties.

The Court concluded that the Parliament had the right to bring proceedings for the annulment of an act adopted by the Council or the Commission where the purpose of the proceedings was to protect the Parliament's prerogatives. Annulment proceedings brought by the Parliament were otherwise subject to the same conditions as such proceedings instituted by the Council or the Commission. Among the Parliament's prerogatives was the right to participate to the full extent contemplated by the Treaty in the legislative process leading to the adoption of a Community act. Since the Parliament claimed that, in the case of the disputed regulation, it had not been allowed to do so, its prerogatives were in issue. The action was therefore admissible.[39]

Although the Court did not expressly overrule "Comitology" in "Chernobyl",[40] it is clear that the two decisions cannot be reconciled, for in the former the Court said that the relevant provisions did not enable the Court to permit the Parliament to bring annulment proceedings. In the latter, that is precisely what the Court allowed the Parliament to do. However, the Court did not depart in "Chernobyl" from the view it took in "Comitology" that Article 173 did not permit the Parliament to bring annulment proceedings. Indeed, in "Chernobyl"[41] the Court cited "Comitology" as authority for that very point. What the Court did in "Chernobyl" was to create a new right of action, analogous to but separate from the right of the other institutions to bring annulment proceedings, in order to preserve the institutional balance created by the Treaties and to enable it to fulfil its task of ensuring respect for the law.

What is worth noting for present purposes is, not only the great boldness of *Les Verts* and "Chernobyl", but also that many of the reasons given by the Court to justify those rulings might also have been thought to justify a relaxed approach to the standing of natural and legal persons. Such an approach would help consolidate the rule of law and make it more difficult for the institutions to avoid review of whether the measures they adopt are compatible with the Community's basic constitutional charter. The possibility that annulment proceedings might be brought by a privileged applicant is purely hypothetical and does not provide an absolute guarantee that the rights of natural and legal persons will not

38 Para. 26.

39 The Parliament's application was subsequently dismissed as unfounded: see [1991] ECR I-4529.

40 It was not until later the same year that the Court expressly departed for the first time from one of its previous decisions: see Case C-10/89, *HAG GF*, [1990] ECR I-3711.

41 See paras. 12-14.

be infringed by unlawful acts of the Community institutions. An interpretation of the Treaty which restricted the right of individuals to bring proceedings would lead to a result contrary both to the spirit of the Treaty and to its system.

III THE ACTION FOR DAMAGES

Although the Court's case law on the action for annulment might appear to be inconsistent, its restrictive decisions on the standing of natural and legal persons find an echo in its case law on the action for damages.[42] The parallel is underlined by the *Plaumann* case, mentioned above. There the applicant also claimed damages for loss arising from the Commission's refusal to authorize a reduction in the duty payable on imported clementines. The Treaty does not say that a successful annulment action must be brought before a claim for damages can be made. Indeed, where the applicant lacks standing to bring annulment proceedings, the case for allowing damages to be sought seems particularly strong. However, the Court took a different view. It observed: "An administrative measure which has not been annulled cannot of itself constitute a wrongful act on the part of the administration inflicting damage upon those whom it affects. The latter cannot therefore claim damages by reason of that measure. The Court cannot by way of an action for compensation take steps which would nullify the legal effects of a decision which ... has not been annulled."[43] The Court subsequently accepted that the action for damages was an independent remedy with a different purpose to the action for annulment.[44] However, it remains the case that an action for damages will not be entertained where its purpose is to secure the same result as an action for annulment which has been found inadmissible.[45]

In claims for damages in respect of loss caused by legislative measures involving policy choices by the institutions, the Court applies a particularly stringent test of unlawfulness known as the *Schöppenstedt* formula. This requires the applicant to show "a sufficiently flagrant violation of a superior rule of law for the protection of the individual".[46] It is not enough to establish liability that the measure in question has been declared void.[47] The Court at one stage went as far as to say that a violation would not be regarded as sufficiently serious for these purposes unless the conduct of the institution concerned was "verging on the arbitrary".[48] The Court subsequently retreated from that extreme posi-

42 See the second para. of Art. 288 (ex 215) EC.
43 [1963] ECR 95, 108.
44 See e.g. Case 4/69, *Lütticke* v. *Commission*, [1971] ECR 325.
45 See e.g. Case 175/84, *Krohn* v. *Commission*, [1986] ECR 753; Case T-514/93, *Cobrecaf and Others* v. *Commission*, [1995] ECR II-621.
46 Case 5/71, *Zuckerfabrik Schöppenstedt* v. *Council*, [1971] ECR 975, para. 11.
47 See e.g. Joined Cases 83 and 94/76, 4, 15 and 40/77, *HNL* v. *Council and Commission*, [1978] ECR 1209, para. 4.
48 Joined Cases 116 and 124/77, *Amylum* v. *Council and Commission*, [1979] ECR 3479, para. 19.

tion[49] and, in *Mulder* v. *Council and Commission*,[50] claims for damages arising out of unlawful legislative acts were upheld notwithstanding the wide discretionary powers enjoyed by the institutions in the field in question and the large number of other claims which would be affected. None the less, the essence of the *Schöppenstedt* formula remains intact.

Where the applicant relies on an act performed by a Community official in the performance of his duties, the Court also applies a strict test. In *Sayag* v. *Leduc*,[51] the Court held that the Community was not liable for an accident caused by a servant while using his private car during the performance of his duties. The Court said that "[o]nly in the case of *force majeure* or in exceptional circumstances of such overriding importance that without the servant's using private means of transport the Community would have been unable to carry out the tasks entrusted to it, could such use be considered to form part of the servant's performance of his duties..." Hartley observes:[52] "It follows from this that the liability of the Community for the acts of its servants is narrower than that of most Member States for the acts of their servants. It is hard to see any justification for this."

Where a claimant suffers damage as a result of the implementation of a Community act at the national level, the Court has held that proceedings under the Treaty will sometimes only be admissible if the claimant has exhausted any cause of action he might have against the national authorities in the domestic forum.[53] Although this is not required where any national remedy would not provide the claimant with an effective means of protection, the claimant is still faced with the difficult task of identifying who bears the primary responsibility for the loss he has suffered. The Court has not been prepared to allow the claimant to choose whether to bring proceedings in the national courts or in the Community Courts.

IV A HIERARCHY OF VALUES?

The case law on damages and the standing of natural and legal persons in annulment proceedings on the one hand and that in which the Court has taken an expansive approach to the action for annulment on the other suggests that it has in the past applied a hierarchy of values. Whatever the Court may have said in *Van Gend en Loos*, individuals do not normally take pride of place in that hierarchy. The Court generally treats enabling the Community and its institutions to

49 See Case C-220/91 P, *Commission* v. *Stahlwerke Peine-Salzgitter*, [1993] ECR I-2393, para. 51.
50 Joined Cases C-104/89 and C-37/90, [1992] ECR I-3061. See also Case C-152/88, *Sofrimport* v. *Commission*, [1990] ECR I-2477.
51 Case 9/69, [1969] ECR 329.
52 *Op.cit.*, p. 453.
53 See e.g. Case 175/84, *Krohn* v. *Commission*, [1986] ECR 753, para. 27.

function effectively as more important. Thus it has sought to shield the institutions from too many actions for annulment or damages, especially in disputes involving legislative measures. In the case of actions for damages, the Court made this explicit in the *HNL* case,[54] where it declared that "... the legislative authority, even where the validity of its measures is subject to judicial review, cannot always be hindered in making its decisions by the prospect of applications for damages whenever it has occasion to adopt legislative measures in the public interest which may adversely affect the interests of individuals."

Enabling the institutions to operate effectively means protecting the prerogatives conferred on them by the Treaties, hence the importance attributed by the Court to the institutional balance. Promoting the smooth functioning of the Community as a whole means securing compliance by the Member States with their obligations. In this respect the Court perceived early on the value of the role which individuals could play, observing in *Van Gend en Loos*[55] that "[t]he vigilance of individuals concerned to protect their rights amounts to an effective supervision in addition to the supervision entrusted by Article 169 [now 226] and 170 [now 227] to the diligence of the Commission and of the Member States." Indeed, it is precisely where the consequence is to enforce compliance by the Member States with their obligations that the Court has seemed particularly enthusiastic about upholding the rights of individuals. A striking recent example of that enthusiasm is provided by the development, since the *Francovich* case in 1991,[56] of the principle of State liability. By contrast, the Court has seemed less keen to protect the rights of individuals where the result would be to interfere with the activities of the institutions and disrupt the smooth functioning of the Community.[57]

It would be misleading not to acknowledge the way the Court's approach has evolved with the passage of time. The increased legislative output of the Community which followed the demise of the Luxembourg Compromise in the early 1980s and the Single European Act may have contributed to some relaxation of the standing rules and even, in due course, to a greater willingness on the part of the Court to entertain claims for damages in cases involving legislative acts. Moreover, the strictness of the standing rules has always to some extent been mitigated by the possibility of challenging the validity of Community acts in the national courts, which are required (where such a challenge seems plausible) to seek the guidance of the Court of Justice under the preliminary rulings

54 Para. 5.

55 [1963] ECR 1, 13.

56 Joined Cases C-6/90 and C-9/90, *Francovich and Others*, [1991] ECR I-5357.

57 Some might argue that this policy also underlies the Court's case law on the general principle of respect for fundamental rights. However, it is submitted that there is no convincing evidence that the Court applies a stricter standard to the actions of the Member States than those of the Community institutions in this respect. See further Arnull, *The European Union and its Court of Justice* (Oxford, 1999), Chap. 6.

procedure.[58] But the Court had become constrained in what it could do by the weight of its own case law and mounting concern about its ability to cope with its growing workload. A concerted effort was made to address the latter consideration in 1988 with the establishment of the Court of First Instance, but that body rapidly encountered problems of its own in handling its workload. It showed no enthusiasm for entertaining significantly increased numbers of annulment actions brought by natural and legal persons when jurisdiction to deal with them was conferred on it in 1993.[59]

V CONCLUDING REMARKS

So the Court's approach to the action for annulment is not beset by double standards at all. On the contrary, the case law of the Court seems consistent, both internally and with its case law in other areas, notably the action for damages. Nor can it be said that it was out of keeping with the expectations of the authors of the EEC Treaty or the needs of the infant legal order of the Community. However, what may have been appropriate in the 1960s and 1970s is no longer so at the beginning of the new millennium. The difficult process of ratification which the Maastricht Treaty underwent in the early 1990s wrought a profound and irrevocable change in the complexion of what is now the European Union. No longer are the peoples of the Member States prepared to leave the governance of Europe in the hands of secretive élites. Transparency and accountability have become the order of the day. The failure of the Santer Commission to recognize the extent to which the climate had changed contributed to the pressure which led to its collective resignation in March 1999. It is inconsistent with this change in mood for the Community to cling to an outdated and paternalistic view of the right of individuals to bring annulment proceedings.

Although the Member States have taken some steps to increase the Union's transparency and accountability, they show few signs of appreciating the link between these matters and the right to bring annulment proceedings. At Amsterdam, Title VI of the Treaty on European Union was revised with a view to providing citizens "with a high level of safety within an area of freedom, security and justice ..."[60] The Council was given the power to adopt binding framework decisions for the purpose of approximating the laws and regulations of the

---

58 See Case 314/85, *Foto-Frost* v. *Hauptzollamt Lübeck-Ost*, [1987] ECR 4199. The preliminary rulings procedure is in many ways a less satisfactory mechanism for reviewing the validity of Community acts than the action for annulment: see AG Jacobs in Case C-188/92, *TWD Textilwerke Deggendorf*, [1994] ECR I-833; Waelbroeck and Verheyden, "Les conditions de recevabilité des recours en annulation des particuliers contre les actes normatifs communautaires", (1995) CDE, 399-441, 433-436.

59 See Dec. 93/350, O.J. 1993, L144/21. The Court of First Instance did not acquire jurisdiction to deal with actions for the annulment of dumping and subsidy measures until the following year (see O.J. 1994, L66/29).

60 Art. 29 TEU.

Member States and binding decisions "for any other purpose consistent with the objectives of this Title". Article 35(6) gives the Court of Justice jurisdiction to review the legality of such measures, but only in proceedings brought by a Member State or the Commission. In the area of freedom, security and justice, individuals are not permitted to ask the Court for justice themselves. The standing rules in Article 230 (ex 173) were left unchanged, even though the Court had specifically pointed out the difficulty of providing individuals with protection against infringements of their fundamental rights by legislative acts[61] and even though a new provision was inserted into the Treaty on European Union[62] proclaiming that the Union is founded on (*inter alia*) respect for human rights and fundamental freedoms and the rule of law.

The charitable might suggest that the Member States were reluctant to add to the Community Courts' already heavy workload. Indeed, this seems to have been one of the reasons for confining the right to request preliminary rulings under the new Title IV of the EC Treaty to national courts of last resort.[63] The problems posed by the Court's workload are notoriously difficult to resolve and equally notoriously unattractive to politicians. An attempt to force the issue onto the political agenda was made by the Community Courts themselves with the publication in the spring of 1999 of a far-reaching discussion paper on the future of the Union's judicial system.[64] It is abundantly clear that the essentially managerial difficulties caused by the Courts' workload cannot be used indefinitely as an excuse for failing to tackle other issues which are vital to the health and legitimacy of the Union.

61 See its report on the application of the Treaty on European Union (Proceedings of the Court of Justice and Court of First Instance of the European Communities, 22-26 May 1995, No. 15/95).
62 Art. 6(1).
63 See Art. 68(1) EC.
64 See http://europa.eu.int/cj/en/pres/aveng.pdf; Arnull, "Judicial architecture or judicial folly? The challenge facing the European Union", 24 EL Rev. (1999), 516-524.

14

PUBLIC INTEREST LITIGATION

Laurence W. Gormley

INTRODUCTION

While the general issues of admissibility have long been the subject of controversy and are dealt with in particular by Arnull in this volume, questions of public interest litigation have attracted surprisingly little academic comment in the English language at least, until the major conference devoted to that subject in Berlin in December 1995.[1] This birthday offering examines some considerations in public interest litigation, in part drawing on some of the issues raised at that conference, taking account of more recent developments in the case-law, and aims to make a modest suggestion or two for future developments. It thus offers a personal present to a special and much-admired friend within the collective birthday cake, which both volumes of this *Festschrift* represent.

AN UNRULY HORSE

Public interest litigation is a horse of somewhat mixed pedigree and temperament. On the one hand, it embraces actions brought by high-minded and often respected groups,[2] which operate, in defence of what clearly is an important public interest or value, such as the protection of the environment or animal welfare, or even the promotion of the interests of consumers.[3] On the other hand,

1 See Micklitz and Reich (eds.), *Public Interest Litigation before European Courts* (Nomos, Baden-Baden, 1996). For a report of the discussion at the conference, see Amtenbrink (1996) 7 EBLR 35.

2 The most celebrated example might be Greenpeace. But today's widespread recognition and acceptance (even if attention to detailed argument is not always a feature of a particular group's arguments) may well be preceded by yesterday's controversies and a reluctance of particular flavours of governing parties to listen to the unpalatable, being minded to seek to rubbish arguments without more ado.

3 In particular BEUC in Brussels has a high profile, but the Commission is not always easily persuaded to adopt a similar view of consumers' interests to that propounded by BEUC: as to an interesting attempt to persuade the Commission to concede in anti-dumping procedures what would in effect be a general interested party status to BEUC, see Case T-256/97 *Bureau Européen des Unions de Consommateurs (BEUC) v. Commission* [2000] ECR I-nyr (27 January 2000), see also Order of February 1, 1999, [1999] ECR II-

D. O'Keeffe (ed.), Liber Amicorum Slynn 191-201 (2000)

what may at first appear to be something in the nature of a public interest organisation is sometimes simply a cover for very much private interests: these may be of a collective or even eccentric nature. Thus a particular association for the promotion of fair competition in a particular sector may in reality be little more than the national or local cartel; or the representative forum for particular trademark owners dressed up as a doughty warrior for higher interest (frequently to the disadvantage of the consumer), or it may even be an *ad hoc* shell association established for a particular instance of cooperation. This at once highlights the difficulty with opening up standing to such organisations: where should the line be drawn, and at what stage does the vaunting of an alleged public interest in fact cease to be an activity in the public interest as such and become declassified to mere private special pleading?

As will become apparent, the Court of Justice's and the Court of First Instance's willingness to find group actions admissible has been very much limited to particular sectors and extremely particular circumstances. As was so elegantly put by that great Community lawyer the late Gerhard Bebr, the purpose of the criteria of direct and individual concern (for actions for annulment brought by non-privileged applicants who are not the addressees of acts of the Community Institutions) is clear: the Community legal order has set its face against an *actio popularis* or the torpedoing of acts of the Community administration.[4] Indeed, given that much of Community administrative law has been developed in the agricultural sector, the most highly developed of the Community's common policies, it is not surprising that the Court of Justice has shown particular caution in its approach to *locus standi* in general.[5] Nevertheless, the Court has not been afraid on occasions[6] to undertake Houdini-like contortions in order to convince itself (but scarcely all academics or practitioners) that a particular litigant fits

---

169. BEUC succeeded in establishing that the Commission could not automatically exclude consumer organisations from the circle of interested parties by applying a general criterion such as the distinction between products sold at the retail level and other products. The Commission was thus obliged to decide on a case-by-case basis whether a party was an interested party in the light of the particular circumstances of each case: it could not exclude consumer organisations from an anti-dumping proceeding without giving them an opportunity to show their interest in the product in question. However, the attempt to obtain a ruling conferring standing to any consumer organisation to have access to the non-confidential file in any anti-dumping proceeding dealing with products not commonly sold at retail level was found inadmissible. The Court of First Instance clearly struck a balance, requiring the Commission to consider each application on its individual merits.

4 Bebr, *Development of Judicial Control in the European Communities* (Nijhoff, The Hague, 1981) 21.

5 See, generally, Barents, *The Agricultural Law of the EC* (Kluwer, European Monographs 9, Deventer, 1994).

6 *E.*g. Case C-358/89 *Extramet Industrie SA v. Council* [1991] ECR 2501 at 2532 (cf. A.G. Jacobs at 2514) and Case C-309/89 *Codorniu SA v. Council* [1994] ECR I-1853 at 1886. As to the latter judgment, see Kapteyn & VerLoren van Themaat (ed. Gormley), *Introduction to the Law of the European Communities* (3rd. ed., London, 1998) 486.

into the judicial straight-jacket which the celebrated *Plaumann* criteria[7] have become. This approach resembles nothing less than pulling an equitable rabbit out of the proverbial hat, making even the yardstick of the length of the Lord Chancellor's foot appear conceptually certain.

THERE'S A TIME AND A PLACE FOR EVERYTHING

In *Greenpeace,* both the Court of First Instance[8] and the Court of Justice[9] made it clear that the traditional hostile stance to public interest litigation would be maintained. Thus where 'the specific situation of the applicant was not taken into consideration in the adoption of an act, which concerns him in a general and abstract fashion and, in fact, like any other person in the same situation, the applicant is not individually concerned by the act. The same applies to associations which claim to have *locus standi* on the basis of the fact that persons whom they represent are individually concerned.'[10] The Court observed that it was the national decision to build the power stations, which was liable to affect the environmental rights concerned, not the Community decision to grant ERDF assistance for the building of the power stations. This really amounts to an argument of *forum non conveniens*: that attempts to block the construction of power stations belong in the national courts. On the other hand, it is possible to analyse this approach as being disingenuous in practical terms, as it ignores the question whether the power stations would have been built at all without Community funding. It also means that there was no possibility at all of challenging the Commission's assessment of the desirability and impact of the project. Against that, it may of course be objected that it is not for the Commission to re-undertake a substantive examination of all projects and their implications; it is rather for the Commission to see whether the conditions for the grant of assistance are satisfied.[11] Despite the clear sympathy in *Greenpeace* of Advocate General Cosmas for the importance of environmental protection,[12] he too was concerned about the consequences of relaxing the criteria of admissibility.

---

7 Case 25/62 *Plaumann & Co. v. Commission* [1963] ECR 95 at 107.

8 Case T-585/93 *Stichting Greenpeace Council (Greenpeace International) et al. v. Commission* [1995] ECR II-2205 at 2230-2232.

9 Case C-321/95 P *Stichting Greenpeace Council (Greenpeace International) et al. v. Commission* [1998] ECR I-1651 at 1715-1716.

10 *Ibid.* at 1715.

11 Krämer in Micklitz & Reich (eds.), *op.cit.* (see note 1, *supra*) 297 at 304-307 discusses the degree of evaluation undertaken and the various problems in ensuring genuine examination of compatibility with Community environmental law and policy. See also the discussion by A.G. Cosmas in Case C-321/95 P *Stichting Greenpeace Council (Greenpeace International) et al. v. Commission* [1998] ECR I-1651 at 1676-1678.

12 *Ibid.* at 1693-1696.

> '[A] relaxation to the extent sought, of the criteria of admissibility could be abused and lead to aberrant consequences. Natural persons without *locus standi* .... could circumvent [the procedural impediment of direct and individual concern] by setting up an environmental association. Moreover, while the number of natural persons, that is to say citizens of the European union, however high it may be, none the less remains limited, the number of environmental associations capable of being created is, at least in theory, infinite. But, even if that obstacle could be overcome, for example by conferring *locus standi* only on associations constituted prior to the adoption of the contested measure, account would have to be taken of the fact that, within the European Union, the number of legal persons which have as their object the protection and conservation of the environment is today particularly high. If the Court were ultimately to follow the proposal of the appellant associations, in future every measure of a Community institution concerning the environment or having an impact on it could be expected, on each occasion, to form the subject-matter of proceedings brought by a plethora of environmental associations.'[13]

This prospect, combined with the clear fact that Article 230 (ex 173) EC is clearly narrower than Article 33 ECSC, made it inevitable that the Court should resist invitations to engage in judicial creativity in this instance.

In other areas and circumstances, though, efforts of associations to obtain standing have often met with a more favourable approach. In Cases T-481 & 484/93 *Exporteurs in Levende Varkens et al. v. Commission*[14] the Court of First Instance conveniently summarised earlier case-law, finding that an association which was not the addressee of a measure would have standing in two circumstances: *first*, where it had a particular interest in acting, especially because its negotiating position was affected by the measure involved; and, *secondly*, where, by bringing the action, it substituted itself for one or more of its members whom it represented, provided that those members were themselves in a position to bring an admissible action. *In casu,* the applicants were not found to satisfy this test as far as their actions for annulment were concerned. But associations which had 'been active in relation both to the general policy on State aid and to specific aid projects in the textile sector in the interests of their members or of members of their members operating in the same sector as the recipient undertaking'[15] will have standing on the first limb of this test: their position as interlocutors of the Commission was affected by the contested decision.[16] The mere attendance at meetings, without any clear negotiating role of more import will not confer standing on an association.[17] The second situation (substitution) may well occur when a trade association takes on board a complaint by one of its

13 *Ibid.* at 1699-1700.

14 [1995] ECR II-2941 at 2965.

15 Case T-380/94 *Association Internationale des Utilisateurs de Fils de Filaments Artificiels et Synthétiques et de Soie Naturelle (AIUFFASS) et al. v. Commission* [1996] ECR II-2169 at 2188.

16 The earlier case law in the field of State aids is examined by Gormley in Micklitz & Reich, *op.cit.* (see note 1, *supra*) 159-167.

17 *E.g.* Case T-86/96 *Arbeitsgemeinschaft Deutscher Luftfahrt-Unternehmen et al. v. Commission* [1999] ECR II 179, at 201.

members who is a direct competitor of a recipient of State aid,[18] or when an association has taken on board a complaint originally brought by a single undertaking, so that (as in anti-dumping cases) it becomes easier to present the complaint as being by or on behalf of Community industry. A *third* situation in which associations will have standing was recalled by the Court of First Instance in Case T-122/96 *Federazione Nazionale del Commercio Oleario (Federolio) v. Commission,*[19] namely when a legal provision expressly grants them a series of procedural rights. In this case, the measure concerned acts as a *lex specialis* in relation to Article 230 (ex 173) EC. The Court of First Instance prefaced its observations, however, by referring to 'at least three types of situations.' Of particular importance is the statement there that even if national law confers on an applicant specific tasks and duties with capacity to bring actions before national courts, that will not justify a change in the system of remedies which Community law has established: otherwise the admissibility of an action for annulment would no longer depend on the desire of the Community legislature to include certain traders and/or associations in the process of Community decision-making, but on the autonomous decision of national authorities based on national rather than on the Community interest.[20] The arguments adduced by Federolio on the other two grounds noted were equally unsuccessful on the facts.

It now seems clear that neither the Court of Justice nor the Court of First Instance is willing to heed calls for a relaxation of the *Plaumann* criteria, particularly in relation to public interest litigation, taking the view that it is up to the Member States in their role during an intergovernmental Conference, and only then, as *Herren der Verträge*, to liberalise standing requirements if they so wish. In the current political climate that is understandable, but it might be observed that the Court is perfectly capable of constructing the EC Treaty so as to permit it to do something other than that which is expressly provided for.[21] The Court has also been willing to be creative with the Treaty provisions when it suited its purpose, while suddenly being strict when it found it convenient to be so.[22] Be-

---

18 See now Reg. 659/1999 (O.J. 1999 L 83/1), Arts. 1(h); 6, and 20.

19 [1997] ECR II-1559 at 1580.

20 *Ibid.* at 1581-1582.

21 *E.g.* Art. 231 (ex 174) EC confers power on the Court to decide which effects of an annulled regulation shall be considered definitive, but the Court has interpreted it by analogy to give itself the same power in relation to directives: *e.g.* Case C-295/90 *European Parliament v. Council* [1992] ECR I-4193 at 4236-4237.

22 A comparison of the development of the concept of direct effect for directives with the refusal to accept horizontal direct effect off directives makes this very plain: see *e.g.* Case 9/70 *Grad v. Finanzamt Traunstein* [1970] ECR 825 at 838 and Case C-91/92 *Faccini Dori v. Recreb Srl* [1994] ECR I-3325 at 3356. The Court's conclusion that it had the power by analogy to determine which of the effects of an annulled directive or decision should be declared definitive, while undoubtedly eminently sensible in the circumstances, clearly flies in the face of the restrictive wording of Art. 231 (ex 174) EC, which confers that power only in respect of regulations: see *e.g.* Case C-295/90 *European Parliament v. Council* [1992] ECR I-4193 at 4236-4237; Case C-34/86 *Council v. European Parliament* [1986] ECR 2155 at 2212, and Case C-271/94 *European Parliament v.*

ing confined by the wording of the Treaty is to some extent a misleading argument: the Court itself has restricted the meaning of direct and individual concern by the interpretation given to those terms.

In general or particular? Modest proposals

At the conference referred to above, Zuleeg was invited to come up with some proposals for redrafting Article 230 (ex 173) EC. He proposed *inter alia* the addition of a new paragraph in the following terms:

> 'By legislative act, associations or institutions pursuing a public interest may be entitled to institute proceedings for [the] purpose [of seeking the annulment of an act described in the first paragraph].'

This approach recognises the risks, to which Advocate General Cosmas referred, of a global relaxation of standing requirements. In fact, though, Zuleeg's suggestion is in substance nothing new: the Community legislature can and does grant standing (sometimes for limited purposes such as making representations or granting access to the non-confidential file) to associations or groups (such as representatives of consumers, as in anti-dumping matters).[23] Once this has been done, the Court clearly treats those persons as having standing (at the very least in relation to challenges concerning those purposes) as has been noticed above. There are plenty of precedents for raising case-law developments or legislative developments to Treaty-level requirements. However, in view of the difficulties in drafting a sufficiently tight general public interest litigation clause at Treaty level, it would be more efficient for the Community Institutions to adopt the legislative act solution. This could be done either by adopting a global public interest measure (most likely on the basis of a new provision to be inserted into the EC Treaty) or by tackling the question on a case-by-case basis, inserting specific standing provisions into Community legislation in more areas. Environmental protection is certainly the most obvious of these, although *inter alia* the regulations on the Structural Funds and the Cohesion Fund could well be opened up to ensure at least as a very minimum consultation of public interest groups, and, more desirably, that such organisations could challenge the Commission's assessment of the compatibility of projects with Community environmental law and policy. Given the high priority now accorded to the environment in the EC Treaty, there would for the first time be a clear opportunity to challenge such assessments. Indeed, the extraordinary situation that Community-level assessments have so far in effect been closed to challenge is itself a key

---

Council [1996] ECR I-1689 at 1719.

23 See Reg. 384/96 (O.J. 1996 L 56/1, most recently amended by Reg. 905/98 (O.J. 1998 L 128/18)), Arts. 5(10); 6(6) and (7), and 21(1) and (2). See also Case T-256/97 *Bureau Européen des Unions de Consommateurs (BEUC) v. Commission* [2000] ECR I-nyr (27 January 2000).

justification for the introduction of some form of public interest litigation facility at Community level. When even national constitutional law requirements (such as courts not being allowed to suspend the operation of Acts of Parliament) cannot prevail against a challenge based on Community law, it is wholly unacceptable that the Commission's assessments are so robustly protected.[24]

At the same conference Krämer in fact came up with what in essence is a more developed draft:

> 'Public interest groups may institute proceedings against acts mentioned in Article 173(1). The European Parliament and the Council shall determine the details of the procedure and in particular the conditions, which a group shall comply with in order to be considered to act in the public interest.'

Noteworthy is that Krämer did not specify the actual decision-making procedure which would apply, although the reference to the Parliament and the Council implies that he intended the co-decision procedure to apply.

If the option of a general approach to standing is to be adopted, it would seem appropriate to re-draft the suggestions of Zuleeg and Krämer slightly to bring them more into conformity with present Treaty drafting style, so as to insert a fifth paragraph into Article 230 (ex 173) EC in the following terms:

> 'The Council, acting in accordance with the procedure referred to in Article 251 and after consulting the Economic and Social Committee, may adopt measures conferring upon the Court of Justice jurisdiction under the same conditions, in actions brought by public interest organisations. Such measures shall in particular specify the criteria which must be satisfied by such organisations in order to benefit from those measures.'

Clearly, the word 'may' could be replaced by 'shall' and the proposed draft opts for the most democratic form of participation by the European Parliament in order that it may have the maximum influence on the establishment of the criteria to be satisfied. The Committee of the Regions and indeed the Court of Justice could be added as additional consultees.

What criteria might be appropriate, in view of the fears expressed by Advocate General Cosmas? Certainly, operation at the Community level would appear to be indicated. Thus, an international or at least Community-wide functioning should be required. The obvious objection is that this would exclude all groups, which were established solely in one Member State. This could be overcome by closer liaison between Community-level and national level public interest organisations. Thus, a Community-level criterion need not actually exclude national or regional organisations, as their interests could effectively be represented by a Community-level organisation. In any event, it should be remembered that if one single action is brought by several parties acting together

---

24 Of course, the Council or a Member State could challenge them, but in reality, this does not happen, unless the addressee Member State is unhappy with conditions attached to a decision.

(using one set of pleadings), only one of the parties needs to be admissible to carry the action.[25] At the very least organisations should be more than purely local in nature, and it is submitted that Community-level operation would be the most efficient level to ensure that public interest litigation is not reduced to mere nimbyism.

It may be thought that an association should have legal personality and should have a non-profit or charitable status, or at the very least not be an organisation with economic or commercial objectives.[26] An association should also be financially transparent.[27] It may even be thought that a public interest organisation should be democratically constituted, although this may prove difficult in practice. Certainly, it should be of a permanent nature, not merely established for an *ad hoc* short-term interest. It may be that some suppleness in this permanence criterion could be appropriate, although via judicious recourse to an already recognised organisation even shorter-term *ad hoc* organisations could be catered for without special provisions. In the environmental field, such an organisation should be clearly established in the interest of the protection of the environmental interest concerned (which might be general, or more specific, such as water, air, land, birds, animals, or wetlands). Clearly, these criteria would be more likely to embrace activist organisations than business-related 'pseudo'-organisations' or mere lobby groups pleading for special interests. Thus, an apparently objective body funded by, say, the tobacco industry or the drinks industry would fall outside such criteria, as would organisations for the promotion of regional economic interests or for the promotion of a particular branch of commerce or industry. On the other hand, such bodies could be given standing in more limited fields of specific interest in individual Community acts.

A register of organisations satisfying the prescribed criteria could be maintained by the Community Institutions (perhaps by the Registrar of the Court of Justice or by the Secretary-General of the European Parliament, so that the Commission is not involved in registration decisions), with organisations having to register and renew registration periodically. The onus would be thus on organisations which claimed to fulfil the criteria laid down to make themselves known. Given that organisations may need to seek to register themselves quickly (particularly if they are new organisations set up on a permanent basis but responding to new or threatened developments, or if *ad hoc* organisations were also to be allowed to bring proceedings) registration should be deemed granted

---

25 *E.g.* Case C-212/90 *Comité internationale de la rayonne et des fibres synthétiques (CIRFS) et al. v. Commission* [1993] ECR I-1125 at 1185.

26 Clearly, the intention would be to exclude the sort of private 'public interest' organisations of the type referred to at the beginning of this contribution. However careful drafting will be necessary to ensure that fund-raising activities and campaigning activities would not in themselves jeopardise classification as a public interest organisation.

27 Benjamin Hartmann from Bonn reminded me of the desirability of including this criterion.

unless opposed or refused within one month.[28] The Commission or the Council should have the right to oppose registration, in which case the body responsible for registration would have to take a decision within one further month. Refusal to register (whether within one month at the instance of the register holder or as a result of a decision after opposition) would be open to challenge before the Court of First Instance (with further appeal in the usual manner), and the Commission or the Council could appeal against registration to the Court of Justice.[29] Applications for registration could be made at any time.

The register would be open to the public, which would have the advantage of encouraging transparency. It would also be possible to provide for registration in relation to specific areas of interest. This would also have the advantage of providing the Commission with a more specific ready-made list of obvious consultees[30] even in the informal stages leading to the preparation of its proposals or other actions, as well as a clear list of interested persons acting in the 'public interest' who could, like individuals who satisfy the 'direct and individual concern test, bring actions before the centralised Community courts. Once on the register, admissibility issues would become otiose as regards public interest organisations in individual cases. Re-registration requirements (say every five years) would ensure that lists were periodically pruned of inactive organisations, but such applications for re-registration could only be refused or opposed if there had been a manifest change in the activities or objectives of the organisation concerned.

The approach in Community legislation which presently make provision for involvement of 'interested parties' also leaves it up to associations or groups to make themselves and their interests known,[31] so that the Community Institution concerned may itself decide what weight to attach to their submissions. Although the Community Institutions have not been unresponsive to calls to im-

---

28 Bearing in mind that the time limits for appeals in the Community system are tight, a short time limit would be appropriate for opposition or refusal.

29 Appeals could be expedited, being heard by a single judge: the appropriate procedural amendments would have to be made.

30 The Commission already maintains a Directory of Special Interest Groups, which is meant to be a working tool rather than a means of accreditation. It currently lists some 800 organizations in the electronic version (accessible through the Europa home page on the Secretariat General's page). The Commission regards the directory as not restricting the access of Commission officials to interest groups but as increasing their awareness of the importance of consulting interest parties more systematically and as raising the profile of certain less well-known (and thus less frequently consulted) organizations. See, further, the Communication SEC (92) 2272 Final, *An open and structured dialogue between the Commission and special interest groups* (O.J. 1993 C 63/2). The Directory and the Communication are aimed at providing a framework within which lobbying is conducted, they thus serve a rather different function than the register for litigation purposes which is discussed in this contribution. See, further, Mazey & Richardson in Edwards & Spence (eds.), *The European Commission* (2nd. Ed., London, 1997) 178.

31 As to the minimum standards to be applied in the relations between the Commission and interest groups, see the Communication, *ibid.*, Annex II.

prove the position of interested parties (as the anti-dumping field makes plain), the experience of groups such as BEUC with this system has hitherto been less than wholly encouraging.[32] Accordingly, it is submitted that a more global approach to standing issues is to be preferred in the form of a Community decision, with registration decisions being taken by a person other than the Commission, and being open to review as outlined above.

Of course, it is one thing to provide for standing to seek review, it is quite another thing to persuade the judiciary that an act should be annulled. Given that the judicial control at Community level is still more of a marginal nature (in the absence of manifestly wrong appraisal of a factual situation) the prospect of obtaining substantive review of the merits of Community action is still somewhat elusive. Now, though, environmental protection is so clearly flagged as an integral part of other Community policies, it may become easier to persuade the centralised Community Courts to be more willing to undertake a more far-reaching examination of the assessments made by the Community Institutions. However, at the moment that still very much depends on the equitable rabbit approach, and the portents are not good. The other avenue, of challenging national decisions on the ground of incompatibility with Community law, and seeking an Article 234 (ex 177) EC reference should of course not be overlooked, although that avenue will not avail a party which would have had standing to seek the annulment of a Community act but did not avail itself of that opportunity.[33]

The public interest litigation industry has, like Topsy, grown and grown, as administrative law in the Member States has developed in recent years to cope with new challenges. There is still a feeling that at the Community level the case law is somewhat lagging behind developments in many Member States, and any prospects of serious movement by the centralised Community judiciary are, like reports of Mark Twain's death, greatly exaggerated.

Concluding observations and salutation

Coming as part of a birthday present, these suggestions deserve some wrapping paper. My thoughts as to that represent something (semi-) permeable or accessible, perhaps in the direction of an environmentally friendly filter or even a cork, temporarily confining the merry Widow. But if the bubbles resulting from these thoughts succeed in pointing out that the way to improve public interest litigation is within our grasp already on a sector-by-sector basis, and that a systematic approach could be achieved through a minor amendment of Article 230 EC and

32 See the contribution by Adamantopoulos in Micklitz & Reich (eds.), *op.cit.* (see note 1, *supra*) 359, and *e.g.* Case T-256/97 *Bureau Européen des Unions de Consommateurs (BEUC) v. Commission* [2000] ECR I-nyr (27 January 2000), and Order of February 1, 1999, [1999] ECR II-169.

33 Case C-188/92 *TWD Textilwerke Deggendorff GmbH v. Commission* [1994] ECR I-833 at 852-853.

specific legislation, both the giver and receiver of this individual present will have reason to be pleased. My own preference for a global approach to enlarging public interest standing is clear enough, but even extending the individual sector-by-sector development through amendments to existing legislation would be an improvement on the current situation.

Perhaps the first step might be taken by the European Parliament which could seize the opportunity to make use of its right of quasi-initiative under the second paragraph of Article 192 (ex 138b) EC to call on the Commission to propose a public interest litigation measure, or to propose an amendment of the EC Treaty on the lines set out above. The above suggestions are indicative of the sort of criteria, which could be used to decide on which types of organisations should be granted standing, and in respect of what issues. They do not pretend to be an exhaustive list, but they certainly lay the framework for legislative action. Indeed, it may even be appropriate to introduce at least public interest consultation in the future into comitology procedures to seek to have wider involvement of public interest organisations in Community decision-making at the level of delegated legislation.

The suggested criteria for registering organisations which will have standing has the advantage of encouraging participation of interest groups in the global Community legislative process in a transparent way, ensuring that there is some body which operates in a disinterested fashion to protect wider interests (and not mere lobbying) which may draw attention to unsatisfactory decision-making and seek review of it. This would go a long way to curing the access to justice deficit, which is perceived by many to exist in the Community (and even more so in the Union) system.

With these pleasant thoughts in mind, I wrap up this little present to a most distinguished friend, whose contribution to the development of law in general, and Community law in particular, has been both singular and humane. In particular, his interest in encouraging others to achieve; his tireless devotion to students and young practitioners; his celebrated support of academic institutions, and his boundless energy in promoting the awareness and understanding of Community law should be fondly recalled and celebrated. As indeed should his outstanding contribution to the development of Community law as a member of the centralised Community judiciary (as Advocate General and then Judge at the Court of Justice) and, both before and since, as a member of the decentralised Community judiciary. Very many happy returns of the day to a very good egg indeed.

15

THE EUROPEAN COURT'S PRE-EMPTIVE JURISDICTION: OPINIONS UNDER ARTICLE 300(6) EC

Richard Plender[*]

Two deceptively simple sentences govern the jurisdiction of Court of Justice to determine whether a proposed international agreement is compatible with the EC Treaty. Article 300(6) of that Treaty (formerly 228) reads as follows:

> "The Council, the Commission or a Member State may obtain the opinion of the Court of Justice as to whether an agreement envisaged is compatible with the provisions of this Treaty. Where the opinion of the Court of Justice is adverse, the agreement may enter into force only in accordance with Article 48 of the Treaty on European Union."

The draftsman could scarcely have concealed so many problems in so short a space had he set out to do so deliberately. Does the word "agreement" denote a treaty in the sense of the Vienna Convention on the Law of Treaties between States and International Organizations?[1] Does the Court's jurisdiction under Article 300(6) extend to agreements not concluded in accordance with the other paragraphs of the same Article? In authorising the Court to determine "whether an agreement ... is compatible with ... this Treaty", did the parties invest it with competence to determine whether the Council, Commission of the Member States had the power to enter into that agreement? Are those institutions entirely at liberty to determine whether to request an Opinion or not? In the interval between the request for an Opinion and its delivery, are the institutions and the Member States free to proceed with the conclusion of an agreement? When considering requests for Opinions, should the Court respect the *principe du contradictoire*?

---

* The author gratefully acknowledges the research assistance of Dr Phillip Landolt, barrister.

1 Convention on the Law of Treaties between States and International Organizations or between International Organizations, Vienna, 21st March 1986, Cm. 244 (not yet in force). See Philippe Manin, "The European Communities and the Vienna Convention on the Law of Treaties between States and International Organizations or between International Organizations" 24 CMLRev (1987) 457.

D. O'Keeffe (ed.), Liber Amicorum Slynn 203-220 (2000)

To discover the answers to these questions it is appropriate, as is often the case when a Community text is to be interpreted, to ascertain at the outset the object of the provision.

THE PURPOSE OF THE PROCEDURE

According to the Court of Justice:

> "It is the purpose of [this provision] to forestall complications which would result from legal disputes concerning the compatibility with the Treaty of international agreements binding upon the Community."[2]

This sets it apart from the most closely comparable provisions in the ECSC and Euratom treaties.

The fourth paragraph of Article 95 of the ECSC Treaty invests the Court of Justice with jurisdiction to rule on the conformity of any proposal for minor treaty amendment with the rules governing such amendments. Here the purpose is to ensure that the Council and Commission do not act *ultra vires*, bearing in mind, in particular, the exclusion of Member States from the process for minor revision. This accounts for the observation, made by the Court of Justice in its first Opinion under the ECSC Treaty,[3] that:

> "Derogation from the normal procedure for amendment of the Treaty is permissible only where it does not interfere with the general structure of the Treaty or the relationship between the Community and the Member States, particularly the relationship between the powers transferred to the Community and the powers reserved to the Member States".

The considerations that the Court of Justice there articulated are based on inference. They are not expressed in the third paragraph of Article 95, which fastens attention on "the relationship between the powers of the Commission and those of the other institutions of the Community".

Article 103 of the Euratom Treaty authorises the Court of Justice to rule on the compatibility with that treaty of draft agreements between Member States and third States, international organizations or nationals of third States. The purpose of this procedure is:

> "to ensure that the provisions of the [Euratom] Treaty are not frustrated by agreements or contracts concluded by the Member States with third parties".[4]

Here the focus is on proposed action by Member States. That Article appears to assume by its wording that the Member State is fully competent to enter into the

---

2 Opinion 1/75 of 11th November 1975, [1975] ECR 1355 at 1360-1361.
3 Opinion of 17th December 1959, [1959] ECR 266 at 268.
4 Ruling 1/78 of 14th November 1978, [1978] ECR 2151 at 2165.

genus of agreement or contract but that in substance the latter might impede the application of the Euratom Treaty.[5]

The Court of Justice may forestall complications at the international level either by identifying an element of incompatibility between a proposed agreement and the EC Treaty, so that either of them may be amended, or by declaring the compatibility of the agreement with the EC Treaty. In the former case, the Court's Opinion may provide an incentive to all parties, including the Community's partners, to modify the proposed agreement; for in the absence of such modification, there would be a "manifest" incompatibility with the internal law of one partner, affecting its capacity to give consent to be bound and thereby affording it a ground for failing to apply the treaty.[6]

The potential international efficacy of a decision of the Court of Justice is illustrated by Case C-327/91, *French Republic v Commission.*[7] This was not an Opinion under Article 300(6) of the EC Treaty but a decision on an application for the annulment of an agreement concluded between the Community and the United States governing the application of their competition laws. The Court recognized that the French application was wrongly formulated as an attack on the agreement rather than upon the act whereby the Community sought to conclude it. It annulled the Commission's decision, however, on the ground that it was required to be taken by the Council. Thereafter the United States agreed to repeat the treaty-making process with the Council: a step which it was no doubt prepared to take for the avoidance of complications both practical and legal.

Therefore, an Opinion establishing the compatibility of a draft agreement with the EC Treaty provides for the parties the reassurance that they may well need so that their pact will not be frustrated by legal disputes arising from considerations internal to the Community's legal order.[8] Such an Opinion may be

---

5 Further, Article 105 of the Euratom Treaty appears to be drafted on the premise that the conclusion of such an agreement in violation of the rule in Article 103 would not affect the validity of the agreement since the third party would be entitled to invoke against the Member State the principle *pacta tertiis nec nocent nec prosunt.* On that principle judgments of Judge Huber in the *Island of Palmas* case, (1928) II UNRIAA 831 and of the Permanent Court in *Free Zones of Upper Savoy and Gex*, (1932) PCIJ Ser. A/B No 46 page 141; Convention on the Law of Treaties, Vienna, 23rd May 1969, Cmnd. 7964, Article 34; and as evidence of customary international law, Convention on the Law of Treaties between States and International Organizations or between International Organizations, Vienna, 21st March 1986, Cm. 244, Article 27 (not yet in force).

6 Article 46 of the Convention on the Law of Treaties between States and International Organizations or between International Organizations, Vienna, 21st March 1986, Cm. 244.

7 [1994] ECR I-3461.

8 This was plainly the case with the agreement on trade-related aspects of intellectual property (TRIPS). See Opinion 1/94 of 15th November 1994, [1994] ECR I-5267 and A. Arnull, "The Scope of the Common Commercial Policy: A Coda on Opinion 1/94" in *The European Union and World Trade Law* (Chichester, John Wiley and Sons, 1995) 343. The new paragraph 5 of Article 133 (formerly 113) of the EC Treaty creates an exception to the principle of parallelism established by Case 22/70, *Commission v Council*, [1971] ECR 263. It provides: "The Council, acting unanimously on a proposal from the

particularly valuable in the case of a mixed agreement, which has no precise counterpart in international practice.[9]

The difficulties that the Court of Justice seeks to forestall, when delivering Opinions under Article 300(6), cannot in all cases be avoided by invoking the second paragraph of Article 231 (formerly 174) of the EC Treaty. This authorises the Court to identify certain aspects of a void regulation which shall be declared as definitive. A striking example of the use of this provision, in the context of an international agreement, is given by the decision of 7th March 1996 in Case C-360/93, *Parliament v Council.*[10]

In Opinion 1/94 of 15th November 1994 the Court had determined that certain agreements with the United States, designed to facilitate the opening of the parties' respective public markets, were beyond Article 133 of the EC Treaty in so far as they applied to services. By its decision in the subsequent contentious proceedings, it disposed of an appeal against two Council Decisions approving the conclusion of these agreements. In view of its earlier Opinion, the Court had no option but to annul those Decisions. In accordance with the recommendation of Mr Advocate General Tesauro, however, it maintained in force their effect, invoking what is now Article 231 of the EC Treaty (formerly 174). It did not identify certain effects for preservation but concluded that "all the effects of the annulled decisions should be conserved." This is Procrustes' approach to the interpretation of a text: one whereby Article 231 is construed to meet the exigencies of the situation, not the object of the draftsman.

The purpose of Article 231 is to alleviate the detriment to those who have acted in reliance on a regulation, in the manner of estoppel. It is designed to protect those who have acted in good faith, on the presumption that the Community's act is lawful. Like the principle of good faith itself, it is designed for the protection of the innocent party.[11] It is a different matter to apply this Article to protect parties from the consequences of future behaviour undertaken in the

---

Commission and after consulting the European Parliament, may extend the application of paragraphs 1 to 4 to international negotiations and agreements on services and intellectual property insofar as they are not covered by these paragraphs." See A. Dashwood, "External Relations Provisions of the Amsterdam Treaty", 35 CMLRev. (1998) 1019 at 1022.

9 J.H.H. Weiler, "The External Legal Relations of Non-Unitary Actors: Mixity and the Federal Principle" in *Mixed Agreements*, D. O'Keeffe and H.G. Schermers, eds., (Kluwer, 1983) 35 at 35.

10 [1996] ECR I-1195.

11 E. Zoller, *La bonne foi en droit international public* (Paris, Editions A. Pedone, 1977) and M. Virally, "Good Faith in Public International Law", 77 *Amer. J. of International Law* (1983) 130 at 133: "good faith protects those who trust, reasonably, the appearances created by the behaviour of other international legal actors (who have confidence in the good faith of those actors) or who have truly fallen into error: the innocent victims, in all good faith, of the appearances".

knowledge, actual or presumed, of the incompatibility of the agreement with the EC Treaty.[12]

AGREEMENTS

By contrast with the International Court of Justice, whose advisory jurisdiction is limited solely by the qualification that it is to pronounce on legal issues, the Court of Justice is invested with the competence to give Opinions only on the compatibility of proposed agreements. In an early Opinion the Court of Justice stated that the word "agreement" is used in this context:

> "in a general sense to indicate any undertaking entered into by entities subject to international law which has binding force, whatever its designation".[13]

Consequently the procedure prescribed by Article 300(6) was available in respect of an understanding negotiated within the Organization for Economic Co-operation and Development which would take effect as a resolution of that body. No less an authority than Christian Tomuschat has observed that the term "agreement" does not comfortably apply to one-sided declarations of States, and to decisions to participate in the votes of international organizations.[14] It is thought, however, that the construction placed on the term by the Court of Justice is compelled by the object of the provision: the avoidance of complications arising from inconsistent agreements, irrespective of their form. Moreover Article 300 of the EC Treaty applies generally "where this Treaty provides for the conclusion of agreements between the Community and one or more States or international organisations". Whereas the word "treaty" is defined for certain purposes to mean those concluded in written form,[15] the word "agreement" is wide enough to embrace undertakings expressed by the casting of votes in international organizations, where this binds the Community as a matter of law.[16]

12 Jean Charpentier, "Le contrôle par la Cour de justice de la conformité au traité des accords en vigeur conclus par la Communauté" in *Revue du Marché Commun* (1997) 409 at 419.

13 Opinion 1/75 of 11th November 1975, [1975] ECR 1355 at 1359-60.

14 Christian Tomuschat "Abkommen der Gemeinschaft" in H. von der Groeben et al, eds., *Kommentar zum EU-/EG Vertrag*, 5th ed. (Nomos, 1997) Vol. 5, page 515.

15 Convention on the Law of Treaties, Treaties, Vienna, 23rd May 1969, Cmnd. 7964, Article 1.

16 There probably is no good reason for denying in principle that a state may, in appropriate circumstances, undertake a binding obligation by consenting to a resolution of an international organisation. Ratification of a signed treaty is not the only way of assuming binding obligations in international law. In the *Advisory Opinion concerning Railway Traffic between Lithuania and Poland*, (1931) PCIJ Series A/B No 42, the PCIJ considered that a resolution of the Council of the League of Nations was in the nature of an engagement binding upon members: *Oppenheim's International Law*, by Sir Robert Jennings and Sir Arthur Watts, 9th edition, 1992 page 1208 note 5.

The conclusion of agreements by such votes may find its basis in the Community's implied powers[17] or in Article 302 (formerly 229), which authorises the Commission to maintain appropriate relations with international organizations including the United Nations. On the basis of the text of Article 300(6) it might be contended the jurisdiction to give Opinions is confined to agreements concluded under other paragraphs of the same Article: association agreements governed by the second paragraph; or trade policy treaties, mentioned in the third paragraph; or agreements concluded under other provisions of the EC Treaty which incorporate references to Article 300.[18] Such an interpretation would remove from the Court's special jurisdiction agreements concluded in the exercise of implied powers, or pursuant to Article 302. It is thought, however, that the opening words of the first paragraph of Article 300[19] and the broad language of the sixth paragraph suggest that the special procedure envisaged by the latter extends to all undertakings into which the Community may enter with entities subject to international law, having binding force.

It seems, furthermore, that the exceptional review procedure envisaged by Article 300(6) is available to resolve any uncertainty as to the compatibility with the EC Treaty of agreements concluded under the first, third, fourth and fifth paragraphs of Article 111 (formerly 109). The first paragraph establishes a special procedure, by way of derogation from Article 300, for determining arrangements and concluding formal agreements on an exchange-rate system for the ECU in relation to non-Community currencies. The third paragraph provides, by way of derogation from Article 300, that where agreements concerning monetary or foreign exchange regime matters need to be negotiated by the Community with one or more States or international organisations, the Council shall decide the arrangements for the negotiation and for the conclusion of such agreements. The fourth and fifth paragraphs read as follows:

> "4. Subject to paragraph 1, the Council shall, on a proposal from the Commission and after consulting the European Central Bank, acting by a qualified majority decide on the position of the Community at international level as regards issues of particular relevance

17 See for instance Case 22/70, *Commission v Council*, [1971] ECR 263.

18 The third paragraph of Article 133 provides that "The relevant provisions of Article 300 shall apply." The second paragraph of Article 170 (formerly 130m) reads "The detailed arrangements for such cooperation may be the subject of agreements between the Community and the third parties concerned, which shall be negotiated and concluded in accordance with Article 300." The fourth paragraph of Article 174 (formerly 130r) provides: "The arrangements for Community cooperation may be the subject of agreements between the Community and the third parties concerned, which shall be negotiated and concluded in accordance with Article 300." Article 181, first paragraph (formerly 130y) provides: "The arrangements for Community cooperation may be the subject of agreements between the Community and the third parties concerned, which shall be negotiated and concluded in accordance with Article 300."

19 "Where this Treaty provides for the conclusion of agreements between the Community and one or more States or international organisations..."

to economic and monetary union and, acting unanimously, decide its representation in compliance with the allocation of powers laid down in Articles 99 and 105.

5. Without prejudice to Community competence and Community agreements as regards economic and monetary union, Member States may negotiate in international bodies and conclude international agreements."

In the case of this Article, as in the case of Article 302, there is no reference to Article 300. Moreover, the agreements envisaged by Article 111 are of direct concern to the European Central Bank, which is denied any standing in the exceptional review procedure under Article 300; and certain of the arrangements envisaged by Article 111 are too ephemeral to amount to "agreements" at all.[20] Against that, it must be recalled that the arrangements, formal agreements and agreements envisaged by the first, third and fifth paragraphs are, at least in the ordinary case, binding. The decisions contemplated by the fourth paragraph may not in all cases amount to binding agreements; but where they do so the Court of Justice must have jurisdiction to determine their compatibility with the EC Treaty if it is to discharge its function of forestalling of complications at the international level.[21]

Since the jurisdiction of the Court of Justice appears to depend on the binding nature of the agreement to be concluded,[22] it may be inferred that the Court has no jurisdiction under Article 300(6) to rule on the compatibility with the EC Treaty of any declaration, resolution, communiqué or other instrument of "soft law" not having obligatory effect. Such documents have in recent years proliferated; and their "legal" characters are very varied.[23] Between the political declarations made jointly by the Community and certain third States to cement their cordial relations and the carefully-crafted multilateral instruments published at the conclusion of an international conference on such matters as environmental standards lies a wide spectrum. It appears unwise to offer a single simple test for distinguishing between those that are in some sense binding and those that are not; but it is suggested that an instrument may be binding for the purposes of Article 300(6) although it would not be justiciable before an international tribunal in the event of a dispute between those engaging in it.

20 This is the case, for instance, with the "general orientations" envisaged in the second paragraph. The Council is authorised to formulate such orientations in relation to one or more non-Community currencies, in the absence of an exchange-rate system in relation to these currencies.

21 C. Zilioli and M. Selmayr, "The External Relations of the Euro Area: Legal Aspects", 36 CMLRev 273 at 346.

22 Opinion 1/75 of 11th November 1975, [1975] ECR 1355 at 1360-1361.

23 On the subject see R. Baxter, "International Law in Her Infinite Variety", 29 ICLQ (1980) 549; H. Seidl-Hohenveldern, "International Economic Soft Law", 163 Hague Recueil (1980) 164; C.M. Chinkin, "The Challenge of Soft Law: Development and Change in International Law", 38 I.C.L.Q. (1989) 850.

COMPATIBILITY

Article 300(6) of the EC Treaty appears to owe its origin to Article 54 of the French Constitution which, following its amendment in 1992,[24] reads as follows:

> "*si le Conseil constitutionnel, saisi par le Président de la République, par le Premier ministre ou par le Président de l'une ou l'autre assemblée ou par soixante députés ou soixante sénateurs, a déclaré qu'un engagement international comporte une clause contraire à la Constitution, l'autorisation de ratifier ou d'approver l'engagement international en cause ne peut intervenir qu'après la révision de la Constitution.*"

That Article must be read in its context.

Article 52 of the Constitution confers on the executive broad powers to negotiate, draft and ratify international agreements. Article 53 provides that treaties on certain matters must be ratified by Parliament. The decision as to whether to submit a treaty to Parliament for ratification is ultimately made by the executive (the Minister of External Relations and the Government General Secretary) although the *Conseil d'État* may express an opinion on the matter.[25] The sanction for a wrongful failure to refer the treaty to Parliament for ratification is not legal but political.[26] Legally the failure to refer is considered as a formal defect in the adoption of the treaty whereas the majority view holds that Article 54 applies only to material defects. That view is based on the wording of the Article which invests the Constitutional Council with the function of determining whether the treaty "*comporte une clause contraire à la Constitution*".[27]

The origin of Article 300(6) of the EC Treaty explains the existence, at one time, of the view that the draftsman, when entrusting the Court of Justice with the task of determining "whether an agreement ... is compatible with ... this Treaty", did not mean to authorise it to determine whether the Community institutions had acted in excess of their powers when entering into that agreement. The view was endorsed by the French Republic in the late 1970s, notwithstanding the emphatic affirmation of the Court of Justice itself that:

---

24 The amendment of 1992 adapted the language of the Article to reflect a 1974 decision of the Constitutional Council extending to Parliament the right to make a request thereunder.

25 J. Dhommeaux, "Le rôle du parlement dans l'élaboration des engagements internationaux", 103 *Revue du droit public et de la science politique en France et à l'étranger* (1987) 1448 at 1454-5 note 28.

26 Christopher Pollman, "La révision de l'article 54 de la Constitution: nouvelle avancée de la juridicité, nouvel échec de l'instrumentalisme juridique", 110 *Revue du droit public et de la science politique en France et à l'étranger* (1994) 1079 at 1100.

27 Pollman, *supra* at note 26 at 1094, emphasis added.

> "The compatibility of an agreement with the provisions of the Treaty must be assessed in the light of all the rules of the Treaty, that is to say, both those rules that determine the extent of the powers of the institutions of the Community and the substantive powers".[28]

In the procedure leading to Opinion 1/78 the French Republic challenged the proposition that the Court's relevant jurisdiction extended to an enquiry into the competence of the Community institutions to conclude the agreement in question. The Court of Justice again rejected that argument, stating that:

> "a judgment on the compatibility of an agreement with the Treaty may depend not only on provisions of substantive law but also on those concerning the powers, procedure or organisation of the institutions of the Community".[29]

Article 107 paragraph 2 of the Rules of Procedure of the Court of Justice appears to have been designed to express a view of the jurisdiction of the Court of Justice consistent with the conclusion expressed by the Court itself. It provides that:

> "The Opinion may deal not only with the question whether the envisaged agreement is compatible with the provisions of the EC Treaty but also with the question whether the Community or any Community institution has the power to enter into that agreement".

The wording suggests, however, that the question whether the envisaged agreement is compatible with the provisions of the EC Treaty is distinct from the question whether the Community or any Community institution has the power to enter into that agreement. The phraseology is unfortunate, for by using the formula "not only ...but also", the draftsman implies that the latter is not embraced within the former.[30]

Were the Court's interpretation based on the procedural provision alone, the latter might be subject to challenge on the ground that although contained in Rules of Procedure, it is a provision of a substantive, jurisdictional, character. In fact, the position of the Court of Justice finds independent support. It applies a natural and unrestricted meaning to the word "compatible", consistent with the object of forestalling complications which would arise, should the Community conclude an agreement inconsistent with the founding treaty. The method and result are consistent with the approach to interpretation of Community texts described by Lord Slynn as predominant.[31]

It is consistent also with practicality; for the problem to the alleviation of which Article 300(6) is directed arises most frequently where external legal ob-

---

28 Opinion 1/75 of 11th November 1975, [1975] ECR 1355 at 1360.

29 Opinion 1/78 of 4th October 1979, [1979] ECR 2871 at 2907-8.

30 Jean Boulouis, "Les avis de le Cour de Justice des Communautés sur la compatibilité avec le traité CEE du projet d'accord créant l'espace économique européen", 22 *Revue trimestrielle de droit européen* 457.

31 See Lord Slynn, "They Call it Teleological" in [1994] *Denning L.J.* 225 and "Looking at European Law Texts", 14 *Statute Law Rev* (1993) 12 at 16.

ligations are inconsistent with the Community's internal order. Save in the exceptional case where the invalidity of a treaty arises from a defect in the capacity of the plenipotentiary, or in his coercion, the absence of authority to conclude a treaty results from a violation of the internal rules of a party.[32] It is frequently the opacity of the Community's internal rules rather than ambiguity in the text of the agreement negotiated that calls for clarification by the Court of Justice.

It follows from the same premises that the procedure prescribed by Article 300(6) should be available to clarify the extent of the Member States' obligations arising under Article 10 (formerly 5) of the EC Treaty in relation to any "agreement envisaged". The compatibility of an agreement with the EC Treaty might well depend upon the ascertainment of the obligations of the Member States to cooperate in respect of its application. Indeed, the viability of the agreement itself might do so. The Community's institutions and their negotiating parties may thus have a vital interest in ascertaining the extent of the obligations of the Member States in respect of the agreement. There seems to be no good reason to deny them the guidance of the Court of Justice on such an question.[33]

It appears possible to go further, in view of Opinion 2/91 on the Standards Agreement of the International Labour Organisation. There the agreement in question concerned Member States' dealings with third parties: it did not concern the Community directly, since it was not a member of the Organisation. The underlying question in the request was ascertainment of the respective competence of the Community and the Member States in respect of the agreement. In assuming jurisdiction in that case the Court of Justice went further, perhaps, than it did in Case 12/86, *Demirel v Stadt Schwäbisch Gmünd*[34] where it considered itself competent to respond to questions posed by way of reference for preliminary ruling on an association agreement between the Community and Turkey. In the *Demirel* case there was a framework agreement to which the Community was a party. That was not the case with Opinion 2/91. The latter supports the view that the power of the Court of Justice to determine whether an agreement envisaged is compatible with the provisions of this Treaty is not confined to cases where the Community is to be a party to the agreement. At the request, properly made, of the Council, the Commission or a Member State, the Court of Justice may give an Opinion on an envisaged agreement wherever its entry into force consistently with the EC Treaty depends on its compatibility with the latter.

---

32 Convention on the Law of Treaties, Vienna, 23rd May 1969, Cmnd. 7964, Article 46.

33 Kovar, "La compétence de la Cour de Justice et la procédure de conclusion des accords internationaux par la Communauté economique européenne" in *Mélanges P. Reuter – Le droit international: unité et diversité (1981) 357 at 366.*

34 [1995] ECR I-521 at 553; [1987] ECR 3719.

OBLIGATION TO REQUEST AN OPINION?

By use of the permissive verb "may", Article 300(6) confers on the Council, the Commission and the Member States a discretion as to whether to request an Opinion. The possibility cannot be excluded, however, that the Commission may under certain circumstances be under an obligation to do so.[35] The case for inferring that the Commission may have such an obligation rests on the fact that the Treaty itself imposes on the Commission the obligation, marked by the mandatory verb "shall" to ensure that the provisions of this Treaty and the measures taken by the institutions pursuant thereto are applied.[36] It would fail in this duty if it were to participate in the negotiation of an agreement the application of which was liable to lead to a breach of those provisions. Hitherto, the prospect of being called upon, by another of the Community's institutions, to refer a question to the Court has been rather remote; but it has ceased to be hypothetical, now that an important function in the negotiation of certain international agreements has been conferred on the European Central Bank.

SUSPENSIVE EFFECT OF A REQUEST UNDER ARTICLE 300(6)

Once the Council, the Commission or a Member State has requested the Court of Justice to give an Opinion under Article 300(6) of the EC Treaty, considerations of comity may cause them to refrain from concluding the international obligation in question.[37] Those considerations will not always lead to that result.

No article of the EC Treaty establishes clearly that the institutions and the Member States are bound to refrain from concluding an international agreement pending the delivery of an Opinion which has been requested pursuant to Article 300(6). There is however a case for maintaining that in the case of Member States, such an obligation is an aspect of their duty to abstain from any measure which could jeopardise the attainment of the Treaty's objectives. In the case of the Commission, it might be said to have failed in its duty to ensure that the provisions of the Treaty are applied when it participates in the conclusion of an incompatible engagement.

In particular a Member State might well fail in its duty of loyal cooperation if it were to proceed unilaterally to the conclusion of an agreement while the Court of Justice was seised of a request for an Opinion as to its compatibility with the EC Treaty. It must not be assumed, however, that all the Member States collectively, and the appropriate Community institutions, must be taken to have

---

35 See V. Christianos, "La compétence consultative de la Cour de justice à la lumière du traité sur l'Union européenne", 37 *Revue du marché commun et de l'Union européenne* (1994) 37.

36 Article 211.

37 I. Macleod, I. D. Hendry, and S. Hyett, *The External Relations of the European Communities* (Clarendon, 1995) at 113.

relinquished *pro tempore* their relevant treaty-making powers, once they have referred the matter to the Court. Exceptional cases may arise in which it is necessary to proceed with dispatch and to resolve any complication at a later stage any complication. *Ex hypothesi* the agreement may prove to be compatible with the EC Treaty; and even if it proves incompatible with it, the objectives of the latter treaty may be preserved and pursued following its amendment.

The view that Member States and Community institutions are not deprived of their treaty-making powers, once they have seised the Court of Justice, derives support from Opinion 3/94 of 13th December 1995 *Framework Agreement on Bananas.*[38] In that case the Court made clear that where the agreement is concluded before the Opinion is issued the Court no longer has jurisdiction under Article 300(6). It is not easy to see how such jurisdiction could be excluded if the making of the request led *ipso facto* to an obligation to refrain from further conclusion of the agreement.

It is therefore of some importance to determine whether the Court of Justice may itself require the Community institutions or the Member States to refrain from taking further steps to conclude an international agreement, once it is seised of a request for an Opinion. It is thought that the Court cannot do so on the basis of Article 242 of the EC Treaty. This provides as follows:

> "[a]ctions brought before the Court of Justice shall not have any suspensory effect. The Court of Justice may, however, if it considers that circumstances so require, order that application of the contested act be suspended".[39]

The word "act", when used in this context, is apt to cover a measure authorising the conduct of international negotiations such a decision made by the Council under Article 300 authorising the Commission to open the necessary negotiations with one or more States or international organisations. Such an act cannot, however, be said to be "contested" merely because an Opinion is requested under Article 300(6).

Support for that last view is to be found in Article 83, paragraph 1 of the Rules of Procedure of the Court of Justice. This requires that applications to obtain suspension of a measure under Article 242 of the EC Treaty are "admissible only if the applicant is challenging that measure in proceedings before the Court". The term "challenging" does not seem to contemplate proceedings of the nature of Article 300(6).

Different considerations apply to the powers of the Court of Justice under Article 243 of the EC Treaty. This provides simply that:

> "The Court of Justice may in any cases before it prescribe any necessary interim measures."

---

38 [1995] ECR I-4577.

39 Article 36 of the Statute of the European Court establishes the appropriate procedure for applications under Article 242 of the EC Treaty.

The breadth of the language requires little emphasis. The Court of Justice is sparing in the exercise of its power to prescribe interim measures.[40] It may be safely assumed that the use of those powers would be rare in any case involving a restraint on the conduct of international negotiations; but it is thought that where the special circumstances of the case merit it, the power is available.

Le Principe du Contradictoire

The procedure under Article 228(6) represents a marked departure from the *principe du contradictoire.*[41] In deference to the objective of securing a speedy determination of the issue presented to the Court of Justice,[42] the procedural safeguards which would apply in contentious litigation are modified. Although in practice the interested parties are permitted to make oral submissions, they have a lesser degree of control over what comes to the attention of the Court of Justice. It required an amendment to the Rules of Procedure, on 11th March 1997, to provide that the European Parliament shall be served with any request for an Opinion under Article 228(6).[43] Those served may make written submissions within a time-frame which the President is entitled to set, so as to respond as appropriate to the exigencies of the particular treaty negotiations. There is no express requirement for oral submissions nor even an express entitlement to comment on or even see the submissions of the other parties. The Court of Justice convenes in closed session. The Advocates General are heard[44] but on the premise that this is in closed session, their views are not published with the Opinion of the Court. Indeed, Article 56, paragraph 2 of the Rules of Procedure of the Court of Justice provides "[t]he oral proceedings in cases heard *in camera* shall not be published". The decision is then made in the usual manner.[45] It is conveyed to the parties who were served with the request as well as to the requesting party.[46]

---

40 See Christine Gray, "Interim Measures of Protection in the European Court", [1979] *European Law Rev.* 80 at 81.

41 In *Gate, Dubosc et autres, Perrimond et autres*, 16th January 1976, Recueil pp. 39 *et seq.* the *Conseil d'État* treated the *principe du contradictoire* as a general principle of law in civil proceedings It mandated proceedings, "*dans le respect des principes généraux du droit, notamment de celui selon lequel la procédure doit revêtir un caractère contradictoire*".

42 The Court of Justice can assume jurisdiction under Article 300(6) of the EC Treaty even before a final text of an envisaged agreement is agreed, as it did in Opinion 1/78 of 4th October 1979, [1979] ECR 2871.

43 O.J. L103/1. Note, however, that in Opinion 1/94 of 15th November 1994, [1996] ECR I-1195, the European Parliament, at its request, was permitted to submit observations.

44 Rules of Procedure of the Court of Justice, Article 108, paragraph 2.

45 Article 27 of the Rules of Procedure of the Court of Justice applies here in the manner of a *lex generalis*.

46 Rules of Procedure of the Court of Justice, Article 108, paragraph 3. This includes the European Parliament under the amendment of 11th March 1997.

The Court of Justice has on at least two occasions emphasised that proceedings under Article 300(6) are non-contentious in nature.[47] Its comment appears to have been provoked by the consideration that in French administrative law, the *principe du contradictoire* has not traditionally been applied in *la procédure non contentieuse* on the ground that such application would hamper administrative action.[48] This is a feature that sets the French principle apart from its counterpart in English administrative law, for the principle *audi alteram partem* is of universal application.[49] The distinction that the Court of Justice draws between contentious and non-contentious proceedings does not correspond, however, with the similar distinction in English law.[50] Nor does it correspond with the distinction between contentious and non-contentious proceedings drawn in French administrative law, where the former are characterised by parties asserting rights on equal terms before the law and justice, and the latter feature a party in "a defensive posture", meaning cases where that party's opponent is the State. In French law the traditional position is that there is no right to the protection of the *principe du contradictoire*, but rather to *droits de la défense* which are delimited by that which is necessary to mount the defence.[51]

Plainly the procedure under Article 300(6) is non-contentious in the literal sense that there is not an action or *lis* between two opposing parties. Equally plainly, the exercise of the jurisdiction of the Court of Justice under that Article may be, and commonly is, a means of resolving differences between those interested in the conclusion of the international agreement. It may indeed resolve an acute dispute of a constitutional nature. In the words of Dr Ehlermann:

> "Article 228 [now Article 300] certainly offers a less conflictual procedure than Articles 169 [now Article 226] or 173 [now Article 230] of the EEC Treaty. But if it is used in order to recognize exclusive Community competence, it is nevertheless considered as an instrument of coercion in a struggle for power".[52]

47 Opinion 1/75 of 11th November 1975, [1975] ECR 1355 at 1361; Opinion 2/92 of 24th March 1995, [1995] ECR I-521.

48 See Hocine Zeghbib, "Principe du contradictoire et procédure administrative non contentieuse" in (1998) *Revue du droit public et de la science politique en France et à l'étranger* 467 at 469.

49 *Painter v. Liverpool Oil Gas Light Co.* (1836) 3 A & E 433 at 448-449: "a party is not to suffer in person or in purse without an opportunity of being heard". The principle was generalised in *Cooper v. Wandsworth Board of Works*, (1863) 14 C.B. (N.S.) 180 at 194 where it was stated to be "of universal application and founded on the plainest principles of justice".

50 In English law the distinction is found in the law of probate where non-contentious proceedings pursuant to the Supreme Court Act, 1981, section 128, are those where there is no dispute between parties.

51 See Zeghbib, *supra*, note 48, who points out that no core discrepancy in procedures results.

52 C.-D. Ehlerman, "Mixed Agreements: A List of Problems" in *Mixed Agreements*, D. O'Keeffe and H. G. Schermers, eds., *supra*, note 9, (Kluwer, 1983) at 7.

This being the case, some writers have raised the question whether an Opinion given under that provision is only interlocutory in nature, and subject to revision upon an application under Article 226 of the EC Treaty, or Article 227, or Article 230.[53]

If the Court of Justice is to be faithful to the purpose of Article 300(6) of the EC Treaty, it should regard an Opinion given thereunder as dispositive of any difference that may arise, on an identical question, between parties to contentious litigation, in the same way and to the same extent as a preliminary ruling under Article 234 of the Treaty would dispose of an issue arising in subsequent contentious litigation. The Court would not forestall or avoid complications arising, particularly at the international level, if it were to review in the course of contentious litigation a decision reached under Article 300(6) and to treat the latter as merely interlocutory.

Examination of the text of Article 300(6) of the EC Treaty supports this conclusion. Before the Treaty on European Union, this provided that the Council, the Commission or a Member State "may obtain beforehand the opinion of the Court of Justice". Although the word "beforehand" has now been removed, the remaining text makes it perfectly clear that the Opinion of the Court of Justice is to be anterior to the conclusion of the agreement. The latter is still characterised as "an agreement envisaged". It is the giving of the favourable Opinion that establishes the compatibility of the agreement with the EC Treaty and declares, in the interests of the parties but *erga omnes* that the agreement is not to be impugned on the ground of its incompatibility with that text. For this reason the Court of Justice takes the view that its jurisdiction under that Article terminates once an agreement has been concluded. In Opinion 1/94 of 15th November 1994 it stated:

> "the Court may be called upon to state its opinion pursuant to Article 300(6) of the Treaty at any time *before the Community's consent to be bound by the agreement is finally expressed*".

In the same Opinion it stated that:

> "in the specific case of Article 228 [now Article 300] the opinion given by the Court of Justice has the *binding effect* stipulated in that Article".[54]

Although the strict English law doctrine of *stare decisis* does not bind the Court of Justice, and its pronouncements have what Mr Advocate General Lagrange

53 Charpentier, *supra*, note 12, at 416; Catalano, *Manuel du droit des Communautés européennes* (Paris, 1973) at 73; Radicati di Bròzolo, "La Funzione consultiva della Corte di Giustizia in materia di relazioni esterne" 62 *Rivista di Diritto Internazionale* (1976) 116.

54 Opinion 1/91 of 14th December 1991, [1991] ECR I-6079, emphasis added.

called a "moral force",[55] they carry that force when they take the form of Opinions no less than when they are judgments in the formal sense.

It is of course the case that where the Opinion of the Court of Justice is not obtained in advance, a litigant may raise in contentious proceedings the compatibility with the EC Treaty of an act whereby the Community institutions approve ratification of an international treaty.[56] Where on the other hand the Court of Justice has given its Opinion on the compatibility of the agreement with the EC Treaty, it has discharged the precise function that it might otherwise be asked to discharge in contentious proceedings.[57]

It is possible to arrive at the same result by pursuing the analogy with Article 54 of the French Constitution. As Professor Charpentier has observed:[58]

> "dans le système français, la déclaration de conformité à la Constitution d'un traite examiné par le Conseil interdit toute mise en cause ultérieure, par voie d'exception, de la validité constitutionnelle dudit traité: et surtout, tout traité qui n'a pas été soumis au contrôle du Conseil avant son entrée en vigueur bénéficie d'une présomption irréfragable de validité constitutionnelle [...]".

SOME SUGGESTIONS FOR PROCEDURAL CHANGES

If that is right, it is all the more important that any departure from the *principe du contradictoire* should be the minimum necessary in the interests of speed and confidentiality. It is not easy to see why the pursuit of those interests makes it necessary to refrain from making public the Opinions of Advocates General in the procedure under Article 300(6). In such procedures, more perhaps than in any others, Advocates General perform a role comparable with that of the *commissaire du gouvernement* to whom there is entrusted the vital function of ensuring that the *Conseil d'État* shall take into account the proper concerns of those who have an interest in the outcome but are not parties to the litigation. As Mr Advocate General Reischl put it:[59]

> "I conceive of my office, however, as being to stand up for a European legal order and to support the Court of Justice in its continuing to build up a solid European legal order. I

55 Cases 28 to 30/62 *Da Costa v. Nederlandse Belastingadministratie,* [1963] ECR 31 at 41-43.

56 See Cases 165/87, *Commission v. Council*, [1988] ECR 5545, and C-327/91, *France v. Commission*, [1994] I ECR 3641. See also Opinion 3/94 of 13th December 1995 *Framework Agreement on Bananas*, [1995] ECR I-4577, paragraph 2.

57 It is suggested at vol. 5, p. 517 of von der Groeben *et al.*, eds., *supra*, note 14, that the Court of Justice was mindful of the fact that its supervisory powers under Article 230 of the EC Treaty should not be subject to no-go areas.

58 Charpentier, *supra*, note 12, at 416.

59 "Die Funktion der Generalanwälte in der Europäischen Rechtsprechung" in *Der Europäische Gerichtshof als Verfassungsgericht und Rechtsschutzinstanz* (Nomos, 1984) at 123-124.

am able to do so in complete independence as I am subject to no one's direction. Accordingly, for me in the foreground there stands the principle '*in dubio pro Europa*'".

Since the collegiate Opinion of a Court of Justice must be the subject of consensus or compromise, it will seldom be as comprehensive as that of an Advocate General. Publication of the views of the latter may therefore clarify the issues before the Court of Justice and may provide for the Member States and other interested parties the assurance that their concerns have been taken to consideration.

There may, indeed, be something to be said for going further. Since international agreements may vitally affect the rights of persons other than the Council, the Commission and Member States, is there not a case to be made in favour of enlarging the category of persons capable of requesting Opinions under Article 300(6)? The European Parliament and the European Central Bank may have good reason to seek clarification from the Court of Justice: particularly in the case of the latter of these institutions.[60] In exceptional cases, there may even by other natural or legal persons who are directly and individually concerned be an agreement envisaged. If an Opinion given under Article 300(6) of the EC Treaty is truly to be determinative of issues that may affect such persons, they ought not to be denied an opportunity of seising the Court of their concerns, on the grounds of convenience.

It is obvious that practical difficulties would arise if the conclusion of international agreements could be delayed, and the negotiating process made public, by the institution of litigation by private parties. Such is the stringency, however, of the test of direct and individual concern[61] that those difficulties can easily be overstated. Prospective applicants, not expressly designated in Article 300(6), would have to demonstrate their sufficient interest *in limine*; and the problems of confidentiality arising from this suggestion do not appear insuperable.

CONCLUSION

The identification of the object of Article 300(6) of the EC Treaty is the first step, and frequently the guide, to resolution of the difficulties that arise in its application. It was on the premise that the object of the provision is to avoid complication at the international level that the Court of Justice deduced that its

60 The clear distinction between standing under Article 230 of the EC Treaty and that under Article 300(6) of the EC Treaty is that in the first even parties without privileged standing are expressly mentioned. Nonetheless, there is a precedent where standing was broadened beyond the scope of a text, in that case, Article 230, which before Maastricht did not refer to the European Parliament. See Case 302/87, *European Parliament v. Council*, [1987] ECR 5615.

61 See T. Hartley, *The Foundations of European Community Law*, 4th ed. (Oxford, 1998) at 355 *et seq*.

Opinions must have "binding effect".[62] It appears to follow from the same premise, and from other considerations mentioned in this essay, that the Court's jurisdiction under Article 300(6) is not limited to cases involving treaties, in the sense of Article 1 of the Vienna Convention of 1969, nor even to agreements to be concluded pursuant to other provisions of Article 300. When construing the word "compatibility", as it appears in Article 300(6), Article 54 of the French Constitution proves a *faux ami*. The incompatibility of an agreement with the EC Treaty may arise from its procedural provisions; or from inconsistency between the EC Treaty and the obligations under the agreement of the Member States, not the Community. While the making of a request for an Opinion does not have suspensive effects, it may be open to the Court to invoke, in appropriate cases, its powers under Article 243 of the EC Treaty. Plainly, the *principe du contradictoire* does not apply in cases under Article 300(6); but it appears desirable to limit to the maximum any departures from that principle. On any view, the incidental problems that arise in defining the Court's jurisdiction and procedure under Article 300(6) are at least as challenging as any of the substantive questions that the Court has had to address when exercising its competence thereunder. Those addressing these incidental problems will, however, find some guidance in the case-law of the Court of Justice, to which Gordon Slynn made such an outstanding contribution.

62 Opinion 1/91 of 14th December 1991, [1991] ECR I-6079.

16

STAFF CASES IN THE JUDICIAL ARCHITECTURE OF THE FUTURE

*Timothy Millett**

THE PROBLEM OF STAFF CASES

"Staff cases" is the name for "any dispute between the Community and its servants" over which the Court of Justice and the Court of First Instance have jurisdiction under Article 236(ex Article 179) of the EC Treaty and Article 152 of the Euratom Treaty (the ECSC Treaty contains no express provision in this regard). The limits and conditions of that jurisdiction are laid down in Articles 90 and 91 of the Staff Regulations of Officials, which are applied by analogy to other categories of employees by the Conditions of Employment of Other Servants.

Staff cases thus have a legal basis of their own, distinct from all other categories of case heard by the two Community Courts. Along with cases concerning Community contracts containing an arbitration clause under Article 238 (ex Article 181) of the EC Treaty, staff cases are distinguished from other categories of litigation before the two courts by the fact that they do not concern the law on European integration. Thus, in principle, it can be said that they do not have to be dealt with in the same way as the categories of litigation relating to the law on integration.

Staff cases were dealt with by the Court of Justice alone until 1989, when the Court of First Instance was established and took over jurisdiction in those cases at first instance. Staff cases always represented a substantial proportion of the case load of the Court of Justice, although the exact number of cases brought varied each year. In the 1980s staff cases represented on average about one-fifth of the cases brought before the Court of Justice. They represent an even larger proportion of the cases brought before the Court of First Instance. In the early days they represented more than half the cases brought (from 1989 to 1992). As the jurisdiction of the Court of First Instance has been successively extended this proportion has fallen slightly, and in 1998 staff cases represented one-third of the cases brought before the Court of First Instance (79 out of 238). This is still a substantial proportion of that Court's case load. It should be added that the establishment of the Court of First Instance has not relieved the Court of Justice of

* Opinions expressed are personal to the author and do not engage the European Parliament.

D. O'Keeffe (ed.), Liber Amicorum Slynn 221-231 (2000)

all contact with staff cases as appeals lie to it on points of law. Out of 36 appeals dealt with by the Court in 1998, one-third (12) were staff cases.

Now, however, the Court of First Instance faces a growing load of cases of other types and is beginning to receive the first cases in the field of intellectual property, which are expected to become very numerous. The number of cases pending at the year end before the Court of First Instance is tending to grow (569 pending at the end of 1998) and the length of time taken to dispose of cases is tending to grow as well: in 1998 staff cases were taking 16.7 months on average and other types of cases 20 months. Such a duration may be thought unhealthy in disputes concerning the lives of individuals, where a quick decision is desirable, particularly in cases of a disciplinary character. Not only would a quick decision release the individual from the anxiety of litigation but it would also enable the defendant institution to resolve a situation which has been held in suspense and which may get worse the longer it continues.

In this connection, the advocate pleading a staff case before the Court of First Instance may be struck by the abundance of judicial manpower expended on such cases. Staff cases have usually been dealt with by a chamber of three judges, so that the advocate finds himself before three of Europe's leading administrative or commercial judges. In addition, the Court of First Instance seldom confines itself to rigorous time limits, and in many staff cases the hearing often spreads to an entire half-day.

Yet, these cases concern labour law issues which may be of limited significance. They might typically concern a dispute about grading or the amount of an allowance paid in addition to the basic salary. Even where a case concerns a more important question such as a disciplinary sanction or an appointment, the scope of such cases rarely goes beyond the employment position of the individual concerned. It is sometimes said that general principles of law may be developed in staff cases. Exceptionally this may be so, as in the case of *Razzouk* and *Beydoun v Commission*[1] (in which, incidentally, the Advocate General was Sir Gordon Slynn as he then was) which established the principle that widowers of female officials were as much entitled to a pension as were widows of male officials, notwithstanding the wording of the Staff Regulations. Similar questions of principle may come up from time to time in staff cases as, for example, in the matter of household allowances payable (or not) to same-sex cohabitees.[2] Again staff cases may give an opportunity to explore other human rights issues such as freedom of expression.[3] However, it is submitted that staff cases much more frequently contain mere applications of well-established principles (such as the duty to state reasons or respect legitimate expectations) than serve as a test bed

1 Joined Cases 75 and 117/82 [1984] ECR 1509.

2 Judgment of the Court of First Instance of 28 January 1999 in Case T-264/97 *D v. Council*; on appeal to the Court of Justice in pending cases C-122/99 P and C-125/99 P.

3 E.g. Article 10 of the European Convention on Human Rights discussed in the judgment of the Court of First Instance of 19 May 1999 in Joined Cases T-34/96 and T-163/96 *Connolly v. Commission*, paragraphs 148-156.

to develop new principles. In this author's submission, staff cases seldom raise issues of general impact and, as mentioned above, do not directly concern the general law of European integration. The question therefore arises whether it is the best use of scarce judicial resources to engage three highly-qualified judges in long hearings on such disputes.

This is not to say that staff cases are necessarily easy. On the contrary, this field of law contains complex rules, some of them made harder by poor drafting, for example in areas such as sickness insurance where there is an interface with national arrangements and where it is difficult to keep the rules both up to date and internally consistent. There is also abundant case law which often contains qualifications of principle or even contradictions.[4] The rules are also quite specific: a recruitment procedure or a promotion procedure, and a fortiori a disciplinary procedure or an invalidity procedure, each comprise a number of steps, practical knowledge of which is most useful to grasp the issues raised.

THE SINGLE JUDGE AND THE COURT OF FIRST INSTANCE

In the context of these issues, the Council, at the request of the two Community courts, recently decided to enable the Court of First Instance to have decisions given by a single judge. By Decision 1999/291/EC, ECSC, Euratom of 26 April 1999[5] the Council amended Article 2(4) of the decision establishing the Court of First Instance[6] so as to read:

> *"The Court of First Instance shall sit in chambers of three or five judges. The composition of the chambers and the assignment of cases to them shall be governed by the Rules of Procedure. In certain cases governed by the Rules of Procedure the Court of First Instance may sit in plenary session* or be constituted by a single judge*"*.[7]

This decision entered into force on 16 May 1999.[8] The Rules of Procedure of the Court of First Instance were then amended to specify the way that it would operate in practice.[9] The new rule applies to staff cases along with certain other categories of cases, which can be heard by a single judge of the Court of First Instance where neither the legal or factual difficulty of the cases nor their importance nor any special circumstance justify them being heard by a chamber of three judges.[10] Such cases will initially be attributed to a three-judge chamber

4 For instance the judgments in *Michel v. Commission*, Case 273/83 [1985] ECR 347 and in case *Samara v. Commission*, Case 266/83 [1985] ECR 189.
5 OJ 1 May 1999 L 144, p.52.
6 Council Decision of 24 October 1988 88/591/ECSC, EEC, Euratom; OJ 25 November 1988 L 319, p.1.
7 Emphasis added by the author.
8 Decision 1999/291, Article 2.
9 Amendments to the Rules of Procedure 17 May 1999; OJ 29 May 1999, L 135, p.92.
10 Rules of Procedure of the CFI, Article 14(2), as amended.

and to a reporting judge; then the chamber will decide unanimously whether to delegate the case to the reporting judge alone after hearing representations from the parties.[11] These amendments came into force on 1 July 1999,[12] which brought the system into operation.

The use of this system in staff cases will, it may be hoped, have clear benefits. First, it will release the two non-reporting judges to proceed with other work. In other terms, the judicial manpower involved in such cases will be more proportionate to the object at stake. Secondly, it may speed up the procedure. In that case both the defendant institution and the official concerned would benefit from the quicker resolution of these cases. The official would be relieved earlier from the anxiety of litigation, and the institution would be enabled to resolve suspended situations more promptly. This would be particularly helpful in cases such as recruitment and disciplinary matters.

On the other hand, it is submitted that the rule for a case to be examined by a chamber and then delegated to a single judge comprises certain disadvantages. It means that the cases will wait for a substantial period as at present while the chamber finds the time for all its members to deal with that first decision. For reasons of efficiency it may be thought that the rule should be the reverse: i.e. that every staff case should in principle be attributed to a single judge who could, if he considered the matter so required, refer the case up to a chamber. Such an arrangement would allow the preliminary sift to be done more quickly.

It is not expected that the use of a single judge in staff cases will completely solve the problems confronting the Court of First Instance. The potential saving of judicial time is estimated at some 10%, and the measure is plainly regarded as an intermediate step pending deeper reforms.[13] Accordingly, it is proposed now to survey some other ways in which the treatment of staff cases might be improved, beyond the use of a single judge.

The institution of the single judge could be doubly beneficial if it were linked to specialisation by subject. It may be supposed that staff cases could be dealt with more effectively if those dealing with them worked regularly in that field of law. This could be done, perhaps on a rota basis, either judge by judge or chamber by chamber. Thus staff cases might be allocated only to certain chambers within which the judges could sit as single judges. Alternatively, certain judges could be designated as single judges for staff cases regardless of which chamber they were attached to. In any event, a certain stability would be

11 Rules of Procedure of the CFI, Article 51(2), as amended.

12 Amendments of 17 May 1999, Article 2.

13 Cf. House of Lords Select Committee on the European Communities "The Court of First Instance: Single Judge", 25th Report of Session 1997-1998, in particular paragraphs 85 and 95. See also Recital 2 of Council Decision 1999/291: "To enable the Court of First Instance to cope with this increased workload, it is necessary, before contemplating any increase in the number of the Members of the Court of First Instance, to exhaust all the possibilities of improving the working efficiency of the Court of First Instance as composed at present".

essential over a period of time in order to obtain the benefit of specialisation. This would entail some adjustment to the present practice of the Court of First Instance. Nevertheless, the principle of specialisation by chamber has now been accepted by the Court of First Instance for intellectual property cases (which are initially attributed to only two of its chambers[14]), and it could be extended to staff cases.

A Separate Staff Tribunal

An alternative to specialisation within the Court of First Instance would be to set up a separate staff tribunal to deal exclusively with staff cases. It is noteworthy that several of the experts who gave evidence to the House of Lords Select Committee about the single judge also recommended in the longer term the creation of a separate staff tribunal.[15] This idea is not new. Suggestions for the establishment of a tribunal to take over the jurisdiction in staff cases at first instance date back at least to the early 1970s. The Council agreed on its desirability in 1974 and again in 1978,[16] following which the Commission in 1978 submitted a proposal to the Council for the establishment of an administrative tribunal to deal with staff cases.[17] The jurisdiction arises under Article 236 (ex Article 179) of the EC Treaty and the Staff Regulations. The Commission proposed that such a tribunal could be set up by amending the Staff Regulations, without necessitating the amendment of the Treaty. However, it was not adopted, owing to opposition from France and Ireland, who considered that the establishment of such a tribunal required the amendment of the Treaty.[18] In the end, power to set up a court dealing with staff cases along with other categories of case was included in the Single European Act in 1986 and given concrete form in the decision establishing the Court of First Instance of 1988.[19] In a sense the wheel has now come full circle in that attention is again turned to the establishment of a staff tribunal, this time not to relieve the Court of Justice but to relieve the Court of First Instance of part of its work load.

It is assumed that such a tribunal would not be added on below the Court of First Instance, with appeal lying to that court and then the Court of Justice. Such an appeal structure may be considered excessive, might not sufficiently relieve the work-load of the Court of First Instance and would lengthen rather than

14 See OJ 24 October 1998, C 327, p.17.

15 See the House of Lords Report on the Single Judge, cited above, paragraphs 80-83.

16 See House of Lords Select Committee on the European Communities, "Staff Administrative Tribunal" 17th Report of the Session 1978-1979, paragraph 3.

17 OJ 1978 C 225, page 6. On that proposal see "Staff Administrative Tribunal" (cited in previous footnote).

18 See "Le Tribunal de première instance des Communautés européennes" by R. Joliet and W. Vogel in *Revue du marché commun* 1989, p. 423 at p.425.

19 Council Decision of 24 October 1988, 88/591/ECSC, EEC, Euratom.

shorten the duration of staff cases. It is envisaged that appeal should lie directly to the Court of Justice from the proposed tribunal, which would thus be established at a rank equivalent to that of the Court of First Instance. It emerges from the experience of the 1978 proposal that if this approach was adopted then it should take the form of amendment to the Treaty. Although that is a substantial measure, in these days of regular Intergovernmental Conferences it does not represent such an obstacle as it did in the 1970s.

Different structures may be envisaged for a specialised staff tribunal. Relevant criteria in this regard include not only the quality and speed of justice but also the economical use of resources. Its structure should accordingly be as light as possible. Hence there should be no presumption that the number of judges should be equivalent to the number of Member States; on the contrary, the number of judges should be proportionate to the workload involved. The number could be limited further if it were provided that cases could be heard by a single judge rather than a chamber. This might even be made the norm for such a tribunal.

A basic question is whether its members should sit alone as judges or whether they should sit with lay assessors. The answer is not self-evident, there being no clear precedent within the existing Community arrangements. It would be a matter of weighing the different advantages and disadvantages. If the single judge were the rule, assessors might provide a collegiate element which is sometimes considered desirable. On the other hand, no clear rules exist for the appointment of assessors, who may feel constrained to represent rigidly either the staff side or the administration side, particularly if they remain attached or expect to return to their original jobs after working as an assessor. The way in which they would contribute to a decision would also remain to be defined. In particular, if they could not act as rapporteurs, they might not be able to speed up the disposal of cases. It is to be supposed that they would in some way bring practical experience to bear on the problems submitted to the tribunal. Such a contribution might be purposeful if the judges appointed to the tribunal were generalists. On the other hand, if the judges were appointed for their existing expertise in the field of staff law, the presence of assessors might serve little purpose. It is suggested that the members of the staff tribunal should be selected for their specialist knowledge of the field. On that hypothesis, the preponderance of arguments may be against sitting with assessors. Accordingly the better structure might be that of a tribunal composed of judges only.

The strength of a staff tribunal would be its permanence. Its judges and staff would be dealing all the time with the field of staff law and so could maintain and build up their expertise in this field. The specialisation and difficulty of this field of law has been alluded to above. A staff tribunal could be given latitude to develop rules specifically adapted to staff disputes. In this connection it may be recalled that the Court of Justice has already adopted certain practices which are specific to the field. In particular the judgment in the case of *Oberthür v. Com-*

mission[20] established a remarkable power for the Court. In that case the applicant sought the annulment of all the promotions to grade B2 in a particular year. The Court held that her arguments were well-founded but that it would be excessive to annul the promotion of the 40 officials concerned. The Court therefore held that, although the applicant had not requested payment of compensation, it would order the payment of a modest amount[21] in order to compensate the wrong which it considered she had suffered. This possibility of granting a relief different from that claimed has not been extended to other cases but has been used subsequently in other staff cases. It is submitted that, although surprising, the solution fits the justice of the case. Rules such as this could be developed specifically in the field of staff cases, although it may be wondered whether the Court of Justice would have upheld such an innovation by a lower court if it had been hearing the case on appeal.

For its part, the Court of First Instance has power under Article 64 of its Rules of Procedure to carry out measures of organisation of procedure which include facilitating a settlement between the parties. In recent times the Court of First Instance has made active use of that power by what have come to be called "fast-track procedures". A possible development of that practice could be a compulsory conciliation stage (in all cases or only in cases designated by the tribunal) before full judicial proceedings were opened. It could then be discussed whether specialist conciliators might be brought in under the supervision of the tribunal or whether conciliation should be performed by members of the tribunal itself. If only for reasons of economy a first option might be for the members of the tribunal themselves to conduct any such conciliation. In either case the specialisation of the person leading the conciliation would be the key to the success of such a suggestion. It would also be crucial to have people present with authority to make the final decisions. Hence the agent of the institution concerned would need a mandate from the operational department concerned and from the financial control department, without which he could not commit expenditure. Similarly, it would be unhelpful for the lawyer of the staff member to attend unless his client was also present or had given the necessary mandate beforehand.

The extent to which a staff tribunal, or indeed the Court of First Instance, should be involved in conciliation raises a fundamental question about the nature of the staff disputes arrangements as a whole. As they stand, these arrangements already provide for a pre-contentious process: i.e. the request procedure under Article 90(1) of the Staff Regulations and the complaint procedure under Article 90(2) of the Staff Regulations. Except in certain narrowly defined cases no staff case may be brought before the Court until a complaint has been made and rejected under Article 90(2) of the Staff Regulations. Consistent case law establishes that one of the functions of the complaint procedure is to allow for conciliation between the parties. If it is considered that conciliation is not being

20 Case 24/79 [1980] ECR 1743.

21 20,000 Belgian francs.

adequately ensured at that stage, perhaps attention should be given to ensuring the effective application of that rule or to amending it rather than to postpone the problem to the judicial stage of the dispute process.

INTER-INSTITUTIONAL BOARDS OF APPEAL

In this context, the Court of Justice has put forward a radical new suggestion in the discussion document which it presented to the Council on 29 May 1999. It proposes the establishment of inter-institutional boards of appeal which would have a role of conciliation and decision in staff disputes. Appeal would lie from them to the Court of First Instance, with further appeal to the Court of Justice subject to a filter mechanism. It thus appears that these boards of appeal would take the place of the appointing authority of each institution or body in complaints under Article 90(2) of the Staff Regulations.

This suggestion is original because it does not focus on replacing the Court of First Instance as previous proposals have done, but addresses the pre-contentious phase, leaving the jurisdiction of the Court of First Instance potentially unchanged. This could meet the objection to the establishment of a staff tribunal that it might cut staff cases off from the mainstream of Community law and fragment the Community judicial system. Under the new proposal staff cases would continue to come before the ordinary Community courts (Court of First Instance and Court of Justice) along with all other types of case.

The proposed boards of appeal are apparently seen as non-judicial (like the appointing authority under Article 90(2) of the Staff Regulations). The discussion document primarily stresses conciliation, with decisions to be delivered only "if necessary". This is an important change of emphasis. It is consistent with contemporary trends, in which alternative dispute resolution is attracting more and more attention, not only because of its advantages in terms of speed and cost but also because of its potential to provide more satisfactory results for the parties than adversarial proceedings. If adopted, this approach might restore the conciliation function which the complaints procedure may to some extent have lost.

The discussion document suggests that the boards of appeal could be composed of an independent lawyer and lay assessors enjoying the trust of administration and staff. As the body is not judicial, there is more justification for assessors than in the case of a specialised staff tribunal. Not having the rank of judge, the legally-qualified member of an appeal board would not have the same legitimacy to decide a case as a judge would. Assessors might thus contribute to the authority of the board, particularly if adequate arrangements could be worked out to ensure that they had the respect of both sides.

The proposed structure resembles that of the boards of appeal established for the Community trade mark (where two out of three members must be legally qualified)[22] and Community plant variety rights (composed of a legally qualified chairman and two other members).[23] The Court's suggestion is plainly based on an analogy with these appeal boards, which are established as a first line of appeal against decisions of the Community trade mark office. ("Office for Harmonization in the Internal Market") and the Community Plant Variety Office, before cases can be brought before the Court of First Instance.

Those appeal boards are not wholly independent but are established "within" their respective offices.[24] For staff cases, on the other hand, the Court proposes appeal boards which are inter-institutional, which from a structural point of view suggests a higher degree of independence. It may also be recalled that the Court explicitly suggests that they should include an "independent" lawyer. Such clearly perceptible independence may enhance the effectiveness of the complaint procedure.

The suggested appeal boards could borrow certain procedures from the trade mark and plant variety boards, such as "interlocutory revision". By that procedure the decision in question is referred to the authority which originally took it, which may rectify the decision itself before the appeal board actually commences proceedings. Similarly, the appeal boards might be given power to require the appointing authority to provide, at the outset of proceedings, an explicit decision with a statement of reasons in cases where these are lacking.

If indeed the suggested appeal boards are intended to operate at the stage of the complaint under Article 90(2) of the Staff Regulations and are not judicial bodies, it would appear possible to establish them by simple amendment of the Staff Regulations, which are a Council Regulation, and not by Treaty amendment. This is in principle a less onerous procedure, and subsequent amendments, if necessary, would probably be easier.

If such boards of appeal were introduced and made the examination of law and fact at the pre-contentious phase more effective, it might be justified to envisage a number of measures to streamline proceedings before the Community courts.

First of all it may be considered whether a *de minimis* rule should be introduced where the claim is out of proportion to the amount of effort involved in hearing the case. For example, the case of *Gaspari* was heard at first instance by the Court of First Instance,[25] was overturned on appeal by the Court of Justice[26] and then was returned to the Court of First Instance to be reheard.[27] However,

22 See Council Regulation 40/94 on the Community trade mark (OJ 1994 L 11, p.1), Article 130.
23 See Council Regulation 2100/94 on Community plant variety rights (OJ 1994 L 227, p.1), as amended by Council Regulation 2506/95 (OJ 1995 L 258, p.3), Articles 45 ff; Commission Regulation 1239/95 (OJ 1995 L 121, p.37), Article 11.
24 See Millett "The Community system of plant variety rights", E.L. Rev. 1999, p.231, at p.247.
25 Case T-36/96 *Gaspari v. European Parliament* [1997] ECR-SC II-595.
26 Case 316/97 P *European Parliament v. Gaspari* [1998] ECR I – 7597.
27 Judgment of the Court of First Instance of 8 July 1999, Case T-36/96, *Gaspari v. Euro-*

the point at issue was a single day's leave which had been refused to an official following the report of the staff doctor. It may be wondered whether the time, effort and money involved in the dispute, including the translations, was justified. In this connection it might be conceivable for the Community courts to build a *de minimis* rule by way of case law without any specific provision to that effect in a legislative text, on the basis perhaps of their inherent powers as a court.

Secondly, the existing Rules of Procedure might be amended in order to allow the Court of First Instance to dismiss cases as frivolous and vexatious, in addition to the present powers to dismiss cases as manifestly inadmissible or unfounded.[28]

Thirdly, assuming a thorough and cost-free procedure before the boards of appeal, it might be appropriate to consider extending to staff cases before the Court of First Instance the normal rule whereby the losing party is ordered to pay the costs. In this connection it might be recalled that the normal rule already applies to appeals before the Court of Justice. Such provisions should, however, be accompanied by a saving for cases of oppressive behaviour by the institution concerned or the requirements of equity as assessed by the Community court.

As regards further appeal to the Court of Justice, the latter suggests in its discussion document that such appeals would not lie as of right but could justifiably be filtered inasmuch as the case had already been examined by two independent bodies. In such a context a leave to appeal procedure such as that used for appeals to the House of Lords would not appear inappropriate.

A last point relating to the suggested boards of appeal is that the opportunity might be grasped to clarify the role of the European Ombudsman in relation to staff disputes. The Ombudsman clearly has no jurisdiction over cases dealt with by the Court or Justice of the Court of First Instance;[29] but he claims competence to inquire into staff disputes so long as they have not been brought before those courts, on the basis that they may constitute "instances of maladministration". As a result, he may transmit a report to the European Parliament and the institution involved, but does not issue an individual decision to the person concerned. It may be convenient to consider whether the legislator actually intended to provide two alternative avenues of complaint in staff disputes and, if so, to specify what the relationship is between the different procedures available.

On the whole the suggestion of inter-institutional boards of appeal may be considered a remarkable alternative to the establishment of a specialist staff tribunal. In strengthening the complaint procedure they could achieve a number of the goals ascribed to such a tribunal, in particular the enhancement of conciliation. Such boards might relieve the Court of First Instance of part of its workload, whilst leaving the present judicial structure unaltered.

---

pean Parliament.

28 Rules of Procedure of the CFI, Article 111.

29 EC Treaty, Article 195(1) (ex Article 138e(1)).

CONCLUSION

In conclusion, it is thought that any lasting improvement in dealing with staff cases and in assisting the Court of First Instance to cope with its ever-growing workload depends on the specialisation of those dealing with such cases. The recent decision to allow *inter alia* staff cases to be heard by a single judge is a welcome step in the direction of efficient use of the Court of First Instance's limited judicial resources. But it is submitted that its success could be amplified by the specialisation of the judges or chambers dealing with such cases. The view seems to be widely held that the use of the single judge is not a complete solution to the present difficulties. There are strong arguments that in the medium term a tribunal specialising in Community staff cases should be established. Its judges should be specialists in the field, and it should occupy a rank equivalent to that of the Court of First Instance, with appeal lying to the Court of Justice. Such a tribunal could relieve the Court of First Instance of a substantial proportion of its current case load and allow it to press ahead with the other categories of cases before it. However, a radical new suggestion from the Court of Justice opens up the alternative possibility of reforming the pre-contentious procedure by establishing inter-institutional boards of appeal along the lines of those in intellectual property cases. They might improve the handling of staff cases without upsetting the existing judicial architecture of the Community. Conceivably, they might also be combined with the other reforms envisaged. So, after a pause for reflection, consideration returns – with important variations – to the ideas expressed in the 1970s about setting up a separate staff tribunal. Back to the future in the judicial architecture of the European Communities?

PART 3

FORMS OF JUDICIAL PROTECTION IN THE EUROPEAN LEGAL ORDER

17

THE PRINCIPLE OF EFFECTIVE PROTECTION OF COMMUNITY LAW RIGHTS

John Temple Lang[*]

One striking feature of the whole Community legal order is the extent to which it relies on national courts to apply Community law. This is much more than the legal principle that some rules of Community law are directly applicable. The Community depends on national judges. There are only two Community Courts. Community law could not be adequately enforced unless national courts enforce it. Community law is probably now interpreted and applied more often in national courts than in the Courts in Luxembourg.

Every national court is a Community law court of general jurisdiction, with the power and the duty to apply every rule of Community law which is relevant to the cases coming before it.[1]

Since all national courts must apply Community law rather than national law if the two conflict, every national court now has power to review national legislation for compatibility with Community rules: every national court is in that respect a Community constitutional court. Every national court is first and foremost a Community law court, in the sense that its duty to Community law overrides its usual duty to apply national law.

The principal legal basis for the duties of national courts under Community law is Article 10 [ex Article 5] EC Treaty. At first sight it seems a very general, rather vague, Article merely requiring national authorities to help the Community and not to obstruct it. But Article 10 refers to the whole of the rest of the Treaty. In fact it is probably the most important single Article in the Community legal system. It is the legal basis for some of the most fundamental principles of

* All opinions expressed are purely personal. I am grateful to Robert O'Donoghue, Barrister, for comments on a draft of this paper. This paper is published here with the kind agreement of the Finnish Association for European Law.

1 Case T-51/89, *Tetra Pak*, [1990] ECR II-309; Joined Cases C-430/93 and C-431/93, *van Schijndel* [1995] ECR I-4705, Advocate General Jacobs at p. 4713. In Case 26/62, *Van Gend en Loos*, [1963] ECR I, the Court stressed that direct application meant that private parties could get remedies directly in their own courts. See Lecourt, *L'Europe des juges* (Bruylant, 1979) on the key role of national courts in the Community legal order.

D. O'Keeffe (ed.), Liber Amicorum Slynn 235-274 (2000)

that system, the principles that govern the relationships between national authorities and Community institutions, and the duties of national courts.

It is the duty of the Court of Justice to ensure that in the interpretation and application of the EC Treaty, the law is observed. National courts have similar obligations, because of Article 10. Their obligations are to ensure that they themselves observe Community law fully, and to ensure that national authorities and private parties involved in cases before them are required to observe it fully. Their right, and at times their duty, to refer questions of Community law to the Court of Justice is to enable them to carry out these obligations.

National courts obtain powers as well as duties under Article 10. Most obviously, it gives them the power to set aside national legislation which is incompatible with rules of Community law. This is so even if they have no power to set aside legislation which is incompatible with the national constitution. I suggest that Community law gives national courts the power and the duty to do whatever is necessary to provide effective protection for Community law rights.

In this paper I summarise the specific powers and duties of national courts as explained in the case law of the Court of Justice. I emphasise the cases which I believe illustrate some important general principles. To look at national judicial attitudes to Community law, as I was asked to, it is necessary to summarise what national courts are called on to do, and then to comment on why it may be difficult or controversial, or even why they may be reluctant to do it fully and correctly without first referring questions to the Court under Article 234 [ex Article 177].

It is now clear that a number of specific duties of national courts are based on Article 10:

- the duty to apply Community law fully means that it is for national courts to determine whether and if so how far a rule of national law is inconsistent with Community law, and whether it should be regarded as inapplicable in some individual cases or as no longer effective in any situation;
- national courts must sometimes raise points of Community law on their own initiative, so as to avoid applying national rules which are inconsistent with Community law;[2]
- national courts must not allow State authorities in litigation to rely on national laws which are inconsistent with directives which should have been implemented;[3]

2 Case C-312/93, *Peterbroeck* [1995] ECR I-4599; Case C-72/95 *Kraaijeveld* [1996] ECR I-5403 at p. 5451; Case C-358/95, *Moratello*, [1997] ECR I-1431, paras. 17-20. Since the Court of Justice may raise questions of sufficient reasons on its own initiative, presumably national courts may also do so, with a view to referring a question under Article 177, even though they cannot themselves declare a Community act invalid: see Joined Cases T-371/94 and T-394/94, *British Airways v. Commission*, June 25 1998.

3 Case 148/78 *Ratti* [1979] ECR 1629: Case 286/86 *McDermott and Cotter*, [1987] ECR

- national courts must interpret national laws, if possible, so as to be consistent with Community rules, even if that is not their normal interpretation, and even in litigation between private parties. National courts must always look at a directive when applying a national law which is said to give effect to it. It is not enough merely to read the national legislation;[4]
- the duty to ensure uniform interpretation of Community law. This has been described (by Advocate General van Gerven) as a fundamental requirement.[5] In practice, even a national court which is *not* a court of final appeal may have a duty to refer a question to Luxembourg if there are conflicting national court judgments on the question;
- national courts must apply Community law as effectively as they apply similar rules of national law. This means that they must apply Community law rules under substantive and procedural conditions analogous to those applying to infringements of national law which are similar in nature and importance, and they must apply it as thoroughly and vigorously as national law. Article 10 requires them to eliminate the unlawful consequences of a breach of Community law either directly or, failing that, by ensuring effective reparation of the damage resulting from it.[6]

1453: Case 8/81 *Becker* [1982] ECR 53: Case 71/85, *Federatie Nederlandse Vakbeweging* [1986] ECR 3855, para. 14.

4 Case C-106/89, *Marleasing* [1990] ECR I-4135; Case C-334/92, Wagner Miret, [1993] ECR I-6911, para. 20; Case C-472/93, *Spano*, [1995] ECR I-4321; Case C-54/96 *Dorsch Consult*, 17 September 1997 ("... the requirement that the rights of individuals must be protected effectively ..."). Case C-373/90, criminal proceedings against X, [1992] ECR I-131 para. 7; Joined Cases C-71/94, *Eurim Pharm and others*, [1996] ECR I-3603 para. 26; Case C-352/95 *Phytheron International v. Bourdon*, [1997] ECR I-1729 para. 18.

5 In Case C-271/91 *Marshall v. Southampton Health Authority* [1993] ECR I at p. 4387, Advocate General van Gerven said "The Court has held that such uniformity as regards enforcement of the rights arising under Community law for individuals is a fundamental requirement of the Community legal order in the judgment in the *Zuckerfabrick* case ... the requirement as to the uniform application of Community law ... which requires the same infringement of Community law to be repressed in a sufficiently effective and deterrent manner in *all* the Member States" (pp. 4387, 4389, emphasis in original). See Cases C-143/88 *Zuckerfabrick* [1991] ECR I-415 at para. 25; Joined Cases C-94/95 and C-95/95, *Bonifaci and Berto*, [1997] ECR I-3969, Advocate General Cosmas at p. 3984. See also Case C-334/95 *Krüger* [1997] ECR I-4517 at para. 51 (The duty to refer the question of the validity of an EC act is based on "the necessity to ensure that Community law is applied"): Case C-337/95, *Parfums Christian Dior* [1997] ECR I-6044, at para. 25 (duty to refer under Article 177 to avoid incorrect or conflicting case law).

6 Case C-24/97 *Commission v. Germany* [1998] ECR I April 30, 1998. *Cour Administrative d'Appel de Paris*, 1 July 1992, *Dangeville*, AJDA p. 768 cited by Advocate General Léger in *Hedley Lomas* [1996] ECR I-2553 at p. 2580, and pp. 2582 et seq., p. 2591: also the judgment of the *Conseil d'État* of 28 February, 1992. *Arizona Tobacco Products AJDA*, 1992, p. 210 cited by Advocate General Tesauro at [1996] ECR I, p. 1092: see also *Kirklees MBC v. Wickes*, 1992 3 WLR 170 (House of Lords).

- in fact, national courts sometimes need to go further than this.[7] They must give a remedy which is *effective* to protect the right given by Community law. It is not sufficient to apply national rules if those rules make it impossible or excessively difficult in practice to exercise Community law rights which national courts have a duty to protect. Community law now includes minimum standards for judicial protection of Community law rights. This is the "principle of effectiveness".

EFFECTIVE PROTECTION OF COMMUNITY LAW RIGHTS

This principle needs to be explained by several examples from the case law of the Court of Justice.

The first example concerns a claim made by a Ms. Marshall against the Southampton Health Authority. Ms. Marshall had already succeeded in a claim that she had been discriminated against because she had been compulsorily retired at an age below that at which men in similar employment would have retired. She claimed compensation, with interest. The relevant UK legislation had the effect of limiting her claim for interest. She claimed that a Directive which

7 Case 33/76, *Rewe v. Saarland*, [1976] ECR 1989, para 5; Case 45/76, *Comet v. Produktschap voor Siergewassen*, [1975] ECR 2043, paras. 15-16; Case 130/79, *Express Dairy Foods*, [1980] ECR 887, para. 12; Case 61/79, *Deukavit Italiana*, [1980] ECR 1205; Case 68/79, *Just v. Ministry of Fiscal Affairs*, [1980] ECR 501, para. 25; Case 811/79, *Ariete*, [1980] ECR 2545; Case 826/79, *Mireco*, [1980] ECR 2559; Case 199/82, *San Giorgio*, [1983] ECR 3595, para 12 et seq.; Case 104/86, *Commission v. Italy*, [1988] ECR 1799; Case 240/87, *Deville*, [1988] ECR 3513; Case 331/85, *Bianco*, [1988] ECR 1099, para. 12; Case 79/83, *Harz*, [1984] ECR 1921, para. 21-28 ("compensation must be adequate in relation to the damage sustained"); Case 179/84, *Bozzetti v. Invernizzi*, [1985] ECR 2301, para. 17; Case 309/85, *Barra*, [1988] ECR 355; Case 68/88, *Commission v. Greece*, [1989] ECR 2965, 2984-85; Case 109/88, *Handels og Kontorfunktionaevernes*, [1989] ECR 3199, at 3225-3226; Joined Cases C-430 and 431/93, *van Schijndel*, [1995] ECR I-4705 ("it is sufficient that individuals are given, by the national procedural rules, an effective opportunity of enforcing their rights": Advocate General Jacobs at p. 4715); Case C-208/90, *Emmott*, [1991] ECR I-4269, para. 16; Case C-410/92, *Johnson*, [1994] ECR I-5483, para. 21; Joined Cases C-31/91 to C-44/91, *Lageder*, [1993] ECR I-1761, paras. 27-29 and p.1777; Case 123/87, *Jeunehomme*, [1988] ECR I-4517, para. 17; Case C-96/91, *Commission v. Spain*, [1992] ECR I-3789, para. 12; Case C-62/93, *BP Supergas*, [1995] ECR I-1883 at pp. 1888, 1919 and 1921; Case C-6/90. *Francovich v. Italy*, [1991] ECR I-5357, para. 43; Case C-338/91, *Steenhorst-Neerings*, [1993] ECR I-5475, para. 15: Joined Cases C-46/93 and C-48/93, *Brasserie du Pêcheur and Factortame*, [1996] ECR I at paras. 67-68; Case C-212/94, *FMC v. Intervention Board*, [1996] ECR I-389. Case C-231/96, *Edilizia Industriale*, Sept. 15 1998, para. 34 (the "principle of effectiveness"). See Quigley, *European Community Contract Law* (Kluwer 1997) p. 31.
The requirement of "effective" application of Community law applies to all national authorities, not only to courts: Case C-8/88, *Germany v. Commission*, [1990] ECR I-2321 at p. 2359.

gave a right to pursue claims for equal treatment "by judicial process" implied a right to full compensation for loss.

The Court held that the Directive meant that the national measures "should be sufficiently effective to achieve the objective of the Directive and should be capable of being effectively relied upon by the persons concerned before national courts". The national measures "must be such as to guarantee real and effective judicial protection" and must include measures appropriate to restore equal treatment when it has not been given. Where financial compensation is the remedy, "it must be adequate in that it must enable the loss and damage actually sustained as a result of the discriminatory dismissal to be made good in full in accordance with the applicable national rules". Fixing an upper limit to the compensation payable cannot constitute proper implementation of the Directive because it limits the compensation to a level not necessarily consistent with the requirement of adequate reparation for the loss sustained. Full compensation for loss sustained cannot leave out of account factors such as the passing of time which may reduce its value. The award of interest must therefore be regarded as an essential component of compensation for the purpose of restoring real equality of treatment.

It seems clear from this judgment that there is a substantive principle of Community law to the effect that where Community law gives a right to financial compensation, it must be sufficient to offset the loss sustained in full. This principle was not stated in the words of the Directive, and therefore it must be a general principle of Community law. It is quite distinct from the second, separate requirement of Community law that rights given by Community law must be protected under substantive and procedural rules analogous to those applying to similar infringements of national law–a rule which might involve a significantly different standard of protection, and which plainly would involve a different standard of substantive protection in each Member State. The full compensation principle on the other hand is a minimum standard of protection given by Community law.

Another case to be discussed in this context is *Factortame I*.[8] In that case, Spanish interests argued in the UK courts that UK legislation requiring fishing boats in UK waters to be owned by U.K. citizens was contrary to Community law. In parallel, the Commission in Article 169 (now 226) proceedings against the UK obtained an interim measures order from the President of the Court of Justice ordering the UK to suspend the application of the nationality clauses in the UK legislation. The House of Lords referred to the Court of Justice under Article 177 (now 234) the question whether Community law required a national

---

8 Case C-213/89, "*Factortame I*", [1990] ECR I-2433 ("*Factortame II*" was Case C-221/89, [1991] ECR I-3905). The Court had previously decided that a rule of national law preventing Article 177 from being followed must be set aside: Case 166/73, *Rheinmühlen*, [1974] ECR 33, paras. 2 and 3. "*Factortame III*" is Joined Cases C-46/93 and C-48/93, *Brasserie du Pêcheur and Factortame*, [1996] ECR I-1029.

court to give interim protection by suspending the national legislation. The Court said:

> "the preliminary question raised by the House of Lords seeks essentially to ascertain whether a national court which, in a case before it concerning Community law, considers that the sole obstacle which precludes it from granting interim relief is a rule of national law, must disapply that rule ....".

After referring to *Simmenthal*[9] the Court went on:

> "In accordance with the case-law of the Court, it is for the national courts, in application of the principle of cooperation laid down in Article 5 of the EEC Treaty, to ensure the legal protection which persons derive from the direct effect of provisions of Community law ......
>
> The Court also held that any provision of a national legal system and any legislative, administrative or judicial practice which might impair the effectiveness of Community law by withholding from the national court having jurisdiction to apply such law the power to do everything necessary at the moment of its application to set aside national legislative provisions which might prevent, even temporarily, Community rules from having full force and effect are incompatible with those requirements, which are the very essence of Community law.
>
> ... the full effectiveness of Community law would be just as much impaired if a rule of national law could prevent a court seised of a dispute governed by Community law from granting interim relief in order to ensure the full effectiveness of the judgment to be given on the existence of the rights claimed under Community law. It follows that a court which in those circumstances would grant interim relief, if it were not for a rule of national law, is obliged to set aside that rule.
>
> The interpretation is reinforced by the system established by Article 177 of the EEC Treaty whose effectiveness would be impaired if a national court, having stayed proceedings pending the reply by the Court of Justice to the question referred to it for a preliminary ruling, were not able to grant interim relief until it delivered its judgment following the reply given by the Court of Justice.
>
> Consequently, the reply to the question raised should be that Community law must be interpreted as meaning that a national court which, in a case before it concerning Community law, considers that the sole obstacle which precludes it from granting interim relief is a rule of national law must set aside that rule."

The Court in *Factortame* spoke of the duty of a national court to set aside a rule of national law which prevents it from giving interim relief required by Community law. But that was not the way the case appeared in the UK courts. The House of Lords had said expressly that a UK court "has no power to give interim protection to the rights claimed by suspending the application of the national measure pending the preliminary ruling". There was no specific rule of

9 Case 106/77, *Simmenthal* [1978] ECR 629.

national law to be set aside: it had been accepted for more than three hundred years that, purely under English law, English courts have no power to set aside an Act of Parliament, temporarily or permanently. In substance therefore the Court of Justice was saying that interim relief when necessary is the general principle and that if interim relief is required by Community law, the national court must give that relief, even if it would have no power under purely national law to give relief of that kind. Its power to do what Community law requires comes from Community law itself. There is no need for the national court to have a general power under national law and to set aside a specific, exceptional rule of national law preventing its exercise in specific circumstances. Advocate General Tesauro recognised this.[10] In other words, the Court's reasons understate the importance of its conclusion.

As the Court pointed out, the idea that Community law provides the legal basis for a national court's *power* to give whatever relief is required by Community law had appeared long before, in 1978 in the *Simmenthal* case. In that case, the Court of Justice said that all national courts, and not only special constitutional courts, had a duty to set aside national legislation which was inconsistent with Community law. But national courts in several Member States have no power, under national constitutional law, to set aside national legislation. Their power to do this came from the same sources as their duty to do it – Community law. And the Court said in *Factortame* that the duty of national courts to ensure legal protection of Community law rights comes from Article 5 (now Article 10).

In *Zuckerfabrik*[11] the Court said that national courts could suspend national measures if the Community measure which they are based on is challenged. "In cases where national authorities are responsible for the administrative implementation of Community regulations, the legal protection generated by Community law includes the right of individuals to challenge, as a preliminary issue, the legality of such regulations before national courts and to induce those courts to refer questions to the Court of Justice for a preliminary ruling". This right, the Court said, would be compromised if individuals could not get a decision suspending the national measures enforcing the disputed regulation. "*The coherence of the system of interim legal protection* ... requires that national courts should also be able to order suspension of enforcement of a national administrative measure based on a Community regulation, the legality of which is con-

10 In Joined Cases, C-46/93 and C-48/93, *Brasserie du Pêcheur and Factortame*, [1996] ECR I-1029 at p. 1078 he said that judicial review by the Court "has on several occasions extended even so far as to require the Member State concerned to adopt a judicial remedy not available under its legal system": see also pp. 1092-1095. Directive 98/27/EC on injunctions for the protection of consumers' interests, O.J. No L-166/51, June 11, 1998 is a legislative measure to harmonise procedures to protect rights given by Community law.

11 Cases C-143/88 and C-92/89, [1991] ECR I-415 at paras. 16, 20. See Case C-334/95, *Krüger*, [1997] ECR I-4517; Case C-465/93, *Atlanta*, [1995] ECR I-3761; Case C-68/95, *Port*, [1996] ECR I-6065. In Case T-111/96, *ITT Promedia*, [1998] ECR II-2937, para. 60, the Court of First Instance repeated that judicial review is a fundamental right.

tested" (emphasis supplied). "The interim legal protection which Community law ensures for individuals must remain the same, irrespective of whether they contest the compatibility of national legal provisions with Community law or the validity of secondary Community law, in view of the fact that the dispute in both cases is based on Community law itself".

So, although national courts cannot annul a Community measure,[12] the effective protection principle means that they can suspend national measures based on it, when its validity is challenged.

In the recent case of *Coote v. Granada Hospitality*[13] the question concerned the Directive on equal treatment for men and women on access to employment. The question was whether the Directive required Member States to provide protection for workers whose employer, after the end of the employment relationship, refused to provide references, as a reaction to the fact that the employee had brought proceedings to enforce her rights. The Court said:

> "The requirement .... that recourse be available to the courts reflects a general principle of law that underlies the constitutional traditions common to the Member States and which is also enshrined in Article 6 of the European Convention for the Protection of Human Rights and Fundamental Freedoms ......
>
> By virtue of Article 6 of the Directive, interpreted in the light of the general principle stated above, all persons have the right to obtain an effective remedy in a competent court against measures which they consider to interfere with the equal treatment for men and women laid down in the Directive. It is for the Member States to ensure effective judicial control of compliance with the applicable provisions of Community law and of national legislation intended to give effect to the rights for which the Directive provides ......
>
> The principle of effective judicial control laid down in Article 6 of the Directive would be deprived of an essential part of its effectiveness if the protection which it provides did not cover measures which, as in the main proceedings in this case, an employer might take as a reaction to legal proceedings brought by an employee with the aim of enforcing compliance with the principle of equal treatment. Fear of such measures, where no legal remedy is available against them, might deter workers who considered themselves the victims of discrimination from pursuing their claims by judicial process, and would consequently be liable seriously to jeopardise implementation of the aim pursued by the Directive."

THE *FRANCOVICH* PRINCIPLE

Another even more important judgment is *Francovich.*[14] In that case the Court ruled that national courts must order States to pay compensation for loss caused by failure to implement directives, in certain circumstances. This rule applies,

12 Case 314/85, *Foto-frost* [1987] ECR 4199.
13 Case C-185/97, [1998] ECR I-5199. The paragraphs quoted are 21, 22 and 24.
14 Joined Cases C-6/90 and C-9/90, [1991] ECR I-5357.

whether or not any similar right to compensation exists under national law. The Court said:

> "... the EEC Treaty has created its own legal system, which is integrated into the legal systems of the Member States and which their courts are bound to apply. The subjects of that legal system are not only the Member States but also their nationals. Just as it imposes burdens on individuals, Community law is also intended to give rise to rights which become part of their legal patrimony. Those rights arise not only where they are expressly granted by the Treaty but also by virtue of obligations which the Treaty imposes in a clearly defined manner both on individuals and on the Member States and in Community institutions ...
>
> ... it has been consistently held that the national courts whose task it is to apply the provisions of Community law in areas within their jurisdiction must ensure that those rules take full effect and must protect the rights which they confer on individuals ...
>
> The full effectiveness of Community rules would be impaired and the protection of the rights which they grant would be weakened if individuals were unable to obtain redress when their rights are infringed by a breach of Community law for which a Member State can be held responsible.
>
> The possibility of obtaining redress from the Member State is particularly indispensable where, as in this case, the full effectiveness of Community rules is subject to prior action on the part of the State and where, consequently, in the absence of such action, individuals cannot enforce before the national courts the rights conferred upon them by Community law.
>
> It follows that the principle whereby a State must be liable for loss and damage caused to individuals as a result of breaches of Community law for which the State can be held responsible is inherent in the system of the Treaty.
>
> A further basis for the obligation of member States to make good such loss and damage is to be found in Article 5 of the Treaty, under which the Member States are required to take all appropriate measures, whether general or particular, to ensure fulfilment of their obligations under Community law. Among these is the obligation to nullify the unlawful consequences of a breach of Community law ...
>
> It follows ... that it is a principle of Community law that the Member States are obliged to make good loss and damage caused to individuals by breaches of Community law for which they can be held responsible.
>
> Although State liability is thus required by Community law, the conditions under which that liability gives rise to a right to reparation depend on the nature of the breach of Community law giving rise to the loss and damage.
>
> Where, as in this case, a Member State fails to fulfil its obligation under the third paragraph of Article 189 [now Article 249] of the Treaty to take all the measures necessary to achieve the result prescribed by a Directive, the full effectiveness of that rule of Community law requires that there should be a right to reparation provided that three conditions are fulfilled.

> The first of those conditions is that the result prescribed by the directive should entail the grant of rights to individuals. The second condition is that it should be possible to identify the content of those rights on the basis of the provisions of the directive. Finally, the third condition is the existence of a causal link between the breach of the State's obligation and the loss and damage suffered by the injured parties.
>
> Those conditions are sufficient to give rise to a right on the part of individuals to obtain reparation, a right founded directly on Community law."

In *Francovich*, Advocate-General Mischo said (at p. 5388) "since the judgment ... in ... *Factortame* ... there can no longer ... be any doubt that in certain cases Community law may itself directly confer on national judicial authorities the necessary powers in order to ensure effective judicial protection of those rights, *even when similar powers do not exist in national law* ..... it follows from the judgment of the Court in .... *Zuckerfabrik* .... that Community law may even lay down the conditions governing the exercise of the jurisdiction which it confers on national courts" (emphasis supplied).

I have dealt at length with these cases because they show the consequences of the principle that national courts must give remedies which are effective to protect the rights given by Community law. This principle has led, and will progressively lead the Court of Justice to define more clearly what substantive and procedural rights are given, and to define more clearly what "effective protection" of each Community right means: national treatment is not enough. No doubt the Court of Justice will be cautious. But the principle is now so well established, and so clearly justified, that it is inevitable that it will give rise in due course to a large and important body of case law. The recent cases show that the Court's comment in 1981[15] that "it was not intended to create new remedies" is no longer completely true. Some remedies new to some national laws have been found necessary, and Article 10 gives national courts the power and the duty to provide them. As Advocate General Léger said in Hedley Lomas:[16] "From the principle of cooperation laid down in Article 5 of the EC Treaty, the Court has developed a minimum standard of judicial protection for individuals relying on Community law in a body of case-law which has grown more and more extensive with the passage of time".

AN EFFECTIVE REMEDY OF COMPENSATION FROM THE STATE – THE CASE-LAW AFTER *FRANCOVICH*

For many years, the case law of the Court had visualised the possibility of claims against a Member State for compensation for breach of Community law,

15 Case C-158/80, *Rewe*, [1981] ECR 1805.

16 Case C-5/94 [1996] ECR I-2553 at p. 2569, pp. 2589 et seq. See Tesauro, *La sanction des infractions au droit communautaire*, (Reports for the XVth FIDE congress, Lisbon 1992) General Report, p. 423.

as well as e.g. for recovery of taxes levied contrary to Community rules.[17] However, it was apparently not until the *Francovich* judgment in 1991 that lawyers and civil servants saw the importance of this principle. Since then there have been a number of judgments of the Court of Justice which have significantly clarified the relevant rules of law.[18]

The *Francovich* judgment said, essentially, that a private party can claim compensation from a Member State which has failed to implement a directive if the directive requires rights to be given to individuals, if the rights are sufficiently clear, and if there is a causal link between the breach of the State's obligations and the loss suffered. All the previous case-law had dealt with directly applicable rules, and it would not make sense to have a right to damages only when the Community law rule was not directly applicable. So in fact the judgment showed that compensation could be recovered for any loss caused by a Member State infringing *any* rule of Community law if the rule was for the protection of private parties, if the breach was clear enough, and if it led to the loss complained of. But this was not confirmed until later.

As Advocate General Léger said later[19] "no other decision of the Court has ever generated so much comment".

He added that the *Francovich* principle enables an individual to bring an action for damages where "by reason of the insufficiently precise and unconditional nature of the provisions of a directive, he cannot rely on it directly before his national courts".

---

17 See Case C-6/60, *Humblet v. Belgium*, [1960] ECR 559 at p. 569: Case C-39/72, *Commission v. Italy*, [1973] ECR 101, para. 11: in Case C-70/72, *Commission v. Germany*, [1973] ECR 813 at para. 13 the Court had said "the aim of the Treaty is to achieve the practical elimination of infringements and the consequences thereof, past and future". Case 60/75, *Russo v. AIMA*, [1976] ECR 45, para. 9: Case C-188/89, *Foster*, [1990] ECR I-3313, para. 22; Joined Cases C-46/93 and C-48/93, *Brasserie du Pêcheur*, Advocate General Tesauro at [1996] ECR I, pp. 1080, 1083: Temple Lang, "Community constitutional law: Article 5 EEC Treaty", 27 CMLRev. (1990) 645-681 at pp. 651-653.

18 Case C-6/90 and C-9/90, *Francovich*, [1991] ECR I-5357; Case C-271/91, *Marshall*, [1993] ECR I-4367; Case C-5/94, *Hedley Lomas*, [1996] ECR I-2553; Case C-192/94, *Faccini*, [1994] ECR I-3325; Joined Cases C-46/93 and C-48/93, *Brasserie du Pêcheur and Factortame*, ("*Factortame III*"), [1996] ECR I-1029; Case C-178/94, *Dillenköfer*, [1996] ECR I-4845; Case C-392/93, *Rv. Treasury ex parte BT*, [1996] ECR I-1631; Case C-192/95, *Comateb*, [1997] ECR I-165 (passing on a tax unlawfully levied); Case C-66/95, *R v. Secretary of State ex parte Sutton*, [1997] ECR I-2163; Cases C-94/95, C-261/95 *Bonifaci Palmisani and Maso,* [1997] ECR I-4025; Case C-90/94, *Haahr Petroleum*, [1997] ECR I-4085; Case C-114/95, *Texaco*, [1997] ECR I-4263.

19 In Case C-5/94, *Hedley Lomas*, [1996] ECR I at pp. 2567, 2574. See Case C-91/92, *Faccini Dori v. Receb*, [1994] ECR I-3324, para. 27. See van Gerven, *Bridging the Unbridgeable* (Durham, 1995). Van Gerven, "Non-contractual liability of Member States, Community institutions and individuals for breaches of Community law with a view to a common law for Europe", 1 *Maastricht Journal of European and Community Law* (1994) 6: Waelbroeck, "Treaty violations and liability of Member States: The effect of the Francovich case law", in Heukels and McDonnell (eds.), *The Action for Damages in Community Law* (Kluwer, 1997) 311-337.

The principle also gives a remedy when the directive, if it had been implemented, would have given a remedy against another private party. The basic rule, according to the Advocate General, is that an action for reparation governed by national law "will be compatible with Community law *only if it guarantees effective protection of the interests of the individual relying on Community law*" (emphasis in the original).[20] The damage must be compensated for in full, and there is no need for any previous judgment finding that the State is acting in breach of Community law.[21]

In *Faccini Dori*[22] the Court said that "the Member States' obligation arising from a directive to achieve the result envisaged by the directive and their duty under Article 5 of the Treaty to take all appropriate measures, whether general or particular is binding on all the authorities of the Member States, including, for matters within their jurisdiction, the courts". If the result required by the directive cannot be achieved by way of interpretation,[23] Community law requires the Member States to make good loss caused to individuals through failure to transpose a directive, if the three conditions are fulfilled.

Brasserie du Pêcheur and Factortame[24] confirmed that breach of directly applicable rules also gives rise to State liability, even when the national legislature is responsible for the breach. The duty to make good damage caused cannot depend on national law rules as to the division of powers between different authorities. The right to compensation is a direct result of the principle of direct effects. Liability is not dependent on fault, except that there must be a sufficiently serious breach of Community law. Two Community law principles "form the basis for State liability namely, first, the full effectiveness of Community rules and the effective protection of the rights which they confer and, second, the obligation to cooperate imposed on Member States by Article 5 of the Treaty".[25]

The liability of Member States differs from the liability of the Community under Article 288 [ex Article 215], essentially because Member States usually have much less discretion when carrying out their obligations under Community law. But even where the State has a broad discretion, there is liability, if the three conditions are fulfilled.

---

20 At p. 2595.

21 At pp. 2595-2598.

22 Case C-91/92, *Faccini Dori*, [1994] ECR I, at p. 3357. At p. 3337, Advocate General Lenz said "The public administration is also bound by an obligation to comply with directives which is comparable to that to which national courts are subject" and cited Case 103/88, *Costanzo* [1989] ECR 1839, para. 26; see also Joined Cases C-46/93 and C-48/93 *Brasserie du Pêcheur and Factortame* [1996] ECR I at para. 34.

23 As required by Case C-106/89, *Marleasing*, [1990] ECR I-4135 and Case C-334/92, *Wagner Miret*, [1993] ECR I-6911, para. 20.

24 Joined Cases C-46/93 and C-48/93, [1996] ECR I-1029 (sometimes referred to as "*Factortame III*").

25 [1996] ECR I, at para. 28, 50.

The question whether the Member State "manifestly and gravely disregarded the limits on its discretion" depends on the clarity and precision of the rule breached, the extent of the discretion left to the national authorities by the rule, whether the infringement was intentional or involuntary, whether any error of law was excusable or inexcusable, whether any position taken by a Community institution contributed to the breach, and the adoption or retention of measures contrary to Community law. A breach is always serious if it continues after a judgment declaring it illegal, or if it is clearly illegal in the light of the case law of the Court. In particular, the Court said that several national law rules would make it excessively difficult to recover compensation, and so must be set aside:

- a German rule under which compensation could be paid only if the legislative act or omission in question concerned an individual situation and not the public at large;
- a UK rule under which State liability arose only if there was misfeasance in public office, since such misuse of power is inconceivable in the case of the legislature. Similarly, the Court said that no national requirement of fault could be added to the Community law rule that compensation is payable in cases of serious breach. Intentional fault or negligence is not a precondition of liability;
- "total exclusion of loss of profit as a head of damage for which reparation may be awarded in the case of breach of Community law cannot be accepted".[26] This is because "especially in the context of economic or commercial litigation, such a total exclusion of loss of profit would be such as to make reparation of damage practically impossible".

In general reparation "must be commensurate with the loss or damage sustained.[27]

The Court also said that it would be contrary to the need for an effective remedy if compensation was payable only for loss suffered *after* there had been a judgment of the Court itself ruling that the State had infringed Community law. "Rights arising for individuals out of Community provisions having direct effect in the domestic legal systems of Member States cannot depend on the Commission's assessment of the expediency of taking action against a Member State pursuant to Article 169 [now Article 226]".[28]

In the same case Advocate General Tesauro said[29] that the *Simmenthal* judgment showed that "Member States' autonomy in relation to judicial remedies for the infringement of rights conferred by the Community system .... is subject to considerable derogations .... whenever it is essential ... to ensure ....

26 At p. 1157.
27 At p. 1158.
28 At pp. 1159-1160.
29 At p. 1093. See also p. 1095.

correct effective protection of the rights claimed by individuals under Community law". He later said that "it is vital that it should be Community law itself which lays down at least the minimum conditions determining the right to compensation"[30] and later said that "judicial protection .... must in any event attain a degree of adequacy .... checking that that level has been attained is a matter for the Court".[31] In other words, the Court determines the minimum standards.

In *Hedley Lomas*[32] the Court ruled that a Member State must pay compensation for refusing to issue an export licence, in breach of Article 34. The Court confirmed the three conditions required for liability: a sufficiently serious breach of a rule of Community law, which is intended to confer rights on individuals, and a direct causal link between the breach and the loss suffered. The Court added that if the Member State had little discretion, the mere infringement of the Community rule may be enough to constitute a serious breach. It also pointed out that the existence of the causal link is a question of fact for the national court to decide, and repeated that the national law requirements for recovery of compensation "must not be such as in practice to make it impossible or excessively difficult to obtain reparation".

In *Dillenköfer*[33] the Court confirmed that failure to transpose a directive is in itself a sufficiently serious breach of Community law to give rise to State liability. Such a failure is a manifest and grave disregard of the limits of the State's discretion. If the period provided for implementation is too short, the State concerned must ask the Community institutions to extend it.

In *FMC v. Intervention Board for Agricultural Produce*[34] the Court said that "a rule of national law, by virtue of which a sum paid to a public authority under a mistake of law may be recovered only if it was paid under protest, manifestly fails" to satisfy the requirement of not making it excessively difficult to recover, "in that it is liable to prejudice effective protection of the rights conferred on the traders in question by Community law".

In *Ex parte British Telecommunications*[35] the Court had to decide a more difficult issue: is there a sufficiently serious breach of Community law if an ambiguous directive is incorrectly transposed? The Court decided that in this case it had all the necessary information to decide whether the facts showed a sufficiently serious breach. In deciding whether the breach manifestly and gravely disregarded the limits on the exercise of the State's powers, the clarity and precision of the rule breached is relevant. The directive in question was "imprecisely worded and was reasonably capable of bearing .... the interpretation given

30 At p. 1096.

31 At p. 1121. See Case C-128/92, *Banks v. British Coal*, [1994] ECR I-1209, Advocate General van Gerven at pp. 1253-1255.

32 [1996] ECR I.

33 Joined Cases C-178/94 *and others*, [1996] ECR I-4845.

34 Case 212/94, [1996] ECR I-389 at paras. 71/72.

35 Case C-392/93, *R v. HM Treasury ex parte British Telecommunications*, [1996] ECR I-1631. See also C-292/94, *Denkavit*, [1996] ECR I-5063 para. 47.

to it by the United Kingdom in good faith and on the basis of arguments which are not entirely devoid of substance .... that interpretation, which was also shared by other Member States, was not manifestly contrary to the wording of the directive or to the objective pursued by it".[36] There was no guidance from the Court's case law, and the Commission had not raised the question when the UK's implementing measures were adopted. So the breach was not serious enough to create liability.

In this case, the Court took it for granted, and the Advocate General expressly said, that a State can be liable for loss caused by *incorrect* implementation of a directive, as well as for complete failure to do so.

The next case, *Comateb*[37] concerned the question how far a trader can recover from the State a tax imposed contrary to Community law, when the tax has been passed on to and borne by another person. The Court recognised that even if the tax was fully passed on, and so could not be recovered from the State without unjust enrichment, the trader might have lost sales and profits as a result of the higher price, and this loss could be claimed for. The Court added[38] "traders may not be prevented from applying to the courts having jurisdiction, in accordance with the appropriate procedures of national law, and subject to the conditions laid down in .... *Brasserie du Pêcheur* and *Factortame* .... for reparation of loss caused by the levying of charges not due, irrespective of whether those charges have been passed on".

In *Bonifaci and Berlo*[39] one of the questions asked by the national court concerned the extent of the reparation payable by a Member State when a directive is transposed late. The Court concisely summarised the cases set out here. It noted that the national implementing legislation provided for retroactive application. This should be sufficient, unless the beneficiaries proved some additional loss as a result of not being able to benefit at the appropriate time, in which case that extra loss must be repaid also. It is for the national court to ensure that reparation for the loss sustained is adequate.

SOME IMPLICATIONS OF THE PRINCIPLE OF EFFECTIVE PROTECTION

A number of conclusions can be drawn from the case-law of the Court summarised above:

---

36 At p. 1669.

37 Joined Cases C-192/95 to C-218/95, *Comateb and others*, [1997] ECR I-165. See also Case C-66/95, *R v. Secretary of State, ex parte Sutton*, [1997] ECR I-2163: Case C-132/95, *Jensen*, May 19, 1998 (rules on set-off against companies getting EC aid must not be more stringent than the corresponding rules on national aid).

38 At p. 192.

39 Joined Cases C-94/95 and C-95/95, [1997] ECR I-3969, at pp. 4021-4023 and Advocate General Cosmas at pp. 3984-3988 who said that retroactive, full and express implementation of a directive is "a requirement of the Community legal order" (p. 2988). See also Case C-373/95, *Maso*, [1997] ECR I-4051.

- national courts, like the Court of Justice, have a duty to see that Community law is observed, under Article 220. This means granting judicial review whenever necessary to make sure that Community law points can be raised. It may also mean allowing actions for declarations of rights rather than forcing private parties to run the risk of being prosecuted or sued in order to establish their rights. The *Coote* case shows that individuals should not have to take risks in order to claim their rights.
- Community law guarantees that national courts will give effective remedies to anyone who has suffered loss as a result of any breach of a rule of Community law for the protection of individual rights;
- The Court is willing to decide progressively what constitutes minimum effective protection in Community law;
- Minimum effective protection includes both substantive and procedural elements. Effectiveness means that substantive Community law rights should be complete and without gaps. It also means that national courts must give them complete protection.
- The case-law clearly implies that effective protection must also be given against private parties who infringe directly applicable Community law rules binding on them if the rules are intended to create rights for other private parties.[40] The full range of remedies available under national law must be used to enforce these rules.
- The Court will not accept procedural or substantive arguments against liability that would result in compensation not being available at all in a significant category of situations, or which would lead to compensation being insufficient to cover the full amount of the loss.
  On the other hand, the Court will accept limitation or prescription periods and requirements that oblige claimants to act with reasonable vigilance to protect their interests.[41]
- The Court will not accept any preconditions for liability that are incompatible with the direct effect of the rule guaranteeing compensation, or which add additional conditions to the exercise of the right. The Court has developed fairly detailed tests for determining whether the breach of Community law is serious enough to create liability.

---

40 See in particular Case C-242/95, *GT-Link v. DSB*, [1997] ECR I-4449 paras. 22-27, 56-61: Case C-128/92, *Banks v. British Coal*, [1994] ECR I-1209, Advocate General van Gerven, at pp. 1243-1260. No doubt other questions will arise in claims for compensation against private parties: see Temple Lang, "The duties of national courts under Community constitutional law", 22 European Law Review (1997), 3-18, at pp. 7-8.

41 Case 33/76, *Rewe*, [1976] ECR 1989; Case C-208/90, *Emmott*, [1991] ECR 4269; Case C-261/95, *Palmisani*, [1997] ECR I-4025; Case C-188/95, *Fantask*, [1997] ECR I; Case C-231/96, *Edilizia Industriale*, [1998] ECR I-4951.

So far, the only Community rules which do *not*[42] protect private rights are some imprecise general provisions in environmental protection directives.

- in retrospect, the surprise and controversy over the *Francovich* judgment seems unjustified from a legal viewpoint. It had been clear from the previous case-law that Community law required Member States to pay compensation in case of breach of directly applicable rules. There had never been any reason to believe that this principle was confined to refunds of previously determined amounts. The legal novelty of the *Francovich* judgment lay *only* in making compensation payable for failure to implement rules which are not themselves directly applicable. But the controversy aroused by the *Francovich* judgment was not about this legal point: it questioned the principle which had first been stated by the Court in 1960;[43]
- The controversy over *Francovich* was understandable insofar as it was prompted by the concern of Ministers for Finance worried by the risk of having to pay large and unforeseeable sums of money from national budgets. However, it is significant that since the *Francovich* judgment in 1991, there have been the negotiations which led to the Treaty of Amsterdam. These negotiations give Member States the opportunity to propose a Treaty amendment to modify the principle stated in the judgment. It seems that no Member State proposed this, and certainly there is nothing in the Amsterdam Treaty which affects the principle. It seems therefore that the Member States accept that the principle is indeed, as the Court said several times, a principle inherent in the Community legal system, and do not object seriously to it;
- there are of course still unanswered questions, notably about "remoteness of damage", how far losses caused *indirectly* can be recovered as compensation;
- the *Francovich* principle ought to be, and will certainly become, an important deterrent, discouraging national authorities from infringing Community law. The national authorities which control public expenditure should be extremely critical of any public body which yields to lobbying and adopts a protectionist measure providing temporary gains to private interests, and later has to pay large sums in compensation out of taxpayers' money;
- in deciding whether a Member State has "manifestly and gravely disregarded" the limits on its discretion, the case law of the Court of Justice and of national courts must be looked at. This means that a national

42 Case C-236/92, *Difesa della Cava v. Regione Lombardia*, [1994] ECR I-483 but see Case C-72/95, *Kraaijeveld*, [1996] ECR I-5403; see also Case C-431/92, *Commission v. Germany*, [1995] ECR I-2189. Treaty provisions on agricultural policy do not protect individuals; Case T-571/93, *Lefebvre*, [1995] ECR II-2379, para. 41.

43 In Case 6/90, *Humblet*, [1960] ECR 559 at p. 569.

measure or policy which was not "manifestly" illegal when it began may become manifestly illegal as a result of later judgments. In such circumstances the State might be liable for loss caused after the illegality became clear, even if it was not liable for loss caused before then. Certainly, a State is liable if it delays in acting on the judgment of any court;

- whether a violation of Community law is serious enough to give rise to liability will be judged, in part, in the light of the case law on Article 288, in which seriousness is assessed both from the circumstances relating to the breach and those relating to the damage caused;[44]
- whether a violation is serious enough to create liability will be influenced by any view expressed by the European Commission on the question, whether or not the Member State is obliged to consult the Commission on the point;[45]
- one can expect that disappointed contractors will sue public authorities for compensation if they have not complied with the Community directives on public contracts;
- the number of cases raising these issues has recently increased very much. It is certain that there will be many claims of this kind in national courts in the near future

But the obligations of national courts which result from Article 10 EC are not only those which are derived from the principle of direct effects and the duty to give effective remedies. Article 10 is expressed as two obligations: a duty to help, and a duty not to obstruct. These duties have consequences for national courts which do not fall under any of the rules mentioned above, and which illustrate some of the less obvious implications of Community law. I turn now to some of those consequences.

WHICH NATIONAL AUTHORITY SHOULD PAY COMPENSATION?

At first sight, one would say that, just as it is for national law to say which national authority should implement or enforce any given rule of Community law, it is also for national law to decide which national authority should be defendant and should pay compensation for breach of Community law. Of course, if the breach is committed by the national legislature or the national government, the government is the natural defendant.

The correct result might be different if the breach was committed by a local or regional authority. In this situation, there are strong arguments for the view

44 Case C-104/89, *Mulder* [1992] ECR I-3061, at p. 3104, Advocate General van Gerven.

45 Temple Lang, "The Core of the Constitutional Law of the Community–Article 5 EC", in Gormley (ed.,) *Current and Future Perspectives in EC Competition Law* (Kluwer, 1997), 41-72.

that the primary defendant should be the authority in question, not the central government. There are several reasons for this view. First, the right to sue the Member State for compensation is a residual right if no more appropriate remedy, or no remedy against a more appropriate defendant, is available. Second, the national authority to which national law gave the task of implementing Community law is the most obviously appropriate defendant: it is most likely to be able to make whatever arguments may be appropriate to defend against the claim, and if its internal documents must be disclosed in the court proceedings, it must in any case be involved. Economy of procedure suggests that it should be the principal or the only defendant. Third, the Court has said that Member States must ensure that "infringements of Community law are penalised under conditions, both procedural and substantive, which are analogous to those applicable to infringements of nation law of a similar nature and importance and which, in any event, make the penalty effective, proportionate and dissuasive".[46] There is no reason to confine this statement to payment of penalties as distinct from compensation. It is clearly more effective, proportionate and dissuasive that the defendant which pays the compensation should be the authority whose act has led to compensation being payable.[47] The principle which requires an effective remedy requires that the remedy should be available against the person or authority primarily responsible. A remedy is dissuasive, i.e. is a deterrent, only if it is directly available against the person or authority responsible for the violation. Since it is important for many reasons that Community law remedies should discourage violations as far as possible, this is a crucial argument. Fourth, most cases will begin as proceedings to annul the action of the authority in question, and it would be efficient to combine such proceedings with a claim for compensation against the same defendants.

There are, no doubt, many national law arguments also which I believe would suggest the same conclusion.

46 Case 68/88, *Commission v. Greece*, [1989] ECR 2965 at 2984-2985; Case C-326/88, *Hansen*, [1990] ECR I-2911 at 2935, para. 17; Case C-7/90, *Vandevenne*, [1991] ECR I-4371; Cases 382/92 and C-383/92, *Commission v. UK*, [1994] ECR I-2435 and 2479 at 2475 and 2494; Case C-52/95, *Commission v. France*, [1995] ECR I-4443; Case C-240/90, *Germany v. Commission*, [1992] ECR I-5387, at p. 5410; Cases C-58/95, *Galloti and others*, [1996] ECR I-4345; Case C-341/94 *Allain*, [1996] ECR I-4631.

47 Temple Lang, "New Legal Effects resulting from the failure of States to fulfil obligations under Community law; the Francovich judgment", 16 *Fordham International Law Journal* (1992-93) 1-52. See however Joined Cases C-114/95 and C-115/95, *Texaco and Olieselskabet Danmark*, [1997] ECR I-4263, at paras. 38-43; Case C-180/97, *Regione Toscana*, [1997] ECR I-5245.

STATE LIABILITY FOR FAILURE TO ENFORCE COMMUNITY LAW – AN EFFECTIVE REMEDY

Another question, not yet decided by the Court of Justice, is how far State authorities are liable to pay compensation for their failure to enforce Community law rules, even if the rules have been duly implemented, if their failure causes loss to private parties.

Some comments can be made:

- a Member State may be liable to pay compensation for failure to act, in certain circumstances;[48]
- Member States have a duty to enforce their national laws, when this is necessary to protect Community law rights of private parties (the French farmers case[49]). Article 10 imposes a duty to take all necessary and appropriate measures to ensure respect for fundamental freedoms such as free movement of goods;
- Member States have a duty to enforce Community law as effectively as they enforce corresponding rules of national law;[50]
- it is clear that a Member State cannot plead that it has allocated inadequate resources to enforcement, as a justification for infringing Community law;[51]

However:

- the Member State would be liable only if the Community rule was one giving rights to individuals (the first *Francovich* condition), and was not a rule intended e.g. to protect only the general public interest, or to state the duties of the Community institutions to one another, or the duties of national authorities towards the Community institutions;

48 Joined Cases C-6/90 and C-9/90, *Francovich* [1991] ECR I-5357.

49 Case C-265/95, *Commission v. France*, [1997] ECR I-6959, para. 30-33.

50 Case 68/88 *Commission v. Greece*, [1989] ECR 2965 at 2984-85; Case C-326/88, *Hansen*, [1990] ECR I-2911 at p. 2935, para. 17; Case C-7/90 *Vandevenne*, [1991] ECR I-4371; Case C-382/92 and C-383/92, *Commission v. U.K.*, [1994] ECR I-2435 and 2479, at pp. 2475 and 2494; Case C-52/95, *Commission v. France*, [1995] ECR I-4443; Case 29/82, *Van Luipen*, [1983] ECR 151 ("Considerations of an administrative nature cannot justify derogation by a Member State from the rules of Community law", para. 12); Case C-187/96, *Commission v. Greece*, March 12, 1998.

51 Case 104/75, *De Peijper* [1976] ECR 613 at paras. 17-18; Case 238/82, *Duphar*, [1984] ECR 523 at 542; Case 40/82, *Commission v. U.K.*, [1984] ECR 283 at 301; Case 74/82, *Commission v. Ireland*, [1984] ECR 317 at 346-47; Case 8/88, *Germany v. Commission*, [1990] ECR I-2321 at pp. 2359-61; Case C-48/91, *Netherlands v. Commission*, [1993] ECR I-5611 at 5633. See now also the Case C-191/95, *Commission v. Germany*, [1998] ECR I-5449, para. 68.

- the Community rule would have to be one which was intended to be enforced only or primarily by official enforcement authorities and procedures. If the rule was merely intended to give private parties rights which they could enforce before courts or other appropriate tribunals, the national authorities would have no duty to enforce it, even if national procedures allowed them to do so;
- there must be a sufficiently clear and serious breach by the national authority of its duty to enforce the Community law rule. Presumably, any large-scale failure to enforce a rule stated in a directive is automatically serious, just as a failure to implement any such rule would be. Certainly, any failure to enforce a rule is serious if breach of the rule is inherently likely to have serious consequences for the private parties whom the rule is intended to protect. A national authority may have some discretion in deciding when to enforce a detailed national law rule established, perhaps, more for administrative convenience than for substantive protection of private interests. But it cannot have a discretion (except when a directive deliberately gives a choice) as to whether to enforce a rule of Community law;
- there must be a causal link between the national authority's failure to enforce the Community law rule and the loss to the private party. Causation is primarily a question of fact, for the national court to decide. However, causation is complex when the violation of Community law is an omission or failure by a national authority to apply or enforce a rule against a third party. The precise question about causation may ultimately have to be decided by the Court of Justice. The test must concern both the thoroughness of the enforcement or supervision, and the likelihood of loss of the kind in question as a result of incomplete enforcement. Probably the test is whether the failure to enforce the rule fully is inherently likely to lead to serious losses of the kind suffered by the plaintiff. It would not be necessary to show that such losses would inevitably occur, but merely to show that such losses were the kind of losses which the rule was intended to prevent. It might be important that the State had previously been asked to enforce more thoroughly, if there were reasons to think the enforcement was needed, or if all routine checks had been properly done without any reason for suspicion.

In all this, it is important to remember that the State will not be the primary defendant: the private party which has suffered loss will usually sue the company which was bound by the Community law rule.

Whatever the precise details of the rules about liability for failure to enforce may be, the principle of effective protection of Community law rights (and indeed common sense) suggests that a private party should be able to obtain compensation if its rights were inadequately protected by authorities responsible for enforcement. The Court has made it clear that if Community law rights are not protected, it does not matter whether it is the national legislature or the national executive which is

> responsible.[52] Many rules of Community law, in particular those relating to banks and insurance companies, cannot be applied by private parties, who have got neither the confidential information nor the expertise needed. Mutual recognition requires other Member States to rely on supervision and enforcement by the Member State in which the bank or insurance company is situated. The duty to enforce rules of Community law itself results from Article 10. A private individual could not reasonably be expected to protect his own rights under Community law rules on, e.g., the hygiene of abattoirs, every time he buys a steak.
> So an "effective remedy" for breach of a right given by Community law includes a right to claim compensation from a State authority which has failed to enforce Community law, if the plaintiff cannot recover fully from the company which was bound by the Community law rule.

This principle will in due course give rise to other questions, outside the scope of this paper, e.g. the liability of stock exchanges for failing to enforce Community rules on defective prospectuses, and the liability of competition authorities for failure to enforce Community competition rules.

COMMUNITY LAW GUARANTEES JUDICIAL PROTECTION

In several judgments the Court has said that there must be judicial review of administrative acts when rights under Community law are involved.[53] These judgments and the *Zuckerfabrik* case[54] illustrate a basic principle of Community law: national courts must take whatever judicial action is needed to enable an efficient litigant to raise any issue of Community law which affects its interests directly. This may mean that in some Member States there is *greater* scope for judicial review of administrative or executive acts when questions of Community law are involved. But the fundamental principle is that there must be no gaps in the judicial protection provided by the national courts and the Community courts working together.

To this general principle there is one important qualification. Private parties which wish to raise points of Community law must make use of the opportunities which the Community legal order and national procedures give to them. If

---

52 Joined Cases C-46/93 and C-48/93 *Brasserie du Pêcheur and Factortame* [1996] ECR I-1029; Joined Cases C-6/90 and C-9/90, *Francovich* [1991] ECR I-5357.

53 Case 294/83, *Les Verts*, [1986] ECR 1339; Case 222/86, *Heylens*, [1987] ECR 4097, paras. 14-16.; Case 222/84, *Johnston v. RUC*, [1986] ECR 1651, at 1663; Case C-128/92, *Banks v. British Coal*, [1994] ECR I-1209, Advocate General van Gerven at pp. 1246-1251; Case C-54/96, *Dorsch Consult*, 17 Sept. 1997; Joined Cases T-134/94, NMH *Stahlwerke*, [1996] ECR II-537, para. 69; Case C-185/97, *Coote v. Granada Hospitality*, [1998] ECR I-5199.

54 Case C-143/88, *Zuckerfabrick*, [1991] ECR I-415; Case C-465/93, *Atlanta*, [1995] ECR I-3761; Case C-334/95, *Krüger*, [1997] ECR I-4517.

they fail to sue within the relevant limitation period or within the time limits under administrative law, or if they fail to make their arguments at the right procedural moment,[55] they have no right to insist on being able to correct the consequences of their own mistakes.

Similarly, in cases brought directly before the Community Courts, parties must begin proceedings at the appropriate moment, and not merely whenever they want to. During a Commission procedure leading in due course to a decision attackable under Article 230, once the Commission has defined its position, even if the position cannot itself be challenged under Article 230, a party cannot immediately bring proceedings for inaction under Article 232.[56] It must wait until the end of the procedure before it can go to Luxembourg. A procedural step which itself has no legal effects is not open to challenge under Article 230.[57] On the other hand, a decision taken during a procedure which itself has substantive, non-procedural, effects is open to immediate challenge.[58] Therefore a legal opinion given by or on behalf of the Commission to a national court or a national authority, which is not binding and has no legal effects, cannot be challenged directly and can be criticised only in the course of a challenge under national law to the decision of the national court or authority.[59]

I believe that one can summarise the duties of cooperation resulting from Article 10 EC Treaty by saying that national courts, like other national authorities, have a general duty not to interfere with the way that Community institutions, laws and policies are intended to work, and a duty and a power, when necessary, to make them work that way.

In the case of most Community policies, there are specific Community measures, and lawyers can see how they are intended to work by reading the preambles. But the duties of national courts in the Community's judicial system result from the Community Treaties. They are not concisely summarised anywhere. They are the logical consequences of a rational and effective judicial system in which the national courts must play a major and crucial role.[60] From the case law summarised here the "rational and effective" system means that *all Community law issues can be raised before a court and referred if necessary to the Court of Justice in Luxembourg and, if they are raised at an appropriate*

55 Joined Cases C-430/93 and C-431/93, *van Schijndel* [1995] ECR I-4705; Case C-312/93, *Peterbroeck*, [1995] ECR I-4599; Case C-188/92, *TWD Textilwerke*, [1994] ECR I-833.

56 Case T-105/96, *Pharos*, Feb.17, [1998] ECR II; Case T-38/96, *Guérin Automobiles*, [1997] ECR II-1223; Case T-348/94, *Enso Española*, judgment dated May 14 1998, paras. 60, 63.

57 Case 60/81, *IBM v. Commission*, [1981] ECR 2639.

58 Cases 8-11/66, *Cimenteries*, [1967] ECR 75; Case 792/79, *Camera Care*, [1980] ECR 119; Case 53/85, *Akzo* (confidentiality of documents), [1986] ECR 1965.

59 Case 229/86, *Brother Industries*, [1987] ECR 3757.

60 Temple Lang, "The duties of national courts under Community Constitutional law", 22 *European Law Review* (1997), 3-18 at pp. 4-5. Presumably, national courts must also allow appeals or judicial review of awards of public arbitration systems; see Case C-126/97, *Eco Swiss China Time v. Benetton*, judgment of 1 June 1999, nyr.

time, the courts will make sure that Community law is applied and that effective, prompt and complete protection is given to rights granted by Community law. Community law itself gives national courts, if necessary, all the powers which they need to do this.

SOME OTHER DUTIES OF NATIONAL COURTS UNDER ARTICLE 10

Apart from cases involving the duty to give effective remedies for breach of Community law rules, various other cases have arisen in which national courts have dealt with the relationship between Community law and national law.

One such case was *Hasselblad (GB) Ltd. v. Orbison.*[61] Mr Orbison had written to the European Commission giving evidence of an infringement by Hasselblad (GB) of Article 85 EC [now Article 81]. During the Commission procedure, Hasselblad sued Orbison in the English courts for defamation. The Commission, unusually, was represented before the English Court of Appeal. Hasselblad's claim was dismissed on two grounds. First, defamation actions against witnesses would seriously discourage them from giving evidence to the Commission. Second, national courts and the Commission should not separately decide what conclusions should be drawn from particular evidence, with the possibility of inconsistent results. Therefore, Mr Orbison's evidence could not be the subject of a defamation action unless there was proof of malice or dishonest intent (the rule called "qualified privilege", in English defamation law).

Clearly this case was correctly decided, and there are a number of other cases in which national courts have decided how far they need to go to avoid possible future conflicts with Commission decisions in parallel procedures in competition cases.[62] However, some other problems are more difficult.

Another problem of reconciling different EC and national objectives arose, also in the English Court of Appeal, in *MTVE v. BMG* in 1998.[63] The case was complicated, but the essential question arose because MTVE was sued for royalties on videos it had broadcast. MTVE argued that the recording companies whose videos it had broadcast were using a licensing joint venture which was

---

61 1984 3 CML Rep. 679.

62 Case 14/68, *Walt Wilhelm*, [1969] ECR I; Case 66/86, *Ahmed Saeed*, [1989] ECR 803; Case C-234/89, *Delimitis*, [1991] ECR I-935 at pp. 991-994; Case C-250/92, *Gøttrup-Klim*, [1994] ECR I-5641; Joined Cases C-319/93 and others, *Dijkstra*, [1995] ECR I-4471; *Hasselblad v. Orbison*, [1984] CMLRep. 679; *MTV Europe v BMG Records*, [1997] CMLRep. 867; *Fyffes v. Chiquita*, [1993] FSR 83; *Re Net Book Agreement*, [1997] UK Restrictive Practices Court, 13 March 1997.

63 Court of Appeal, England, March 10, 1998; for an earlier stage of the same Case see *MTV Europe v. BMG* (Records) (UK), [1997] I Common Market Law Reports 867.
On exchanges of information between competitors, see the Commission decision *Wirtschaftsvereinigung Stahl*, adopted in November 1997; Cases T-35/92, *John Deere*, [1994] ECR II-905, 957; Cases C-8/95P, C-7/95P, *New Holland, John Deere*, [1998] ECR I.

contrary to Article 85 and that it was therefore entitled to refuse to pay the royalty demanded by this joint venture, because this would force it to pay more. MTVE also said it was contrary to Article 85 for the video companies to exchange information within the joint venture about their licensing policies. The Commission had written a letter substantially agreeing with these arguments, though not with MTVE's conclusions. But the Court of Appeal ordered MTVE to disclose various documents, including MTVE's agreements with the other video companies, so that MTVE's argument that the joint venture led to high royalties could be assessed. These agreements would normally be highly confidential, and it would normally have been contrary to Article 85 for the video companies to agree to exchange such information.

My purpose is not to argue that the Court of Appeal was wrong. My purpose is simply to point out that in national proceedings a court needs to be very careful to avoid bringing about, even for the purposes of the proceedings, exchanges of confidential information which the companies themselves would not be legally free to arrange, and which would lessen competition between them. This kind of issue could arise in any situation in which a joint venture which is said to be unlawful is in litigation with a company with which it has been or normally would be contracting. If the information exchanged was out-of-date, the problem is less serious: if it is valuable up-to-date information, national courts should be very slow to order it to be disclosed, and certainly not without safeguards to prevent violations of Community competition law. National courts, like all other national authorities, have a legal duty not to deprive Community competition rules of their useful effects.[64]

A third series of cases concerns situations in which it is said that a Member State has granted State aid contrary to Articles 87-89 [ex Articles 92-94] EC Treaty, some provisions of which are directly applicable. Such cases normally arise when a competitor asks the national court to halt the payment of aid which has not been properly notified. In a recent case[65] the Court said "National courts must offer to individuals the certain prospect that all the appropriate conclusions will be drawn from an infringement of ... Article 93(3) [now Article 88(3)] ... in accordance with their national laws, as regards the validity of measures giving effect to the aid, the recovery of financial support granted in disregard of that provision, and possible interim measures". The Court did not explain what it meant by "all appropriate conclusions", but I regard this again as a duty to provide effective remedies. Community law also requires that State aid which

64 See the case law discussed by Advocate General van Gerven in Cases C-48/90 and C-66/90, *Netherlands and PTT Nederland v. Commission*, [1992] ECR I-565 at pp. 614-619.

65 Case C-39/94, *SFEI*, [1996] ECR I-3547 at p. 3590-91; see also Case C-354/90, *FNCE*, [1991] ECR I-5505; Case T-49/93, *SIDE*, [1995] ECR II-2501; Case T-239/94, *EISA*, [1997] ECR II-1839; Case 169/84, *COFAZ*, [1986] ECR 391; cp. Case T-435/93, *ASPEC*, [1995] ECR II-1281; Case C-313/90, *CIRFS*, [1993] ECR I-1125; Case C-301/89, *France v. Commission ("Boussac")*, [1990] ECR I-307.

should not have been paid is recovered from the companies which received it, and there are minimum standards of efficiency in this respect also.[66]

A fourth example of the other duties of national courts concerns "mandatory" Community rules, i.e. rules which override any clause in a contract which is contrary to the rule. It is well known that these include Community rules on equal treatment for men and women[67] and Community competition rules. A similar rule invalidates any clauses in agreements to settle litigation which try to prevent complaints to the Commission about future breaches of Community competition law, or to prevent a company from giving evidence to the Commission. It is convenient to say that such clauses are contrary to Community rules of public policy, or *ordre public*. It is more precise to say that Article 10 obliges national courts to treat as invalid any contractual clause which interferes with the right of any private party to give evidence or information to the Community institutions, or to claim in any appropriate forum rights given to it under Community law, or which would interfere with the activities of the Commission as envisaged by Community law,[68] or which would involve a breach of any mandatory rule of Community law.

I believe there is a broader principle. In *Commission v. France*,[69] the Court decided that the French authorities had failed to fulfil their obligations under Community law because they had not used their normal powers to stop French farmers blocking roads in a protest against private parties exercising their right to move their goods freely within the Community. The Court said that Article 30

---

66 See e.g. Case 205/82, *Deutsche Milchkontor*, [1983] ECR 2633 at p. 2666.

67 Case 43/75, *Defrenne v. Sabena*, [1976] ECR 455, at paras. 32,39; Case C-177/88, *Dekker*, [1990] ECR I-3941; Case C-271/91, *Marshall II*, [1993] ECR I-4387; Case C-324/86, *Tellerup*, [1988] ECR 739, at para. 14 and p. 747 (where the Advocate General used the phrase "public policy"); Case C-189/89, *Nimz*, [1991] ECR I-297 at pp. 320-321; Case C-200/91 *Coloroll*, [1994] ECR I-4389; Case C-305/94, *Rotstart v. Benoidt*, [1996] ECR I-5927; Case C-15/96, *Schöning-Kougebetopoulou*, [1998] ECR I-4771 (a clause in a collective agreement is void if it does not treat equally experience in public service in other Member States); see also Case 102/81, *Nordsee*, [1982] ECR 1095 at p. 1111; Case 58/80, *Dansk Supermarked v. Imerco*, [1981] ECR 181 at para. 17. See also Directive 93/13/EC, O.J. No L 95/29 Article 6(2) and Directive 94/47/EC, O.J. No L 280/83, Article 9, which provide that consumers cannot be deprived of the protection given by the directives by choice-of-law clauses. See also Case C-126/97, *Eco Swiss China Time v. Benetton* (how far arbitrators are obliged to apply Community competition law, and whether national courts should raise the issue if they have not done so) *supra* note 60.

68 Of course, bona fide settlements of claims for loss in the past are permitted. On the duty of public authorities not to interfere with the operation of Community institutions see Case 208/80, *Lord Bruce of Donington*, [1981] ECR 2205; Case 44/84, *Hurd v. Jones*, [1986] ECR 29; Case 230/81, *Luxembourg v. European Parliament*, [1983] ECR 255, 287; under EC law obligations, national courts have the same duties as other national authorities; see e.g. Case C-72/95, *Kraaijeveld*, [1996] ECR I-5403 at p. 5452.

69 Case C-265/95, *Commission v. France*, [1997] ECR I-6959, paras. 30, 32; cp. *R v. Chief Constable of Sussex, exp. International Traders' Ferry*, [1997] 2 Common Market Law Reports 164.

[now Article 28] (on free movement of goods) applies to a Member State's failure to take whatever measures are needed to deal with obstacles even if the State is not itself responsible for them. Article 28, combined with Article 10, imposes a duty to take all measures necessary and appropriate to ensure respect for this fundamental freedom on their territory.

So it seems to be a principle of Community law that private parties must not be allowed to interfere seriously with the rights and freedoms of other private parties guaranteed by Community law, and that the agreements by which they try to do so are void and unenforceable. This principle would call in question, e.g. agreements between a trade union and any company by which the union agreed that its members would not work for any competitor of the company in question, if this would create a dominant position and interfere with the freedom of the competitors to establish themselves, to supply goods and services, and to compete. Such an agreement is not subject to Article 81, since a trade union is not regarded as an "enterprise", but it would clearly be contrary to the principle of "Community public policy" derived from Article 10. I understand that this principle may be of some relevance in Swedish harbours.

These are essentially duties to prevent infringements of Community law by private parties, and to prevent private parties from interfering with the way in which Community law or a clearly defined Community policy is intended to work.

The duty to provide an effective remedy would also give national administrative courts a duty, if the relevant rule of law protects private rights, to make positive orders obliging public authorities to give private parties their rights – their rights to a licence without unlawful conditions, for example.

THE EFFECT ON THE CONCEPT OF "JUSTICE" IN THE NATIONAL ENVIRONMENT OF NON-COMPLIANCE WITH COMMUNITY LAW

When national law does not comply with Community law, national courts are obliged to make sure, in whatever way is most appropriate, that rights given by Community law are protected. "Justice according to law" no longer means merely justice according to whatever the national law happens to be at the time, but justice according to national law, supplemented or modified if necessary to ensure that Community law is fully applied. Of course, this will not be necessary very often. Application of the normal rules of substantive law and procedure of the Member State in question will normally protect Community law rights fully. But it is important to remember that it *may* be necessary: the relevant rule of national law may be insufficient or inappropriate to protect fully a right given by Community law, and if this happens the national courts have the power and the duty, both given by Article 10, to provide the most appropriate remedy, even if it is only compensation on the *Francovich* principle.

So the effect on the national concept of "justice" is to introduce a second body of principles, to be applied when necessary by the same national courts, which occasionally override or add to national law rules. This second body of law includes principles of fundamental human rights, as guaranteed *inter alia* by the European Convention for the Protection of Human Rights. These are "general principles of Community law", so they apply throughout the sphere of Community law, and are directly applicable. They must be applied whenever appropriate by national courts, in the Community law sphere, even if the European Convention has not otherwise been made part of national law, or has not been given constitutional or overriding status in national law.

It follows, among other things, that national courts act in two different spheres: the sphere of Community law, in which they may be required to apply human rights principles and other general principles of Community law, and the purely national law sphere.[70] This may mean that in certain points the rights of individuals or companies are better protected in the Community law sphere than under national law.[71] If this is so (which may not be very often, but it will certainly occur), private parties will strongly argue that Community law applies: the court will need to decide if the case is indeed within the sphere of Community law; and, less clearly, there will be a tendency for the national courts to introduce into national law principles previously found only in Community law. Unless they are obliged to say so, national courts will be reluctant to say that Community law provides a just and fair remedy and national law does not.

So the most important lesson to be drawn about the concept of "justice" is that Community law requires the remedies available to individuals to be "effec-

---

70 Case C-2/92, *Bostock*, [1994] ECR I-955; see Temple Lang, "The sphere in which Member States are obliged to comply with the general principles of law and Community fundamental rights principles", 1991/1992, *Legal Issues of European Integration*, pp. 23-36. See *R v. Ministry of Agriculture ex parte First City Trading*, [1997] I Common Market Law Reports 250 (fundamental Community law principle of equal treatment not applicable to a national agricultural aid scheme differentiating between UK companies but not adopted under a duty or power or exemption given by Community law; Community law is stricter than UK law). First City Trading distinguishes between Treaty provisions such as the prohibition on discrimination on the grounds of nationality, which apply to all sectors of the Common Market, and "general principles" which are said to apply to powers exercised pursuant to Community law. See *also R v. Customs and Excise, ex parte Lunn Poly*, English Court of Appeal, April 2 1998. There is not space available to consider this issue fully, but fundamental rights principles must apply throughout all sectors of the Common Market. I believe that all "general principles" apply to all national measures which affect rights given or protected by Community law (including freedom of movement of goods, services, persons, capital, and freedom of competition) and even if the legal basis of the power (or the duty) to adopt national measures is national law rather than Community law. The Court in First City Trading said that general principles apply to "measures adopted pursuant to Community law", (which is ambiguous) but later explains this as meaning measures "taken so as to implement Community law, or [which] must necessarily rely on it (as in the Article 3b example)" which it is submitted is correct (at p. 269).

71 See for the situation in the UK, *R v. Chief Constable of Sussex, ex parte International Traders' Ferry*, [1997] 2 Common Market Law Reports 164; *R v. Ministry of Agriculture, ex parte First City Trading*, [1997] 1 Common Market Law Reports, 250.

tive": it creates a common European minimum standard which may require national remedies to be supplemented.

FUNDAMENTAL LEGAL CONCEPTS OF NATIONAL LAWS ARE REFLECTED IN COMMUNITY LAW AND THE PRACTICE OF THE COMMUNITY COURTS

All this will not mean extensive modifications to national remedies or procedures. Community law is broadly similar to national administrative laws (even if a different vocabulary is used, which is intended to be independent from the vocabulary of any one Member State). Community law has now been in force long enough for the Community Courts to rely, in most cases, on the Court's own case law: it is only when a new question arises that the Courts now need to turn again to national law rules and concepts . But the Court, from the beginning, looked to the national law rules and concepts of the original six Member States as sources of Community law.[72] In particular, the Court drew on the national administrative laws of the original Six. Article 230, which sets out the grounds on which a Community act can be annulled, is similar to French administrative law. From national administrative and constitutional laws the Court drew what we now regard as the Community law principles of proportionality,[73] legal certainty and legitimate expectations. More important still, from national constitutional laws comes also the Court's case law on fundamental human rights. Article 6(2) of the Treaty on European Union reads:

> "The Union shall respect fundamental rights, as guaranteed by the European Convention for the Protection of Human Rights and Fundamental Freedoms signed in Rome on 4 November 1950 *and as they result from the constitutional traditions common to the Member States, as general principles of Community law*". (emphasis supplied)

---

72 Schwarze, *Europäisches Verwaltungrecht* (Baden Baden 1988); Kutscher, "Methods of interpretation as seen by a Judge at the Court of Justice", in *Reports of the Judicial and Academic Conference* 1976, Luxembourg (a Court of Justice publication) passim; see in particular Case 7/56, *Algera* [1957] ECR 83; Schwarze, "Tendencies towards a Common Administrative Law in Europe", 16 *European Law Review* (1991) 3-19; Lord Mackenzie Stuart, *The European Communities and the Rule of Law* (Hamlyn Lectures, London, 1977), pp. 31 ff.; van Gerven, Bridging the unbridgeable (Durham, 1995); Wyatt, "European Law and Public Law in the UK", in Markesinis, *The Gradual Convergence: Foreign ideas, Foreign Influences and English Law on the Eve of the 21st Century* (Oxford, 1994), 188-201. Usher, "Influence of National Concepts on Decisions of the European Court", 1 *European Law Review* (1976), 359. Edward and Robinson, "Is there a place for private law principles in Community law?" in Heukels and McDonnell (eds.), *The Action for Damages in Community Law* (Kluwer, 1997) 339-349. The second volume of the European Court Reports, for 1957-58, contains many references to national law.

73 Emiliou, *The Principle of Proportionality in European Law: A Comparative Study* (Kluwer, 1996). Jowell, "Is proportionality an alien concept?" 1996 *European Public Law* 401; Himsworth, "Legitimately expecting proportionality", 1996 *Public Law* 46.

This confirms, but does not alter, the case law of the Court of Justice.[74]

It is perhaps more obvious from conclusions of Advocates General than from the Court's own judgments, but the Court often considers the national law solutions to a question in order to decide which is most appropriate in Community law. This was done, strikingly, in the *AM&S* case[75] on confidentiality of communications between lawyers and clients. In *AM&S* the Court said:

> "... Community law, which derives from not only the economic but also the legal interpenetration of the Member States, must take into account the principles and concepts common to the laws of those States concerning the observance of confidentiality, in particular, as regards certain communications between lawyer and client. That confidentiality serves the requirements, the importance of which is recognized in all of the Member States, that any person must be able, without constraint, to consult a lawyer whose profession entails the giving of independent legal advice to all those in need of it.
>
> As far as the protection of written communications between lawyer and client is concerned, it is apparent from the legal systems of the Member States, that, although the principle of such protection is generally recognized, its scope and the criteria for applying it vary, as has, indeed, been conceded both by the applicant and by the parties who have intervened in support of its conclusions.
>
> Whilst in some of the Member States the protection against disclosure afforded to written communications between lawyer and client is based principally on a recognition of the very nature of the legal profession, inasmuch as it contributes towards the maintenance of the rule of law, in other Member States, the same protection is justified by the more specific requirement (which, moreover, is also recognized in the first-mentioned States) that the rights of the defence must be respected.
>
> Apart from these differences, however, there are to be found in the national laws of the Member States common criteria inasmuch as those laws protect, in similar circumstances, the confidentiality of written communications between lawyer and client, provided that, on the one hand, such communications are made for the purposes and in the interests of the client's rights of defence and, on the other hand, they emanate from independent lawyers, that is to say, lawyers who are not bound to the client by a relationship of employment.
>
> Viewed in that context Regulation No 17 must be interpreted as protecting, in its turn, the confidentiality of written communications between lawyer and client subject to those two conditions, and thus incorporating such elements of that protection as are common to the laws of the Member States."

Something similar was also done, I believe, in *Emmott*[76] on the question when a limitation or prescription period begins if the person entitled cannot be certain what his rights are.

---

74 See most recently Case T-348/94, *Enso Española*, [1998] ECR II-1875, para. 55.

75 Case 155/79, *AM&S v. Commission*, [1982] ECR 1575, at pp. 1610-1611. See also the opinion of Advocate General Warner at pp. 1621-1623, 1631-1636 and Advocate General Slynn especially at pp. 1651-1658.

76 Case C-208/90, *Emmott v. Minister for Social Welfare*, [1991] ECR I-4269; Cp Case

In *Mulder*[77] the Court referred to "a general principle common to the legal systems of Member States to the effect that the injured party must show reasonable diligence in limiting the extent of his loss or risk having to bear the damage himself".

One of the most striking examples of the extent to which Community law draws on the principles of national law is Article 288 [ex Article 215] EC Treaty, which says:

> "In the case of non-contractual liability, the Community shall, in accordance with the general principles common to the laws of the Member States, make good any damage caused by its institutions or by its servants in the performance of their duties".

The Court referred to this recently in the context of the liability of Member States.[78]

> "Since the Treaty contains no provision expressly and specifically governing the consequences of breaches of Community law by Member States, it is for the Court, in pursuance of the task conferred on it by Article 164 of the Treaty of ensuring that in the interpretation and application of the Treaty the law is observed, to rule on such a question in accordance with generally accepted methods of interpretation, in particular by reference to the fundamental principles of the Community legal system and, where necessary, general principles common to the legal systems of the Member States.
>
> Indeed, it is to the general principles common to the laws of the Member States that the second paragraph of Article 215 of the Treaty refers as the basis of the non-contractual liability of the Community for damage caused by its institutions or by its servants in the performance of their duties.
>
> The principle of the non-contractual liability of the Community expressly laid down in Article 215 of the Treaty is simply an expression of the general principle familiar to the legal systems of the Member States that an unlawful act or omission gives rise to an obligation to make good the damage caused. That provision also reflects the obligation on public authorities to make good damage caused in the performance of their duties.

C-188/95, *Fantask*, [1997] ECR I-6783.

77 Case C-104/89, *Mulder*, [1992] ECR I-3061, para. 33: repeated in Joined Cases C-46/93 and C-48/93, *Brasserie du Pêcheur and Factortame* [1996] ECR I-1029 at para. 85; see also Case C-152/88, *Sofrimport*, [1990] ECR I-2477 at para. 32: "As the claim relates to the non-contractual liability of the Community under the second paragraph of Article 215 [288], it must be considered in the light of the principles common to the legal systems of the Member States to which that provision refers. According to those principles a claim for interest is, as a general rule, permissible".
See also Joined Cases 83/76, *HNL v. Council and others*, [1978] ECR 1209 at para. 5; and see generally Case T-120/89, *Stahlwerke Peine-Salzgitter*, [1991] ECR II-279 at p. 389.

78 Joined Cases C-46/93 and C-48/93, *Brasserie du Pêcheur and Factortame* [1996] ECR I-1029 at p. 1144; see also Joined Cases C-94/95 and C-95/95, *Bonifaci and Berto*, [1997] ECR I-3969, at p. 3984 Advocate General Cosmas.

> In any event, in many national legal systems the essentials of the legal rules governing State liability have been developed by the courts.
>
> In view of the foregoing considerations, the Court held in *Francovich and others,* at paragraph 35, that the principle of State liability for loss and damage caused to individuals as a result of breaches of Community law for which it can be held responsible is inherent in the system of the Treaty"

Later on the Court said:

> "... Article 215 ... refers ... to the general principles common to the laws of Member States, *from which, in the absence of written rules, the Court also draws inspiration in other areas of Community law*" (emphasis supplied).

It is interesting in this context to contrast the situation in one of the cases already cited, *Hedley Lomas*. In his conclusions[79] the Advocate General said that "as far as State liability for legislative action is concerned, there are no general principles which are truly common to the Member States". That being so, no conclusions could be drawn. Similarly, in *Brasserie du Pêcheur*[80] the Court commented that "the concept of fault does not have the same content" in the legal systems of Member States, and the Advocate General pointed out[81] that in several Member States the question whether compensation could be paid for loss caused by an unconstitutional law was not clearly resolved.

There is a further example of how the Court prefers to rely on a principle of national law rather than merely using the general words of the Treaty. Article 10 is the legal basis for the rule that a State may not rely on a national law which is inconsistent with the directive which it should have implemented.[82] But for years the Court described this rule as a result of the principle, found in all national laws, that a party cannot be allowed to take advantage of its own unlawful act or failure. The Court clearly felt that this was a more practical and convincing explanation for the rule than the very general words of Article 10 (the two are, of course, perfectly compatible).

In *Johnston v. R.U.C.*[83] and *Heylens*,[84] the Court held that there must be a judicial remedy against any decision of a national authority refusing an individual the right to employment. This "requirement reflects a general principle of Community law which underlies the constitutional traditions common to the Member States and has been enshrined in Articles 6 and 13 of the European Convention for the Protection of Human Rights and Fundamental Freedoms".

---

79 [1996] ECR I at p. 2579.

80 At p. 1155.

81 At p. 1089. See also pp. 1097, 1105, 1133.

82 Case 190/87, *Moorman*, [1988] ECR 4689, at p. 4722.

83 Case 222/84, *Johnston v. R.U.C.*, [1986] ECR 1651; see also Case C-345/95, *France v. Parliament*, [1997] ECR I-5215 at p. 5223, Advocate General Lenz.

84 Case 222/86, *Heylens*, [1987] ECR 4097; see Case T-348/94, *ENSO Española*, *supra* note 60.

To permit satisfactory exercise of this right, the individual must be given the reasons for the decision which he or she may wish to challenge.

Another example of how the Court has drawn on national laws, also in the area of procedure, is *Transocean Marine Paint Association*.[85] The question was whether the Commission could grant an individual exemption under Article 81(3) but impose a condition on which the parties had not been given an opportunity to comment. The Advocate General made a careful analysis[86] of the national laws of the Member States and concluded that there is a right to be heard on the terms of any decision affecting legal rights, even if the decision is substantially favourable. The Court agreed.

Many more examples could be given.[87] There is no doubt that the Court deliberately draws on national laws when it considers it useful to do so. Also, it is certain that each Member of the Court must be influenced by his or her own national background and experience. This is obvious in the case of Advocates General: it is certain, even if it is not obvious to outsiders, in the case of the judges.

It is not possible to say how the case law of the Court would have developed if the Nordic countries and the UK and Ireland had joined the Community in 1952 or in 1958. Presumably, the Treaties themselves would have been rather differently written. What *is* certain is that the Nordic countries have *already* influenced Community law, in at least two striking respects: the creation of the Community Ombudsman, and the move towards more open government.[88] There is no doubt, also, that the case law of the Court has been influenced by English, Scots and Irish law, though perhaps in less obvious ways. The members of the Court whose experience had been in those countries certainly introduced the

85 Case 17/74, [1974] ECR 1063.

86 [1974] ECR at p. 1082.

87 See Case T-194/94, *Carvel and Guardian Newspapers*, [1995] ECR II-2765 concerning the interpretation of the Council Decision on public access to Council documents.

88 See the Opinion of Advocate General Slynn in [1982] ECR 1575 at 1649, where he said: "Mr Advocate General Lagrange adopted a comparable approach in Case 14/61 *Hoogovens v High Authority* (1962) ECR 253 at pp. 283-4 and it is reflected elsewhere (see for example Case 5/71, *Zuckerfabrik Schöppenstedt v Council* [1971] ECR 975 at 989 and Cases 63 to 69/72, *Werban v Council* [1973] ECR 1229 at pp. 1259-1260....... That national law may be looked at on a comparative basis as an aid to consideration of what is Community law is shown in many cases of which Cases 3/54, *Assider v High Authority* [1954-1956] ECR 63, 28/76, *LTU v Eurocontrol* [1976] ECR 1541 at para. 3, 814/79, *Netherlands v Rüffer*[1980] ECR 3807, 4/73, *Nold v Commission* [1974] ECR 491 at para. 13; 3/65, *Espérance-Longdoz v High Authority* [1965] ECR 1065 at 1090 may be taken as examples. Such a course is followed not to import national laws as such into Community law, but to use it as a means of discovering an *unwritten* principle of Community law (see for example Case 18/57, *Nold v High Authority* [1959] ECR 41 at 73-74, Case 36-38 and 40/59 *Geitling v High Authority* [1960] ECR 423 at p. 438 and at p. 450 (Mr Advocate General Lagrange); Case 11/70 *Internationale Handelsgesellschaft v Einfuhr- und Vorratsstelle Getreide* [1970] ECR 1125 at paragraphs 3 and 4 and pp. 1146-1147, (Mr Advocate General Dutheillet de Lamothe)."

now general practice of asking lawyers questions during oral hearings in Luxembourg.

The general approach of the Court has been described by Advocate General Slynn as follows:[89]

> "In looking at national laws it does not seem to me that it can be a pre-condition of the existence of a rule of Community law that the principle should be expressed identically, or should be applied in identical form, in all of the Member States. Unanimity, as to a subject which is relevant to a Community law problem, may well be a strong indication of the existence of a rule of Community law. Total unanimity of expression and application is not, however, necessary. It is at best unlikely, not least as the Community grows in size. It seems to me highly probable that there are differences in the various Member States in the application of the principles of "la bonne administration de la justice", rejection of "un deni de justice" and in the "principe de proportionalité". ....Yet such differences do not prevent such principles from being part of Community law. Indeed, in Case 17/74 *Transocean Marine Paint Association v Commission* [1974] ECR 1063 it was accepted that a right to be heard existed even though Mr Advocate General Warner found, in the relevant context, that the rule *audi alteram partem* existed only in some of the Member States. The fact that proceedings in one Member State may be criminal, in others civil, that judicial procedures differ, that for historical reasons different practices are adopted, different conditions apply, makes divergence inevitable. In my opinion, what has to be looked for is a general principle, even if broadly expressed. If that is widely accepted then it may, if relevant, be found to be part of Community law. It is then for the Court to declare how that principle is worked out in the best and most appropriate way, to use Judge Kutscher's words, in the context of Community proceedings. Nor is the fact that in some Member States the general principle may have been modified or excluded, in certain contexts covered by legislation, fatal to the existence of the principle. It is for the Member States and (within their various powers) those who make the Community legislation to decide whether the general principle which exists should be modified or excluded.
>
> Because of these divergences in procedure and practice, it is, in my view, important not to fasten too closely on a detailed comparison of particular labels or rules. What matters is the overall picture. Thus the question is not whether "legal professional privilege" (a misnomer and the right of the client) is identical with "le secret professionnel" (the duty, *inter alia*, of the lawyer), which plainly it is not, but whether from various sources a concept of the protection of legal confidence emerges, e.g. in England from the "privilege" and any rules as to the protection of confidentiality, in France from an amalgam of "le secret professionnel", "les droits de la défence" and rules applicable to "le secret des lettres confidentielles"."

COMPLIANCE WITH COMMUNITY LAW AND GENERAL ACCEPTANCE OF THE LAW

It is well known that at times there has been temporary opposition in certain Member States to certain specific rules of Community law, in particular, some of the rules discussed in this paper. The Conseil d'Etat in France was reluctant

89 In *AM&S*, [1982] ECR at p. 1650.

for some years to accept the principle that private parties could rely, against the State, on a directive which had not been implemented. In Italy, the Constitutional Court before *Simmenthal* thought that a later Italian law prevailed over a Community law rule. In the UK, the idea that Community law might require suspension of an Act of the UK Parliament was criticised, (although apparently by people who had never understood or never accepted the principle that Community law overrides national law in case of conflict). The principle that a Member State might have to pay compensation for its failure to comply with Community law also caused shocked surprise. More generally, there has been criticism (not very well informed) of the Court of Justice for "judicial legislation".

Several things should be said about these reactions:

- it is human nature that after an unfavourable decision, the referee becomes less popular;
- the French *Conseil d'Etat* and the Italian Constitutional Court finally changed their minds;
- in the UK, the adverse reaction to the *Factortame* judgment did not come from the best-informed people, and was certainly influenced by prejudices against the Community in general (euphemistically called "Euroscepticism");
- it was understandable that civil servants and politicians would be concerned about the risks of State liability for large amounts of compensation. Similar concerns had been expressed, for similar reasons, when the Court ruled that the Treaty Article on equal pay for men and women was directly applicable;[90]
- the case law of the Court on direct application has been well known for many years;
- the Court of Justice may have exposed itself unnecessarily to accusations of "judicial legislation" by failing to refer to Article 10 as the legal basis for some of its most important judgments;
- even national courts, in particular constitutional courts, find that some of their judgments are controversial or unpopular;
- several features of the Community legal system make it inevitable that some of its implications, when they become clear, will cause surprise: it is a new legal system, doing things which no treaty or legal system even tried to do before, and on the basis of a framework Treaty which was not drafted as a constitution and which therefore did not state clearly many things which would be said in the constitution of a federation;
- members of governments of Member States have not been as ready as would have been desirable to explain judgments of the Court which, in retrospect, were clearly correct;

90 Case 43/75, *Defrenne v Sabena*, [1976] ECR 455.

- some of the misunderstandings of Community law have been due merely to unfamiliar language, not to the unfamiliarity of the underlying concepts;
- Member States in recent years have had two opportunities, in the negotiations leading up to the Treaties of Maastricht and Amsterdam, to alter the Articles in the Community Treaties dealing with the Court of Justice. They have not done so;
- nobody criticises the most striking piece of judicial legislation ever undertaken by the Court of Justice, the finding that fundamental human rights are part of Community law.[91]
- the Community is built on the rule of law. The single market could not function without the principle of direct application of Community law.[92] When the Court decides what that principle implies in a particular situation, one can discuss whether it is correct in that specific case, or one can protest against a principle which, sometimes, has inconvenient consequences. Those who protest against the principle sometimes do so because they have not understood the previous case law. In any case, they have never been able to suggest an *effective* legal system based on different principles.

  But it is certainly important that all lawyers should understand why the Single Market and the Community legal system need the principle of direct applicability of Community law and the principle of effective protection of Community law rights. Understanding is necessary for acceptance. In brief, these principles are needed because without them there would be endless scope for protectionist and discriminatory national measures, delaying tactics and obstruction, and rights given by Community law would go unprotected. These two basic principles must be applied by national courts: they could not be applied in any other way. The Community relies on its national courts to understand, accept and act on these principles.

General Acceptance of Community Law and the Evolution of the Communities

The principle that some rules of Community law are directly applicable in national courts was always clear from Articles 234 and 249, EC Treaty, and nobody now questions that principle. It was foreseeable, and inevitable, that this principle would lead the Court of Justice to say what national courts should do

91 See Mancini, "The Making of a Constitution for Europe", 26 *Common Market Law Review* (1989), 595-614 at 608-612; Temple Lang, "The development of European Community Constitutional Law", 25 *The International Lawyer* (1991), 455-470.

92 Temple Lang, "The duties of national courts under Community constitutional law", 22 *European Law Review* (1997) 3, at pp. 4-6.

to apply the rules in question correctly. This is all unquestionably sound judge-made law. But there is a disadvantage in having such a large body of case law built, however firmly in logic and in practical needs, on two general Treaty Articles, however fundamental. The disadvantage is that those who are prejudiced for any reason against the Court of Justice or against the Community or against the consequences of any particular judgment will, however incorrectly, accuse the Court of "judicial activism".[93] I believe that this criticism is unfounded. However, it is a criticism which was always foreseeable because of the way the Community Treaties are drafted. They were drafted so that they would gradually evolve, in due course, into the constitution of a wholly new kind of association of States.[94] Because the Treaties were intended to evolve in this way, they did not include many of the provisions which would naturally be included in a constitution which was thought of as a constitution from its beginning, and which was not intended to evolve further than all constitutions should be designed to do. Because basic principles such as the primacy of Community law were not stated in the Treaties, they had to be developed by judge-made law. Having such a large and important body of judge-made law made several things necessary, or at least desirable. First, the Court itself and the Advocates General could have done more to stress the legal basis in the Treaties of what the Court was doing, (in particular by referring expressly to Article 10 whenever it is in fact the legal basis for a judgment[95]) and by repeating in full the legal and policy reasons which have led it to its more far-reaching conclusions.[96] Second, the Member States, when they were drafting the series of Treaties by which the original Treaties have been amended, could have confirmed and embodied in the Treaties some of the legal principles which have developed in the case law.[97] I think I know why this was not done. Both the Court and the Member States thought it wise to "leave well alone" – not to start a perhaps controversial public discussion about what *they* at least knew was necessary, and was working well. But the result of *not* writing, say, the principle of primacy of Community law or the duty of national courts to give effective protection for Community law rights into the Treaties, is to make it more necessary for the Court to set out in full all the legal and policy reasons behind these principles, as a means of educating and in-

93 Edward, "Judicial Activism – Myth or Reality", in *Legal Reasoning and Judicial Interpretation of European Law: Essays in honour of Lord Mackenzie-Stuart* (Trenton, 1998), 29-67.

94 Temple Lang, "The Development of European Community Constitutional Law", 25 *International Lawyer* (1991), 455-470; Temple Lang, "Community constitutional law", in Laffan (ed.), *Constitution-building in the European Union (Institute of European Affairs*, Dublin, 1996), 124-139 and 217-223.

95 See e.g. Case 190/87, *Moorman*, [1988] ECR 4689 at p. 4722.

96 See Temple Lang, "The duties of national courts under Community constitutional law", 22 *European Law Review* (1997) 3-18, at pp. 4-6.

97 See the observations of the Commission to the Intergovernmental Conference leading up to the Maastricht Treaty: Curtin, "The Constitutional structure of the Union: a Europe of bits and pieces", 30 *Common Market Law Review* (1993), at pp. 31-34.

forming politicians, and as a way of protecting the Court from ill-informed criticism. The Court in my view does not need to defend itself. But it does need to explain itself more fully to the public, as well as to the judges and lawyers who read its judgments who are, of course, the Court's principal audience.

So, why do we need to summarise the powers and duties of national courts in the Community legal order in this way? There are several, closely related, reasons.

First, although there is no master plan or blueprint, and the Court is not always willing to make general statements, it has always acted in this sphere on the basis of a coherent and logical set of principles. The case law in this area is a consistent whole, not a miscellaneous collection of responses to particular questions, and needs to be understood as a result of a clear conception of the Community legal order.

Second, it needs to be understood so that lawyers can see what new issues it will be right to raise in future cases, and so that national judges can see how they should be decided. This is essential because, among other reasons, the Court of Justice has not got any power corresponding to that of the US Supreme Court to refuse to hear a case because it believes that the issue raised is not yet ready to be decided, or that a given case is not a suitable case on which to base an important judgment. In other words, the Court of Justice has to be prepared for anything. So lawyers who may have to appear before it, which means every lawyer who appears in *any* national court, need to be as well prepared, in advance, as they can. The judgments of the Court of Justice will be more fully considered and more far-sighted if the issues have been well understood and thoroughly argued before national courts. The clearer the whole vision which we all have, the wiser and more consistent our contributions to it will be. Unless busy people have an overall view already, they may not be able to develop a sufficient one *ad hoc* for the purposes of a particular case. And since few lawyers outside the Community institutions appear regularly before the Court and many lawyers may have to do so, it is important that this overall view of the whole Community system of judicial protection should be understood as widely as possible by lawyers throughout the Community.

The Community judicial system – not only the Community Courts in Luxembourg, but the whole system of national courts and Community courts working together – is a system which will be build by developing consensus, and not by fiat. That consensus is developing between the courts themselves – nearly all the cases analysed here have been cases referred by national courts to Luxembourg under Article 234. The Commission is slow to being cases against a Member State under Article 226 criticising judgments of national courts, although there have been situations in which it might well have done so.[98] The

98 See the judgment of the Spanish Supreme Court criticised by Creus in his national FIDE paper (XVIII Fide Congress, Stockholm, 1998), p. 97. See also the judgment of the Swedish Supreme Court of 1997 after the judgment of the Court of Justice in Case C-43/95, *Data Delecta*, [1996] ECR I-4661.

Commission often prefers that national courts should reconsider their own judgments when they seem to be open to criticism. This is so especially in a sphere of law so pre-eminently judicial, rather than legislative, as the operation of national courts.

Another reason is that lawyers and national judges need to have some general principle, however briefly and generally stated, to guide them in deciding whether a new issue is one which ought to be referred to the Court of Justice under Article 234, or is one which the national court could decide itself with confidence. Broadly, it seems that issues covered by the two principles (that it must always be possible to bring a Community law question before a national court and to get an effective remedy) need not necessarily be referred. However, a question whether a particular substantive or procedural remedy is necessary to protect the essence of the right given by Community law is one which is more likely to need a reference under Article 234, because each right may need separate definition.

An overall view is also needed to prevent the kind of ignorance and misunderstandings which unnecessarily led to unjustified criticisms of the Court's judgments in *Factortame* and *Francovich*. In retrospect those judgments can be seen to be inevitable and logical results of the Community's legal order, which could have been foreseen since, respectively, *Simmenthal*[99] and *Humblet*.[100] The later judgments would have been more widely accepted if the earlier ones had been better understood. The Community system of judicial protection necessitates this kind of understanding. In my view,[101] Article 10 is the legal foundation of all these principles, and this paper shows that all the elements of such a closely reasoned argument are now available.

There are two other reasons. The lessons of referendum campaigns in Denmark and Ireland, and impressions of the situation in other Member States, are clear. The Community's institutional structure and legal system, and above all the amendments made by successive Treaties, are too complex for the general public to accept or to understand readily. The Community Treaties, initially well drafted, are now far too complicated. This is seriously affecting public acceptance of the Community. It is therefore essential that lawyers, whose duty it is to understand Community law, should be able to understand it and explain it simply and clearly, wherever possible. The subject of this paper can indeed be explained simply and attractively: *Community law gives many rights to individuals, and national courts everywhere in the Community must give these rights, including fundamental human rights, prompt and complete protection.* It is this

---

99 Case 106/77, *Simmenthal*, [1978] ECR 629.

100 Case 6/60, *Humblet v. Belgium*, [1960] ECR 559: see Schermers, *Active or hyper-active European Courts* (Oxford, 1997), p. 16, who says that all these consequences result from *Van Gend en Loos*.

101 Temple Lang, "The core of Constitutional law of the Community, Article 5 EC", in Gormley (ed.), *Current and Future Perspectives in EC Competition Law* (Kluwer, 1997) 41-72.

kind of explanation which is now needed: young people are no longer interested by being told that war is no longer possible in western Europe, because to them war is no longer conceivable. Europe needs an ideal, and the Community legal order offers a dignified and a worthy ideal.

The last reason is that if this ideal is to be achieved in practice, national courts should not regard Community law as simply a few more, slightly unusual, rules to be applied. National courts need to regard themselves as part of the judicial system of the Community, together with the national courts in all the other Member States.

As I said at the beginning of this paper, the Community depends on national courts.

18

THE SANCTION OF MEMBER STATES' SERIOUS VIOLATIONS OF COMMUNITY LAW

Denys Simon

The issue of reforming the Community judicial system is again high on the European agenda.[1] Both the Court of Justice and the Court of First Instance have drawn Community institutions' and Member States' attention to the growing structural imbalance affecting the functioning of the Community system of justice. Likewise, they have highlighted the challenges facing the system as a consequence of the prospect of enlargement of the European Union.[2] In this context, the Prodi Commission's decision in favour of the global opening of negotiations with applicant countries, instead of the so-called "progressive wave" accession policy, makes it even more urgent to consider the difficulties which are challenging the Community judicial system. Discussions on these problems focus most of the time on preliminary reference procedure, appeals against the Court of First Instance's judgments, and direct actions (action for annulment, failure to act), which are deemed to represent the most heavy burden for the Community judicial bodies.[3] On the other hand, non-compliance with judgments of the Court which find against Member States' violations of their EU obligations is seldom considered.[4] Nonetheless, this is one of the crucial activities of the Court of Justice and, lately, measures have even been adopted to improve its effectiveness:

---

1 See, for instance, R.Mehdi ed., *L'avenir de la justice communautaire, enjeux et perspectives*, La Documentation française (Paris, 1999).

2 See in particular the reflection paper of the Court of Justice and the Court of First Instance, *The future of the judicial system of the European Union*, no.8208/99, which was presented by the President of the Court of Justice to the Justice and Internal Affairs Council of 28 May 1999 (available on the Court's web site at www.curia.eu.int).

3 See for instance the 13th Report of the Select Committee on the European Communities of the House of Lords, *Enlarging the jurisdiction of the Court of First Instance* (July 1999).

4 See, however, the brilliant study realized under the *aegis* of the British Institute of International and Comparative Law, *The role and future of the European Court of Justice*, A report by the Members of the EC Section of the British Institute's Advisory Board chaired by the Rt.Hon. Lord Slynn of Hadley (1996).

D. O'Keeffe (ed.), Liber Amicorum Slynn 275-286 (2000)

therefore it is worth reflecting upon this question in the context of the future of the judicial system of the European Union.

This contribution aims to highlight the changes to Articles 226-228 (ex Article 169-171) EC and to evaluate, also in the light of subsequent practice, the functioning of one of the most peculiar remedies of the Community legal order.[5] Three elements appear to have mostly improved the effectiveness of enforcement proceedings in recent times: firstly, the imposition of financial penalties introduced by Article 228 (ex-article 171) (2) EC of the Maastricht Treaty is starting to be implemented; secondly, enforcement proceedings have been completed by special procedures aiming at sanctioning certain Member States' behaviour, either because of their exceptional seriousness, or because of the need for an expedited proceeding; thirdly, the case law of the Court of Justice has progressively seen national courts playing a supplementary role in order to make Member States' compliance more effective.

I DIRECT ENFORCEMENT: THE MECHANISM OF ARTICLE 228 (2) (EX ARTICLE 171)

The declaratory nature of the Court's judgment stating a Member State's breach of its obligations under the Treaty is well known. Indeed, in this context, the Court of Justice concentrates on any violation of Community law, while Member States are required "to take the necessary measures to comply with the judgment of the Court of Justice". Contrary to the highest jurisdictions in federal legal orders, the Court does not have the power to declare void the national legislation which is incompatible with Community law,[6] nor does it have the power to deliver injunctions to national courts.[7] Owing to their institutional and procedural autonomy, it is up to national judiciaries to take all necessary measures to give full effect to the judgment. Admittedly, the Court has declared its competence to frame Member States' enforcement powers in order either to clarify the consequences of its judgments,[8] or to specify the period within which Member States are required to adopt the enforcement measures to comply with the judg-

5 On this point see, for instance, D.Simon, *"Recours en manquement", Juriclasseur Europe* no.380; Articles 169-171 EC in Constantinesco, Jacqué, Kovar and Simon, eds., *Traité instituant la CEE, Commentaire article par article* (Economica, Paris, 1992); D.Simon, *Le système juridique communautaire* (PUF, Paris, 2nd ed., 1999), at para. 426 et seq.

6 Case 6/60, *Humblet*, [1960] ECR 559.

7 The Court had suggested that it be granted such a power of delivering injunctions (Supplement 9/75 – Bull.EC, 17). However, the idea seems to have been withdrawn since it was no longer mentioned in the preparatory report of the Court of Justice for the 1996 Intergovernmental Conference.

8 Case 192/79, *Commission* v. *Belgium*, [1980] ECR 1473; joined Cases 314 and 316/81 and 83/82, *Waterkeyn*, [1982] ECR 4337.

ment of the Court.[9] Thus, the late compliance, or the voluntary non-compliance, with a judgment, could only be sanctionable through proceedings for failure to give effect to it brought by the Commission before the Court of Justice. In its role as a "guardian of the Treaty" (Article 211, ex-Article 155 EC), the action of the Commission is based on a double infringement: the first is the persisting violation of EC law; the second (or derived breach) consists in the failure to comply with the *res judicata* and with the obligations following from Article 228 (2) (ex-Article 171) EC. Though exceptional at the beginning of the Community integration process,[10] these hypotheses are becoming, at least for certain Member States, more and more a reality.[11] Reasons for non-compliance may derive either from carelessness, for which Member States are held responsible, or from their deliberate non-compliance with the Court's final decision. This is why a new paragraph has been added to Article 228 (ex-Article 171) EC providing for the imposition of financial penalties in case of non-compliance. Such a device is expected to fill the *lacunae*[12] which the Court claimed to affect the binding nature of its judgments.

The penalty mechanism has been thoroughly discussed,[13] but always before its practical implementation. It is now starting to be applied, though slowly, and this on-going process has already raised certain relevant questions.

First of all, the Commission, through a series of communications, has determined in advance how it means to recruit the Court's intervention in imposing penalty payments. In a first Communication of 21 August 1996,[14] the Commission favours the mechanism of the penalty payment instead of that of a lump sum, both provided for pursuant to Article 228 (ex-Article 171) EC. The Communication also establishes the criteria according to which the Commission shall set the amount of the financial penalty, that is the seriousness and the length of the infringement, as well as the dissuasive nature of the sanction. The second

---

9 See for instance joined Cases 227-230/85, *Commission* v. *Belgium*, [1988] ECR 1. As a rule, Member States are given a "reasonable" period of time; but the interest in the immediate and uniform application of Community law requires that the process of compliance with a judgement must be initiated immediately and must be completed as soon as possible. (See for instance Case C-328/90, *Commission* v. *Greece*, [1992] ECR I-425).

10 The first case of enforcement proceeding for failure to give effect to a judgement of the Court dates back to 1972 (Case 48/71, *Commission* v. *Italy*, [1972] ECR 529, commentary of Gayet and Simon, CDE (1973), 301). For more recent example see Simon and Medhi, *Justice communautaire*, *Justices*, no.1 (1995), 172, particularly at 174-175.

11 The refusal of France to enforce the judgment *"Code maritime"* (Case 167/73, *Commission* v. *France*, [1974] ECR 359), which has been followed 22 years later by another one stating the non-compliance with the first one (Case C-334/94, *Commission* v. *France*, [1996] ECR I-1307) is particularly scandalous.

12 Suggestions from the Court of Justice on the European Union, Supplement 9/75 – Bull.EC, 17.

13 See for instance D.Ritleng, Article 171, in Constantinesco, Kovar, Simon, *Traité sur l'Union européenne, commentaire article par article* (Economica, 1995, Paris), 571 et seq.

14 O.J. 1996, C 242/6.

Communication, of 28 February 1997, sets more explicitly the method of calculating the penalty payment.[15] The Commission considers itself bound by the obligation of predictability of the sanction for Member States, as well as by the principles of proportionality and equal treatment for all the Member States. The penalty to be paid is the sum of the amounts due in respect of each day's delay starting from the day on which the Court's second judgment stating the non-compliance was brought to the attention of the Member State concerned and ending when the latter complies with the judgment itself. The amount of the daily penalty is based on a uniform flat-rate amount[16] multiplied by two coefficients, one relating to the seriousness of the infringement[17] and the other to its duration.[18] The result is then multiplied by a special factor (n), variable from one State to the other, and reflecting, on the one hand, the ability to pay of the Member State concerned and, on the other, the number of votes it has in the Council.[19]

The first case applying the mechanism of Article 228 (ex-Article 171) (2) EC is currently pending before the Court. The Advocate General having presented his conclusions, a few interesting features may already be drawn from the pending case concerning the functioning of the mechanism itself. It is an action against Greece for failure to comply with a Court's seven-year-old judgment concerning the implementation of the Directive on the disposal of toxic and dangerous waste in the Greek region of Chania.[20] In spite of several letters of notice and a "package-deal meeting",[21] Greece did not take any measures effectively to enforce the judgment of the Court. On 6 August 1996 the Commission delivered a reasoned opinion fixing the time limit for enforcement to two months and expressing its intention to ask the Court to condemn Greece to a penalty payment. The Commission, unsatisfied with the answers of the Greek government, brought an action before the Court for a fine of 24600 Euros to be imposed on Greece. The case at issue is interesting as it raises a range of legal questions which are fundamental to the subsequent application of the mechanism of financial penalties provided by Article 228 (ex-Article 171) (2) EC. These questions concern, firstly, the application of the mechanism under examination to non-compliance cases which took place and/or were reported before the entry into force of the European Union Treaty; secondly, the compact or fragmented nature of the infringement, and therefore the individualization or the

---

15 O.J. 1997, C 63/2.

16 The amount has been set at ECU 500 per day.

17 The coefficient on the seriousness of the infringement is calculated on a scale going from at least 1 to no more than 20.

18 The coefficient on the duration of the infringement is calculated on a scale going from at least 1 to no more than 3.

19 For a table establishing the situation of each Member State with respect to this method of calculating the penalty payment see *Europe* (February 1997), no.39.

20 Case C-45/91, *Commission* v. *Greece*, [1992] ECR I-2509.

21 About this procedure see D.Simon, *Le système juridique communautaire*, *loc.cit.*, para.446.

globalization of the penalty payment; and, finally, the respective responsibility of both the Commission and the Court in setting the amount of the penalty payment. Advocate General Ruiz Jarabo Colomer's conclusions are very useful in clarifying these issues. In particular, these conclusions are relevant with respect to the Advocate General's approach, which consists in posing a "preliminary question" about the nature of the sanctions. In practice, the Advocate General considers the arrangement established by Article 228 (ex-Article 171) (2) EC not as a sanction mechanism *stricto sensu*, aimed at "punishing" Member States in way which, by analogy, pertains more to penal law, but rather as a special system for compliance aimed at encouraging Member States to remove the breach of Community law in the shortest possible delay. This opinion is acceptable since it fits with the logic of the enforcement proceedings, whose function is not to punish, but to re-establish compliance with Community law.[22] This conclusion is even more relevant since it shows the extent of the guarantees provided to the condemned Member State. If the granting of certain procedural guarantees logically derives from the principle of a Community based on the rule of law, it would be excessive to grant them an absolute presumption of innocence. This will be a paradox, if it is taken into account that Member States have voluntarily refused to recognize the value of *res judicata* of the judgment of the Court. Following from these preliminary considerations, the Advocate General concludes that the principle of non-retroactivity of penal legislation does not prevent the new Article 228 (ex-Article171) (2) EC mechanism from applying, since the latter introduce neither a punishment, nor a new sanction, but only establishes a new additional enforcement procedure completed by a financial penalty. Therefore, contrary to situations previously settled by the Court, the immediate application of the penalty payment procedure to non-compliance found out before the entry into force of the Maastricht Treaty, does not "confer *ex post facto* a binding character on measures which were not binding", and, therefore, it infringes neither the principle of *nulla poena sine lege*, nor the principle of the protection of legitimate expectation.[23] From the analysis of the enforcement proceeding inserted by the Maastricht Treaty, it also follows that the Commission is competent to decide on whether or not to bring an action before the Court, on the kind of sanction and on the amount of the penalty payment. Conversely, the Court's control over the procedure is limited since it applies only in case of flagrant mistake and misuse of powers. However, the extent of the Court's jurisdiction means it is the Court's duty to impose respect of the

22 On this point see also H.Calvet, *Encyclopédie Dalloz, Répertoire de droit communautaire V° manquement*, in particular at para. 1 to 6. The mechanism of Article 171(2) is, thus, more similar to both the "Zwangsvollstreckung" of Article 888 of the German Code of civil procedure (Zivilprozessordnung) and the mechanism of penalty payment established by the French Act of 16 July 1980 (JORF 17 July 1980, 1799; for a commentary to this text see D.Linotte, JCP (1981) I, 3011; J.Tercinet, AJDA (1981) 3), than to the Anglo-Saxon rule of contempt of court, in which the penal nature is much more evident.

23 Case 14/81, *Alpha Steel Ltd. v. Commission*, [1982] ECR 749.

principle of equal treatment for all Member States and the principle of proportionality of the sanction. The transparency requirement, all the more relevant in these procedures, is considered satisfied as a consequence of the two communications of the Commission establishing the guidelines to which this institution will conform when acting on the basis of Article 228 (ex-Article 171) (2) EC. The guarantee follows from the fact that, as the Advocate General affirms, these acts, though non-binding, are held to bind their own author on the basis of the principle "*venire contra factum proprium*", except when a different, and adequately reasoned, proposal is presented for a specific case. Finally, if he agrees with the criteria organizing the coefficients used by the Commission to calculate the penalty payment, the Advocate General disagrees on the method of calculating the divisibility of the infringements cumulated in the main litigation. Most probably, the judgment of the Court will set the case law in this respect.

In any event, it is worth considering the extent to which the mechanism of financial penalties may finally force Member States to comply with the judgments of the Court, and this notwithstanding the doubts which such a mechanism raised at the time of its introduction in the Treaty.[24] Moreover, it must be noted that, eventually, the threat of the sanction is even more effective than the sanction itself. It is enough to glance at the Report on monitoring the application of Community law[25] presented on a yearly basis by the Commission to the European Parliament to see that, most of the time, when a procedure ex Article 228 (ex-Article 171) EC has been initiated, Member States have rapidly complied with Community law, so that 11 cases out of 16 have been withdrawn. From this perspective, political and media pressure may prove to be very effective in persuading "bad classmates" to respect their obligations. A good example of the indirect effect of the threat of imposing a penalty payment is the French debate about the scandal following the voluntary breach of Community law by the French Parliament, where the latter refused to implement the Directive on the conservation of wild birds.[26] Likewise, it may be relevant for a Member State not to hold the record of non-compliance with Community directives.[27]

---

24 For an opinion raising doubts about the "growing" relevance of the mechanism see J.Diez-Hochleitner, RMUE no.2/1994, 111.

25 Sixteenth Annual Report on monitoring the application of Community law, Com(99)301 final of 9/7/1999.

26 After having reduced the penalty payment from 105500 to 26375 Euros, the Commission brought an action in front of the Court on 16 October 1998 (Case C-373/98). About the new legal order created by the Act of 3/7/1998 on hunting see, in particular, Rigaux and Simon, *Palinodies politiciennes et légalité communautaire*, *Europe* (July 1998), Repères, 1; Cassia and Saulnier, *La loi du 3 juillet 1998 sur la chasse et le droit communautaire: "error communis facit jus"?*, *Europe* (July 1997), chronique, 7.

27 Including when it appears in widely diffused newspapers; see for instance R.Rivals, *La France tarde à transposer les directives européennes*, *Le Monde* (15 October 1999), 17.

II SPECIFIC ENFORCEMENT: PARALLEL MECHANISMS

Two additional procedures complement the classical enforcement proceedings. They either aim at sanctioning very serious violations of rights protected by Community law, or at allowing the Commission to initiate expedited proceedings to safeguard the unity of the internal market.

A The political sanction mechanism: Articles 7 (ex-Article F.1) TEU and 309 (ex Article 236) EC

It is known that the Amsterdam Treaty introduces a remarkable novelty as regards the sanctioning mechanism against Member States breaching the founding principles of the Union. Articles 7 (ex-Article F.1) TEU and 309 (ex Article 236) EC provide the Council with the power of sanctioning Member States for serious and persistent violations of one or more of the principles mentioned in Article 6 (ex-Article F) (1) TEU, i.e. "the principles of liberty, democracy, respect for human rights and fundamental freedoms, and the rule of law". These procedures, showing "la lente, progressive et inexorable montée en puissance des droits de l'homme dans le système de la Communauté et de l'Union",[28] finally provide for the suspension of the rights deriving from EC membership. Though common to many other international organizations,[29] such a mechanism was so far unknown in the Community context.[30] Admittedly, this procedure differs very much from the enforcement proceedings as far as both the object and the intensity of the violation are concerned. In order to apply Article 7 (ex-Article F.1) TEU, there must be a breach of the European Union fundamental principles, and it must also be a very serious and persistent one.[31] Moreover, the procedure differs from the enforcement proceedings: the provisions of Articles 7 (ex-Article F.1) TEU and 309 (ex Article 236) EC provide for a strictly political sanction,[32] which, at least with respect to the evaluation of the situation origi-

---

28 P.Wachsmann, *Les droits de l'homme*, special issue on the Amsterdam Treaty, RTDE (1997), 883.

29 V.C.Leben, *Les sanctions privatives de droits ou de qualité dans les organisations internationales spécialisées* (Bruylant, 1979, Bruxelles). See also J.M.Lavieille, *La procédure de suspension des droits d'un Etat membre des Nations Unies*, RGDIP (1977), 431.

30 On the innovative nature of the Article 7 (ex-Article F.1) TEU procedure, see, for instance, P.Y.Monjal, *Le traité d'Amsterdam et la procédure de constatation politique de manquements aux principes de l'Union*, LPA, no.69 (10 Juin 1998), 8; N.Neveux, *La suspension des droits d'un Etat membre*, Mémoire DEA Université Robert Schuman de Strasbourg, 1999.

31 Enforcement proceedings of general jurisdiction, on the contrary, are not subject to the *de minimis* principle; see on this point D.Simon, *Le système juridique communautaire*, *loc.cit.*, 452.

32 F.Sudre, *La Communauté européenne et les droits fondamentaux après le traité d'Amsterdam, vers un nouveau système de protection des droits de l'homme?*, JCP (1998) I, 9.

nating the decision of applying a sanction, is beyond the jurisdiction of the Court. In addition, the main actors deciding about the outbreak of the procedure and the determination of the sanctions are the European Council and the Council of Ministers of the European Union, whereas with regards to the enforcement proceedings, the main actors are the Commission and the Court of Justice. However, apart from the specific nature of the procedure provided by Articles 7 (ex-Article F.1) TEU and 309 (ex Article 236) EC, it nonetheless complements the classical enforcement proceedings in order to sanction particularly serious breaches of the Union founding principles.

B The immediate intervention: the Regulation of 7 December 1998

Because of the deficiencies of the classical enforcement proceedings,[33] for many years the Commission has been lobbying for the introduction of an expedited proceeding to remedy flagrant restrictions to free movement of goods which could lead to grave disruption to the proper operation of the internal market. The European Council of 16 and 17 June 1997 required the Commission to examine means of guaranteeing, in an effective manner, the free movement and the proper functioning of the internal market, " including the possibility of imposing sanctions on Member States". The "strawberry judgment",[34] delivered by the Court of Justice in December 1997, has definitely pushed in favour of the adoption of a special proceeding. In this judgment the Court condemned the French Republic for failure to fulfil its obligations under Article 28 (ex-Article 30) EC in conjunction with Article 10 (ex-Article 5) EC because it did not prevent the obstructions to the free movement of goods coming from other Member States carried out by French farmers who intercepted the lorries transporting such products in France. However, the fact that these situations keep occurring, shows the need to adopt a mechanism for immediate intervention by Community authorities. The proposal of the Commission[35] aimed at establishing a special enforcement proceeding applicable in these situations.[36] According to the proposed procedure, the Commission should be able to intervene to find Member States' non-compliance by way of decisions ordering them to take the necessary and proportionate measures to remove the obstacles to free movement of goods.

33 See in particular A.Mattera, *La procédure de manquements et la protection des droits des citoyens et des opérateurs lésés*, RMUE no.3/1995, 122; R.Munoz, *Comment pallier les manquements du recours en manquement?*, *Europe* (February 1999) chronique 2, 4.

34 Case C-265/95, *Commission, supported by Spain and the United Kingdom v. France*, [1997] ECR I-6990; commentary by Rigaux and Simon, *Europe* (February 1998), 55; L.Dubouis, *La "guerre des fraises", l'impuissance publique sous la toise du droit communautaire*, RFDA (1998), 120.

35 Com(97)619 final of 26/11/1997.

36 It was out of the question for the Commission to propose an amendment to the enforcement proceedings requiring the revision of Article 226 (ex-Article 169), since it would have meant the convening of an Intergovernmental Conference.

Such a procedure looks very much like the enforcement proceedings provided by the Treaty of Paris (Article 88 ECSC). The Commission's proposal being rejected by the Council, the latter, after a complex negotiation process carried out under the British presidency, adopted another solution contained in Regulation 2679/98EC of 7 December 1998 and in a resolution adopted on that same day.[37] This is not the place to examine in details the rules established by the above mentioned regulation.[38] Suffice it to say that the regulation's legal basis is Article 308 (ex-Article 235) EC, that it applies in case of obstacles which, according to Article 1 of the Regulation, are attributable to a Member State "whether it involves action or inaction on its part", and that its implementation must not affect the exercise of fundamental rights, including the right to strike. When an obstacle occurs or when there is a threat thereof, Member States must immediately transmit all the relevant information to the Commission, which must transmit it to all other Member States ("alert mechanism"). The Member State concerned shall answer the requests for information from the Commission and from other Member States concerning the nature of the obstacle and the action it proposes to take. In case the obstacle occurs, the Member State shall take all necessary and proportionate measures so that free movement is assured. Where the Commission is first to consider that there is an obstacle in a Member State, it shall "notify" to the Member State the reasons which led to such a conclusion and request it to adopt all necessary measures. The Member State, then, has five working days to inform the Commission of the measures which it has taken or to communicate the reasons as to why there is no breach of Community law. The added value, if any, of this regulation in comparison with the classical procedure consists in the fact that, however ambiguous its legal scope may be, the notification has a stronger political meaning than the formal letter of notice to comply. Taking into account that the "notification/injunction" is similar to the formal notice provided for by Article 226 (ex Article 169) EC, as well as the short response time given to the Member State concerned, the Commission may immediately deliver a reasoned opinion, completed in a relatively short time, and bring the matter before the Court more quickly than if it had to follow the administrative phase of the classical enforcement proceedings.[39] Once again, only subsequent practice will allow observers to evaluate the effectiveness of this new procedure.[40]

---

37 O.J. 1998, L 337/8.

38 For a detailed analysis see R.Munoz, *loc.cit.*; A.Mattera, *Un instrument d'intervention rapide pour sauvegarder l'unicité du marché intérieur: le réglement 2679/98. De nouveaux pouvoirs pour la "Commission Prodi"*, RMUE no.2/1999, 9.

39 It is known that in the ordinary procedure the Court of Justice requests the Commission to give Member States sufficient time to prepare their defence; see for instance Case 293/88, *Commission* v. *Belgium*, [1988] ECR 305.

40 Along the same line see R.Munoz, *loc.cit.*, 6 and A.Mattera, *loc.cit.*, 32.

III Indirect Enforcement: The Sanction of Non-Compliance by National Courts

At the risk of being accused of yielding to the wicked pleasure of paradox, it is tempting to conclude by wondering whether the true guarantee of the enforcement proceedings lies as much, if not more, in the hands of national courts as in those of the Court of Justice. At the end of the day, is not the national judge the true judge of enforcement proceedings? If the goal of the different existing procedures aimed at obliging Member States to respect Community law is "to achieve the practical elimination of infringements and the consequences thereof, past and future",[41] does the sanctioning of violations not ultimately rely for effectiveness on the role that national courts, acting as "Community courts of general jurisdiction",[42] are called to play?

It may also be worth wondering whether this was not what the Court of Justice's prediction meant when, in *Van Gend en Loos*, it affirmed that "the vigilance of individuals concerned to protect their rights amounts to an effective supervision in addition to the supervision entrusted by Articles 169 and 170 to the diligence of the Commission and of the Member States".[43] The recent developments of the case law concerning Member States' responsibility towards their own national courts in case of violation of Community law, clearly confirm what initially could have been considered as a hazardous prediction.[44] Taking into account that, according to the *Francovich* case law,[45] "the Member States are obliged to make good loss and damage caused to individuals by breaches of Community law for which they can be held responsible", such an obligation will further support this development, once the violation has already been affirmed by a non-compliance judgment of the Court. Admittedly, the prior judgment of the Court finding an infringement is not a necessary pre-condition to the establishment of the Member State's responsibility before the national courts.[46] As

---

41 Case 70/72, *Commission* v. *Germany*, [1973] ECR 813.

42 According to the long time formulation used by the "doctrine' (see for instance, A.Barav, *La fonction communautaire du juge national*, Thesis Strasbourg 1983; *La plénitude de compétence du juge national en sa qualité de juge communautaire*, Mél.Boulouis, 1; Grévisse et Bonichot, *Les incidences du droit communautaire sur l'organization et l'exercise de la fonction juridictionnelle dans les Etats membres*, Mél.Boulouis, 297; D.Simon, *Les exigences de la primauté du droit communautaire, continuité ou métamorphose*, Mél.Boulouis, 483) and, finally, recognized by the Community judiciary itself (Case T-51/89, *Tetra Pak*, [1990] ECR II-309, in particular 364).

43 Case 26/62, *Van Gend en Loos*, [1963] ECR 25.

44 See for instance Simon and Barav, *La responsabilité de l'administration nationale en cas de violation du droit communautaire*, RMC (1987), 165. For a premonitory vision see P.Pescatore, *Responsabilité des Etats membres en cas de violation du droit communautaire*, *Foro Padano* (1972), 10.

45 Joined Cases C-6/90 and 9/90, *Francovich and Bonifaci*, [1991]ECR I-5357.

46 Joined Cases C-46/93 and 48/93, *Brasserie du Pêcheur and Factortame*, [1996] ECR I-1029, in part. para.93, I-1159; see also the conclusions by Advocate General Tesauro, I-1123.

the Court clearly affirmed, "to make the reparation of loss or damage conditional upon the requirement that there must have been a prior finding by the Court of an infringement of Community law attributable to a Member State would be contrary to the principle of the effectiveness of Community law, since it would preclude any right to reparation so long as the presumed infringement had not been the subject of an action brought by the Commission under Article 226 (ex-Article 169) of the Treaty and of a finding of an infringement by the Court. Rights arising for individuals out of Community provisions having direct effect in the domestic legal system of the Member State cannot depend on the Commission's assessment of the expediency of taking action against a Member State pursuant to Article 226 (ex-Article 169) of the Treaty or on the delivery by the Court of any judgment finding an infringement".[47] However, though the prior judgment of the Court finding an infringement is not an essential condition, it is nonetheless considered by the Court as "determinative".[48] When the infringement is *res judicata* by the Court, the breach of Community law is sufficiently serious, that is to say "manifest and grave", if the violation persists despite a judgment finding the infringement.[49] In such a situation the Member State is then obliged to give reparation of loss or damage which they have caused to individuals as Community subjects. Thus, a Member State's responsibility before its own courts either strengthens the effectiveness of the prior judgment of the Court of Justice finding an infringement according to Articles 226 to 228 (ex-Articles 169 to 171) EC, or replaces the lack of a Community judgment sanctioning the breach of Treaty's obligations. Apart from the reparation of loss and damage, it is clear that the finding of the infringement implies, in any event, for the national courts a "prohibition having the full force of law"[50] against applying a national rule recognized as incompatible with the Treaty by the Luxembourg Court. But this obligation is imposed, first as a consequence of the supremacy of Community law, independently of any prior judgment finding an infringement of Community law. Thus, also in this respect, the national judge either strengthens the effectiveness of the prior judgment of the Court, or takes over the task of controlling the respect of Community law obligations by national authorities.

At the end of this analysis of the current situation concerning the procedures for sanctioning serious violations of Community law by the Member States, clearly shorter and not as deep as originally intended to be, it would seem that there is in the Community legal order a complete and particularly effective system of means to ensure the respect of the rule of law by the Member States. In practice, however, this turns out to be an overestimation. A careful reading of

---

47 Ibid. para.95. Along the same line see joined Cases 314/81, 315/81, 316/81 and 83/82, *Waterkeyn and Others*, [1982] ECR 4337.

48 Ibid. para.93.

49 Ibid. para.55 to 57.

50 According to the well known formulation of the Court; see Case 48/71, *Commission* v. *Italy*, [1972] ECR 527; commentary by Gayet and Simon, CDE (1973), 301.

the annual report of the European Commission to the European Parliament on monitoring Community law application shows that the application of Community law by the Member States is far from being beyond reproach and, furthermore, that sanctioning procedures are not always fully effective. Therefore, without any doubt, it would be very useful, in view of the next Intergovernmental Conference, further to consider the means to strengthen the efficiency of existing procedures, or to create new ones.[51]

51 It has been proposed that the European Community return to the infringement procedure by way of a Commission's reasoned opinion, which the Member States could bring before the Court of Justice by an application to find the infringement. Or, more simply, to make the proceedings lighter in case of non-contested breaches of law.

19

PUBLIC LIABILITY IN U.S. COURTS AND *BRASSERIE DU PÊCHEUR* AND *FACTORTAME* IN THE EUROPEAN COURT

*Cynthia Crawford Lichtenstein**

In 1924, the then great Professor of International and Comparative Law at Yale, Edwin M. Borchard,[1] published a three part piece in the Yale Law Journal urging "a repeal by legislation of the antiquated and unjust rules of [government] immunity in tort cases."[2] Professor Borchard was exercised by the anomaly in Anglo-American law that "[T]he common law and the political theory underlying both British and American constitutional law have been regarded as a bulwark protection to the individual in his relations with the Government. . . . Yet it requires but a slight appreciation of the facts to realize that in Anglo-American law the individual citizen is left to bear almost all the risks of a defective, negligent, perverse or erroneous administration of the state's functions, an unjust burden which is becoming graver and more frequent as the Government's activities become more diversified and as we leave to administrative officers in even greater degree the determination of the legal relations of the individual citizen. . . . Yet there is no reason why the most flagrant of the injuries wrongfully sustained by the citizen, those arising from torts of officers, should be allowed to rest, as they now generally do, in practice if not in theory, at the door of the unfortunate citizen alone."[3] As a professor of comparative law, Borchard was keenly aware that ". . .[O]n the continent, steeped in legal tradition and juristic conceptions of corporateness, that [legislative] consent was assumed. We adopted a rule of jurisdictional immunity; they did not. Both are rules of law to which the state is subject. The problem in Europe is pragmatic – how far does public policy and social theory require that the State and other public corpora-

* My sincerest thanks are due to my research assistant for June 1998 to May 1999, Mr. Douglas Wood, J.D. expected May 2000, for his preliminary research into the *Gaubert* case.

1 Professor Borchard was the predecessor to Professor Myres McDougal at Yale Law School and a prolific scholar whose subjects of interest have a most contemporary ring: see his two-volume treatise on state debt.

2 Borchard, Government Liability in Tort, 34 Yale L.J. 1, 129, 229 at 19 n.68 (1924-25).

3 *Id.*, at 1.

D. O'Keeffe (ed.), Liber Amicorum Slynn 287-302 (2000)

tions shall assume responsibility for the injuries inflicted by its agents on private individuals, a problem which requires no metaphysical speculations into the nature of sovereignty, of law and of the State. Is it expecting too much to invoke such emancipation from dogma and metaphysics for the United States?"[4]

Borchard's complaints were directed purely to non-contractual liability; the United States had by federal legislation subjected itself to liability for its delicts sounding in contract since 1855.[5] Moreover, he was in no way arguing for reparation for legislative torts; he viewed the federal and state ". . . procedural devices, such as mandamus, certiorari and judicial safeguards of various kinds designed to nullify the wrongful act . . . without pecuniary compensation"[6] as sufficient protection to the individual against the tortious exercise of governmental power. Borchard, as demonstrated by his "popular" plea for "Governmental Responsibility in Tort – A Proposed Statutory Reform" published in the American Bar Association Journal[7] was primarily interested in overcoming the jurisdictional (and total) hurdle of the doctrine of sovereign immunity to claims for compensation for harm caused by negligence or wrongful act or omission of the government's "servants within the scope of their duties or authority," tort claims based on "the universally accepted and elementary principle of the employer's responsibility . . ."[8] for such torts. The balancing issue so brilliantly set out by Duncan Fairgrieve in his and Mads Andenas' chapter in *English Public Law and the Common Law*,[9] the tension between "the basic right of an injured party to have a wrong set right" and "the judicial reluctance to encroach upon the policy-making function of public bodies" as Fairgrieve puts it[10] was of no concern to Borchard because he seems to have focused solely on the lack of redress for ordinary garden variety harm inflicted by the negligence of public servants. Indeed, his policy argument offered in the Bar Association Journal piece for the proposed legislative reform was that in the absence of a public doctrine of *respondeat superior*, it would be harder for the government to attract good officials because of the fear of personal liability for negligence.[11] In proposing an

4 Borchard, "Governmental Responsibility in Tort", 36 Yale L.J. 1, 757, 1039 at 1100 (1926-1927).

5 See H.R. Report No. 1287 to accompany H.R. 181, 79th Cong., 1st Sess. (1945) at 2. After 1855 and the legislative permission to sue the Federal government *on contracts* in the Court of Claims, it became possible, as Borchard notes, to make the U.S. constitutional mandate that private property may only be "taken" for a public purpose and upon the payment of just compensation effective, but even then, Borchard subsequently notes, the Supreme Court narrowly construed the 1855 Act so as to provide no recovery if the Federal "taking" were tortious. Borchard, *op.cit.* n. 2 at 28, 30.

6 Borchard, *op.cit.* n. 4 at 2.

7 11 Am. Bar Assoc. J. 495 (1925).

8 *Id.*, at 500.

9 Andenas and Fairgrieve, "Sufficiently Serious? Judicial Restraint in Tortious Liability for Public Authorities and the European Influence," Chapter 14 in Andenas (ed.) *English Public Law and the Common Law of Europe* (London 1998) at 285-326.

10 *Id.* at 285.

11 *Op.cit.* n. 7 at 496. "If the underpaid, subordinate employee is alone responsible in law,

end to the use of the "antiquated" doctrine of sovereign immunity as an absolute bar to governmental non-contractual liability, Borchard simply was not dealing with the profoundly difficult delimitation issues involved in the question of just when a public authority with some discretion should be liable for its acts that cause harm to individuals.

The legislation that the United States ultimately (in 1946, more than twenty years after Borchard's campaign) passed, reflected this reluctance to deal with the problems of harm caused by administrative and legislative acts as opposed to harm caused by the negligence or wrongful acts of individual officers. The Federal Tort Claims Act of 1946[12] was considered in 1991 to effect a "relatively broad waiver"[13] of sovereign immunity for the Federal government, but as enacted and today contains an exception[14] usually referred to in the literature as the "discretionary function exception" or, as the exception to the waiver of sovereign immunity will be referred to hereafter, the DFE section of the FTCA.[15] This DFE section of the FTCA provides that the waiver of sovereign immunity in the

---

the risk of accepting public employment is unduly burdensome upon all excepting the financially irresponsible, and the detriment to public service is great." In fairness to Borchard, the second series of pieces published in the Yale L.J., *op cit.* n. 4 is a fascinating jurisprudential exploration of the then Continental law of the subject where, as Borchard puts it, ". . . the subject has greatly occupied the public mind, for or against the responsibility of the state or minor political group," *id.* at 1 and ". . . the interest there lay in establishing the exceptions to the rule by virtue of the peculiar functions of governmental agencies." *Id.* at 780.

12 Federal Tort Claims Act of 1946, 60 Stat. 843, codified at various sections including 28 U.S.C. § 1346(b), 2671-2680 (1982).

13 The phraseology is that of Ronald Cass, in his contribution "Official Liability in America: Actors and Incentives," pp. 110-144 at 114 in Bell and Bradley, eds. Governmental Liability: A Comparative Study (Glasgow 1991). The Cass chapter was written before the decision of *United States* v. *Gaubert*, 499 U.S. 315, 111 S. Ct. 1267 (S. Ct. 1991), the U.S. Supreme Court case analyzed in this contribution. Cass's view of the effect of the Federal Tort Claims Act was a fair description of the effect, up to *Gaubert*, of prior Federal Court interpretation of that Act. The entire piece by Dean and Professor Cass, a truly first class overview of the state of official liability in United States law in 1991, obviates any need for a further survey by this author, except to delineate in detail the profound sea change in that law made by *Gaubert*, which, although harshly criticized by commentators, the best piece being Peterson and Van Der Weide, "Susceptible to Faulty Analysis: United States v. Gaubert and the Resurrection of Federal Sovereign Immunity", 72 Notre Dame L. Rev. 447 (1997) and, when possible, distinguished away by lower federal courts and state courts desiring to allow injured plaintiffs to go to trial, remains the law of the United States, at least so far as the "discretionary function exception" to the Federal Tort Claims Act and the swallowing of the Act by the exception are concerned.

14 28 U.S.C. § 2680 (a) (1982).

15 Two lawyers working in the federal government legal office defending suits against the government under the FTCA surveyed the major cases under the DFE section up to 1989 and once again, the cases to which they refer will not be reanalyzed here, see Fishback and Killefer, "The Discretionary Function Exception to the Federal Tort Claims Act; Dalehite to Varig to Berkovitz", 25 Idaho L. Rev. 291 (1988-1989).

FTCA does not apply to "[a]ny claim based upon an act or omission of an employee of the Government, exercising due care, in the execution of a statute or regulation, whether or not such statute or regulation be valid, or based upon the exercise or performance or the failure to exercise or perform a discretionary function or duty on the part of a federal agency or an employee of the Government, whether or not the discretion involved be abused."[16]

The contemporary legislative history of the DFE section is scant, as the exceptions to the historic waiver of sovereign immunity in the FTCA were not debated on the floor of the House where the original bill for the Federal Tort Claims Act that was passed (with no $10,000 top limit on the amount of the claim) by the Senate as part of the 1946 Legislative Reorganization Act[17] was debated. (The debate was purely concerned with whether or not the Federal Government *should* enact such a waiver, whatever the exceptions that might be provided for.[18]) The House Report[19] is more helpful. The House Report summarizes the then existing law providing for federal government liability in contract, other claims "not sounding in tort," for patent infringement and for admiralty and maritime torts and adds: "On the other hand, no action may be maintained against the Government in respect to any common-law tort."[20] The Report finds that this exemption of liability for common-law torts is "incongruous" and its "only justification . . . historical."[21] The Report then goes to say (echoing Borchard's view of twenty years before): "With the expansion of governmental activities in recent years, it becomes especially important to grant to private individuals the right to sue the Government in respect to such torts as negligence in the operation of vehicles."[22]

The proponents of the bill (and there is appended to the Report the Minority Views signed by seven members of the reviewing Committee on the Judiciary who believed that the then existing system of private bills to be reviewed by the Claims Committee of Congress had resulted in "fair and equitable determinations to the claimants and to the Federal Government")[23] make quite clear in their discussion of Title IV of the bill, the limitations on the suits provided for, that there was no intention to permit suit in instances any broader than a government employee's negligence or tortious act. The Report describes the DFE section as

> ". . .a highly important exception, intended to preclude any possibility that the bill might be construed to authorize suit for damages against the Government growing out of an authorized activity, such as a flood-control or irrigation project, where no negligence on

16 Sec. 421 (a) of 60 Stat. 842 at 845, 28 U.S.C. § 2680 (a) (1982).
17 See Fishback and Kellefer, *op.cit.* n. 15 at 152.
18 92 Cong. Rec. 10991-10993, 79th Cong. 2d Sess. (1946).
19 H. Rep. No 1287 on H.R. 181, 79th Cong., 1st Sess. (1945).
20 *Id.* at 3.
21 *Id.*
22 *Id.*
23 *Id.* at 11.

the part of any Government agent is shown, and the only ground for suit is the contention that the same conduct by a private individual would be tortious, or that the statute or regulation authorizing this project was invalid. It is also designed to preclude application of the bill to claim against a regulatory agency, such as the Federal Trade Commission or the Securities and Exchange Commission, based upon an alleged abuse of discretionary authority by an officer or employee, whether or not negligence is alleged to have been involved. To take another example, claims based upon an allegedly negligent exercise by the Treasury Department of the blacklisting or freezing powers are also intended to be excepted. The bill is not intended to authorize a suit for damages to test the validity of or provide a remedy on account of such discretionary acts even though negligently performed and involving an abuse of discretion. Nor is it desirable or intended that the constitutionality of legislation, or the legality of a rule or regulation should be tested through the medium of a damage suit for tort."[24]

When the bill was enacted the following year, the language of the DFE section was that of the section so described by the House Judiciary Committee. In 1945 and 1946, in the United States, at least, the notion that the remedy of compensation for damage caused by state action is an ineluctable component of the legal protection of the individual's rights in the face of the State was not a developed concept.

However, as the years passed and case after case for compensation for harm was brought in federal courts under the FTCA, the lower federal courts' understanding of the effect of the DFE section moved quite far from what one might deduce as to Congress' intention in placing the section in the Act,[25] even if the three major Supreme Court cases discussed in Fishback and Killefer[26] continued

24 *Id.* at 5-6.

25 Fishback and Killefer, *op.cit. supra* n. 15 at 294 indicate that in the years immediately following the enactment of the FTCA, the scope of the DFE was "the subject of dispute" and that "some saw the exception as severely limiting what otherwise would have been a very broad waiver of sovereign immunity." As they discuss, at 294, the seminal case interpreting the DFE, *Dalehite* v. *United States*, 346 U.S. 15 (1953) read the legislative history of the section as we have suggested, to not permit suit in the case of governmental activities (here a program of government-manufactured fertilizer being shipped to Europe as part of a post-war aid program which, bagged in easily-ignitable paper containers without warning labels, was loaded onto steamers adjacent to a cargo of explosives, ignited, with resulting explosions that leveled the port area of Texas City, Texas) involving some measure of discretion or judgment. The Court is quoted (at 295) as saying in *Dalehite*: "[w]here there is room for policy judgment and decision there is discretion," and the fact that actual cause of the Dalehite explosions, the bagging, was on the level of carrying out the operation did not make that operation actionable. As noted by Fishback and Killefer (at 296) the language of *Dalehite* "was broad and potentially encompassed just about everything except the most routine postal truck injury-type cases." However, as we noted in the text at n. 13, by 1991 the FTCA was labeled as being a "relatively broad waiver[s] of sovereign immunity." Curiously also, Cass, *supra* n. 13, describes the *Dalehite* case as the derivation of the "dominant test" for whether the DFE applies, "whether the tortious conduct occurred at the 'planning level' of government or at the 'operational level'," Cass, *supra* n. 13 at 119.

26 *Op.cit.* n. 15 *supra*.

to attempt to maintain the presumed purpose of the exception, ". . . to prevent judicial 'second-guessing' of legislative and administrative decisions grounded in social, economic and political policy through the medium of a tort suit."[27]

The problem, of course, is that of delimitation: just where is the line between an operation which is the carrying out of policy decision, a planning decision (protected by the DFE) and an act that does not implicate any "planning" or any "policy," short of the negligent driving of a government vehicle? In practice, the "planning v. operational level distinction"[28] as to when the DFE section applies and when it does not has not provided in the United States federal courts a useful methodology of delimitation.[29] As Professor Cass noted in his 1991 survey of the American law of governmental liability,[30] ". . . the more or less random application of the FTCA exception in cases implementing the policy-making-versus-routine-decision-making test reveals that it, too, lacks a litmus quality. . . . The doctrine has generated a mass of conflicting decisions applying confusing tests."[31] Interestingly, Professor Cass here calls the DFE section of the FTCA a "doctrine," seemingly forgetting that the exception is a statutory mandate attempting to insulate the Federal Government from liability other than simple *respondeat superior*.

While the three Supreme Court cases interpreting the DFE section of the FTCA[32] up to 1991 did not prevent the lower federal courts from attempting to use the policy-making-versus-routine-decision-making test to make "distinctions that resist all efforts at clarification,"[33] one of the three, *Berkovitz* v. *United States*,[34] made a significant interpretatory exception to the DFE exception.[35]

---

27 *United States* v. *S.A. Empressa De Viacao Aerea Rio Grandense (Varig Airlines)*, 467 U.S. 797, 814 (1984).

28 The phrase is that used by Reynolds, "The Discretionary Function Exception of the Federal Tort Claims Act: Time for Reconsideration", 42 Okla. L. Rev. 459 (1989), asserting that the "distinction was applied in numerous decisions by lower federal courts," *id.* at 460. Reynolds points out that the distinction has been "attacked as producing inconsistent results in application, as illustrated by one case that found that dredging of irrigation canals involves planning while another case ruled that faulty construction of a sewage disposal system is operational." *Id.* at 462.

29 Two other United States commentators, Bagby and Gittings, "The Elusive Discretionary Function Exception From Government Tort Liability: The Narrowing Scope of Federal Liability", 30 Am. Bus. L.J. 223 (1992), note that ". . . the guidance that has emerged from nearly 50 years of common law, legislative history, and theoretical analysis is satisfactory in only the simplest of cases. It falls short particularly in the increasingly complex governmental functions that parallel private sector activities." *Id.* at 224. Unfortunately, their article does not resolve the delimitation dilemma, and only calls for an ad hoc inquiry into each case (including whether policy was in fact inquired into) and further research into the area.

30 Cass, n. 13 *supra*.

31 *Id.* at 120-121.

32 The three cases are those in the title of Fishback and Killefer, *op.cit. supra* n. 15.

33 Cass, *op.cit.* n. 13 at 133.

34 486 U.S. 531, 108 S. Ct. 1954 (1988).

Berkovitz concerned an infant who contracted polio from an oral vaccine licensed by the government's Division of Biologic Standards and from a lot whose release was approved by another government agency. The controlling statute authorized the issuance of a license to produce a polio vaccine only upon a showing that standards 'prescribed in regulations' and 'designed to insure the continued safety, purity and potency of such products' were met and the government agencies concerned had not required certain tests before issuing the licence. The Supreme Court held that the DFE section does not apply ". . . when a federal statute, regulation, or policy specifically prescribes a course of action for an employee to follow. In this event, the employee has no rightful option but to adhere to the directive. And if the employee's conduct cannot appropriately be the product of judgment or choice, then there is no discretion in the conduct for the discretionary function exception to protect."[36] In short, a plaintiff can avoid having its FTCA suit dismissed on motion by alleging a failure to comply with specific and mandatory regulations; under *Berkovitz* the DFE does not protect violations of specific and mandatory regulations.

Unfortunately, however, for the clarity of the law of governmental liability, the *Berkovitz* gloss on the DFE section was of no help when the governmental employee was *following* regulations and harm resulted. If the law was as the lower courts insisted, then an inquiry needed to be made into whether the employee's actions were on the planning level or the operational level and the court would be back into the delimitation swamp. At this point, the Supreme Court weighed in again with *United States* v. *Gaubert*.[37]

Mr. Gaubert was the largest shareholder and Chairman of the Board of Independent American Savings Association ("IASA"), a Texas state-chartered and federally-insured savings and loan association, a type of depository institution that in the 1980s was the source of the United States' savings and loan crisis. Numerous such institutions over the country were failing and the Federal Government's insurance scheme for deposits therein was at risk, leading to efforts by the federal regulator concerned, the Federal Home Loan Banking Board ("FHLBB") to stabilize the situation by merging institutions, closing others down and, in effect, directing the operations of still others. IASA became involved with the FHLBB and its local representative, Federal Home Loan Bank-Dallas (FHLB-Dallas) in 1984 when FHLBB wanted it to merge with a failing Texas thrift, Investex Savings. FHLBB and FHLB-Dallas assisted IASA in the merger and by 1986 sought the replacement of IASA's management and Board of Directors and "persuaded" the Board to resign, with the new Board and officers being searched for and selected by FHLB-Dallas.[38] According to the Circuit

35 The relationship of the addition to DFE jurisprudence in *Berkovitz* to the jurisprudence of State liability in European law will be discussed in the text when the possible implications of the U.S. law for extensions of *Brasserie du Pêcheur* are taken up subsequently.

36 108 S. Ct. at 1958-1959.

37 499 U.S. 315, 111 S. Ct. 1267 (1991).

38 The statement of facts is taken from the Fifth Circuit's opinion, *Gaubert* v. *United States*,

Court's opinion, thereafter ". . . officials at FHLB-Dallas actively involved themselves in IASA's affairs and played an increasingly larger role in the day-to-day operations."[39] As important, the new directors announced that IASA had over a $400 million negative net worth; the old Board had believed IASA to be about $74 million in the black at the end of 1985.[40] By May 1987, the savings and loan association was in receivership and Gaubert filed suit in the District Court for the Northern District of Texas under the FTCA for $100 million alleging negligent selection of directors and officers and negligent involvement in day-to-day operations by federal officials. The District Court dismissed the complaint for lack of subject matter jurisdiction on September 28, 1988.[41]

The Court of Appeals for the Fifth Circuit on appeal from the District Court decided the ". . . distinction [between policy decisions and operational actions] still retains its force today and is dispositive of this case"[42] and reversed the dismissal of Gaubert's "claims which concerned the regulators' activities after they assumed a supervisory role in IASA's day-to-day affairs."[43] The Court of Appeals necessarily had to resort to the manipulable policy decision/operational action dichotomy if it was to allow Mr. Gaubert his day in court; it had already found that, unlike the agencies in *Berkovitz*, ". . . the actions of the FHLBB and FHLB-Dallas were not as closely guided by statute. . . . The FHLBB and FHLB-Dallas officials did not have regulations telling them, at every turn, how to accomplish their goals for IASA; this fact, however, does not automatically render their decisions discretionary and immune from FTCA suits."[44]

If, however, the FHLBB officials' "operational in nature" actions to attempt to save IASA from receivership were *not* immune under FTCA, the agency could look forward to a torrent of suits springing from its efforts to resolve the S&L crisis. Clearly the Fifth Circuit's decision was a challenge to the government and naturally when the government appealed to the Supreme Court, the Supreme Court responded so as to try to clear up the use of the policy/operational dichotomy once and for all, at least in the case of agency action.

---

885 F.2d 1284 (1989) and the Circuit Court makes clear its opinion that the "persuasion" was accomplished by a threat to close IASA if it did not cooperate with FHLB-Dallas' plans for it.

39 *Id.* n. 39 at 1286.

40 *Id.*

41 Technically, the FTCA is a waiver of the Federal Government's sovereign immunity, a bar to the jurisdiction of the federal courts. If the trial court accepts that the DFE applies to the case, it will grant a motion to dismiss for lack of subject matter jurisdiction. If the DFE or other exception to the FTCA is not thought to apply, the plaintiff is given the opportunity to try to prove the case. The larger the scope of the DFE section is understood to be, the fewer tort suits need be defended by the government under the Act.

42 *Op.cit.* n. 38 at 1287.

43 The description of the claims allowed to go to trial by the Court of Appeals is that of the Supreme Court in *United States* v. *Gaubert*, *op.cit.* n. 37 at 322 which reversed the Court of Appeals' reversal of the District Court's dismissal of those claims as well as all others in the complaint.

44 *Op.cit.* n. 38 at 1289.

The Supreme Court, after recital of the litigation history of the case, turned, interestingly, not to the legislative history of the DFE section, but to its own precedents interpreting the section (the three cases, *Dalehite*, *Varig* and *Berkovitz*), and stressing that *Varig* taught that the purpose of the exception ". . . is to 'prevent judicial "second-guessing" of legislative and administrative decisions grounded in social, economic, and political policy through the medium of an action in tort,"[45] added that ". . . when properly construed, the exception 'protects only governmental actions and decisions based on considerations of public policy,'" citing *Berkovitz*.[46]

So how is a lower court to determine *which* actions and decisions are those? Where, says the Court, Congress has delegated to an independent agency or to the Executive Branch the authority to implement a regulatory statute and to issue regulations to that end, ". . . there is no doubt that planning-level decisions establishing programs are protected by the discretionary function exception . . ."[47] unless the Berkovitz exception to the exception, failure to follow the specific directions contained in the applicable regulations, applies. The Court then makes a significant leap and declares: "Under the applicable precedents, therefore, if a regulation mandates particular conduct, and the employee obeys the direction the Government will be protected because the action will be deemed in furtherance of the policies which led to the promulgation of the regulation. . . . [I]f a regulation allows the employee discretion, the very existence of the regulation creates a strong presumption that a discretionary act authorized by the regulation involves consideration of the same policies which led to the promulgation of the regulations. . . . [W]hen established governmental policy, as expressed or implied by statute, regulation, or agency guidelines, allows a Government agent to exercise discretion, it must be presumed that the agent's acts are grounded in policy when exercising that discretion. For a complaint to survive a motion to dismiss, it must allege facts which would support a finding that the challenged actions are not the kind of conduct that can be said to be grounded in the policy of the regulatory regime. The focus of the inquiry is not on the agent's subjective intent in exercising the discretion conferred by statute or regulation, but on the nature of the actions taken and on whether they are susceptible to policy analysis."[48]

So are there any governmental tortious acts left for which the government will be liable if the case is proved? Yes, says the Court in Footnote 7 appended to the words "susceptible to policy analysis."

> "There are obviously discretionary acts performed by a Government agent that are within the scope of his employment but not within the discretionary function exception because these acts cannot be said to be based on the purposes that the regulatory regime seeks to

---

45 *Op.cit.* n. 37 at 323.
46 *Id.* at 323.
47 *Id.*
48 *Id.* at 324-325.

> accomplish. If one of the officials involved in this case drove an automobile on a mission connected with his official duties and negligently collided with another car, the exception would not apply. Although driving requires the constant exercise of discretion, the official's decisions in exercising that discretion can hardly be said to be grounded in regulatory policy."[49]

So the Court has returned to the example given in the House Report: the federal government's sovereign immunity is waived by the FTCA "in respect to such torts as negligence in the operation of vehicles."[50]

Having claimed to have set out its prior jurisprudence, the Court went on to make absolutely clear that the planning/operational dichotomy should no longer be used: ". . . it is clear that the Court of Appeals erred in holding that the [DFE] exception does not reach decisions made at the operational or management level of the bank involved in this case."[51] . . . "The Court of Appeals misinterpreted *Berkovitz*['s] . . . as perpetuating a nonexistent dichotomy between discretionary functions and operational activities."[52]

The decision in *Gaubert* has been bitterly criticized in Peterson and Van Der Weide,[53] a 1997 commentary on the case, who say that the key phrase of the Court's decision ". . . susceptible to policy analysis" was "unexpected and unexplained."[54] They maintain that "[T]his phrase is now raised by the government's lawyers in countless negligence lawsuits against the United States, and it has greatly restricted the federal government's tort liability for all but the most mundane transgressions."[55] Quite apart from the quantitative analysis of plaintiff success (or rather, lack thereof) under the *Gaubert* revised interpretation of the DFE section, the article is useful because it reviews in detail recent United States jurisprudence in torts, including a synopsis of the law and economics approach to the theoretical need for governmental tort liability.[56] Peterson and Van

---

49 *Id.* at n. 7 at 325.

50 See text at n. 22 *supra.*

51 *Op.cit.* n. 37 at 325.

52 *Id.* at 448.

53 *Op.cit.* n. 13 *supra.*

54 *Id.* at 448.

55 In Part III of the article, the authors review all of the post-*Gaubert* cases up to March of 1994 as well as the DFE cases decided during the period between *Berkovitz* and *Gaubert* and found that the plaintiff success ratio had declined from 43% to 23%. *Id.* at 466.

56 Part IV of the article is entitled "Real Policy Decisions: A Better Test for Discretionary Function Immunity," *id.* at 474 and the authors plunge into torts jurisprudence as the necessary back drop to their proposal as to how the delimination job should be done. (The issue of governmental tort liability and adequate jurisprudential underpinnings therefore has fascinated United States scholars as well as British and continental ones. Cass, *op.cit.* n. 13, having written about the intellectual incoherence of the policy/operations distinction as applied by the U.S. courts, finishes his survey of official liability in America by a general jurisprudential excursion into "the problems encountered in ordinary tort law [which] look a good deal like many of those encountered in official liability law in the United States. *Id.* at 133, stating the "gut" issue of both branches of tort law as ". . . how one influences the actions of an organization or individual to reduce

Der Weide understand Congress' intention in the DFE section to be what *Varig* declared it, an insurance against "judicial second-guessing" of legislative and administrative decisions grounded in policy, that is, what Duncan Fairgrieve calls in his and Andenas' Chapter in *English Public Law and the Common Law of Europe*[57] a "public law filter" designed to exclude "sensitive polycentric issues" . . . "from the ambit of judicial enquiry."[58]

Accepting this exclusion of polycentric issues from judicial second guessing as the purpose of the DFE section, Peterson and Van Der Weide see the susceptibility test of the *Gaubert* decision as seriously overinclusive, in Fairgrieve's analogy, words as using far too fine a mesh in the filter. After an extensive law and economics analysis of why the effects of decisions implicating policy are not quantifiable,[59] and other "[R]eflection upon the economic bases of tort law and the theoretical foundations of sovereign immunity,"[60] Peterson and Van Der

---

the harm likely to flow from those actions and whether the possible adverse consequences of harm-preventing incentives exceed the gains." *Id.* at 133-134. Cass then completes his piece by trying to delineate the "difficulty of applying these lessons [from ordinary tort law] to official liability." *Id.* Peterson and Van Der Weide believe it necessary to do this because they have roundly criticized the Supreme Court for having ". . . adopted susceptibility analysis with none of the jurisprudential underpinnings that usually support a significant shift in the law. . . .[T]he Supreme Court in *Gaubert* offered no justification for its unexpected leap in the direction of a more capacious sovereign immunity." Peterson and Van Der Weide, *op.cit.* n. 13 at 464.

57 *Op.cit.* n. 9.

58 *Id.* at 293.

59 *Op.cit.* n. 13 at 479. "Fault cannot be assessed where an unquantifiable policy variable is involved."

60 Basically, Peterson and Van Der Weide are against sovereign immunity in all cases *except* those which do implicate a "sensitive polycentric issue," in Fairgrieve's phrase. *Op.cit.* n. 9 at 293. They would hold the government liable in any case, for example, where the government is acting as "a proprietor rather than as a regulator," Peterson and Van Der Weide, *op.cit.* n. 13 at n. 92, because "The use of susceptibility analysis is particularly hard to justify when the government is acting as a proprietor rather than as a regulator. Even though the government as landlord, employer, health care provider, or auto fleet manager could conceivably make decisions based on large questions of public policy, it usually tries to get the most value for the least expenditure – as would any private actor. Little is to be gained by wrapping this kind of government conduct in the cloak of susceptibility analysis" *id.*, even though, from Borchard's point of view, when the government acts as proprietor, and there is an accident, the social issue arises, who is to pay the costs of that accident, the individual or the group? Peterson and Van Der Weide see an accident arising from government negligence (if proved) as a form of tortious "taking" for which the group should pay the individual; Borchard would seem to take the view that first an inquiry should be made into the social reasons behind the assignment of the proprietorship function to the collective. Another way to put this idea is contained in the Introductory Chapter to Bell and Bradley, *eds. Governmental Liability: A Comparative Study* (Glasgow 1991): "Risks undertaken for the common good do not fall into the same category as those undertaken for private advantage, and special rules are commonly imposed, at least where the activity in question is specific to public authorities." Bradley and Bell, Governmental Liability: A Preliminary Assessment,

Weide conclude with their own method of delineation: "The government should be immune . . . only when it can produce evidence that an official whose responsibilities include the weighing of social, economic, or political policy actually relied on a true policy factor in making the challenged decision."[61]

It is certainly correct that the Court in *Gaubert* did not articulate any justification for its shift towards a much more frequent application of the doctrine of sovereign immunity. As is described above,[62] the Court simply insisted that its precedents were to be so read and did not support the use of a policy-making/operational distinction for the purpose of deciding when an action falls into the "discretionary function or duty"[63] referred to in the DFE section of the FTCA and when the allegedly tortious action does not. But the Supreme Court could have reminded its readers that the process of delineation under the DFE section is a process of *interpretation of a statute*. It is true that the particular statute was passed in 1946; it is true that the particular statute, the FTCA, was changing the long established common law of federal government sovereign immunity from liability for its torts, but a statute it is and consequently it is the legislature that has made the decision as to what should be the scope of the possibility of reparation to the individual for harm caused to him or her wrongfully by the state.

Although the Supreme Court did not so state, it could have justified its narrowing of Federal Government liability in tort by its susceptibility analysis[64] as an interpretation of the intention of Congress in passage of the FTCA with the DFE section, an interpretation which its own jurisprudence had consistently adhered to. In this light, *Berkovitz* fits in nicely; the government was subject to suit on those facts because the relevant statute concerning the licensing of the vaccine had not left the agency any discretion. From this point of view, the Peterson and Van Der Weide approach is wrong-headed; they may have proposed an excellent line of demarcation for when the judiciary should or should not exercise restraint in second-guessing the administration through the medium of a tort suit, a line for which their article fully sets out the theoretical justification,[65] but it is not the line Congress would seem to have chosen when in 1945 it carved out, from the waiver of sovereign immunity provided for by the FTCA, the cases covered (under a fair reading) by the DFE section. Peterson and Van Der Weide

---

Chap. 1 in *op.cit.* n. 13 at 4.

61 Peterson and Van Der Weide, *op.cit.* n. 13, at 474.

62 See text at n. 45.

63 See text at n. 16.

64 A narrowing which certainly worked: Peterson and Van Der Weide, *op.cit.* n. 13, state that fifty-one of the eighty-nine separate cases in the pre-*Gaubert* sample went to trial; twenty-one of the eighty-eight post-*Gaubert* sample did. *Id.* at 473.

65 In this author's opinion a much better line of demarcation than the attempted use of the operational-policy distinction recommended by Fairgrieve as "a means of judicial restraint in relation to negligence actions," *op.cit.* n. 9 at 295. Professor Cass's review in 1991 of the U.S. cases demonstrated the intellectual incoherence of that particular public law filter, see Cass, *op.cit.* n. 13.

should have addressed their arguments to Congress as Borchard did, so long ago, not used the Supreme Court's decision in *Gaubert* as a whipping boy. The DFE section is not a "doctrine," it is not common law; it is a statutory gate.

Now, in what way may this United States history of Federal Governmental non-contractual liability under the FTCA illuminate the present debate about the scope of Member State non-contractual liability in European law, particularly as that law was created by the European Court of Justice in its decision in *Brasserie du Pêcheur/Factortame III*[66] ("*Brasserie*") and subsequent major cases on State liability?[67] Perhaps the first light relates importantly to the judicial function in the area of public liability. From the lens of legal method, the legal elements of responsibility for fault have always been defined by the courts, whether in Continental (working from very abbreviated sections of civil codes) or common law systems. So while Art. 288(2) (formerly Article 215) EC directs the Community "[I]n the case of non-contractual liability . . ." to ". . . make good any damage caused by its institutions or by its servants in the performance of its duties," the delineation of the parameters of this direction was naturally up to the European Court of Justice under its authority to interpret the Treaty. Art. 215(2) EC's only help to the Court in carrying out this task, the Article's specification that the "mak[ing] good" shall be ". . . in accordance with the general principles common to the laws of the Member States," thus referring the European Court to, presumably, the special torts jurisprudence governing claims against public authorities, created either by Member State courts and/or statutory authority in the Member States. Neither space here nor the author's own capacity in European law permits any attempt at recapitulation[68] of the ECJ's jurisprudence under Art. 215(2) EC, but it may be remarked that at least the Treaty does provide for non-contractual liability of the Community institutions in circumstances to be defined by the Court in the light of Member State common general principles, just as the FTCA provided in 1946 for the non-contractual liability of the United States Federal Government for the commission of common-law torts by that government's servants. (Of course, unlike Art. 215(2), the FTCA was explicit in *not* providing for legislative or administrative (execution of a regulation) torts.) So in both legal systems, the European Court and the federal courts had the authority of the Treaty in one case and the statute in the other for any finding of liability for harm to persons injured by Community or Federal Government acts.[69]

66 [1996] ECR I-1029.

67 The cases are listed in n. 147 of Andenas and Fairgrieve, *op.cit.* n. 9.

68 I have used for my own introduction Van Gerven, "Bridging the Unbridgeable: Community and National Tort Laws After Francovich and Brasserie" (1996) 45 ICLQ 507 and have briefly looked at Heckels and McDonnell, *eds.*, *The Action for Damages in Community Law*, Kluwer 1996.

69 A possible explanation for the U.S. Supreme Court's failure to justify its *Gaubert* decision on the basis of statutory interpretation might be the general mindset of all courts as the creators of the general principles of tort law.

In both cases the ECJ and the Supreme Court used that authority to take a very strict view of when the Community and the Federal government would be liable for harm caused by its acts. The correspondence between the *Schöppenstedt* formula and the *Berkovitz* exception to the DFE section is striking. Under the ECJ's jurisprudence, if the Community organ has a ". . . wide discretion, liability should arise only in case of a 'sufficiently flagrant [or serious] violation of a superior rule of law for the protection of the individual' (as the famous *Schöppenstedt* formula puts it)."[70] Under *Berkovitz*, as reiterated in *Gaubert*, since the DFE protects administrative discretionary action, an agency will only be held liable if the plaintiff can show that it has clearly violated its own mandatory governing regulation or statute – in short, a flagrant violation of law. Presumably the *Schöppenstedt* formula also implies that if a Community institution clearly violates its own mandate, it will also be held liable a la *Berkovitz*, that is to say, the ECJ also would not[71] in this case look into any issue of discretion.

In both judicial narrowings of the statutory mandate, one suspects that what was really motivating both the ECJ and the Supreme Court is the matter mentioned extrajudicially by Lord Browne-Wilkinson and quoted by Fairgrieve:[72] that in authorizing suit for non-contractual liability against the Community and against the Federal Government, neither the governments party to the Treaty nor the U.S. Congress wished the interpreting courts to ignore the financial health of public authorities. Whatever the human right to receive reparation for wrong, social policy requires that those acting for the collective good should *not* be ruled liable for their harmful errors unless those errors were flagrantly a violation of law. Borchard's issue of who must pay, in cases *other* than ordinary automobile accidents judged on the usual negligence principles, the individual or the collective, remains a prime consideration. In effect, in both Community law and U.S. law, there will not be liability unless there is a flagrant violation of the governing law or a garden variety species of *respondeat superior*.

The second light cast by the U.S. cases is upon the problem of delimitation in the cases of *some* discretion, and what *Gaubert* may presage for further development of *Brasserie* in European law. *Gaubert* has definitely rejected the policy/operational distinction and broadened the scope of federal sovereign immunity. What has the ECJ done with respect to suits for damages against Member States for violations of Community law that cause harm to individuals or

70 Van Gerven, *op.cit.* n. 68 at 518.

71 Just as the ECJ had no difficulty holding Italy strictly liable in *Francovich* for non-implementation of the directive within the mandated time limits.

72 Fairgrieve quotes from Lord Browne-Wilkinson's address to the Education Law Association, op.cit. n. 9 at 288, as follows:
". . . it is not really in the interests of society as a whole if you spend your time concentrating on rights of individuals to damages – because that is what we are talking about, financial compensation – against public authorities who are charged with looking after society as a whole and doing its best to perform a social welfare function; the creation of ever more duties giving rise to financial compensation is actually counterproductive in a society."

entities? It is first necessary to emphasize that in the case of the liability of Member State authorities or legislatures, the Treaty itself does not provide for such liability nor has the Community harmonized the law by a Directive. The European Court first announced the susceptibility of Member States to a duty to pay compensation to individuals or legal entities harmed by state action breaching Community law (in circumstances to be further defined in the future) in *Francovich.*[73] As Mads Andenas has elaborated,[74] the further circumstances through 1998 have been misimplementation of directives, administrative acts and legislative acts. It is notable that in the first important case to follow on *Francovich*, *Brasserie*, concerning whether or not the United Kingdom and Germany could be held liable in damages to individuals and corporations harmed by legislative violations of Community law (in Germany's case, by failure to amend the offending statutes; in the case of the United Kingdom, by passage of offending legislation), Germany argued to the Court that it should not create the cause of action in these cases without the authorization of the Community "legislature," or the Member States by Treaty, that it should be for the legal equivalent in the Community structure of the legislature, the Council, to determine the circumstances under which persons harmed by Member State acts should receive compensation in addition to their rights to have the Member State action annulled.[75]

The Court determined otherwise – not even mentioning the argument – and held that the possibility of suit in national court for damages was necessary to effectuate Community law. It then went on to lay out the conditions necessary for liability for breach of EC law: (a) the rule of law that was breached must be intended to confer rights upon individuals; (b) the breach must be "sufficiently serious" and (c) the appropriate causal link must be found.[76]

So how is a national court to know when a breach is "sufficiently serious"? If the situation is the same as in the *Schöppenstedt* situation, that is, the rule-making body has a very wide discretion, then the case falls into what we in the United States would see as a *Berkovitz* analysis: the legislature or other body acting must have "manifestly and gravely disregarded the limits on its powers" for liability to occur.[77] This test would seem to differ not at all from the *Berkovitz* rule that if the agency has violated its own mandatory regulations, it may be held liable. What the plaintiff must show in the first instance is that the public authority violated its governing statute.

But what if the governing statute is not explicit, the Community law claimed to be violated ambiguous? What if the defendant agency has some discretion,

73 *Francovich* [1991] ECR I-5357, pp. 37 and 38.

74 Andenas and Fairgrieve, *op.cit.* no. 9 at 315.

75 [1996] All ER (EC) 301, Report for the Hearing p. 27. "[The German Government] points out that during the negotiations concerning the Maastricht Treaty the Member States did not adopt any rules in that regard."

76 *Op.cit.* n. 9 at 316.

77 Andenas and Fairgrieve, *id.*

but not a wide discretion? Has the Court then given national courts a coherent rule with its "sufficiently serious" standard?[78] The history of the United States Court's struggles with the DFE section of the FTCA suggests that courts' attempts to deal with the issues when an agency with some discretion, some policy making function, commits an act that causes harm, end up with no clearly discernable line of demarcation between cases where the agency is held liable and where it is not; that the policy/operational distinction has not helped nor will the "sufficiently serious" standard.

Both the United States and the Community commentators have tried to offer methods of delimitation.[79] Yet the problem remains of *who* in society should make the ultimate balance in official liability between "[T]he remedy of compensation . . . as an essential element of the legal protection"[80] of individuals and the need of the state to have its "special responsibilities . . . reflected in the scope of its liability."[81]

This piece has suggested that the United States Supreme Court in its bitterly criticized *Gaubert* decision may have been looking back to Congress' attempt to draw the line in the FTCA and trying to draw it in accordance with its understanding of the legislative intention. Might one suggest that the Community might wish to consider a Community pronouncement on the conditions for Member State liability for breaches of Community law, if, as this piece foretells, more and more national court decisions are unable to draw a coherent line with the "sufficiently serious" standard. Might one also suggest that it should be a legislative function, not a judicial one, to build Van Gerven's bridge. Sometimes judges can use a "statute" to guide them, particularly where the balance between individual rights and social welfare is concerned.

---

78 Walter Van Gerven in his Chapter, "Taking Art. 215(2) EC Seriously," in Beatson and Tridimas, *eds.*, *New Directions in European Public Law* (Oxford 1998) at 43, refers to "the 'sufficiently serious breach' test" as an "obscure standard" and criticizes the Court in its post-*Brasserie* case law for its failure "to define *and* differentiate the liability conditions for breaches by Member States according to the type of situation involved." *Id.* at 42.

79 See text at n. 61 for Peterson and Van Der Weide's method of delimitation. Van Gerven in "Bridging the Unbridgeable: Community and National Tort Laws After Francovich and Brasserie", *op.cit.* n. 68 at 518 suggests that ". . . the public authority should behave as a normally reasonable and diligent authority being placed in the same kind of circumstances . . .". Van Gerven thinks that the "sufficiently serious" standard, since it is being applied to cases of interpretation of Community legal rules, is both over and under inclusive. *Id.* at 519.

80 Van Gerven, *op.cit.* n. 78 at 516.

81 Bradley and Bell, *op cit.* n. 60 at 2. "[The state]'s] activities, being intended for the welfare of society, must not be unduly restricted or encumbered." *Id.* The quotation from Lord Browne-Wilkinson at n. 72 was expressing the same idea.

20

THE "EU HUMAN RIGHTS CHARTER" AND THE UNION LEGAL ORDER: THE 'BANNS' BEFORE THE MARRIAGE?

Deirdre Curtin

I INTRODUCTION

Gordon Slynn in his capacity as Chairman of the European Communities Committee of the House of Lords when it reported on *Europol* (a European Police Office)[1] revealed, while taking evidence on the subject, a characteristic concern for the rights and interests of individuals when faced with the creation of new bodies operating within a constitutional no-mans land. Such bodies also include, for example, the Executive Committees established under the terms respectively of the Schengen Implementing Agreement, the Dublin Convention on Asylum as well as the External Borders Convention and the Customs Information Convention. Europol, moreover, is integrated neither into the national system of law enforcement nor into a system of law enforcement at the European level where it will operate.[2] Lord Slynn explicitly queried the UK reluctance in particular to involve the ECJ in Luxembourg in the resolution of disputes which could arise in that context: "Why is the United Kingdom so frightened about giving the European Court jurisdiction? This is the second or third time in recent months that we have had the United Kingdom saying: "We do not want the Court of Justice involved".[3] He continued: "We are very interested and keen in seeing to what extent a citizen who is wrongly recorded or where information is wrongly used should be given redress."[4]

The point was – and to some extent at least still is – that the nascent "area of freedom, security and justice" takes shape as a "non-law area".[5] The "non-law" element refers to the fact that the "cooperation" affects in practice the rights and

1 Select Committee on the European Communities, *Europol*, Session 1994-5, 10th Report (HL Paper 51).
2 See, Swart, "Cooperation in the field of criminal law: some comments" in Monar and Morgan (eds.) *The Third Pillar of the European Union* (College of Europe, 1994), 193, at 198.
3 Minutes of Evidence, Wednesday 23 November 1994, para. 71, p.11, *op.cit.*
4 Ibid. at para.90, p.13.
5 See, European Parliament resolution on the progress made in 1996 in the implementation of cooperation in the fields of justice and home affairs pursuant to Title VI of the Treaty on European Union, OJ C 20/185, (20.1.1997).

D. O'Keeffe (ed.), Liber Amicorum Slynn 303-318 (2000)

interests of individual citizens but they have no possibility of challenging either the policy decisions or attacking questionable operational decisions. The concern is basically about a lack of separation of powers, in particular that the new executive and police structures are not embedded in those other structures inherent to democratic states, namely those guaranteeing parliamentary control and supervision by an independent judiciary *inter alia* of human rights protection. The fact that rule-making relating for example to police cooperation increasingly takes place at the European level means that the scrutiny of *national* judicial and parliamentary organs is to a considerable extent by-passed[6] without any adequate substitute at the European level. This disembedment process results in the reinforcing of the executive power at the expense of both the legislative and the judicial power and has been referred to as an "insult to democracy".[7] For example, the transborder application of certain modern investigative methods, such as controlled delivery, deployment of undercover agents and the interception of various forms of telcommunications is now regulated at the European level.[8] Europol already effectively cooperates with the American FBI on a more or less equal footing.[9] The difference between Europol and the FBI is however that the American FBI is subject to democratic control in the national sphere whereas Europol has been "liberated" from analogous control. The absence of accountable executive action in the structures currently under construction presents a difficult challenge to those concerned about the quality of Europe's future.

Lord Slynn's concern that the rights and interests of individuals be protected within the judicial architecture of the Europe in evolution is one which found ultimate expression in the Report issued by the Committee on the important and novel topic of Europol, albeit within the confines of the existing legal framework at that time. The House of Lords Committee concluded to the effect that:

> "where the individual seeks redress in the courts it should normally be in the national courts and the majority of cases will not require any further consideration. We are not persuaded that there should be direct access by the citizen to the European Court of Justice....Even giving full weight to the distinction between the Community pillar and the Home Affairs and Justice pillar the Committee take the view that the European Court is

6 A significant exception is the Dutch parliament's right to insist in certain circumstances that Dutch Ministers obtain the assent of the Parliament before agreeing to putatively (legally) binding decisions. See, Rijkswet 17 December 1992, Stb. 1992, 692. In practice however the procedure has been labelled a "farce" (TK 23 490., nr. 23, p. 1) due to the fact that Council documents are frequently only made available at the last moment and often untranslated. See also, R. Schutz, *Europaweite Freizugigkeit ohne democratische Kontrolle?* 120 *Archiv des Offentlichen Rechts* (1995) 509 and House of Lords Select Committee on the European Communities, *Enhancing Parliamentary Scrutiny of the Third Pillar,* Session 1997-98, (HL, Paper 25).

7 See, C.A. Groenendijk and E.Guild, "Admission for Employment" in Standing Committee of Experts in International Immigration,Refugee and Criminal Law, *A New Immigration Law for Europe?* (Utrecht,1993),40,43.

8 High Level Action Plan, *op.cit.*

9 *NRC Handelsblad*, 28 May 1997.

> perfectly capable of applying this Convention as an inter-state agreement outside the Community pillar.... We would not support a compromise which left the European Court with uneven jurisdiction in regard to the Member states....by an optional protocol. There is no precedent...".

From the vantage point of the "brave new world" of the EU anno 2000 we must now view these conclusions as somewhat dated. The constitutional penumbra of the EU is increasingly populated with extra-EC bodies and organs with no clear constitutional status (unidentified international organisations such as Europol?) either in the national legal systems or in the European legal system (SIS, Eurodac, Eurojust etc.). Moreover, the distinction between the Community Pillar and the 'Third Pillar' has rescinded quite dramatically both in the practices which developed post-Maastricht and in the terms of the Amsterdam Treaty itself.[10] The fact that some limited provisions were made in the Europol Convention for the settlement of disputes between Member States and optionally for national courts to refer questions to the Court of Justice in Luxembourg does not mean that an effective and authoritative mechanism for settling disputes and interpreting the Convention once it has become a living instrument was created.[11] For example, the Court of Justice had no competence to deal with disputes between Europol and the Member States nor is there any direct access to the ECJ for individual persons detrimentally affected by Europol's actions.The optional protocol finally included in the Europol Convention (granting Member States the right to "opt out" of the ECJ preliminary reference jurisdiction) has in fact functioned as a 'precedent' for other Conventions adopted subsequently on justice and home affairs but, moreover, very similar provisions were actually included in both the EC Treaty and the EU Treaty as a result of the changes introduced by the Treaty of Amsterdam. Finally, 'flexibility' in terms of policy-making and decision-making is part of the vista both of the present (Schengen) and of the future (title on enhanced cooperation pursuant to the provisions of the Amsterdam Treaty).[12]

A changed legal environment in some respects is thus the result of these various nuances introduced or consolidated by the Treaty of Amsterdam. At the same time some features of the Community/Union legal order remain defiantly the same. Most importantly the question of direct access to the Court of Justice by individuals: here the classic and restrictive limitations as developed by the Court itself in the early days of the European *Economic* Community remain as if writ in stone. Even in the midst of a prolific debate on the current judicial architecture of the EU in which the Court itself very actively participates, no serious suggestions have been made to reassess the validity of these restrictive *locus*

10 See, Dekker and Curtin, "The EU as a 'Layered' International Organization: Institutional Unity in Disguise" in: P.Craig and G.de Burca (eds.), *The Evolution of EU Law*, (OUP, 1999), 83-136.

11 See, in general, S.Peers, "Who's Judging the Watchmen? The Judicial System of the 'Area of Freedom, Security and Justice" (1998) *Yearbook of European Law*, nyp

12 See, in general, A.Albors-Llorens, "Changes in the Jurisdiction of the European Court of Justice under the Treaty of Amsterdam" 35 CML Rev. (1998) 1273-1294.

standi conditions (the dreaded "direct and individual concern" in particular) in the light of the evolving nature of the wider European Union and its ever-expanding remit (police, security, criminal law, environment....).[13] There seem to be no immediate plans to include reform of justiciability requirements in the agenda for the upcoming Treaty of Paris. This is a shame (see, *infra.).*

At the same time, and here is the nub of the matter, very different fora are discussing the content of a so-called "Charter on Fundamental Rights of the Citizens of the European Union" which the European Council has already placed on the agenda of the newly opened IGC as one of the few non-institutional adaptation topics brought about by the enlargement to the East, left open at Amsterdam. One of the main purposes of this proposed Charter is the political drive to appear to do something concrete for the citizen in the EU, something he or she can directly relate to. Another purpose must be, in the light of recent fraud and corruption scandals at the level of the EU, to address concerns about the lack of accountability of EU institutions as actors in the political and administrative decision-making process. Finally there is the expressed wish to codify in the context of the text of the EU Treaties themselves a list of the applicable fundamental rights provisions in the application of Community and or Union law. This would address concerns about the structural lack of transparency of the system of fundamental rights protection which essentially relies upon the role of the Court of Justice in Luxembourg in "discovering", interpreting and applying these norms. It is of course impossible for the citizen to understand at present how precisely the provisions at national level, in the European Convention on Human Rights and the Court's case-law interact nor what the practical consequences of such interaction might be.

But do we really need another Charter at the international level in order to fulfill these functions? Is the risk not that an additional "Charter of Human Rights" at the European level will not only undermine the position of the European Convention on Human Rights but will also considerably add to the fragmentation of human rights protection at the international level? And how would the provisions of an EU Charter be enforced in practice and by whom? Will the provisions be binding in law? Will individuals be given direct access to the European Court where their fundamental rights, as enshrined in the EU Charter, have been infringed? Will the EU Charter apply in the context of the multitude of ad-hoc bodies and organs being created on the fringe of EU activity and will individuals have (direct) access to the ECJ when they claim that their rights have been violated as a result of their rule-making or operational decisions? If so according to what conditions? And finally is the risk not that there will be a reduction in standards of human rights protection compared to currently prevailing ones if a new chapter is drafted and subjected to the normal EU process of dip-

13 See, *Access to Justice. A record of thoughts and ideas dealing with the interrelationship between national law and courts and Community law and courts.* (Helsinki,1999). See also, for example, the recent *Report of the Working Party on the Future of the European Court of Justice*, not yet published.

lomatic negotiation and compromise? Are the risks in this regard not even greater once the formal accession takes place of the Central and Eastern European countries?

These and other questions need to be teased out carefully in advance of the headlong rush to agree an EU Charter at the next IGC. The purpose of this short essay is not to supply authoritative answers at this stage of the debate but rather to situate some of the more key questions within the current stage in the evolution of the EU legal order and to consider its putative relationship with the general (European) system of human rights protection. This short essay is dedicated to Gordon Slynn and the interest he has consistently displayed in ensuring that adequate redress was available to citizens adversely affected by the decisions and practices of various national and European institutions and their satellites in whatever shape or form. Moreover, this essay seeks to start the process of bringing together two important contemporary legal debates, the debate on reform of EU judicial architecture and the debate on the desirability, content and positioning of an EU Charter on Fundamental Rights. Both debates must of course be taken seriously, but they should not be artificially isolated from one another, and the guaranteeing of the rights and interests of individuals in practice must be a common *leitmotiv*.

II THE *STATUS QUO* IN TERMS OF EU HUMAN RIGHTS PROTECTION

The EU has acknowledged in diverse ways that it has an important role to play in promoting respect for human rights of those resident within the Union and of ensuring those rights are fully respected. The Amsterdam Treaty proclaims that "the Union is founded on the principles of liberty, democracy, respect for human rights and fundamental freedoms and the rule of law" while making it obvious that the Member States remain the principal guardians of human rights within their own territories.[14] Moreover, the Union attempts to staunchly defend human rights in its external affairs by *inter alia* insisting that those States seeking admission to the Union and those seeking cooperation agreements or aid or benefit from trade preferences undertake to respect human rights.[15] If that undertaking is breached then the agreement in question can be suspended. Moreover, since the Amsterdam Treaty, any Member State violating human rights in a "serious and persistent" way can lose its rights under the Treaty.

That said, the epicentre of human rights *protection* in Europe is without doubt the ECHR and the supervisory system it sets in place. The ECHR was drafted on the presumption that all implementation and applicability of the law is the responsibility of a single (clearly identified) state.[16] The question arose decades ago with

14 See further, P.Alston (ed.), *The EU and Human Rights,*(Oxford, 1999).

15 See, in general, E.Riedel and M.Will, "Human Rights Clauses in External Agreements of the EC" in P.Alston (ed.), *ibid.*

16 See Article 25 of the original version of the Convention: "The Commission may receive

regard to the European Community, that since the Community is itself not a party to the ECHR, does that imply that, by transferring power to the Communities, it was possible for the Member States to *de facto* deprive their citizens from the very protection previously enjoyed by virtue both of the terms of the ECHR itself as well as by virtue of their national constitutions? The answer by now is well known, and national constitutional courts, the Court of Justice and the supervisory organs in Strasbourg all ultimately adopted a tandem approach accepting the pivotal (and exclusive) role of the Court of Justice in ensuring the protection of human rights within the scope of Community law as a specific instance of a "general principle" of Community law.[17]

Despite the absence of any reference in the original constituent treaties to the protection of fundamental rights, the European Court of Justice has thus played a pivotal role in affirming that respect for such rights was part of the legal heritage of the Community. The Court of Justice, in the absence of any express provision in the Treaties themselves, "incorporated" in a certain sense the provisions of the ECHR as well as principles gleaned from the constitutional traditions of the Member States into the Community legal order.[18] The Court thereby successfully fought off the threat posed by rebellious constitutional courts in various Member States as well as the risk that the Strasbourg organs would assume human rights jurisdiction over matters falling within the scope of Community law. Measures incompatible with fundamental human rights were deemed to be unacceptable and judicial protection of those rights took root in the Community legal order. Respect for human rights became a condition of the lawfulness of *Community* acts[19] and is supervised by the Court of Justice itself. Moreover, national acts or measures in so far as they have effects falling within the scope of Community will also be scrutinised for their compatibility with the human rights norms developed by the Court of Justice.[20] As is well known, the European Commission on Human Rights responded to the Court of Justice's established line of case law by asserting that it had no jurisdiction in actions brought by private individuals, directly or indirectly, against the European Communities. One of the major factors in prompting

petitions... claiming to be a violation by one of the High Contracting Parties..." (of Article 34 of the Convention as amended by Protocol No. 11).

17 See further, F.Mancini and V.di Bucci, "Le developpement des droits fondamentaux en tant que partie du droit communautaire" *Collected Courses of the Academy of European law*, vol I, (1990), 35.

18 See, in general, Rodriguez Iglesias, "The protection of fundamental rights in the case law of the Court of Justice of the European Communities" 1 *Columbia Journal of European Law* (1995) 169.

19 Court's Opinion 2/94 of 28 March 1996, para. 34. Decision of 9 December 1987, *Tete v. France*, No. 11123/84.

20 An example is the activist interpretation of the principle of equality and the consequent very wide reach of the relevant provision of Community law see: Case C-13/94, *P. v. S.* [1996] ECR I-2143.

this reply by the European Commission on Human Rights was the protection provided by the Court of Justice in the Community legal system.[21]

Over the years however much criticism has been voiced as to the approach of the Court of Justice in this regard. The criticism ranged from worry as to the possibility that the two courts in question (Strasbourg and Luxembourg) could give divergent interpretations of the same provision of the ECHR despite the so-called "incorporation" of the ECHR into the Community legal order[22] to the more aggressive accusation that the Court of Justice did not take human rights seriously.[23] The complexity and unclear nature of the institutional system for the individuals affected (Strasbourg incorporated in Luxembourg and applied by the Luxembourg judges but only within the scope of application of Community law) was also emphasised.[24] It is not so surprising therefore that the subject of the Community simply acceding, as such, to the ECHR has featured prominently over the years in institutional debates about the reform of the EC. Indeed, it has long been assumed that accession by the EC to the ECHR would be the best way forward, both symbolically but also in terms of ensuring control by an *external* judge.[25] The accession option has however become much more unlikely since the Court of Justice's opinion to the effect that the Community did not currently possess the legal capacity to accede, largely on institutional-technical grounds.[26] What seems to have *sotte voce* been a key consideration was the fact that upon accession the Strasbourg Court would have had the last word on human rights matters and that this might prove in-

21 See the decisions of 10 July 1978, *CFDT v. European Communities*, No. 8030/77, DR 13, p. 231; decision of 19 January 1989, *Dufay v. European Communities*, No. 13539/88 and decision of 9 February 1990, *M and Co v. Federal Republic of Germany*, No. 13258/87, DR 64, p. 138.

22 See, for example, R.Lawson, "Confusion and Conflict? Diverging Interpretations of the European Convention on Human Rights in Strasbourg and Luxembourg" in R.Lawson and M.de Blois (eds.) *The Dynamics of the Protection of Human Rights in Europe. Essays in Honour of H.G.Schermers,* Vol.III, (Dordrecht, 1994), p. 219-252.

23 See, J.Coppel and A.O'Neill, "The European Court of Justice: Taking Rights Seriously?" 29 CML Rev. (1992), p. 669, 692.

24 See, A.Clapham, "A human rights policy for the European Community" in *Yearbook of European Law,* vol. 10 (1990), p. 309-366.

25 See, for example, the President of the Court of Justice himself, Rodriguez Iglesias, *op.cit.*

26 See, Opinion 2/94 of 28 march 1996, ECR 1996, pp. 1759; see for further comments N. Burrows, "Question of Community Accession to the European Convention Determined", E.L. Rev. 22 (1997), pp. 58-63; G. Gaja, "ECJ-Opinion 2/94: Accession by the EC to the ECHR", CMLR 33 (1996), pp. 973-989; T. Jaag, "Beitritt der EG zur EMRK?", Aktuelle Juristische Praxis 5 (1996), pp. 980-984; S. O'Leary, "Accession by the European Community to the European Convention on Human Rights – The Opinion of the EJC", EHRLR (1996), pp. 362-377; H.G. Schermers, "Toetreding van de EG tot het EVRM: Het Hof van Justitie adviseert", NJCM-Bulletin 21 (1996), pp. 874-883; C. Vedder, "Anmerkung zum Gutachten 2/94, EMRK, des EuGH", EuR 31 (1996), pp. 309-319; P. Wachsmann, "L'avis 2/94 de la Cour de justice relatif à l'adhésion de la Communauté européenne à la Convention de sauvegarde des droits de l'homme et des libertés fondamentales", RTD eur. 32 (1996), pp. 467-491.

compatible with the Court of Justice's perception of the entire system of EU judicial remedies.

One of the key problems in the current approach to human rights protection at the EU level is *the lack of structural visibility* of fundamental rights in the legal order of the European Union. It can reasonably be argued that fundamental rights can only fulfill their function if citizens are aware of their existence and conscious of their ability to enforce them. It is consequently crucial to express and present fundamental rights in a way that permits the individual to know and access them: fundamental rights must be visible. They are not elaborated in the text of the Treaties as such, with a few almost haphazard exceptions (right of access to information, right of non-discrimination and right to equal pay). This makes it extremely difficult for individuals to know what rights are entitled to protection in the Community legal order and by what means they are to be enforced. This structural invisibility was only rectified to a limited extent in the Treaty of Amsterdam. That Treaty essentially affirmed the practice of the Court by providing that the Union "shall respect fundamental rights, as guaranteed by the European Convention [on Human Rights] ... and as they result from the constitutional traditions common to the Member States, as general principles of Community law". This approach displays once more the uncertain status of fundamental rights in the Community legal order: they are to be qualified as "general principles" of Community law, on a par with other judicially developed general principles such as the principle of proportionality and the principle of legitimate expectations but with no clear hierarchy in the Community legal system. Moreover, it is clear from the wording used that the provisions of the ECHR are not binding as such, but rather a source of inspiration for the Court, alongside the national constitutional traditions, in working out what are the applicable standards at the Community level.[27]

At the last IGC, the Dutch Addendum to the Dublin Draft Treaty involved the reinforcement of the role of the Court of Justice in the protection of human rights within the European Union. It entailed the amendment of the EU Treaty so that the EU would be *bound* by the terms of the ECHR as such and not merely as discretionary elements of the "general principles" of Community law (the current situation). This would have involved some alteration of what the late Federico Mancini famously termed the ECJ's "genetic code".[28] Instead the Amsterdam Treaty in its final form rather more weakly provided that its terms must be "guaranteed" as "general principles of law" which represented essentially the *status quo*. Indeed the Amsterdam Treaty epitomises what I have previously referred to as the "'LAT' relationship" ('LAT' is a Dutch synonym for "living apart together") of the EU system and the EC system.[29] In other words, the European Convention system

27 See further, the contribution by P.Oliver in this volume.

28 F.Mancini and D.Keeling, "Language, Culture and Politics in the Life of the European Court of Justice" 1 *Columbia Journal of European Law* (1995) 397.

29 D.Curtin and Y.Klerk, "De Europese Unie en het Europese Verdrag voor de Rechten van de Mens: een nieuwe fase in een LAT-relatie?" 72 *Nederlands Juristen Blad* (1997)

remains intact and there are no structural or institutional links between the two systems: in that sense they are "apart" and conveniently located in entirely separate (albeit reasonably adjacent) housing. But the systems are "together" by virtue of the obligation on the EU institutions and Member States and enforced by the European Court of Justice to ensure that the provisions of the ECHR are "guaranteed" in the Union legal system. Experience has shown that this does not mean that its provisions are binding as such and without further ado in the Union legal system but rather that due account will be taken of the provisions and the interpretation given by the Strasbourg supervisory organs without interfering with the discretion of the ECJ in the final instance with regard to its inimitable tailoring of the (now) Union legal order. Up until recently the Strasbourg organs have tended to stress the apartness of the two systems provided that some (judicial) supervision was being provided within the international institution in question.

Recent events show however some fairly dramatic developments in the ongoing relationship between the two systems which indicates a renewed intensity. The first surprising indication came from the revamped Strasbourg organs themselves in the form of the judgment in *Matthews v. United Kingdom*.[30] This case arose from the fact that Gibraltar was excluded from participating in the direct elections to the European Parliament. The United Kingdom was of the opinion that it was not liable for this exclusion under the terms of the ECHR since Community law was at the origin of this exclusion. The Court disagreed and concluded to the effect that the United Kingdom had indeed violated article 3 of the First Protocol to the Convention and was responsible for the violations caused to the Convention, even where the power in question had been transferred to an international organisation. It ruled that:

> "The suggestion that the United Kingdom may not have effective control over the state of affairs complained of cannot affect the position, as the United Kingdom's responsibility derives from its having entered into treaty commitments subsequent to the applicability of Article 3 of Protocol No. 1 to Gibraltar".

This seems to be quite a clear signal from the Court in Strasbourg that it is entering a new phase in its relationship with international organisations in general, and the European Union in particular.

The second development indicative of some increasing intensity has come from the Court of Justice itself. Recently it has developed quite stringent case-law with regard to the respect of fundamental rights by the EC institutions themselves, in particular with regard to the securing of the principle of good administration within the EU institutions and the fact that everyone is entitled to a fair legal process. In so doing it has relied very explicitly on the provisions of the

---

202-210.

30 ECHR, judgment of 18 February 1999.

ECHR and applied them directly.[31] Moreover, it appears that the Court is, within the limits of its current jurisdiction, contributing to the securing of the EU citizens' right of participation in an "effective political democracy". In other words, the Court has, in a number of test cases, already made a significant contribution to a citizens' right to obtain information about the decision-making processes from a number of EU institutions and bodies (the Council, the Commission and "comitology" committees).[32] In an effective political democracy, the idea of an informed citizenry, the free expression of opinion of the people in the choice of the legislature and the possibility to complain about one's government and administration must indeed be secured as fundamental rights. The Court is responsible for the development and application of these ideas in the context of the EU. It provides an excellent example of the ECJ going further than the minimum provisions in this regard provided in the ECHR.

However the question of access to information also arises as it relates to the procedure before the Court of Justice itself. One can reasonably ask *shouldn't the Court itself be leading by example*? And this is something which the Court seems to be refusing to consider at present. It is for example the *only* EU institution which has to date not adopted a legal instrument giving citizens access to information as it relates to its judicial and administrative documents. Even Europol, which is under no constitutional or legal obligation to do so, has recently announced its intention to adopt a provision governing citizens access to information contained in its documents and archives. But shouldn't the ordinary citizen or his/her representatives, be they parliamentary or in the form of active public interest groups, be able to know what arguments are being raised before the Court in what are often very crucial cases with enormous implications in the national legal sphere by various intervening governments, the EU institutions themselves as well as the parties to the case? Of course the judicial process is different to the legislative or administrative process and I am not suggesting that the deliberations of the Court itself in reaching its actual decision be made public, only the arguments put before it, as an important aspect of ensuring an effective political democracy. In several Member States of the EU this is quite common practice and does not give rise to insurmountable problems. Moreover this issue acquires a particular relevance at the moment given the fact that the Court has restricted significantly in the past years the information it gives on the arguments and observations presented to it.

III Does the Proposed EU Human Rights Charter Have Added Value?

The current idea of a Charter is above all to be seen to do something for the citizen and to make the protection of human rights in the EU legal order more visible.

---

31 See further, the contribution by P.Oliver in this volume.

32 See further, D.Curtin, "Citizens' Fundamental Right of Access to EU Information: An Evolving Digital *Passepartout?*" 37 CML Rev. (2000) 7-41.

From this perspective the proposal to elaborate a Charter in the context of the EU could be viewed as a positive development. At the same time the elaboration of such a Charter should not present Member States with the opportunity to agree with less far-reaching standards than those currently prevailing within the European Convention on Human Rights or national constitutional systems. Any such Charter should therefore, as a starting point, *incorporate all the substantive provisions (Articles 1-18) of the European Convention on Human Rights into the Treaty on European Union together with the relevant protocols.* The idea could be that incorporation of the provisions of the ECHR in this manner would provide a more effective integration of the Convention into the Community/Union legal system than accession by the EC/EU to the ECHR. These rules would then have formal and visible constitutional status in the Union and would be fully and directly integrated into the Community legal order and there would no longer be any need to rely on the concept of "general principles of law" as developed by the Court of Justice on a case-by-case basis.[33]

Conferring *full jurisdiction upon the Court of Justice* over the interpretation and application of the Convention would be a necessary consequence of its incorporation into the Treaties. Otherwise the Convention would remain unenforceable in Community law and its incorporation would achieve nothing. This step would ensure the full integration of the Convention into the Community system of remedies. The provisions of the Convention would be interpreted and enforced in the same manner as those of the EC Treaty. This would have a number of important consequences. First, it could be expected that in due course the Court would confirm either on an article-by-article basis or by way of general interpretation that all the substantive provisions of the Convention are capable of producing *direct effect* in the national legal systems. What is more the Court could, by a bold interpretation, conceivably rule that certain provisions of the Convention even have horizontal direct effect and are thus capable of being invoked by one individual against another just like Article 141 TEC (previously Article 119 EC) at present.[34]

Second, the provisions of the Convention would enjoy *supremacy* over national law in the same way as the provisions of Community law and irrespective of the national systems of incorporation (monist or dualist systems). It is easy to see that the combined application of the principles of direct effect and supremacy could enormously enhance the effectiveness and efficiency of the enforcement of the Convention's provisions. The long, complicated, time-consuming

---

33 See further, A.Toth, "The European Union and Human Rights: The Way Forward", 34 CML Rev (1997) 491-529.

34 Toth *ibid.* refers to the example of Article 8 of the Convention in this sense where he argues that if it were to have horizontal direct effect that could have tremendous implications for the protection of privacy against unjustified intrusion by other individuals (for example, the Media). This would considerably extend the scope of the Convention. At present the Convention can only be invoked by individuals against violations committed by States.

and expensive Convention machinery would be replaced by much faster and simpler proceedings before national courts. Individuals would be able to invoke the Convention at the earliest possible opportunity in both civil and criminal cases instead of having to go all the way to Strasbourg after having gone right through the national appeal system. The result would be *a truly decentralised system of protection* in which national courts would play the leading role. They could of course refer any question of interpretation to the Court of Justice under the preliminary reference procedure.

This brief discussion has thus squarely departed from the premise that the proposed EU Human Rights Charter would include, as a minimum, all the substantive rights contained in the ECHR; its provisions would be binding in law within the Union legal system and would be applied and enforced by the ECJ in cooperation, as appropriate, with the national courts. The difference with the *status quo* would be that the ECJ would be applying the provisions of the ECHR as such and that they would be binding as such within the legal order of the EU. One advantage of this approach compared to the *status quo* would be the fact that the substantive provisions would apply as such in a horizontal fashion to all the institutions and organs and independent agencies operating under the auspices of the EU. This would mean in principle that, for example, Europol and other such agencies which currently do not fall under the jurisdiction of the ECJ in a proper fashion and which are arguably also excluded from Strasbourg review, would be subject to a fundamental rights review. Moreover, the binding nature of the provisions of the ECHR would once and for all be squarely recognised within the EU system and inevitably their supremacy over relevant provisions of national constitutions, which presumably would retain their current status of a source of inspiration for the ECJ's further development of its "general principles".

The weak point in the manner in which the EU Charter on Human Rights would fit into the EU institutional architecture lies in the fact that for it to have a real added value it is dependent on application and enforcement by the ECJ. If this is not to be the case then not only will the ECHR system as such be substantially undermined but the addition of such a Charter to the EU system will represent a step backwards in terms of the current *status quo* of protection of human rights by the Court of Justice itself. Assuming, therefore, only the best case scenario of full enforcement by the Court of Justice, a significant problem still remains. The EU Charter could only represent a genuine added value as compared to the current situation if the related questions of *access to justice* and in particular access directly to the Court itself by individuals and by public interest groups interested in pursuing so-called "test cases" on the interpretation and application of certain issues is simultaneously pursued and achieved. The concepts of "direct and individual concern" are not defined by the Treaty but their restrictive scope is the result of the Court's own case-law. These conditions are such that individuals or groups representing individuals are for the most part shut out from direct challenges to offensive measures before the ECJ.[35] This situation is of course particularly grave when the challenges in question concern alleged violations of human rights by Union institutions or bodies or by Member States operating on behalf of the Community. The issue of access to justice in the field of human rights requires review both by the ECJ itself and by the Intergovernmental Conference. The *locus standi* requirements of Article 230 (ex Article 173) TEC could in the first instance be reinterpreted by the Court so as to allow an individual to challenge any act of an institution of the Union or one operating under its auspices, capable of producing legal effects which directly affect a specific right or legal interest of that individual.

Access to the ECJ should always be available where no other guaranteed judicial route is available before national courts, or where national courts have refused to make a reference.[36] This is not part of the *status quo.* Not only do we now post-Amsterdam have different conditions governing the operation of preliminary reference mechanisms as they operate in different policy-making contexts (and optional conditions such as in the Europol protocol) but there is a vivid debate being led by the Court of Justice itself as to how this mechanism should/can be modified as a result of the hugely increasing work pressure on the Court itself. Much of this debate is preoccupied with finding solutions that will reduce the numbers of references made to the Court and the manner in which they will be dealt with as a matter of practice. Little account seems at present to be taken of the very legitimate perspective of the individual whose rights and interests have been affected by European Union law as broadly understood and embracing in any event the acts of those various organs, entities, data-banks which operate under the auspices of an institution of the EU (European Council, Council, Commission etc).

There is much however that the ECJ can do itself in "leading by example" with regard to its own access rules. It could for example revisit its case law and, if necessary request a revision of its Statute, in order to facilitate intervention by recognised public interest groups. As the "Agenda for Human Rights" expressed it:

> "The current automatic right of intervention of Member States must be balanced by a right of intervention by other public groups which may better inform the Court of sensitive societal concerns in the field of human rights."

Revising the judicial architecture can never only address legitimate concerns by the courts themselves that they are over-burdened (or operating inefficiently in terms of time and publication management). It must also include the perspective of potential individual litigants whose rights and interests are affected by the legal order in question. The perspective of civil society in the broad sense is not best represented only by the Bar or the judiciary or EU institutions: it needs a

35 See further the contribution by L.Gormley in this volume.

36 See, in the same sense, P. Alston and J.H.H. Weiler, *The European Union and Human Rights: Final Project Report on the Agenda for 2000*, (Florence, 1999), paragraph 181.

wider cast which could (should) include and recognise the role which public interest and civil liberty groups can have to play in stimulating and focussing the debate. After all, the increasing recognition given to, and value placed upon, a role for so-called 'civil society' should not only be restricted to the realm of consultation in the policy-making realm but should include debates on institutional reform in general and reform of judicial architecture in particular.[37]

An alternative to leaving it to the Court, and from the viewpoint of legal certainty the preferable alternative, is to include these and related points in the coming amendment process of the Treaties themselves. Prior to the Treaty of Amsterdam, specific proposals were made that the terms of Article 173 EC (now Article 230 TEC) be amended so as to enable individuals to initiate actions for annulment against all acts of the Union, whatever their form, prejudicially affecting their rights or interests. This exemplary approach ensures that in each case where the civil rights of individuals are affected or where their rights under the ECHR are violated by an act of the Union they would be granted a right to a tribunal even if they are not direct "addressees" of this act.[38]

IV Conclusion

My base-line is incorporation of the existing European instrument, the ECHR, into the proposed EU Human Rights Charter. This approach would not exclude, in addition, developing certain further-reaching rights which may be of particular or specific importance in the context of the rule-making activity of the EU (for example social rights, or rights relating to a citizens access to (digital) information[39]). The EU Charter should in any event be subject in its entirety to the full jurisdiction of the ECJ over its interpretation and application. Moreover, the Court of Justice should make a serious attempt to itself *lead by example* with regard to the precepts of good administration. It would follow that it should introduce access to information for citizens to certain of its own judicial and administrative documents. Moreover, certain procedures before the Court should be revised, either by the Court itself or by the IGC itself, in particular the standing requirements to bring direct and indirect actions before the Court. Public interest and other groups should also be enabled to initiate such actions. Further, the

---

37 See further in general on the role of "civil society": D.Curtin, "Civil Society and the European Union: Opening Spaces for Deliberative Democracy" *Collected Courses of the Academy of European Law*, 1997 (Kluwer, 1999).

38 The Court of Justice itself queried some time ago whether the current limitation on the right to bring an action for annulment under Article 173 EC (now Article 230) which individuals only enjoy in regard to acts of direct and individual concern to them "is sufficient to guarantee for them effective judicial protection against possible infringements of their fundamental rights arising from the legislative activity of the institutions". See, Report by the Court of Justice of May 1995 on certain aspects of the application of the Treaty on European Union, unpublished.

39 See further, D.Curtin, *op.cit.* n. 32.

preliminary reference procedure should not be too restrictively amended and in any event account must be taken, in that context, of the proposed revamped role for the ECJ regarding fundamental rights jurisdiction both with regard to national courts and Union institutions.

If the European Convention is incorporated into the TEU and is, in its entirety, brought within the jurisdiction of the ECJ, is there a point in the Member States remaining subject to the Convention's control machinery? It has been argued that this would be unnecessary (since the Convention would become fully enforceable under Community law) but moreover that the simultaneous application of the enforcement procedures could lead to conflicting decisions since they would operate independently of one another. The ultimate advantage, it has been argued, of withdrawal from the European Convention on Human Rights by all the Member States of the EU would be that the protection of human rights in the EU and its Member States would be brought within a single system of enforcement under the final authority of a single court (the ECJ in Luxembourg).[40] But there is in my view a better way of reaching the same result (a single system of enforcement under the final authority of a single court) and that is to propose a *marriage between the two systems* rather than effectively a divorce between the Member States of the EU and the ECHR system. The latter after all can justly be considered " a part of the cultural self-definition of European civilisation" which has become more than simply a legal safety net to be discarded at will.[41]

The EU Charter on Human Rights in my view must only be considered as a small first step. The real goal to be achieved remains Union accession to the ECHR system itself. The proposed marriage is (like many such ventures) fraught with difficult hurdles to be taken one at a time and requiring both tenacity and patience (long, complex and technical negotiations and an uncertain outcome in that any one Member State out of a total of 42 Council of Europe members can potentially block accession even at the last minute). But it is in my opinion where the real challenge lies. After all, only the option of accession by the EU to the ECHR will ensure that the EU system as such is subject to a truly *external* judge just like the national systems and national highest courts. And why shouldn't the ECJ itself, in the final analysis, be subject to the same scrutiny as its national counterparts? Otherwise who will guard the watchers and the independent actors on the European stage?

Some commentators worry that even an explicit Treaty amendment permitting accession might not be sufficient to overcome the hurdle of satisfying the Court of Justice as to the ultimate compatibility of accession by the EC(EU) to the ECHR with the Community/Union system. It is in any event worth stressing that the general situation is different to the rejection of the European Economic Area Court by the ECJ in 1991. The EEA was a new creation by the Member States of the EC and EFTA and the question of supervision was therefore able to be solved within the legal sphere of the EC and the Contracting States as such. It was acceptable for all

40 See, A.Toth, *op.cit.* n. 33.
41 See, P. Alston and J.H.H.Weiler, Final project report, *op.cit.* n. 36, paragraph 93.

the parties concerned that the ECJ was the only court interpreting the law of the EC. With regard to the ECHR, the situation differs in several respects. First, the ECHR is an earlier treaty covering a wide field of human rights questions and the European Court of Human Rights is hence not subject to other judicial supervision without the consent of the Council of Europe. Second, the EC does not have substantive competence in this field (and its putative Charter will take the provisions of the ECHR as its minimum starting point). The supervision of Community acts by the Strasbourg Court does not run counter to the primacy of the ECJ to interpret EC law, provided that the Strasbourg court limits itself to the protection of human rights as such and does not impinge upon the Community sphere. Under these circumstances, future EC/EU accession would be a challenge for the ECJ. Moreover, more recently the Court accepted the dispute resolution mechanisms of the World Trade Organization without a problem: why should it object to the jurisdiction of the European Court of Human Rights?

At the end of the day the EU itself has to lead by example in the field of human rights and not just engage in a megaphone rhetoric on the subject, and what better way of so doing than accepting for itself an external judge and not just imposing that obligation on others? This is the only credible and serious message for individual citizens as well as for third parties at the beginning of the new millennium. Moreover, the accession option ensures at the very least that the wider and at times fragmented Europe which is emerging is a Europe of, in any event, civil and political rights. This of course does not exclude at the same time the development of a Europe of social rights. In the perspective of *enlargement* as well, the Central and East European states (and others) would join a European Union which, instead of relying on vague general principles, has an up to date Constitution incorporating a set of precisely defined fundamental rights which are binding on and are directly enforceable in *all* the Member States in a uniform manner. The new Member States will have adhered to the ECHR prior to accession and their obligation to respect human rights, which will not only be a precondition for accession but an ongoing condition for enjoying the rights and benefits of membership of the Union, will also *exist towards the Union itself*. The proposed EU Charter on Human Rights can thus in certain circumstances (see above) be viewed in a positive light as the formal "banns" declaring a (long-term) intent to marry (accession by the EU to – in any event – the ECHR).

21

FUNDAMENTAL RIGHTS IN EUROPEAN UNION LAW AFTER THE TREATY OF AMSTERDAM

*Peter Oliver**

I INTRODUCTION

Among the many and varied fields on which Lord Slynn has made his mark in the course of his distinguished career are European Community law and fundamental rights. This makes an examination of the place of human rights in European Union law especially apt.[1] What is more, a number of significant developments have occurred in this field very recently; and the enactment of the Human Rights Act 1998 in the United Kingdom indirectly lends a further sprinkling of topical spice to this highly important subject.

Particular emphasis will be placed here on the European Convention of Human Rights (ECHR), since that convention has been held to have "special significance" as a source of inspiration when it determines the fundamental rights which "form an integral part of the general principles whose observance the Court ensures".[2] Other international human rights instruments are referred to in the Treaty on European Union (TEU) and the Treaty of Rome establishing the European Community (EC) as well as the case-law of the European Court of Justice (ECJ),[3] but they cannot be discussed within the confines of this paper;[4]

---

* The author wishes to thank Tim Eicke of the English Bar, Allan Rosas, Principal Legal Adviser at the European Commission, Paul Mahoney, Deputy Registrar of the European Court of Human Rights and Dean Spielmann of the Luxembourg Bar, for their most helpful comments on an earlier draft of this paper. However, the views expressed here are personal to the author, and any errors made are attributable to him alone.

1 The terms "fundamental rights" and "human rights" will be used interchangeably here. However, the tendency in the European Union institutions is to use the former term in relation to internal matters, and the latter with respect to the Union's relations with third countries.

2 Case C-260/89 *ERT v Dimotiki Etaira* [1991] ECR I-2925, point 41; Opinion 2/94 [1996] ECR I 1759, point 33; Case T-10/93 *A v Commission* [1994] ECR II-183, point 48.

3 For present purposes, the term "ECJ" will be used to include the Community's Court of First Instance.

4 The ECJ has also taken cognisance of the European Social Charter signed under the auspices of the Council of Europe in 1961: Cases 24/86 *Blaizot v University of Liège* [1988] ECR 379, 149/77 *Defrenne v SABENA* [1978] ECR 1365 and point 28 of the Opinion of Advocate General Lenz in Case 236/87 *Bergemann v Bundesanstalt für Arbeit* [1988]

D. O'Keeffe (ed.), Liber Amicorum Slynn 319-342 (2000)

nor can the Constitutions of the Member States, which have also acted as a source of inspiration to that Court.

After briefly discussing the ECJ's case-law on human rights and the provisions on the subject in the Single European Act and the Treaty of Maastricht, our attention will turn to the ECJ's Opinion 2/94, before focussing on the European Court of Human Rights (EctHR) and its recent rulings on the European Community. Finally, we shall consider the Treaty of Amsterdam and subsequent developments.

II Human Rights in the European Communities Prior to Maastricht

Originally, the Treaties establishing the European Communities contained no human rights provisions, and the ECJ showed little interest in such rights. However, pressure began to build up from two directions: first, five of the six original Member States of the Community had ratified the ECHR before the Treaty of Rome, and were therefore bound to observe their prior obligations under the Convention, as was recognised by Article 307 (ex Art 234) EC;[5] second, it gradually became clear that the courts of some Member States would baulk at Community law overriding national law unless the Community respected fundamental rights.[6]

ECR 5125. See generally: S. Sciarra "From Strasbourg to Amsterdam: Prospects for the Convergence of European Social Rights Policy" in P. Alston (ed.) *The EU and Human Rights* (1999) p. 473; E. Szyszczak "Social Rights as General Principles of Community Law" in N. Neuwahl and A. Rosas (eds) *The European Union and Human Rights* (1995) p. 207.
Equally, the ECJ has referred on a number of occasions to the International Covenant for Civil and Political Rights: Cases 297/88 and C-197/89 *Dzodzi* [1990] ECR I-3763, 374/87 *Orkem v Commission* [1989] ECR 3283, C-249/96 *Grant v South-West Trains* [1998] ECRI-621 and point 30 of the Advocate General's Opinion in *Bergemann*. See T. Eicke, "Human Rights in the European Community: Past, Present and Future" 1997 *European Current Law*, Focus p. liii.
(Health warning: reading all the literature on human rights and the EU could seriously damage your eyesight. No attempt will be made here to set out anything approaching an exhaustive list of the relevant sources.)

5 The Articles of the Treaty of Rome were re-numbered by the Treaty of Amsterdam. The first paragraph of Article 307 reads as follows: "The rights and obligations arising from agreements concluded before 1 January 1958 … between one or more Member States on the one hand, and one or more third countries on the other, shall not be affected by the provisions of this Treaty." The first person to have suggested that, as a result of this Article, the Community must take cognisance of the Convention appears to have been M. Waelbroeck "La Convention européenne des droits de l'homme lie-t-elle les Communautés européennes?" in *Droit communautaire et droit national* Semaine de Bruges (1965).

6 Notably the German and Italian Constitutional Courts; see generally the judgments of the German Constitutional Court in *"Solange I"* 37 BverfGE 271, [1974] 2 CMLR 540 and *"Solange II"* 73 BverfGE 339, [1987] 3 CMLR 225; and those of the Italian Constitu-

The first reference to fundamental rights in the case-law of the ECJ came in *Stauder v City of Ulm,*[7] but it was no more than a passing reference. This idea was then developed in *Internationale Handelsgesellschaft v EVGF,*[8] where the Court stated: "... respect for fundamental rights forms an integral part of the general principles of law protected by the Court of Justice. The protection of such rights, whilst inspired by the constitutional traditions common to the Member States, must be ensured within the framework of the structure and objectives of the Community". The first indirect mention of the ECHR came in *Nold v Commission,*[9] where it stated:

> " ... fundamental rights form an integral part of the general principles of law, the observance of which it ensures.
>
> In safeguarding these rights, the Court is bound to draw inspiration from constitutional traditions common to the Member States, and it cannot therefore uphold measures which are incompatible with fundamental rights recognised and protected by the Constitutions of those States. Similarly, international treaties for the protection of human rights on which the Member States have collaborated or of which they are signatories, can supply guidelines which should be followed within the framework of Community law".

That judgment was delivered a matter of days after the last of the then Member States – France – had ratified the Convention.[10] It should also be noted that the first sentence quoted here is an implicit reference to Article 220 (ex 164) of the Treaty of Rome, which provides: "The Court of Justice shall ensure that in the interpretation and application of this Treaty the law is observed".

Although the ECJ has been criticised for merely paying lip service to fundamental rights,[11] the fact remains that on occasion it has struck down Commu-

---

tional Court in *Frontini* 1973 Giurisprudenza cost. 2401, [1974] 2 CMLR 372, *Granital* 1984 Foro Italiano 2062 (partial English translation in 1984 CMLRev. 757) and *Fragd* (1989) 72 RDI, and. See P. Craig and G. de Búrca *EU Law: Text, Cases, and Materials* (2nd. ed., 1998), p. 264 and A. Oppenheimer *The Relationship between European Community Law and National Law: the Cases* (1994).

7 Case 29/69 [1969] ECR 419.

8 Case 11/70 [1970] ECR 1125 at p. 1134.

9 Case 4/73 [1974] ECR 491 at p. 507.

10 Yet subsequently in Case 36/75 *Rutili v Minister of the Interior* [1975] ECR 1205, the ECJ referred *inter alia* to the Fourth Protocol to the Convention, which a number of Member States had not yet ratified – although France, the Member State concerned in that case, had done so after the material facts arose but before the ECJ's judgment. Also, in Case C-370/90 *The Queen v Surinder Singh ex parte Secretary of State for the Home Department* [1992] ECR I-4265, paragraph 22, the ECJ referred, albeit tangentially, to Protocol 4 to the Convention; this was despite the fact that the United Kingdom, the Member State concerned in that case, has never ratified that Protocol. As to the current state of ratification of the Protocols, see note 45 below.

11 See e.g. J. Coppel and A. O'Neill "The European Court of Justice: Taking Rights Seriously" 1992 CMLRev. 669; *contra* J. Weiler and N. Lockhart "'Taking Rights Seriously' Seriously: the European Court and its Fundamental Rights Jurisprudence" 1995

nity and national measures on these grounds. Suffice it to mention two examples: in *R v Kirk,*[12] the Court issued a wrecking interpretation of a Community Regulation, which purported to create a retroactive criminal offence contrary to Article 7 of the Convention; and in *Johnston v Chief Constable of the RUC*[13] a Minister's certificate excluding judicial review was held to be incompatible with the fundamental principle of the right of access to the courts enshrined *inter alia* in Article 6 of the Convention. It should also be noted that, although the Court has insisted that it only takes account of the Convention as a "source of inspiration", in practice it has striven to respect the case-law from Strasbourg.[14]

The judgment in *Wachauf v Germany*[15] is that best known for the principle whereby Member States are bound to observe the "requirements of the protection of fundamental rights in the Community legal order", when implementing Community provisions.[16] Also, in *ERT v Dimotiki Etaira*[17] the Court held that the powers of Member States to impose restrictions on the provision of services under the public policy, public security and public health exceptions set out in

---

CMLRev. 51 and 579.

12 Case 63/83 [1984] ECR 2689.

13 Case 222/84 [1986] ECR 1651.

14 One exceptional case in which the case-law of the ECJ diverges from that of the EctHR relates to the question as to whether the protection of private life under Article 8 of the Convention extends to business premises: unlike the ECJ in Cases 46/87 *Hoechst v Commission* [1989] ECR 2859, the EctHR held that that provision applies to such premises (judgment of 16 December 1992, *Niemetz v Germany* Series A 251-B, (1993) 16 EHRR 97). There is also a discrepancy between the case-law of the two courts as to whether the right not to incriminate oneself is enshrined in Article 6 of the Convention (compare Case 374/87 *Orkem v Commission* [1989] ECR 3283, point 30, and *Funke v France*, judgment of 27 January 1993, paragraph 44, Series A 256-A, (1993) EHRR 297).
It is a moot point whether the ECJ has ever disregarded pre-existing authority from Strasbourg, since it is sometimes suggested that the ruling in *Hoechst* was at variance with the earlier judgment of the EctHR in *Chappell,* (judgment of 30 March 1989, Series A, vol. 152). See J. Andriantsibazovina "Chronique des droits de l'homme: Réflexions à propos de la jurisprudence de la Cour européenne des droits de l'homme de 1988 à 1995" 1997 CDE 655 at pp. 729-739; R. Lawson "Confusion and Conflict? Diverging Interpretations of the European Convention on Human Rights in Strasbourg and Luxembourg" in *Essays in Honour of Henry G. Schermers* (1994) vol III; R. Lawson and M. de Blois (eds.) *The Dynamics of the Protection of Human Rights in Europe* 219; and D. Spielmann "Human Rights Case Law in the Strasbourg and Luxembourg Courts: Conflicts, Inconsistencies and Complimentarities" in P. Alston, *op.cit.* at 757.
In a number of more recent cases, the ECJ has also referred to judgments of the EctHR: e.g. Cases C-13/94 *P v S and Cornwall County Council* [1996] ECR I-2143, point 16, C-129/95 *Criminal Proceedings v X* [1996] ECR I-6609, point 25, C-368/95 *Familiapress v Bauer Verlag* [1997] ECR I-3689, point 26, and *Grant* (note 4 above), points 33-34.

15 Case 5/88 [1989] ECR 2609, point 19.

16 In fact, the Court had already ruled to this effect in Case C-249/86 *Commission v Germany* (migrant workers) [1989] ECR I-1263, point 10.

17 See note 2 above.

Articles 46 and 55 (ex 56 and 66) of the Treaty of Rome must be determined in the light of fundamental rights, including the freedom of expression enshrined in Article 10 ECHR.[18] The same applies to the equivalent exceptions to the other basic freedoms laid down in that Treaty.[19] On the other hand, the Court has consistently held that it had "no power to examine the compatibility with the European Convention on Human Rights of national rules which do not fall within the scope of Community law".[20]

By the mid-1970s, the inevitably unpredictable and piece-meal development of the ECJ's case-law led to a wide-spread debate on whether the Community should draw up a Charter of fundamental rights and/or accede to the ECHR.[21] Neither step would have entailed general powers with respect to fundamental rights being conferred on the Community, beyond the areas for which it was responsible. Nor would accession to the Convention have restrained the ECJ from extending its case-law on fundamental rights beyond the bounds set by the Convention.[22]

The benefit of the first option was perceived to be that it would create a "home-grown" catalogue of rights designed to meet the special needs of the Community. Its obvious shortcoming lay in the political difficulty of achieving

18 This ruling was confirmed in Cases C-288/89 *Collectieve Antennevoorziening Gouda v Commissariaat voor de Media* [1991] ECR I-4007, point 23, and C-148/91 *Veronica Omroep v Commissariaat voor de Media* [1993] ECR I-487, point 10.

19 On Article 30 (ex 36) on the free movement of goods, (see *Familiapress,* note 14 above); Article 39(3) (ex 48(3)) on the free movement of workers (see *Rutili* note 10 above); and Article 58 (ex 73(d)) relating to the free movement of capital. Although the Court was too coy to admit it, the ruling in *ERT* in effect reversed the rather surprising decision in C-61/84 *Cinéthèque v Fédération Nationale des Cinémas Français* [1985] ECR 2605 where the Court, declining to follow Lord Slynn (then Advocate General Sir Gordon Slynn), had held that the ECHR was not relevant in interpreting Article 30 (ex 36). The *Cinéthèque* ruling may perhaps be explained by the dearth of authority from Strasbourg about the point at issue.

20 Cases C-12/86 *Demirel v Stadt Schwaebisch Gmund* [1987] ECR 3719, paragraph 28, *ERT* (note 2 above), C-159/90 *Society for the Protection of Unborn Children v Grogan* [1991] ECR I-4685, C-299/95 *Kremzow v Austria* [1997] ECR I-2629 and C-309/96 *Annibaldi v Lazio* [1997] ECR I-7493.

21 Judge Lenaerts ("Fundamental Rights to be Included in a Community Catalogue" 1991 ELRev. 367 at p380) suggested a variant of the first option whereby the ECHR and the EC Treaty would be amended so as to permit the ECJ to request a preliminary ruling from the EctHR on the interpretation of the Convention.

22 Article 53 (ex 60) provides: "Nothing in this Convention shall be construed as limiting or derogating from any of the human rights and fundamental freedoms which may be ensured under the laws of any High Contracting Party or under any other agreement to which it is a Party". In some respects, the ECJ has gone further than the Convention. Thus, pursuant to Article 6 everyone has the right of access to the courts for the determination of his "civil rights"; in contrast, such a right exists with respect to all directly applicable rights deriving from Community law (see the Opinion of Advocate General Colomer in Cases C-65 and 111/95 *The Queen v Secretary of State for the Home Department ex parte Shingara and Radiom* [1997] ECR I-3343 at p. 3363).

an acceptable degree of consensus on a catalogue of rights, especially as regards those of a social and economic nature.[23] Meanwhile, it was generally considered that the clear advantage of accession was that it would ensure that the case-law of the ECJ was in line with that of the EctHR. The main problems of accession were felt to be the institutional complexities of grafting the Community on to the already intricate structure of the Council of Europe.

As long ago as 1979, the Commission proposed that the Community should accede to the Convention.[24] It renewed that suggestion in 1990.[25] In view of the lukewarm attitude or even hostility of some Member States,[26] the Council of Ministers ultimately sought an Opinion from the ECJ as to whether the Treaty of Rome empowered the Community to accede to the ECHR. That Opinion is discussed below.

As to the idea of drawing up a Charter of Fundamental Rights, Judge Lenaerts advocated a model based on concentric circles:[27] the rights enshrined in the Convention and the Protocols thereto would constitute the nucleus of such a Charter, the other circles consisting respectively of the general principles of Community law, the rights of citizens and finally "aspirational" fundamental rights (economic and social, cultural and educational, environmental and consumer rights and so forth).

Before considering the Treaty of Maastricht, we should point out that the preamble to the Single European Act, which came into force on 1 July 1987,

---

23 In addition, the House of Lords Select Committee on the European Communities also objected that "the establishment of a separate catalogue would undermine the position of the Convention" ("Human Rights", 71st Report 1979-80, paragraph 33; and "Human Rights Re-examined", 2nd. Report 1992-3, paragraph 76). However, the basis for this view is no means clear: in this respect, the creation of a Charter of fundamental rights is no different from the adoption of a Bill of Rights by a Contracting Party to the Convention (see further note 83 below).

24 Supplement 2/79 to the Bulletin of the European Communities.

25 SEC(90)2087 final.

26 The House of Lords Select Committee on the European Communities examined this issue twice, and found accession undesirable on both occasions (see the reports referred to in note 23 above). Nevertheless, the Committee did not rule out accession "at some future date" (first report, paragraph 32). At all events, it regarded the solution as lying in a strengthening of the Convention and the procedures for applying it (this has now occurred, as explained below). The Committee also welcomed the case-law of the ECJ on human rights and took the view that the best solution lay in the continuing development of that case-law. However, in its second report on the matter, the Committee made two more limited proposals: first, closer links between the institutions in Luxembourg and Strasbourg should be established so as to "remedy potential gaps in protection of individual rights"; second, the rules of *locus standi* for actions for annulment under Article 230 (ex 173) EC should be widened. On the latter point, see also Judge Lenaerts "Respect for Fundamental Rights as a Constitutional Principle of the European Union" 1999-2000 Columbia Journal of European Law (forthcoming).

27 *Op.cit.* note 21 above.

contained the very first mention of fundamental rights in the Community Treaties.[28] It was a small step, but a significant one nevertheless.[29,30]

III The Treaty of Maastricht and its Aftermath

The Treaty on European Union signed at Maastricht, which came into force on 1 November 1993, effected a number of significant amendments to the Treaty of Rome. In addition, it established the Union, which was "founded on the European Communities, supplemented by the policies and forms of cooperation established by this Treaty" (Article A (now Article 1) TEU[31]). The latter "policies and forms of cooperation" were the Common Foreign and Security Policy and – more importantly from the human rights point of view – cooperation in the fields of justice and home affairs. In contrast to the European Communities, these "policies and forms of cooperation" were implemented on an intergovernmental basis.

For the first time, a number of human rights provisions were introduced into the body of the Treaties. In particular, Article F(2) TEU read as follows: "The

---

28 The third recital in that preamble stated simply that the Heads of State were "determined to work together to promote democracy on the basis of the fundamental rights recognized in the constitutions and laws of the Member States, in the Convention for the Protection of Human Rights and Fundamental Freedoms and the European Social Charter, notably freedom, equality and social justice". The Court was to refer to this recital in point 10 of its judgment in Case C-249/86 (note 16 above).

29 See J. Pipkorn "La Communauté européenne et la Convention européenne des droits de l'homme" 1993 Rev. Trim. Dr. H. 221 at p. 229.

30 In addition, the following "soft law" instruments were adopted during this period: Joint Declaration of the European Parliament, the Council and the Commission on Fundamental Rights of 5 April 1977 (1977 OJ C103/1); the European Parliament's Declaration of Human Rights and Fundamental Freedoms of 12 April 1989 (1989 OJ C120/52); and the Resolution of the European Parliament of 11 March 1993 on respect for human rights in the European Community (1993 OJ C115/178); Resolution of the European Parliament of 21 April 1993 on the resurgence of racism and xenophobia in Europe and the danger of right-wing extremist violence (1993 OJ 150/127). The ECJ has recognised that such instruments are not deprived of all legal effect and must be taken into account by the courts (Case C-322/88 *Grimaldi v Fonds des Maladies Professionnelles* [1989] ECR I-4407, point 18). Also, in Case 44/79 *Hauer v Land Rheinland-Pfalz* [1979] ECR 3727, point 15, the ECJ referred in passing to the Joint Declaration of 5 April 1977.
Moreover, a Community Charter of the Fundamental Social Rights of Workers was concluded by eleven Heads of State or Government of the Member States of the European Community meeting in Strasbourg on 9 December 1989. However, at paragraph 137 of his Opinion in Case C-67/96 *Albany International* (judgment of 21 September 1999), Advocate General Jacobs said of this Charter: "[it] has very limited legal effects. It is not a legal act of the Community but a solemn political declaration adopted by Heads of State or Government of 11 of the then 12 Member States, and it has not been published in the Official Journal".

31 The Articles of the TEU have also been renumbered by the Treaty of Amsterdam.

Union shall respect fundamental rights, as guaranteed by the European Convention for the Protection of Human Rights and Fundamental Freedoms signed in Rome on 4 November 1950 and as they result from the constitutional traditions common to the Member States, as general principles of Community law".[32] Despite being contained in the TEU, this provision was probably intended to apply to the Community; at any rate, it was so construed by the Court.[33] In the light of the last phrase ("as general principles of Community law"), it is manifest that the Union was not bound by the Convention *as such*. With the entry into force of the Treaty of Amsterdam, this highly important provision has become Article 6(2), but its wording has been left unaltered.

Article L TEU, which listed the provisions subject to the jurisdiction of the ECJ, did not include Article F(2) in that list. However, this omission was presumably to be seen as excluding human rights issues from the Court's jurisdiction in relation to the Union. It could scarcely have been intended to preclude the Court from continuing to develop its case-law on human rights as regards the Community, which it had initiated at a time when the Treaties contained no mention of this matter whatsoever. After all, that case-law was based on Article

---

32 As D. Spielmann has pointed out (*op.cit.* at p. 759), the reference to the Convention must be regarded as implicitly extending to the Protocols thereto. It will be recalled that the ruling in *Hauer* (note 30 above) was concerned with the right to property under the First Protocol to the Convention, while that in *Rutili* (note 10 above) related to the Fourth Protocol.
On another point, Lenaerts ("Respect for Fundamental Rights ...") sees significance in the fact that the ECHR is mentioned first, and the constitutional traditions common to the Member States second. This indicates, he suggests, that one must primarily have regard to the Convention and that "it is only in so far as the Member States of the Union, representing a narrower range of legal traditions, have enough in common to add to it, that the Union is also bound ... to require its institutions to respect such additional protection".

33 Case C-415/93 *Union Royale Belge des Sociétés de Football v Bosman* [1995] ECR I-4921, point 79; see also generally *A v Commission* (note 2 above), points 47 to 49; *Familiapress* (note 14 above); and Case T-113/96 *Dubois et Fils v Council and Commission* [1998] ECR II-125, points 73-4. Equally, in Case C-84/95 *Bosphorus Hava v Minister for Transport* [1996] ECR I-3956 at pp. 3971-2, Advocate-General Jacobs said: "Article F(2) ... gives Treaty expression to the Court's case-law. Article F(2) appears in Title I of the Treaty, and therefore does not fall within the jurisdiction of the Court in so far as it extends to the Union Treaty as a whole. In relation to the EC Treaty, it confirms and consolidates the Court's case-law, underlining its paramount importance of respect for fundamental rights".
As Pechstein has pointed out ("Die Justitiabilität des Unionsrechts" 1999 EuR 1 at p.4), it follows that Article M (now 47) TEU should not altogether be taken at face value. That article reads as follows: "Subject to the provisions amending the Treaty establishing the European Economic Community with a view to establishing the European Community [i.e. Article G (now 8) TEU] ... nothing in this Treaty shall affect the Treaties establishing the European Communities or the subsequent Treaties and Acts modifying or supplementing them". The ruling of the ECJ in Case C-170/96 *Commission v Council* (visas) [1998] ECR I-2763, point 16, appears to imply that the provisions of the TEU other than Article 8 (ex Article G) must not encroach on the EC Treaty or its application.

220 (ex 164) EC, which continues to be subject to the jurisdiction of the Court. What is more, the Court had had regard in the past to other international agreements falling outside the limits of its jurisdiction.[34] Thus it was not surprising to find the Court continuing to build on its human rights case-law with respect to the Community.[35]

At Maastricht, new provisions were also inserted into the EC Treaty on citizenship of the Union, which is enjoyed by all nationals of the Member States (Articles 8 to 8E, now 17 to 22).[36] These provisions relate to such matters as the right to move freely between Member States and to reside in other States and to vote in municipal and European elections in the host State.

Finally, a reference to human rights was introduced into the Treaty provisions on external relations, in that Article 130U(2) (now 177(2)) EC stipulates that Community development aid "shall contribute to the general objective of developing and consolidating democracy and the rule of law, and to that of respecting human rights and fundamental freedoms".[37]

---

34 Case 44/84 *Hurd v Jones* [1986] ECR 29 (the Statute of the European School of 1957 and the 1962 Protocol thereto).

35 See note 33 above.

36 In Case C-168/91 *Konstantinidis* [1993] ECR I-1191 at pp.1211-2, Advocate General Jacobs voiced his support for a wide conception of citizenship of the Union when he said: "In my opinion, a Community national who goes to another Member State as a worker or self-employed person … is entitled not just to pursue his trade or profession and to enjoy the same living and working conditions as nationals of the host State; he is in addition entitled to assume that, wherever he goes to earn his living in the European Community, he will be treated in accordance with a common code of fundamental values, in particular those laid down in the European Convention on Human Rights. In other words, he is entitled to say '*civis europeus sum*' and to invoke that status in order to oppose any violation of his fundamental rights."
Similarly, the Court has held that Article 17(2) (ex 8(2)) EC "attaches to the status of citizens of the Union the rights and duties laid down by the Treaty, including the right, laid down in Article 6 of the Treaty, not to suffer discrimination on grounds of nationality within the scope of application *ratione materiae* of the Treaty" (Case C-85/96 *Martinèz Sala v Freistaat Bayern* [1998] ECR I-2691, point 62, commented by S. O'Leary 1999 ELRev. 68). Lenaerts ("Respect for Fundamental Rights ..") points out that if this provision were construed too widely, it would transform citizenship of the Union into a vehicle for the ECJ to review questions of human rights otherwise falling outside the scope of Community law. See generally D. O'Keeffe and A. Bavasso "Fundamental Rights and the European Citizen" in M. La Torre (ed.) *European Citizenship: An Institutional Challenge* (1998), and A. Rosas "Electoral Rights and the European Union: a Broader Human Rights Perspective" in N. Neuwahl and A. Rosas, *op.cit.*

37 See Case C-268/94 *Portugal v Council* [1996] ECR I-6177. See also Council Regulation 975/1999 relating to the promotion of human rights and democracy in the Community's development policy (1999 OJ L 120/1), based on Article 179 (ex 130w) EC; and Council Regulation 976/1999 (1999 OJ L120/9), which is based on Article 308 (ex 235) and relates to other non-member countries, especially those in Europe; and B. Brandtner and A. Rosas "Human Rights and the External Relations of the European Community: an Analysis of Doctrine and Practice" 1998 EJIL 468 and "Trade Preferences and Human Rights" in P. Alston, *op.cit.*

IV Opinion 2/94

As we noticed earlier, after many years of prevarication the Council decided to seek an Opinion from the ECJ as to whether the Community was empowered to accede to the Convention. The Council, the Commission, the European Parliament[38] and a large number of Member States argued that Article 308 (ex 235) of the Treaty of Rome constituted a sufficient legal basis for such a step. A significant minority of Member States – France, Ireland, Portugal, Spain and the United Kingdom – claimed that no provision in the Treaties conferred such power on the Community.

In Opinion 2/94,[39] the Court endorsed the latter approach. After a brief reference to the Treaty provisions concerned and its own case-law on human rights and after recalling the "special significance" of the ECHR in this regard, it continued as follows:

> "Respect for human rights is ... a condition of the lawfulness of Community acts. Accession to the Convention [on Human Rights] would, however, entail a substantial change in the present Community system for the protection of human rights in that it would entail the entry of the Community into a distinct international system as well as integration of all the provisions of the Convention into the Community legal order.
>
> Such a modification of the system for the protection of human rights in the Community, with equally fundamental institutional implications for the Community and for the Member States, would be of constitutional significance and would be such as to go beyond the scope of Article 235 [now 308]. It could be brought about only by way of Treaty amendment.
>
> It must therefore be held that, as Community law now stands, the Community has no competence to accede to the Convention."

This reasoning has been widely criticised as being both evasive and laconic.[40] In particular, commentators have drawn attention to the fact that the real

38 On 18 January 1994, the Parliament had passed a resolution in favour of the Community acceding to the Convention (1994 OJ C44/32).

39 See note 2 above.

40 For particularly critical comments, see O. De Schutter and Y. Lejeune "L'adhésion de la Communauté à la Convention européenne des droits de l'homme – A propos de l'avis 2/94 de la Cour de justice des Communautés" 1996 CDE 555, G. Gaja casenote 1996 CMLRev. 973; P. Wachsmann "L'avis 2/94 de la Cour de justice relatif à l'adhésion de la Communauté européenne à la Convention de sauvegarde des droits de l'homme et des libertés fondamentales" 1996 RTDE 467; M. Waelbroeck "La Cour de justice et la Convention européenne des droits de l'homme" 1996 CDE 549. In contrast, R. Errera ("La fin d'un songe: l'avis de la Cour de justice des Communautés européennes sur l'adhésion de la Communauté à la Convention européenne des droits de l'homme" 1996 *Gazette du Palais III* p. 1467) and C. Vedder (casenote, 1996 EuR 309) consider the Opinion to be unquestionably correct in its result, while conceding that its reasoning leaves something to be desired.

reason for the Court's decision is a fear that its jurisdiction would be diluted.[41] Yet the Court had declined to rule on whether accession would be compatible with Articles 220 and 292 (ex 164 and 219) EC – the very provisions which relate to that issue – on the grounds that it had insufficient information as to the precise arrangements envisaged.

However, it must be pointed out that, even if the Court had reached the opposite conclusion, formidable obstacles would have stood in the way of the Community acceding to the ECHR. In the first place, acts adopted under the TEU could also have human rights implications, but the European Union, taken as a separate entity from the Community, is not generally considered to possess legal personality;[42] so it is not easy to see how the Union could become party to the Convention. Second, either the ECHR or the Statute of the Council of Europe would need amending: Article 59 (ex 66) ECHR[43] provides that any member of the Council of Europe may sign that Convention, while Articles 2 and 4 of the Statute of that organisation restrict membership of that organisation to European "States".[44]

In addition, other more technical nettles would have to be grasped, of which we can only name a few within the confines of this paper. In the first place, the Member States have not ratified all the Protocols to the ECHR.[45] They have also

41 As in Opinion 1/91 [1991] ECR I-6079 (the first Opinion on the European Economic Area) and Opinion 1/92 [1992] ECR I-2821.

42 For the prevailing view, see e.g. De Schutter and Lejeune, *op.cit.* p. 600; J-V Louis "Le traité d'Amsterdam: une occasion perdue?" 1997 2 RMUE 5 at p.9; Pechstein *op.cit.* p. 2. While admitting that the Treaties contain no express provision to this effect, S. van Raepenbusch contests the prevailing view as far the Union's position on the international stage is concerned; thus he argues that the Union possesses external legal personality ("L"émergence de l'Union européenne dans l'ordre juridique international" in *Mélanges en hommage à Michel Waelbroeck* 1999). Also, A. von Bogdandy argues that the Union and the Community are to be treated as single entity ("The Legal Case for Unity: the European Union as a Single Organisation with a Single Legal System" 1999 CMLRev 887).

43 The articles of the Convention were renumbered by the 11th Protocol thereto, which came into force on 1 November 1998. That Protocol abolished the European Commission of Human Rights, thereby streamlining the procedure before the EctHR; it also provided for mandatory and permanent acceptance by the Contracting Parties of the right of individual application before the Court.

44 In its submissions to the ECJ prior to Opinion 2/94, the Council stated that only the ECHR should be amended, since it was not intended that the Community should become a member of the Council of Europe. Also, see generally Article 303 (ex 230) of the EC Treaty, which provides: "The Community shall establish all appropriate forms of cooperation with the Council of Europe".

45 All the Member States are party to Protocols 1, 6 and 11; in any event, the latter instrument is applicable *erga omnes*. On the other hand, Greece, Spain and the United Kingdom have not ratified Protocol 4; and Belgium, Germany, Ireland, the Netherlands, Portugal, Spain and the United Kingdom have yet to ratify Protocol 7. (This information, which has been gleaned from the database of the Council of Europe, reflects the situation as it stood on 23 June 1999.) The other Protocols have lapsed with the entry into force of

entered a variety of reservations to the Conventions and the Protocols thereto. Given the need for the uniform application of Community law, it seems hard to imagine how these reservations could subsist in matters governed by Community law after accession, although the Community could put in its own reservations at the time of signature or ratification.[46] Having said that, this difficulty could arise in any event under the present system whereby human rights in Community law is developed solely by the ECJ. Second, how would the "European Community judge" on the EctHR be appointed? Third, a special arrangement might have to be devised to ensure that the Member States and the Community were not precluded from litigating amongst themselves on human rights matters before the courts of the Community.[47] Lastly, problems would ultimately arise in relation to acts taken by the Community and one or more Member States; but then the issue of joint liability is by no means new.[48,49]

Protocol 11. G. Cohen-Jonathan "L'adhésion de la Communauté européenne à la Convention européenne des droits de l'homme" 1995 JTDE 49 maintains that the Community should only ratify those Protocols to which all its Member States are party, while at the same time advocating a coordinated approach by those States to the ratification of the Protocols. See also generally footnote 10 above.

46 Reservations are governed by Article 57 (ex 64) of the Convention, and similar provisions in each of the Protocols thereto; see generally S. Spiliopoulou Åkermark "Reservations: breaking new ground in the Council of Europe" 1999 ELRev. 499.
The Commission's initial memorandum of 1979 seemed to indicate that the continued application of national reservations would be tolerated within the scope of Community law. In contrast, the Council took the opposite view in its submissions to the ECJ prior to Opinion 2/94. Fortunately, the Member States have exercised considerable restraint in entering reservations, unlike some other Contracting Parties such as Russia and Switzerland.

47 De Schutter and Lejeune, *op.cit.* p. 602. Article 55 (ex 62) ECHR reads as follows: "The High Contracting Parties agree that, except by special agreement, they will not avail themselves of treaties, conventions or declarations in force between them for the purpose of submitting, by way of petition, a dispute arising out of the interpretation or application of this Convention to a means of settlement other than those provided for in this Convention." There appears to be some doubt as to the ambit of this provision (P. van Dijk and G. van Hoof, *Theory and Practice of the European Convention on Human Rights* (3rd. ed., 1998) pp. 6-7), which is the counterpart to Article 292 (ex 219) EC. In any case, it is surely arguable that the TEU and the Treaty of Rome are to be regarded as "special agreements" for these purposes.

48 See G. Gaja "Some Reflections on the European Community's International Responsibility" and P. Oliver "Joint Liability of the Community and the Member States", both in *The Action for Damages in Community Law* (1997) ed. T. Heukels and A. McDonnell.

49 On another point, it seems clear that requesting a reference for a preliminary ruling under Article 234 (ex 177) EC is one of the steps which must be taken by a litigant so as to exhaust his domestic remedies pursuant to Article 35(1) (ex 26) ECHR prior to commencing proceedings in Strasbourg: see Advocate General Jacobs in *Konstantinidis* (note 36 above) at p. 1213. (Admittedly, in *Pafitis v Greece*, judgment of 26 February 1998, (1999) 27 EHRR 566, paragraph 95), the EctHR found that Greece could not be held responsible under Article 6 of the Convention for the delay of the ECJ in delivering a preliminary ruling, as this would "adversely affect the system instituted by Article 177 of

Nevertheless, complex and delicate though these problems may be, none of them is insuperable.

V The Case Law of The European Court of Human Rights

In *M. & Co v Germany,*[50] the European Commission of Human Rights issued its first warning to the Community. There an application concerning the execution of a fine imposed pursuant to Article 81 (ex 85) of the Treaty of Rome was held inadmissible on the following grounds: " ... the Convention does not prohibit a member State from transferring powers to international organisations. ... The Commission considers that a transfer of powers does not necessarily exclude a State's responsibility under the Convention with regard to the exercise of the transferred powers. ... The Commission notes that the legal system of the European Communities not only secures fundamental rights but also provides for control of their observance. ..." Few realised at the time that this reasoning was a two-edged sword,[51] as was shown subsequently by the same body's decision in *Procola v Luxembourg.*[52]

Then came the ruling of the EctHR in *Cantoni v France.*[53] The plaintiff was the manager of a supermarket, who had been convicted for selling pharmaceutical products in his shop contrary to Article L. 511 of the French Public Health Code. Article L. 512 prohibited the sale of such products by persons other than qualified pharmacists. The French courts rejected Mr. Cantoni's defence to the effect that the products concerned did not constitute pharmaceutical products. Mr. Cantoni claimed that the definition of "pharmaceutical products" in Article L. 511 was so imprecise and left such a wide margin of discretion to the courts that he could not be reasonably expected to have known that the products concerned fell within it. Accordingly, in his view that provision was in breach of Article 7 of the Convention.

The French Government relied *inter alia* on the fact that the contested definition of pharmaceutical products was virtually identical to that in Article 1 of Council Directive 65/65 on proprietary medicinal products.[54] It followed, so the argument ran, that a finding that Article L. 511 was incompatible with Article 7

the EEC Treaty and work against the aim pursued in substance by that Article".)

50 Decision of 9 February 1990, DR 64 p. 138 at p. 145.

51 One exception was J-P Jacqué "Communauté européenne et Convention européenne des droits de l'homme" in *Mélanges Boulouis* (1991) 325 at p. 339.

52 Decision of 1 July 1993, DR 75 p. 5, (1996) 22 EHRR 193. The European Commission of Human Rights indirectly examined the compatibility of the Community's milk quota scheme with Article 1 of Protocol 1 to the ECHR (right to property); it found that the scheme was justified on public interest grounds.

53 Application 17862/91, judgment of 15 November 1996 (reports 1996-V), noted by D. Spielmann 1997 Rev. Trim. Dr. H. 689 and S. Winkler 1999 EuGRZ 181.

54 1965 OJ 369, as amended.

of the Convention would necessarily imply a similar finding with respect to the Directive. The ECtHR rejected that submission in the following forthright terms:

> "The fact, pointed to by the Government, that Article L. 511 of the Public Health Code is based almost word for word on Community Directive 65/65 ... does not remove it from the ambit of Article 7 of the Convention."

This may perhaps be taken as the first indication that the Court now reserves the right to question Community legislation in an action directed against a Member State. If so, this statement – which may be a reaction to Opinion 2/94, which had been delivered a few months before – is all the more striking in that the Court found that in any event there had been no breach of Article 7 of the Convention. The Court could therefore have skirted around the fact that the same definition of "proprietary medicinal products" is to be found in Directive 65/65 – especially as that Directive does not even require such products to be sold by qualified pharmacists in any case!

The plaintiff in *Matthews v United Kingdom*[55] was contesting the fact that, despite being within the European Community,[56] Gibraltar was not represented in the European Parliament. This followed from Annex II to the Act of 1976 on direct elections to that Parliament, which in turn was endorsed unanimously by Council Decision 76/787.[57] By Article 138(3) (now Article 190(4)) of the Treaty of Rome, that instrument was required to be ratified by all the Member States. Accordingly, neither the Act nor the Decision is open to challenge before the ECJ or the courts of Member States. At all events, Annex II to the Act consists simply of the following wonderfully enigmatic sentence: "The United Kingdom shall apply the provisions of this Act only in respect of the United Kingdom." This was in fact a coded way of excluding Gibraltar, the only British colony within the European Community: as a matter of domestic law, the colonies are not regarded as part of the United Kingdom.[58] Accordingly, Annex II is to be understood to mean: "The Member State known as the United Kingdom shall apply this Act only to the territory defined as "the United Kingdom" in its domestic law".

The EctHR – sitting as the Grand Chamber of 17 judges, rather than the normal Chamber of 7 judges – upheld Ms Matthews' complaint that this state of affairs constituted a breach by the United Kingdom of Article 3 of Protocol 1 to

---

55 Application 24833/94, judgment of 18 February 1999, noted by H. Schermers 1999 CMLRev. 673.

56 Article 299(4) (ex 227(4)) EC. However, various provisions of the Treaty do not apply to Gibraltar: see Article 28 of the Act of Accession of Denmark, Ireland and the United Kingdom and Article 3 of the Common Customs Code (Council Regulation 2913/92, 1992 OJ L197/1), which excludes the colony from the Community's customs territory.

57 1976 OJ L278/1.

58 By virtue of s. 5 Interpretation Act 1978 read with Schedule 1 thereto "United Kingdom" means Great Britain and Northern Ireland, unless the context otherwise requires. The same definition is to be found in earlier enactments.

the ECHR, which requires the High Contracting Parties to "hold free and fair elections at reasonable intervals by secret ballot, under conditions which will ensure the free expression of the opinion of the people in the choice of the legislature".[59] The Court found that, since its powers were enhanced by the Treaty of Maastricht, the European Parliament must be regarded as "the legislature" with respect to Gibraltar for these purposes – although Judges Sir John Freeland and Jungwiert dissented on this point.[60] As to whether the United Kingdom was "required to 'secure' elections to the European Parliament notwithstanding the Community character of those elections", the Court ruled:

> " ... acts of the EC as such cannot be challenged before the Court because the EC is not a Contracting Party. The Convention does not exclude the transfer of competences to international organisations provided that Convention rights continue to be 'secured'. Member States' responsibility therefore continues even after such a transfer."[61]

Read in isolation, this statement would suggest that the Court may be claiming jurisdiction over *all* Community acts. However, it then went on to state:

> "... The Council Decision and the 1976 Act ... and the Maastricht Treaty ... all constituted international instruments which were freely entered into by the United Kingdom. Indeed, the 1976 Act cannot be challenged before the European Court of Justice for the very reason that it is not a 'normal' act of the Community, but is a treaty within the Community legal order. The Maastricht Treaty, too, is not an act of the Community, but a treaty by which a revision of the EEC Treaty was brought about. The United Kingdom, together with all the other parties to the Maastricht Treaty, is responsible *ratione materiae* under Article 1 of the Convention and, in particular, Article 3 of Protocol No. 1, for the consequences of that Treaty."[62]

---

59 That Protocol applies to Gibraltar by virtue of a declaration made by the United Kingdom on 25 February 1988 pursuant to Article 4 of the Protocol.

60 Back in 1987, the European Commission of Human Rights had ruled that the European Parliament could not yet be regarded as "the legislature" for these purposes, in view of its limited powers (*Tête v France* Application 11123/84, decision of 9 December 1987, DR 54, p. 52).
However, the Court had already held that bodies other than national parliaments could constitute "the legislature". Thus, the Flemish Council (the Parliament of Flanders) was held to be a constituent part of the Belgian "legislature", alongside the French Community Council and the Walloon Regional Council (*Mathieu-Mohin and Clerfayt v Belgium*, judgment of 2 March 1987, paragraph 53, Series A n° 113 p. 23, (1988) 10 EHRR 1). The two dissenting judges in *Matthews* chose to ignore that ruling and concentrated instead on a range of other issues such as: the use of the definite article in Article 3 ("*the* legislature"); the fact that several parts of the EC Treaty do not apply to Gibraltar (see note 56 above); and the fact that the European Parliament has no power to initiate or adopt legislation.

61 The Court ruled to the same effect with respect to the European Space Agency in two other judgments delivered on the same day (*Waite and Kennedy v Germany* (Application 26083/94) and *Beer and Regan v Germany* (Application 28934/95)).

62 Paragraph 33 of the judgment. According to Schermers (*op.cit.* at p. 680), by declaring

Article 1 of the Convention provides: "The High Contracting Parties shall secure to everyone within their jurisdiction the rights and freedoms defined in Section I of this Convention". Accordingly, the Court has taken the view that the acts concerned fall "within the jurisdiction" of the United Kingdom.

Ironically, it is strongly arguable that Annex II to the 1976 Act did not *require* the United Kingdom to exclude Gibraltar from elections to the European Parliament: on this view, it simply conferred on that Member State the power to define the extent of its territory subject to such elections.

In any event, what matters is that the Court now appears to reserve the right to review the compatibility of a Community instrument with the ECHR, where there is a clear nexus with one or more Member States which have actively participated in its adoption.

Whether the Court would rule to the same effect in the absence of such a nexus remains a matter of speculation. An action lodged with the ECtHR by a bankrupt company against all 15 Member States of the European Community in September 1999 may possibly clarify this matter.[63] It claims that the Commission failed to act on its complaint under Article 81 (ex 85) of the Treaty of Rome. Plainly, this action is directed against the Commission as such, and no single Member State is involved. Hence the applicant's decision to attack all 15 Member States.[64]

Might not this line of case-law be regarded as tipping the balance in favour of the Community, or possibly even the Union, acceding to the ECHR? The shortcomings of a system in which parties are constrained to attack "men of straw" in the form of the Member States in respect of acts of the Community institutions are plain: the States concerned will find themselves in the invidious position of having to defend measures which they did not take; the Community institutions will be reliant on the States to present arguments on their behalf, without even having the advantage of a Community judge on the EctHR; and this could also lead to the dissatisfaction of other litigants and of the EctHR itself. True, pursuant to the new Article 36(2) of the Convention read with Article 61(3) of the revised Rules of the Court, it is open to the President of the Court to invite "any person concerned who is not the applicant" to "submit written comments or, in exceptional cases to take part in an oral hearing"; no doubt, those provisions could be applied in favour of the Community.[65] That would alleviate

---

that the United Kingdom is responsible "together with all the other parties to the Maastricht Treaty", the Court has indicated that Spain has its share of responsibility in ensuring that free and fair elections to the European Parliament are held in Gibraltar.

63 Application n° 51717/99.

64 The Applicant may also have been encouraged to follow this course by the statement in paragraph 33 of the ruling in *Matthews* that the United Kingdom "together with all the other parties to the Maastricht Treaty" is responsible for the consequences of that Treaty.

65 The new Article 36 was introduced into the Convention by the 11th Protocol (see note 43 above); the Rules of Procedure were amended to take account of that Protocol. Even if the European Union is not a "person" (see above), it is probably still entitled to intervene, since the EctHR has adopted a liberal attitude to third party intervention under the previ-

the problems, but it would not solve them. These difficulties will become particularly acute if the EctHR further extends its jurisdiction to cases having no nexus with any particular Member State and relating to the Community institutions.

VI THE TREATY OF AMSTERDAM AND SUBSEQUENT DEVELOPMENTS

The Treaty of Amsterdam, which was signed on 2 October 1997[66] and came into force on 1 May 1999,[67] has effected a number of significant changes to the TEU and the Treaty of Rome.

In the first place, Article 6(1) (ex Article F(1)) TEU has now been replaced by the following wholly new paragraph: "The Union is founded on the principles of liberty, democracy, respect for human rights and fundamental freedoms, and the rule of law, principles which are common to the Member States". Should any Member State commit a serious and persistent breach of these principles, then some of its rights may be suspended pursuant to the new Article 7 TEU. This may occur even where the breach concerned relates to matters falling outside the scope of European Union or Community law. In addition, that provision makes it clear that this may include the suspension of that State's right to vote in the Council; if such a decision is taken, then by virtue of Article 309(1) EC that State's voting rights in the same institution will also be suspended automatically in relation to European Community matters. Article 309(2) EC goes further still, in that it empowers the Council to suspend other "rights deriving from the application of this Treaty to the Member State in question", although that institution is required to "take into account the possible consequences of such a suspension on the rights and obligations of natural and legal persons".[68]

---

ous, and essentially similar, Rules of Court. Thus, various sections of national Bars and associations of advocates were allowed to intervene in *Pham Hoang v France* (judgment of 25 September 1992, Series A-243, (1993) 16 EHRR 53) and *Capuano v Italy* (judgment of 25 June 1987, Series A-119, (1991) 13 EHRR 271). Equally, in *Tinnelly & Sons v United Kingdom* (judgment of 10 July 1998, (1999) 27 EHRR 249), the Standing Advisory Commission on Human Rights, an independent statutory body based in Northern Ireland, was permitted to intervene. On third party intervention before the EctHR, see generally O. De Schutter *Fonction de juger et droits fondamentaux* (1999) pp. 1082-1094.

66 The text is to be found in 1997 OJ C340.

67 1999 OJ L114/56.

68 From a reading of Article 46 (ex Article L) TEU, it would appear that a suspension adopted pursuant to Article 7 of that Treaty may not be reviewed by the ECJ. Article 309(1) EC merely lays down the consequence of such a decision with respect to votes in the Council on EC matters, and does not provide for a separate decision, which could be quashed by the ECJ. In contrast, a decision taken pursuant to Article 309(2) EC would presumably be open to review, in so far as such a manifestly political act is justiciable at all. The Court's task will undoubtedly be facilitated by the enactment of a Charter of

As one might expect, Article 49 (ex Article O) TEU also provides that respect for the principles set out in Article 6(1) is a condition for a European State to become a member of the Union in the future.[69]

Article 6(2) (ex Article F(2)) TEU has been left unaltered. It follows that the ECHR still does not apply as such; instead the fundamental rights guaranteed by that Convention merely apply to the European Union "as general principles of law". Nevertheless, as we noticed earlier, the ECJ has taken care for many years to abide by the Convention, at least in the face of clear case-law from Strasbourg.[70]

Article 46 (ex Article L) now extends the jurisdiction of the ECJ to "Article 6(2) with regard to action of the institutions, insofar as the Court has jurisdiction under the Treaties establishing the European Communities and under this Treaty." While this undoubtedly constitutes a (largely symbolic) step forward, it should be noted that the acts of Member States are not mentioned here. Yet, it seems scarcely conceivable that the ECJ would regard such language as reversing the principle set out in *Wachauf,* just as Article L of the Maastricht Treaty did not restrain it from continuing to develop its case-law on fundamental rights.

Furthermore, the Treaty of Amsterdam has considerably extended the ECJ's jurisdiction over (i) police and judicial cooperation in criminal matters and (ii) visas, asylum and related issues – areas of law in which human rights issues are especially likely to arise. Although the first of these fields continues to be a matter for intergovernmental cooperation and is thus still governed by Title VI of the TEU, Article 35 of that Treaty confers limited jurisdiction on the ECJ with respect to instruments adopted pursuant to that Title.[71] In contrast, the second area is now governed by new provisions of the Treaty of Rome, but Article 68 EC restricts to courts of last instance the right to make references for preliminary rulings in this regard. What is more, the same article stipulates that "the Court of Justice shall not have jurisdiction" over measures or decisions relating to controls at the Community's internal borders taken so as to maintain law and

---

Fundamental Rights (see below), particularly if it is incorporated into the Treaties.

69 By an anomaly, Article 49 is one of the provisions of the TEU over which the ECJ does have jurisdiction by virtue of Article 46! On the quirks of the latter provision, see Pechstein, *op.cit.*

70 Note 14 above. On paper, the United Kingdom will be one step ahead of the EU when the Human Rights Act 1998 comes into force: British courts will then be *required* to apply the substantive provisions of the Convention and the Protocols thereto, albeit without setting aside primary United Kingdom legislation; but they will only be bound to "take into account" the case-law and declarations of the European Commission of Human Rights and the EctHR (s.2(1)). It may be argued, however, that the situation under Article 6(2) TEU is not very different in practice.

71 In particular, the Court's jurisdiction to deliver preliminary rulings pursuant to this Title is subject to the Member State accepting that jurisdiction. All but four Member States (Denmark, France, Ireland and the United Kingdom) did so prior to 1 May 1999 when the Treaty of Amsterdam entered into force. The other four are at liberty to do so at a later date.

order and safeguard internal security. In short, while the Court's jurisdiction has been extended, some of the most sensitive issues remain beyond its remit; many would regard it as unfortunate that any measures taken under the Treaty of Rome should be excluded from the Court's jurisdiction.[72]

In addition, the Treaty of Rome now contains a new Article 13, which reads: "Without prejudice to the other provisions of this Treaty and within the limits of the powers conferred by it upon the Community, the Council, acting unanimously on a proposal from the Commission and after consulting the European Parliament, may take appropriate action to combat discrimination based on sex, racial or ethnic origin, religion or belief, disability, age or sexual orientation".[73]

Amongst the other amendments to the Treaty of Rome with human rights overtones, the following deserve special mention: a revised Article 2 and a new Article 3(2) on equality between the sexes, and not just in the workplace. Moreover, Article 141 (ex 119) has been amended so as to contain a legal base for legislation on sex discrimination in the labour market and to allow for affirmative action;[74]

- a new provision granting to "any natural or legal person residing or having its registered office in a Member State" the right of access, subject to exceptions, to documents of the European Parliament, the Commission or the Council (Article 255);[75] and

---

72 A. Albors-Llorens "Changes in the Jurisdiction of the European Court of Justice under the Treaty of Amsterdam" 1998 CMLRev. 1273; M. Colvin and P. Noorlander "Human Rights and Accountability after the Treaty of Amsterdam" 1998 EHRLR 191; P. Wachsmann "Le traité d'Amsterdam: les droits de l'homme" 1997 RTDE 883.

73 The Commission's proposals for implementing this article are contained in the following documents: COM(99) 565(4), COM(99) 566(4) and COM(99) 567(4). See also the Commission's Communication on the subject (1999 OJ C 369/3) and. L. Flynn "The Implications of Article 13 EC – After Amsterdam, Will Some Forms of Discrimination be More Equal than Others?" 1999 CMLRev. 1127.

74 The new Article 141(4) reverses the ruling in Case C-450/93 *Kalanke v Bremen* [1995] ECR I-3051, which had in fact already been qualified by the judgment in Case C-409/95 *Marschall v Land Nordrhein-Westfalen* [1997] ECR I-6363. See C. Barnard "Gender Equality in the EU" in P. Alston, *op.cit.*

75 The legislation to be adopted pursuant to that provision will replace the current measures, which the Commission, the Council and the Parliament have imposed upon themselves: Commission Decision 94/90 (1994 OJ L46/58), amended by Commission Decision 96/567 (1996 OJ L 247/45); Council Decision 93/371 (1993 OJ L340/43), amended by Council Decision 96/705 (1996 OJ L325/16); and (rather belatedly) European Parliament Decision 97/632 (1997 OJ L263/27). In addition, the Court of Auditors (which is not covered by the new Article 255) has adopted Decision No 18/97 laying down internal rules for the treatment of applications for access to documents held by the Court (1998 OJ C295/1).

– a new provision on protection of data held by the Community institutions and other bodies established pursuant to that Treaty (Article 286[76]).[77]

While these amendments are to be welcomed, the Treaty of Amsterdam has provided neither for the drawing up of a Charter of fundamental rights nor accession to the Convention – omissions which have not failed to attract widespread criticism.[78]

At all events, the Community institutions have not been idle since the Treaty of Amsterdam was signed. In February 1999, the expert group on fundamental rights established by the European Commission under the chairmanship of Professor Simitis submitted its report. The group was particularly critical of the patchwork of human rights provisions and references to international human rights provisions in the Treaties as amended by the Treaty of Amsterdam, saying:

> "The ... system of references is confusing and counterproductive. While, for instance, the ECHR is cited twice in the EU Treaty, there is not a single mention in the EC Treaty. In contrast, both the European Social Charter and the Community Charter are quoted in each of these documents. But their explicit mention in the Preamble of the EU Treaty is not followed by an equally outspoken reference in Art. 6 where only the ECHR is cited. The opposite is the case in Art. 136 of the EC Treaty. It cites the European Social Charter and the Community Charter but not the ECHR, despite the impact of fundamental rights, such as freedom of association, respect for private and family life, or freedom of expression, on employment relationships."

The report therefore recommended that a Charter of Fundamental Rights be incorporated into the Treaties in a prominent position. Recognising that achieving a consensus on a wholly new Bill of Rights would be fraught with difficulty, the authors of the report suggested that all the rights enshrined in the ECHR and the Protocols thereto should be incorporated into this text together with some others.[79]

---

76 The Commission's proposal for implementing this new provision (COM(99)337/6) is modelled on Directive 95/46 of the Parliament and the Council on data protection (1995 OJ L281/31). This was in turn based on the Council of Europe's Convention of 1981 for the Protection of Individuals with regard to Automatic Processing of Personal Data.

77 In addition, in Declaration no° 1 annexed to the Treaty, the Inter-governmental Conference recalled that Protocol 6 to the ECHR provides for the abolition of the death penalty. While this Declaration appears to be primarily political, it is significant that the three Member States which had not ratified that Protocol at the time – Belgium, Greece and the United Kingdom – have done so in the interim.

78 P. Gallagher "The Treaty of Amsterdam and Fundamental Rights" 1998 IJEL 21; J-V Louis *op.cit.*; P. Wachsmann, *op.cit.* note 73 above; J. Weiler and P. Alston "An 'Ever Closer Union' in Need of a Human Rights Policy: the European Union and Human Rights" in P. Alston, *op.cit.* 4 at pp 30-31.

79 The report thus harks back to the suggestion of Judge Lenaerts ("Fundamental Rights to be Included in a Community Catalogue", note 21 above) that the Convention rights

In keeping with this, the Heads of State and Government of the Member States of the Community made the following declaration at the close of their summit held in Cologne in June 1999:

> " ... There appears to be a need, at the present stage of the Union's development, to establish a Charter of fundamental rights in order to make their overriding importance and relevance more visible to the Union's citizens.
>
> The European Council believes that this Charter should contain the fundamental rights and freedoms as well as basic procedural rights guaranteed by the European Convention for the Protection of Human Rights and Fundamental Freedoms and derived from the constitutional traditions common to the Member States, as general principles of Community law. The Charter should also include the fundamental rights that pertain only to the Union's citizens. In drawing up such a Charter account should furthermore be taken of economic and social rights as contained in the European Social Charter and the Community Charter of the Fundamental Social Rights of Workers (Article 136 TEC), insofar as they do not merely establish objectives for action by the Union.
>
> In the view of the European Council, a draft of such a Charter of Fundamental Rights of the European Union should be elaborated by a body composed of representatives of the Heads of State and Government and of the President of the Commission as well as of members of the European Parliament and national parliaments. ...
>
> This body should present a draft document in advance of the European Council in December 2000. The European Council will propose to the European Parliament and the Commission that, together with the Council, they should solemnly proclaim on the basis of the draft document a European Charter of Fundamental Rights. It will then have to be considered whether and, if so, how the Charter should be integrated into the treaties. ..."

The term "Charter of Fundamental Rights of the European Union" clearly indicates that the envisaged Charter is to apply to the European Union, and not merely the European Community.

The drafting of this solemn act will coincide with the Intergovernmental Conference for the amendment of the Treaties which, according to the Cologne declaration, is also set to conclude its work by the end of the year 2000 so as to pave the way for further enlargement of the Union. Accordingly, it is sincerely to be hoped that the opportunity will not be lost to confer treaty status on the Charter, as the German Government in particular is urging.[80] In particular, should it be relegated to the rank of a mere resolution or other instrument of "soft law", its legal value will be limited.[81]

---

should constitute the core of a Community Charter.

80 Regrettably, the Dehaene report on *The Institutional Implications of Enlargement*, so bold on many other issues, expressly left this question open (at p.4). This report, which was submitted to the Commission on 18 October 1999, was drafted by the former Prime Minister of Belgium together with the former President von Weizsäcker of Germany and Lord Simon of Highbury.

81 See note 30 above.

Following their meeting held at Tampere in October 1999, the Heads of State and Government of the Member States announced the composition and working methods of the group drafting the Charter. This group is to consist of one representative of the Government of each of the 15 Member States, one representative of the Commission, 30 MEPs and 36 national MPs. Two representatives of the ECJ are to participate as observers, as well as two delegates of the Council of Europe (including one judge of the EctHR). In principle – *transparence oblige* – the group's debates are to be made public, as are all the documents presented to it.

No mention is made in either the Cologne or the Tampere declaration of the possibility of accession to the European Convention of Human Rights. Indeed, since the ECJ's Opinion 2/94, no serious attempt has been made to revive this idea which would still require an amendment to the Treaties.[82] That may be regarded as surprising in view of the recent case-law of the EctHR, which we noticed earlier. While it is sincerely to be hoped that the enactment of a Charter of Fundamental Rights will enable the courts within the Community to ensure human rights protection in the overwhelming majority of cases, that will not obviate the need for external judicial control in exceptional circumstances.[83]

---

82 An unofficial, but highly authoritative, appeal in favour of such a move was made at the Conference held at Vienna in October 1998 by Judge Antonio Cassese, Mme Catherine Lalumière, Professor Peter Leuprecht and Mrs. Mary Robinson in point 19(g) of their memorandum entitled "Leading by Example: A Human Rights Agenda for the European Union for the Year 2000"; (that document is annexed to P. Alston *op. cit*, and is also available on the website of the European University Institute at http://www.iue.it/AEL/documents/report.rtf).

83 According to H. Schermers (editorial, 1998 CMLRev. 5), the prospect of accession to the Convention is now more remote than ever, especially because it is unlikely to be supported by the attitude of the Contracting Parties to the East, including Russia. In contrast, G. Gaja advocates this course as a preferred alternative to a Charter of the Union; in his view, to pursue both options at once would serve only to create conflicts ("New Instruments and Institutions for Enhancing the Protection of Human Rights in Europe" in P. Alston, *op.cit.* 781).
In the same editorial, H. Schermers argues that the adoption of a Charter of the Union would operate to the detriment of the other European countries – essentially those in Eastern Europe. Surely such a fear would only be well-founded if the Member States of the Union were to withdraw from the Convention, which is absolutely not envisaged. As already mentioned (note 23 above), it is hard to see how the establishment of a Charter within the European Union in itself could result in a two-speed approach to human rights in Europe, any more than the adoption of a Bill of Rights by any Contracting Party could have such an effect.
At the other end of the spectrum, A. Toth ("The European Union and Human Rights: the Way Forward" 1997 CMLRev. 491) advocates transferring the protection of human rights to the Union under the control of the ECJ, with its Member States withdrawing from the ECHR altogether. This approach is unlikely to find much favour in practice, since it would scarcely be regarded by the more recent Contracting Parties in Eastern Europe as a gesture of solidarity from their counterparts in the West.

VII CONCLUSION

Thanks to the dynamism of the ECJ, it is by now axiomatic that "respect for human rights is ... a condition of the lawfulness of Community acts"[84] and presumably also of acts adopted pursuant to the Treaty on European Union. Moreover, great strides were made at Maastricht and Amsterdam in enshrining certain fundamental rights into the Treaties. Nevertheless, the case-law of the ECJ has inevitably been developed in a piecemeal and unpredictable manner which leaves much to be desired. At the same time, the Simitis Report is no doubt right to point to the haphazard patchwork of human rights provisions in the Treaties as they now stand.

Some who may have felt in the past that talk of the Community adopting its own Charter or acceding to the European Convention of Human Rights was premature may now feel that the time is now ripe for such moves. The last decade has seen three significant developments: (i) the powers of the Community (and the Union) have now been extended to cover some highly sensitive areas such as visas, asylum and immigration from third countries; (ii) the collapse of Communism in Europe, and the ensuing prospect of many East European countries acceding to the Community, lends a new urgency to human rights issues; and (iii) the EctHR is in effect applying that Convention by the back door to some Community acts.

In these circumstances, the decision to draw up a Charter of Fundamental Rights of the European Union deserves a warm welcome, although it will prove to be less than a half-measure unless it enjoys treaty status.

Meanwhile, although official talk of the European Community (or perhaps even the Union) acceding to the Convention has now dwindled to a murmur, this idea can surely not be ruled out for ever, in view of the judgment in *Cantoni* and *Matthews*. Should this trend in the case-law of the EctHR continue, the prospect of accession may well come to the fore once again.

Plainly, it would be naïve to think that these two steps can constitute an absolute panacea.[85] Yet it is manifest that together they would achieve a higher level of protection of fundamental rights than is at present the case in the Union, while at the same time avoiding conflicts between the ECJ and the EctHR.

---

84 Opinion 2/94 (note 2 above).

85 For instance, difficulties would continue to arise where a Member State has a "higher" standard than the Community; see L. Besselink ""Entrapped by the Maximum Standard: on Fundamental Rights, Pluralism and Subsidiarity in the European Union" 1998 CMLRev. 629 and J. Weiler "Fundamental Rights and Fundamental Boundaries: on Standards and Values in the Protection of Human Rights" in N. Neuwahl and A. Rosas, *op.cit.*

POSTSCRIPT

The following noteworthy development occurred too late to be incorporated into the body of this paper:

In its Order of 4 February 2000 in Case C-17/98 *Emesa Sugar (Free Zone) v Aruba*, the ECJ dismissed an application by the plaintiff in the main case to submit written submissions after the Advocate General had delivered his Opinion. That party claimed to have such a right by virtue of Article 6 of the Convention, citing a number of ECHR judgments in support of this proposition (*Lobo Machado v Portugal* (judgment of 20 February 1996), 1996-I, p. 195; *Vermeulen v Belgium* (judgment of 20 February 1996) 1996-I, p.224; *Van Orshoven v Belgium* (judgment of 25 June 1997) 1997-III, p. 1040; *J.J. v Netherlands* (judgment of 27 March 1998) 1998-II, p. 604; *K.D.B. v Netherlands* (judgment of 27 March 1998) 1998-II, p. 621).

After rehearsing its own case-law on fundamental rights and referring to the new Article 46 TEU, the ECJ rejected Emesa's contention. It distinguished the case law of the ECHR on the grounds that the role and status of its Advocates General differed in several material respects from that of the supposedly equivalent magistrates in those cases. The ECJ also pointed to its power under its Rules of Procedure to re-open the oral procedure in certain circumstances. Subsequently, in its judgment on the substance of the case delivered on 8 February, it upheld the validity of the Community legislation attacked by Emesa.

22

SHIFTING THE GRUNDNORM (AND OTHER TALES)

David Anderson

INTRODUCTION[1]

Any practising lawyer must have a certain amount of fellow-feeling for Miss Brass, one of the minor stars of Charles Dickens's "The Old Curiosity Shop". From her earliest youth she devoted herself to the study of the law:

> "not wasting her speculation upon its eagle flights, which are rare, but tracing it attentively through all the slippery and eel-like crawlings in which it commonly pursues its way".[2]

Time spent in the courts is sadly no substitute for the high degree of jurisprudential expertise that usually characterises discussions of such matters as sovereignty, competence and the clash of legal orders. However there may be occasional value in such subjects, fit for the eagles, being addressed by someone whose experience and aptitudes are more those of the eel.

The first part of this article looks at two questions of some general interest: has the United Kingdom Parliament already signed away its sovereignty to the European Community; and is it our own courts, or those of the Community, which can ultimately decide the limits on the Community's powers? The second part examines the way in which similar questions are being asked about the control of the powers of the Community by the European Convention of Human Rights.

I EUROPEAN UNION LAW AND UNITED KINGDOM LAW

Has Parliament Signed Away its Sovereignty?

When the Divisional Court in *Factortame* first gave its injunction suspending the operation of the Merchant Shipping Act 1988,[3] I passed a copy of the Order round my undergraduate seminar, convinced – as were my clients, the fishermen

1 This contribution is based on the author's inaugural lecture as Visiting Professor at King's College London, delivered on 18 January 2000.

2 Chapter 33.

3 *R v Secretary of State for Transport ex p Factortame Ltd.* [1989] 2 CMLR 353.

D. O'Keeffe (ed.), Liber Amicorum Slynn 343-360 (2000)

– that it must be of historic importance. Other people certainly seemed to think so. When the Court of Justice (counting Lord Slynn among its members) ruled that the domestic legal impediments to the grant of an injunction must be disregarded,[4] and when the House of Lords eventually confirmed the injunction,[5] the reaction was dramatic. The front-page of *The Independent*, on the day after the ruling of the Court of Justice, proclaimed "EC Rewrites British Constitution".[6] Lord Denning, in a reference to his celebrated dictum from *Bulmer v Bollinger,*[7] stated:

> "No longer is European law an incoming tide flowing up the estuaries of England. It is now like a tidal wave bringing down our sea walls and flowing inland over our fields and houses – to the dismay of all."[8]

Professor Wade, similarly, wrote of a "constitutional revolution", expressing the view that:

> "The House of Lords elected to allow the Parliament of 1972 to fetter the Parliament of 1988 in order that Community law might be given the primacy which practical politics obviously required."[9]

Ten years after these developments, it is time to reflect on whether *Factortame* did shift the *Grundnorm*, in the sense of heralding a change to the ultimate legal principle or "top rule" which in our domestic legal system determines the validity of all other legal rules.

Others have debated at length how exactly that top rule is to be formulated. A working definition was provided by Chief Justice Holt, almost exactly 300 years ago:

> "an Act of Parliament can do no wrong, though it may do several things that look pretty odd."[10]

In simple terms, the question is this: has the sovereignty of Parliament been modified by judicial recognition of the special and privileged position of European Community law?

---

4 *The Queen v. Secretary of State for Transport ex parte: Factortame and others* [1990] ECR I-2433.

5 [1991] 1 AC 603 (9 July 1990).

6 20 June 1990.

7 [1974] Ch 401.

8 Introduction to Smith, *The European Court of Justice: Judges or Policymakers* (Bruges Group, 1990).

9 "Sovereignty – Revolution or Evolution" (1996) 112 LQR 568.

10 *City of London v Wood* (1702) 12 Mod. 669, 687; 88 ER 1592. CJ Holt's position was in fact more interesting than that modern-sounding passage implies. He went on to state, relying on *Bonham*'s case that if an act of Parliament ordained that a person should be judge in his own cause, it would be void.

In my opinion it has not. It is true that on the second occasion that *Factortame* came before the House of Lords, Lord Bridge spoke briefly and in broad terms about what he called the loss of sovereignty accepted by Parliament when it enacted the European Communities Act 1972.[11] That speech has given encouragement to those who believe that the *Grundnorm* may be on the move.[12] But as recently as November of last year, a unanimous House of Lords in *ICI v Colmar*[13] endorsed the fuller explanation given by Lord Bridge in the first *Factortame* case of what he believed Parliament to have been doing when the United Kingdom joined the European Communities.[14]

In the first *Factortame* case, Lord Bridge gave primacy to Community law without reference to the idea that the Parliament which took the United Kingdom into the Community was purporting to bind its successors. Rather, he saw it as an exercise in construing two statutes consistently with each other. Section 2(4) of the European Communities Act provides that any enactment passed or to be passed shall be construed and have effect subject to the enforceable Community rights referred to in section 2(1). Section 2(4), as interpreted by Lord Bridge, no more shifts the *Grundnorm* than does the Interpretation Act. Its effect is as though a section were incorporated into the later Act, stating that its provisions were without prejudice to directly enforceable Community rights.[15]

In the absence of a clear statutory intention to depart from its Community obligations, statutes will be interpreted so as to conform with those obligations or, if they cannot be so interpreted, disapplied. However if Parliament were to decide that we should leave the Community, or even state expressly and unambiguously that the provision of a new statute were to prevail over any contrary provision of European Community law, the courts would give effect to what Parliament said, because their first allegiance is still owed to the United Kingdom rather than to the Community. That, at any rate, was the view expressed by Lord Denning, 21 years ago, in *Macarthys v Smith*,[16] and despite some academic doubts[17] there has been no judicial sign, either in *Factortame* or in any case since, that the position is about to change. Parliament was not restricting its fu-

11 *R v Secretary of State for Transport ex p Factortame Ltd.* [1991] 1 A.C. 603, 658-659.

12 See, notably, P. Craig, "Sovereignty of the United Kingdom Parliament after *Factortame*" (1991) 11 YEL 221.

13 Judgment of 18 November 1999.

14 *R v Secretary of State for Transport ex p Factortame Ltd.* [1990] 2 A.C. 85, 140 B-D; cf. Lord Keith in *R v Secretary of State for Employment ex p Equal Opportunities Commission* [1995] 1 AC 1 at 27 D-E.

15 See Sir J. Laws, "Law and Democracy" [1995] *Public Law* 72. At 89: "The law of Europe is not a higher-order law because the limits which for the time being it sets to the powers of Parliament are at the grace of Parliament itself."

16 [1979] 3 All ER 325, 329.

17 Craig, "Report on the United Kingdom" in *The European Courts and National Courts*, Slaughter, Sweet and Weiler, eds., (1998), p. 195 at 204.

ture powers, save, perhaps, concerning the manner in which it would have to express itself.[18]

Is there any prospect that the United Kingdom courts will, of their own volition, introduce a change to the "top rule" that would acknowledge the primacy of a European federation, irrespective of anything that Parliament said to the contrary? In one sense they are in a good position to do so, for like all courts in the Community they function as courts both of national and of Community law. The *Grundnorm* can shift without there being blood on the streets: in Professor Wade's phrase, the necessary revolution can be "quiet and legal" in nature.[19]

It is difficult to predict the circumstances in which our courts might effect such a quiet revolution. At the moment, the idea hardly seems a plausible one. The Italian correspondent in London was only half joking when he said of the British that if asked whether they feel part of Europe they will agree, but only after:

> "a long thoughtful pause in which all other continents are mentally evoked and regretfully discarded".[20]

But Parliamentary sovereignty is ultimately founded on the notion that, as Dicey expressed it:

> "The permanent wishes of the representative portion of Parliament can hardly in the long run differ from the wishes of the English people ..."[21]

The day may come when the people endorse, in a referendum, a Treaty amendment which makes the European Union into a truly participative democratic federation. In that event, it would be open to our courts to decide that the popular will now finds a more perfect expression through the institutions of the Union than through the United Kingdom Parliament. In those circumstances – but not, perhaps in any others – the sovereignty of Parliament really would be dead.

Who Decides the Limits on the Community's Powers?

So for the moment, the United Kingdom Parliament has retained the ultimate power to take us out of the Community or even – though at risk of sanctions from the Community itself – to legislate in defiance of our Community obligations. But sovereignty that can be expressed only in such an extreme way is perhaps of limited practical value.[22] A question just as important as whether we

18 T. Hartley, *Constitutional Problems of the European Union*, p. 173.

19 H.W.R. Wade, "The Basis of Legal Sovereignty" [1955] CLJ 172.

20 Luigi Barzini.

21 A.V. Dicey, *An Introduction to the Study of the Constitution*, 10th ed. (1967), p. 83, cited by P. Craig, "Sovereignty of the United Kingdom Parliament after *Factortame*", (1991) 11 YEL 221.

22 There is, in other words, some force in Professor Wade's view that if the low-key inter-

have signed away the sovereignty of Parliament, and one to which it is perhaps more useful to know the answer, is whether there are grounds on which United Kingdom courts may refuse to give effect to Community laws which they consider to lie outside the powers of the Community. In other words, who decides the limits on the Community's powers?

For the European Court of Justice, sitting in Luxembourg, that question can be answered, quite unambiguously, "we do". In the case-law of that court, the power to decide the limits of Community power, or *Kompetenz-Kompetenz* as the eagles call it, lies with the Community itself. The Treaties, it is true, state that the Communities must act within the limits of the powers conferred upon them by the Member States.[23] But in its *Foto-Frost* decision of 1987,[24] the Court of Justice held that it had a monopoly over the final determination of whether or not any act or measure of the Community was valid. In other words, it is the Community's court, and not those of the Member States, which is alone competent to determine whether the Community has exceeded the powers that it has been given.

A different answer has emerged from the constitutional courts of a number of Member States – notably France, Germany and Italy.[25] National constitutional courts tend to look at Community law as something which must be measured against national constitutional rules, and if found invalid, given no effect. That was the approach taken, most famously, by the German Federal Constitutional Court in its decision on the constitutionality of the Maastricht Treaty.[26] In a direct repudiation of the European Court's *Foto-Frost* doctrine, it stated that *Kompetenz-Kompetenz* lies with Germany and that *ultra vires* acts of the Communities, for constitutional reasons, may be inapplicable in Germany. There are strong echoes of this approach in the decisions of a number of lower courts in Germany, particularly in relation to the sensitive subjects of tax, labour law and bananas.[27] The Italian Constitutional Court also locates *Kompetenz-Kompetenz* in Italy; and the French *Conseil d'Etat* is said to have reserved to itself the power to defend certain core values, namely the respect for republican institutions, the continuity of the life of the nation and the guarantee of civil rights and

---

pretation of *Factortame* advanced above is correct, the House of Lords was providing "camouflage for the fundamental change which has evidently occurred": (1996) 112 LQR 568, 575.

23 Article 5 (ex 3b) EC. Cf. also Article 48 (ex N) of the TEU, providing that amendments to the Treaties shall enter into force only after being ratified by all the Member States *in accordance with their respective constitutional requirements*".

24 Case 314/85; [1987] ECR 4199

25 In relation to the law of these jurisdictions I am indebted to the ground-breaking comparative survey contained in *The European Courts and National Courts*, Slaughter, Sweet and Weiler, eds., (1998).

26 *Brunner v European Union Treaty* [1994] 1 CMLR 57.

27 J. Kokott, "Report on Germany" in *The European Courts and National Courts*, Slaughter, Sweet and Weiler, eds., (1998), pp. 112-117.

liberties.[28] More recently, the Danish Supreme Court has held that there are exceptional circumstances in which the Danish courts could hold a Community act inapplicable in Denmark, even after it has been specifically held to be valid by the Court of Justice.[29]

The issue of whether the European Court is to be followed when it claims the power to determine the limits on the Community's own competence has never arisen in the United Kingdom, just as, apparently, it has never arisen in the Netherlands, another country without a Constitutional Court.[30] If it did, though, I have little doubt that as matters stand, the English courts at least would give full effect to the *Foto-Frost* doctrine, and thereby concede *Kompetenz-Kompetenz* to the Community court. Some may now regret having granted to the Community such powers as the Community's court shall at any time declare it to have: but that certainly appears to be the effect of section 3(1) in particular of the European Communities Act 1972.

A practical example of this is afforded by the recent litigation on the tobacco advertising Directive.[31] The Directive purports to be an internal market measure but has been widely perceived as a measure predominantly motivated by public health concerns; public health being an area in which the competence to issue directives was specifically excluded by the former Article 129 EC (now Article 152). The Court of Appeal entertained grave doubts as to the Community's competence to adopt the Directive in issue. Lord Justice Laws, in particular, would have suspended the implementing regulations on the basis that the Directive was certainly *ultra vires*. Yet the question of the Directive's validity has been referred to the Court of Justice for its ruling, and neither the Court nor the parties have sought in any way to question the competence of the Court of Justice to make the final determination of the limits on the Community's competence.

A series of litigants have sought to resist the encroachments of the Community in the English courts – Blackburn, Smedley, Rees-Mogg[32] – but in the absence of a constitution upon which to rely, they have not been able to get around the point that Parliament can do as it likes. The upshot has been that in contrast to the other large Member States of the Community, the United Kingdom has

28 See, generally, A. Sweet, "Constitutional Dialogues in the European Community" in *The European Courts and National Courts*, Slaughter, Sweet and Weiler, eds., (1998), p. 305, 322-323.

29 *Carlsen v Rasmussen* [1999] 3 CMLR 854; see T. Hartley, *Constitutional Problems of the European Union* (1999), pp. 157-159.

30 M. Claes and B. De Witte, "Report on the Netherlands" in *The European Courts and National Courts*, Slaughter, Sweet and Weiler, eds., (1998), p. 171.

31 *R v Secretary of State for Health and ors. ex p.* Imperial Tobacco and ors., Judgment of 16 December 1999 (Court of Appeal). At the time of writing an appeal was pending to the House of Lords. The reference to the Court of Justice is Case C-74/99.

32 *Blackburn v Attorney-General* [1971] 1 WLR 1037; *R v HM Treasury ex p Smedley* [1985] QB 657; *R v Secretary of State for the Foreign and Commonwealth Office, ex p. Rees-Mogg* [1994] QB 552.

never qualified its acceptance of the supremacy of Community law. That is not necessarily a bad thing. Perhaps it simply demonstrates the truth of Justice Scalia's dictum that:

> "The whole *purpose* of a constitution – old or new – is to impede change, or pejoratively put, to obstruct modernity."[33]

Nonetheless, the absence of any domestic constitutional challenge to the Community's power to determine its own competence has certain consequences from a national viewpoint.

First, it deprives the United Kingdom of the kind of leverage that some other national courts have managed to apply to the Court of Justice. The emergence of a fundamental rights doctrine in Community law in response to threats from the German and Italian Constitutional Courts is the best-known example. Another example is the restrictive interpretation given by the Court of Justice in Opinion 2/94 to the Community's jurisdiction under the old Article 235 (new 308), seen by some as a response to the decision in the German Maastricht case about the need for integration to proceed predictably.[34]

Secondly, the absence of constitutional defence against the supremacy of Community law gives the Court of Justice liberty to lead the Member States in some very awkward directions. One might take two hypothetical but perhaps not entirely implausible examples. What if the Court interpreted Community law as imposing certain strict limits on national doctrines of state sovereignty? Or what if it proclaimed that a power to annul Treaty amendments was inherent in the *acquis communautaire*,[35] thereby removing the Treaties from the control of the Member States? The constitutional implications of such rulings would be immense. But it is difficult to see what the courts of the United Kingdom could do other than accept them.

II EUROPEAN UNION LAW AND THE ECHR

The story of the discovery of fundamental rights by the European Court of Justice, under pressure from the constitutional courts of Germany and Italy, and their subsequent assimilation into European Community law, has often been told and can be shortly summarised.

The European Court first held, in 1959, that it was without power to review Community acts by reference to fundamental rights.[36] Ten years later it suggested for the first time, in the case of *Stauder*,[37] that fundamental rights might

---

33 A. Scalia, "Modernity and the Constitution" in *Constitutional Justice under Old Constitutions*, ed. E. Smith, (1995), 315.

34 [1994] ECR I-1759.

35 T. Hartley, *Constitutional Problems of the European Union* (1999), p. 151.

36 Case 1/58 *Stork v High Authority* [1959] ECR 17.

37 Case 29/69 *Stauder v City of Ulm* [1969] ECR 419, 425.

form part of the general principles of Community law. In May of 1974, whether by accident or design, things began to speed up. On 3rd May, France ratified the European Convention: the only Member State not already to have done so. Eleven days later, in the case of *Nold*,[38] the Court of Justice felt able to make its first ever explicit reference to the European Convention of Human Rights. That in turn preceded by 15 days the *Solange I* judgment, in which the German Federal Constitutional Court reserved its right to ensure that Community law, as applied by the Court of Justice, was applied in a manner consistent with the catalogue of fundamental rights in the German Basic Law.

All those cases in the Court of Justice concerned the acts of Community institutions. The next step, in 1989, was for the Court to apply the doctrine of fundamental rights to the acts of the Member States, to the extent that they come within the scope of Community law.[39] They will, of course, not always be within that scope. Courts in England are instinctively attracted by the case of *Kremzow*, perhaps because of their sympathy for the applicant – a judge who had confessed to murdering a lawyer. He persuaded an Austrian court to ask human rights questions of the Court of Justice relating to his appeal against sentence and a claim for compensation, but he received no answer because there was no Community connection.[40]

In defining fundamental rights, the Court continues to claim inspiration from "the constitutional traditions common to the Member States", as well as from international human rights treaties. But the human rights treaties are referred to more than the constitutional traditions; and among those treaties, the European Convention of Human Rights is now held to be "of special significance",[41] in keeping with the specific references to it in the Community Treaties. Adherence to the Convention case-law is now taken very seriously in Luxembourg. In the sexual orientation discrimination case of *Grant*,[42] the Court went so far as to cite even unreported decisions of the European Commission of Human Rights, provided to it by the United Kingdom Government, in order to demonstrate that its conclusion – which some have sought to characterise as illiberal – was in accordance with the law of Strasbourg.

The position of the Court of Justice was informally summarised by Advocate General Jacobs in the *Bosphorus* case:[43]

> "For practical purposes the European Convention of Human Rights can be regarded as part of Community law and can be invoked as such both in this Court and in national courts where Community law is in issue."

38 [1974] ECR 491.
39 Case 5/88 *Wachauf* [1989] ECR 2609, 2639.
40 Case C-299/95 *Kremzow v Austrian State* [1997] ECR I-2969.
41 *Ibid.*, at 2645.
42 Case C-249/96 *Grant v South West Trains* [1998] ECR I-621.
43 Case C-84/95 [1996] ECR I-3953.

To be sure, human rights in Luxembourg sometimes come out looking a little different from the way they do in Strasbourg; just as in certain fields there is a distinctively British strain of Community law. In keeping with the economic nature of much of the Community Court's case law, there is a much greater emphasis on property rights, such as Article 1 of Protocol 1 and the right to a business, though few, if any, violations of these principles have been found. Competition law has been an unexpectedly fertile ground for human rights points, owing partly to what seem to modern eyes the inadequate procedural safeguards of Regulation 17. But members of the Court have made their own substantial contributions to the corpus of Convention case-law: in particular Advocate-General Jacobs, who in *Konstantinidis*[44] advanced the jurisprudence on the right to a name and personal identity, and further suggested, in an idea that seems to have been before its time, that any breach of the fundamental rights of another Community national should automatically be classed as an unlawful impediment to free movement.[45]

So far, a harmonious picture has been painted of Luxembourg and Strasbourg marching hand in hand, perhaps in the direction of the European Common Law which, if the legal journals had been frivolous enough to publish predictions for the new Millennium, would no doubt have featured among them. But it is not always as simple as that. There have been a number of cases, many of them in the field of competition law, in which the Luxembourg court has simply failed to take the human rights position properly into account. They include, in particular, the *Hoechst* case,[46] in which the Court wrongly held that Article 8 of the Convention does not apply to companies, and the *Orkem* case,[47] in which the Court of Justice was specifically identified in a later judgment of the European Court of Human Rights as having given insufficient scope to the right not to incriminate oneself in Article 6 of the Convention.[48]

Each of those conflicts can be understood as inadvertent. The public position of the Luxembourg court is supportive of the Strasbourg case-law, even if Advocate General Darmon was at pains to indicate, in the *Orkem* case, that the Luxembourg court was free to adopt an interpretation of the Convention which does not coincide with that given in Strasbourg.[49] But there is potential for much

44 Case C-168/91 *Konstantinidis v Stadt Altensteig-Standesamt* [1993] ECR I-1191

45 That idea was not taken up by the Court, and disapproved of as "too far-reaching" by Gulmann A-G in *Bostock* [1994] ECR I-955, fn. 12.

46 Joined Cases 46/87 and 227/88 *Hoechst v Commission* [1989] ECR 2859. The Court took no account of the earlier decision of the European Court of Human Rights in *Chappell* (1989) Series A, Vol. 52. See also the later decision in *Niemietz* (1992) Series A Vol. 251-B.

47 Case 374/87 *Orkem v Commission* [1989] ECR 3283.

48 *Funke* (1993) Series A Vol. 256-A. The Court of First Instance however continued to rely upon the *Orkem* test, without reference to *Funke* – to which they had been referred by the applicants – in Joined Cases T-305/94 *LVM and others v Commission* ("PVC II"), Judgment of 20 April 1999, paragraphs 443-459.

49 Case 374/87 *Orkem v Commission* [1989] ECR 3283, Opinion at paragraph 140.

more serious conflict between the Community and Council of Europe systems: conflict not over the interpretation of specific Convention provisions, but at the level of jurisdiction and powers.

I had my first hint of this when sitting in the Luxembourg court during the oral hearing of Opinion 2/94:[50] the case which decided that for the moment at least, the Community lacks the necessary competence to accede to the European Convention of Human Rights. As the afternoon wore on, one of the Advocates General interrupted the Commission's lawyer with a question that went more or less as follows: "Are you really saying that we should surrender the ultimate power over our own Treaty to an international court sitting in Strasbourg – some of whose members are not even nationals of Member States of the Community?" The question sounded familiar: I had once heard something like it in a small county court in the Midlands, when witnessing an attempt to persuade one of the older breed of Circuit Judges to give effect to a decision of that "foreign" court in Luxembourg.

There has however not, so far, been any open rebellion in Luxembourg against the authority of Strasbourg. Partly, no doubt, that is because the Community has not acceded to the Convention, and currently shows no signs of having the political will to do it. It therefore follows the Convention because it wishes to, or because the courts of its Member States expect it to, and not because it is in a subordinate relationship with the Court of Human Rights. But the relatively peaceful co-existence that has characterised relations between the two courts must owe something, also, to the tact with which the European Court of Human Rights has dealt with the Community. There are signs, as will be seen later on, that this tact may be wearing rather thin.

Until last year there were two categories of case in which the European Community had been involved in Strasbourg.

The first category is complaints brought in relation to *acts of the Community*, whether against the Community itself or its Member States. Such complaints are routinely rejected as inadmissible.[51] In *Dufay*, a decision of 1989 concerning the redundancy of a European Parliament employee, the Commission left open the question of whether a Community act could engage the responsibility of the Member States. The application was rejected on the basis that the applicant had failed to exhaust the remedies available to him in the Community legal system – remedies which would have included the opportunity to plead a breach of his fundamental rights in the Community's own courts.

The second category of case is where complaints are brought in relation to *acts of the Member States* which are taken in pursuance of Community obligations. Here, the classic case is *M & Co. v Germany*.[52] The company, having

---

50 [1996] ECR I-1759.

51 See e.g. Application No. 8030/77 *CFDT v European Communities and their Member States* 13 DR 231; Application No. 13539/88 *Dufay v European Communities and their Member States* (Decision of 19 January 1988).

52 Application No. 13258/87; 64 DR 138.

failed to overturn a Commission competition decision addressed to it, was faced with enforcement in Germany of the judgment of the European Court of Justice. It challenged the warrant of execution issued by the German authorities on the basis that the underlying judgment of the Luxembourg Court violated Article 6 of the Convention. The application was declared inadmissible.[53]

This category of cases shows the Court of Human Rights balancing two important principles. On the one hand, it adheres to the principle of public international law whereby:

> "if a State contracts treaty obligations and subsequently concludes another international agreement which disables it from performing its obligations under the first treaty it will be answerable for any resulting breach of its obligations under the earlier Treaty."[54]

On the other hand, it recognises that a Member State cannot be prohibited from transferring powers to international organisations; and that it would be contrary to the very idea of such a transfer if the Strasbourg institutions were to examine in every case whether the decision of the international organisation which gave rise to the national action was in itself Convention-compliant.

Conflict between these two principles has been averted by what the Commission described in *M & Co.* as:

> "the generally accepted principle that the Convention did not apply to the European Communities and would become binding for them only if they formally adhered to it".[55]

The basis for this self-denying ordinance on the part of the Strasbourg institutions was its finding that the legal system of the European Communities not only secured fundamental rights but also provided for control of their observance. In other words, rather like the German Federal Constitutional Court in its *Solange II* judgment,[56] the Council of Europe institutions were prepared to exempt the Community from their scrutiny for as long – but only for as long – as the Court of Justice gave effective protection to basic rights.

That position was effectively confirmed by the old Court of Human Rights in its *Pafitis* judgment of 1998.[57] The case concerned the Article 6 requirement of trial within a reasonable time. The applicant's case had been delayed for 5 ½ years in the Supreme Administrative Court of Greece, and for one year – in-

53 The "safe haven" for national action taken in pursuance of Community obligations is, however, not limitless. In *Cantoni v France* (15 November 1996) RJD 1996-V, No. 20, the fact that a domestic provision was based almost word for word on a Community directive was held not to remove it from the ambit of Article 7 of the Convention.

54 No. 235/56, Dec. 10.6.1958, Yearbook 2 p. 256 (300), cited in *M & Co. v Germany* 64 DR 138 (1990).

55 64 DR 138 at 141.

56 73 BVerfGE 339 (1986): for the evolution of the German case law see J. Kokott, "Report on Germany" in *The European Courts and National Courts*, Slaughter, Sweet & Weiler eds., (1998), 77.

57 RJD 1998-I, No. 66.

triguingly – by a strike on the part of members of the Athens Bar. A further delay of 2 years 8 months was caused by a reference to the European Court under the old Article 177, now Art. 234. The Strasbourg Court commented that the delay caused by the reference appeared "relatively long" – a notable example of the pot calling the kettle black – but did not take that period into account, on the basis that to do so would adversely affect the system of references for a preliminary ruling, and work against the aim pursued by Article 177 (new 234).[58]

The deference of Strasbourg towards the Community ended with the old century in *Matthews v UK,*[59] one of the first cases to be heard by the new European Court of Human Rights as reconstituted by the 11th Protocol to the Convention. The facts could scarcely have been less attractive to a court entrusted with the protection of human rights. Gibraltar, for whose external relations the United Kingdom is responsible, is for relevant purposes a part of the European Union. The question arose, back in 1976, of how, if at all, its people should participate in direct elections to the European Assembly as it was then known, the European Parliament as it has now become. With only 30,000 inhabitants, the Government considered that Gibraltar was too small to make up a Euro-constituency on its own. Equally, it was thought undesirable to lump Gibraltar in with a mainland constituency, not least because the political parties and the political issues in Gibraltar are quite different from those in the United Kingdom. The result was that the people of Gibraltar, uniquely among citizens of the European Union, were deprived of the right to vote in European elections.

This was no doubt a pragmatic solution, but one which came to look increasingly unjust as the powers of the European Parliament grew, notably in consequence of the Maastricht Treaty, and its activities came to have more and more influence on the people of Gibraltar.

The applicant was a young Gibraltarian who had asked for the right to vote and been refused. Article 3 of Protocol 1 to the Convention guarantees the free expression of the people in their choice of the legislature. Once she had established that the European Parliament was a legislature for the purposes of that Article – as she did in the Court, though not in the Commission – it was difficult to see why she should not be given the vote.

The United Kingdom's defence, for which I must take some responsibility, was the familiar one, in other contexts, of blaming the European Community. The exclusion of Gibraltar from the franchise may have been a British idea, but it was enshrined in the 1976 Act on Direct Elections – a provision which, as was common ground, had the status of a Treaty in the Community legal order. The Act was adopted pursuant to specific requirements in the Community's founding Treaties, and was an integral part of what the Court of Justice has referred to as "the constitutional charter of a Community based on the rule of law".[60] It concerned elections to an assembly which, as the French *Conseil Constitutionnel*

58 Paragraph 95.
59 Judgment of 18 February 1999.
60 Opinion 1/91[1991] ECR I-6097, p. 6102 at para 21.

had held, did not belong to the institutional order of the Member States, and did not participate in the exercise of national sovereignty.[61] Finally, and most importantly, the exclusion of Gibraltar could be removed only by proposal of the Parliament itself, consented to by all 15 Member States. There was therefore nothing the Government could do, on its own, to extend the franchise to Gibraltar. The defect which the applicant had identified was in the constitution of the European Community, not that of the United Kingdom. The Community had chosen not to accede to the Human Rights Convention. In those circumstances, neither the Community nor the Member States on its behalf could be condemned for a violation of the Convention.

By the time the hearing came round, that argument had a grounding in political reality. Since the Labour victory of 1997 and the introduction of proportional representation for European elections, the Government has wished as a matter of policy to include Gibraltar in the franchise. But it has always been clear that the opposition of Spain will make that impossible to achieve.

The United Kingdom's argument was rejected, by 15 votes to 2. The Court repeated the established principles that acts of the EC as such cannot be challenged before the Strasbourg Court, and that the Convention does not exclude the transfer of competences to international organisations. But it noted also that Member States' responsibility continued even after such a transfer, and could be invoked in the event that the international organisation in question failed to secure the Convention rights.[62] In this case, the fact that a Treaty provision was at stake meant that the Community courts had no jurisdiction to correct a violation of Article 3 of Protocol 1. The fact that the United Kingdom was in no position to reverse the breach complained of was accepted by the Court but treated as irrelevant.[63] The United Kingdom was at fault for entering into international Treaties that made it impossible for it to carry out its prior obligations under the Convention, notably the Maastricht Treaty which by increasing the powers of the European Parliament had turned it into a "legislature" for the purposes of the Convention.

The Court of Human Rights has thus gone further than the German or Danish Supreme Courts in their *Maastricht* decisions, by holding that the Maastricht Treaty, viewed in conjunction with its predecessors, conflicts with one of those fundamental rights which the Community itself, as well as its Member States, purport to give effect. What conclusions should the Community and its Member States draw from this? One possible means of complying with the judgment – which not even the most extreme of Eurosceptics has so far advanced – would be to denounce the Maastricht Treaty. More realistically, one might expect to

---

61 Decision of 30 December 1976; JORF 31.12.76 p. 7651.

62 Judgment, paragraph 32, *supra* note 59.

63 Compare *Drozd and Janousek v France and Spain* (1992) Series A No. 240, establishing that the responsibility of a State will be engaged under the Convention only when that State has a power of effective control over the act complained of: Commission's Report, paragraph 5; Judgment, paragraphs 92-96.

see an amendment to the Act of 1976 that was at the root of the trouble. But no such amendment has yet been made – and it is here that the full extent of the constitutional implications of the *Matthews* judgment become apparent.

The United Kingdom, keen both to comply with the judgment and, now, to extend the franchise to Gibraltar, has proposed the necessary change to the 1976 Act. Spain continues to object. Spain is of course subject to the jurisdiction of the Human Rights Court; and the Court went out of its way to stress that all the Member States, not just the United Kingdom, were responsible.[64] But Spain has available to it an answer to that, grounded not only on political convenience but on constitutional principle. How can the Community or any of its Member States accept the *Matthews* judgment, the argument goes, when it is predicated upon the invalidity of the Community constitution itself – something which the Court of Justice has no competence to decide? That indeed was the line taken by Spain in Opinion 2/94, where – alongside the United Kingdom – it argued that Community accession to the Convention would contravene the Treaty by calling into question the autonomy of the Community legal order and the Court of Justice's monopoly of jurisdiction.[65] Increasingly frustrated by the Spanish position, the United Kingdom has publicly threatened to extend the franchise unilaterally, and without the consent of Spain that the Treaty appears to require.

The interesting question for a constitutional lawyer is: what if the issue comes before the European Court of Justice, as it could quite conceivably do? The Luxembourg Court, as we have seen, feels obliged to follow its Strasbourg counterpart in all things. It is under pressure to do so both from States such as Germany, who acknowledge its authority only for so long as it ensures full protection of human rights, and from Strasbourg itself, whose self-denying ordinance in relation to measures giving effect to Community secondary legislation is predicated upon its Luxembourg counterpart effectively protecting the Convention rights.

But how could the Court of Justice follow the Court of Human Rights down the road that it took in *Matthews*? The Treaty provision in issue appears unambiguous, and on the basis of the Court of Justice's own case-law could not be interpreted against its plain meaning. Equally, the Court of Justice has no power to ignore it or set it aside. The two senior courts of Europe would appear to be on a collision course. The Human Rights Court has declined the chance in *Matthews* to avert a conflict. Perhaps the politicians will succeed in resolving what is currently an intractable problem. But if they do not, it is difficult to see how a collision could be avoided, save by a change in the "top rule" or rule of recognition in the Community, from "the Community has the powers attributed to it in the Treaties" to "the Community has the powers attributed to it in the Treaties, to the extent that those Treaties are compatible with fundamental rights". That would be a shift in the *Grundnorm*, indeed.

---

64 Judgment, paragraph 33.
65 [1994] ECR I-1759, pp. 1780-1782.

It is not only the European Court of Justice but the courts of the Member States that would be affected by such a conflict between the legal order of the Community and that of the Convention. The key provision here is article 307 (ex 234) of the EC Treaty, which states that agreements concluded by one or more Member States and third countries, prior to the accession of the Member States to the Community, shall not be affected by the provisions of the EC Treaty. For most, though not all, of the Member States, Article 307 would allow them to give primacy to the Convention over the law of the Community as it was declared by the Community court. If the showdown ever comes, that Article might serve to concentrate the mind of the Community court. Article 307 suggests that in a battle of norms between Strasbourg and Luxembourg, it is not necessarily Luxembourg that would come off the best.

When the consequences of a conflict between Luxembourg and Strasbourg are so unpredictable and potentially damaging, it is small wonder that the subject of co-operation and co-ordination between the Luxembourg and Strasbourg Courts has been receiving some overdue attention in recent years.

The circulation of judges between the two courts would be a useful practical step, though hardly a complete answer. The same is true of the proposal to create a Chamber of Human Rights to sit in the ECJ.[66] There is much to be said for the Judges of each Court having a greater familiarity with each other's legal systems than perhaps exists at present. An interesting foretaste is provided by the recent decision of the European Court of Human Rights in *Pellegrin v France*,[67] in which the Strasbourg Court looked to an analogy drawn directly and in detail from Community law in order to help resolve the intractable problem of when public service employees have civil rights for the purposes of Article 6.

Both an Advocate-General of the European Court, a Judge of the Court of First Instance and a Commissioner of Human Rights have gone further still, suggesting a system, modelled on Article 234 (formerly 177) of the EC Treaty, of references from Luxembourg to Strasbourg for preliminary rulings on issues of human rights.[68] Within the Community, that system, as operated between national courts and Luxembourg, has proved adept in supplying a degree of central guidance without threatening the jurisdiction of national courts. But in the context of the current demands on the time of both courts, that hardly seems a practical option. Those taking cases to Luxembourg, whether directly or by way of reference from the national court, are already deterred by the period of two years or so that is necessary for their decision. An additional excursion to Strasbourg

66 Proposed by C. Turner, "Human Rights Protection in the European Community: Resolving Conflict and Overlap Between the European Court of Justice and the European Court of Human Rights" (1999) 5 *European Public Law*, 453-470.

67 Judgment of 8 December 1999, paragraphs 37-41, 66.

68 Warner AG in Case 130/75 *Prais v Council* [1976] ECR 1589; K Lenaerts, "Fundamental rights to be included in a Community catalogue" (1991) 16 *European Law Review* 367 at 380; H. Schermers, "The Scales in Balance: National Constitutional Court v Court of Justice" (1990) 27 *Common Market Law Review* 97-105.

could only add further time to the process, with the result that litigants and national courts would be disenchanted, and justice could be denied.

Finally, and intriguingly, there is last year's decision by the European Council – the heads of State and Government of the Community's Member States – to commission its own Charter of Fundamental Rights. In its Decision on Drawing up a Charter, the Member States have specified that the Charter should contain fundamental rights and freedoms and basic procedural rights guaranteed by the European Convention of Human Rights, as well as rights derived from the constitutional traditions common to the Member States and rights established as general principles of Community law.[69] Interestingly, it was also determined that the Charter should contain economic and social rights – the elderly relative in the European attic to whom lip service is paid but with whom meaningful contact is generally avoided by the Member States.

A Drafting Body has been set up. Its first act, in February 2000, was to christen itself a Convention. Each Member State is represented by the Head of State and two Members of Parliament. Representatives of the European Parliament and the Commission also serve on the body, as – in the capacity of observer – do two representatives from the Court of Justice and two from the Council of Europe, including one from the Court of Human Rights. The United Kingdom delegation is led by the former Chairman of the Bar, Lord Goldsmith. A draft is to be prepared in advance of the European Council summit in Paris in December 2000.

It would not be surprising if different Member States and Community institutions turn out to have different reasons for, and expectations of, this German initiative. Indeed some of them may already be experiencing cold feet. The United Kingdom Prime Minister has stated that the Charter:

> "should take the form of a political statement, rather than a legal text to be incorporated into the Treaties".[70]

But as envisaged by the committee of wise persons that promoted the idea, the Charter is intended to protect and promote the human rights of all Community residents, and to provide an integrated framework for what is generally acknowledged to be the fragmented and marginalised nature of the Community's human rights policies. Others have stressed that the acquisition of its own Charter of Fundamental Rights should not be viewed as a replacement for Community accession to the European Convention, but rather as a supplement to it.[71]

It is difficult to resist a comparison between the human rights debate that raged in the United Kingdom during the 1990s and that which is now taking place in the Community. Incorporation of the European Convention into United

69 Presidency conclusions, Cologne European Council, 3 and 4 June 1999, Annex IV.
70 Answer to Written Question of Mr. Mitchell M.P., 30 November 1999.
71 Note for Belgian Parliament prepared by E. Bibosia, O. De Schutter, K. Lenaerts and P. Magnette.

Kingdom law was driven by an unlikely but effective coalition of interests: those who saw it as a way of improving the substantive protection of human rights, and those who saw it rather – in the words of the Government's White Paper – as a way of "bringing rights home". The support of the legal and political establishment owed much to the argument that by giving our own judges the power to apply the Convention, the influence of the foreign judges in Strasbourg would be – though not excluded – at least diminished. Put bluntly, there were votes in ensuring that constitutional human rights protection in the United Kingdom was secured, in the first instance at least, by United Kingdom judges. If unpalatable things need to be said, we would rather hear them from the English courts – or, as we are already doing, from the Court of Session in Scotland – than from an international court with members drawn from 41 states in western Europe, Eastern Europe, Anatolia and the former Soviet Union.

Taken to its extreme, that view translated into a desire to disengage from the Convention system altogether. In a comment inspired by the *Osman* decision on the liability of public authorities, Lord Hoffmann has issued a thinly coded call for the United Kingdom, having brought the Convention home, to remove the right of individual petition to Strasbourg.[72] That suggestion perhaps pays insufficient regard to the importance of setting an example to those new and restored democracies in the east which have themselves been induced by their western neighbours to join the Council of Europe and submit to the jurisdiction of the Strasbourg court. But it is an idea that resonates strongly in many quarters.

Perhaps similar reasons will play their part in persuading the Community that there would – contrary to the Government's view – be merit in giving Treaty status to the Community's own Charter of Fundamental Rights. Obedience to the Convention case law – even without formal accession to the Convention – has been a useful way for the Court of Justice to defuse criticism from national constitutional courts of the failings in human rights protection within the Community, and thus preserve the supremacy of Community law. But once the Court has a Community Charter to apply, negotiated by the Member States themselves and affording protection of at least an equivalent standard to that provided for by the Convention, the necessity of following every twist and turn in the Convention case-law would be much reduced. Perhaps as the Charter takes shape, some European equivalent of Lord Hoffmann will suggest that the references in the Treaties to the European Convention of Human Rights be replaced by references to the European Charter. Rights would be "brought home" from Strasbourg to Luxembourg.

To give Treaty status to a free-standing catalogue of fundamental and other rights would undoubtedly assist those who see the European Union developing into an autonomous federal State on the traditional model, dependent upon the constitutional rights protection neither of the Council of Europe nor of the Member States. It might also have far-reaching implications for the balance of

---

72 (1999) 62 MLR 159.

power within the Union. In particular, a catalogue of fundamental rights could provide a benchmark by which the Court of Justice could examine the constitutionality not only of secondary legislation and action within the scope of Community law, but of subsequent Treaty amendments proposed by the Member States – and perhaps even of existing Treaty provisions.[73] In that event, it would no longer be true to say of the Member States that they are, in the well-known phrase of the German Federal Constitutional Court, "the Masters of the Treaties". The Charter may prove to have a more dramatic effect upon the constitution of the European Union than upon the effectiveness of human rights protection within it.

CONCLUSION

It will be seen that there is no consistency between the courts of the European states, the European Community and the European Convention, as regards what eagles call the hierarchy of norms. Indeed – though one should not overemphasise it – there is a degree of more or less friendly competition between different courts in Europe, not so different from the competition that took place in a different age between the King's Bench and the Common Pleas.

Such competition, though jurisprudentially untidy, is not necessarily a bad thing.[74] It has certainly produced valuable results in terms of human rights protection in the Community, the development of which owes nothing to the original Treaties, and everything to the pressure exerted on the Court of Justice by a combination of national constitutional courts and, more recently, the European Court of Human Rights.

But it seems unlikely that these conflicts and inconsistencies identified will be allowed to go unresolved for ever. The constitution of Europe still has much evolving to do. It is to be hoped that Lord Slynn, with his unrivalled judicial experience in two legal orders, and his enthusiasm for Europe north, south, east and west will play a leading role in that debate.

---

73 Compare Bieber [1993] RMC 343, Cruz Vilaça and Piçarra [1993] CDE 3; T. Harrley, *op.cit.*, p. 146, n. 75.

74 See Neil MacCormick, "Beyond the Sovereign State" (1993) 56 MLR 1.

PART 4

EUROPEAN LAW BEFORE THE NATIONAL COURTS

23

DANISH PRELIMINARY REFERENCES

Ole Due

INTRODUCTION

It was with great pleasure that I received the invitation to contribute to the *Liber Amicorum* for Lord Slynn of Hadley, or, as he is better known to his former colleagues in the EC Court of Justice, Sir Gordon or simply Gordon. During the ten years he served at the Court, he made a great impression on all of us. Many of the opinions which he presented as Advocate General are still important for the present day development of Community Law. Possibly he found it more difficult to adapt himself to the more anonymous role of a judge at the Court, without being able to express his views in a personal opinion, but he greatly contributed to the collective work of the bench. And first of all he was – and is – an eminent and loyal colleague and a wonderful friend.

Gordon has had the opportunity to experience the value of preliminary references both from the perspective of a national judge and from that of the EC Court. This very special feature of Community judicial procedure therefore seems an appropriate topic for an essay in his honour. I shall concentrate on the preliminary references made by Danish courts. There are in fact considerable variations in the use which courts in different Member States make of this procedural instrument, with regard to the frequency of references, the way in which they are drafted and the area of law which they concern. Many of these variations may be explained by differences in the judicial systems of the Member States, by different procedural rules or traditions, or by differences in the material law.

Before addressing the promised topic of this essay, I shall therefore begin by giving a short explanation of the Danish judicial system, then go on to some specific features of Danish judicial procedure and finally touch on some other areas of Danish law which may have an influence on the use of preliminary references by Danish courts.[1]

1 For a more comprehensive review of the Danish judicial system and of Danish law in general, see Dahl, Melchior, Rehoff and Tamm (ed.), *Danish Law in a European Perspective* (GadJura, 1996).

D. O'Keeffe (ed.), Liber Amicorum Slynn 363-375 (2000)

THE DANISH JUDICIAL SYSTEM

The structure of the judicial system is relatively simple. The ordinary courts are organized in a three tier system: City courts, Courts of Appeal/High Courts and a Supreme Court.

The country is divided into about 80 city court districts, many of them held by only one judge dealing with civil as well as criminal cases or by two judges, one for civil cases, the other for criminal procedures. In bigger towns the city court may consist of several judges, often headed by a president. Besides cases between parties, the Danish city courts also handle matters which in other countries are dealt with by notaries or solicitors. For these purposes the judges are assisted by deputy judges who may also deal with police court cases and some civil cases. The deputy judges enjoy practically all the guarantees of independence that the Constitution and the Code of Procedure confer upon judges and most of them will later be nominated as judges. Taking into account the variety of tasks performed by deputy judges, the total number of lawyers hearing civil and criminal cases at the city court level may correspond to 5-600 full time judges, a number which in relation to the population is smaller than in most Member States. Except for a few areas of law in which a specialisation other than legal expertise is considered to be required on the bench, a city court judge or deputy judge sits alone in civil cases. In criminal cases he or she is assisted by two lay judges, except for police court cases and cases where the accused pleads guilty. Juries are not used at this level.

The second tier consists of two courts of appeal, one in Copenhagen and one in Viborg (Jutland), with about sixty and thirty judges respectively. They are divided into chambers of three judges, who in criminal appeal cases are assisted by three lay judges. These courts also function as high courts, i.e. as first instance courts for some civil cases and for the most serious criminal cases in which a jury decides the question of guilt.

The Supreme Court is composed of seventeen justices. Cases are heard by chambers of five or more justices, but they are prepared for the hearing by a body consisting of three justices. It is not a court of cassation but an appellate court for judgments rendered by the two appeal courts and by the Maritime and Commercial Court in Copenhagen, which is the only specialized High Court in Denmark.

There are no administrative courts in Denmark. Disputes between public authorities and citizens are brought before the ordinary courts, but in many fields quasi-judicial boards of appeal are inserted between the normal administrative authorities and the courts. Some of these bodies probably qualify as courts or tribunals in the sense of Article 234 (ex 177) of the EC Treaty, but until now they have not referred preliminary questions to the Court of Justice. Because of the existence of these appeal boards the number of disputes concerning administrative law which reach the ordinary courts is relatively small.

There are a few specialized courts of first instance dealing with cases in specific areas of law. A good example is the Labour Court which, in particular, deals with disputes concerning violations of collective agreements and where the judges are nominated by the Minister of Labour following recommendations from the parties on the labour market. Other industrial disputes are normally settled by a permanent court of arbitration which, in spite of its denomination, has the character of a tribunal.[2]

In principle a case may only be tried at two instances. Further appeal requires special permission from a board consisting of judges, a practising lawyer and a professor in law. In civil cases the appellate courts, including the Supreme Court, may try questions of fact as well as questions of law and new evidence may be produced.

The vast majority of cases, civil as well as criminal, are heard by the city courts. However, the appeal courts act as high courts in certain types of cases, e.g. cases against the central State authorities. Of special interest is a rule, inserted in the Code of Procedure after accession to the Communities, according to which a city court, on the request of one of the parties, may transfer a civil case concerning Community law to the High Court.

Some specific features of Danish judicial procedures

In general, the Danish procedure is closer to that of the Common Law countries than it is to the typical continental procedure. By far the greatest weight is placed on the oral hearing.

In criminal cases the investigation is the task of the police or other prosecuting authorities. The courts are addressed only if coercive measures against the defendant are requested.

In civil cases the parties are the masters of the litigation and must produce both the evidence and the legal arguments. The decision of the court cannot go beyond the claims of the parties and the evidence produced. However, the judge may put questions both to the parties and to witnesses. The judge may also draw the attention of the parties to possible legal arguments in order to clarify their positions and he must apply mandatory rules of law in order to avoid wrong decisions. This is of particular importance in relation to rules of Community law. In lower courts especially, only scant attention is paid to strict observance of procedural formalities and it is a common joke among practising lawyers that invoking the Code of Procedure amounts to unfair practice.

It is in conformity with this relaxed view on procedural formalities that a practice of conciliation has developed – without any foundation in the Code of Procedure. Both in the city courts and in the two courts of appeal, the court often tries to conciliate between the parties not only during the preparatory stage, but also following the closure of the oral hearing. If the judges are able to form an opinion on the dispute immediately after hearing the evidence and the pleadings,

---

2 This character has been recognized by the Court of Justice in Case 109/88, *Danfoss*, [1989] ECR 3199.

they may ask the parties whether they would be interested in hearing the conclusion of the court and the grounds for this conclusion – in general on the understanding that the orally presented opinion would also form the conclusion of a written judgment. The parties are of course free to ask for such a judgment either before or after hearing the oral presentation of the opinion of the court. In the latter case, a party which is considering an appeal will certainly do so. But in about one third of cases, the parties accept the opinion as a settlement which is then entered in the records of the court and becomes enforceable as a judgment but is not published in the Court Reports. This practice, together with the many settlements entered into by the parties during the preparatory stage of the litigation, explains how a large volume of civil litigation can be dealt with by the relatively small number of Danish judges.

In all collegiate courts each judge is free to express his views in a dissenting or concurring opinion which is published as a part of the judgment with an indication of the name of the judge. This faculty is often used by the justices of the Supreme Court, more rarely by the appeal court/high court judges. Therefore, dissenting opinions in judgments from one of these courts will often be understood as an invitation to bring the case before the Supreme Court by an appeal or by requesting leave to appeal.

Although judgments of the Supreme Court deciding legal problems of general importance carry a considerable weight when similar cases are heard by lower courts, precedents have no binding effect. Legal certainty should in principle be created by the legislator and Danish courts have a tendency to concentrate their judgments on the specific circumstances of the case and not decide questions of principle if it can be avoided. This tendency also leads to relatively brief judgments giving rather succinct grounds for the result which the judges, normally in agreement with the parties, consider the most important part. In these respects – just as in relation to procedural formalities – the attitude of Danish judges is pragmatic.

OTHER RELEVANT FEATURES OF DANISH LAW

The Danish *Constitution* contains no explicit rule on the effect in Denmark of international agreements ratified by Denmark, but it is a legal tradition of long standing that only Danish authorities can adopt acts having direct effect within the country, at least if the acts impose obligations on natural or legal persons. Thus, Denmark adheres to the so-called dualist doctrine concerning the relationship between national law and rules of international law. To become directly applicable in Denmark such rules, as well as acts adopted by international organizations, must be transformed into Danish law by an act adopted by Danish authorities pursuant to Danish constitutional law. This may be done by an act simply incorporating the international rules as they stand. For instance, the European Convention on the Protection of Human Rights has been transformed in this way. But rules thus transformed have no higher rank within the hierarchy of Danish norms than the act transforming them.

International rules not transformed into Danish law may nevertheless influence the way in which Danish law is applied. Danish courts will normally try to avoid interpreting Danish law in a manner that may conflict with the international obligations of Denmark, even if the wording of the Danish rules can hardly be understood in conformity with these obligations.

By these means Denmark has avoided the strict consequences of its dualist approach to international law. This structure, however, was not sufficient to implement Community law correctly. The effect of Community rules and acts is a question of interpretation of Community law to be finally decided by the Court of Justice, not by national legislators or national courts.

Therefore the latest modification of the Danish Constitution in 1953 included the insertion of a new section 20 according to which powers vested in the Danish authorities under the Constitution may "to such an extent as shall be provided by statute" be delegated to international authorities set up by mutual agreement with other States for the promotion of international rules of law and cooperation. The adoption of such a statute requires either a majority of five-sixths in the Parliament or a simple majority followed by the direct approval of the electorate in a referendum. The 1972 statute on Danish accession to the Communities as well as the later amendments implementing the modifications in the treaty system all provides that powers vested in Danish authorities under the Constitution may "to the extent specified in the treaties" be exercised by the institutions of the European Communities.

Eurosceptics found this simple reference to the treaties to be contrary to the Constitution. The statute should itself specify the powers delegated and, in particular, not refer to open-ended authorizations like Article 235 (now Article 308) of the EC Treaty. However, according to long-standing case law, judicial review of acts of Parliament required that the act was of immediate and specific interest to the applicant and it wasn't until 1996 that the Supreme Court admitted an action brought by twelve citizens against the Danish Prime Minister claiming the statute implementing the Treaty on European Union to be unconstitutional.[3] In its final judgment on the merits of this case, the Supreme Court dismissed the claim as unfounded.[4] In particular, the Supreme Court found that the extent of powers delegated pursuant to section 20 of the Constitution may be defined by reference to the powers conferred on the international authority by a treaty, if the treaty itself specifies these powers. In principle this was the case with the EC Treaty which is based on a principle of conferred powers. As to Article 235, the Supreme Court quoted points 29 and 30 in the Opinion of the Court of Justice considering the eventuality of an accession by the Communities to the European

3 Ugeskrift for Retsvæsen (hereafter: UfR) 1996 p. 1300.

4 UfR 1998 p. 800. For a thorough discussion of this judgment, see the contribution to this book by Professor Hjalte Rasmussen.

Convention on the Protection of Human Rights.[5] Interpreted in the way stated in these points, Article 235 was also found to be in conformity with section 20 of the Constitution. But the Supreme Court made an important reservation: Under Danish constitutional law, Community acts draw their direct effect in Denmark from the delegation of powers made by Danish statutes pursuant to section 20 of the Constitution. Therefore, a Danish court cannot apply such acts if they go beyond the powers delegated by the statutes or trespass on the limits for delegation of powers under the Constitution, and Danish courts cannot be deprived of their right to review Community acts in those respects. However, before a Danish court may declare such an act inapplicable in Denmark, it must obtain a preliminary decision from the EC Court of Justice on the validity of the act according to Community law and, in the view of the Supreme Court, the Danish court can normally follow the ruling of the Court of Justice when deciding whether the act is within the limits of the delegation of powers.

Even if this reservation clearly contradicts the case law of the Court of Justice according to which Community law is an autonomous legal system independent of the constitutional systems of the Member States, the judgment of the Supreme Court is in fact in line with the general tendency of Danish courts to show *judicial restraint when reviewing the constitutionality of acts of Parliament.* The same *restraint* may, although to a lesser extent, be seen *in the case law on the legality of administrative acts* which, as it happens, do not often come before the courts because of the many administrative appeal boards.

Another area of Danish law which may be of interest in relation to the topic of this essay is *labour law*. Since 1899, when a general conflict between workers and employers was ended by the conclusion of a basic agreement between the Confederation of Trade Unions and the Danish Employers' Confederation, sometimes referred to as the "Constitution for the Labour Market", collective agreements have been the major source of law within the labour market. The basic agreement recognized the right of the workers to unionize and the legally binding effect of collective agreements not only between the organizations but also between workers and employers who are members. The use of collective actions was regulated and a judicial system set up to solve disputes between the organizations. At the same time, the workers recognized the employers' discretionary power to recruit and dismiss workers and their right to direct and allocate the work – rights which have ensured a considerable mobility on the Danish labour market, the effects of which have later been alleviated by relatively high unemployment benefits. This system has lead to unionization of the great majority both of wage earners and of employers. On the other hand the individual protection of wage earners who are not members of a trade union or who cannot persuade their union to take action on their behalf is weaker than in countries where the labour market is essentially regulated by statutory instruments and where disputes are normally brought before the ordinary courts.

---

5 Opinion 2/94, [1996] ECR I-1759.

At the time when Denmark joined the Communities, the main organizations in the labour market were concerned that the tendency within the EC to regulate the rights of wage earners by way of directives, intended to confer rights on the individual, would threaten their position. However, this attitude is slowly changing, most unions having seen an advantage in having a number of problems removed from collective bargaining.

The relatively high level of mobility on the Danish labour market and the considerable freedom for the participants in this market to regulate their mutual relations and those of their members by collective agreements must be seen against the background of the comprehensive *social welfare system* for the whole population, which is generally financed by tax revenue. The general social security schemes for old age pensions, pensions in case of incapacity to work and family allowances are not dependent on the attachment of the person to the labour market but cover all Danish nationals resident in Denmark, conditions from which derogations are made for EU citizens by EC regulations and for citizens in other Nordic countries by mutual agreements. Even special insurance schemes which are linked to the labour market, like cash benefits in case of unemployment or sickness, are to a large extent co-financed by the State. The administration both of the general social security schemes and of social assistance and care are normally left to the municipal authorities, but a system of administrative appeal boards deals with the complaints which rarely arrive before the courts.

The strain which the funding of this comprehensive social security system puts on the public finances presupposes a high level of *taxation*. Income taxation, as well as VAT, which is levied at a flat rate of 25 % with a minimum of exemptions, are among the highest in the world. The registration tax for motor vehicles would appear prohibitive to most foreigners – but the number of private cars proves the opposite. The inventiveness of Danish governments when it comes to finding goods and services on which taxes could be imposed is legendary. So is, of course, the ability of the citizens to find loopholes in the tax legislation which, also for that reason, becomes more and more complicated. In spite of a number of administrative or quasi-judicial appeal boards in this area, a relatively large number of tax disputes find their way to the ordinary courts.

DANISH PRELIMINARY REFERENCES 1973-98

With this background it is possible to explain the development and many of the peculiarities of Danish references.

Up to January 1, 1999 Danish courts had made 78 references to the Court of Justice which had given 59 rulings covering 62 of these references. The number of references conceals very few overlapping or repetitive questions. This is probably due to the fact that the great majority of references came from the two appeal courts and from the Copenhagen Maritime and Commercial Court, and that each of these courts is able to keep itself informed of the Community law problems decided by or pending before the other two courts.

It took three years from the Danish accession before the first reference arrived at the registry of the Court of Justice, and during the seventies only a trickle of Danish references – seven in all – found its way to this court. However, this was not very different from what happened in the two other new Member States, the United Kingdom and Ireland. In all three countries the courts were unaccustomed to such a procedural instrument and judges, as well as counsels, had little knowledge of Community law.

In Denmark, the situation changed at the beginning of the eighties and the number of references rose during the following years to the present level of 5-8 annual references. In relation to the number of inhabitants, this places Danmark above the average number of references from the Member States. Probably this has something to do with the teaching of Community law as well as with the judicial system. The Danish law schools included obligatory courses in Community law in their curriculum many years ago and post-university courses in this law for advocates and judges have been abundant since the Danish accession to the Communities. The relatively small number of judges in Denmark means that a majority of them have now taken part in one of the meetings to which the Court of Justice invites national judges twice a year. Finally, the fact that nearly all court cases are handled by the ordinary courts has the consequence that these courts must be prepared to hear cases in which Community law issues are decisive and where it may be necessary to refer preliminary questions to the Court of Justice.

In the rest of this essay I shall concentrate on the references on which the Court of Justice had ruled before January 1, 1999. Of these cases 13 were referred by the Supreme Court, 26 by the Eastern Court of Appeal in Copenhagen (which in 22 cases acted in its capacity as High Court), 4 by the Western Court of Appeal in Viborg (acting as High Court in one of the cases), 8 from the Maritime and Commercial Court in Copenhagen, 3 from the City Court of Copenhagen, 3 from city court criminal judges and 2 from city court civil judges outside Copenhagen, 1 from the Labour Court and 2 from the permanent court of arbitration for industrial disputes.

This seems to indicate a difference in the handling of Community law issues in the two courts of appeal. However, 15 of the references from the Eastern Court of Appeal concerned actions brought against central State authorities whose seats are in Copenhagen. According to the Code of Procedure these cases had to be brought before this court in its capacity as High Court and they were of a type which often necessitates a reference in order to enable the national court to decide whether a rule of national law should be set aside as being contrary to Community law.

Compared with references from courts in other Member States the amount of references introduced by the Supreme Court is rather high, just as the amount coming from civil judges of first instance outside Copenhagen is small. The small number of city court references in civil cases may be explained as a consequence of the rule in the Code of Procedure permitting the judge, at the request of one of the parties, to transfer a case concerning Community law to the High Court. Seen together with the high number of references from the Supreme Court and the fact that the two courts of appeal have made seven of their references in their capacity as appellate courts there is, however, a reasonably good case for concluding that Danish judges of first instance have a tendency to leave preliminary references to possible appeal proceedings. Their reticence may have something to do with the general position of the parties in the Danish civil procedure as masters of the litigation. When the parties do not agree on the desirability of a reference, the judge of first instance may well hesitate to delay his decision a couple of years when knowing that, if he does not refer, an appellate court will have to refer the question if it finds an answer necessary in order to decide the appeal. This reticence is understandable and probably saves the Court of Justice from a certain number of useless questions. But it is of course deplorable when a Danish citizen, residing and working in Germany, whose Mercedes registered in Germany had been seized by the Danish customs authorities, because he used it when visiting his girlfriend north of the Danish-German border, had to go from the City Court to the Appeal Court and, after leave to appeal, to the Supreme Court in order to obtain the reference of a question the answer to which finally made the authorities release his car after several years of judicial fighting.[6] At the Court of Justice the case was referred to as "the case on the free movement of lovers"

Many references include a number of questions which may concern different areas of Community law. An examination of the questions reveals a considerable variation in this respect. Within the EC Treaty itself references have concerned the general prohibition of discrimination on the basis of nationality in Article 6, now Article 12 (1 reference), the prohibition of customs duties and charges having equivalent effect in Articles 9-16, now Articles 23-27 (6 references), the prohibition of quantitative restrictions in Articles 30-36, now Articles 28-30 (6 references), the rules on agriculture in Articles 38-47, now Articles 32-38 (2 references), the rules on competition applying to undertakings in Articles 85 and 86, now Articles 81 and 82 (5 references), the prohibition of discriminatory or protectionist internal taxation in Article 95, now Article 90 (9 references), the requirement of equal pay for male and female workers in Article 119, now Article 141 (3 references) and the exemption of Community officials from national taxes on their salaries in the Protocol on privileges and immunities (1 reference).

Danish courts have put questions to the Court of Justice on the general principles for reimbursement of taxes levied in violation of Community law (6 references), on the liability of Member States for loss caused by their failure to apply Community law (1 reference), on the relationship between EC regulations on fisheries and the rules of international law (1 reference), on the possibility of a Member State to plead a set-off against Community agricultural subsidies (1

6 Case 297/89, *Ryborg*, [1991] ECR I-1943.

reference), and conversely on its right not to reclaim Community subsidies unlawfully paid (1 reference).

Altogether 11 references asked questions on the interpretation of regulations. Five of these concerned agriculture and three fisheries. No fewer than 27 references concerned the interpretation of directives; two of them also questioned the validity of the directive. The directives which caused the greatest number of questions were those on the protection of workers in the cases of transfer of undertakings (seven references) and of collective redundancy (three references), the directives on equal pay and equal treatment of men and women (four references) and the VAT directives (also four references).

In some respects this pattern differs from the ones found in other Member States. It is often possible to explain these differences by special features in Danish law and social culture as described in the first part of this essay.

The many references within the area of labour law (16 in all) shows, on the one hand, that the parties in the labour market, and especially the trade unions, have become well aware of the possibility of invoking Community rules in this field, and on the other, that Danish courts are unaccustomed to finding the solution to industrial disputes in legislative instruments instead of in collective agreements and therefore have difficulties in interpreting the rules. In particular, this is true in relation to rules concerning the protection of workers against dismissal, where Danish courts account for a major part of the references made to the Court of Justice. In this respect the Danish labour market has been characterized by a considerable freedom for the employer.

The many questions concerning problems of taxation (26) may to a great extent be explained by the high level of taxation in Denmark and the inventiveness of the Danish legislator in this field. This conclusion is reinforced by the fact that, of the 22 references which at least in part intended to enable the Danish court to evaluate the compatibility of a Danish act with the Community rules, no fewer than 15 concerned the Danish tax legislation.

That none of the Danish references concerned the complicated Community rules on the coordination of the social security systems in the Member States may, in part, be explained by the fact that social security disputes rarely reach the Danish courts. Another reason which may also explain the absence of references concerning the free movement of persons is the fact that the great majority of migrant workers in Denmark are nationals of third countries .

As already mentioned 22 references intended, at least in part, to inform the Danish judge on the compatibility, with Community law, of the Danish act which in principle was applicable in the main proceedings. In 11 of these cases the Danish court, having received the answer to its questions, could base its decision on the Danish act, while in the other half of the cases it had to set aside this act. It is interesting to compare these statistics with the number of direct actions brought by the Commission against Denmark for having failed to fulfil its obligations. In the same period there were 15 judgments in such cases and the Court followed the Commission, at least essentially, in 9 of them. Even though some of these judgments were rendered at the same time as the ruling on a preliminary question concerning the same problem, this comparison shows the importance of the preliminary references as a supplement to the direct actions – in particular as the ruling of a national court on the basis of an answer to a preliminary question may well have a more immediate effect than the judgment in a direct action before the Court of Justice.

In connection with their references concerning the interpretation of Treaty articles and of provisions in directives, Danish courts normally have not put questions to the Court of Justice on the direct effect of such rules. Probably they have found it more natural to find the solution by an interpretation of Danish law in the light of Community law, thus following the traditions of Danish courts when trying to make Danish law conform to Denmark's obligations under international law. Although few Danish judgments expressly point to the supremacy of Community law, this principle does not seem to have created problems for Danish judges so long as the cases only concerned Danish legislative or administrative acts.

Only in two of the references has a Danish court asked a question on the validity of a Community act. In none of the cases has the Court of Justice found the act invalid. This reticence of Danish courts may well be connected to their judicial restraint when reviewing the legality of Danish administrative acts and, in particular, the constitutionality of acts of Parliament. In no cases have Danish courts questioned the validity of a Community act in relation to a fundamental right or a general principle of law. This may also be due to the modest number of fundamental rights embodied in the Danish Constitution. The recent incorporation into Danish law of the European Convention on the Protection of Human Rights, combined with the fact that the Court of Justice applies the rights embodied in this convention, as interpreted by the Strasbourg Court, when reviewing the legality of Community acts, may change the attitude of Danish courts. So may the recent judgment of the Supreme Court which reserved the right of Danish courts to try questions as to whether a Community act exceeds the limits for the powers delegated to the Community institutions by the statutes adopted pursuant to section 20 of the Danish Constitution. This judgment may give rise to references to the Court of Justice questioning the validity under Community law of acts both in relation to the Treaty rules on the competences of the institution which has adopted the act and to fundamental rights.

An examination of the semi-official Danish Court Reports[7] (which contains all Supreme Court judgments and a considerable part of the final judgments from the two appeal courts and the Maritime and Commercial Court of Copenhagen) does not seem to reveal cases where Danish courts of last instance have clearly violated their obligation to refer questions to the Court of Justice. In Danish legal literature there has been a certain tendency to criticize the courts for being too reticent in this respect. In particular, it has been regretted that no preliminary questions were asked in the many cases on reimbursement of the very considerable amounts which had been levied before the Court of Justice

7 Ugeskrift for Retsvæsen.

found the so-called AMBI tax contrary to Article 33 in the sixth VAT directive.[8] However, the Danish courts found sufficient elements of interpretation concerning the obligation to reimburse taxes levied in violation of Community law in the earlier case-law of the Court of Justice. In these cases, as in a number of others, they simply drew a reasonable line between interpretation of Community law, which is the task of the Court of Justice, and application of Community law, as already interpreted by this court, which is the role of the national court. Whether their application was correct, is another problem.

It is also difficult to find references from Danish courts which were clearly unnecessary – maybe with the exception of the anecdotal case of the prohibition on the importation of bees to the small island of Læsoe, a prohibition which had been introduced in order to protect the very special species of brown bees that had been preserved on the island because of its isolated geographical situation and which was clearly justified in order to maintain biodiversity.[9]

The Danish court and the parties concerned will always discuss whether to make a reference and the drafting of the decision to refer, and, in particular in civil cases, the court will often leave it to the parties to agree on the text whenever possible, although of course the court will reserve the final decision for itself. The influence of the parties can often be seen in the text of the reference, which may contain a number of supplementary questions on the importance, for the ruling on the main question, of different facts or legal arguments advanced by one or the other party. This may complicate the proceedings before the Court of Justice which, for that reason, prefers that the facts are established and that pure problems of national law are decided before the reference is made.[10] However, the Danish procedural rules and traditions are not well suited for this purpose, unless the parties are in complete agreement on these points. If they are not, it presupposes an interlocutory judgment after a special oral hearing. This is time-consuming but possible in other courts than the Supreme Court, in which the small composition of three justices preparing the case has no jurisdiction to make a ruling.

In the confusion of the first years after accession we find a few preliminary questions of the type "Do any provisions of the EEC Treaty or of acts adopted in pursuance thereof prevent the application of the Danish statutes on [...] in the present case?".[11] Since that time, Danish courts have become accustomed to the technique of drafting preliminary questions and, in general, the questions are precise and the decision includes a full explanation of their context and the reasons for asking them.

I am not aware of any case in which a Danish court has not followed the ruling of the Court of Justice, unless the main proceedings afterwards have

8 Case C-234/91, *Commission v. Denmark*, [1993] ECR I-6273.

9 Case C-67/97, *Ditle v. Bluhme*, [1998] ECR I-8033.

10 See for instance joined Cases 36 and 71/80, *Irish Creamery*, [1981] ECR 735.

11 See for instance the first question asked by the Suprene Court, Case 58/80, *Dansk Supermarked v. Imerco*, [1981] ECR 181.

shown that the case could be decided on other grounds. In cases where no question has been asked, it is more and more common to see references to the case-law of the Court of Justice, although there is no tradition for references to earlier Danish case-law. Rulings of the Court of Justice have even influenced Danish law outside the scope of application of Community law. An example can be found in the case-law of the Supreme Court. Until recently the Danish code of procedure was generally understood to the effect that no court could issue an interim order in the form of an injunction to suspend the application of a measure adopted by an authority in its official capacity. However, in two cases where the applicants challenged the compatibility of such measures with Community law, one case even concerning the construction of the bridge between Denmark and Sweden, decided by act of Parliament, the Supreme Court, referring to the judgment of the Court of Justice in the *Factortame* case,[12] ruled that such orders could be issued under exceptional circumstances – without in any way limiting this possibility for cases concerning Community law.[13]

CONCLUSION

It can safely be concluded that the cooperation between Danish courts and the Court of Justice under the system of preliminary references has functioned smoothly. The Danish courts have kept to the division of tasks provided for in the Treaty, in their decisions in the main proceedings they have invariably followed the interpretation given by the Court of Justice and they have until now avoided the pitfalls which may be found in the difference between Danish constitutional law and the principles stated by the Court of Justice as to the effects of Community law within the legal systems of the Member States. The only dark cloud on the horizon is the reservation in the recent judgment of the Supreme Court on the constitutionality of Denmark's implementation of the Treaty on European Union. The traditional pragmatic attitude of Danish courts may, however, prove to offer the best security against that gathering storm.

12 Case C-213/89, [1990] ECR I-2433.
13 UfR 1994 p. 823 and UfR 1995 p. 634.

24

CONFRONTATION OR PEACEFUL CO-EXISTENCE? ON THE DANISH SUPREME COURT'S MAASTRICHT RATIFICATION JUDGMENT

Hjalte Rasmussen

I INTRODUCTION

It was an honour for me to be asked to contribute to the *Liber Amicorum* for Lord Slynn of Hadley irrespective of the fact that I do not know him very well personally. In fact, I have met him only rarely, but I retain very clear and pleasant memories of those occasional instances where I have profited at first hand from his always challenging and inspiring company; be this on a conference panel with him and other distinguished and learned colleagues; at the occasion of a tête-à-tête exchange of views over some jurisprudence of the European Court; or at a lunch or dinner table. In sum, it was with the greatest pleasure that I accepted an invitation to put down the following ideas on paper in order to honour Lord Slynn of Hadley.

The editors of the *Liber Amicorum* invited me to write about the Danish Supreme Court's ruling in the *Maastricht Ratification Case* (hereinafter also: *The 1998 Maastricht Ruling*).[1] Accepting, as I said, the invitation without hesitation, I must admit that it soon became clear to me that the road to meeting this new commitment was not the pastoral thoroughfare I initially took it for. One of the reasons was that Professor Ole Due of the Law Faculty of the University of Copenhagen and former President of the European Court of Justice, had already finished writing an article about the judgment and was in the process of publishing it in a *Liber Amicorum* for Professor Michel Waelbroeck. Ole Due's article not only says almost everything worth knowing about the Supreme Court's ruling; the article also reproduces *in extenso* all the important parts of the judgment.[2] Against this background, I do not have very much new to say. I do enjoy

1 The ruling was handed down on April 6, 1998; it is recorded in *Ugeskrift for Retsvæsen*, a weekly law report: UfR 1998.800 H. I refer in what follows to this ruling as 'The Case' or 'The Maastricht Case' or 'The 1998 Ruling'. The case dealt with *Lov nr. 281 af 28. april, 1993, Lovtidende 1993, ss. 1157*, a parliamentary statute adopted following the final yes-vote at the 1993 referendum on the ratification of the Maastricht Treaty.

2 The Danish ratification of the Maastricht Treaty before the Danish Supreme Court in *Mélanges en hommage à Michel Waelbroeck*, (Bruylant, Bruxelles, 1999); an unofficial

D. O'Keeffe (ed.), Liber Amicorum Slynn 377-390 (2000)

the advantage, however, that the following pages are written almost a year after Professor Due finished his article. Thus, I may profit both from his and others' learned analyses[3] and from a body of scholarship which has emerged since then.

I will first present, in brief, this article's theoretical framework (II). It centres on the competition for primacy between the Community's legal order – as personalised by the European Court – and the Member States' legal systems, in this article epitomized by the Danish Supreme Court. Next, I present briefly the Maastricht ratification litigation, placing it in its Danish constitutional framework (III). The article then comments on the Supreme Court's *1998 Maastricht Ruling*. These comments focus on what I consider to be the judgment's internationally most important pronouncements (IV-V). My closing remarks are about the potential for 'Confrontation or Peaceful Co-existence' between the legal systems of the Community and those of Member States (VI).

II The Legal Theoretical Framework

During the first 25 years or so of the EC Treaty, a recurrent theme of numerous meetings of specialists in Community law was this: how long will it take before the Member States acknowledge that they have to accept unconditionally the supremacy of Community law over their own constitutions? The theoretical assumption underlying this question was the European Court of Justice's conception of the nature of Community law and of its relationship to national law.[4] Community law was, in this conception, a legal order *sui generis*. The Court[5] and its judges[6] contended that the norms of this order derived their validity exclusively from the order's own sources of law, the peak of which was the Treaty. In this judicial view, the nature of Community law resulted from a permanent, irrevocable transfer of sovereignty from the Member States to the institutions of the Community and not only a limitation of their sovereignty or a simple transfer of limited competencies.[7] To make this sound more persuasive, the Court, in

translation of the judgment is available on the internet address: www.um.dk/udenrigspolitik/europa/domeng.

3 Harck, Sten and Henrik Palmer Olsen, 'Decision Concerning the Maastricht Treaty', *The American Journal of International Law*, vol.93, No. 1, 1999, pp. 209-214; and Henning Koch, Dansk forfatningsret i transnational belysning, *Juristen*, 1999, pp. 372-412; Ole Spiermann, 'Hvad kommer efter tyve? En analyse af Højesteretsdommen i "Grundlovssagen"', UfR 1998.B.325.

4 Hereinafter: the Court or, if necessary, the European Court.
It all began in Case 26/62, *van Gend en Loos* [1963] ECR 1. Another landmark ruling is that in Case 35/76, *Simmenthal* [1976] ECR 1871.

5 Here, *van Gend en Loos* and *Simmenthal* are in issue (both are cited in note 4) but also Case 6/64, *Costa* [1964] ECR 585 and Case 11/70, *Internationale Handelsgesellschaft* [1970] ECR 1125.

6 An outstanding example is P. Pescatore, *The Law of Integration*, (Sijthoff, Leiden, 1974).

7 For this view, see Diarmuid Rossa Phelan, *Revolt or Revolution – The Constitutional*

some of its judgments, expressly referred to the Treaty as the Community's constitutional document, and sometimes even as the Community's supranational, written constitution.[8] It was implied in this legal-ideological construction that the responsibilities of the supreme and/or constitutional courts of the Member States were – at least in the last resort – for Community law to resolve, and not for the national constitutions.[9] Thus, in the logic of the Court's – and in the genuine Kelsenian sense, pure – theory of Community law, once the Court had declared that a Community legal act was valid under Community law, the supreme and/or constitutional courts of the Member States had to acquiesce. In this revolutionary, monist and hierarchical construction of the relationship between Community law and national law, there was no room for national judicial margins of discretion or choice-making. National courts had to comply unconditionally with the Court's rulings, even if compliance necessitated that one or more of the provisions of a national constitution, including its most fundamental ones, had to be left unapplied. The Court did not postulate that it was given an open-ended authority to develop Community law, but it demonstrated in case after case that it felt quite free in this respect. Some of the most wide-ranging and profoundly important of the Court's expansions of the Community's competencies occurred in its case law on the EC's external relations powers.[10] As a consequence of these and other potent expansions of Community competencies, a fairly open-ended and far-reaching arsenal of empowerments were at the disposal of the political processes when they re-activated themselves by the mid-1980's. The empowerments are wide in scope and very often essentially undelineated, so that it will be hard to identify a case before the Court, direct or preliminary, in which the plaintiff found it worth while to argue that the disputed Council enactment was *ultra vires*. In any event, the Court has not as yet struck down a Council enactment for that reason. The principle of enumerated powers (*pouvoirs d'attribution*) has, in other words, been seriously and perhaps even definitively eroded as a result of a sort of activism by "passivism" (hereinafter: the Community Sovereignty Friendly Theory).

By the end of the 20th Century, the diametrically opposed question has come into currency. At this point in Community history it is regularly asked

---

Boundaries of the European Community, (Sweet & Maxwell, 1998), at p.72.

8 For example in: Case 294/83, *Les Verts, Parti Ecologiste* [1986] E.C.R. 1339 and in Opinion 1/91, *EEA* [1991] E.C.R I-6079. Some examples of authors using the constitution terminology are: F. Mancini, 'The Making of a Constitution for Europe' (1989) 26 CMLRev, 595-614); and Professor S. Weatherhill, *Law and Integration in the European Union*, (Clarendon Press, Oxford, 1995), p. 210 *et seq*; and J. Temple Lang, 'The development of European Community constitutional law', (1991) 25, *The International Lawyer*, pp 455-470.

9 This has been clear since for example Case 48/65, *Lütticke* [1966] E.C.R. 19 and Case 28/67, *Molkereizentrale* [1968] E.C.R. 143 which were precursors to the landmark case, *Simmenthal* (cited in note 4).

10 The first of these Big Bang judgments was in Case 22/70, *Commission v. Council (AETR)* [1971] E.C.R. 41. The other cases are all well known.

when Community law and its Court will acknowledge that most state constitutional provisions remain, as a matter of principle, forbidden land for Community law's claim to an exception-free supremacy for the Treaty and all the laws deriving thereof. The pure theory of Community law has been given up by all but a small coterie of die-hard Community law idealists, whose views are based on what seems to be a striking disregard for sociological reality: today, the validity of the national constitutional orders is not deemed to be a consequence of, or mediated by, Community law. Far from this, the national constitutional law perspective emphasises that the Community institutions exercise only those powers that have been delegated to them by the Treaties and which in return derive their authority from national constitutional law. The EC institutions are therefore not in the final analysis the ultimate authorities (hereinafter: The State Sovereignty Friendly Theory).[11]

III THE FACTS AND THE DANISH CONSTITUTIONAL FRAMEWORK OF THE CASE

The litigation surrounding the Danish ratification of the Maastricht Treaty led to four Danish judicial pronouncements: First, a High Court ruling from 1995 which dismissed twelve Danish citizens' claim that they had standing to bring an action against the Prime Minister claiming that his ratification of the Maastricht Treaty constituted a violation of the Constitution's Section 20.[12] Second, the Supreme Court's virtually revolutionary *1996 Maastricht Ruling* which, in flagrant contradiction of a century old jurisprudence on standing in constitutional cases, granted those citizens a right to bring a class action.[13] Explaining this volte-face the Supreme Court stressed that,

> adhesion to the Treaty on the European Union implies a transfer of legislative competence within a number of general and important fields of life and, accordingly, in itself is of radical significance for the Danish population in general. In this way this case is different from usual cases relating to an examination of the compatibility of acts with the Constitution. Due to the general and vital significance of the Act on Adhesion the Appellants have a major interest in having their claims examined.[14]

It is not easy to explain convincingly why the Act of Ratification of the Maastricht Treaty is so dramatically different from many other statutes and acts of

11 The views just expressed match quite well those of Professor Neil MacCormick in a conference paper, presented at the CORE conference on 'Rethinking Constitutionalism in the European Union', March 19-20, 1998, at Schæffergården, Copenhagen, Denmark, at pp. 13 and 26 (under publication: Oxford University Press).

12 See text of this Section in note 17 and text above it, below.

13 The situation on standing before the *1996 Ruling* is described below in Section III.

14 UfR 1996. 1300 H (italics added by me). I have analysed this judgment in 'Denmark's Maastricht Ratification Case: Some Serious Questions About Constitutionality', *European Integration*, 1998, Vol. 21, pp. 1-35.

ratification as to justify the *1996 Maastricht Ruling*'s truly radical turn-about.[15] The effect of the judgment was that the Supreme Court remitted the case for a hearing on its merits by the High Court. Third, this Court, in a short-sighted and unprincipled decision, acquitted the Prime Minister of the charges brought against him.[16] Fourth, closing the Maastricht ratification litigation, the Supreme Court on April 6, 1998, ruled that (a) the Prime Minister had not violated the Constitution when he ratified the Maastricht Treaty; that (b) Denmark's membership of the Community was constitutionally valid; and that (c) the text of Section 20 compels a distinction to be made between those of its elements which are legal and open to judicial intervention; and those which are of a political nature. The Supreme Court entrusted to the country's political processes the task of functioning as Section 20's *primus motor*. These processes, the Court ruled, enjoy a fairly wide margin of discretion when deciding how much, and how imprecisely delineated, sovereignty can lawfully be transferred to the Union. The present article deals only with the judgment of 6 April, 1998; hereinafter *The 1998 Maastricht Ruling*.

First, however, the main procedural and constitutional points of the standing-issue as it stood before 1996 must be recapitulated. During those years, if the plaintiff of a constitutional case was not able to show that he/she had a concrete and individual interest in a court decision about the constitutionality of a specific statute, standing was always denied.

Next, although Danish courts repeatedly asserted that they were empowered to perform constitutional review, they never actually decided to repeal a statute for the reason that it was unconstitutional. In the wake of these developments, potential plaintiffs slowly began to realise that in order to win a constitutional case in court they had to overcome a strong judicial presumption of constitutionality of parliamentary enactments. It was not a realistic perspective, even for those who had a concrete and individual cause to fight for, successfully to contest the constitutional validity of the statute in question. Complainants with this motivation stopped asking the courts for help. The inevitable consequence of all this was that the courts never took an active part in defining what the constitution meant but left, I assume quite deliberately, the initiative in this matter to the country's political processes.

This judicial hands-off attitude produced unfortunate side-effects. One such was an indirect result of the fact that the procedural conditions which the Constitution in its Section 88 prescribes for amending it, are among the Western World's most difficult to meet in practice. Because transfer of powers falling outside those authorised by Section 20 will have to be adopted by a Section 88-amendment, constitutional change and modernisation could not in practice be accomplished by constitutional amendment. Nor was judicial constitutional in-

15 So also Ole Due, who clarifies why the Supreme Court took nonetheless its historical decision to admit a class action, in the article cited in note 2 above.

16 The judgment is recorded together with the Supreme Court's Maastricht ratification ruling in: UfR 1998.800 H.

terpretation and adaptation to changing international conditions available for these purposes.

The requirements for constitutional change set out in Section 88 are directly to be blamed for the government's failure, in 1939, to ensure the passage of a project of constitutional reform, the political wisdom of which virtually all Danish political parties and voters acclaimed. After the Second World War, in 1953, the government, out of political necessity, had to try its hand again at constitutional reform. This time, the reform barely obtained enough yes-votes to pass the required referendum. Since 1953, successive governments have all preferred to leave the Constitution, though in many ways outdated, unchanged in order not to run the risk renewed failure.

IV About Section 20 on Sovereignty Transfers and the Ratification of the Maastricht Treaty

The provision of paramount importance to this article, Section 20, which authorises transfer of Danish sovereignty to international bodies like the Community, was inserted into the Constitution in 1953. Section 20 reads as follows, in the semi-official translation of it from Danish into English:

> § 20, (1) Powers vested in the authorities of the Realm under this Constitutional Act may, *to an extent specified by statute*, be delegated to international authorities set up by mutual agreement with other states for the promotion of international rules of law and co-operation.
>
> (2) For the enactment of a Bill dealing with the above, a majority of five-sixths of the members of the Folketing shall be required. If this majority is not obtained, whereas the majority for the passing of ordinary Bills is obtained, and if the Government maintains it, the Bill shall be submitted to the electorate for approval or rejection in accordance with the rules for referenda laid down in section 42.[17]

The core issue of the *1998 Maastricht Ruling* turned on the meaning of the words "to an extent specified by statute". These words are in Danish "*i nærmere bestemt omfang*" which, if translatable into any foreign language at all, should in English be "to a more specified extent". Yet, the meaning of those five words is, even in Danish, uniquely opaque. From the earliest debates about Danish mem-

---

17 (Italics added by me). In Danish, Section 20 stipulates the following:
Stk. 1. Beføjelser, som efter denne Grundlov tilkommer rigets myndigheder, kan ved lov *i nærmere bestemt omfang* overlades til mellemfolkelige myndigheder, der er oprettet ved gensidig overenskomst med andre stater til fremme af mellemfolkelig retsorden og samarbejde (Italics added by me).
Stk. 2. Til vedtagelse af lovforslag herom kræves et flertal på fem sjettedele af folketingets medlemmer. Opnås et sådant flertal ikke, men dog det til vedtagelse af almindelige lovforslag nødvendige flertal, og opretholder regeringen forslaget, forelægges det folketingsvælgerne til godkendelse eller forkastelse efter de for folkeafstemninger i § 42 fastsatte regler.

bership of the Community, the meaning of these words attracted massive legal and political attention and dispute.

In these debates, proponents of what could be termed 'Denmark in the heart of Europe' argued that Section 20 authorised that virtually all legislative, judicial and administrative powers could be transferred to the Community – piece by piece – on the condition that every single transfer was defined in a satisfactory manner by statute;[18] a view to which Section 20's legislative history lends notorious support. Proponents moreover emphasised that transfers of sovereignty, which five-sixths of the members of Parliament, or a simple parliamentary majority plus a sufficient majority of the voters at a referendum, could agree upon, could not in the normal course of events be *ultra vires* Section 20.

Disagreeing, Danish Euro-sceptics responded that the proponents' analysis was flawed, because it could not be true that Section 20 authorised successive power-transfers which eventually could divest the authorities of the Realm of all their powers. Unfortunately, due essentially to the Supreme Court's hands-off policy, an authoritative answer to the question about which was the better view could not be obtained. Eventually, change came, but belatedly, when some Eurosceptic plaintiffs in the *1996 Maastricht Case* successfully urged the Supreme Court to assume responsibility for coming out with its views of the matter. Of these views I purport in the remaining part of this Section IV, to highlight and explain five. Two more points will be developed in Section V.

First: the Court ruled that Section 20 authorises transfers of sovereignty to such an extent only that it can be said that Denmark still exists as a '*selvstændig stat*'. The English language equivalent for '*selvstændig*' is 'independent'.[19] Yet, 'independent' can also be translated into Danish as '*uafhængig*', the meaning of which is: not dependent. The Supreme Court used the term '*selvstændig stat*' in the sense of a self-governing (if not fully independent) state. 'Self-governing' implies that the Danish state remains in possession of societally adequate quantities and qualities of non-transferred regulatory powers. Although the Supreme Court did say so expressly, it seems safe to assume that the following rationale underlies this part of the judgment. The Court's view seems to be that it will only be meaningful to organise, as the constitution requires, general elections, form governments and the like in order to govern municipal Danish affairs, if Parliament is still in possession of a substantive amount of non-transferred powers.

By taking the position that Section 20 imposes a substantively defined limit to how many powers can be transferred, the Supreme Court followed the submissions of the plaintiffs. In spite of this, however, their legal victory was not of much avail to them and their cause because the Court also found that, even after the government's ratification of the Maastricht Treaty, the total transfer of powers still clearly lay on the safe side of Section 20's demarcation line. The Court,

18 See details below.

19 'Independent' is the term used in the semi-official translation of the judgment which is reproduced *in extenso* in Ole Due's article, cited in note 2 above.

moreover, added that the determination of the location of Section 20's so-far-and-no-further boundary is a question almost exclusively of a political nature. Therefore, although it is by now clear that a justiciable boundary exists, beyond which further transfers of powers will be declared unconstitutional, the Supreme Court also signalled that it is intent on following events at a distance and that it should not be expected to censure a sovereignty-transferring statute unless it is seriously flawed.

Second: every time Denmark has transferred Section 20 sovereignty to the Community, the extent of the transfer has been defined by statute. These statutes all used the same technique for the purposes of defining the scope and content of the proposed transfer of powers. The technique consisted in inscribing in the statute itself a reference to the texts and Articles of the to-be-ratified Community Treaties which describe those powers.[20] This technique was arguably problematic, however, in so far as the stipulations of the treaties are often open to argument about what they mean. However, as soon as one or more stipulations are open to interpretation, it can be argued that the sovereignty-transfer does not meet Section 20's requirement of sufficient specification.

In the *1998 Maastricht Ruling* the Supreme Court nonetheless found this technique constitutionally acceptable, explaining that, even though Section 20 imposes a condition of positive delimitation of a transfer of powers, interpretative doubts do not suffice to make the transfer *ultra vires*. The delimitation may leave room for political discretion and legal interpretation, but this requirement excludes that a power be transferred to an international institution, authorising it to define its own competencies.[21]

The Court based these two findings on the legislative history of Section 20, which informs us that the words '*i nærmere bestemt omfang*' were inserted into the Constitution in a situation where it was impossible for the drafters of the constitutional amendment to predict in which directions and with which legal and political intensity certain future forms of international legal and political integration and cooperation would develop. Because the major aim of the drafters of Section 20 was to facilitate, not to render difficult, Danish participation in these new forms of international cooperation, the drafters did not – so the Supreme Court argued – specify in Section 20 itself a precise location of the limits to how much sovereignty Denmark can consent to give away.[22]

Third: only powers vested in the ordinary Danish authorities can be transferred. Since these authorities cannot adopt acts contrary to the Constitution, neither can the institutions of an international organisation be entrusted with such powers.[23]

---

20 'Confer' is the term used by the Treaty in for example Article 234 (ex Article 177); the Court thinks in terms of 'transfer' of sovereignty.

21 So also Ole Due in the aforementioned article (note 2); UfR 1998. 800 H.

22 This is the generally shared view of Danish constitutional scholarship, see for this my article cited in note 14 *in fine*.

23 Advocate General Warner argued along the same lines in his conclusions in Case 7/76,

Fourth: if a Community institution proposes to adopt a legal act for which there is, according to the Supreme Court's reading of Section 20 and the Danish Act of Accession, no legal basis in the Treaty, this will have two legal consequences. The first is that Danish ministers, other Danish officials and, perhaps, even commissioners, judges and Community staff with a Danish passport, cannot lawfully participate in the adoption and/or implementation of such an act. The second is that the Supreme Court, under conditions to be specified below, will refuse to enforce the act on Danish territory because it will be invalid under Danish law. "Similar interpretations", the Supreme Court noted, "apply with regard to Community law rules and legal principles which are based on the practice" of the European Court.[24]

To this possibility of non-application of a Community legal enactment a few notes should be added. The first is that the Supreme Court's legal-theoretical frame of reference is the State Sovereignty Friendly conceptualisation of the relationship between the Community's and the Member States' legal orders.[25] In this view, the Treaty is not ultimately an independent source of law. Instead, Community law derives in the last resort its validity from (*inter alia*) Danish constitutional law.

The second note is that the Supreme Court assuaged the difficulties to which the latter conclusions subjected the Community legal order in two respects. First, the Supreme Court made it clear that the European Court must have been given an opportunity to rule on whether the act under attack, in its view, is *ultra vires* in relation to the Treaty. Second, Danish courts can as a rule base their decisions concerning the applicability in Denmark of Community law on that of the European Court.[26] An exception to this applies only if a Danish court "with the required certainty" finds that an act upheld by the European Court is *ultra vires* Section 20 of the Danish Constitution.

Fifth: the Supreme Court found no real difficulty in ruling that the scope of each individual head of authority in the EC Treaty, and therefore also the sum of all of them, meets the requirement of a constitutionally satisfactory, positive delimitation. It was with less ease that the Court managed to explain that the open-

---

IRCA [1976] E.C.R. 1213 but was not followed by the Court which, as early as in Case 44/79, *Hauer* [1979] E.C.R. 3727 explained that a Community enactment's validity was conditioned by its conformity with Community law only. Next, in *Foto-Frost*, the Court declared that national courts can under no circumstances declare a Community enactment invalid, Case 314/85 [1987] E.C.R. 4199. The Supreme Court was not respectful of any of these commandments, see right below.

24 See for all this UfR 1998.800 H. These parts of the judgment are, of course, remindful of what the German Constitutional Court said in its Maastricht Ratification ruling of October 12, 1993, *Entscheidungen des Bundesverfassungsgerichts* [1993] 89.

25 Which I explained above in Section II.

26 This part of the judgment seems to accept the authority of *Foto-Frost* when it stipulates that the European Court must always be given an opportunity to pronounce its opinion about the attacked enactment's validity under Community law before the Danish court can take action.

ended powers provided for by Articles 220 [164] and 308 [235] meet this requirement. I shall in my observations below deal with the transfer-of-competencies problem raised by these two articles in turn, beginning – as did the Supreme Court – with Article 308.

V Specifically about Section 20 and Articles 220 [164] and 308 [235]

In order to rule on the relationship between Article 308 and Section 20, the Supreme Court first enumerated the conditions to which any application of Article 308 are subject (Common Market, Articles 2 and 3, etc.). These conditions are admittedly vague but, as the Court said, not open to any possible political use or application. The Court was quite satisfied that this interpretation was confirmed by the EC Court's *Opinion 2/94* on Union membership of the ECHR.[27] The Supreme Court next emphasised that Article 308 is part of an institutional system which is founded on the principle of conferred powers. The Court continued by observing that this article, therefore,

> cannot be applied as authority for an expansion of the scope of jurisdiction of the Community in excess of the general scope which follows from the provisions of the Treaty as a whole, particularly the provisions whereby the tasks and operation of the Community are determined. Under no circumstances can the Article be applied as authority for the determination of provisions the actual consequence of which is that the Treaty is altered without the prescribed procedure being followed.
>
> The stated interpretation of Article 235 must be taken as the basis *even though, prior to the amendment of the Treaty, the provision may have been applied on the basis of a wider interpretation.* [...]
>
> Against the background of the objective which Article 235 is intended to support, it is unavoidable that the precise delimitation of the scope of application of the provision may give rise to doubts. In view of this, it is considered that the Act of Accession grants the Government a not insignificant margin.[28]

In the section of the pronouncement I have italicised, the Court deals with the Council's legislative practices under Article 308, which date from the period before the Maastricht Treaty was ratified by Denmark.

The brevity with which the Court expresses itself on this point invites us, in my view, to take a closer look at the Court's underlying motivation. The brevity becomes no less interesting if one places the short pronouncement in its procedural context . This context is that the twelve plaintiffs had expended a great deal of energy in their attempt to persuade the Supreme Court to address the issue of the Council's pre-Maastricht practices under Article 308, and to address, more specifically, the issue of whether the Council had abused this provision for

27 (1996) E.C.R. I-1759.
28 UfR 1998.800H.

political purposes legally outside the scope of Article 308.[29] The plaintiffs had moreover invited the Supreme Court to rule, if the latter question was answered in the affirmative, that *ultra vires* acts were inapplicable in Denmark. The plaintiffs, having argued rather persuasively that the Council's application of Article 308 might in some cases have been beyond what that Article could be used for, had produced a list of alleged irregularities.

The Court, the quotation shows, refused to follow the applicant's line of argument. Yet it is not quite clear why. The reason might have been procedural, the Supreme Court assuming that the period prior to Maastricht was not part of the litigated issue. If this is correct, the italicised words are an *obiter dictum*. Be this as it may, the Court's observation, although it does not say so plainly, can only be taken to mean that the Supreme Court was tempted to think, if not persuaded to think, that the Council had from time to time used Article 308 for political purposes, for which this Article offers no legal basis.

A different point can be made about the Court's evaluation of the Danish constitutional situation as it emerged after Maastricht. Without exhibiting the slightest sign of doubt, the Court found that after Maastricht, Article 308 does not pose a problem in relation to Section 20's requirement of positive delimitation. In so finding the Court relied, as noted, heavily on the EC Court's ECHR-Opinion 2/94.

This reliance amounts to building on quick-sand if, upon a closer look, the European Court's sole or major concern in this case was not to uphold respect for the principle of legality – although this was what the European Court explained in its Opinion. I, for one, am inclined to believe that observance of this principle was not the most important concern for all of the thirteen judges – or even of the majority of them – who took part in the decision in this case. Space constraints bar me from corroborating this view in the present article.

Second, concerning the relationship between Article 220 [164] and Section 20 the Supreme Court said:

> The fact that the detailed determination of the powers vested in the institutions of the Community may give rise to doubts, and that the jurisdiction to give rulings concerning the interpretation of such questions is transferred to the EC Court of Justice cannot in itself be regarded as incompatible with the requirement for specification in sect. 20 of the Constitution.
>
> *The fact that the EC Court of Justice in its interpretation of the Treaty also attaches importance to factors of interpretation other than the wording of the provisions, including the objectives of the Treaty, is not in violation of the assumptions on which the Act of Accession was based, nor is it in itself incompatible with the demand for specification in sect. 20 (1) of the Constitution. The same applies to the law-making activities of the EC Court of Justice within the scope of the Treaty.*[30]

29 See article mentioned above in note 3.
30 UfR 1998.800 H.

The italicised, crucial part of the Supreme Court's pronouncement on the relationship between Article 220 and Section 20 merits a closer look, short and laconic as the dictum is. The pronouncement contrasts with the lengthy, well-documented, articulate and often quite persuasive arguments presented to the Court by the plaintiffs. In this argument, they sat out to demonstrate that the European Court in an occasionally uncontrolled, pro-integrationist, spirit of judicial policy-making, had frequently trespassed on to powers vested by the Treaties in one or more of the other Community institutions, or on to powers not transferred to the Community at all. I propose to present three observations in what now follows to explain what I think the Supreme Court had on its mind.

The first observation addresses the EU Court's use of the methods of interpretation available to it. In this respect, the Supreme Court makes a very tenable point. This is so especially where the Supreme Court says that the European Court can make use of other methods of interpretation than the one based on the wording of the disputed provision without violating the assumptions on which the Act of Accession was based. Of course, all national, international and supranational courts make use of a subtle variety of methods of interpretation, including methods based on the objectives of, for example, a Treaty. Those who adopted the Act of Accession must surely have known this.

My second observation takes issue with the Supreme Court's pronouncement to the effect that the European Court's use of a variety of methods is not "in itself incompatible with the demand for specification in sect. 20". In contrast to the Court's first point, this second one is not so flawless. In fact, a closer examination of this pronouncement discloses that the Supreme Court side-stepped addressing the plaintiffs' activism argument, which did not criticise the European Court's *neutral* use of a variety of methods of interpretation. Their concern was instead about the Court's *systematic* reliance on a few sovereignty-absorbing, pro-integrationist methods of interpretation. This reliance was systematic in so far as it was part of a judicial-methodological pattern, identifiable almost whenever the Court, over a period of twenty-odd years running from the mid-1960's, had to decide cases turning on the scope of application of transferred competencies and/or treaty-prohibitions against unilateral Member State actions. In case after case, as I have already explained above, the Court ruled to expand the reach of the Community's powers and reduced the scope of the exceptions to the said bans on unilateral actions.

My third observation is that the last sentence of the italicised quotation is a truism. This follows because a law-making activity "within the scope of the Treaty" cannot be in violation of Section 20 because it is, precisely, this provision which defines the scope of the transferred competencies. The European Court's action within the scope of these competencies, and more specifically inside Article 220, cannot therefore by definition constitute an infringement of Section 20. Nor did the plaintiffs, incidentally, focus on the Council's activities *within* the scope of the Treaty. Before the Supreme Court they had produced handsome evidence to corroborate their contention that many of the European Court's lawmaking activities had been taking place outside the powers which

Denmark had entrusted to the Community and its Court to exercise. Yet, if the plaintiffs were right in their contention on this point, the European Court's action could occasionally have been in blatant violation even of Section 20.

If the Supreme Court was not persuaded by the plaintiffs' argument and evidence, why did the Court not offer a far more analytically potent line of reasoning in order to show that they were wrong in their contentions? I can think of only one answer. This is that the plaintiffs' argument and evidence had convinced the Supreme Court: there had been too much unwarranted judicial activism. However, as with what seemed to be the Supreme Court's tacit recognition that the Council had sometimes acted *ultra vires* Article 308 – which the Court preferred not to admit in so many words – the Court balked at finding an EC judicial violation of Section 20. Why? Presumably because of the dire legal, political and economic consequences which a ruling finding violation of Section 20 would have entailed, nationally as well as internationally. What these consequences would be will have to be the theme of some future article.

VII Confrontation or Peaceful Co-existence? Some Closing Remarks

The Danish Supreme Court declared unequivocally that the day could come when it would have to disapply a Community legal act because it was *ultra vires* Section 20 or in violation of a fundamental right protected by the Danish Constitution – although the European Court had ruled to uphold the same act because it was adopted in conformity with the Treaty. Five years before, the German Constitutional Court said more or less the same, targeting, of course, possible violations of the German Constitution.[31]

Will these threats be carried out one day? I am convinced they will – if certain conditions are met.

One Danish condition is, as has been pointed out, that the constitutional infringement is established with 'sufficient clarity'.

It will be far more important, if such a traumatic disapplication is to be avoided, that the European Court changes its outlook: it must begin to pursue a far more intensive review of politically important acts adopted by the Council and the EP to ensure that they observe the limitations which the individual legal bases, invoked by the Community legislator, impose on its application.

At present, both the German government and the German Tobacco Industry have brought cases before the Court arguing that the Directive on the Ban of Tobacco Products is *ultra vires* the invoked legal bases. Exceptionally, sixteen EC law specialists, several of them of distinguished professional reputation, have, independently of each other, concluded that the Directive is without a legal basis in the Treaty. Even more exceptionally, the legal service of the Council

---

31 See reference to the German judgment in note 24.

is known to have shared in this opinion.[32] The EC Court's rulings in these cases are therefore awaited with considerable interest.

This Court can help to avoid the crisis between the Community and several national legal systems exploding into an actual confrontation if it invalidates the Directive. The sole alternative to this will be to explain thoroughly in the judgments why the experts and the legal service were all wrong in this case.

The Court ought not to reach its interpretative judgments without regard to their potential impact on national constitutions. National courts ought not to interpret laws or constitutions without regard to the resolution of their compatriots to take full part in the European Union or European Community.[33] "If conflicts despite this come into being through judicial decision-making and interpretation, there will necessarily have to be some political action to produce a solution."[34]

32 See Schneider, Hans-Peter and Torsten Stein (eds.) *The European Ban on Tobacco Advertising*, Nomos Verlag, Baden-Baden, (1999).

33 Harck and Palmer Olsen discuss the potentiality for conflict or peaceful co-existence in their article cited in note 3, p. 214.

34 See Neil MacCormick, article cited in note 11 above.

25

COMMUNITY LAW AND NATIONAL COURTS – AN ITALIAN PERSPECTIVE

Giuseppe Tesauro

I Relationship between Community and National Judges as a Factor of Consolidation and Development of the Community System. Some Shadows in the Most Recent Community Case Law

The contribution made by national courts to the consolidation of the Community legal system has always been a noticeable element in the Community experience as a whole. The most important steps in the development of Community law, from direct effect to supremacy, from interim measures to the State liability in damages, from the protection of fundamental rights to the autonomy of national judicial systems, have in fact been based on a continuous dialogue between national judges and the Court of Justice. Indeed, the instrument of preliminary references and rulings has proven to be an irreplaceable mechanism for the development and consolidation of the system.

It is true that there have been some shadows in the most recent case law of the Court of Justice, both on the limits placed on dialogue between national and Community courts and on the more general and not always marginal aspects of the existence and the effects of Community law. Regarding the first, we may consider the long series of decisions in which the Court on one hand refused preliminary questions which were not precise enough, or had no real link to Community law; and on the other, somewhat contradictorily, provided answers to questions where there was no Community law, or even where Community law could not be applied to the case in point.[1] Certainly, one could be disappointed if one compares this state of affairs with the limitless generosity shown in the past, accompanied by widespread favour, the "whim" of Foglia-Novello aside. However, to take a more optimistic view, it is evident that the system has reached maturity, requiring more attentive collaboration of national courts and, ultimately, that they play the more active role of "natural judges" of Community law.

Optimism seems more unwarranted, by contrast, for some of the more recent positions taken by Community judges on important aspects of the Community's legal system. The old optimism has been substituted, not only by distress at the

---

1 C-7/97, *Oscar Bronner*, [1998] ECR I-7791.

D. O'Keeffe (ed.), Liber Amicorum Slynn 391-405 (2000)

ease with which indications of substantial changes in a solid case law are justified, but also by the concern that the level of integration reached with such effort, particularly with the stimulus of the Court of Luxembourg, might be subject to too many or unmindful attacks by the same Court. To take an example, there have been some clear signals of the need for verification of the actual effects of obstacles to trade or restrictions on competition, after a wise and consolidated case law for decades taught and pushed people to teach that "all trading rules enacted by Member States, which are capable of hindering directly or indirectly, actually or potentially, intra-Community trade"[2] are incompatible with the Common Market. In another case, the challenge of a contract subject to Community regulations by a company that did not previously enjoy freedom of establishment or free movement of services has been qualified as a purely internal situation, precluding the application, not only of the rules on establishment and services, but even of article 86 (formerly article 90) of the Treaty (sic!).[3] Finally, one has the general impression of an "acritical" approach, set within uncertain borders, to the use by member States of the national interest as a general limit to the functioning of the Community legal system.[4]

Long-distance dialogue fed by preliminary references remains irreplaceable, especially if we resist the temptation to introduce *ex tempore* novelties which can only weaken the system: for example, excluding the dialogue with lower court judges who have made the "freest", most meaningful contribution to the realisation of a true Community of law, or the idea of creating national filters with specialised regional judges. There is a clear risk (or a precise strategy?) of widening the distance between Luxembourg and individuals and therefore the system's factor of "internationalism", so that the meaning and achievements of the Community legal experience up to the recent past will be significantly reduced, to the level of a "normal" organised co-operation between States. We should not forget that the mechanism of preliminary references, as it has worked until today, allowed for reinforced compliance with Community law and the

---

2 This was the historical *Dassonville* formula (Case 8/74, [1974] ECR 873). It is enough to compare this formula with the rapid, lapidary affirmation of the *Laara* judgment of 21 September 1999, Case C-124/97, according to which "given a lack of sufficient information regarding the real consequences of the *de qua* regulations on importing of equipment, the Court is unable to give its opinion on the question as to whether article 30 of the Treaty opposes the application of regulations of that king" (para. 26). In competition matters, it has been always very clear that the agreement must not necessarily have an actual effect on trade it it suffices that is "capable of constituting a threat" (Cases 56-58/64, *Consten and Grundig*, [1966] ECR 299); but see, specifically on injury to trade, Joined Cases C-215 and 216/96, *Bagnasco*, [1999] ECR I-135.

3 Case C-108/96, *RI.SAN* , judgment of 9 September 1999, paras. 21-22 and 25-26.

4 This is an approach that appears with adequate clarity in some significant, relevant passages of the recent case law, from *COMATEB* (Case C-192/95, [1997] ECR I-165; see also, with respect to different cases with the same state-centred approach, Case C-188/95, *Fantask*, [1998] ECR I-165; *Bagnasco*, mentioned above), until the *Laara* decision mentioned above and also the very recent C-67/98, *Zenatti* judgment, 21 October 1999.

protection of rights of individuals granted by that law within national legal orders.

II THE DIALOGUE BETWEEN THE ITALIAN CONSTITUTIONAL COURT AND THE COURT OF JUSTICE ON RELATIONS BETWEEN COMMUNITY LAW AND NATIONAL LAW

Given this premise, I would like to recall the main passages in the dialogue, particularly between Italian judges and the Court of Justice.

The time when the Italian Constitutional Court rejected any consideration of an act enacted for the execution of the Rome Treaty other than as an ordinary law, thus excluding the *de facto* supremacy of Community Law and settling all inconsistencies on the basis of *lex posterior derogat priori*, seems today prehistoric.[5] Albeit through a different theoretical approach, the Italian Constitutional Court did pay due attention to the concern of the Court of Justice regarding the pursuit of integration through a construction of the relations between legal systems where Community law actually prevails through its own force over conflicting internal laws.[6] In its decisions during the Seventies, the Court, moving away from the autonomy and dissociation of the two legal systems, asserted coordination by virtue of the "limitations of sovereignty" allowed by Article 11 of the Italian Constitution. In this way, the conflict between subsequent national legislation and prior Community legislation was a constitutional conflict, with the further consequence that the scrutiny was the exclusive power of the Constitutional Court itself.[7]

While this guaranteed the supremacy of Community law and the certainty of juridical situations, it took place, first, by substantially preserving control of Community compatibility with national legislation for the Italian Constitutional Court, with the clear risk of a conflict with the Court of Justice. Second, control was exercised through a procedure that reduced the useful effect by delaying it, in particular preventing judges from immediately applying Community law and effectively protecting the rights conferred on individuals by the directly effective Community law. These needs were promptly met in the *Simmenthal* ruling of the Court of Justice,[8] which was at the same time a response to the aforementioned Italian point of view.

---

5 Constitutional Court, 7 March 1964, n. 14 in *Giurisprudenza Costitutzionale*, 1964, p. 129 and 27 December 1965, n. 98, 1965, p. 1322.

6 Case 6/64 *Costa/Enel*, [1964] ECR 1127.

7 Judgment of the Constitutional Court of 27 December 1973, n. 183, in *Giurisprudenza Costituzionale*, 1973, p. 2405. and the following decision of 30 October 1975, n. 232, in *Giurisprudenza Costituzionale*, 1975, p. 232. The legislation was confirmed in the later decisions of 26 October 1981, n. 176 and 177, in *Foro italiano*, 1982 I, 359.

8 Case 106/77, *Simmenthal* [1978] ECR 629, paras. 13-24.

It is well-known that, as a result of the *Simmenthal* judgment, while the Constitutional Court showed its concern at remaining faithful to the axiomatic separation of national and Community legal systems, in *Granital* it elaborated a theoretical model whose greatest importance lies in its practical effects.[9] It allows normal judges to grant immediate protection to the individual rights deriving from a directly effective Community rule, without the need for prior judgment of constitutionality. It is then not so important if that happens since Community law impedes the conflicting national law to be used, relegating it to a grey area of "non-application" from which it could only emerge should Community law lose its effectiveness;[10] or because the directly applicable Community law, as an integral of the whole legal system but with a superior rank *vis-à-vis* national law, prevents the valid creation of an incompatible national rule (i.e. the *Simmenthal* formula).[11] What is important, is the ultimate goal of both theoretical approaches: the guarantee of the effectiveness of full and immediate protection provided to individual rights of Community law origin.

Moreover, the positions of the two courts, Luxembourg and Rome, do not seem so distant, even as regards the theoretical approach. With respect to a specific case (control of a regional law before it enters into force), the Constitutional Court once again proposed the thesis of unconstitutionality of national legislation in conflict with Community law, without that solution being in serious conflict, at least from the viewpoint of immediate effects in the judicial procedure, with Simmenthal. In decision n. 384/94, in the context of a "principal" procedure, when the Court is the only and principal judge (e.g., in a conflict between a region and the State), the Constitutional Court declared that the national law was incompatible with the Community law and that there was a violation of Article 11 of the Italian Constitution.[12] This solution does not contradict the principle of "non application" by ordinary judges, as long as it is integrated into the context of a procedure, where the role of direct guardian of correct ad-

---

9 Judgment of 8 June 1984, n. 170, in *Giurisprudenza Costituzionale*, 1984, p. 1098 .

10 The *Granital* decision speaks of preventing the ascendancy of domestic law for the definition of the controversy before the national judge. The Constitutional Court, 11 July 1989, n. 389, in *Foro italiano*, 1991, I, 1076, and 18 April 1991, n. 168, *ivi*, 1992, I, 660, speak respectively of "disapplication" and not "non-application" so as to avoid evoking defects of the national law that actually do not exist because of the separateness of the legal systems of the various sources. The second decision was preceded by a decision of the Constitutional Court, 14 June 1990, n. 285, denying that the conflict between national and Community regulations was settled as a defect of legitimacy of the first. In the same sense, see, for example, the Court of Cassation, 11 July 1997, n. 8313.

11 Case 106/77, *Simmenthal* [1978] ECR 629, para 17.

12 Judgment of 10 November 1994, n. 384, *Foro Italiano*, 1994, I, 3289. The principle was later confirmed in the following judgment of 30 March 1995, n. 94 where it was actually extended to all "principal" judgments and not limited, as it was in virtue of decision 384/94, to the question of constitutional legitimacy of the regional law before promulgation in accordance with article 127 (4) of the Italian Constitution. In the same sense, cf. the subsequent decisions of 7 November 1995, n. 482, *Rivista ital. diritto pubblico comunitario*, 1996, 749, and 28 December 1995, n. 520, *ibid.*, 768.

aptation of national law to Community law can only be assumed by the Constitutional Court itself.

While the latest developments move in the direction of a substantial co-ordination with Community practice, some perplexities arise in decision n. 146/96, delivered within the sphere of an incidental judgment.[13] Here, the Constitutional Court seemed to see the question of constitutional legitimacy of a national law conflicting with a Community regulation as admissible, as in the case mentioned before, through the parameter of Article 11 of the Italian Constitution. If this decision were not limited, as I believe it is, to the peculiar circumstances of the case in point, it would take on the significance of a return to a solution where the control of constitutionality interferes with the immediate application of the Community law involved, including cases where that law is directly applicable. Actually, this solution should be limited to situations of conflict between national law and Community law not producing direct effects, either because it lacks precision, clarity and the unconditional nature to which those effects are subordinate, or because it was made to regulate "horizontal" relations.[14]

In fact, the case law framework defined above shows very well that, while it has a different approach to the theoretical aspects of relations between Community and national law, the Constitutional Court wanted to guarantee the current functioning of the Community legal system, consistent with the practice of the Court of Justice, and has shown how to do so. Here it made a valuable contribution, especially in relation to some issues, even at the cost of creating some friction, more apparent than real.

III Competence relating to fundamental rights. Reverse discrimination

As is commonly known, the Constitutional Court reserves its right to intervene in two situations. The first is to censure constitutional illegality of a *national rule* when it is "aimed at preventing or damaging continuing observance of the EC Treaty in relation to the system whole or essential nucleus of its principles".[15] The second, parallel, situation is that of a *Community rule* which violates the basic principles of the Constitution or fundamental rights. In this way, national legislation opens up to Community legislation but with some limitations.

13 Judgment of 7 May 1996, n. 146, *Rivista ital. diritto pubblico comunitario*, 1996, 1300.

14 The exclusion of horizontal direct effects is, rightly or wrongly, an acquired element given in the Community's present jurisprudence: cf. Case C-91/92, *Faccini Dori*, [1994] ECR I-3324. The Court of Cassation aligned itself with this, not without some uncertainty: cf. judgment of 27 February 1995, n. 2275, *Giurisprudenza italiana*, 1996, I, 1, 100.

15 *Granital*, *cit.*, on this point, later confirmed by the order 16 April 1987, n. 141, in *Giurisprudenza Costituzionale* 1987, I, 964.

While these cannot be inferred directly from Article 11 of the Italian Constitution, they are justified by the overall system, which acknowledges implied limitations, as far as its revision is concerned, relating to the supreme values that said limitations define. The national legal system cannot avoid acknowledging limits to the integration of Community laws.

On the other hand, there is only a relative risk of "challenge" by provisions of the Treaty[16] or of Community secondary legislation[17] to the fundamental rights protected by the Constitution. The case law of the national constitutional courts, the Italian and German courts in particular,[18] believing that a scrutiny of constitutionality *vis-à-vis* Community law for the protection of the basic values expressed in their respective constitutions is feasible, had the inestimable merit of making the need to guarantee and reinforce the safeguarding of human rights visible and topical, even at a Community level. Indeed, the Court of Justice,[19] and subsequently the member States, undertook to guarantee that protection, in particular during later modifications of the treaties.[20] In the concrete definition of rights to be protected, the Court of Justice, in the absence of explicit provisions, is required to refer to the Constitutional traditions common to the Member States and the international instruments regarding protection of human rights to which Member States are parties. The parameter of fundamental rights, which arises in relation to control of the legality of institutional acts, became also a way of evaluating national legislation, at least wherever it came within the sphere of Community law.[21]

The Constitutional Court's call for respect of fundamental rights has apparently become an important stimulus in the construction of Community jurisprudence in this sphere and represents, moreover, one of the clearest examples of the mutual influence of the two courts, as well as the extremely important results

16 Cf. judgment n. 183/73 *cit.* and, more pertinently, the following of 21 April 1989, n. 232, in *Giurisprudenza Costituzionale*, 1989, I, p. 1154.

17 Judgment n. 509/1995, in *Giurisprudenza Costituzionale* 1995, 1.

18 In particular, the decision of the *Bundesverfassungsgericht* of 29 May 1974, *Solange I*, in *BverfGD*, 37, 271, should be recalled.

19 This case law is well known. Moving from initially negative positions, underlining the Community law's lack of competence to regulate protection of fundamental rights (Case 1/58, *Stork*, [1959] ECR, p. 41), to the full affirmation of the fundamental rights as an integral part of the EC legal system (cf. the Opinion 2/94 of 28 March 1996, regarding the Community's adhesions to the Convention for Protection of Human Rights, [1996] ECR I-1759).

20 Consider, first of all, the Preamble of the Single European Act, above all Article 6 of the European Union Treaty which coded the jurisprudence of the Court of Justice on this point. Moreover, even the Union's not strictly Community sectors are bound to respect of human rights: see, regarding co-operation in the sector of justice and internal affairs, the measures set forth in Article 30 of the EUT. The Amsterdam Treaty, in its new formulation that contains for Article 6, confirms the Union's complete solidarity with those values, stating that the respect of human rights is one of the Union's foundations.

21 Case 260/89, *ERT*, [1991] ECR I-2925; 29 May 1997, Case C-299/95, *Kremzow,* [1991] ECR I-2629.

of the dialogue between courts. At present, following the highly visible operation of integration carried out in this sphere by the Court of Justice, also with the aim of avoiding centrifugal tendencies by national bodies, Constitutional judges consider the protection of fundamental rights guaranteed by the Community legal system as adequate. In particular, while confirming, in judgment n. 509/95, the scrutiny of constitutionality of Community law in relation to fundamental rights, the Constitutional Court censures the judges *a quo* for not having raised, prior to the question of constitutionality, a preliminary question with the Court of Justice as far as the parameter of fundamental rights is concerned, fundamental rights being an integral part of the Community legal system. It is clear that, if the dialogue between Community judges and judges of the Constitutional Court has brought about an acceptable level of protection of fundamental rights, the national legal system appears "reassured" by the protection that the Court of Justice can provide. Indeed, any initiative of the national Constitutional judge is reserved for extreme, not easily imaginable, cases.[22]

Again, in relation to respect of fundamental rights, we should stress an important aspect that led constitutional judges to concern themselves with the equal treatment principle *vis-à-vis* "reverse discrimination" determined by the application of Community law. It is commonly known that Community law, normally applied to situations which have some connection to the legal system to which they belong (free movement of goods or persons, intra-Community exchanges), may ultimately highlight negative treatment, from the viewpoint of the material interests underneath, in situations that have nothing in common with Community law. In other words, the exercise of rights attributed by Community provisions may be such as to create inequality of treatment with respect to those involved in an apparently identical, but solely internal situation. In such circumstances, discrimination that occurs, not noticeable at the Community level, is only important in light of the principle of equality set out in the Italian Constitution.[23]

In seeking a remedy to this problem, the Constitutional Court has at times gone beyond utilisation of the mere national principle of equal treatment (Article 3 of the Italian Constitution) in order to directly influence the sphere of application of relevant Community law. In decision n. 249/95,[24] the Court saw a similarity between the internal and the Community situations. From this, it gleaned reasons to apply the Community law and Court decisions to the internal situation

22 Even the German Constitutional Court, taking into account the case law of the Court of Justice, has come to overturn its sceptical position of 1974; cf. the decision of 22 October 1986, *Solange II* in *BverfGE*, 73, 339. However, reserve of principle has been maintained even in subsequent decisions: see the decision of 12 May 1989, in *EuR*, 1989, or 270 in *Rivista di. Diritto Internazionale*, 1990, p. 424. In the same direction also the *Maastricht-Urteil,* decision of 12 October 1993, in 1994, 1 CMLR 57.

23 Case C-132/93, *Steen*, [1994] ECR. I-2715, and Joined Cases C-64 and 65/96, *Uecker,* [1997] ECR I-3171. On this point, see also the Constitutional Court, decision 16-30 December 1997, n. 443, point 5, *Foro italiano*, 1995, I, 2363.

24 Judgment of 16 June 1995, n. 249, *Foro italiano*, 1998, I, 697.

as well. It is difficult to say whether this is the best way of finding a solution to the problem of reverse discrimination. Certainly, the Court in the aforementioned case showed its sensitivity towards the problem, although it invaded the jurisdiction of the Court of Justice in defining the field of application of Community law.

On another, more recent occasion, the Constitutional court more properly underlined the importance of the problem for national law. The solution was then found in the consideration, for the purposes of a judgment of equality entrusted to the Constitutional Court, of the "discriminatory effects that the application of Community law is capable of provoking", and in the consequent need to give the benefit to all individuals involved.[25] In any event, the problem of reverse discrimination shows the impact, albeit indirect, of the Community system on national legislation, and underlines the continuous, fruitful dialogue between the two courts.

IV The Constitutional Court and the notion of court or tribunal in Article 234 (ex 177) of the EC Treaty

As we have seen, this dialogue has developed over time, in the sense that the Constitutional Court has always been attentive to the jurisprudence of the Court of Justice and vice versa. One wonders whether this kind of relationship will ever take the form of direct dialogue through the mechanism of co-operation provided for in Article 234 (formerly Article 177) of the Treaty. On this point, it is important to note that, with order n. 536/95,[26] the Constitutional Court performed a clear *u-turn* with respect to a precedent which was not very old,[27] excluding the possibility of a preliminary reference to the Court of Justice simply because of the lack of quality of court or tribunal, consequently meaning that the Community law allowing reference to the sole "court or tribunal of one of the member States" was not applicable. This solution is somewhat perplexing: this is not true so much in relation to the specific case where, since it is a preliminary ruling, so that the *a quo* judge remains the principal judge and will be able to (or will have to) make use of the instrument of preliminary reference to Luxembourg. It is perplexing for the legal reasoning which the constitutional judges employed, reasoning equally suited to negating the nature of "court or tribunal" in accordance with Article 234 of the Treaty, even if resorted to in a principal case, where the Constitutional Court is the only judge involved. The result is that, lacking an *a quo* judge, the Community court is definitively denied an interpretative role.

25 Constitutional Court, decision n. 443 of 30 December 1997, in *Foro Italiano* 1998, I, 697.

26 Order of 29 December 1995, n. 536, *Foro italiano*, 1996, I, 783.

27 Judgment of 18 April 1991, n. 168, in *Foro italiano*, 1992, I, 660.

Actually, and first, the notion of court or tribunal in accordance with Article 234 is a Community concept and the Court of Justice is the only arbiter. Secondly, it appears impossible to say that the Constitutional Court does not fulfil the prerequisites that Community case law uses as parameters to define jurisdiction in accordance with Article 234 – i.e. the independent, permanent nature of that body, the obligatory nature of its jurisdiction, the adversarial nature of procedure, the legal basis and, at least when it is the unique judge, its appropriateness in establishing effective, definitive judgment for the parties involved in the dispute. Third, the orientation of the Constitutional Court is in singular contrast to a clear tendency of the European Court to enlarge the number of national courts or tribunals entitled to resort to preliminary reference. Thus it would seem to be a paradox to exclude the judges of the Constitutional Court when the case law of the Court of Justice includes among courts and tribunals, bodies which clearly do not fall under that definition: the examples of the German body for public procurement or the Spanish competition commission are well known.[28] Fourthly, this approach of the Court of justice gives good reasons to the Italian Constitutional Court for not feeling itself to be in the appropriate club of courts and tribunals in accordance with article 234 anymore.

V SOME THOUGHTS ON THE RELATIONS BETWEEN COMMUNITY LAW AND ITALIAN LAW

Having achieved the practical result that Community law normally prevails over conflicting national law, we are still faced with the basic contrast on the theoretical reconstruction of the nature of relations between Community law and internal law. In fact, this contrast is apparently a chapter of the long story of monism and dualism as far as the relations between international and national law are concerned. We can also state, however, that it combines with the effort to define as much as possible the Community's experience of integration among sovereign States, something not easy to compare.

Moreover, we are uncertain of the usefulness of lingering too long over these issues. There is the risk of reducing serious examination to a purely dialectic exercise. In addition, while it is not easy, it is appropriate to resist the temptation of using stimulating, undeniable and yet juridically incorrect terms such as supranational, federal, pre-federal *et similia*. Another temptation to avoid is the use of other terms of comparison, mainly those of the United States, still far from the Europe of today. A few comments of some elements often ignored are sufficient and can contribute to defining the current situation in concrete terms.

---

28 C-54/96, *Dorsch Consult*, [1997] ECR I-4961; C-67/91, *Asociación Española Banca Privada*, [1992] ECR I-4785. See also Joined Cases from C-69/96 to C-70/96, *Garofalo*, [1997] ECR I-5603.

First, we should consider that the phenomenon of the Community has highly original aspects which often require a different use of some traditional legal categories. Thus, the approach to relations between the Community system and national systems can only be different from other phenomena of organised co-operation between sovereign states. Indeed, the very concept of sovereignty should be reconsidered in the light of such a substantial attribution of legislative power to the Community, even in "intimate" sectors of the State such as, for example, taxes or economic and monetary policy.

Having made this obligatory methodological introduction, we should also clarify that, from the viewpoint of relations between laws in the strict sense, which is neither a unique nor decisive aspect, the diversity of the Community phenomenon cannot and should not lead to a consideration of the problems that, far from being measured on the basis of the phenomenon's originality, is only simplistic and lacks rigour, and is perhaps inspired by dialectics or by emotional factors. For example, the international aspect, which is the first level of the Community juridical system as a whole, cannot yet be eliminated, whatever the dialect expedients used. At the same time, negotiations and international agreements are still the instruments used to mark the basic phases in the division in principle of the respective powers between the States and the Community institutions, and to define the methods of implementing the legislation made pursuant to their competence, the legislative power in particular, and the goals to pursue and improvements or corrections to be made to the Community structure. The process of elaborating the resulting Community laws is still substantially a contractual one, despite the progress made with a growing use of the majority criterion and a more intense involvement of the Parliament, giving a more "organic" connotation to the legislative process.

Ultimately, the constitutional instruments of adaptation and execution of the Member States, rapid and automatic, establish and regulate relations between Community law and internal law.[29] The case of Italy is a confirmation of this. Italy has been, for a long time, far behind in transposition of Directives and, in general, adaptation of internal legislation to the modifications decided by Community regulations. It has, however, managed to keep up with the average Member State by creating for itself the instrument of the so-called Community law Statute, which annually takes care of adopting all the required Community laws "en bloc".

At the same time, the practice is to be excluded of Member States' verifying, once jurisdiction has been attributed to the Community, the correct exercise, except with the specific mechanisms set forth in the Treaty. In this sense, it would be at least strange (and against the *pacta sunt servanda* rule) that, as sup-

29 Just as the Court itself acknowledged in its first rulings in this area: see, for example, Case 20/59, *Italy v. High Authority*, [1960] ECR 325, at 335, para. II which justified the immediate application of these regulations to the ECSC Treaty with the condition that "said regulations be included in the law of Member States in virtue of the ratification of the Treaty."

posed by the German constitutional court, a national or even a Constitutional judge could have the power to verify if the exercise of jurisdiction by a Community institution was legitimate with respect to the conventionally defined limits; with the consequence that there would be a resulting lack of obligation in national law of a Community law that did not comply with those limits.[30] The judicial control of the legitimacy of Community acts *vis-à-vis* the Treaty is within the jurisdiction of the Court of Justice, to the exclusion of the national judges. At the most, the latter may request the Court's control through preliminary reference. This is obviously not a singularity, nor even a *diminutio* for the national judges since jurisdiction was in any event conferred upon the Court through the first level of national legislative instruments.

Ultimately, reconstruction of the effectiveness of Community law within national legal systems as the result of its own authority is certainly a stimulating formula and one to be hoped for, but it is also most certainly incorrect from the viewpoint of general legal theory. Nor does it properly represent the real existence and function of the mechanisms created for this purpose. It is therefore to be appreciated, but *cum grano salis*.

Moreover, it is not a necessary description. Actually, that the effect of Community law comes out of its own force or because it was conferred with the said force and will continue to be conferred on a permanent basis by certain national laws or mechanisms, does not seem to make the slightest difference. The important thing is that the effects of that law must come about in the way, and according to the timetable, the law itself prescribes, without any condition for further formal intervention by any national body, except when required by Community law itself.[31]

This way, the directly effective law must and does produce its effects, even for individuals, from the very moment it comes into force, without any obstacles being placed in its way by national laws or procedures. On the other hand, any law lacking this prerequisite requires that member States create, modify or abrogate national laws according to the requirements for its observance. Otherwise, there will be a violation of obligations by the State and certainly not the nullity of the conflicting national law. This nullity is neither intentional, foreseen nor necessary, even if it is mentioned in some nonchalant statements of doctrine and judgments. For this reason, the Community system includes both non-application of the national law conflicting with the direct effective Community law and infringement procedures and the State's obligation to take all necessary steps when the Community rule has no direct effect.

---

30 *Bundesverfassungsgericht*, Maastricht Urteil, 12 October 1993, n. 213/92, in 1994, 1 CMLR 57.

31 See Constitutional Court, order 7 March 1990, n. 144, Buitoni, in *Giurisprudenza Costituzionale* 1990, p. 812, where it is reconfirmed that Community law comes into and remains in effect in the domestic legal order without having its effectiveness conditioned each time by a national law.

The Court itself recently, actually with a too rapid and not reasoned re-examination of a leading decision such as *Simmenthal*, stated that, from this case on, it is not allowed to deduce the non-existence of the subsequent national law incompatible with Community law. On the contrary, the national judge is required to not apply it.[32]

If this is the reality, as we strongly agree, it is not possible, except for the sake of purely academic discussion, to define Community law from the viewpoint of its own force with regard to relations with national law and in a strictly regulatory manner. Other considerations notwithstanding, this definition does not match the following elements:

- any integration and/or modification of the Treaty requires normal constitutional procedures of ratification and adaptation by the member States.
- Community powers and competences are only those attributed by the Member States through the Treaty and no others; this is also true for their methods and effects, including the direct effect of some acts when some conditions are met; at the same time, case law in this sphere is a result of the Court's being assigned, by Article 164 (now 220), the task – general and exclusive – of ensuring that "in the interpretation and application of this Treaty the law is observed", according to the specific jurisdiction and the procedures set forth by the present provisions of the Treaty;[33]
- the efficacy of non-directly applicable Community laws is conditioned by the times and methods of the adjustment, transposition and enactment mechanisms set forth by national constitutional systems, however automatic they might be;
- a domestic law inconsistent with Community law is not, nor could or should be, null; when necessary it should be repealed, modified or substituted by the States; non-application or disapplication is totally different and in any event is only used in case of directly applicable Community laws.

Regarding the legal principle according to which directly effective Community laws prevail over national legislation, we need to simply and realistically admit that the national legal system attributed an external position, but prevailing over national laws regulating the same questions, even constitutional questions, to the Community laws provided with direct effect, and will continue to

32 Joined Cases C-10-22/97, *INCOGE v. Ministry of Finance*, [1998] ECR I-6307, para. 16.

33 It should also be underlined that the fact that the Member States are still "Herren der Verträge" has nothing to do with Community institutions exercising the powers attributed by the Member States, something whose legitimacy can only be decided by the Community judge in virtue of the express will of the Treaty. For that, there was a mistake in the judgment of the *Bundesverfassungsgericht* mentioned in note 30.

do so on a permanent basis. Moreover, it is not a privilege but simply a fact that the regulation of certain relationships are entrusted to Community law, thus excluding the applicability (or legal relevance if one prefers) of national laws.[34] It is an open question as to whether, in Italy, this is derived from a principle inherent to the system or a rule of positive constitutional law. That is less important, however, as long as we remain at the primary level of the national legal system which only allows the legitimisation and coverage of those "novelties" that the Community treaties and even, at times, the resulting Community law have undoubtedly introduced with respect to the Constitution, inasmuch as the ordinary law of execution of the Treaty is not sufficient from this specific point of view.

VI Impact of Community Case Law on Italian Judicial Practice

The evolution of Italian constitutional practice regarding relations with Community law has kept up with the growth of this legal system, which has now reached full maturity. Moreover, it appears meaningful that some of the basic steps taken by Court of Justice case law have ultimately had a profound influence on national law. They have even brought into question principles deeply rooted in the Italian tradition, which has no meagre history, principles that had been considered very difficult, if not impossible to alter. The effect that the decisions of the Court of Justice has had on the State's liability in damages for the violation of Community law through regulatory acts or omissions is emblematic. This is an important topic in Italy's experience, both because it undermines solid categories and distinctions (see, for example, the dichotomy between right-legitimate interest) and because the Italian system is certainly one of the most sophisticated from the point of view of judicial guarantees for the individual.

Following the well-known *Francovich* judgment of the Court of Justice regarding the consequences of Italy's not having transposed in good time a Community directive into national law, the legislature intervened to implement the financial results imposed by the decision, applying it to an already existing mechanism of workers' guarantees run by the public social security body (INPS).[35] Either because the employer's insolvency was prior to enactment of the directive or because intervention came afterwards, the burden of payment of damages was borne by INPS and generically defined as "indemnity": both the Constitutional Court[36] and the Court of Cassation[37] ruled in this sense. In par-

34 Constitutional Court, judgment 11 July 1989, n. 389, Province of Bolzano, in *Foro italiano*, 1991, I 1076; and the former judgment of 19 November 1987, n. 399, Regions of Emilia Romagna and Liguria, in *Foro italiano*, 1989, I 1018.

35 Joined Cases C-6 and 9/90, *Francovich*, [1991] ECR I-5357.

36 Judgment of 16 June 1993, n. 285, in *Foro italiano*, 1993, I, 2393 and 31 December 1993, n. 512, in *Foro italiano* 1994, I, 316.

37 Court of Cassation, Labour Section, 11 October 1995, n. 10617, in *Foro italiano*, 1996, I, 503.

ticular, it is worthwhile recalling that while the arguments used by the Court of Cassation led to a satisfactory practical result in the case in point – compensation of the individual as a result of the behaviour of the State and its legislature – it is at the very least debatable from the point of view of legal construction and therefore more generally.

After having underlined that the Community legal system imposes a result on the Member States but that the definition of the individual's subjective position is the task of the national law, the Court of Cassation stresses that exercise of the legislative function is removed from judicial control and that "in the face of the exercise of political power subjective protected situations for the individual are not conceivable." The result is that the Court of Cassation deems it inadmissible to speak of illicit action or configure a right of the individual to indemnity in relation to the legislator's activity or inactivity. On the other hand, the individual enjoys "the right to receive indemnity for reduction of assets suffered as the result of the exercise of a power that courts cannot verify."

This motivation is perplexing, at least to the extent that the individual is not allowed to demand full compensation for damages sustained because of the State's behaviour, the legislature in this case, which was incompatible with Community law. While we can agree with the general premise, according to which Community law leaves the task of defining the individual legal position to the national systems, the Supreme Court still seems to forget that Community law requires full and effective judicial protection for the positions it confers. From this point of view, while it is certainly true that national judges can make use of instruments that national legislation has made available, they must also acknowledge that they are required to remove any obstacles to achieving the results desired by Community law without waiting for further legislative measures or initiatives. This is the lesson to be learned from the *Simmenthal* to the *Factortame* rulings,[38] a lesson which the Constitutional Court has also adopted.

On the other hand, in the face of precise obligations imposed on the Member States arising from the very fact that they belong to the European Community, obligations that translate into a limitation of sovereignty (Article 11 of the Italian Constitution) which the State accepted, the idea that the exercise of the legislative function as an "expression of political power" is always and in any case removed from judicial verification seems unacceptable. Ultimately, when the legislature is no longer free but is under a precise obligation to legislate in one way rather than another and does not respect this obligation, it is difficult to comprehend why its behaviour should not be subject to control. Careful study reveals that this verification already exists *vis-à-vis* the constitutional parameter of legitimacy and, in substance and procedure, is not unlike the verification carried out based on the Community parameter.

For this reason, the solution of the Court of Cassation with respect to the *Francovich* case cannot be considered satisfactory from a general point of view.

38 Case C-213/89, *Factortame*, [1990] ECR I-2433.

In that case, satisfaction of the substantial interests involved was derived from the fact that non-enactment of the directive was followed by a specific law, which attributed additional burdens of providing indemnity from the State to an already existing public body. In other situations, however, this might not be possible. Examples from cases with which Community jurisprudence has already dealt include a situation involving violation of directly applicable Community law where an incompatible national law also exists.[39] Another was the situation where there was an obligation to guarantee a certain economic result to a certain category of operators but in the absence of a pre-existing public fund to assume the burden.[40]

In the light of the above, I feel that, in order to adapt fully to the principles of Community law on the liability of the States, the Court of Cassation will have to take original steps, certainly more sophisticated but drawn up in a purely national context prior to Community integration. It is simply a question of admitting that the State must assume the obligation of compensating individuals who suffered damage to their assets due to the effect of violation by the State itself of a precise Community obligation.

Another possibility recently appeared with a judgment of the Court of Cassation which finally sanctioned the principle of compensation for damages for disregard of so called "legitimate interests" through a novel reading of Article 2043 of the Italian Civil Code.[41] This is a first step towards the affirmation of the importance of this provision, also in terms of the State-legislature. This step is also motivated by the impulse of Community case law, always indifferent to national classifications but careful that subjective positions determined by Community law, however they are defined, receive equal and adequate judicial protection.

In conclusion, I believe that, as the entire Community history has shown, the difference in approach and the friction that has arisen, and will continue to arise in the future on some points, are destined to weaken and disappear through the common attempts made by Community and national judges to give growing force to the process of integration and, in this way, to protect common values. Set in this perspective, the relationship between Community and national judges is therefore destined to be the central, irreplaceable element of the process of integration in the future as well. I would add that this process cannot avoid being at the same time both new and old: the growth process, albeit with some pauses and stalling that might make one think of a return to the past, inevitably means adjustments which both Community and national judges must make. The important thing is that their dialogue should continue, taking advantage of new dimensions which can only lead to mutual enrichment.

---

39 Joined Cases C-46 and C-48/93, *Brasserie du Pêcheur and Factortame*, [1996] ECR I-1029.

40 Joined Cases C-178/94 and others, *Dillenkofer*, [1996] ECR I-4845.

41 Court of Cassation, Joined Sections, n. 500 of July 22, 1999.

26

JUDICIAL REVIEW IN ENGLISH COURTS: AN IDEAL FORUM FOR COMMUNITY LAW?

David Vaughan and Margaret Gray

INTRODUCTION

It is well established that two of the essential characteristics of the Community legal order are its primacy over the law of the Member States and the direct effect of a whole series of provisions which are applicable to the Member States themselves and to individuals.[1] Member States and their institutions are responsible for the full and effective enforcement of any rights derived from Community law. In particular, pursuant to Article 10 of the Treaty, it is the duty of national courts to ensure the legal protection of rights which individuals derive from the Treaty. This principle has been repeatedly underscored both by the European Court of Justice and by national courts themselves.[2]

The European Court of Justice has particularised this general obligation of ensuring the protection of rights created by the Treaty and the Community legislature to emphasise that Member States must provide, through national courts and tribunals, an effective means of judicial review. In *Parti écologiste 'Les Verts' v. Parliament*[3] it held that the Community:

> "...is a Community based on the rule of law, inasmuch as neither its Member States nor its institutions can avoid a review of the question whether the measures adopted by them are in conformity with the basic constitutional charter, the Treaty."

Further refinement of this principle has required that Member States must also provide a national system of review which is not merely apparent, but real. In *Johnson v. Chief Constable of the Royal Ulster Constabulary*[4] the Court recog-

1 Opinion 1/91 (Opinion concerning the draft Treaty on a European Economic Area) [1991] ECR I-6079.

2 See in particular Lord Bingham CJ in *R v. Secretary of State for the Home Department, ex p Gallagher* [1996] 2 CMLR 951 para. 10 where he held that "[i]t is a cardinal principle of Community law that the laws of Member States should provide effective and adequate redress for violations of Community law by Member States where these result in infringement of specific individual rights conferred by the law of the Community."

3 Case 294/83 [1986] ECR 1339 para. 23.

4 Case 22/84 [1986] ECR 1651.

D. O'Keeffe (ed.), Liber Amicorum Slynn 407-415 (2000)

nised as a general principle of law the requirement of effective judicial control as regards the compliance of national legislation intended to give effect to relevant rights with applicable provisions of Community law.[5]

The effect of these demands on national courts and of the fact that by far the most part of litigation in the Community involving Community law issues is dealt with at national court rather than European Court level,[6] is that national legal systems either must have already had installed national procedures for judicial review which were adept at addressing novel points of Community law raised, or must have been sufficiently adept at adapting their existing procedures.[7] It is acknowledged that 'judicial review procedures are perhaps the most nationally idiosyncratic aspects of administrative law'.[8] Some mechanisms of the procedures of review differ considerably from Member State to Member State.

BLUEPRINT FOR AN EFFECTIVE NATIONAL LEGAL SYSTEM

There are, however, certain constants which a national legal system must exhibit in order to fulfil its role as an effective enforcer of Community law: efficiency, economy and speed, and the capacity to deal conclusively with points of Community law. Combined with access to a respected and possibly specialised judiciary that is eminently capable of developing an authoritative and respected jurisprudence in the field, any national legal system that displays the above principles would be truly indispensable to the Community legal structure.

If follows that the ultimate test of the effectiveness of a national legal system as an essential component of the Community legal order must be its ability to handle efficiently and definitively cases raising points of Community law. In the context of the complementary working relationship between the Court of

5 *Ibid.* paras. 17 to 19. The Court went on to conclude that a national provision which requires that a certificate signed by or on behalf of the Secretary of State be treated as conclusive evidence that conditions for derogating from the principle of equal treatment are fulfilled has the effect of permitting the competent authority of depriving an individual of the possibility of asserting by judicial process the rights conferred by the relevant directive. Such a provision, therefore, was considered contrary to the principle of effective judicial control laid down in the directive itself.

6 It is the national courts of the Member States which are the proper fora for disputes involving issues of Community law which arise between individuals and national authorities.

7 For a comprehensive analysis of the application of EC law by national courts in the existing Member States and the interaction of the demands of EC law with the constraints imposed by national legal orders see Slaughter, Sweet and Weiler (eds), *The European Courts of Justice and National Courts – Doctrine and Jurisprudence* (Oxford, Hart, 1998).

8 See John Bell, *Mechanisms for Cross-Fertilisation of Administrative Law in Europe* at chapter 11, p.165 of Beatson and Tridimas (eds) *New Directions in European Public Law* (Oxford, Hart, 1998).

Justice and national courts, a network of systems displaying these properties could also have the effect that most of the important cases are decided in national courts and tribunals, and only exceptional cases, namely where there is no guiding precedent, are referred to the Court of Justice pursuant to Article 234 (ex 177) of the Treaty.[9] Of course these is always the danger that the misapplication of Community law may result in legal heresies developing in national courts.[10] However, the existing case law of the Court of Justice, even at present, amounts to some 4,000 judgments, including over 3,200 preliminary rulings. This should provide sufficient detail to allow national courts and tribunals (at least at first instance), to decide many cases with the necessary degree of confidence and without requiring a reference.

In this contribution, judicial review in English courts will be tested against the above benchmarks of efficiency, economy, speed and definitiveness to see whether it provides a satisfactory service to parties raising Community law issues in public law cases. By reference to the procedures of the Crown Office and a limited number of cases it will be shown that the High Court is a well-equipped forum for the effective application and enforcement of Community law. This is further enhanced by the pragmatic and malleable approach taken by English courts to the making of references.

CHARACTERISTICS OF JUDICIAL REVIEW IN ENGLISH COURTS

The English courts have developed certain principles which are particular to judicial review, characterised by the role of the court in relation only to a limited class of administrative acts and decisions, and in reviewing those acts and decisions, in most cases, on grounds of unreasonableness, irrationality or procedural unfairness. The court undertakes this limited review rather than substituting its own decision for that of the administrative decision-maker in question. It also provides certain peculiar remedies. A number of procedural practices are associated in particular with judicial review proceedings: the need for leave, speed, limited discovery and disclosure, and limited use of cross-examination of deponents. The judges on the Crown Office list have considerable expertise in public law matters, and also frequently deal with cases drawn from a wide spectrum of subjects.

Where judicial review proceedings are brought for the enforcement of Community law or against public authorities in the English Courts, the normal

---

9 For some of the alternative propositions of how this balance might be achieved by other means see Kennedy, T., 'First Steps towards a European Certiorari' (1993) ELRev. *121* and de la Mare, 'Article 177 and Legal Integration' at chapter 6 pp. 246-249 of Craig and de Búrca *The Evolution of EU Law* (Oxford University Press, 1999).

10 See David Anderson, *References to the European Court* (London, Sweet & Maxwell, 1995), sects. 6-047 – 6-052; A. Arnull, 'The Use and Abuse of Article 177 EEC' (1989) 52 MLR 622.

principles of English law have had to adapt to accommodate the demands of Community law.[11] In addition to providing for challenges both to primary legislation and administrative acts, even where they are not dependent for their authority on the Treaty but have been adopted solely by virtue of domestic law,[12] and to granting appropriate remedies,[13] English judicial review proceedings have responded to the need to alter some procedures and judicial approaches with regard to the resolution of applications.

Procedural Adaptability: Efficiency, Economy and Speed

Often the resolution of Community law issues has required the analysis by the Court of considerably more written evidence than is customary in domestic judicial review matters. In many instances this involves consideration of highly technical documents concerning complex issues of both law and fact. The various judicial review proceedings in the *Factortame* litigation have each spawned a vast amount of court bundles let alone court proceedings. Yet while the *Factortame* proceedings themselves have stretched for over a decade, each part of the judicial review application itself was dealt with efficiently and economically. As an illustration, on 12 December 1988, leave was granted in the first *Factortame* action. The Divisional Court gave its judgment on 10 March 1989, granting interim relief and ordering a reference.[14] The Court of Appeal gave judgment on 22 March 1989, overturning the interim relief[15] and the House of Lords (following a hearing lasting some 8 days) gave judgment on 18 May 1989 declining to grant at that stage interim relief but ordering a reference on that point.[16] Following the preliminary ruling of the European Court of Justice on 19 June 1990,[17] the House of Lords, on 10 July 1990,[18] notified the parties of its decision in principle to grant interim relief, with the judgment following on 11 October 1990.

Another good example of the ability of the English courts to accede to the need to deal efficiently with cases raising a point of Community law, the resolution of which has important economic, political, social or other consequences, is the recent litigation involving the challenge to the legal validity of Directive

11 See de Smith, Woolf and Jowell, *Judicial Review of Administrative Action*, (5th edn., London, Sweet & Maxwell, 1995) at 21-116 – 21-204; Lewis, *Judicial Remedies in Public Law*, (2nd edn., London, Sweet & Maxwell, 2000) at 15-91.

12 Laws J in *R v. MAFF, ex p First City Trading* [1997] EuLR 195 at 210C.

13 *R v. Secretary of State for Transport, ex p Factortame Ltd (No 2)* [1991] 1 AC 603 at 658A-E.

14 [1989] 2 CMLR 353. This was the substantive hearing with full evidence.

15 [1989] 2 CMLR 292.

16 [1990] 2 AC 85. The House of Lords requested the ECJ to deal with this matter with expedition.

17 Itself an exceptionally speedy determination in a case of such complexity.

18 Following a hearing of five days.

98/43/EC on the approximation of laws, regulations and administrative provisions relating to the advertising of tobacco products. At the leave hearing, Turner J made a reference, stating that there were advantages in establishing at an early stage whether the Directive would be implemented.[19] On 29 October 1999, following a further application, judgment at the hearing was given by Turner J in favour of granting injunctive relief to the applicant tobacco companies, following an extensive survey of the case-law relating to the legal basis of Community acts and to the availability of interim relief in English courts.[20] An application for an expedited appeal was granted and on 16 December 1999 a majority of the Court of Appeal allowed an appeal against the grant of interim relief, Lord Justice Laws dissenting.[21]

Judicial Approach: Definitiveness

Definitiveness of national judicial control in the field of law concerning European Community issues is integrally bound with the degree of competence and confidence of national courts in applying Community law. With an increasing emphasis by the Community on subsidiarity it must be welcomed that the English Courts have proven themselves highly capable of both applying conclusively Community law and taking difficult decisions touching the validity or possible invalidity of Community law.[22] Of course there remains the worry that this may be at the expense of uniformity or correctness of interpretation or application. This is a genuine concern where there is a series of cases running simultaneously in different national courts where the same point is repeatedly at issue.[23] However such situations may be regarded as exceptional and should not

19 *R v. Secretary of State for Health ex p Imperial Tobacco Ltd* [1999] EuLR 582. The fact that Article 230 (ex 173) proceedings had already been taken in the Court of Justice by the Republic of Germany was a factor taken into consideration in making the reference. See also *R v. Secretary of State for the Environment, Transport and the Regions, ex p Omega Air Limited* [2000] EuLR n.y.r. and Case T 165/99 *Omega Air Ltd v. Council.*

20 [2000] EuLR vol. 4:1.

21 [2000] EuLR vol 4:1. Permission has been given for the case to be heard on appeal by the House of Lords.

22 In Case 314/85 *Foto-Frost v. Hauptzollamt Lübeck-Ost* [1987] ECR 4199 the Court of Justice established that although national courts have the power to declare that acts of the Community institutions are valid, they do not have the power to declare such acts invalid. However a national court does have jurisdiction to order the suspension of national measures which give effect to Community law where it is persuaded that there are serious doubts as to the validity of the Community provision: Joined Cases C-143/88 and C-92/89 *Zuckerfabrik* [1991] ECR I-415 and Case C-465/93 *Atlanta Fruchthandelsgesellschaft* [1995] ECR I-3761.

23 One example is that for a number of years in the English courts (including the Court of Appeal) there had been a series of cases concerning the application of Article 81 and the impossibility of a remedy for damages by way of enforcement of potential Community law rights in the context of tied agreements between breweries and tenants of public houses. See for example *Gibbs Mew v. Gemmell* [1998] EuLR 588 (the others are re-

detract from the generally high success rate of the application of Community law, particularly in courts of first instance.

One aspect of this process of the conclusive application of Community law without the aid of a preliminary reference for a specific case, is whether there should be a judicial standard of review in addition to that of irrationality, unreasonableness, or procedural unfairness. It seems to be accepted that there is little difference between the approaches of a national court and that of the Court of Justice when evaluating factual matters.[24] The same goes for the application of the law on proportionality. Proportionality is one of the guiding principles employed by the Court of Justice itself to test the validity of a Community act.[25] Although in some circumstances the application of a test of proportionality may require a slightly different examination by the national court, *Wednesbury* and European review are 'different models – one loose, one tighter – of the same juridical concept, which is the imposition of compulsory standards on decision makers so as to secure the repudiation of arbitrary power'.[26] In some respects, therefore, the difference may be regarded as no more than a matter of labelling. This was emphasised by Lord Slynn in the House of Lords judgment in *R v. Chief Constable of Sussex, ex p. International Trader's Ferry Ltd.*:[27]

> "In *Reg. v. Secretary of State for the Home Department, Ex parte Brind* [1991] 1 AC 696 the House treated *Wednesbury* reasonableness and proportionality as being different. So in some ways they are though the distinction between the two tests in practice is in any event much less than is sometimes suggested. The cautious way in which the European Court usually applies this test, recognising the importance of respecting the national authority's margin of appreciation, may mean that whichever test is adopted, and even allowing for a difference in onus, the result is the same."

As regards the need to consider a wide range of substantive areas and diverse subject matters of Community legislation the English courts have proven themselves notably adroit. Although this technique is not recent – the High Court has for some time been considering points of Community law in fields as

---

ported in the same volume of EuLR at pp. 483-587). On 27 May 1999 the Court of Appeal gave judgment referring the issue to the Court of Justice (*Courage Ltd v. Crehan* [1999] EuLR 834 now Case C-453/99).

24 See for example *Royal Society for the Protection of Birds v. Secretary of State for Scotland* (*The Times*, 14 December 1999) per Lord Johnson citing Case C-120/97 *Upjohn Ltd v. Licensing Authority* [1999] ECR I-223.

25 There has been much academic comment on the use of this technique, in particular, Ellis (ed) *The Principle of Proportionality in the Laws of Europe* (Oxford, Hart, 1999). See also J. Jowell and A. Lester, "Proportionality: Neither Novel nor Dangerous" in J. Jowell and D. Oliver (eds), *New Directions in Judicial Review* (London, Stevens, 1988), at 51-73; S. Boyron, "Proportionality in English Administrative Law: A Faulty Translation?" (1992) OJLS 237.

26 See Laws J. (as he then was) in *R v. MAFF, ex p First City Trading Ltd.* [1997] EuLR 195 at 219 D-F.

27 [1999] 3 WLR 1260 at p.1277B-D.

diverse as sex equality in employment,[28] agriculture,[29] pharmaceuticals,[30] and treaty ratifications[31] – as the competence of the Community grows and its jurisprudence matures the fields have become wider and yet the English courts have been fortified in making conclusive findings either at first instance or on appeal. Two recent cases where the Court of Appeal has taken conclusive decisions on technical questions of state aid taxation are good examples of this. In *R v. Commissioners of Customs and Excise ex p. Lunn Poly Ltd and another*[32] the Court of Appeal, after giving consideration to the Treaty provisions on state aid, Articles 87 and 88 (ex 92 and 93), held that since on a purposive construction, the aim of Article 87 was to prohibit aid which threatened to distort competition, it was the substance rather than the form of the matter which controlled whether there was a state aid. On the facts, the Court of Appeal concluded that the state had conferred a benefit on the lower rate taxpayer and, as this had distorted or threatened to distort competition, therefore there had been such an aid. In *R v. Commissioner of Customs and Excise ex p. Shepherd Neame Ltd*[33] the applicant's complaint was that the United Kingdom had breached its alleged obligations under Articles 10 and 93 (ex 5 and 99) to avoid further divergence from reference rates by reason of increases in excise duty. After giving consideration to the degree of fiscal sovereignty enjoyed by Member States and to the fact that no harmonisation measures beyond minimum rates of duty specified in Council Directive 92/84/EEC had ever been agreed, the Court concluded that there was no such obligation placed on the United Kingdom. In both of these cases, the Court of Appeal competently and conclusively applied Community law in relatively unexplored fields, without reference to the Court of Justice.[34]

References

A brief comment on the making of references by the English courts, particularly in the judicial review context, serves to enforce the conclusion that the litigant in the English court is being well-served. In cases concerning courts and tribunals which are not courts of last resort and which have a discretion to refer if a decision on a question of Community law is necessary to enable it to give judgment, national judicial proceedings have proven to be well-equipped for making refer-

---

28 *R v. Secretary of State for Employment, ex p Equal Opportunities Commission* [1995] 1 AC 1.

29 *R v. Ministry of Agriculture, Fisheries and Food ex p Bell Lines and An Bord Bainne* [1984] 2 CMLR 502.

30 *R v. Pharmaceutical Society of Great Britain, ex p Association of Pharmaceutical Importers* [1987] 3 CMLR 951.

31 *R v. Secretary of State for Foreign Affairs, ex p Rees-Mogg* [1994] QB 552.

32 [1999] EuLR 653. There was no appeal from this decision.

33 [1999] EuLR 522.

34 See also in the VAT field, *Marks and Spencer plc v. Customs and Excise* [1998] EuLR 154, 164 (VAT Trib), [1999] EuLR 450 (Moses J) and [2000] EuLR vol. 4:2 (CA).

ences in an appropriate situation and at an appropriate time. In a number of cases either where there was unresolved conflict on factual matters,[35] or where the issues of fact are not substantially in dispute[36] the English courts have exercised their discretion to make a reference. References have also been made at early stages in proceedings.[37]

Some commentators have interpreted the practical and pragmatic approach of the English courts regarding the referral for interpretation by the Court of Justice of points of Community law as a greater readiness or willingness to refer.[38] This is certainly true in real terms – compare one reference by United Kingdom courts collectively in 1974 with 21 references in 1996 – but it is unclear whether, in the context of a massively increased and increasing number of cases which raise potentially referable points, the trend to refer would be so marked. This is a point worthy of further consideration.

Others have been prepared to measure the success of a national system by the number of references. However, given the delays often associated with making a reference, receiving a preliminary ruling, and applying it in the national court, it is considered that a far better test of the success of a system is the proportion of cases involving points of Community law decided at first instance in national courts, and for references to be made only when the issues of Community law raised are novel, complicated or important. This is particularly true where a substantial number of the references made to the Court of Justice do not meet that test.[39] On that test the United Kingdom courts can be said to have been particularly successful.

CONCLUSION

The above should not be taken as discouraging national courts from making references to the Court of Justice in cases where references are considered necessary, but rather as encouraging the development of national systems where cases raising points of Community law can be decided conclusively, particularly at first instance. This short survey of cases indicates that the English courts at least are not daunted by the prospect of deciding questions of Community law according to the body of established case-law and legal doctrine rather than with

---

35 *R v. Pharmaceutical Society of Great Britain, ex p Association of Pharmaceutical Importers* [1987] 3 CMLR 951.

36 *R v. Plymouth Justices, ex p Rogers* [1982] QB 863.

37 *R v. Minister of Agriculture, Fisheries and Food, ex p FEDESA* [1988] 3 CMLR 207; see also *ex p Imperial Tobacco* (see above, n. 19).

38 See in particular Craig, *Report on the United Kingdom*, Chapter 7 at pp. 220-222 in Slaughter, Sweet and Weiler (eds) (see above n. 7).

39 See A.G. Jacobs in Case C-388-985 *Weiner v. Hauptzallant Emmerlich* [1997] ECR I-6495 in which the Advocate General called for "self-restraint" by national courts in referring questions. A possibly more appropriate call could be for national courts to show "self-confidence" in deciding questions.

the help of a preliminary ruling from the of the Court of Justice. This may be a realistic recognition of the stark fact that if all questions of Community law that were not entirely clear were referred, the Court of Justice itself would become administratively unworkable.

It may also be a manifestation in the English courts of what was perceived by Lord Mackenzie Stuart in the 29th Series of Hamlyn Lectures[40] as one of the 'essentials of a continuing Community legal order', namely the complementary role of the Court of Justice in creating standards and the national courts in applying them. The processes of judicial review in the English courts have shown themselves to be more than capable of absorbing principles derived from the jurisprudence of the Court of Justice into the judicial system and of applying them.

40 *The Hamlyn Lectures* 29th Series, Lord Mackenzie Stuart, 'The European Communities and The Rule of Law' (London, Stevens, 1977).

27

THE ATTITUDE OF FRENCH COURTS TOWARDS ECJ CASE LAW

Jacqueline Dutheil de la Rochère

In 1987, in a book devoted to "The effect of treaties in domestic law",[1] we concluded a contribution on France by saying that we awaited the day when, under the double pressure of Community law and the *Conseil Constitutionnel,* the French *Conseil d'Etat* would decide to embark on the course opened by the *Cour de Cassation*, that is to say, accept that Community law provisions should take priority over conflicting subsequent national legislation. Indeed the revolution occurred on 20 October 1989, with the *Nicolo* case: the *Conseil d'Etat* handed down a judgment which reversed its previous case law and ensured, in conformity with the prescriptions of Community law, the primacy of Community law over French statute law, even if the national law was of a later date. This judgment of great importance has opened a new era in the attitude of French courts – namely administrative courts – towards ECJ case law: although they will keep on trying to protect the coherence of the French legal system, French courts will take more and more into account the prescriptions defined by the ECJ as regards the relationship between EC law and national law. Furthermore, the improvement of the dialogue between the Luxembourg Court and French courts has meant that French case law appears, sometimes, to be influenced by substantive concepts and principles developed by ECJ case law.

I THE *NICOLO* REVOLUTION

In a number of Member States, the founding statement in ECJ case law, according to which the supremacy of EC law over national law is a necessary consequence of the very nature of EC law,[2] did not match with the national rules – constitutional provisions and case law – concerning the relationship between treaties and national law. Adaptation by French courts proved to be quite difficult; the difficulties have

1 The effect of treaties in domestic law, *United Kingdom National Committee of Comparative Law*, Volume 7, edited by Francis G. Jacobs and Shelley Roberts, London, (Sweet & Maxwell, 1987).

2 Case 6/64 *Costa v. ENEL* [1964] ECR 1141.

D. O'Keeffe (ed.), Liber Amicorum Slynn 417-431 (2000)

concentrated on the question of the priority of treaties, including EC Treaties, over subsequent statute law. The long resistance of the administrative courts has not yet been entirely extinguished.

1 The traditional situation

It must be recorded that, before 1958, under French law, both the principle of the sovereignty of Parliament and that of the supremacy of treaties over statute laws were traditionally accepted. Equally traditionally, when a court was faced with a problem of incompatibility between a statute law and a treaty, it tried to solve it through a "harmonizing" interpretation. If the conflict could not be resolved in this manner, according to the case law of the French supreme courts – *Conseil d'Etat* and *Cour de Cassation* – the treaty prevailed over the law only if the treaty was of a later date; if the statute law was of a later date than that of the treaty, the courts made the statute law prevail – it being admitted that the most recent expression of the will of the Parliament had to be applied as the law.

The French Constitution of 1958 maintained and even strengthened the principle of the supremacy of treaties over statute laws through the new provisions of Article 55,[3] and instituted a *Conseil Constitutionnel,* charged with reviewing the constitutionality of legislation, something very new in the French legal system, which had never before known any proper mechanism of control of constitutionality. It might have been expected that the *Conseil Constitutionnel* would consider that it was its task to uphold the constitutional rule of the supremacy of treaties over statute laws, and that it would declare incompatible with the Constitution any law passed by Parliament which would prove to be incompatible with treaty obligations, whatever the respective date of the laws and treaties.

However, in a judgment of 15 January 1975,[4] widely criticized, the *Conseil Constitutionnel* interpreted its role as reviewer of the constitutionality of statute law in a narrow sense, as including the review of the conformity of laws with provisions of the Constitution, but not the conformity of laws with provisions contained in a treaty, whatever Article 55 of the Constitution said. In subsequent judgments, the *Conseil Constitutionnel* indicated that it was the task of the various organs of the State to ensure the application of international conventions within the framework of their respective competences. Therefore, it was up to the courts, either ordinary courts or administrative courts, to ensure that the primacy of treaties was respected.

Taking advantage of the loophole left open by the *Conseil Constitutionnel,* the *Cour de Cassation,* in a judgment of 24 May 1975 – "*Société des cafés Jacques*

---

3 Article 55 of the Constitution provides:
"Treaties or agreements duly ratified or approved shall, upon their publication, have an authority superior to that of (domestic) legislation, subject, for each separate agreement or treaty, to reciprocal application by the other party".

4 Judgment on "Voluntary interruption of pregnancy", in Favoreu and Philippe *Les grandes décisions du Conseil Constitutionnel* (Paris, 1989).

Vabre"[5] – decided to opt in favour of the primacy of treaties over conflicting national statute laws, even those of a later date.

In his opinion Advocate General Touffait explained that Article 55 of the Constitution provided sufficient basis for a judge to ensure the primacy of a treaty over a law, and reminded the court that the *Conseil Constitutionnel* had left this task to the judiciary. However, the Advocate General suggested that the Court should not rely on Article 55 of the Constitution, but on the principle of the primacy of Community law over national law, as had emerged from the case law of the ECJ. The *Cour de Cassation* declined to follow him on this point, considering that the Treaty of 25 March 1957 had gained an authority higher than that of legislation "by virtue of Article 55 of the Constitution". A precedent was thus established in the French judiciary case law. Since then, when the occasion arises, French courts have made EC provisions prevail over subsequent legislation, usually making express reference to Article 55 – but not always. This applies not only to Treaty provisions but also to secondary legislation, which is seen by French courts as taking its legal value from the EC Treaty.

The French administrative courts did not follow the same line. The *Conseil d'Etat* first pronounced upon the question of conflict between the EC Treaty and a subsequent national statute law in 1968, in the "*Syndicat général des semoules de France*" case,[6] and, along with the traditional approach, made the subsequent national legislation prevail. The 1975 judgment of the *Conseil Constitutionnel* and the reversal of the case law of the *Cour de Cassation* did not influence it to modify its position which, after that, it confirmed on several occasions.[7] The reasons given by Madame Questiaux in her opinion on the *Semoules* case remained those supporting the administrative courts' case law. While recognizing the existence of the principle of the primacy of the Treaty over statute laws, the *Conseil d'Etat* has no competence to ensure the application of such a principle, as it is the judge of the executive and not of the statute law; it cannot refuse to enforce a statute law, even to ensure the application of Article 55 of the Constitution. It was sometimes said that the reversal of the position of the *Conseil d'Etat*, perhaps desirable, could only take place as a consequence of a legislative measure or even a constitutional one.

---

5 *Chambre mixte*, with opinion by advocate general Touffait, Dalloz-Sirey, 1975 p.497.

6 CE 1 March 1968, Rec. Lebon 1968 p.149.

7 For example, CE Ass 22 October 1979, *Union démocratique du travail*, Rec. Lebon p.383. Furthermore the *Conseil d'Etat* has refused to censure decrees – acts of the executive – which were in conflict with a treaty if they were based on a statute law itself in conflict with the treaty but adopted at a later date. This qualifies as the "*loi-écran*" doctrine. The limits of this doctrine were clarified in subsequent judgment: the screen of the law works if the content of the decree is the necessary consequence of the statute law posterior to the treaty (CE 8 February 1985 *Association des centres distributeurs Edouard Leclerc* Rec. Lebon p.25).It does not work if the law posterior to the treaty gives a wide habilitation to the executive; then the administrative court will be entitled to control the compatibility of the deccree with the earlier treaty: the screen has become transparent (CE 13 December 1985 *Sté International Sales and Import Corporation*, AJDA 1986 p.178, Opinion Martine Laroque, Rec. Lebon p.174; CE 19 November 1986 *Société Smanor*, AJDA 1986 p.683).

Meanwhile, the European Court of Justice had firmly established its case law on the necessary primacy of EC law over any conflicting rules of national law of the Member States with its various consequences and implications in terms of substance and procedure. In most countries, including Germany and Italy, the supreme courts had admitted the primacy of Community law over national law, a principle which, according to the *Simmenthal*[8] ruling should be applied by any national judge. The position of the French *Conseil d'Etat* was in direct contradiction with the ECJ case law Article 5 (now Article 10) EC, by which any Member State is obliged to comply.[9] Furthermore, and even more embarrassing at national level, the administrative courts, by virtue of the case law of the *Conseil d'Etat*, did not ensure the supremacy of treaties – and therefore of Community law – over subsequent national statute laws whilst ordinary courts did; so that it depended on purely internal reasons of partition of judicial competences between ordinary courts and administrative courts whether, in an individual case situation, EC law would prevail or not. It is in this context that the *Nicolo* case occurred.

2 *The Nicolo case*

The applicant – Mr Nicolo – brought his appeal before the *Conseil d'Etat* concerning the annulment of the French elections to the European Parliament of June 1989. In support of his action, he claimed that the French overseas departments and territories (DOM and TOM) should be excluded from the electoral territory used as a basis for these elections. He stated that, in so far as a French statute law had incorporated these territories in the French electoral territory in view of the elections to the European Parliament, it was contrary to Article 227 (now Article 299) of the Rome Treaty and should therefore be declared inapplicable.[10] The *Conseil d'Etat* rejected the appeal in one sentence, considering that the French law which had included the DOM -TOM in the one constituency for elections to the European Parliament was "not incompatible with the clear requirements of Article 227(1)" of the EEC Treaty.

The *Conseil d'Etat* did not explain the reasons for its change of attitude. In line with its habit of concision of language, the *Conseil d'Etat* said that nowhere was it upholding the principle of the primacy of a treaty over subsequent statute law; but this could be inferred without any doubt from the fact that for the first time it consented to examine the plea raised of the compatibility of a statute law and an earlier treaty.

8 Case70/77 *Simmenthal* [1978] ECR 1453.

9 The breach by France of its obligations under the treaty remained potential as the Commission never brought an action on the basis of Article 169 (now Article 226) EC with reference to such a violation of ECJ case law.

10 See Philippe Manin, "The *Nicolo* case of the *Conseil d'Etat*: French Constitutional Law and the Supreme Administrative Court's acceptance of the primacy of community law over subsequent national statute law", 28 CML Rev. (1991) 499-519.

Fourteen years after the *Cour de Cassation*, the *Conseil d'Etat* decided to enter the area left open by the 1975 judgment of the *Conseil Constitutionnel*. The *Commissaire du Gouvernement*, Mr Patrick Frydman, insists in his opinion that in so doing the *Conseil d'Etat* does not carry out a "constitutional review" of the law, which is the exclusive task of the *Conseil Constitutionnel*, but a control of compatibility of legislation with a treaty which any judge is entitled to carry out.[11]

The *Conseil d'Etat* did not clearly indicate on which legal basis it founded the supremacy of the EEC Treaty over national law. The only indication which can be found in this respect appears in the "visas" (preceeding mentions) of the judgment which refer to "the Constitution, more specifically, Article 55". According to most commentators[12] this reference implies that the *Conseil d'Etat* has accepted the arguments presented by its *Commissaire du Gouvernement*, namely that the basis for the primacy of the treaties – including EC treaties – over national statute law can only be found in Article 55 of the Constitution and not in the very nature of EC law as expressed by the ECJ case law.

There is a positive aspect in that reference to Article 55: the reversal operated by *Nicolo* in the *Conseil d'Etat* case law concerns any treaty and not only EC law. On the other hand, by proposing Article 55 as the only legal basis for ensuring the priority of the EC Treaty over French laws and rejecting Community law as another possible basis, Mr Frydman is quite far from the spirit of the Community law system. He expresses himself very strongly, stating in his opinion: "We are well aware ... that the ECJ which, as we know, accords Community law an absolute supremacy over rules of national law, even if they are constitutional, has not for its part hesitated to affirm the obligation to annul, in every case, laws which conflict with Community norms...But we do not believe you can follow the Court in this "pretorian" case law which to tell the truth seems to us to be at least susceptible of criticism".

The author of this opinion seems to forget that, by entering the EEC Treaty, the Member States have agreed to comply with its various provisions, including those establishing the authority of the Court and of its judgments. However, the *Cour de Cassation* had not adopted a different approach in 1975 in the *Jacques Vabre* case: domestic courts feel safe when they refer to the national Constitution and, up to now, have preferred not to add any reference to the general principle of primacy of Community law as defined by the ECJ case law.[13] Through the banalisation of EC

11 The review made by a judge of the compatibility of legislation with a treaty on the basis of an article of the Constitution which gives primacy to treaties has been qualified by a member of the *Conseil d'Etat* as an "indirect" control of constitutionality; see on that: Ph. Manin, *op.cit.* p.508.

12 The *Nicolo* case has been the object of a large number of commentaries, generally favourable. See the list quoted by Ph.Manin, *op.cit.* p.499; footnote n°1.

13 The Belgian *Cour de Cassation* in its judgment *Le Ski* is really the only example of a national judge who could have relied on a provision of the Constitution and deliberately chose to refer to the "natural" supremacy of Community law. See *Olmi*, "Les hautes juridictions nationales, juges du droit communautaire" in *Liber amicorum Pierre Pescatore*, (1987) p.499, quoted by Ph. Manin *op.cit.* p.510.

law and its assimilation with international conventions, the risk of a drift towards a recognition of prevalence of Community law over constitutional rules seems averted.

If Article 55 of the French Constitution provides a clear basis for the supremacy of treaties over national law, it does not provide equivalent certainty as regards the relationship between international rules other than treaties and national law. There comes the question of the status of secondary law of international organisations, namely that of EC secondary legislation.

Soon after *Nicolo* the *Conseil d'Etat* decided in the *Boisdet* case that an EC Regulation should prevail over national legislation of a later date.[14] The *Conseil d'Etat* had previously assimilated an EC Regulation into an international convention; therefore the extension to regulations of the *Nicolo* ruling was to be expected. However, in substance, a regulation – like any other act of EC secondary legislation – is different from an international convention. It is adopted in the framework of the Treaty and, therefore, according to a procedure accepted by the Member States, but which allows wide room for discretion by the various institutions involved; secondary legislation in the EC system is not of the same nature as the Treaty. Therefore it would be more coherent with the nature of such secondary legislation to establish its priority over national law as a consequence of the general principle of primacy of Community law over national law.

This would be of equal value as regards directives. The *Conseil d'Etat* in two very important cases of 28 February 1992, *Rothmans International* and *Arizona Tobacco,*[15] decided to give priority to a directive over conflicting subsequent legislation. We understand through the opinion of Madame Laroque that, as one might have expected, it did it in line with the *Nicolo* ruling, the directive being assimilated into an international convention. No reference was made to the general principle of primacy of Community law over national law.

If *Nicolo* is the result of a mode of reasoning which is not exactly in line with the ECJ case law, the decision itself marks a decisive shift from the approach traditionally adopted by French administrative courts. It has had subsequent significant consequences on the attitude of French courts towards ECJ case law.[16]

---

14 CE 24 September 1990, *Boisdet*, AJDA 1990 p.906.

15 CE Ass *SA Rothmans International France et SA Philip Morris France (1ère espèce), Sté Arizona Tobacco Products et SA Philip Morris France (2ème espèce)* 28 February 1992, concl. Laroque, AJDA 1992 p.210; 30 CML Rev. (1993) 187-198.

16 Since then, things have evolved even further. In a case of 3 December 1999, the French *Conseil d'Etat*, referring to the obligation for national authorities to implement EC law, and without mentioning article 55 of the French Constitution, has interpreted provisions of the French Constitution in order to ensure their compatibility with EC law (CE, Sect., *AOSML et Rassemblement des opposants à la chasse*, req. n°164789 et 165122).

II THE RELATIONSHIP BETWEEN COMMUNITY LAW AND NATIONAL LAW: NEW OPENINGS AND SOME ASPECTS OF RESISTANCE

A more significant evolution appears in the administrative courts' case law. As regards the *Cour de Cassation*, since 1975 it has followed a steady path regarding ECJ case law. It takes scrupulous account of the interpretations and evaluations of Community law to which the Luxembourg Court proceeds either through preliminary rulings, actions for annulment or enforcement actions against Member States.[17] It does not hesitate to quash a judgment of a court of appeal which would appear to be in contradiction with an ECJ decision.[18] Judgments of the *Cour de Cassation* sometimes reproduce part of the statements of reasons of the ECJ.[19] It also happened that a reversal in the case law of the *Cour de Cassation* took place as a consequence of a judgment of the European Court of Justice: this occurred in connection with the interpretation of the principle of continuity of a labour contract in case of transfer of undertakings.[20] The *Cour de Cassation* has even agreed to the liability of the State, on the basis of a fault, in order to compensate damages caused by the failure of a Minister of Justice's decision to take into account a judgment of the Court of Justice;[21] this is quite exceptional as ordinary courts have few occasions to examine questions of State liability. In the same way, ordinary courts will not normally have to face the question of direct effect of directives, as they are mostly confronted with horizontal situations. More generally, the ordinary courts, including the *Cour de Cassation,* are essentially confronted with questions of compatibility of the substance of national law with Community law and they have entirely accepted the consequences of the principle of priority of Community law as interpreted by the ECJ. The administrative courts have to adjudicate cases in which public authorities are involved and where the complex question of boundaries between Community and national competences in the implementation of Community law necessarily arises.

During the past ten years, very much as a consequence of the *Nicolo* trend, the *Conseil d'Etat* has experienced a noticeable evolution in the direction of an opening to EC law: no barrier seems to be insuperable anymore. However, without exerting any systematic resistance, the administrative courts tend to protect the coher-

17 See Georges Le Tallec "La Cour de Cassation et le droit communautaire" in *L'Europe et le droit, Mélanges en l'honneur de Jean Boulouis*, Dalloz (1991) p.363.

18 Cass.com. 11 February 1986, *Barbier c. Directeur général des impôts,* Bull.civ. 1986, 4ème partie p.6 n°7; Cass.com et fin. 16 January 1990, *Société Knoll international et Gavina c. Société Aliota diffusion e.a.,* Bull. civ. 1990, 4ème partie p.9 n°14.

19 Cass.Ass. plénière 6 March 1992, *Société Bachelot- Tessier et a. c. Société Sogramo* Carrefour et a., Europe, December 1992 p.9 n°447, to compare with: Case 112/89, *Upjohn v. Farzoo,* [1991] ECR I-1703.

20 Cass.Ass.plénière, 16 March 1990, *S.A. Nîmoise de tauromachie et de spectacle c. Mme Bodrero Sereu e.a., Droit social* 1990 p.416 note X.Pretot.

21 Cass. com. 21 February 1995, *Sté United Distillers c. Agence judiciaire du Trésor,* RTDE 1995 p.116.

ence of the French legal system when it appears that it could be threatened by some consequences of the supremacy of Community law.[22]

In the *Rothmans* case,[23] the *Conseil d'Etat* took into account two Article 169 (now Article 226) judgments of the Court of Justice condemning France for non-compliance of its legislation on the price of tobacco with an EC Directive; but the supreme administrative court, following the opinion of its *Commissaire du Gouvernement*, reaffirmed its competence to define the consequences under French law of such incompatibility. We may observe this sort of balance between consideration for EC case law and care for the logic of the French legal system in connection with questions such as the direct effect of directives, the public order value of EC law or the State liability for non compliance with EC obligations.

1 Direct effect of directives

The traditional antipathy of the *Conseil d'Etat* towards the ECJ case law is well known in relation to the possible invocation in national courts of provisions of a directive a Member State has failed to transpose in domestic law. Since the famous *Cohn Bendit* case,[24] the supreme administrative court sticks to its interpretation of Article 249 (ex189) EC according to which the Member States have an obligation to take the appropriate measures to apply a directive; in the absence of such measures, individuals cannot gain rights from the directive which they cannot invoke in national courts. The clearer result of that heterodox position is that the *Conseil d'Etat* refuses to pronounce the nullity of a decision of a public authority for the reason that such a decision would infringe the provisions of a non-transposed directive. Paradoxically enough, when a regulation exists on the basis of which the individual decision is adopted, administrative courts agree to pronounce the nullity by way of exception, if the regulatory measure, on the basis of which the individual measure has been adopted, does not comply with the directive.[25] This distinction is not very convincing, as the directive creates obligations for all public authorities,

---

22 On the general change of attitude of the *Conseil d'Etat,* see *Conseil d'Etat*, Rapport public 1992, "Sur le droit communautaire", Etudes et Documents n°44 La Documentation Française.

23 See above note 15. In the *Rothmans* case the question was that of the legality of a Minister of Finances' decision refusing to increase the price of tobacco. As a consequence of *Cohn Bendit* this decision could not be directly confronted with the EC directive France had been condemned by the ECJ for non-compliance with. The *Conseil d'Etat*, following the opinion of Mme Laroque, decided nevertheless to quash the Minister's decision which applied a regulation taken to enforce a statute law, itself incompatible with the EC directive and, for that reason, declared by the *Conseil d'Etat* as being deprived of legal value; this as a consequence of *Nicolo.* In the *Philip Morris* case of the same date the *Conseil d'Etat* draws the consequences on the ground of liability and compensation of the annulment of the Minister's decision.

24 CE 22 December 1978, *Ministère de l'Intérieur c. Cohn Bendit,* Rec. Lebon p.524.

25 TA Lyon 25 October 1979, *Stasi,* Rec.Lebon p.535; CE 8 July 1991, *Palazzi,* AJDA 1991 p.827.

including those taking individual measures, and compliance with the directive should be compulsory for all of them, whatever measures they take.[26]

Although the *Conseil d'Etat* has never renounced its traditional attitude as regards direct effect of directives,[27] its case law demonstrates important steps in the direction of the case law of the Court of Justice, with the practical result that the *Cohn Bendit* approach is now deprived of part of its efficiency. Administrative courts' case law has for the first time allowed that an individual could bring an action against a regulatory measure of transposition for non-compliance of those measures with a directive.[28] More generally, it has admitted the possibility, once the period allowed for transposition has expired, of invoking the non-compliance of any regulatory measure with the provisions of a directive.[29] Finally, it has been judged that an individual was entitled to ask the regulatory authorities to repeal a regulation incompatible with a directive and to introduce an action in judicial review against a refusal by public authorities to do so.[30]

Furthermore, in line with the case law of the Court of Justice (Case 14/83, *Von Colson & Kamann,* (1984) ECR 1891) the *Conseil d'Etat* applies the principle of compliant interpretation: in the case *Cercle militaire mixte de la caserne Mortier*[31] a decision of taxation was declared null because it was founded on an interpretation of the French General Tax Code (statute law) which was not compatible with the 6th VAT directive. There is little difference between this approach, which is allowed, and the possibility which is not open to an individual to invoke in court, the provision of a directive against an individual measure.

Following *Nicolo* the administrative courts' case law went even further in the direction of ECJ case law. It is now admitted that a non-regulatory measure founded on a statute law which is incompatible with a directive is illegal: this was outlined in 1992 in *Rothmans International* and *Philip Morris France* and confirmed in 1996 in *Revert et Badelon*[32] where it was decided that a refusal of exemption of VAT taxation was illegal as it was based on a provision of the General Tax Code which was incompatible with the 6th VAT directive. Now, as long as a

---

26 See D. de Bechillon, "L'applicabilité des directives communautaires selon la jurisprudence du Conseil d'Etat", *Revue du Droit Public* 1991 p.759.

27 Recent examples of the traditional attitude: CE 14 June 1999, *Fédération Nationale des Associations d'Usagers des Transports*; CE 28 July 1999, *Coordination des associations contre le tracé autoroutier urbain du sud d'Avrillé e.a. Revue Europe* October 1999 n°318.

28 CE 28 September 1984, *Confédération des sociétés de production des animaux de France,* Rec.Lebon, tables p.512.

29 CE 7 December 1984, *Fédération française des sociétés de protection de la nature et autres,* Rec. Lebon p.410.

30 CE Ass. 3 February 1989, *Compagnie Alitalia,* Rec. Lebon p.44.

31 CE 22 December 1989, AJDA 1990 p.328, Opinion Mme Hagelsteen.

32 *CE Ass.* 30 October 1996, *Revert et Badelon,* Opinion Goulard, RTDE 1997 p.171. In *Rothmans* a statute law and a regulation came between the directive and the Minister's decision; in *Revert et Badelon* only a statute law came between the directive and the refusal of tax exemption.

regulatory or statute law provision may be considered to be the legal basis of an individual decision, the test of compatibility with an EC directive may operate.

It is interesting to note in *Revert et Badelon* the insistence of the *Commissaire du Gouvernement* in convincing the supreme administrative court that it should comply with the ECJ case law. This is even more obvious in *Tête,*[33] a case decided in 1998 relating to the validity of the authorisation to build a motorway around the city of Lyon, where the difficulty lay in the absence of any national measure, either legislative or regulatory, to found the decision of the local authority which, the plaintiff argued, was contrary to the EC directive on public procurement procedures because of a lack of any measure of publicity. After having recalled the main lines of the ECJ case law on direct effect of directives and the administrative court case law, the *Commissaire du Gouvernement* advised the *Conseil d'Etat* that in the absence of any specific text it should consider (1) that the general principles of French law interposed between the directive and the administrative decision, (2) that these general principles were not compatible with the directive, and (3) that the administrative decision was null as it was founded on principles incompatible with an EC directive. This audacious reasoning was almost entirely adopted by the *Conseil d'Etat* which decided that "the national rules applicable at the date of the decision under review ...which did not provide for any publicity measure were not compatible with the objectives of the directive" and therefore the decision was illegal.

A new generation of *Commissaires du Gouvernement* have prompted the Supreme Administrative Court to align its case law with that of the Luxembourg Court. They maintain in their opinions a sort of deferential reference to the *Cohn Bendit,* precedent but they seem to be absolutely convinced that a total alignment will come with time. Some recent examples of traditional attitudes show that this time has not come yet.[34]

2 *Public policy value of EC law rules*

On that question there appears to exist quite a remarkable similarity between ECJ case law and administrative courts' case law. In the *Morgane* case decided by the *Conseil d'Etat* on 11 January 1991,[35] the *Commissaire du gouvernement* in her opinion advised the Supreme Administrative Court to examine *ex officio* the question of the compatibility of a tax regulation with the objectives of a directive, an argument which had not been clearly articulated by the plaintiff. The opinion stated that the principle of primacy and efficient implementation of Community law, as developed by the ECJ case law, implied that the national judge should examine the question of compatibility of national law with EC law even if the interested party

33 CE Ass. 6 February 1998, *Tête*, Opinion Savoie, *Revue Française de Droit Administatif* 1998 p.406.

34 See note 26.

35 CE Sect. 11 January 1991, *Société Morgane,* Rec.Lebon p.9; Opinion Mme Hagelsteen AJDA 1991 p.149.

had failed to use that ground; it quoted *Simmenthal*. The *Conseil d'Etat* did not follow, implicitly refusing to consider that the question of compatibility of a national regulation with a directive was a public policy matter.

Soon afterwards, the European Court qualified its case law. In *Verholen* (11 July 1991)[36] it judged that "the recognized right of an individual to rely, in certain conditions, before a national court, on a directive where the period for transposing it has expired, does not preclude the power for the national court to take that directive into consideration even if the individual has not relied on it"; it is a possibility for the national judge and not an obligation. Two well-known subsequent decisions of 14 December 1995 have completed the case law of the Court.[37] In *Peterbroeck* it was judged that Community law prohibits the application of a national rule of procedure forbidding the national judge to raise *ex officio* the question of the compatibility of a rule of national law with Community law if this question of compatibility has not been raised within a certain lapse of time. In *Van Schijndel* the Court judged that Community law does not require national courts to raise *ex officio* the question of a possible violation of Community law when the examination of this question would have the effect of making the judicial debate go beyond the limits defined by the parties.

In a judgment of 1996[38] the *Conseil d'Etat* maintained its careful previous position: not to make a rule that the question of compatibility of national law with Community law should automatically be raised by the national judges if this has not been done by the parties. This position is very much in line with that of the Luxembourg Court; both value the importance of taking into account the specificities of procedural rules applicable in each Member State, procedural rules which are usually inspired by the desire for a fair trial.

3 *Non-compliance with Community law and State liability*

This is another area where French courts' case law has developed in parallel with ECJ case law. French courts are quite ready to accept that the State must repair the damaging consequences of its violations of Community law, irrespective of whether such violations have been established by the ECJ or not. French administrative courts' case law has long been open to the principle of liability of public authorities for damages resulting from their regulatory activities, either on the basis of a fault – when, for instance, a regulation proves to be illegal – or for breach of equality – when a regulation causes very specific damages to a limited number of people. These principles apply when the reason for illegality is a breach of Community law; however, difficulties appear in connection with statute laws.

36 C-87 to 98/90, *Verholen*, [1991] ECR I-3783,at p.3789 n°15.

37 C-312/93, *Peterbroeck*, [1995] ECR I-4599; C-430 & 431/93, *Van Schijndel*, [1995] ECR I-4705.

38 CE 28 February 1996, *Megel et Petit, Revue Europe* 1996 n°273 p.8.

French law excludes the idea that the legislator could be responsible of any illegality – or fault – as he makes the law. However there is a tradition in administrative court case law[39] according to which the State may, in the absence of any illegality, compensate damages caused by a statute law if (1) the damage is especially important and specific, and (2) the legislator has not explicitly or implicitly intended to exclude compensation. These conditions are particularly difficult to apply to situations where Community law is in question, for instance, where the legislator has failed to transpose a directive.

At first, the *Conseil d'Etat* established the liability of the State for non compliance with Community law as a liability without fault:[40] it was strongly criticized and gave up this solution in the *Philip Morris* case of 28 February 1992. In this case, which was ruled on soon after *Francovich*, Mme Laroque in her opinion considered that, by not complying with the directive on the price of tobacco, the State had committed an illegality, the damaging consequences of which it should repair; however, very skilfully, Mme Laroque made the responsibility for such illegality fall on the regulatory authority and not on the legislator as, in the circumstances, a regulatory measure had been adopted to implement the law.

That sort of "legal hypocrisy"[41] is not always possible: the time will come when, in order to be in line with *The Brasserie* case law, the French Supreme Administrative Court will have to accept that the legislator is at fault when he does not comply with EC law. Lower courts have already paved the way. The Administrative Court of Appeal of Paris has decided[42] that the State was responsible for a failure to implement certain provisions of a VAT directive, using in its reasoning the exact formulations of *Francovich;* it is an implicit recognition of the fact that a failure to comply with EC law constitutes a fault of the legislator. The *Dangeville* judgment of the Paris Administrative Court of Appeal was quashed by the *Conseil d'Etat*[43] because, on a fiscal matter, the plaintiff should have opted for the special type of action provided by the Tax Code; however, in his opinion, the *Commissaire du Gouvernement* seemed to admit the reasoning of the Court of Appeal as regards the possible liability of the State as a consequence of the faulty non-compliance of a statute law with Community law.

As for the *Cour de Cassation,* which usually has no jurisdiction as regards public authorities' liability, it had to adjudicate a question related to the functioning of the public service of justice and decided that the adoption by the Minister of Justice of an instruction which was incompatible with the terms of an ECJ judgment constituted a gross negligence, for the consequences of which the State should

39 CE Ass. 14 January 1938, *Société Anonyme des produits laitiers "La Fleurette"*, Rec.Lebon p.25.

40 CE 23 March 1984, *Alivar,* Opinion Denoix de Saint-Marc, AJDA 1984 p.396,

41 Denys Simon "Le Conseil d'Etat, la directive, la loi, le droit: ad augusta per angusta", *Revue Europe* April 1992, chr.p.1-4.

42 CAA Paris, 1 July 1992, *Dangeville,* AJDA 1992 p.768; same court and same reasoning: 12 November 1992, *Société J.Walker and sons, Droit administratif* March 1993, n°130.

43 CE Ass. 30 October 1996, *SA Jacques Dangeville*, Opinion Goulard RTDE 1997 p.171.

compensate.[44] One may conclude that, as regards the liability of the State for non-compliance with community law, French courts are progressing very much in line with ECJ case law.

III Influence on French Courts of Substantive Concepts Developed by ECJ Case Law

Administrative courts' case law has evolved considerably during the past ten years, not only as regards the relationship between EC law and national law, but also as regards general principles of EC law.

The ECJ case law has developed over the years an impressive corpus of general principles, most of them common to the legal traditions of the Member States. However some are less familiar than others to the French legal system: this is especially true of the principles of legitimate expectation and legal safety, which until recently remained unknown in French courts' case law.

Although Article 55 of the Constitution does not make any reference to the general principles, in 1987, the *Conseil d'Etat* expressly considered for the first time the "general principles of international law" as sources applicable in domestic law;[45] it seemed that it could include in future the general principles of Community law. In 1995, the Supreme Administrative Court had to examine a request concerning the validity of the elections of 1994 to the European Parliament: the *Commissaire du Gouvernement* delivered a very clear opinion in favour of the application of the general principles of Community law and, in the particular case, the principle of equality. The *Conseil d'Etat* followed in principle, making an express reference in its judgment to Article F.2 (now 6) TEU.[46] One might wonder if this express recognition of the general principles of Community law as a source of law, which parties can refer to in administrative courts, would bring in new guarantees in comparison with the general principles already applied by these courts. The answer is probably in the affirmative: although French administrative courts have a long tradition of referring to general principles of procedures and to the principles developed by reference to the European Convention of Human rights, it is likely that the ECJ case law has contributed and will contribute to reinforce general principles recognised under French law.[47] We will give two examples.

The principle of proportionality is far from being foreign to French law. As early as 1909 the *Conseil d'Etat* established the rule according to which a public authority can limit civil liberties only to the extent which is strictly necessary for

---

44 See note 20.

45 CE 23 October 1987 *Société Nachfolger navigation Cy,* Rec. Lebon p.319; in fact it was a customary rule to which the *Conseil d'Etat* gave the qualification of general principle.

46 CE Ass. 17 February 1995, *Meyet e.a.* Rec. Lebon p.79; Opinion Toutée AJDA 1995 p.233.

47 See Yves Galmot, "L'apport des principes généraux du droit communautaire à la garantie des droits dans l'ordre juridique français", *Cahiers de Droit Européen* (1997) p.67.

the protection of public order.[48] This case law, inaugurated in relation to the freedom of worship, was subsequently extended to any civil liberty, including those granted by the European Convention of Human Rights. However, the *Conseil d'Etat* never presented these solutions as the application of a general principle of law; it never required as a general rule that any regulatory or individual decision should not exceed what is necessary to achieve the contemplated end. It is likely that the reference to the general principle of proportionality as established by Community law would reinforce the control of French administrative courts over public authorities' decisions, whenever they exert a discretionary power.

The formulation as well as the content of a principle of legitimate expectation is ignored by French administrative law. The ECJ case law, as we know, tries to reconcile between the legitimate confidence of individuals in the regulations which are applicable to them and the necessary flexibility of the rules in economic matters: when certain conditions are met, the Court requires that modifications to existing regulations incorporate transitory measures, so that the legitimate interests of individuals are protected.

Until recently, French administrative courts never considered that the absence of transitory measures could be a cause of illegality. The situation may change in the future, following a judgment of the Administrative Court of Strasbourg.[49] The existence of a company active in the recycling of domestic waste, namely waste imported from Germany, was severely threatened as a consequence of the adoption of a regulation which prohibited the importation of such waste, even from another EC Member State. The company asked for compensation for damages caused by the abruptness of the modification operated by the regulation. In its judgment of 1994, the Administrative Court of Strasbourg decided that, on the basis of the EC general principle of legitimate expectation, the State was responsible and should repair the damage incurred. This is a total innovation in French law.

Subsequently the case law of the *Conseil d'Etat* gave some signs that the signal given by the Administrative Court of Strasbourg would at some time be recognised. In a judgment of 16 March 1998[50] where a change in the curriculum for students of veterinary surgery was in question, the *Conseil d'Etat* refused to apply the EC principle of legitimate expectation as it considered the matter to be purely domestic. In another judgment of 5 March 1999, the *Conseil d'Etat* decided again, following the opinion of its *Commissaire du Gouvernement*, that the principle of legitimate expectation could not be referred to as long as no rule of Community law was in question.[51] The importance of this last case is underlined by the fact that the *Conseil*

48 CE 19 February 1909, *Abbé Olivier*, Rec. Lebon p.181.

49 TA Strasbourg 8 December 1994, *Entreprise Freymuth c. Min. de l'Environnement*, AJDA 1995 p.555, subsequently quashed by the Administrative Appeal Court (CAA Nancy 17 June 1999) which judged that the principle of legitimate expectation did not apply as the matter was purely domestic.

50 CE 16 March 1998, *Association des elèves, parents d'élèves et professeurs de classes et Mlle Poujol*, req. n°190768.

51 CE Ass. 5 March 1999, *M.Rouquette et Mme Lipietz e.a.*, *Revue française de droit*

d'Etat pronounced its judgment in *Assemblée.* For the time being the case law of the Supreme Administrative Court seems to be that the reference to the principle of legitimate expectation could be considered in relation with Community law matters.

This evolution shows that French administrative courts, pushed by the plaintiffs, are ready to use the new possibilities opened by the general principles of Community law, even those which are most unfamiliar to the French legal tradition. After noticeable evolution in the relationship between EC law and French law, the long term effect of the *Nicolo* case will continue to be felt in substantive matters.

administratif 1999 p.357.

28

COMPARATIVE LAW IN A TEXTURE OF COMMUNITARIZATION OF NATIONAL LAWS AND EUROPEANIZATION OF COMMUNITY LAW

*Walter van Gerven**

A lot of water has flowed under the bridges of the River Thames since Lord Denning wrote, in 1974, that Community law is "like an incoming tide. It flows into the estuaries and up the rivers".[1] He was referring to British rivers, but the same holds true of all Member States. More importantly, however, incoming and outgoing tides alternate ... which means that water from the Thames flows into the sea and becomes part of the incoming tide flowing into the estuaries and up the rivers in other Member States.

INCOMING ... AND OUTGOING TIDES: CROSS-FERTILIZATION[2]

Community law and national laws of the EU Member States pervade each other as much as water from the rivers in these Member States flows into the sea and from there into each others' estuaries. Not only does Community law modify the domestic laws of the Member States, in very diverse areas of the law, but national laws or, in the words of Article 288, ex 215, para. 2 EC, "general principles common to the laws of the Member States" also have an impact on, and contribute to the creation of, Community law.[3] The latter is exemplified by a 1986 judgment of the ECJ, in the case of *Leussink-Brummelhuis,*[4] rendered in

* The author apologizes for the many references hereafter to articles of his own. Those articles, relating to various aspects of the same theme, were published in different locations and are now difficult to oversee, even for the author. Hence, the present effort of coordination.

1 *Bulmer v. Bollinger* (1974) 2 All E.R. 1226, (1974) 3 W.L.R. 202.

2 See further J. Bell, "Mechanisms for Cross-fertilisation of Administrative Law in Europe", in *New Directions in European Public Law* (ed.) J. Beatson and T. Tridimas, (Hart Publishing, Oxford, 1998), 147-167 and in the same volume, J.W.F. Allison, "Transplantation and Cross-fertilisation", 169-182.

3 See further my article, "Bridging the unbridgeable: Community and National Tort Laws after *Francovich* and *Brasserie*", (1996) 49 ICLQ, 507-544, at 532 ff.

4 Cases 169/83 and 136/84 [1986] ECR 2801.

D. O'Keeffe (ed.), Liber Amicorum Slynn 433-445 (2000)

conformity with the Opinion of Advocate-General Sir Gordon Slynn (as he then was), and relating to a simple traffic accident. In that case two Community civil servants were involved, riding in a Community-owned car, one as a driver, the other as a passenger. In its judgment, the ECJ granted the injured passenger civil servant, Mr. Leussink, damages to an amount of BEF 2 million to be paid by the Commission, which was held liable for poor maintenance or inadequate inspection of the vehicle, or negligent use by the driver civil servant. However, the claims of Mr. Leussink's spouse and children were dismissed because their damage was indirect. The judgment rendered on the basis of Article 288 (then 215), para 2, EC was founded, as required by that Article, on principles common to the legal systems of the Member States, which the Court explicitly recognized in dismissing the claims of the spouse and the children by holding that "the legal systems of most Member States make no provision for compensating such effects".[5]

Extra-contractual liability of Community Institutions, referred to in Article 288 (ex 215) EC, is not the only area where the ECJ looks at the national legal systems to find Community law. It also sets out to do so in the area of extra-contractual liability of Member States for breaches of Community law (the so-called *Francovich* liability).[6] This implies, moreover, as the ECJ recognizes,[7] that both Community tort law systems, the one for breaches committed by Community Institutions and the one for breaches committed by Member States' institutions, are to be developed harmoniously, as they are both based on general principles common to the Member States' legal systems. In other areas of Community law as well, especially in the area of fundamental rights and freedoms, the ECJ has founded its case-law on common general principles, embodied in constitutional traditions common to the Member States (as well as, obviously, in the provisions of the ECHR).[8] As explained elsewhere,[9] the ECJ in its case-law as well as other EU institutions in their legislative tasks should increasingly draw inspiration from the national legal systems to develop rules of Community law. Indeed, for the European institutions not to take account of the legal concepts and principles which the national legal orders have in common –

5 *Ibid.* Excerpts from the judgment and the Advocate General's Opinion are reproduced, and discussed, in W. van Gerven, J. Lever, P. Larouche, C. von Bar and G. Viney, *Scope of Protection of Tort law on the national, supranational and international level, Casebooks for a common law of Europe*, (Hart Publishing, Oxford, 1998), at 409-412.

6 As the Court acknowledges in joined cases C-46/93 and C-48/93, *Brasserie du Pêcheur and Factortame*, [1996] ECR I-1029, paras. 27 and 41.

7 *Ibid.*, para. 42.

8 Thus e.g. the ECJ judgment in Case 4/73, *Nold v. Commission* [1974] ECR 491, para 13. The principle is now explicitly laid down in Article 6 (ex Art. F), para. 2 TEU.

9 W. van Gerven, "Taking Article 215 EC seriously" in the volume, edited by J. Beatson and T. Tridimas, referred to in footnote 2, at 35-47 as well as: "From Communitarisation of National Tort Rules to Europeanisation of Community Tort Law: The Invader Invaded" in R. Schulze (ed.) *Auslegung europäischen Privatrechts und angeglichenen Rechts*, (Nomos, Baden-Baden, 1999), 179-192.

and which legal research can and should bring to the fore – would, in the long run, lead to a loss of credibility, and legitimation, for the legal order of the European Union. As can be inferred from the foregoing, such legal concepts and principles also include concepts and principles derived from the ECHR and the Strasbourg Court's case law.

Obviously, drawing inspiration from the general principles common to the laws of the Member States does not mean that the ECJ is under an obligation to look for "some sort of arithmetic mean", or for "the lowest common denominator", of the solutions adopted by all of the Member States.[10] Nor does it mean that the Court may choose freely the national solution which it considers the most appropriate at its own discretion.[11] The Court's task is rather to look at the national legal systems for general principles (not specific rules) which are common to, and thus present in, systems, and which are capable of founding the interpretation of Community law rules which accords best with the structure and the fundamental principles of Community law.[12]

COMPARATIVE LAW CHALLENGED: A NEW TASK OF STRATEGIC IMPORTANCE

The cross-fertilization between Community and national legal systems leads to Communitarization of national laws – understood as overturning national rules inconsistent with Community law and therefore substituting Community law for national rules – on the one hand, and to Europeanization of Community law – understood as procuring for Community law a firm foundation in the concepts and principles which the legal orders of the EU Member States have in common – on the other. All this transforms comparative law radically from a purely persuasive branch of the law into one which has to fulfill a task of strategic importance.

The classic role of comparative law was, and still is, to compare legal systems of different countries, which in itself has many advantages.[13] Thanks to comparative law, legislators should be able to make better laws for their own jurisdiction; lawyers interpreting national laws may, in case of gaps or ambiguities, draw on solutions functioning in other countries in order to improve their own legal system; teachers may use comparative law to give students and them-

10 See Gand AG in his Opinion, in Joined Cases 5, 7 and 13-24/66, *Kampffmeyer* [1967] ECR 245; Roemer AG in his Opinion in Case 5/71, *Schöppenstedt*, [1971] ECR 975.

11 F. Schockweiler, G. Wivenes and J.M. Godart, "Le régime de la responsabilité extra-contractuelle du fait d'actes juridiques dans la Communauté européenne" (1990), Rev. trim. dr. eur., 27 ff.

12 Gand AG: "[*faire*] *oeuvre de comparaison et de création*", in his Opinion, *supra*, n. 10; see also J. Mertens de Wilmars, "Le droit comparé dans la jurisprudence de la Cour de Justice des Communautés Européennes" 1991 J.T. 37 ff. See further my article, *supra* n. 9, at 44-45.

13 See Zweigert/Kötz, *An Introduction to Comparative Law* (2nd ed., translation T. Weir, 1987), at 2 ff., esp. 11-27.

selves a better insight into their own legal system; and, finally, comparative law can and will be of assistance in preparing projects for the international unification of law. All these functions and aims are useful but not indispensable, in that they *assist* legislators, lawyers and teachers to carry out their work – which can also be performed, albeit presumably less well, without the assistance of comparative law. They are all of a "persuasive nature".[14]

Due to the cross-fertilization between Community law (and other European supranational law, more particularly the law of the legal order of the ECHR) and the national laws of the Member States of the EU (respectively of the ECHR), comparative law has taken on a new dimension which will reinvigorate comparative law research. That dimension is "a private law common to the whole of Europe".[15] To understand that task properly one must keep in mind that comparative law is presently understood to encompass both external and internal comparative law.[16] Whilst the former refers traditionally to a comparison of legal systems existing in different countries, the latter refers to the comparison of legal orders existing within the same country, either because different legal orders (such as international, supranational, national, regional and local legal orders) function alongside one another on the same territory, or because different sets of rules (such as common law and equity law, civil and administrative tort liability rules) relating to similar problems function within the same national legal order in that country.[17]

Understood in that double sense, comparative law becomes of strategic importance as it constitutes an indispensable tool (i) to enable the *harmonization between* the national legal systems of the EU Member States (external dimension) to be carried out efficiently: only when the harmonization of rules is effected and the harmonized rules interpreted on the basis of genuine comparative research, will those rules have a chance not to be regarded as *Fremdkörper* in each of the legal systems of the Member States, (ii) to preserve *homogeneity within* each national and each supranational legal order (internal dimension) which must be maintained between rules dealing with identical or similar issues in that legal order, and (iii) to maintain *coherence within and between* the na-

14 J. Vranken in *Algemeen Deel*, Asser-series, 1995, at 140.

15 Zweigert/Kötz in *An Introduction to Comparative Law*, translated by Tony Weiz (1998), 16 and 28-31. See also Kötz, "Comparative Legal Research and its Function in the Development of Harmonized Law. The European perspective" in M. Jareborg (Ed.), *Towards Universal Law* (1995), 21-36.

16 Vranken, *op.cit.*, at 132.

17 *Idem*, at 124 *et seq.* There is, of course, a nuance: international, supranational and national rules, applicable within the same territory, belong to different (but intertwined) legal orders; national, regional and local (e.g. municipal) rules pertain to the same legal order but function, vertically, on a different level; common law and equity, civil and administrative rules function vertically on the same level but, horizontally, in different compartments. See further: W. van Gerven, "Mutual Permeation of Public and Private Law at the national and supranational level" (1998), 5 *Maastricht Journal of European and Comparative Law*, 7-24.

tional and Community legal orders (internal and external dimension), which is needed to preserve (sufficiently) equal treatment of citizens before the law, within each Member State and throughout the Community, as well as equal judicial protection in the enforcement thereof.

To fully assess the need to maintain homogeneity within the national legal system of each Member State, it must be recalled that the legislative harmonization process – which in the EC is carried out mainly by way of directives – is substantially of a limited and specific nature. The reason for this lies in the limited scope of powers conferred upon, and objectives assigned to, the Community (Art. 5, ex 3b, EC), and in the allocation of such powers among a variety of directorates-general within the Commission.[18] The effect of this is that the individual directives are not always supported, not even when they relate to the same or a similar branch of the law, by a consistent and comprehensive view at the level of the Community as a whole. Moreover, and more importantly so, whilst those directives tend to bring together national laws within specific areas of (basically) economic law, they are at the same time responsible for growing disparities, within each Member State, between national rules affected by Community law and those, albeit relating to similar issues, which are not affected by Community law.

The same state of affairs arises in practice as a result of case-law of the Community judiciary where it interprets fundamental Treaty provisions which take effect throughout the Community. The harmonizing effect of such case-law may also result in additional disparities both at the level of the Community, that is between different areas of Community law, and at the level of each Member State, that is between areas of that Member State's law which are affected, and those, dealing with similar issues, which are not affected by Community law. The phenomenon can be perceived in the field of remedies which are intended to enable Community citizens to enforce rights which they derive from Community law before Community and/or national courts. Thus, for example, in the field of the remedy of compensation, the ECJ's case-law contains, as already mentioned, two different Community law regimes to make good harm which individuals have sustained as a result of breaches of Community law by, respectively, Community institutions (Art. 288, para 2, EC) and Member States (*Francovich* liability). At the same time, the ECJ's *Francovich* case-law has the effect of modifying the rules, and related remedies, on State liability within each Member State but *only* in so far as breaches of Community law by State agencies are involved, and not for breaches of purely national law by the same agencies. The result of all this is the co-existence, not only at the level of Community law but also within each Member State, of two different tort liability sets of rules for public law legal entities (and their civil servants). Moreover, in common law countries, and in some continental systems, where tort rules do not differentiate

18 See my article "Community and national Legislators, Regulators, Judges, Academics and Practitioners: living together apart?" in *Law Making, Law Finding and Law Shaping*, ed. B.S. Markesinis, (Oxford University Press, 1997), 13-35.

between tortious behaviour of private and public law persons, the disparities which affect the national legal system as a result of Community law may spread throughout the whole of national tort law. The same would occur in the other continental legal systems as well if, as should be expected,[19] the ECJ were to decide that a remedy for compensation must also be made available, under conditions to be determined by it, for breaches by private law persons or entities of directly applicable Community rules, such as Articles 81 and 82 (ex 85 and 86) EC.

To remedy the disruptive effect which Community legislation and case-law may have at the Community and national level, it is an absolute requirement to pursue homogeneity of rules at both levels. Such an effort is needed if one wishes to avoid the unhappy situation that citizens are governed by different rules, although they find themselves in similar situations, and/or must rely on different actions of law before the courts when such rules are breached. As the ECJ held in *Brasserie* regarding the application of the two Community tort law regimes:

> "the conditions under which the State may incur liability for damage caused to individuals by a breach of Community law cannot, *in the absence of particular justification*, differ from those governing the liability of the Community in like circumstances. The protection of the rights which individuals derive from Community law cannot vary depending on whether a national authority or a Community authority is responsible for the damage" (italics added).[20]

It is obviously a matter for the Community legislator, or judiciary, to eliminate, or at least reduce, such disparities in rules and their enforcement, when Community rules are concerned, such as the two Community tort law regimes referred to above. But, where disparities are involved resulting from national rules governing similar situations, of which some are affected by Community law and others not, it is a matter for the national legislature, or judiciary, to bring about homogeneity by virtue of principles inherent in their own legal system, such as the principle of good governance or the requirement to treat citizens equally when they seek relief from the courts. In some countries, for example, national legislatures have undertaken to make national competition rules dealing with purely domestic cartel agreements, abuses of a dominant position, or concentrations, fully consistent and sometimes identical to EC competition rules dealing with the same practices in the context of inter-State commerce.[21] An example of an effort to achieve homogeneity on the part of a national judiciary is the judgment of the House of Lords in *M. v. Home Office*, where the rule of im-

19 See my Opinion in Case C-128/92, *Banks v. British Coal Corp.*, (1994) ECR I-1209.

20 *Brasserie*, *supra*, n. 6, para 42. Not to eliminate, or at least reduce, such differences would result in a too large unequal treatment of individuals in respect of judicial protection: see F.J. Jacobs, "Remedies in National Courts for the Enforcement of Community Rights" in *Liber Amicorum for Don Manuel Diez de Velasco*, (1993), at 969 and 982.

21 That effort has been undertaken by the Belgian, Dutch and U.K. legislature.

munity of the Crown was set aside also in purely national law matters as, in Lord Woolf's words, it would be "an unhappy situation" if the rights of individuals risk being less protected in pure national law than in areas affected by Community law.[22]

It may be apparent from the foregoing that to preserve a sufficient degree of coherence in the legal order of each Member State as well as in the Community legal order (including relevant ECHR principles which are part of Community law)[23] and between all of these legal orders, poses an immense challenge for legislators, practitioners and academics. The plurality of legal systems which are closely intertwined with each other, to the point of being sometimes an integral part of each other, both at the national and the supranational level, and the fact that they are to be enforced by a plurality of courts with different mentalities, backgrounds and procedural rules, are factors which may cause any legal system, alone and in conjunction with others, to become unmanageable because of intrinsic inconsistencies and unjustified disparities. This situation necessitates a new way of approaching comparative law, which (i) focuses on differences and similarities between *concepts* and general *principles* belonging to different national and supranational legal orders and, within each legal order, to different branches of the law; (ii) examines differences and similarities in substance and style, between judicial and legislative *solutions* applied to similar factual situations, and analyses the legal issues arising therefrom and the value judgments inherent therein; (iii) explains how such differences and similarities in solving similar issues are influenced by differences and similarities in concepts used and principles adhered to; (iv) examines and explains the impact on the traditional differences in legal reasoning and mentalities of the fact that Member States of the EU have decided to live together under the same roof, with all the exchanges this entails in the legal field (as in others) between practitioners, teachers and students.

To promote this new way of (practicing and teaching) comparative law, the project of case-books for a common law of Europe was launched in 1994 by the author, in cooperation with many others,[24] and the first case-book was published in 1998[25] with others to follow. Each of these case-books tend to reproduce legal materials, mainly case-law from the three major national legal systems and the two supra-national legal orders (EU and ECHR), accompanied by short comments and followed by comparative overviews. The idea is not to give a complete overview of the systems concerned – a case-book is not a textbook – but to

---

22 (1993) 3 All ER 537, (1993) 3 WLR 433. See further M. Brealy and M. Hoskins, Remedies in EC law, 2nd ed., (Sweet and Maxwell, 1992), at 153, footnote 24.

23 As for Community law, see also N. Fennelly, "Preserving the Legal Coherence within the New Treaty", 5 *Maastricht Journal*, 1998, 185-199.

24 For an early presentation of the project, see 4 *European Review of Private Law* (1996), 67-70. See also the project's website: http://www.unimaas.nl/-casebook.

25 See the book referred to *supra*, n. 5. The second and extended edition will be published in the course of 2000.

supply materials to be used in universities as well as by practitioners (in the first place judges), within and outside the EU, at the user's discretion, that is without imposing the authors' own views. These case-books are intended to be complementary to other initiatives looking to develop a European *ius commune.*[26]

JUDICIAL REMEDIES AT THE CROSSROADS BETWEEN COMMUNITY AND NATIONAL LAW: PERMEATION BACK AND FORTH

The emergence of judicial remedies in the national legal orders of the EU Member States to enforce rights which individuals can derive from Community law, is a prime example of how Community law influences national laws, and *vice versa*. It is the consequence of the Community law principle of judicial protection which requires Member States to put judicial remedies at the disposal of persons who seek to enforce their Community rights in national courts. The requirement of judicial protection as an overriding principle of Community law has its origin in the far reaching (and ever further reaching) doctrine of direct effect, but goes now beyond it, as is demonstrated by the ECJ's *Francovich* and *Brasserie* judgments relating to the remedy of compensation.[27]

There are, at present, four remedies which are available in the national courts to allow plaintiffs to enforce their Community rights: one general remedy to set aside national measures, including legislation, which are inconsistent with directly applicable Community law; and three specific remedies, implementing and complementing the general remedy, which tend to obtain, respectively, restitution, compensation and interim relief. For each of these remedies, the ECJ has laid down the principle, but also, and increasingly so, the conditions under which those remedies can be put into operation before a national court. These conditions concern the type and extent of redress to be obtained, the persons entitled to initiate the remedy and the persons against whom it can be brought, the burden of proof and the time limits, foreclosures and statutory limitations to which the remedy may be subjected. Obviously, not all those aspects have already been spelled out in the ECJ's case-law for each of these remedies. But, the existence of each remedy has been acknowledged by the Court as a principle of Community law (now also, it would seem, for the remedy of restitution[28]) as well as the constitutive conditions, under which each of them can be brought in a national court. Moreover, the ECJ has recognized, as the "bottom line" of judicial protection, that no national law or measure of a procedural nature may ren-

26 On that subject, see recently J. Basedow, "The Renascence of Uniform Law-European Contract Law and its Components" in 2 *Europarättslig Tidskrift* 1999, 44-71.

27 See further my article "Bridging the gap between Community and National Laws: towards a Principle of Homogeneity in the field of legal Remedies", 32 CMLRev. 1995, 679-702; and the later article on "Bridging the unbridgeable ...", *supra*, n. 3.

28 See the ECJ's judgment in Case C-188/95, *Fantask A/S and others v. Industriministeriet (Erhverusministeriet)* [1997] ECR I-6783, para 38.

der the initiation of the remedy concerned practically impossible or excessively difficult; a "minimal efficiency" guarantee which, in my view, would be better replaced, or implemented, by an "adequacy test" according to which the remedy should allow plaintiffs to obtain *adequate* redress, that is commensurate with the nature of, and the degree of interference with, the plaintiff's Community right.[29]

The specific remedies for which the ECJ, so far, has given most indications regarding the content and extent of the remedy are the remedies of compensation and of interim relief.[30] It is also in connection with these two remedies that the Court has endeavoured to bring homogeneity to the two remedial systems existing in Community law, one to be initiated before the Community judiciary itself and the other before a national court.[31] Furthermore, as already mentioned, it was in connection with the remedy of interim relief that the House of Lords enlarged the scope of the remedy under national law by setting aside the rule of immunity of the Crown in view of treating plaintiffs equally, regardless of whether their claim is based on national law only or on national law as modified by Community law.

Communitarization of national remedial law, leading to the replacement of existing national rules that are inconsistent with Community law, by new national rules intended to enforce Community rights in a sufficiently uniform way throughout the Community, goes – and should go more systematically – hand in hand with the *Europeanization* of Community law.

The Communitarization of national remedies, by replacing old with new, Community friendly, national rules can be very radical, as is demonstrated by the remedy of compensation. In that regard, Community law has not only modified the conditions for State liability to arise within each Member State's legal order, by imposing three constitutive conditions: serious breach, (of) norms conferring rights, and (direct) causation between breach and harm, but has also specified the scope of compensation by also including pure economic loss (which is not contingent on loss to property or to the person) as a head of damage to be compensated for.[32] As said, such changes may affect the tort laws of countries where public and private defendants are subject to the same rules on tort liability, even more drastically than in other countries. But in the latter

29 W. van Gerven, "Of Rights, Remedies and Procedures", to be published in the April 2000 issue of CML Rev.

30 For an overview of the ECJ's case-law regarding those general and the specific remedies, see T. Trimidas, *The General Principles of EC Law*, (Oxford University Press, 1999); M. Brealy and M. Hoskins, Remedies in EC Law, 2nd ed., (Sweet and Maxwell, 1998).

31 See for the remedy of compensation, Article 288, para 2 EC and *Francovich*, *supra* note 20 and accompanying text, and for the remedy of interim relief, Article 242 (ex 185) EC and Joined Cases C-143/88 and 92/89, *Zuckerfabrik Suderditmarschen and Zuckerfabrik Soest*, [1991] ECR I 415.

32 In a recent judgment of 1 June 1999 in case C-302/97, *Konle v. Austria*, nyr, the ECJ held that in Member States with a federal structure, reparation need not necessarily be granted by the federal State itself provided that there is a public authority which is made responsible for making good the harm.

countries further changes may also have to be made if the need is felt to treat plaintiffs equally in similar circumstances regardless of the public or private law nature of the perpetrator of the breach of Community law.

The more drastic those changes are, the more imperative the need for Europeanization of Community law, in the sense that changes brought about by Community law must be founded as much as possible on concepts and principles which show a large degree of commonality between the legal orders of the Member States. As pointed out elsewhere,[33] the aforementioned constitutive conditions of serious fault, causation and, even more importantly, that the norm breached must confer rights, and in that connection the issue of *ius standi* of for example environmental organizations, are all issues which urgently need to be determined in a sufficiently uniform manner. They are decisive for the question of whether, for example, a breach of (sufficiently clear and unconditional) directive provisions, as they exist in the environmental area, may give rise to damage claims from anyone having sustained harm as a result of such a breach. Comparative research should lead the way and enlighten the Community judiciary which sooner or later will have to decide these issues. In the absence of such research, the solution chosen by the Court may add confusion rather than clarify the legal situation.

EMERGING CONSTITUTIONAL LAW PRINCIPLES ON ACCOUNTABILITY AND RESPONSIBILITY

The rules on remedies to enforce Community rights before Community and national courts are an example of the mutual permeation of Community and national laws in an area where Community law is already well developed, thanks to extensive case-law of the ECJ. There are other areas of Community law where such development has not yet taken place, but where it is in an early stage only, making it even more desirable for Community law to draw benefit from general principles which are common to the legal systems of the Member States. One such area relates to the emergence of constitutional rules regarding the political responsibility and accountability of the European Commission towards the Community legislature, in particular the European Parliament, i.e. the directly elected branch of the legislature. The subject has been analysed in two reports which the Committee of Independent Experts[34] designated by the European Parliament to examine allegations of fraud, mismanagement and nepotism in the

33 See case-book cited *supra* in n. 5, at p. 480-483 and W. van Gerven, "The ECJ's recent case-law in the field of tort liability; towards a European *Ius Commune*?" in Jansen *et al.* (eds), *European Ambitions of the National Judiciary,* (Kluwer, 1997), pp 91-110 and, somewhat expanded, in N. Reich/R. Heine-Mernik (eds), *Umweltverfassung und nachhaltige Entwicklung in der Europäischen Union*, (Nomos, 1997), pp 177-194 (with a summary in English by R. Heine-Mernik, at pp 203-205).

34 The Committee consisted of five members of which the author was one.

European Commission, has made public on 15 March 1999 and 10 September 1999 respectively. After having focused in its first report[35] on the collective responsibility of Commissioners (which provoked the resignation of the Santer Commission) the Committee analysed, in chapter 7 of its second report, the issues of accountability and (personal and political) responsibility of Commissioners in connection with their duties of integrity in public life and of leadership and sound management as members of the Executive branch of the European Community.[36]

The broad issue underlying the question of accountability and responsibility concerns the constitutional relationship between the top of the Executive, that is the cabinet of Ministers in a national context and the Commission as a body in the European Community, *and* the elected Parliament acting as the legislature, or in the Community as part of the legislature. The issue turns around the constitutional, or political, responsibility of Ministers or Commissioners on the one hand and their personal, or managerial responsibility, individually or collectively, on the other hand. Sub-questions concern the extent to which members of the Executive have a duty to inform Parliament, the sanctions for not complying with that duty, and the scope of political responsibility; that is, whether it exists not only for personal and managerial conduct for which those members can be blamed, but also, possibly, for conduct of officials for which they cannot be blamed but for which they are politically responsible.

Political responsibility of cabinet Ministers raises problems in all Member States and exists in different forms and at different levels depending on the constitutional structure of the legal system concerned. Differences exist as to the scope of political responsibility, as mentioned, but also, obviously, as to the nature of the political consequence to be drawn, and by whom it should be drawn. In its second report the Committee came to tentative conclusions regarding the political responsibility of members of the Commission. It found that collective responsibility is, in the present state of Community law (Article 201, ex 144 EC), a matter for Parliament whilst individual political responsibilities are a matter for the President of the Commission to decide, but that his hand must be strengthened.[37] The Committee also discussed at length the standards of integrity to be observed in public life generally and, in particular, by members of the Commission.[38] It recommended the institution of a Committee on Standards in Public Life.[39]

35 *First Report on Allegations regarding Fraud, Mismanagement and Nepotism in the European Commission* (15 March 1999), p. 144.

36 *Second report on reform of the Commission. Analysis of current practice and proposals for tackling mismanagement, irregularities and fraud*, Vol. I and II, 10 September 1999, p. 138 and p. 140.

37 See para. 7.14.15 through 7.14.22. See also the Recommendations in para. 7.16.14 and 7.16.15.

38 Para. 7.4.1 through 7.4.8 respectively para 7.5.1 through 7.5.13 and the Recommendations in para 7.16.1 ff.

39 Para. 7.7.1 through 7.7.5 and Recommendations in para 7.16.9.

These findings are tentative and reflect the present state of Community law. They should be implemented by extensive comparative research concerning the constitutional principles and traditions applicable in the Member States, and carried out with the intention of reaching conclusions which support the future development of the Community's constitutional structure. Such conclusions must, also, be based on principles common to the constitutional systems of the Member States while taking into account the characteristics of the European Union itself.

CHANGES IN THE METHODOLOGY OF COMPARATIVE LAW

The new dimension of comparative law, as a result of the developments mentioned above, may well be responsible for changes in the methodology of comparative law. The most important change, as already mentioned, is the emphasis on comparing rules which do not necessarily belong to legal systems functioning in different countries, but belong instead to systems which function alongside each other, sometimes as an integral part of each other, within the same territory, be it at different levels and/or in different areas of the law. Such emphasis goes hand in hand with the need to analyse basic concepts and general principles which different systems or branches of the law have in common, in order to maintain a sufficient degree of coherence without which the large variety of legal developments can no longer be overseen. It is also responsible for the need to give more attention to case-law, particularly of the supreme courts in the different national and supranational legal orders, in which basic concepts and general principles come more frequently to fruition than in statutory provisions.

The increased attention for the role of case-law emanating from various supreme courts is responsible in turn for the need to explore the phenomenon of rule-making activities of such courts in a context of (internal and external) comparative law. It can indeed no longer be denied that supreme courts do have such a rule-making function, which finds its main expression in the development of general principles as a result of freer teleological methods of interpretation and analytical application of existing rules to situations involving new issues of law. The Court of Justice in Luxembourg, as well as the European Court of Human Rights in Strasbourg, both operating within a recent legislative environment, have very much contributed to the recognition of such new methods of interpretation and the rule-making function they imply. That is so because of the prominence, in those Courts' case-law, of basic rights and fundamental freedoms which are in permanent need of creative implementation. To recognize the reality of such a rule-making function is most imperative if one wishes to avoid supreme courts acting as legislators without being subjected to the checks and balances which accompany law-making activity in a democratic society. Such checks and balances imply, more particularly, that enough insight is given in the legal reasoning and underlying value assessments that have led the judges to reach their conclusion. It also implies that some device is developed, in those courts' case-law, to limit the retroactive character of important jurisprudential changes.

The subject of rule-making activity of supreme courts is closely related to the way in which these courts view their function themselves. In that respect, there is a marked difference between, for example, the French *Cour de cassation* and the German *Bundesgerichtshof*. This is *not only* a difference in style: *Cour de cassation*-decisions are remarkably succinct and offer little insight to the reader, whereas *BGH*-decisions are very much elaborated and often contain an extensive discussion of prevailing case-law and even legal writings. That is *also,* and even more importantly so, a difference in the approach taken in respect of the legal issues to be determined by those Courts: the French *Cour de cassation* considers many questions as questions of fact coming within the trial courts' "pouvoir souverain", whereas the German BGH considers many such questions as questions of law to be determined by the supreme court itself. The House of Lords, on the other hand, not unlike the BGH, speaks out on many issues which the French *Cour de cassation* would consider to be questions of fact, but deals with those questions in a much more pragmatic way than the BGH, and also in a language which is easier understood. It is interesting to see how the ECJ and the ECHR have developed their own style, which is somewhere in the middle.

A final point to be mentioned here is the impact which the case-law of both the ECJ and the ECHR have on the constitutionalisation of substantive and procedural domestic laws. For the ECJ that is more specifically the case in the area of 'remedial' law, where, as seen above, the requirement of adequate judicial protection has played a considerable role in the shaping of that Court's case-law.[40] As for the ECHR case-law, such constitutionalisation is seen in very different areas of civil, administrative and criminal law, both substantive and procedural, where the respect of human rights is in issue. Such constitutionalisation is no longer limited to public law, but also "invades" important areas of private law, such as family law, and contract and tort law.

TRIBUTE TO A GREAT JUDGE AND AN EVEN GREATER FRIEND

I had the privilege of knowing Gordon Slynn at the European Court of Justice. During our pleasant encounters, sometimes at the occasion of often tedious 'administrative' meetings, I learned to know him as a great Judge and an even greater friend. And also after his, and my, departure from Luxembourg friendship remained, a symbol as so many of a unifying Europe.

40 See also H.P. Nehl, *Principles of Administrative Procedure in EC Law*, (Hart Publishing, Oxford, 1999), p. 214 where the emergence of procedural law principles is examined, in a context of good administration (and not, as here, in a context of full judicial protection). Those are mainly the principle of access to information and the right to be heard and, more generally, the principle of care (diligence).

29

THE ROLE OF THE EUROPEAN COURT OF JUSTICE IN SHAPING LEGAL STANDARDS FOR ADMINISTRATIVE ACTION IN THE MEMBER STATES. A COMPARATIVE PERSPECTIVE.

*Jürgen Schwarze**

INTRODUCTION

> "There is in the air – even amongst lawyers – what the great politician Harold Macmillan called the 'wind of change'; and people – whatever the outcome will be – are looking at these ideas with a view to the future."[1]

This statement made by the Right Honorable Lord Slynn of Hadley about the English attitude towards a European constitution at our first meeting at an international conference in Hamburg over sixteen years ago shall be the starting point of my essay in honour of Lord Slynn, because it is a perfect description of the development of legal standards for administrative action by the European Court of Justice.

In my article, I will describe and analyse this development. An attempt shall be made to contribute towards making those "winds of change" stronger, bearing in mind the words of Lord Scarman in his Hamlyn Lecture, that the law "is resistant to change: encapsulated in the forensic process, jealously guarded by those tireless workers in the legal hive, the teachers and the practitioners, it can have no greater sensitivity to the winds, let alone the gentle breezes, of change than have the judges and the profession who administer it".[2]

In the first part, I will explain the dichotomy of European administrative law and Europeanized administrative law. I shall then deal with those two parts separately, analysing their development (parts two and three). The fourth part will focus on the impact of the European Court of Justice on the Europeanization of national administrative law. Finally, I will discuss the possibility of a

---

* The author is grateful to Ms Corinna Bölhoff for her assistance in preparing this article.

1 G. Slynn, Statement, in: J. Schwarze/R. Bieber (ed.), *Eine Verfassung für Europa, Von der Europäischen Gemeinschaft zur Europäischen Union*, (Baden-Baden 1984), at p. 122.

2 L. Scarman, *English Law – the new Dimension,* (London 1974), at p. 7.

D. O'Keeffe (ed.), Liber Amicorum Slynn 447-464 (2000)

codification of European administrative rules for indirect administration (part five).

I "EUROPEANIZATION OF ADMINISTRATIVE LAW" VS. "EUROPEAN ADMINISTRATIVE LAW"

In the past decades, a set of rules has developed in the European Union that could well be termed a "European administrative law". It is a well-known fact, that neither the treaties nor secondary Community law contain a fully-fledged administrative law system, but leave the enforcement of Community law largely to public authorities in the Member States according to their own rules of procedure. Detailed written secondary Community law prevails only in some fields of direct administration executed by Community authorities, such as competition policy, anti-dumping matters or the rules relating to the Community's own civil service. The predominant factor in this evolution, therefore, has been the European Court of Justice. Through its case-law, it has built a widely ramified system of European administrative law on the basis of the general principles common to the laws of the Member States, a method which is expressly provided for in Art. 288 para. 2 (ex-Art 215 EC Treaty), though only for the development of rules in the field of non-contractual liability.[3]

For several decades, this development from national to European administrative law has been the main object of legal practice as well as academic debate. It was only after a while that the awareness has grown that this is only one side of the coin. Meanwhile, there has evolved an interactive system in the opposite direction – from Community law to a Europeanization of national administrative law – as well.[4] Thus, there is now a two-way process of cross-fertilisation between national and Community legal systems: in the first place, a new European administrative law has developed by way of comparative analysis of the general legal principles in the Member States, and now this newly created Community law begins to reverberate and to have a modifying influence on national law. As a consequence, European administrative law in its traditional sense and a "Europeanised" domestic administrative law, i.e. a European administrative law in the sense of an *ius commune* of the Member States, now stand side by side.

3 See J. Schwarze, *Die Befugnis zur Abstraktion im europäischen Gemeinschaftsrecht*, (Baden-Baden 1976), pp. 224 *et seq.*

4 *See J. Rivero*, "Vers un droit commun européen – nouvelles perspectives en droit administratif", in: M. Cappelletti (ed.), *New perspectives for a common law in Europe*, (Florence 1978), p. 405.

II THE DEVELOPMENT OF A EUROPEAN ADMINISTRATIVE LAW

1 *Methods in the jurisdiction of the Court*

Over the years, the European Court of Justice has sought to fill the lacunae in primary and secondary Community law by developing and establishing general principles of European administrative law. The landmark decision at the very beginning of its case law was the famous *Algera* case,[5] where the Court had to deal with the revocation of an administrative act. Although at that time the legal system of the European Community had never been confronted with this legal construction, the legal orders of all the Member States knew very well how to handle such a case. The Court, by using the French Civil Code as a sort of guideline, was able to deal with the case in an appropriate manner. By referring to the French idea of the "refusal of justice", the Court established certain rules on the revocation of administrative acts.

The Algera case was decided in the fifties under the Treaty of the Coal and Steel Community. Since then, the European Court of Justice has acknowledged a substantial number of such general principles of administrative law:[6] for instance, the fundamental principle of legality of administrative action,[7] the requirements of a due process of law, especially the right to be heard,[8] the principle of equal treatment[9] and the principles of proportionality,[10] of legal certainty[11] and of the protection of legitimate expectations,[12] to mention but a few principles of fundamental importance.

These basic principles, derived from domestic law, were developed by the Court with the aim of safeguarding subjective rights of citizens and enterprises in the Community in the absence of explicit provisions in the Treaties.[13] In a

---

5 Joined Cases 7/56 and 3-5/57, *Algera v. Common Assembly*, [1957-1958] ECR 39; see also J. Schwarze, "Tendencies towards a Common Administrative Law in Europe", ELR 1991, 3 at p. 5.

6 For a detailed description of the general principles of European law see J. Usher, *General Principles of EC Law*, (London 1998).

7 See Cases 42 and 49/59, *SNUPAT v. High Authority*, [1961] ECR 53; Case 113/77, *NTN Toyo Bearing v. Council*, [1979] ECR 1185 at 1209.

8 See Case 17/74, *Transocean Marine Paint Association v. Commission*, [1974] ECR 1063 at 1080 *et seq.*; Case 85/76, *Hoffmann-La Roche v. Commission*, [1979] ECR 461 at 511; Case 136/79, *National Panasonic v. Commission*, [1980] ECR 2033 at 2058.

9 Case 52/79, *Debauve* [1980] ECR 833 at 858; Case C-269/90, *Technische Universität München v. Hauptzollamt München-Mitte*, [1991] ECR 5469 at 5499.

10 Case 11/70, *Internationale Handelsgesellschaft*, [1970] ECR 1125 at 1137; Case 136/79, *National Panasonic*, [1980] ECR 2033 at 2059.

11 Case 13/61, *de Geus v. Bosch/van Rijn*, [1962] ECR 45 at 52; Case 98/78, *Racke*, [1979] ECR 69 at 86.

12 Case 111/63, *Lemmerz Werke*, [1965] ECR 677 at 690; Case 74/74, *CNTA*, [1975] ECR 553 at 548; Case C-177/90, *Kühn v. Landwirtschaftskammer Weser-Ems*, [1992] ECR 35 at 62 *et seq.*

13 See J. Schwarze, "Tendencies towards a common Administrative Law in Europe", ELR

broader perspective, the protection of fundamental human rights was to be promoted by the introduction of procedural guarantees as well.[14]

In the early stages of the development of Community law, the Court's chief aim seemed to be to guarantee the objective lawfulness of administrative action. However, in the course of time the notion of protecting the subjective rights of individuals as an additional aspect has gained increasing importance. By emphasizing the lawfulness of administrative procedure, the Court has also recognized the importance of a fair procedure for individuals and commercial enterprises affected by Community measures. In this context, it is characteristic for the emerging legal order of the Community, that there has been no clear distinction between the general principles of constitutional and administrative law. The European Court of Justice has developed and elaborated the general principles for administrative action on an "ad hoc basis", thereby following the example of the French *Conseil d'Etat*.[15]

In order to determine these general principles, the Court has recourse to the method of comparative law.[16] Comparative law encounters its own difficulties and has sometimes been challenged with regard to the compatibility of different administrative law systems. In terms of comparative administrative law, it can in fact turn out that in the various administrative systems, functionally similar legal principles may be quite differently categorized and defined from the point of view of legal doctrine. Therefore, a functional approach must be the cardinal method when applying comparative law methods in the field of administrative law.[17]

2 *Difficulties arising from the method of comparative law*

Difficulties arise mainly from the role and special situation of the Court. It is constantly seeking a new perspective, aiming at the protection of individual rights by defining legal constraints for administrative discretion: how should it be able to review the great number of principles of national laws, which in their turn protect individual rights, sufficiently? Moreover, the collision of different legal systems of the Member States may lead to the painful result that a certain jurisdiction will be welcomed in one Member State while in another, it will be deemed unlawful. Therefore, the task of establishing common administrative law principles in Community law is a rather complex and difficult one. The principles have to be extracted from, at present, fifteen different national legal systems of administrative law, which are not at all easy to compare. Neverthe-

1991, 3 at p. 5.

14 See J. Schwarze, "The Administrative Law of the Community and the Protection of Human Rights", CMLR 23 (1986), p. 401.

15 J. Schwarze, *op.cit.* (footnote 13), p. 5.

16 Y. Galmot, "Réflexions sur le recours au droit comparé par la Cour de justice des Communautés européennes", *Revue française de droit administratif* 6 (2), 1990, 255.

17 J. Schwarze, *European Administrative Law*, (London 1992), p. 1445.

less, the Court has been quite successful in dealing with this problem. As the Court's case law shows, it has been able to integrate specific ideas and principles of British legal thinking into European administrative law, such as the idea of a fair procedure and the strict observance of procedural guarantees for the protection of individual rights.[18] Thus, it has created a synthesis between common law standards and principles of Continental administrative law.

This influence of British ideas began as early as 1973, when Advocate General Warner in his conclusions described the restrictive approach of English and Scots law towards the possibility of self-imposed limitations on the exercise of discretion by the administration in detail.[19] To illustrate the point, I would like to refer to the well-known *AM & S*[20] case where the Court found a compromise solution to protect legal privilege – the right to confidential correspondence between advocate and client – and to the *Nakajima*[21] case. In this anti-dumping case, the Court was confronted with the principle of estoppel, which derives from the Anglo-American legal tradition and has no direct equivalent in Continental Europe. By integrating this principle into existing legal concepts and notions, notably those of legal certainty and legitimate expectations, the Court handled the problem in its own characteristic and successful way. This clearly underlines its intention to find a balanced synthesis between different legal concepts of national law and to use this technique to promote an adequate standard of civil rights protection and procedural guarantees in Community law.

III WAYS AND MEANS OF INFLUENCE OF COMMUNITY LAW UPON NATIONAL ADMINISTRATIVE LAW

I shall now turn to the examination of the other side of the coin, the Europeanization of the domestic administrative law of the Member States. Upon close examination, the process of Europeanization of national administrative law is characterized by the impact of Community law upon national law on three different levels:

The first and most eye-catching of these are the changes to the administrative laws of the Member States caused by binding secondary Community law. The duty to implement Community directives especially requires important changes within national law. However, the influence of Community legislation

18 Case C-294/90, *British Aerospace and Rover*, [1992] ECR 493.

19 Case 81/72, *Commission v. Council*, [1973] ECR 575, Opinion of AG Warner at p. 587, see p. 592 *et seq*. For further details and the effect on the case law of the ECJ see J. Schwarze, *Die Befugnis zur Abstraktion im europäischen Gemeinschaftsrecht*, (Baden-Baden 1976), at pp. 66 *et seq*.

20 Case 155/79, *AM & S Europe v. Commission*, [1982] ECR 1575, at 1611 *et seq*.

21 Case C-69/90, *Nakajima All Precision Co. Ltd.* [1991] ECR I-2069 at 2202.

is confined to specific fields that the Community may regulate within the limits of the powers conferred upon it by the EC Treaty.[22]

The European Court of Justice, on the other hand, has established in its case-law general principles of a more comprehensive and widespread application. Preliminary rulings under Art. 177 EC (now 234) Treaty especially, which have so vividly been described by Jowell and Birkinshaw as the "engine room for the development of some of the key concepts of EC law",[23] enable the Court to set up landmarks or reference points for the legal orders of the Member States. The impact of the Court's jurisdiction upon national administrative law is often regarded as even more important than Community legislation.[24]

However, modifications of domestic administrative law caused by Community legislation as well as the case law of the European Court of Justice are binding upon the Member States only where matters of Community law are concerned. The creation of a "Europeanized" administrative law in the Member States is essentially due to a third level of cross-fertilization between European and national law. This is the assimilation of domestic administrative law to European administrative law by voluntary adoption of Community law standards. Such an assimilation is most important for a European *ius commune* in the field of administrative law, insofar as the rules based on voluntary and unconstrained reception invariably apply to Community law matters as well as to matters of national law. The impetus for this reception may either come from Community legislation or from the case-law of the European Court of Justice. Such impulses and initiatives are to be explained by the desire to prevent the perpetual creation of two distinct legal orders for national and Community law matters.

IV Tendencies towards a Europeanization caused by the case law of the European Court of Justice

As the principles created by the Court's case law tend to be of a more widespread and comprehensive applicability, a few examples of the influence of European jurisdiction on national administrative law may be allowed. This – considering the limited space – can only be a short and abbreviated outline of existing tendencies without laying claim to completeness or full detail. Therefore, I will confine myself to a few principles, which in my eyes illustrate the above mentioned development particularly well. They come from substantive as

22 Art. 7 (ex-Art. 4 para. 1, 2nd. sentence EC Treaty).

23 J. Jowell/P. Birkinshaw, "English Report", in: J. Schwarze (ed.), *Administrative law under European influence: on the convergence of the administrative laws of the EU member states*, (London 1996), p. 318.

24 J. Schwarze (ed.), *Administrative law under European influence: on the convergence of the administrative laws of the EU member states*, (London 1996).

well as procedural administrative law and from the field of legal protection of the rights of individuals.

1 Substantive administrative law

It is important to note, first, that the area of substantive administrative law can be divided into the two fields of general administrative law and special administrative law. Each field is influenced by European Community law in its own way. Because of its extensive importance, however, the following examples shall focus on the field of general administrative law only.[25] It is mainly in this field that in recent years the common law systems of the United Kingdom and Ireland especially, but also – if to a lesser extent – the administrative law systems of the Continental Member States have been subject to a remarkable change, caused by the influence of European law.

a) The powerful influence of the general principles of European administrative law as developed by the jurisdiction of the European Court of Justice on the domestic law of the Member States is shown first and foremost by the *protection of legitimate expectations*. This principle has for a long time been recognized in the case law of the European Court of Justice as a general principle of law.[26] It is closely linked to the principle of legal certainty[27] and has gained practical importance at Community level notably through the revocation and withdrawal of administrative acts by direct administration and the recovery of unlawful Community payments by indirect administration.[28] Moreover, it has played an important role for the legal control of legislative acts, especially in connection with the problem, if and to what extent retroactive statutes may be lawfully enacted.[29]

In the Member States, however, the principle of legitimate expectations was originally by no means generally recognized. For a long time, the British legal order had no counterpart to this principle[30] and French law is also traditionally very hesitant to restrict administrative powers under the aspect of the protection of legitimate expectations.[31] Under the influence of Community law, the legal

---

25 To the changes of special administrative law see J. Schwarze, "The Europeanization of national administrative law", in: J. Schwarze (ed.), (footnote 24), at pp. 789 (798 *et seq.*).

26 A "claim to the protection of legitimate expectations" is mentioned for the first time in Case 111/63, *Lemmerz-Werke* [1965] ECR 677 at 690. From the following case law see esp. Case 1/73, *Westzucker GmbH v Einfuhr- und Vorratsstelle für Zucker* [1973] ECR 723 at 730, note 10 & 13; Case 112/77, *August Töpfer & Co. GmbH v Commission* [1978] ECR 1019 at 1032, note 19.

27 See J. Schwarze, *European Administrative law*, (London 1992), pp. 867 *et seq.*; for its conditions see C. Crones, *Selbstbindungen der Verwaltung im europäischen Gemeinschaftsrecht*, (Baden-Baden 1997), pp. 112 *et seq.*

28 For details see J. Schwarze (footnote 25), at pp. 895 *et seq.* and 942 *et seq.*

29 *Ibid.*, pp. 1113 *et seq.*

30 *Ibid.*, at pp. 901 *et seq.*

31 See J. Flauss, "French Report", in: J. Schwarze (ed.), (footnote 24), at p. 107; see also C.

orders of both Member States have experienced changes, which have proved to be more fundamental in British than in French law, however.

In England, the doctrine of legitimate expectations was first introduced in an *obiter dictum* by *Lord Denning M.R.* in the case *Schmidt* v. *Secretary of State for Home Affairs*.[32] In the meantime, the protection of legitimate expectations has been invoked and granted several times.[33] The Continental as well as European provenance of this principle has to this day not been expressly recognized either in England or in Ireland, where the Irish Supreme Court has acknowledged in 1987 that the notion of legitimate expectations limits the discretion of administrative bodies.[34] The following statement of *Lord Mackenzie Stuart*, the former President of the ECJ, has remained uncontested, however:

> "Can one here detect the influence of Community law or at least some of the Member States? It is at least possible to suggest that the answer is yes. The concept of recognising that a failure to respect legitimate expectations may give rise, in public law, to a remedy is a novelty in English law and lacks discernible English parentage. To find the true ancestry one does not have to look far beyond the Channel."[35]

In France, on the other hand, there are only a few early signs of the possibility that the doctrine of legitimate expectations may find its way into French administrative law one day. Those indications also point to influences from the case-law of the European Court of Justice. The *Tribunal administratif de Strasbourg*, for example, allowed an action for damages in 1994 while expressly acknowledging a "principe de confiance légitime".[36] The Tribunal was seized with a claim by an importer of waste who had suffered damages through the alteration of a statute by "décret". While the statute had formerly allowed the import of household waste, it now prohibited the import subject to the strictly limited possibility of granting exceptions. By recognizing the principle of legitimate expectations, the Tribunal followed the opinion of the *Commissaire de gouverne-*

Crones (footnote 27), at p. 36.

32 *Schmidt* v. *Home Secretary* [1969] 2 W.L.R. 337, see C. Crones (footnote 27), at p. 41.

33 See *Council of Civil Service Unions* v. *Minister for Civil Service* [1985] A.C. 374 (HL) esp., further J. Jowell/P. Birkinshaw, "English Report", in: J. Schwarze (ed.), (footnote 24), at pp. 298 *et seq*.

34 See *Webb* v. *Ireland* [1988] IR 353, and G. Hogan/A. Schuster, "Irish Report", in: J. Schwarze (ed.), (footnote 24), at pp. 446 *et seq*.

35 Lord Mackenzie Stuart, *Recent developments in English administrative law – The Impact of Europe?*, in: Capotorti *et al.* (ed.), *Liber Amicorum Pierre Pescatore*, (Baden-Baden 1987), at p. 417. Note in this context also the decision by the Manchester Crown Court in the case R. v. *Ministry for Agriculture, Fisheries and Food, ex parte: Hamble Fisheries* [1995] 2 All ER 714, QBD, where the court expressly referred to European standards when interpreting the doctrine of legitimate expectations. See P. Craig "Substantive Legitimate Expectations and the Principles of Judicial Review" in: M. Andenas (ed.) *English Public Law and the Common Law of Europe* (London 1998) at pp. 23 *et seq*. See also the recent *ex parte Coughlan*, Court of Appeal, 16 July 1999

36 For the decision and the Opinion of the *Commissaire de gouvernement* see AJDA 1995, 555 *et seq*.

ment, M. J. Pommier, who had – while mentioning the European provenance of the protection of legitimate expectations – supported the incorporation of this principle into French law.[37]

European influences on the doctrine of legitimate expectations can also be traced in those Member States where it is part of the domestic law, even in matters without any Community relevance. Among these countries are the Netherlands and Germany.[38] Frictions between national and Community principles are particularly likely to occur in this context. This shows that the process of Europeanization of national administrative law does not necessarily lead towards an amelioration of the standard of protection of individuals' rights.

In the Netherlands, the concept of the protection of legitimate expectations was initially developed in the context of the recovery of civil servants' salaries paid without a legal basis.[39] Today, it plays a role in a variety of cases. Contrary to the legal situation at Community level, there is the peculiar feature in Dutch law that legitimate expectations may warrant protection even where a promise has been unlawfully made or the administration practice has not complied with legal standards.[40] However, in cases involving Community law this possibility usually has to give way to the principle of effective enforcement of Community law.[41] At the end of the day, European influences may restrict rather than expand the scope of the legal protection of legitimate expectations at national level.

In Germany, too, the scholarly discussion on the impact of Community law on the principle of legitimate expectations has focused mainly on the decline of the national level of protection. At the forefront of this discussion stands the question if, and to what extent, the mechanisms of the protection of legitimate expectations as provided in § 48 of the German federal and regional rules on administrative procedure (*Verwaltungsverfahrensgesetze des Bundes und der Länder*) may be applied where state aids are found to be contrary to Community law. I should like to add that this question is the object of an extensive as well as heated debate which is still in progress and to which I shall refer for further details.[42]

---

37 *Ibid.*, at pp. 558 *et seq.*

38 See J. Schwarze (footnote 27), at pp. 886 *et seq.* and pp. 926 *et seq.*

39 See R. Widdershoven, "Dutch Report", in: J. Schwarze (ed.), (footnote 24), pp. 568 *et seq.*

40 To the legal situation at Community level see Joint Cases 303 and 312/81, *Klöckner-Werke AG v. Commission* [1983] ECR 1597, 1530 at note 34 and C. Crones (footnote 27), at pp. 145 *et seq.*

41 For the Court's case law see R. Widdershoven, "Dutch Report", in: J. Schwarze (ed.), (footnote 24), pp. 570 *et seq.*

42 See H. G. Fischer, "Zur Rückforderung von unter Verstoß gegen Art. 92, 93 EWGV gewährten nationalen Beihilfen", DVBl. 1990, 1089; D. Triantafyllou, "Zur Europäisierung" des Vertrauensschutzes (insbesondere § 48 VwVfG) am Beispiel der Rückforderung staatlicher Beihilfen", NVwZ 1992, 436; J. Kokott, "Nationales Subventionsrecht im Schatten der EG", DVBl. 1993, 1235; C.-M. Happe, "Zur innerstaatlichen Wirkung von Beihilfeentscheidungen gem. Art. 93 Abs. 2 EWGV", NVwZ 1993, 32; F. Schulze,

b) One, if not the most important part of the developing European *ius commune* in the area of administrative law is the *principle of proportionality*. It has been recognized in the Court's case-law since 1970[43] and is now an established concept in the legal orders of various Member States. It can now be found also in those states where it was traditionally limited to specific fields or even completely unknown.[44] Despite this, the principle of proportionality is mentioned here only in the second place due to the fact that its propagation in the Member States of the European Union can less clearly be attributed to the influence of the ECJ's case law. It is true that in Italy, the principle of proportionality has under this name attracted attention only in the wake of the case-law of the European Court of Justice, and the direct influence of its jurisdiction may be safely assumed.[45] In other Member States, however, such a provenance cannot be clearly established.

Again, the French and English legal orders provide distinct examples for this. In England, administrative acts could originally, according to the "*Wednesbury*" principle, only be successfully challenged on the ground that they were "so unreasonable that no reasonable decision-maker, properly directing himself as to the law, could have arrived at it".[46] The mistake had to be evident and "on the face of the record". Today, however, the courts do control the proportionality of administrative action, employing criteria that resemble in content the concept of proportionality as it underlies the ECJ's case-law. Although the principle of proportionality is still not expressly recognized in British law, nor even directly linked to its possible European provenance, it seems to be only a question of time until it will also formally be introduced into British administrative law.[47]

"Vertrauensschutz im EG-Recht bei Rückforderung von Beihilfen", EuZW 1993, 279; E. Pache, "Rechtsfragen der Aufhebung gemeinschaftswidriger Beihilfebescheide", NVwZ 1994, 318; T. S. Richter, "Rückforderung gemeinschaftswidriger Subventionen nach § 48 VwVfG", DÖV 1995, 846.

43 Case 11/70, *Internationale Handelsgesellschaft* [1970] ECR 1125, at 1135, note 3 *et seq.*; further Joint Cases 41, 121 & 796/79, *Testa u.a. v. Bundesanstalt für Arbeit* [1980] ECR 1979, at 1997, note 21; Case 265/87, *HS Kraftfutter GmBH & Co. KG v. Hauptzollamt Gronau* [1989] ECR 2237, 2269, note 21.

44 In addition to the states mentioned infra, see R. de Lange, "Dutch Report", in: J. Schwarze (ed.). pp. 551 *et seq.*

45 G. M. Ubertazzi, "Le principe de proportionnalité en droit italien", in: H. Kutscher u.a. (ed.), *Der Grundsatz der Verhältnismäßigkeit in europäischen Rechtsordnungen*, (Heidelberg 1985), p. 79; J. Schwarze, (footnote 27), at pp. 692 *et seq.*

46 *Associated Provincial Picture Houses Ltd. v. Wednesbury Corp.* [1948] 1 K.B. 223, see M. Supperstone/J. Goudie, *Judicial Review*, (London 1992), p. 73 for further details.

47 For details on the application of the principle of proportionality in British law see J. Jowell/P. Birkinshaw, "British Report", in: J. Schwarze (footnote 24), pp. 282 *et seq.*; further J. Jowell/A. Lester, "Proportionality: Neither novel nor dangerous", in: J. Jowell/D. Oliver (eds.), *New Directions in Judicial Review*, (London 1988), p. 51, at pp. 59 *et seq.* See also Lord Hoffmann "A Sense of Proportion", in M. Andenas and F. Jacobs, *European Community Law in English Courts* (Oxford 1998), pp. 149.
In Irish law, the principle of proportionality has already been adopted and its European

An indication of this may be the recent decision of the House of Lords in the case *Reg. v. Chief Constable of Sussex, Ex parte ITF Ltd.*[48] where the House had to determine whether the decision of a Chief Constable to restrict the policing of lorries owned by ITF had been lawful. The appellants, a group of farmers and hauliers, had incorporated their own company for the purpose of carrying livestock through a port in Sussex across the channel. From the start, large numbers of animal protesters tried to prevent the lorries from moving through the port and the police had to provide escorts at considerable cost. When, after a few months, the Chief Constable restricted the policing level to two days a week because he found he did not have the resources to provide effective and efficient police services in other areas of the county, ITF sought to quash those decisions. The House of Lords upheld the Chief Constable's decision, stating that "in a case like the present where the Chief Constable had statutory and common law duties to perform, it was required to ask whether he did all that proportionately and reasonably he could be expected to do with the resources available to him." When dealing with the relationship between Wednesbury reasonableness and the proportionality test required by Community law, Lord Slynn stated that,

> "in *Brind v Secretary of State for the Home Department, Ex parte Brind* [1991] 1 All ER 720 the House had treated Wednesbury reasonableness and proportionality as being different. So in some ways they were, though the distinction between the two tests in practice was much less than was sometimes suggested. The cautious way in which the European Court usually applied that test, recognising the importance of respecting the national authority's margin of appreciation, might mean that whichever test was adopted, and even allowing for a difference in onus, the result would be the same."[49]

Thus, while *prima facie* the tests applicable under domestic and Community law are still different, the acceptance seems to grow that these two tests correspond with each other and that in practice, the results will often be the same. A further step towards their convergence has been taken.

In France, on the other hand, the increasing control of administrative decisions may safely be assumed to be due to European influences. The case law of the European Court of Justice was only one of several factors in this. Over and above that, the legal practice of the ECHR Convention authorities has proved to be of paramount importance, as can be seen in the cases dealing with the deportation of aliens. Where an EU national is concerned, the administrative courts have subjected deportation orders to a full proportionality test as early as 1990.[50]

---

provenance expressly recognized in 1988, see G. Hogan/A. Schuster, "Irish Report", in: J. Schwarze (footnote 24), pp. 463 *et seq.*

48 *R v Chief Constable of Sussex, ex parte International Trader's Ferry Ltd* NLJ Practitioner of Nov. 27th 1998, pp. 1750 *et seq.*

49 *R v Chief Constable of Sussex, ex parte International Trader's Ferry Ltd*, (footnote 48), p. 1750.

50 *Conseil d'Etat*, decisions of 24.10.1990 (*Ragusi*) and of 19.11.1990 (*Raso*), AJDA 1991, 322 *et seq.*

Contrary to its former established case-law,[51] the *Conseil d'Etat* now also controls the proportionality of exportation measures against non-EU nationals where they fall within the scope of Article 8 of the ECHR.[52] Here, the proportionality test includes the ECHR criterion, which provides that a measure violating the rights granted in the Convention must be "necessary in a democratic society".[53] Such a test shows that the search for "European" influences on national administrative law has to bear in mind not only the actions of the Community authorities but also the reverberating effects of the legal practice dealing with the ECHR.[54]

The increasing influence of Community law on national law strongly manifests itself in a rather recent decision by the European Court of Justice on the control of discretionary acts by the Member States: in the case *Commission v. France*, it had to deal with the protest movement of French farmers against the import of agricultural products from other Member States and the alleged passivity of the French authorities in adopting effective measures against those violent acts. The Court held that although the Member States enjoyed a margin of discretion as to how they maintain public order and safeguard internal security, it fell to the Court "to verify, in cases brought before it, whether the Member State concerned had adopted appropriate measures for ensuring the free movement of goods." [55]

2 *Procedural administrative law*

Procedural administrative law is an area where – similar to the organization of administrative bodies – national peculiarities manifest themselves in a special and distinctive way. This is due to the fact that principles of administrative procedure determine whether a legal order attaches greater importance to the complete protection of the individual or to the demands of rapid and effective administration. Nowadays, there are tendencies towards a convergence of the national legal systems in this field as well, even though differences between the Member States still remain. After the analysis of their own legal orders, a considerable number of reporters of a research project on this topic even came to the

51 For example, see decision of 25.7.1980 (*Touami Abdeslem*), Recueil p. 820.

52 See decisions of 18.1.1991 (*Beldjoudi*), Recueil p. 18 and of 19.1.1991 (*Belgacem*), AJDA 1991, 551, for instance.

53 To this criterion see J. Frowein, in: J. Frowein/W. Peukert, *EMRK-Kommentar*, (2nd ed., Kehl 1996), note 14 before Articles 8-11.

54 See the House of Lords decision in *Barrett* [1999] 3 W.L.R. 79 where the *Osman* decision of the European Court of Human Rights contributed to the expansion of rights of compensation against public authorities.

55 Case C-265/95, *Commission v. France*, [1997] ECR 6959, at p. 6999. Thus, the Court subjects national measures to a limited judicial review that is similar, if not severer than that of discretionary acts of Community authorities, see case C-120/97, *Upjohn Ltd and The Licensing authority*, [1999] ECR I-223, at p. 251 *et seq.*, note 34.

conclusion that their respective administrative procedures did not show any discrepancies with the principles for the field of indirect execution as developed in the case-law of the European Court of Justice that were worth mentioning.[56]

The reasons for this convergence of the national legal orders are manifold. Notably the growing importance of the ECHR and the common roots of various national procedural rules in German as well as French administrative law have been mentioned as a probable reason.[57] But also the case-law of the European Court of Justice has had an important effect. This has become apparent in the context of the problem, if and to what extent reasons for an administrative decision have to be given.

The Belgian legal order, for example, for a long time did not know a general duty to give reasons for a decision as it is laid down in § 39 of the German Federal Rules for Administrative Procedure (VwVfG). In 1992, however, the duty to give reasons for individual administrative decisions was introduced by statute. This legislation may well have been triggered off by the *Heylens* case, where the European Court of Justice held that a statement of the grounds for the decision was a requirement for a legal administrative procedure as well as for effective judicial protection.[58]

Similarly, there was traditionally no duty in France, either, to give reasons for administrative decisions imposing a burden on the citizen. The predominant objective there was the effective enforcement of statutes and that seemed to be endangered by the additional burden of giving reasons.[59] By the statutory introduction of such duties for certain administrative decisions, however, the French authorities now find themselves compelled to state the reasons for their decisions. It is true that even now the "principe de non-motivation" continues to exist. Legal experts predict, however, that – considering the importance of this principle in the jurisdiction of the European Court of Justice – the French legal order will not be able to maintain this proportion of rule and exception.[60]

---

56 See E. Garcia de Enterria/L. Ortega, "Spanish Report", pp. 701 *et seq.*; S. Flogiatis, "Greek Report", p. 428; M. Chiti, "Italian Report", p. 248; R. Widdershoven, "Dutch Report", p. 603; M. Thewes, "Luxembourgian Report", p. 503, all in: J. Schwarze (footnote 24).

57 M. Thewes, "Luxembourgian Report", in: J. Schwarze (footnote 24), p. 503 calls the Luxembourgian administrative law for this reason a "mosaïque juridique".

58 Case 222/86, *Union nationale des entraîneurs et cadres techniques professionels du football (UNECTEF)* v. *Georges Heylens et al.*, ECR [1987] 4097, to the possible impact of this case on the aforementioned Belgian statute see M. Boes/J. Stuyck, "Belgian Report", in: J. Schwarze (footnote 24), at p. 353.

59 See G. Braibant, *Le droit administratif français*, (3iéme ed., Paris 1992), at p. 241.

60 J. F. Flauss, "French Report", in: J. Schwarze (footnote 24), at p. 75.

3 Judicial protection

Another basic requirement of European Community law – in addition to the demands following from the substantive principles of legitimate expectations and proportionality – is the judicial protection of individuals against the wrongful infringement of their fundamental rights.[61]

The duty to be loyal to the Community's aims and objectives stemming from Art 10 EC Treaty (ex-Art 5) compels the national courts to grant effective legal protection to all citizens of the European Union whenever Community law infringes their rights. Confronted with Community law standards, the courts used to find themselves faced with conflicts that national law could not solve adequately from the point of view of Community law. Interim relief is surely the legal area that was influenced the most by European Community Law. Here, there is paramount evidence of the genesis of common European standards.

The Community law standards for the granting of interim relief have often been described.[62] They can be summarized in the following way: the Member States are compelled by European Community law to grant provisional remedies for the protection of rights granted by Community law, even in those cases where national law used to deny them.[63]

This principle, which was established by the *Factortame* decision in 1991, corresponded with the legal situation in a significant number of the Member States as before 1991.[64] Where it had an influence on national law, however, it led to profound changes in the field of interim relief. This has been the case rather strikingly in England, the starting-point of the *Factortame* decision. Before *Factortame*, the notion of a Court repealing a statute without violating "Supremacy of Parliament" was unthinkable. Now, interim relief is granted even in cases where Community law has no bearing.[65] Therefore, the field of interim re-

61 See Case 222/84, *M. Johnston v. Chief Constable of the Royal Ulster Constabulary*, ECR [1986] 1651, 1682, note 18.

62 See F. Schoch, "Die Europäisierung des Verwaltungsrechts", JZ 1995, 109; F. Krumbacher, *Vorläufiger Rechtsschutz vor nationalen Gerichten in Fällen mit Gemeinschaftsbezug*, (Frankfurt am Main *et al.* 1998).

63 Case C-213/89, *The Queen v. Secretary of State for Transport, ex parte: Factortame Ltd.* ECR [1991] 2433, 2473 at note 19 *et seq.* On the other hand, national law has to provide for the possibility to declare administrative acts as immediately enforceable in order to prevent the suspensive effect of national legal remedies taken against them, see case C-217/88, *Commission v. Germany* ECR [1990] 2879, 2908 at note 34.

64 See for the respective countries: R. Widdershoven, "Dutch Report", p. 634, M. Chiti, "Italian Report", p. 250; both in J. Schwarze (ed.) footnote 24. In Germany, too, the question whether there should be interim relief does not present itself, as this is expressly provided by §§ 80 V and 123 VwGO. The discussion focuses on the question, how far the Community standards may influence the interaction between the suspensive effect of preliminary proceedings (*Widerspruchsverfahren*), immediate enforceability and interim relief, see F. Schoch, in *loco cit.* (footnote 6).

65 See *M. v. Home Office* [1993] 3 All ER 537 (HL), where the House of Lords declared itself competent to issue temporary measures against a minister in proceedings that had no

lief has justly been described as "one of the areas most heavily influenced by European Public law".[66]

In France, Community law standards have influenced the internal legal system as well. According to the established case law of the *Conseil d'Etat*, and similar to the situation in England, provisional measures did not belong to the instruments of national administrative courts.[67] At the beginning of the nineties, however, Art. L 22 of the *Code des Tribunaux administratifs* introduced the possibility of issuing an injunction in matters with Community relevance.[68] Meanwhile, this provision has been extended by the Anti-Corruption Act 1993 insofar as it now allows administrative judges to take provisional measures in a number of strictly domestic matters as well. Art. L 22 of the *Code des Tribunaux administratifs* is therefore one of the still relatively rare examples of the voluntary reception of Community standards into French law. Thus, Community law – as my French colleague *Flauss* has critically put it – has contributed "à contaminer des matières n'èntrant pas directement dans le champ d'application du droit communautaire".[69]

V CODIFICATION?

Let me return briefly to the first part of my analysis, the administrative law of the European Union. The question has arisen whether the codification of its procedural rules would not further its administration. Codification already exists in a few separate fields of European law; the most notable example is the Customs Code.[70] As far as the recovery of unlawful state aids is concerned, the discussion about a codification of its rules – possibly based on Art. 89 (ex-Art. 94 EC-Treaty) – has started again after the *Alcan II*-decision.[71] In this field, a new Council Regulation "laying down detailed rules for the application of Art. 93[72] of the EC-Treaty" has now been passed.[73] The recovery of unlawful aids, however, is still left to the authorities of the Member States to be effected in accordance with the procedures under their national law. With regard to the modes of recovery, Art. 14 of the regulation confirms the case-law of the ECJ that stressed the importance of an immediate and effective execution. Moreover, the aid to be recovered shall include interest at a rate fixed by the Commission.

EC relevance whatsoever.

66 J. Jowell/P. Birkinshaw, "English Report", in J. Schwarze (footnote 23), p. 302.

67 See e.g. *Conseil d'Etat*, Decision of 15 Feb. 1978, *Plantureux*, AJDA 1978, p. 501 *et seq.*

68 This is a result of the implementation of the Community Directive 89/665/EEC of 21 Dec. 1989, OJ L 395 p. 33, see J. F. Flauss, "French Report", in: J. Schwarze (footnote 24), p. 83.

69 J. F. Flauss, in *loco cit.*, p. 84.

70 Council Regulation No. 2913/92/EEC of 12.10.1992, OJ L 302, p. 1 of 19.10.1992.

71 Case C-24/95, *Rheinland Pfalz v. Alcan GmBH Deutschland*, ECR [1997] 1591.

72 The new Art. 88.

73 Council Regulation 659/1999 of 22.3.1999, OJ L 83, p. 1 of 27.3.1999.

On the other hand, some areas are at a much earlier stage that could, none the less, eventually lead to codification as well. There are, as Lord Slynn during his time as Advocate General at the ECJ pointed out, administrative principles that are not always legally enforceable:

> "Nor do I consider, as is submitted, that there is any generalised principle of law that what is required by good administration will necessarily amount to a legally enforceable rule. To keep an efficient filing system may be an essential part of good administration but is not a legally enforceable rule. Legal rules and good administration may overlap (*e.g.* in the need to ensure fair play and proportionality); the requirements of the latter may be a factor in the elucidation of the former. The two are not necessarily synonymous. Indeed, sometimes when courts urge that something should be done as a matter of good administration, they do it because there is no precise legal rule."[74]

A current example for such rules that are not legally enforceable is the suggestion of a code of conduct for the Commission that was submitted by the Committee of Independent Experts in its Second Report on Reform of the Commission.[75] Such a code would not impose legally binding obligations, but it is hoped to exert a high degree of moral persuasion, and should be supervised not by the Court but by a Committee that will convene either ad hoc or take a more permanent form. These rules of conduct with their widely accepted ethical content[76] may at a later date become true, enforceable European administrative law.

Returning to the question of codification, one has to note that there is only a hesitant and cautious debate about the possibility of a *general* codification of the rules governing the indirect administration of Community law by the authorities of the Member States. However, the above-mentioned convergence of the national legal orders may give rise to a new assessment of this. While, realistically, a comprehensive codification of European general administrative law is out of the question, a partial codification of the most important procedural rules could be a workable compromise. While gaps and inconsistencies still exist, today there should be a sufficient and undisputed corpus of administrative law principles. A catalogue of these principles could consist of a mixture of purely procedural principles, such as the duty to give reasons, the principle of legal clarity and the significance of procedural defects and more material principles, such as the protection of legitimate expectations.

Even now, after the ratification of the Treaty of Amsterdam, the European Treaties do not offer a legal basis for a comprehensive codification of administrative principles.[77] Such a codification would therefore require a change of the

---

74 Case 64/82, *Tradax Graanhandel v. Commission* [1984] ECR 1359, Conclusions by AG Slynn at pp. 1381 *et seq*. For a detailed analysis see J. A. Usher, "The 'Good Administration' of European Community Law", *Current Legal Problems* (1985), 269 *et seq*.

75 *Second Report on Reform of the Commission*." Analysis of current practice and proposals for tackling mismanagement, irregularities and fraud" 10. September 1999.

76 *Loc.cit.*, chapt. 7.7.1.

77 For a detailed analysis see J. Schwarze, "Konvergenz im Verwaltungsrecht der Mitglied-

Treaties. This problem notwithstanding, on balance the arguments for a codification seem to me to outweigh those against it. A deficit of convergence of the legal systems of the Member States especially, nowadays would not hinder an agreement on common procedural rules for indirect administration. The argument that a codification would halt further development does not convince me either, considering the limited extent of such a codification. Although this is one of the classical drawbacks of codification as such, its consolidating effect would outweigh this disadvantage. The transparency and the acceptance of the Community's legal system, in particular, would be improved by such a project. Without seeing a codification as a panacea, in my view it would further the uniform enforcement of Community law and contribute towards equal conditions for competition in the European Union.

CONCLUSION

National administrative law today is no longer an impermeable, autonomous legal system. Though presumably it will – despite European integration – keep its respective peculiarities and its dominant role for the regulation of internal legal proceedings, it has, under the auspices of Europe, been opened up to new influences. The standards for indirect administration of Community law by national authorities thus have inspired the national legal orders in certain fields to adopt solutions for their own systems that were jointly worked out at Community level. European law not only opens up the domestic legal orders, but also stimulates them to improve on their own solutions. By setting up common fundamental principles that have been developed by a comparative analysis of the various European legal systems as reference points and yardsticks for comparison, it occasionally even forces their self-justification.

However, it would be desirable if this effect worked in the other direction as well: not only should national legal orders develop themselves and converge with each other under the influence of Community law, but Community law also should be influenced by the solutions found for specific problems under national law. As Walter van Gerven says, "paraphrasing Lord Denning's famous statement: time has come for the "incoming tide" of Community law to be reversed. That is to say it in warrior's terms of the past: time has come for the Community invader to be invaded by the legal orders of the Member States."[78] Thus, a third level of cross-fertilization between Community law and the national laws of the Member States would evolve: while, at the beginning, European administrative law was developed from, especially, the general principles common to the laws of the Member States, and then, in a second stage, started to reverberate and to

staaten", DVBl. 1996, 881, at p. 886 *et seq.*

78 W. van Gerven, "The invader invaded or The need to uncover general principles common to the laws of the Member States", in: G. Rodríguez Iglesias (ed.), *Mélanges en hommage à Fernand Schockweiler*, (Baden-Baden 1999), p. 593, at p. 598.

influence the domestic administrative laws in its turn, this modified domestic law would then lead to changes within Community law and force it to self-criticism and to a continuous control and improvement of its solutions. To use a catch phrase, this would lead to a "Europeanization of Community law" (Walter van Gerven again). To take this point even further, it is conceivable that a steady flow between the two levels of Community law and national law could develop, a constant cross-fertilization between jurisdictions in this respect. It is important to note, however, that such a process of mutual influence could take place only within the limits imposed by the constitutional cornerstones of the European Community: the autonomy and the predominance of Community over national law. It could therefore only serve to improve Community law in substance and to firmly root it in the domestic law of the Member States.

Only time will tell whether the developing convergence of domestic administrative laws will be able to trigger off the codification of the rules governing the indirect administration of Community law. I shall not deny a certain widespread reservation concerning this project. As early as in 1981, Hans Peter Ipsen considered such a codification to be even more daring than a European constitution.[79] In 1997, scepticism still prevailed: Judge Koen Lenaerts noted that the question arose at the 17. F.I.D.E conference, "whether the European Community should have [...] comprehensive legislation on administrative procedures. I did not hear a single voice in the room arguing in favour of that position. There was far more sympathy with the common law tradition of fairness, natural justice, or natural and constitutional justice [...]. In this field the European Community may well be closer to the common law than to Continental legal traditions."[80]

It is not easy to voice the demand for a (partial) codification in the face of such important voices. However, let me hope at least for "a little puff of change"[81] in this context.

---

79 See J. Schwarze (ed.), *Europäische Verwaltungsrecht im Werden*, (Baden-Baden 1982), at p. 123.

80 Résumé by Koen Lenaerts, "Report on the Proceeding of Working Group 3", in: J. Schwarze (ed.), *17. F.I.D.E.-Kongress – Erlebnisse und Perspektiven*, (Baden-Baden 1997), p. 180.

81 G. Slynn, "Statement", in: J. Schwarze/R. Bieber (footnote 1), at p. 123.

30

ENFORCING COMMUNITY RIGHTS IN NATIONAL COURTS: SOME RECENT DEVELOPMENTS

Takis Tridimas[*]

THE EVOLUTION OF THE CASE-LAW: NON-INTERVENTION, EFFECTIVENESS, AND SELECTIVE DEFERENCE

The Community legal order is supported by a decentralised system of justice. Although Luxembourg is undoubtedly the most dramatic witness to judicial power, the primary venue for the assertion of Community rights are the national courts whose rôle remains pivotal even in relation to policies, such as competition law and state aid, which are administered centrally by the Commission.[1] Community measures rarely prescribe the remedies available for the breach of Community rights so that, where such rights fall to be enforced in national courts, in principle, the national rules of procedure apply. Within the last twenty years, however, the law of remedies has undergone a transformation. One could distinguish three phases in the Court's case-law. Initially, the Court took the view that remedies were a matter for the national laws and relied on national rules of procedure and remedies subject to the dual requirement of equivalence (or non-discrimination) and minimum protection.[2] The *locus classicus* of this early stage is the *Rewe*[3] and *Comet*[4] case law. The Court's approach was encapsulated in *Rewe v Hauptzollamt Kiel* decided in 1981, where it was stated that the EC Treaty "was not intended to create new remedies".[5] As the case-law progressed, the emphasis shifted from the requirements of non-discrimination and

---

* This paper is based on a talk delivered in the 5th EC/International Law Forum on the *Future of Remedies in Europe* which took place at the University of Bristol on 13-14 May 1999. It will be published also, subject to minor amendments, as part of the conference proceedings in C. Kilpatrick, P. Skidmore *et al.* (Eds), *The Future of Remedies in Europe,* Hart Publishing, forthcoming.

1 See e.g. Case C-234/89 *Delimitis* [1991] ECR I-935; Case C-39/94 *SFEI and Others* [1996] ECR I-3547. Note also the Commission's White Paper of May 1999 on the Modernisation of the Rules implementing Articles 85 and 86 (ex 89 and 90) of the EC Treaty which proposes the decentralisation of the administration of EC competition rules, OJ 1999, C 132, p. 1.

2 See below p. 467.

3 Case 33/76 *Rewe v Landwirtschaftskammer für das Saarland* [1976] ECR 1989.

4 Case 45/76 *Comet v Productschap voor Siergewassen* [1976] ECR 2043.

5 Case 158/80 [1981] ECR 1805, para. 44.

D. O'Keeffe (ed.), Liber Amicorum Slynn 465-479 (2000)

minimum protection to the need to provide effective remedies for the breach of Community rights. Indeed, one of the key features of judicial constitution-building at Community level has been the derivation from the general principles of primacy and direct effect of a specific duty on national courts to provide full and effective protection of Community rights. This, more interventionist, approach of the Court is evinced by cases such as *Johnston*,[6] *Factortame*[7] and *Peterbroeck*,[8] and reached its apex in the establishment of State liability in damages and the cognate right to reparation for private parties.

Currently, the case law seems to have entered a third period, the chief feature of which is selective deference to the national rules of procedure. This trend is exemplified in particular by the following developments:

- the post-*Emmott* case-law;
- recent developments on State liability in damages, especially, the judgment in *Brinkmann*;[9]
- the tendency of the case-law to leave discretion to national courts in determining whether the national rules of procedure provide a sufficient level of protection for the Community rights in issue.

The above developments should not be taken as evidence of retreat on the part of the Court. Rather, they illustrate the directed use of judicial power as the legal system matures. The underlying rationale seems to be that, since the general principles of the law governing remedies have now been established, the Court can entrust national courts to apply those principles and be more selective with regard to the national rules with which it takes issue. The purpose of a remedy is to stop the breach of a legal norm and undo its detrimental effects or, to put it in a different way, "to make constitutional ideas into living truths".[10] The starting point of the Court's approach remains the universality of remedies. Where there is a right, there must be a remedy (*ubi jus ibi remedium*), so that national courts must in principle provide a remedy for the protection of Community rights, and offer individuals the opportunity to assert rights derived from Community law.[11]

6 Case 222/84 *Johnston v Chief Constable of the Royal Ulster Constabulary*. [1986] ECR 1651.

7 Case C-213/89 [1990] ECR I-2433.

8 Case C-312/93 *Peterbroeck v Belgian State* [1995] ECR I-4599.

9 Case C-319/96 *Brinkmann Tabakfabriken GmbH v Skatteministeriet*, [1998] ECR I-5255. In that case, the Court held that, where a Member State fails to take implementing measures to transpose a directive into national law, the national authorities may present as a valid defence in an action for damages that they themselves attempted to comply with the directive. In such a case, liability arises only if the incorrect transposition of the directive by the national authorities amounts to a serious breach. *Brickmann* is the first case where the Court denied State liability on grounds of lack of causation.

10 *Cooper v Aaron* 358 US 1, 20 (1958).

11 For a recent example in the field of sex equality, see Case C-185/97 *Coote v Granada Hospitality Ltd*, [1998] ECR I-5199; see further Case C-167/97 *R v Secretary of State for*

This association between rights and remedies, which is much clearer in German law,[12] is not as foreign to common law as it is sometimes assumed.[13]

The purpose of this paper is not give an exhaustive account of the case law.[14] It intends rather to focus on two issues: the dual requirements of equivalence and effectiveness especially as applied by the Court in selected recent cases, and the post-*Emmott* case law. This paper does not cover state liability in damages.[15]

THE PRINCIPLES OF EQUIVALENCE AND EFFECTIVENESS

According to the established case-law,[16] in the absence of Community rules, it is for the domestic legal system of each Member State to designate the courts and tribunals having jurisdiction and to lay down the detailed procedural rules governing actions for safeguarding the rights which individuals derive from Community law, provided that such rules satisfy two conditions:

- they are not less favourable than those governing similar domestic actions (the principle of equivalence); and
- they do not render virtually impossible or excessively difficult the exercise of rights conferred by Community law (the principle of effectiveness).

The two principles operate cumulatively, so that in order for a national rule to be compatible with Community law, it must comply with both. For example, a rule of evidence[17] or a time-limit[18] which renders the protection of Community

---

Employment, ex parte Seymour Smith and Perez, judgment of 9 February 1999 and, on judicial review, Case C-120/97 *Upjohn Ltd v The Licensing Authority established by the Medicines Act 1968 and Others*, [1999] ECR I-229.

12 See Ruffert, *Rights and Remedies in European Community Law: A Comparative View* (1997) 34 307 at 332-333.

13 See the dissenting judgment of Oliver LJ in *Bourgoin SA v Ministry of Agriculture* [1986] 3 All ER 585.

14 For a more extensive treatment and further bibliography, see Tridimas, *The General Principles of EC Law* (OUP 1999), Ch. 8.

15 For a discussion, see Tridimas, *op.cit.*, Ch. 9 and for recent cases, see *Brinkmann, op.cit.*; Case C-302/97 *Konle v Republic of Austria*, judgment of 1 June 1999; Case C-140/97 *Rechberger and Greindl v Republic of Austria*, judgment of 15 June 1999; Case C-127/95 *Norbrook Laboratories limited v Ministry of Agriculture*, [1998] ECR I-1531.

16 See e.g. *Rewe v Landwirtschaftskammer für das Saarland, op.cit.*, para. 5; *Comet, op.cit.*, para. 12 to 16; Case 199/82 *Amministrazione delle Finanze dello Stato v San Giorgio* [1983] ECR 3595, para. 14; Joined Cases C-6 & C-9/90 *Francovich and others v Italian Republic* [1991] ECR I-5357, para. 43; Case C-312/93 *Peterbroeck v Belgian State* [1995] ECR I-4599, para. 12; Case C-231/96 *Edis v Ministero delle Finanze*, [1998] ECR I-4951, para. 19.

17 See e.g. *San Giorgio, op.cit.*

18 See e.g. *Peterbroeck, op.cit.*

rights virtually impossible must be set aside by the national court even if it applies equally to similar claims arising from an infringement of national law.

In *Peterbroeck*[19] the Court held that, in order to ascertain whether the principle of effectiveness is complied with, the following enquiry should be pursued:

> ... a national procedural provision ... must be analysed by reference to the role of that provision in the procedure, its progress and its special features, viewed as a whole before the various national instances. In the light of that analysis the basic principles of the domestic judicial system, such as protection of the rights of the defence, the principle of legal certainty and the proper conduct of procedure, must, where appropriate, be taken into consideration.[20]

Similarly, in order to ascertain whether a provision complies with the principle of equivalence, account should be taken of the function of that provision in the procedure as a whole, as well as the operation and any special features of that procedure before the various national courts.[21]

The principle of equivalence requires that the rule in issue must be applied without distinction, whether the infringement alleged is of Community or national law, "where the purpose and cause of actions are similar".[22] In principle, it is for the national court to ascertain whether the national rules of procedure comply with the principle of equivalence, since it is the national court alone which has direct knowledge of those rules.[23] Thus, it is primarily for the national court to ascertain what claims under national law may be considered to be comparable to the claim based on Community law in issue in the proceedings. The Court of Justice, however, may provide guidelines. The determination of comparable claims is by no means a mechanical exercise. In some cases, it may not be necessary to carry out a detailed search for a comparable claim under national law. An example of this is provided by *BP Supergas v Greek State*,[24] a case concerning overpaid VAT contrary to the Sixth Directive. The Advocate General opined that, where a taxable person is entitled to a refund of tax in respect of a particular tax year on grounds recognized by national law, that possibility must extend to grounds based on Community law without need the to find a comparable claim under national law. In particular, where national law provides for revision of a tax assessment on the ground that the taxpayer made an excusable error, it must be open to the taxpayer to claim revision on the ground that the national law, in accordance with which he calculated the tax applicable to him, is incompatible with Community law. This is because, in dealing with the tax

---

19 *Ibid.*

20 *Peterbroeck*, *op.cit.*, para. 14; see also Joined Cases C-430 and C-431/93 *Van Schijndel and Van Veen v SPF* [1995] ECR I-4705, para. 19.

21 Case C-326/96 *Levez v Jennings (Harlow Pools) Ltd*, [1998] ECR I-7835, para. 44.

22 *Levez*, *op.cit.*, para. 41; *Edis*, *op.cit.*, para. 15.

23 *Levez*, paras. 39- 43; Case C-261/95 *Palmisani v Istituto Nazionale della Previdenza Sociale (INPS)* [1997] ECR I- 4025, para. 33.

24 Case C-62/93 [1995] ECR I-1883.

authorities, an individual is entitled to assume that the State has correctly implemented all Community directives and complied with Community obligations.[25] In such a case, "[i]t is not, in my view, necessary to engage in the difficult and somewhat artificial exercise of seeking a comparable claim under national law".[26] The claims, however, must not be wholly unrelated. Thus the fact that, under domestic law, a national court may exceptionally take into account certain pleas of its own motion even if they have not been raised by the parties, such as the issue that the dispute is *res judicata* or that the action is time-barred, does not mean that the national court may also raise of its own motion any plea based on Community law.[27]

In order to determine whether the principle of equivalence has been complied with, the national court must consider "the purpose and essential characteristics" of allegedly similar domestic actions.[28] In *Palmisani*[29] it was held that an action to recover the loss suffered as a result of the belated implementation of a directive is comparable to a claim for the non-contractual liability of the State brought under ordinary national law and therefore the two claims may be subject to the same limitation period. By contrast, in that Case, the Court decided that an action to recover the loss suffered as a result of the failure to implement Directive 80/987[30] is not comparable with an action to claim the benefits guaranteed to employees by that directive, so that the time-limits applicable to the two actions need not be compared. In *Singhara and Radiom*[31] it was held that the right of nationals from other Member States to enter the host Member State cannot be equated with the right of the host State's own nationals to enter the national territory and therefore the remedies for breach of the two need not be the same.

It should be accepted that the requirement of equivalence prohibits not only direct but also indirect discrimination against claims based on Community law. Where a procedural rule applies to certain categories of claims, most of which are claims based on Community law, and a more favourable rule applies to other categories of claims, most of which are claims based on national law, the first rule may run counter to the requirement of equivalence unless it is objectively justified.

The principle of equivalence does not require Member States to extend their most favourable rules to all actions based on Community law. The Court has had the opportunity to elaborate on this issue in a series of recent cases arising as a result of the imposition by the Italian authorities of corporate registration

25 *Op.cit.*, p. 1904 per Jacobs AG.
26 *Op.cit.*, para. 58 of the Advocate General's Opinion.
27 See *Peterbroeck*, *op.cit.*, paras. 23-27 of the Advocate General's Opinion.
28 *Levez*, *op.cit.*, para. 43; *Palmisani*, *op.cit.*, para. 34-38.
29 Case C-261/95 *Palmisani v Istituto Nazionale della Previdenza Sociale (INPS)* [1997] ECR I- 4025.
30 Directive 80/987 relating to the protection of employees in the event of the insolvency of their employer, OJ 1980 L 283, p. 23.
31 Joined Cases C-65 and C-111/95 *The Queen v Secretary of State for the Home Department, ex parte Mann Singh Shingara and Abbas Radiom* [1997] ECR I-3343.

charges incompatible with Directive 69/335 concerning indirect charges on the raising of capital.[32] In *Edis v Ministero delle Finanze*,[33] an Italian company sought recovery of unduly paid corporate registration charges but, under the case-law of Italian courts, the registration charge fell within the scope of Article 13(2) of Decree No 641/72, according to which the taxpayer may request repayment of charges wrongly paid within a period of three years from the date of payment. The referring court questioned the compatibility of that time-limit with Community law, pointing out that, under the ordinary rules provided for in the Italian Civil Code, an action for the recovery of sums paid but not due is subject to a ten year limitation period. The Court held that Community law does not preclude the legislation of a Member State from laying down, alongside a limitation period applicable under the ordinary law to actions between individuals for the recovery of sums paid but not due, special detailed rules, which are less favourable, governing claims and legal proceedings to challenge the imposition of charges and other levies. The position would be different only if those detailed rules applied solely to actions based on Community law for the recovery of such charges. In the case in issue, the three year time-limit applied not only in relation to repayment of the contested registration charge but also to that of all government charges of the same kind. A similar time-limit applied to actions for repayment of certain indirect taxes, and also to actions for repayment of charges or dues levied under domestic laws declared incompatible with the Italian Constitution.[34]

On the basis of similar reasoning, the Court held in *Ansaldo Energia SpA v Amministrazione delle Finanze dello Stato*[35] that Member States may calculate the interest payable, in respect of the recovery of fiscal charges paid to the national authorities contrary to Community law, in accordance with methods of calculation which are less favourable than those applicable to actions between individuals for the recovery of sums paid but not due, provided that the method in question applies without distinction to actions against national authorities based on Community law and those based on national law.[36]

The reasoning in the above cases seems persuasive. In general, a claim against the national authorities to recover a sum levied contrary to Community law can better be equated to a claim to recover a sum levied contrary to a superior rule of national law, such as the national constitution, rather than to claims

32 OJ, English Special Ed.1969 (II), p. 412. For other aspects of those cases, see below p. 474.

33 Case C-231/96 [1998] ECR I-4951; See also Case C-260/96 *Ministero delle Finanze v SPAC* [1998] ECR I-4997; Case C-228/96 *Aprile v Amministrazione delle Finanze dello Stato*, [1998] ECR I-7141; Joined Cases C-10 to C-22/97 *Ministero delle Finanze v IN.CO.GE'90 Srl*, [1998] ECR I-6307.

34 *Edis*, *op.cit.*, paras. 37-38; *SPAC*, *op.cit.*, paras. 21-22.

35 Joined Cases C-279 to C-281/96 [1998] ECR I-5025.

36 *Op.cit.*, para. 30. The Court left open the question whether it makes any difference that the method of calculating the interest is fixed by the authority responsible for the breach of Community law which gave rise to the claim for repayment. See paras. 31-35.

of recovery against other individuals. The public – private law distinction reasserts itself and assists the search for comparability. More subtle distinctions, however, may need to be made if other factors are entered into the equation, e.g. the restitutionary or otherwise nature of the claim.[37] Further enquiry may also need to be pursued if national law provides for a variety of procedures for the recovery of levies charged in breach of national law, depending for example on whether the levy was simply miscalculated, or *ultra vires*, or even contrary to a fundamental constitutional norm. In general, however, the Court is unwilling to interfere with the way legal relations between the individual and the national authorities are classified under national law.[38]

THE JUDGMENT IN *LEVEZ*

A case which gave rise to interesting issues concerning the requirements of effectiveness and equivalence was *Levez.*[39] Mrs Levez took up employment as manager of a betting shop replacing a male employee. Her employer falsely told her that she received the same salary as her predecessor although in fact she was paid less. When she found out, she sought to recover arrears of equal pay but her claim to full recovery was obstructed by s. 2(5) of the Equal Pay Act 1970. That provision limits a woman's entitlement to arrears of remuneration or damages for breach of the principle of equal pay to a period of two years prior to the date when proceedings are instituted. The Court examined first the requirement of effectiveness. It held that a national rule under which entitlement to arrears of remuneration is restricted to the two years preceding the date on which the proceedings were instituted is not in itself open to criticism. Mrs Levez, however, was late in bringing proceedings precisely because of the misleading information provided by her employer. The Court held that the application of s.2(5) in the circumstances would be manifestly incompatible with the principle of effectiveness. It would facilitate the breach of Community law by an employer whose deceit caused the employee's delay in bringing proceedings.[40]

It would be difficult to disagree with the ruling of the Court. Basic principles of justice require that a deceitful employer should not deny a remedy to one of his employees nor obtain an unfair advantage over an honest employer, precisely as a result of his deceit.[41] It is notable that the judgment placed emphasis on the deceit of the employer. The Advocate General, by contrast, formulated his re-

---

37 Compare, for example, Case C-271/91 *Marshall II* [1993] ECR I-4367 with Case C-66/95 *R v Secretary for Social Security ex parte Sutton* [1997] ECR I-2163, and see further Tridimas, *op.cit.*, p. 347.

38 See e.g. *IN.CO.GE'90*, *op.cit.*, para. 26.

39 Case C-326/96 *Levez v Jennings (Harlow Pools) Ltd*, [1998] ECR I-7835.

40 *Levez*, *op.cit.*, para. 31-32.

41 See Barnand and Hervey, European Union Employment and Social Policy Survey, (1998) 18 YEL 613 at 640.

sponse to the question referred in slightly wider terms. Section 2(5) is a strict rule in that it does not grant any discretion to the national court to extend the backdating of payment beyond the two-year period in special circumstances. In the view of Léger AG, what ran counter to the principle of effectiveness was not s.2(5) itself but the lack of flexibility in its enforcement. The fact that the national court had no power to extend the time-limit set, and thus mitigate its application in order to take into account special circumstances, made it excessively difficult to enforce a Community law right.[42] The Advocate General therefore appeared to leave the door open to setting aside s.2(5) in other cases where its application would be inequitable.

Levez raised also the issue of the inter-relationship of domestic remedies, which so far has not been examined by the case law in any detail. The UK Government argued that Mrs Levez could have recovered full compensation by bringing proceedings against her employer based on the tort of deceit before the County Court. In such proceedings, she could have relied both on the Equal Pay Act and the deceit of her employer and s. 2(5) would not have applied. The Court accepted that, where an employee can rely on the rights derived from Article 119 (now Article 141) of the Treaty and the Equal Pay Directive before another court, s. 2(5) does not compromise the principle of effectiveness.[43] It then turned to examine whether, in the circumstances, proceedings such as those brought before the County Court would comply with the principle of equivalence. The order for reference suggested that claims similar to those based on the Equal Pay Act may include those linked to a contract of employment, to pay discrimination on grounds of race, to unlawful deductions from wages, or to sex discrimination in matters other than pay. The Court left the determination of whether any of those forms of action could be considered similar to a claim under the Equal Pay Act brought before the County Court to the national court. If any of them were found to be similar, the national court would need to determine whether the claim brought before the County Court was governed by procedural rules or other requirements which were less favourable. It would be appropriate to consider whether, in order to assert fully her Community rights before the County Court, an employee in the position of Mrs Levez would incur additional costs and delay by comparison to a claimant of a similar right based on national law, who could bring an action before the Industrial Tribunal, which is simpler and, in principle, less costly.[44] Also, it was of relevance that s.2(5) applied solely to claims based on equal pay without discrimination on grounds of sex, whereas claims based on similar rights under domestic law were not limited by such a rule and therefore could be adequately protected by actions brought before the Industrial Tribunal.[45]

42 Opinion of the Advocate General delivered on 12 May 1998, at paras. 96-97.
43 *Levez*, *op.cit.*, para. 38.
44 *Op.cit.*, para. 51.
45 *Op.cit.*, para. 52.

Levez establishes that a rule of national law which makes the protection of Community rights excessively difficult is precluded even where an alternative remedy is available, if the latter is likely to entail procedural rules or other conditions which are less favourable than those applicable to similar domestic actions. This illustrates the inter-relationship between the principles of effectiveness and equivalence which, taken together, provide a double shield. However, the Court's apparent readiness to accept that proceedings before the County Court based on the tort of deceit were a viable alternative to proceedings before the Industrial Tribunal (now the Employment Tribunal), and therefore satisfied the principle of effectiveness, may be problematic. The reason why the Court did not enter into that enquiry appears to be twofold, namely, the way the preliminary questions were formulated by the national court and the Court's general tendency not to interfere with the national rules of procedure more than it is necessary.

Suffice to say in this context that the natural forum for a claim based on equal pay irrespective of sex is the Employment Tribunal. An action before that specialist tribunal compares favourably both in terms of access to justice and in terms of substance with an action before the County Court.[46]

In general, it should be accepted that a rule of domestic law, such as s.2(5), which in certain circumstances makes excessively difficult the protection of Community rights is not incompatible with Community law, if, on the facts, the applicant can have recourse to another remedy before another national court. However, such an alternative remedy must be effective and equivalent. That is particularly important where the alternative remedy is a substitute for the remedy specifically introduced by implementing legislation for the protection of a Community right.

RULES SPECIFICALLY INTRODUCED TO RESTRICT COMMUNITY CLAIMS

The case law takes a much stricter view with regard to rules which are introduced by a Member State specifically to restrict claims for the recovery of a charge which has been found by the Court of Justice to be incompatible with Community law. In *Barra*[47] it was held that Community law precludes a national provision which restricts repayment of a duty held to be contrary to the Treaty by a judgment of the Court solely to plaintiffs who brought an action for repayment before the delivery of that judgment. Such a provision renders impossible the exercise of the rights conferred by Community law for those persons who

46 In an action before the County Court, the prospective plaintiff would have to overcome the problem of legal aid; she would have to establish the tort of deceit as an independent cause of action and also argue the sex equality point occupying valuable judicial time in an unsuited forum.

47 Case 309/85 *Barra v Belgium and Another* [1988] ECR 355.

initiate proceedings after the Court's judgment. Similarly, in *Deville*[48] it was held that a Member State may not, subsequent to a judgment of the Court from which it follows that certain legislation is incompatible with the Treaty, adopt a procedural rule which specifically reduces the possibilities of bringing proceedings for repayment of charges unduly levied under that legislation. More recently, the Court has had the opportunity to revisit the judgments in *Barra* and *Deville* in a series of cases arising as a result of preliminary references made by Italian courts.

As we saw above, *Edis v Ministero delle Finanze*[49] arose as a result of the imposition by Italian law of an annual fee in respect of the registration of companies in the corporate register. In its judgment in *Ponente Carni*,[50] the Court had held that the payment of such a fee ran counter to Directive 69/335 concerning indirect charges on the raising of capital.[51] Following the judgment in *Ponente Carni*, Edis sought repayment of unduly paid registration charges, but a dispute arose as to the applicable limitation period. Under Article 13(2) of Italian Decree No 641/72, the taxpayer may request repayment of charges wrongly paid within a period of three years from the date of payment. Traditionally, the case law of Italian courts interpreted that provision as applying only in cases where a sum had been unduly paid owing to an error in the calculation in the tax. Claims for the recovery of unduly paid corporate charges were subject to the ten-year limitation period provided for in the Italian Civil Code. In 1996, however, after the judgment in *Ponente Carni* was delivered, the *Corte Suprema di Cassazione* departed from its previous case law, holding that repayment of the registration charge was subject to the three-year time limit provided for in Decree No 641/72. The Commission argued that, by departing from its previous case law, the *Corte Suprema di Cassazione* specifically curtailed the opportunity for the persons concerned to bring proceedings to secure repayment of charges levied in breach of Community law. The Court rejected that argument, distinguishing the case in issue from *Barra* and *Deville*. It held that a Member State is prohibited from adopting provisions making repayment of a tax held to be contrary to Community law, subject to conditions relating specifically to that tax which are less favourable than those which would otherwise be applied.[52] The case in issue was distinguishable on two grounds. First, the interpretation given by the *Corte Suprema di Cassazione* related to a national provision which had been in force for several years when judgment was delivered in *Ponente Carni*. Secondly, that provision was concerned not only with repayment of corporate registration charges, which were in issue in *Ponente Carni*, but also with all

48 Case 240/87 *Deville v Administration des Impôts* [1988] ECR 3513.

49 *Op.cit.* n. 33.

50 Joined Cases C-71/ and C-178/91 *Ponente Carni and Cispadana Construzioni* [1993] ECR I-1915.

51 *Op.cit.*

52 *Edis, op.cit.*, para. 24.

registration charges levied by the Italian Government.[53] The Court expressly left open the issue under what conditions the *Deville* principle might apply to judicial authorities.[54]

In *Aprile Srl v Amministrazione delle Finanze dello Stato*,[55] the applicant sought to recover inspection fees charged by the Italian authorities on the importation of goods, which in *Aprile I*,[56] on a previous reference for a preliminary ruling, the Court had found to be incompatible with Community law. The right to reimbursement, however, had become statute-barred by virtue of Article 29 of Italian Decree Law No 428/1990. That Decree Law introduced a special time-limit of three years for all actions for reimbursement of customs charges instead of the ordinary ten-year limitation period laid down for actions for the recovery of sums paid but not due provided for in the Italian Civil Code. The change in the law was prompted by the case-law of the *Corte Suprema di Cassazione* which had held that an action for sums paid but not due under Community law was subject to the ten-year limitation period provided for in the Civil Code and not the shorter period provided for in the customs legislation which applied only to actions for the recovery of sums overpaid as a result of an error of calculation or the incorrect application of a tariff.

Recalling *Edis*,[57] the Court held that Community law does not preclude the legislation of a Member State from laying down, alongside a limitation period applicable under the ordinary law to actions between individuals for the recovery of sums paid but not due, special detailed rules, which are less favourable, governing claims and legal proceedings to challenge the imposition of charges and other levies. The position would be different only if those detailed rules applied solely to actions for repayment based on Community law.[58] In the case in issue, the time-limit provided for by Decree-Law No 428/1990 applied without distinction to all actions for recovery of indirect levies and therefore complied with the principle of equivalence. The Commission argued, however, that by making repayment subject to a three-year time limit rather than the ten-year time limit provided for under ordinary law, Article 29 of Decree law No 428/1990 specifically curtailed the opportunity for the persons concerned to bring proceedings, thereby disregarding the judgments in *Barra* and *Deville*. The Court did not accept that argument. It stated that, although Article 29 reduced significantly the period within which reimbursement of unduly paid sums could be claimed, it set a time limit which was sufficient to guarantee the effectiveness of the right to reimbursement. That provision did not have retroactive effect. Also, the time limit in issue was applicable not solely to a specific kind of charge which had previously been declared incompatible with Community law, but to a

53 *Op.cit.*, para. 25.
54 *Ibid.*
55 *Op.cit.*, above n. 33. See also Case C-343/96, *Dilexport*, judgment of 9 February 1999.
56 Case C-125/94 [1995] ECR I-2919.
57 *Op.cit.*, above n. 33.
58 *Aprile*, *op.cit.*, para. 26.

whole range of internal charges and taxes for which the legislation had standardised the rules on time-limits. The Court also pointed out that the adoption of the contested law preceded its judgment in *Aprile*.

It appears therefore that a Member State is prohibited from adopting provisions governing the repayment of a tax which has been held to be contrary to Community law where those provisions,

- (a) relate specifically to that tax;
- (b) are less favourable than those which would otherwise apply.

It remains open whether a Member State may adopt, subsequent to a judgment of the Court declaring a national levy incompatible with Community law, provisions which are less favourable than those which would otherwise apply but which relate not specifically to the recovery of that levy but also to comparable national levies. Arguably, if such provisions are an integral part of a general reform of the regulations governing recovery of sums unduly paid to the national administration and there is no element of discrimination against Community claims, they could be compatible with Community law.

THE POST-*EMMOTT* CASE LAW

In *Emmott*,[59] decided in 1991, the Court held that so long as a directive has not been properly transposed into national law, individuals are unable to ascertain the full extent of their rights. Consequently, until a directive has been properly transposed, a defaulting Member State may not rely on an individual's delay in initiating proceedings against it in order to protect rights conferred upon him by the directive, and a period laid down by national law within which proceedings must be initiated cannot begin to run before that time. *Emmott* was hailed as introducing a new, more assertive, approach on the part of the Court. In subsequent cases, however, the scope of the ruling was restricted. In *Steenhorst-Neerings*[60] it was held that the failure of a Member State to transpose properly Article 4(1) of Directive 7/79 [61] did not preclude it from relying on a rule of national law according to which benefits for incapacity for work were payable not earlier than one year before the date when benefit was claimed. The Court held that the national rule in issue applied equally to claims based on national law and claims based on Community law, and did not make virtually impossible the exercise of rights conferred by Community law. *Emmott* was distinguished on the ground that the rule of Irish law in issue in that case fixed a time-limit for

59 Case C-208/90 [1991] ECR 4269.

60 Case C-338/91 *Steenhorst-Neerings v Bestuur van de Bedrijfsvereniging voor Detailhandel, Ambachten en Huisvrouwen* [1993] ECR I-5475.

61 Directive 7/79 on the progressive implementation of the principle of equal treatment between men and women in matters of social security, OJ 1979 L 6, p. 24.

bringing actions and made it impossible for the applicant to rely on Article 4(1). By contrast, the rule in issue in *Steenhorst Neerings* did not affect the right of individuals to rely on Directive 7/79 but restricted the retroactive effect of claims for benefits. That restriction was justified by the need to ensure that the claimant satisfied the conditions for eligibility and the need to preserve the financial balance of the social security system.[62] *Steenhorst-Neerings* was confirmed in *Johnson*[63] where the benefit in issue, unlike that in issue in *Steenhorst-Neerings*, was non-contributory and consequently that there was no need to preserve the financial balance of the system.

Thus, in the above cases the Court distinguished between national rules which prescribe time limits within which proceedings must be brought, and national rules which limit the period prior to the bringing of a claim in respect of which arrears of benefit may be claimed. The two types of rules, however, may lead in practice to the same result. In *Steenhorst-Neerings* and *Johnson*, the Court focused on whether the applicable national rules made it impossible to exercise rights based on Community law rather than on whether an individual suffered as a result of late transposition. The judgments do not require that an individual should be put in the same position that he would have been, had a Member State transposed Directive 7/79 properly into national law within the requisite period of implementation. They thus leave open the possibility that a Member State may derive a benefit as a result of its failure to implement a directive in time.[64]

The trend towards a restrictive interpretation of *Emmott* reached is climax in *Fantask a/S and Others v Industriministeriet (Erhvervsministeriet)*.[65] The case concerned charges on the registration of companies levied by the Danish authorities which were found to be contrary to Directive 69/335. Danish law made the recovery of such claims subject to a limitation period of five years, but the applicants argued, pursuant to *Emmott*, that a Member State could not rely on that limitation period as long as Directive 69/335 had not been properly transposed into national law. Confirming *Johnson* and *Steenhorst-Neerings*, the Court stated that the solution adopted in *Emmott* was justified by the particular circumstances of that case where the time bar had "the result of depriving the applicant of any opportunity whatever" to rely on her right arising from the directive in issue. The five-year limitation period imposed by Danish law was reasonable and applied without distinction to domestic claims and those based on Community law and was therefore compatible with Community law.

Fantask gave a fatal blow to *Emmott* and it is now settled that the latter must be read on its facts. It applies only in relation to directives and only given the

---

62 Cf the "dissenting" Opinion of Darmon AG, *op.cit.*, pp. 5492-5493.

63 Case C-410/92 [1994] ECR I-5483.

64 But see Case C-66/95 *R v Secretary of State for Social Security ex parte Sutton*, [1997] ECR I- 2163, according to which the individual concerned may recover any loss suffered by bringing an action for damages against the State.

65 Case C-188/95, [1997] ECR I-6783.

specific circumstances of that case.[66] As a general rule, a limitation period imposed by national law starts from the date specified therein rather than the date when national legislation has complied with the Community obligation in issue. This was reiterated more recently in *Edis*, where the Court held that Community law does not prevent a Member State from resisting actions for repayment of charges levied in breach of a directive by relying on a time-limit under national law which begins to run from the day of payment of the charges in question, even if the directive concerned had not yet been properly transposed into national law.[67]

The case law focuses on whether the time limit imposed by national law is adequate, in the sense that it offers the individual the opportunity to protect rights derived from Community law, and whether it complies with the principle of equivalence. An example of the Court's policy of selective deference is provided by *Magorrian v Eastern Health and Social Services Board*.[68] The applicants were women employed as mental health nurses. They were refused additional pension benefits payable under a voluntary contracted-out pension scheme on the ground that they did not have the status of full-time workers at the time of their retirement. The national court held that their exclusion from the additional benefits amounted to indirect sex discrimination. The question then arose from which date their periods of service as part-time workers should be taken into account for the purpose of calculating the additional benefits to which they were entitled. In response to a preliminary reference, the Court held that the appropriate date as from which periods of service of part-time workers who have suffered indirect sex discrimination must be taken into account is 8 April 1976, the date of the judgment in *Defrenne*.[69] The claim of the applicants, however, encountered an obstacle posed by national law. Regulation 12 of the Northern Ireland Occupational Regulations[70] provides that, in proceedings concerning access to membership of occupational schemes, the right to be admitted to the scheme is to have effect from a date no earlier than two years before the institution of proceedings. The Court held that Regulation 12 deprived the applicants of the additional benefits under the scheme to which they were entitled to be affiliated, since those benefits could be calculated only by reference to periods of service completed by them as from 1990, that is to say two years prior to their commencing proceedings. The Court distinguished *Steenhorst-Neerings* and *Johnson*

66 See Case C-90/94 *Haahr Petroleum v Åbenrå Havn and Others* [1997] ECR I-4085, paras. 52-53; Joined Cases C-114 and C-115/95 *Texaco and Olieselskabet Danmark* [1997] ECR I-4263, paras. 48-49; and see also Case C-2/94 *Denkavit International and Others v Kamer van Koophandel en Fabrieken voor Midden-Gelderrland and Others* [1996] ECR I-2827, at 2851 per Jacobs AG.

67 *Edis*, *op.cit.*, paras. 45-48; *Aprile*, *op.cit.*, paras. 40-45; *SPAC*, *op.cit.*, paras. 28-32; *Ansaldo Energia*, *op.cit.*, paras. 19-23.

68 Case C-246/96, [1997] ECR I-7153.

69 Case 43/75 *Defrenne* [1976] ECR 455.

70 Occupational Pension Schemes (Equal Access to Membership) Regulations (Northern Ireland) 1976, No. 238.

on the following grounds. The rules in issue in those cases limited the period, prior to commencement of proceedings, in respect of which backdated benefits could be obtained. By contrast, Regulation 12 prevented the entire record of service completed by those concerned after 8 April 1976 until 1990 from being taken into account for the purposes of calculating the additional benefits which would be payable even after the date of the claim. Consequently, Regulation 12 was such as to strike "at the very essence of the rights conferred by the Community legal order".[71] Also, the effect of the regulation was to limit in time the direct effect of Article 119 (now Art. 141) of the Treaty in cases where no such limitation has been laid down either in the Court's case-law or in Protocol No 2 annexed to the Treaty on European Union. The distinct feature of Regulation 12 was that it restricted claims for future benefits based on past service. Are all national rules which have such restrictive effects caught by the ruling in *Magorrian*? Given the generality of the ruling one may venture to suggest that that is so, but it is to be noted that in a recent case where the same issue of principle has arisen, the House of Lords has made a further reference to the Court of Justice.[72]

CONCLUDING REMARKS

The Court's approach to national rules of procedure and remedies in recent years can perhaps best be described as being one of selective deference. As Advocate General Jacobs has observed, the case law in this area seeks to draw a balance between the effectiveness of Community law and the autonomy of national procedural systems.

It may be said that, overall, the case law has drawn that balance successfully. The Court sees the development of the law in this area as a dialectical process which results from a constant dialogue with the national courts. Indeed, the development of no other area of Community law depends as much on the cooperation of the national courts as the law of remedies. The principles of effectiveness and equivalence force national courts to view national remedies under the prism of Community law. An incidental effect of their application is expose possible inconsistencies and a lack of coherence in the national system of remedies and, at times, to lead to a rethinking of national remedies as they apply to areas unconnected with Community law.[73] This infusion of Community standards into national legal systems by the Court of Justice may yet prove the most powerful centripetal force towards a *jus communae europeum*.

---

71 *Magorrian*, *op.cit.*, para. 44.

72 *Preston v Wolverhampton NHS Trust* [1998] 1 ALL ER 528.

73 See e.g. *M v Home Office* [1994] 1 AC 3777.

31

A CASE STUDY IN JUDICIAL ACTIVISM IN THE 1990s: THE STATUS BEFORE NATIONAL COURTS OF MEASURES WRONGFULLY UN-NOTIFIED TO THE COMMISSION

Stephen Weatherill

I Introduction

The ruling of the European Court in *CIA Security International SA* v. *Signalson SA and Securitel SPRL*[1] provides a reminder that any proposed diagnosis of a recent decline in its capacity for innovative and imaginative rulings should be examined with some caution. Although the decade of the 1990s has witnessed some wariness on the part of the European Court when invited to deliver expansionist rulings at the outer margins of Community competence, such reticence has not noticeably troubled the Court when invited to sharpen the pain of failure to abide by agreed rules which fall unquestionably within the sphere of Community competence. The famous *Francovich* ruling, in which the Court established that failure to transpose a Directive might lead to liability to compensate injured parties, and its high-profile offspring in which the matter has been examined in the light of violation of provisions of the Treaty itself, fit this description, but so too does *CIA Security International*. The Court was asked whether a draft technical regulation which had not been notified to the Commission by the public authorities of a Member State in breach of the obligation imposed by Directive 83/189 was enforceable in proceedings before national courts involving third parties (Part 2 of this paper, below). The Court ruled that such measures were *not* enforceable for want of notification (Part 3). This sanction of unenforceability in proceedings involving third parties constitutes a vigorous method for inducing Member States to comply with their obligation of notification of draft technical regulations. The purpose of this paper is to trace the implications of the Court's enhancement of the judicial protection of rights to trade in the European internal market in its ruling in *CIA Security International*. This demands that the decision be placed in the context of, first, the regime of notification instituted by Directive 83/189 and, second, the wider pattern of transparency and administrative co-operation which underpins the Commission's post-1992 quest for stability and reliability in the management of the internal market (Part 4). It is also

1 Case C-194/94 [1996] ECR I-2201.

D. O'Keeffe (ed.), Liber Amicorum Slynn 481-503 (2000)

relevant to inquire how far beyond the system instituted by Directive 83/189 the rather dramatic penalty of unenforceability for unnotified measures may reach (Part 5). In addition, the paper seeks to use the decision in *CIA Security International* to demonstrate the ingenuity of the European Court and its allies in litigation (*in casu*, and not untypically, commercial interests and the Commission) and the persisting aptitude of European Community law to be propelled into realms in which national acts and omissions are subjected, often unexpectedly, to judicial control at European level. Subsequent case law has already illuminated how a high-profile ruling such as *CIA Security International* inevitably generates further unforeseen attempts by ingenious litigants to exploit the Court's reasoning (Part 6). This invites consideration of anxieties that European Community law, although unquestionably dynamic in its evolution, has the tendency to be *over*-stretched and thereby to suffer a potential diminution in the respect in which it is held (Part 7). In conclusion (Part 8), it is suggested that any account of the judicial activism of the European Court in the 1990s demands an analysis characterised by subtle nuance.

II DIRECTIVE 83/189 AND THE BACKGROUND TO THE RULING IN *CIA SECURITY INTERNATIONAL*

Directive 83/189 requires prior notification to the Commission of draft technical standards and regulations introduced in the Member States.[2] The Directive was twice extended by amendment[3] before the regime was the subject of consolidation by Directive 98/34[4] in accordance with the Commission's preoccupation to simplify Community legislation.[5] The establishment of this "early warning" system permits a more intensive supervision of proposed national initiatives that may impede product market integration than is feasible under the orthodox system for securing the free movement of goods, which emphasises reactive enforcement by the Commission or by private parties relying on Community law before national courts. The aim is the establishment of a more reliable and predictable basis for the management of the internal market. In pursuit of this objective the Member States have therefore accepted procedural limitations on their freedom to regulate their markets in supplement to their substantive Treaty obligations to respect, *inter alia*, free movement.[6] The system initiated by Di-

2 O.J. 1983, L109. See Weatherill, "Compulsory Notification of Draft Technical Regulations: the Contribution of Directive 83/189 to the Management of the Internal Market", 16 YEL (1996) 129-204; Fronia, "Transparenz und Vermeidung von Handelshemmnissen bei Produktspezifikationen im Binnenmarkt" EuZW [4/1996] 101-109; Fronia and Casella, "La procedure de controle des reglementations techniques prevue par la nouvelle directive 83/189/CEE" RMUE [2/1995] 37-84.

3 By Dir.88/182 O.J. 1988, L81 and Dir.94/10 O.J. 1994, L100/30.

4 O.J. 1998, L204/37, itself amended by Dir. 98/48 O.J. 1998, L217/18.

5 O.J. 1996, C224/5.

6 See discussion in this vein by Jans, "National Legislative Autonomy? The Procedural

rective 83/189 requires Member States to postpone the adoption of a draft technical regulation for a stipulated period, allowing the Commission time to examine the circumstances. It was the consequence of neglect of this "standstill" obligation that was at stake in *CIA Security International SA* v. *Signalson SA and Securitel SPRL*.

The background to the ruling deserves attention for it is germane to this paper's thesis that the Court is a key player in the dynamic evolution of EC law but that it is dependent for pathbreaking opportunities on the support supplied by other actors who, in turn, rely on the Court to nurture their own ambitions. The text of Directive 83/189 and subsequent amendments is barren of reference to the legal consequences before national courts of a failure to comply with the obligation of notification. However, in 1986 the Commission had published a communication "concerning the non-respect of certain provisions of Directive 83/189/EEC of 28 March 1983 laying down a procedure for the provision of information in the field of technical standards and regulations".[7] This summarised the nature of the obligations introduced by the Directive and identified them as significant methods for preventing the creation of new obstacles to trade. It commented that the failure of a State to observe the "clear and unequivocal" obligations to notify and to observe the standstill period would damage the construction of the internal market. So, in the view of the Commission, an enactment of a technical regulation falling within the scope of Directive 83/189 in breach of these obligations did not merely amount to a Treaty violation capable of leading to infringement proceedings but also deprived the regulation of enforceability against third parties in the legal system of the State in question.

Subsequently the Commission chose frequently to repeat its view of the legal consequences of non-notification in documentation relevant to the development of the system instituted by Directive 83/189.[8] It received criticism for its perceived extravagance. The ECOSOC's opinion on the Commission's report of activities between 1984 and 1987 commented that it was for the Court to decide the point and criticised the 1986 communication as "a precedent which should not be repeated unless there is a sound legal presumption that it will be upheld in the Courts".[9] Nevertheless, the Commission sought to persuade the Court to adopt its own view. Success was delayed until 1996 as the Court declined to take the increasing number of opportunities presented to it to rule on the point. For example, in a pair of Article 169 (now 226) infringement proceedings against the Netherlands which reached the European Court[10] the Commission submitted that non-notification at draft stage renders a technical regulation unen-

Constraints of European Law" LIEI [1998/1] 25-58.

7 O.J. 1986, C245/4.

8 E.g. Report on the Directive's operation in 1984-1987, COM (88) 722, pp.10,43,54; O.J. 1989, C67/3, O.J. 1993, C237/3, O.J. 1994, C3/2, C8/2, C129/5. See also W.Q. 39/86 (de Vries) O.J. 1986, C270/22; W.Q. 1376/86 (Rogalla) O.J. 1987, C143/12.

9 O.J. 1989, C298/19, para. 4.6.

10 Cases C-52/93, C-61/93 [1994] ECR I-3591.

forceable but Advocate General Van Gerven expressed the view that it was inappropriate to answer the question in the context of infringement proceedings, stating that "The Court's task is to decide whether or not the Member State in question has failed to fulfil its obligations under Community law." It was not for the Court "to decide on the consequences that a finding of such failure may have in the national legal systems of the Member States". The European Court confirmed that a violation of the obligations created by the Directive had been established, but it ignored the legal status of the non-notified measures before national courts.[11] It is accordingly clear that when the Court eventually came to rule on the matter a fund of institutional aspiration had already been invested in it.

III The ruling in CIA Security International

The Commission's view of the status of non-notified measures before national courts was ultimately vindicated by the European Court in its April 1996 ruling in *CIA Security International SA* v. *Signalson SA and Securitel SPRL*.[12] The Court insisted on the purpose of Directive 83/189 to "protect, by means of preventive control, freedom of movement for goods, which is one of the foundations of the Community".[13] The pattern of notification plus suspension under the Directive allows examination of the implications for trade of planned national measures. The Court, repeating the point that the Directive is designed to protect the free movement of goods, then added that "the effectiveness of Community control will be that much greater if the Directive is interpreted as meaning that breach of the obligation to notify constitutes a substantial procedural defect such as to render the technical regulations in question inapplicable to individuals".[14] Pursuit of this end allowed the Court to leap beyond the absence of express provision in the Directive relating to effects of failure to notify and it took this bold approach, notwithstanding contrary submissions presented by the German, Dutch and British governments, contending that, in the absence of any express provision in the Directive, any breach should lead to consequences only at the level of Commission/Member State. This is a ruling which deepens incentives for Member States to participate actively in the system of notification envisaged by the Directive.

The vigour of the ruling is striking. It was surely open to the Court to rule that the infraction should have been addressed only by infringement proceedings

11 See similarly Advocate General Ruiz-Jarabo Colomer in Case C-273/94, *Commission* v. *Netherlands,* [1996] ECR I-31 in which the Court also preferred to remain silent on the point. A Dutch court in 1991 decided the point contrary to the Commission's view but made no preliminary reference under Art. 177 (now 234); see Jans *supra* note 6.

12 Case C-194/94 *supra* note 1.

13 Para. 40 of the ruling.

14 Para. 48 of the ruling.

initiated by the Commission (slow though these doubtless would have been) and/ or by proceedings at national level for compensation based on the *Francovich* principle initiated by traders whose commercial freedom had been impeded (albeit that elements such as the establishment of a causal link between breach of an obligation to notify and loss would militate against the successful pursuit of such a claim). The analogy is admittedly inexact, but this line of reasoning puts one in mind of the approach adopted by the Court to national time limits, which it does not insist must be disapplied even though they may serve to defeat a claim based on inadequately implemented Community law provided that they operate without discrimination against the claimant basing him- or herself on Community law rather than national law and provided that they are not so short as to defeat access to an effective remedy. The Court instead acknowledges the contribution of time limits to the preservation of legal certainty and a litigant wishing to rely on Community rules whose claim is time-barred but who has suffered loss as a result of faulty implementation of Community law should have recourse to an action for compensation of the type envisaged by the Court in *Francovich* and subsequent cases. The State will then be in a position to defend itself with reference to the circumstances of the default, for only a sufficiently serious breach of Community law will trigger a responsibility to compensate the applicant. In this way the competing interests at stake may be balanced.[15] Not so in the case of draft technical regulations which fall within the scope of application of Directive 83/189. Left unnotified, they must not be applied by national courts in proceedings involving third parties.[16]

One may interpret this chain of events as an example of the propensity of the Court and the Commission to by-pass the legislature. The sanction of unenforceability could have been stipulated in the legislation. It was not. The Commission had made amending proposals to this effect to no avail.[17] Yet the Court added it. The Commission gleefully began to accompany published material relating to the Directive with reminders that the Court's ruling in favour of the unenforceability of non-notified measures against individuals confirmed its own longstanding view on the matter.[18] The Court is not slow to thicken the constitutional impact of agreed rules. The landmark ruling in *Francovich*, in which the Court established the competence as a matter of Community law of national courts to

15 This is a necessarily abbreviated, and somewhat simplified, portrayal of a complex line of case law. The Opinion of AG Jacobs in Case C-188/95, *Fantask A/S*, [1997] ECR I-6783 is especially illuminating in depicting the trends. See further Weatherill and Beaumont, *EU Law*, 3rd ed. (Penguin Books, 1999), pp.404-5.

16 In appropriate circumstances *Francovich* liability may be incurred *in addition*: Jans *supra* note 6.

17 In the process which eventually led to Dir. 94/10 *supra* note 3 the first Commission proposal, O.J. 1992, C340/7, included a reference to the point in a recital, but in an amended proposal, COM (93) 444, the Commission accepted deletion in the light of the Parliament's Opinion (see PE DOC A3-153/93 of May 1993), although the Commission stated that it maintained its position on the principle of unenforceability.

18 E.g. O.J. 1998, C9/2.

award damages in cases of loss caused by breach of EC law,[19] conforms to this pattern. The Court was not deterred from intruding further on the remedial and procedural autonomy of the national legal system in relation to matters falling within the scope of application of Community law. Indeed, in mapping these trends, one could go back as far as the ruling in *Van Gend en Loos* itself[20] and identify the assertion of the direct effect of Community law as evidence of the Court's anxiety to make real and immediate the enforcement of obligations agreed by the Member States.

The community of interest between Court and Commission in sharpening incentives to comply with Community law is striking in *CIA Security International*. This carries echoes of the celebrated *Cassis de Dijon* ruling.[21] There too the Court and the Commission's work was visibly intertwined as the shaping of the internal market took a new twist. The Commission immediately welcomed the ruling.[22] *Cassis* allowed the Commission to use the principle of (non-absolute) mutual recognition and home country control as a platform on which to build its internal market strategy, permeating both its interpretation of the Treaty provisions governing free movement and the pattern of secondary legislation which, in pursuit of integration, has increasingly come to exercise a re-regulatory influence over the Community marketplace to the partial or total exclusion of national competence in the occupied fields. Moreover, the Court's readiness to move beyond the hints dropped in *Dassonville*[23] and to make unambiguously clear that the Treaty provisions on the free movement of goods are capable of catching technical standards which cause market fragmentation simply because they vary State by State exerted a direct impact on the context in which the legislative contribution to market-building came to be shaped. The applicability of (what was then) Article 30 even to non-discriminatory measures removed the need to promote a harmonisation programme on the comprehensive scale previously envisaged. The Commission was able to focus its legislative ambitions on those areas where barriers to trade persisted because of the existence of justifications recognised under the *Cassis de Dijon* "mandatory requirements" formula and areas in which mutual recognition alone was seen to provide an inadequate basis for reliable integration. But many areas were deleted from the harmonisation agenda, allowing greater leeway for continuing diversity in the market, subject to the competitive discipline of mutual recognition. The inter-institutional cause-and-effect may be persuasively tracked yet further. The harmonisation programme as conceived prior to the *Cassis* ruling deserved criticism for its over-regulatory influence. In addition the supply of measures by the Community's legislature was simply too slow. The laborious and technical na-

19 Joined Cases C-6, C-9/90 [1991] ECR I-5357.

20 Case 26/62 [1963] ECR 1.

21 Case 120/78 [1979] ECR 649. See at length Weatherill and Beaumont *supra* note 15 Ch.17.

22 Commission Communication, O.J. 1980, C256/2.

23 Case 8/74 [1974] ECR 837.

ture of the exercise was in part culpable, but also highly significant was the requirement of unanimity in the Council attached to the adoption of measures under Article 100 EEC which, until the entry into force of the Single European Act in 1987 and the release of opportunities provided by qualified majority voting under Article 100a, provided the motor of the harmonisation programme. The legislative route was frequently blocked. In the light of this political background, it is not fanciful to see the Court's subtle and innovative ruling in *Cassis de Dijon* as a conscious contribution to altering the environment in which the Commission was operating.[24] In turn the Court's willingness to propel Article 30 into territory thought to belong to the legislature affected its own role (and that of national courts). The type of intensely sensitive judgements about the balance between interests in market integration and those of regulatory protection expressed through national choices, previously thought to be allocated to the Community legislator, were transferred into the judicial arena in the guise of the *Cassis de Dijon* formula. It is this swoop which has drawn the Court into its high-profile judgments of recent years which have pitted integration against national preferences for, *inter alia*, environmental protection,[25] the maintenance of Press diversity[26] and protecting the economic interests of consumers.[27] The ruling in *Keck and Mithouard*[28] represents only a partial retreat from this deep involvement in adjudicating on the validity of local regulatory choices in the context of European market re-structuring.

IV *CIA Security International* and Post-1992 Market Management

The days of intense legislative activity across a range of sectors in pursuit of integration are past. The Commission focuses its endeavours on "better laws", not more laws; and it is dedicating an increased proportion of its resources to improving enforcement of the legislative bedrock of the internal market.[29] The "better not more" slogan initially assumed prominence after the Edinburgh European Council of December 1992 and the Interinstitutional Agreement of October 1993. The rise of subsidiarity and the expiry of the deadline for the

---

24 Other candidates for examination from this perspective abound; e.g. in the field of mergers and related transactions, Cases 142, 156/84, *BAT and Reynolds* v. *Commission*, [1987] ECR 4487 and in relation to postal services, Case C-320/91, *Paul Corbeau*, [1993] ECR I-2533.

25 E.g. Case C-2/90, *Commission* v. *Belgium*, [1992] ECR I-4431.

26 E.g. Case C-368/95, *Vereinigte Familiapress Zeitungsverlags und -vertriebs GmbH* v. *Heinrich Bauer Verlag*, [1997] ECR I-3689.

27 E.g. Case C-470/93, *Verein gegen Unwesen* v. *Mars GmbH* [1995] ECR I-1923.

28 Joined Cases C-267 and C-268/91 [1993] ECR I-6097.

29 For a critical account, see Armstrong, "Governance and the Single European Market" Ch.21 in Craig and De Burca (eds.), *The Evolution of EU Law* (OUP, 1999); also Mortelmans, "The Common Market, the Internal Market and the Single Market, What's in a Market?" 35 CMLRev. (1998) 101-136.

completion of the internal market combined to create a new regulatory environment. This may be traced from the Commission's first annual report on the subsidiarity principle[30] through subsequent reports and other related documentation.[31] It is placed on a more formal constitutional footing by the Amsterdam Treaty's innovation, the Protocol on subsidiarity and proportionality.

In this climate of changing emphasis on the instruments appropriate for managing the internal market as "deadline 1992" recedes into history, transparency has assumed an increasingly prominent role. The Commission is determined to improve patterns of notification and to deepen structures for administrative co-operation. It aims to breed trust in the viability of the internal market. To some extent perception is reality; if the rules underpinning the market are believed to be the subject of more-or-less reliable enforcement across the territory of the Union, the market will be treated as a credible arena in which to operate by both traders and consumers. Absent such trust, the ambitions of the integration project will remain unfulfilled.

As a general observation, the Commission's quest to develop new strategies for the management of the internal market is built around the notion that litigation can form only one component of a comprehensive strategy. Case law establishes the legal obligation imposed on public authorities in the Member States to "assist in bringing about a relaxation of the controls existing in intra-Community trade".[32] The direct effect of Articles 28-30 (ex 30-36) of the Treaty empowers private parties to police infractions of the principles of free movement by taking action before domestic courts, in addition to the separate possibility of Commission intervention under the Article 226 (ex 169) infringement procedure. But litigation is both *ad hoc* and *ex post facto*. The Commission has placed an increasing emphasis on devising a framework within which practical administrative co-operation may be deepened and actual or potential obstacles to integration brought to light in order that problems may be addressed with expedition. The prior notification system instituted by Directive 83/189, now consolidated in Directive 98/34 and buttressed by the Court's ruling in *CIA Security International*, examined above, forms part of this pattern. The "standstill" period envisaged by the Directive allows the Commission to examine draft measures with a view to halting their introduction at national level should it conclude that a violation of Article 28 (ex 30) would follow. The drive to improve transparency and to establish supervisory mechanisms that are more sensitive than litigation was extended beyond Directive 83/189 (now 98/34) by Decision 3052/95,[33] which has operated since the start of 1997 at the more detailed level of control exer-

---

30 COM (94) 533.

31 E.g. COM (97) 626, COM (98) 715.

32 E.g. Case 272/80, *Biologische Producten*, [1981] ECR 3277, para. 14 of the judgment.

33 O.J. 1995, L321/1. See Fournier and La Pergola, "La nouvelle procédure d'information mutuelle sur les mesures nationales dérogeant au principe de libre circulation des marchandises à l'intérieur de la Communauté" *Revue du Marché Unique Européen* 145 [4/1996].

cised by national authorities over the marketing of a particular model or type of product lawfully produced or marketed in another Member State. Action taken must be notified to the Commission. The Decision sets up an attractive new element in market management. It will induce greater transparency and, by compelling States to think harder before they refuse market access to imports, it should foster among public authorities a greater awareness of the demands of an integrating market. This generates appealing visions of networks of horizontal (national/national) and vertical (Commission/national) administrative co-operation. At a more general level, such initiatives highlight the diminishing space allowed to the autonomy of proposed legislative and administrative acts within the Member States of the EU.

The Commission is also intent on using softer forms of intervention to improve patterns of co-operative market management. The influential Sutherland Report of 1992[34] stressed the desirability of arranging administrative partnerships between Community and national authorities. Subsequently, two Commission communications have prompted Council Resolutions on the development of administrative cooperation in the implementation and enforcement of Community legislation in the internal market. The first, adopted in June 1994, expressed general support for the aims of improved transparency and mutual confidence between administrative authorities.[35] A practical edge was added by the invitation to Member States to notify to the Commission contact points for enforcement activities in a range of stated areas. The follow-up resolution adopted in July 1996 maintained the thematic insistence on transparency and co-operation and invited Member States to complete the supply of contact points and to ensure that lists are kept up-to-date.[36] In June 1997, energised by Mario Monti, the Commissioner holding responsibility for the internal market, the Commission published an "Action Plan for the Single Market".[37] A theme of transparency as a basis for creating a reliable environment for commercial activity in the internal market underpins the Action Plan. It is insisted that "The Single Market stands or falls on confidence". The Plan was submitted to the European Council in Amsterdam in the same month of June, where it was firmly endorsed as a basis for renewed effort to eliminate remaining obstacles to realisation of the full benefits of the single market programme. In 1999 the Commission, reviewing the achievements of the Action Plan, has asserted continuing success in "making the Single Market a reality for citizens and business" and now looks to "fine-tune" the process.[38]

---

34 *The Internal Market after 1992: Meeting the Challenge* (Report to the EEC Commission by the High Level Group on the Operation of the Internal Market).

35 O.J. 1994, C179/1.

36 O.J. 1996, C224/3.

37 "Action Plan for the Single Market, Communication of the Commission to the European Council", CSE(97)1, final, 4 June 1997.

38 IP/99/128.

Both Commission and Court have made valuable efforts to improve transparency in relation to national regulatory practice as part of the general quest to secure effective management of the internal market. Admittedly, administrative heterogeneity is a phenomenon that will continue to impede the growth of effective co-ordination, leaving gaps and unevenness in the practical impact of Community law across the territory of the Union. One might suppose that clarifying the nature of the notification obligation, as has been achieved by successive amendments of Directive 83/189 combined with the Court's ruling in *CIA Security International*, will make States more likely to comply with the requirements of transparency in future. But in so far as the impediment is caused by administrative heterogeneity and unfamiliarity, rather than deliberate cheating, the problems cannot be overcome simply by increasing top-down structures and strengthening sanctions. Administrative heterogeneity among the Member States operates as a persisting barrier to the "Europeanisation" of networks of information gathering and sharing.[39] However, although the process is gradual and one should caution against over-reliance on transparency as an instrument of market management, the Commission is to be commended for its energetic thinking on how to shape a "post-1992" agenda for market management. In this regard, it has enjoyed support from the Court.

V *CIA SECURITY INTERNATIONAL* AND OTHER REGIMES BASED ON NOTIFICATION

The question to be addressed in this section is whether the reasoning on which the *CIA Security International* ruling is based is properly confined to the system of notification set up by Directive 83/189 or whether the sanction of unenforceability threatens any national authority which defaults on an obligation of notification under Community law. If the latter, the Court has made a truly dramatic contribution to making real the need for Member States to comply with legislative promises to act in a transparent manner.[40]

The parallel that is most immediately apparent is with Article 88(3) (ex 93(3)) in the field of State Aids. This provision requires that the Commission be informed in advance of "any plans to grant or alter aid". Where the Commission considers the plan is not compatible with the common market, "it shall without delay initiate the procedure provided for in [Article 88(2) ex 93(2)]", which is a special infringement procedure which derogates from Article 226 (ex 169 EC). Article 88(3) (ex 93(3)) concludes "The Member State concerned shall not put

39 For examples drawn from the area of product safety, see Micklitz, Weatherill and Roethe (eds.), *Federalism and Responsibility: a Study on Product Safety Law and Practice in the EC* (Graham and Trotman, 1994). See also Weatherill *supra* note 2 pp.153-166 on the patchy patterns of notification, sector by sector, State by State, under Dir. 83/189.

40 This Part represents an up-dated version of the arguments presented in the article cited *supra* at note 2. See also Fournier and La Pergola *supra* note 33, pp.172-179; Jans *supra* note 6, pp.40-50.

its proposed measures into effect until this procedure has resulted in a final decision". It is not made explicit whether applying new aid in breach of these procedural requirements of notification and standstill has any impact on the lawfulness of the aid itself, but the Court has ruled on the matter. As far the Commission is concerned, the aid is not rendered illegal *per se* because of the procedural flaw;[41] the Commission must examine the substance of the case. However, the Court has declared that a national court should rule aid illegal where it has not been notified under Article 88(3) (ex 93(3)), which is directly effective and creates rights in favour of individuals which national courts must protect in the event of implementation of aid without notification.[42] Any subsequent Commission Decision that the aid must conform to the substantive criteria within Article 87 (ex 92) EC cannot carry retrospective effect for the purposes of proceedings before national courts. Accordingly, it is not open to a State which has failed to adhere to the obligation to notify to submit before a national court that the aid is in any event compatible with the common market and therefore valid. The Court has thus elaborated a delicate pattern whereby the Commission and the national courts fulfil separate but complementary roles.[43] The Commission deals with the impact of aid on the common market, while national courts safeguard individual rights by granting appropriate legal protection against the consequences of procedurally flawed implementation of aid.[44] The allocation of this tough control to national courts provides a strong incentive to national authorities to comply with their procedural obligations, which should in turn optimise the Commission's capacity to manage the market on the basis of full and transparent information. It is this same concern which underpins the Court's treatment of the consequences before national courts of failure to notify draft technical regulations under Directive 83/189.

However, it does not seem that the ruling in *CIA Security International* is a pointer to a general notion of unenforceability of rules that have not been notified in violation of obligations imposed by Community law. There are features of the regime governing notification of State Aids and of draft technical regulations that are distinct from those applying to other notification-based systems. On these differences hangs the margin between unenforceability as a penalty for failure to notify and more orthodox remedial methods under Community law

---

41 E.g. Case C-301/87, *France* v. *Commission*, [1990] ECR I-307.

42 Case 120/73, *Lorenz* v. *Germany*, [1973] ECR 1471, confirmed and explained fully in Case C-354/90, *Fédération Nationale du commerce extérieur des produits alimentaires* v. *France*, [1991] ECR I-5523. See also Case C-39/94, *SFEI and others* v. *La Poste and others*, [1996] ECR I-3547.

43 The Commission expounded its interpretation of law and practice in the Notice on cooperation between national courts and the Commission in the State Aid field, O.J. 1995, C312/8.

44 This may embrace not only an order requiring repayment in accordance with domestic procedures, but in appropriate circumstances also an award of damages against awarding public authorities; see e.g. Case T-239/94, *EISA* v. *Commission*, [1997] ECR II-1839 (concerning the ECSC). Cf. *supra* note 16.

which fall short of the brutal sanction of unenforceability. The key lies in the relatively detailed nature of the system of control envisaged by Directive 83/189. This is touched on by the Court in *CIA Security International*[45] but is the subject of fuller treatment by Advocate General Elmer, with whose Opinion there seems no reason to suppose the Court disagreed on this point.

In his Opinion, Advocate General Elmer drew on the ruling in *Bulk Oil*,[46] which dealt with a Council decision envisaging that a State contemplating a change in the state of trade with third countries must inform the other States and the Commission. Notification would be followed by consultation before final adoption. The regime lacked detailed procedural rules or time-limits. The Court in *Bulk Oil* decided that the system affected only the State/Community relationship and that it did not create rights which individuals could call on national courts to protect in the event of non-notification. Mr Elmer also referred to the ruling in *Enichem Base*, to which the Court too paid explicit attention in *CIA Security International*.[47] He commented on Advocate General Jacobs's Opinion in the case, which distinguished Directive 75/442 on waste from Directive 83/189 on the basis that the latter, but not the former, contained detailed arrangements for Commission and State comments on notified drafts combined with standstill periods arising in specified circumstances. In *Enichem Base* Mr Jacobs had been of the view that, given the absence of a standstill procedure and Community control, a failure to comply with the notification obligation imposed by Directive 75/442 could not render the measures unlawful, but he had seemed inclined to adopt a different view of the consequences of non-notification arising under Directive 83/189. The Court had reached the same conclusion as its Advocate General in *Enichem Base* after reference to the omission of any procedure for Community monitoring of the planned rules and of provisions making implementation conditional on Commission agreement or non-objection.

In *CIA Security International* Advocate General Elmer summed up the principle he derived from the accumulated case law in the following terms:

> "... a rule which merely lays down an obligation to notify a draft national rule without linking that obligation to a subsequent formal procedure does not of itself confer rights on individuals. If, however, the obligation to notify is linked to a procedure under which the draft must be examined at Community level and the Member States are bound not to implement a notified draft before that procedure has been terminated, rights will ensue that can be relied upon by individuals. In that connection no requirement can be implied that the procedural provision in question should expressly confer rights on individuals. It is the content and object of the provision in question that are decisive."

Therefore the rather well-developed structure for comment combined with standstill of up to twelve months[48] under Directive 83/189 was properly treated

45 Paras. 49-50 of the ruling.
46 Case 174/84 [1986] ECR 559.
47 Case 380/87 [1989] ECR 2491; see para. 49 of the ruling in *CIA Security International*.
48 The relevant time periods have been extended on amendment; see *supra* note 3.

in a fashion comparable to that operative in the field of State Aids, but differently from the Community measures at stake in *Bulk Oil* and *Enichem Base*. It is important to appreciate that Mr Elmer was not merely engaged in a search for dry formal reasons to limit the wider impact of the penalty of unenforceability. He observed how the system instituted by Directive 83/189 allows comments by traders on notified drafts, the existence of which is publicised in the Official Journal. Their ability to influence rules that they may encounter in export markets would be undermined were the relevant provisions requiring notification and standstill to be denied direct effect.

The adoption of the "Elmer test" would cause failure to notify rules of consumer protection and environmental protection in accordance with Articles 153(5) and 176 (ex 129a(3) and 130t) EC respectively to lead to consequences on the Community/Member State plane, but the absence of notification would not of itself lead to the unenforceability of the measures in proceedings before national courts involving third parties. The provisions of the Treaty concerned establish duties to notify *simpliciter* and they lack the more complete programme of examination which characterises the regime instituted by Directive 83/189. Similarly, it seems improbable, though not inconceivable, that disregard for the obligations set out in Decision 3052/95[49] could render any national action unenforceable at national level. The system involves an obligation to notify action taken and it envisages some dissemination of detail with a view to eliciting comment. But no standstill is imposed on Member States. Infringement of the Decision should probably be remediable only at the level of Commission/ Member State.[50] And, in a fine example of how the ruling in *CIA Security International* inspires similar submissions in areas of Community remote from product market integration, the Court in *AGS Assedic Pas-de-Calais* v. *Francois Dumon*,[51] invited to hold that a Member State which fails to notify the Commission of any ceilings it chooses to set to liability for employers' outstanding claims under Directive 80/987 may therefore not rely on any such ceiling, pointed out that the duty to notify was not accompanied by any monitoring procedure nor any requirement of Commission authorisation. The Court referred to its ruling on an "analogous provision" in *Enichem Base*[52] and concluded that this was an obligation to notify *simpliciter*, breach of which did not attract a penalty of inapplicability before national courts.

---

49 *Supra* note 33.

50 If this analysis is correct, then in a case where an intervention has not been notified, the determination of whether the national act is properly treated as falling within Dir. 83/189 or Dec. 3052/95 could become a definitional issue of sharp significance before a national court.

51 Case C-235/95, [1998] ECR I-4531. See Jans *supra* note 6 for a collection of secondary legislation imposing notification requirements which may generate comparable litigation in future.

52 Case 380/87 *supra* note 47, cited at para. 30 of the ruling in Case C-235/95 *supra* note 51.

Would a failure to notify rules stricter than a harmonised standard in accordance with what was Article 100a(4) and what is now, post-Amsterdam, the more elaborate procedure found in Article 95(4) et seq. have any impact on the enforceability at national level of the stricter measure independent of assessment of conformity with the Treaty provisions governing free movement?[53] That is, is the procedural flaw of non-notification enough to disallow reliance on the stricter measure before national courts? Article 100a(4) seems to establish a control mechanism which is less complete than the more precise structures found in Directive 83/189 and Article 88(3) (ex 93(3)). However, the Court has recently ruled that even a notified measure may not be applied at national level until it has been confirmed by the Commission, and so presumably an unnotified measure is *a fortiori* inapplicable. *Antoine Kortas*[54] was a preliminary reference from Sweden arising out of criminal prosecution of a trader for infringement of provisions concerning the use of additives in food. Kortas had sold products imported from Germany containing a colorant banned in Sweden but permitted under Directive 94/36, which has Article 100a (now 95) as its legal base. In November 1995 Sweden had requested the Commission for a derogation pursuant to Article 100a(4) and had maintained its ban on the colorant. No reply had been received from the Commission although, in response to a question from the Court in connection with the proceedings in *Antoine Kortas*, it indicated in July 1998 that it would provide one shortly. The status of the stricter Swedish rules, as yet unconfirmed by the Commission, was therefore vital to the prosecution. The Court emphasised the damage that would be inflicted on the harmonisation process were States allowed to apply rules in derogation without having secured Commission authorisation in accordance with the strict criteria set out in Article 100a(4). The Court declined to rule that Commission silence over such an extended period should be treated as deemed authorisation. No time limit was imposed on the Commission, nor would the Court invent one. The Court accepted only that the Commission should act with due diligence and in co-operation with Member State authorities, as envisaged by Article 5 EC, but any breach of such duties should be remedied by recourse to judicial review, most obviously the action for failure to act under Article 232 (ex 175). The provisions of the Directive should in the meantime apply once the deadline for transposition into national law has expired, unaffected by notification of stricter local standards pursuant to Article 100a(4).

If a State cannot apply the measure after it has notified it pending Commission authorization, it cannot apply it if it has not notified it at all. Both notification and authorisation are required, which places all the cards in the hands of the Commission as market manager. Probably this is justified because of the exceptional situation envisaged by this procedure, which is that Member States may

53 On Commission mishandling of a notification, allowing the Court to insist on the narrow scope to be allowed to Art. 100a(4), see Case C-41/93, *France* v. *Commission*, [1994] ECR I-1829.

54 Case C-319/97 judgment of 1 June 1999.

apply stricter rules even in areas subject to agreed levels of harmonisation. In such circumstances, the Court appears to insist on careful compliance with the supervisory mechanism established by the Treaty as a strict pre-condition to the application of national rules that derogate from the harmonised standard on which integration is to be built. This approach emerges particularly clearly from the Opinion of Mr Saggio, Advocate-General in *Antoine Kortas*, who draws a distinction between Article 100a(4) and the State Aid procedure, on the one hand, and, on the other, the less complete system of notification *simpliciter* under Article 130t (now 176).[55] It denies to Member States the luxury of applying the notified derogation even where the Commission drags its feet in responding. However, it should be appreciated that the long delay suffered by Sweden in *Antoine Kortas* will not recur, because the Amsterdam Treaty amendments now provide a cut-off six months after notification, whereupon the Commission is deemed to have approved the national provisions. The Court in *Antoine Kortas* referred to this imminent prospect and was doubtless aware that it was not dealing with a case the detail of which would trouble it again in future. The new system found in Articles 95(4) et seq. post-Amsterdam now shares with Directive 83/189 the feature of a standstill which is not of indefinite duration, which was not the position at the time *Antoine Kortas* fell to be decided by the Court in accordance with Article 100a(4).

It is submitted that the case law begins to disclose a workable basis for distinguishing between the impact at national level of rules establishing a "simple" obligation to notify a draft (where violation does not of itself confer rights on individuals) and rules imposing an obligation to notify which are supported by a fuller procedure involving a period of examination at Community level during which Member States must observe a "standstill" (where violation triggers rights that can be relied upon by individuals). In the latter instance, a sanction of unenforceability against individuals attached to unnotified rules is highly significant in ensuring the system operates properly. However, it is submitted that where individuals are given rights to enforce the "standstill", it is vital that States are permitted a system to respond to urgent problems, especially involving health and safety. That is to say, where the risk of a regulatory vacuum is real (which it was not under Directive 83/189 in *CIA Security International* by virtue of the procedure for urgent cases which is available under that Directive[56]), States must be allowed leeway to act and should not be held to a rigid standstill. If this is missing from the explicit text of a relevant Community measure, then it should be reflected in the Court's interpretation of the impact of the measure at national level. It should be carefully considered whether the contribution in a particular case of a sanction of unenforceability to effective market integration is of sufficient value to outweigh any disadvantage caused by suspension of regulatory

55 This adds a further practical twist to the notoriously complex task of choosing the correct legal base for a measure affecting both market-building and the environment, on which see Weatherill and Beaumont *supra* note 15, pp.1054-57.

56 See now Art. 9(7) Dir. 98/34 *supra* note 4.

coverage. Naturally, it would be preferable to see this choice made explicit by the legislature in adopting particular measures, but it is probably unrealistic to suppose that this will become standard practice.[57]

VI Case law since CIA Security International

The Court's ruling in *CIA Security International* places a premium on the definitional question of whether or not a particular national measure falls within the material scope of Directive 83/189 (with the result that it is unenforceable against third parties if unnotified). This runs in parallel to the extra significance attached to the definition of an "aid" since the Court's assertion of the illegality before national courts of procedurally flawed State aid, discussed above. Were the matter dealt with as a *Francovich* claim, reasonable doubt about the need to notify a particular measure might protect the State from liability for loss caused by its default, but as the Court's jurisprudence currently stands no such fault-related threshold appears to dilute the sanction of unenforceability in proceedings before national courts involving third parties. The centrality of these definitional questions may be appreciated from inspection of the proliferation of cases referred to the Court since the *CIA Security International* ruling was handed down. It is of particular interest that once the Court offered the prize of unenforceability to commercial operators able to show that rules obstructing their trading freedom fell within the scope of Directive 83/189 but had not been notified, ingenious lawyers were not slow to seize the opportunities available. This provides a vivid illustration of the way in which new trends in European Community law may be exploited with vigour to challenge apparently established features of national systems. So, for example, in *Bic Benelux* v. *Belgian State*[58] orders requiring that distinctive marking be attached to disposable razors subject to an eco-tax were ruled to constitute "technical regulations" within the meaning of Directive 83/189. Although the initiative was part of a broader environmental policy involving use of fiscal instruments, the marking requirement affected the composition of goods and therefore fell within the Directive. Prior to the Court's ruling in *CIA Security International* a failure to notify such a measure at draft stage would have meant no more than exposure to the laborious *ex post facto* infringement procedure instituted by the Commission under Article 169 (now Art. 226) EC, but today the consequence of the apparently technical finding that the measure fell within the ambit of the notification obligation laid down by Directive 83/189 is that it is unenforceable before national courts. In the late 1990s several other cases have been decided on such definitional questions;[59] more again await the Court's determination.

---

57 Cf. Jans *supra* note 6, pleading for a general Dir. at pp. 40, 58.

58 Case C-13/96 [1997] ECR I-1753.

59 E.g. Case C-279/94, *Commission* v. *Italy*, [1997] ECR I-4743; Joined Cases C-425/97 – C-427/97, *Adrianus Albers, Martinus van der Berkmortel and Leon Nuchelmans*, judg-

It is no coincidence that a disproportionately high number of these cases emerged from the Netherlands, where the *CIA Security International* ruling provoked a far more intense degree of anxiety than elsewhere. And the most remarkable of the post-*CIA Security International* cases also began life in the Netherlands. It is *Johannes Martinus Lemmens*[60] and it serves as a glorious example of the capacity of EC law to invade areas of national law which may seem remote from its sphere of influence. Even though the point based on Directive 83/189 ultimately did not avail Lemmens, this conclusion was reached only after an intriguing process of legal reasoning, conducted amid a uniquely high-profile debate in the Dutch media about the consequences in Dutch society of long-term neglect by the public authorities of obligations to notify draft norms under Directive 83/189.[61]

Lemmens was charged with driving a vehicle while under the influence of alcohol. In short, he failed a breathalyser test. Breathalysers are used in the Netherlands pursuant to ministerial regulations stipulating the necessary specifications. But these regulations had not been notified to the Commission, as was required by Directive 83/189. Lemmens relied on the Court's ruling in *CIA Security* in submitting that they were therefore unenforceable before national courts; that accordingly use of the breathalyser was tainted by the underlying unenforceability of the regulations governing its use; and that he was entitled to plead a "Euro-defence" to the criminal charge which he faced.

The Court was unpersuaded by submissions that the field of criminal law escapes the scope of application of Community law. This is entirely consistent with its case law[62] and unsurprising. The EC enjoys no explicit competence to adopt legislation which imposes criminal penalties, but the provisions of the EC Treaty and the general principles of Community may affect the exercise of national competence in the field of criminal justice. Consistently with *Bic Benelux*, the Court also maintained a broad interpretation of measures subject to Directive 83/189, the amendments to which have in any event been directed at expanding its material scope.[63] Having concluded that the Dutch measure had improperly been left unnotified, the Court turned to examine the consequences of this default before a national court.

---

ment of 11 May 1999; Case C-33/97, *Colim NV* v. *Bigg's Continent Noord NV*, [1999] ECR I-4743. It is by no means the case that the Court in these cases has always found the matter to fall within the ambit of the notification system instituted by Dir. 83/189.

60 Case C-226/97 judgment of 16 June 1998.

61 The matter was discussed extensively on television and in newspapers in the Netherlands, e.g. 'Richtlijn 83/189 zaait paniek', *NRC Handelsblad* 6 June 1997, p.3. See also Jans *supra* note 6, pp.34-36; Timmermans, "Rapport Communautaire: Community Directives" in *Proceedings of the FIDE Conference*, Topic I: Les Directives Communautaires: Effects, Efficacite, Justiciabilite (Stockholm, 1998), paras. 32, 33; and, by the same author, "Community Directives Revisited" 17 YEL (1997) 1, 21-22.

62 E.g. Case 34/79, *R* v. *Henn and Darby*, [1979] ECR 3795; Case 186/87, *Cowan* v. *Le Tresor Public*, [1989] ECR 195.

63 Dirs. 88/182, 94/10 *supra* note 3; Dir.98/48 *supra* note 4.

The Court, referring to its ruling in *CIA Security International*, stated that the purpose of the Directive is to protect freedom of movement for goods by means of preventive control. Failure to notify renders regulations inapplicable in as much as they hinder the use or marketing of a product which is not in conformity therewith. But it does not have the effect of rendering unlawful any use of a product which is in conformity with regulations which have not been notified. The use of the breathalyser by the Dutch authorities was not liable to create an obstacle to trade which could have been avoided if the notification procedure had been followed. So an importer of a breathalyser who fell foul of the specifications imposed under the unnotified measure would have been able to rely on the *CIA Security International* ruling to require Dutch courts to set aside the obstructive measure. Lemmens, however, was in a quite different situation. The regulations applicable to him prohibited driving while under the influence of alcohol and required a driver to exhale into a breathalyser.

Notification enhances the Commission's capacity to fulfil its role as supervisor of potential hindrances to market integration. In *CIA Security International*, the Court reasoned that the effectiveness of Commission control would be enhanced if the Directive were interpreted as meaning that breach of the obligation to notify constitutes a substantial procedural defect such as to render the technical regulations in question inapplicable. The ruling induces faithful observance of the obligation to notify. It would not be such a large step to conclude that the Member States will be all the more likely to respect their duty of notification, thereby further enhancing the Commission's power of control, if absence of notification were to carry consequences that slice deep even into competence to regulate matters of criminal justice in so far as reliance on technical regulations is at stake. However, that pugnacious approach, built on a determination to maximise incentives for Member States to comply, did not find favour with the Court in *Lemmens*. It merely observed that the process of free movement would not be directly accelerated by the disapplication of the Dutch rules. Indeed, had the Court upheld Lemmens' submission, it would have merited criticism for recklessness. Supervision of the process of integration in the post-1992 internal market is of profound significance, but so too are matters such as the effective application of criminal law. The Court's ruling in *Lemmens* places the interest in promoting structures for building and maintaining the internal market in its wider context, alongside, not above, other interests in society. The ruling in *CIA Security International* has accordingly not been stretched beyond its proper scope, which is tied to the pursuit of a stable integrated market. The Court in *Lemmens* was right to reject the ingenious proposed manipulation of its ruling in *CIA Security International*.

VII EC LAW AS A "JACK IN THE BOX"

The Finnish scholar Thomas Wilhelmsson has described the "Jack in the Box" effect in EC law.[64] Wilhelmsson demonstrates how recourse to EC law by imaginative litigants can spring surprises within national legal systems. EC law is less systematic than a national legal order; indeed it has different ambitions from those of national legal orders. It is a Jack in the Box whose appearance cannot always be readily foreseen but whose vigour can startle. There are many examples of the vitality of this metaphor. This paper has provided one. The ruling in *CIA Security International* was mildly surprising but not unforeseeable, but it paved the way for the astonishing deployment of EC law in *Lemmens* to challenge a drunk-driving conviction. Ultimately the Court closed that Jack-in-the-Box, and, as explained above, rightly so. The "Sunday Trading" saga provides another glorious example of a "Jack in the Box". Who would not admire the flamboyant ingenuity required to deploy Article 30 (now 28) to challenge laws governing shop hours? The litigation ultimately failed in the sense that the laws were held compatible with EC law,[65] but the UK Parliament, influenced by the pressure brought to bear, chose to pass legislation liberalising the legal regime applying to Sunday shop hours. This was the Sunday Trading Act 1994. The retreat sounded by the European Court in *Keck and Mithouard*,[66] doubtless provoked more by the "Sunday Trading" fiasco than by any other single incident of over-indulgence in the rich nourishment to litigation provided by Article 30, was an attempt to slam shut this irritating "Jack in the Box". The Court generally deserves credit in *Keck* for indicating that Article 28 (ex 30) is not designed to supervise local regulatory choices unconnected with patterns of trade integration, thereby declining to succour the rise of a "European Economic Constitution" which would have deeply threatened the fabric of national legal orders. But its reproof to the tendency of commercial operators to spring or to try to spring Jacks in the Box surprises when one recalls that one of the Court's long-term strategies has been to coil the springs of Jacks in the Box and to expect them to be used by litigants to invigorate the process of market adaptation in Europe. As discussed above in Part 3, the ruling in *Cassis de Dijon* already propelled the Court into sensitive areas of adjudication involving competing policy goals. *Keck* adjusts, but does not overturn, this pattern, and, especially when read in conjunction with its cousins in the area of the law of persons and services, *Bosman* and *Alpine Investments*,[67] will itself breed further litigation de-

64 "Jack-in-the-Box Theory of European Community Law" in Kramer, Micklitz and Tonner (eds.), *Law and Diffuse Interests in the European Legal Order* (Nomos, 1997); and see also Tuori, "EC Law: an Independent Legal Order or a Post-Modern Jack-in-the-Box" in Cameron and Simoni (eds.), *Dealing with Integration Volume 2* (Iustus Forlag, 1998).

65 Case 145/88, *Torfaen BC* v. *B&Q plc*, [1989] ECR 765; Case C-169/91, *Stoke on Trent and Norwich City Councils* v. *B & Q plc*, [1992] ECR I-6635.

66 Cases C-267/91, 268/91 [1993] ECR I-6097.

67 Respectively Case C-415/93 [1995] ECR I-4921, Case C-384/93 [1995] ECR I-1141.

signed to tease out the space left for traders wishing to use the law of free movement to challenge national regulatory choices.[68]

Wilhelmsson's "Jack-in-the Box" offers more than merely a brilliant image, drawing our attention to the shiny new cards held by the EC lawyer, which, thanks to the principle of supremacy, operate as trump cards. Wilhelmsson's more serious point was that the very expansion of the scope of the EC legal order has sharpened anxiety about its continued legitimacy. The more EC law there is, the more it intrudes into national competence and the more critics it may attract. Anxiety may be especially acute where the spread of EC law is attributable to judicial or legislative innovation which surpasses the explicit formal reach of the Treaty. Wilhelmsson reminds us that a Jack in the box "startles". It may be treated as a "frightening or annoying destroyer of the secure life". It lies far beyond the scope of this paper even to begin to sketch the many areas in which this thesis could be tested. It is a perspective that invites nervous consideration of the very constitutional shaping of the EU system, which has generated a partially discordant, occasionally unsettling form of indirect dialogue between national supreme courts and the European Court in recent years.[69] And, as suggested above, the "Jack-in-the-Box" metaphor helps us to understand aspects of the ebb and flow of internal market law. It escapes the ambitions of this paper to do more than pass brief comment, but it is submitted that some aspects of the Court's decision-making during the 1990s reflects a concern to interpret Community law in a less expansionist manner than has been the norm in the past when the political and legal context within which the law was shaped was quite different. Most of all, it is the rise of Treaty revision as a regular feature of the EU's development combined with the availability of qualified majority voting in replacement for unanimity in the Council across many fields of Community activity that has changed the Court's working environment. So, for example, in *IHT Internationale Heiztechnik Gmbh* v. *Ideal Standard GmbH*[70] the Court observed that the result pressed on it (rendering void under national law assignments made for part only of the Community) could be achieved only by a Directive adopted under Article 100a and not by the application of Article 30. In *Grant* v. *South West Trains*[71] the Court declined to extend the law of discrimination to catch discrimination based on sexual orientation, referred explicitly to the potential for legislative action in the field adopted under a provision in the Amsterdam Treaty which was at the time of the ruling not even yet in force (it is

68 For discussion see Weatherill and Beaumont, *EU Law*, *supra* note 15, pp.608-619.

69 Most strikingly, see *Brunner* v. *European Union Treaty* [1994] 1 CMLR 57, a decision of the BverfG but one heard beyond German borders both by the European Court and by courts in other Member States, cf. e.g. the Danish Supreme Court's similarly structured ruling in *Carlsen and others* v. *Rasmussen* judgment of 6 April 1998. For a survey see Slaughter, Sweet and Weiler, *The European Courts and National Courts: Doctrine and Jurisprudence* (Hart Publishing, 1997).

70 Case C-9/93 [1994] ECR I-2789.

71 Case C-249/96 [1998] ECR I-621.

now Article 13 EC). In its Opinion on *Accession by the European Community to the European Convention on Human Rights and Fundamental Freedoms* the Court observed that "as Community law now stands, the Community has no competence to accede to the Convention",[72] preferring to leave developments to the realms of Treaty revision rather than exorbitant use of Article 235 (now 308). And finally, in *Silhouette International Schmied GmbH & Co. KG* v. *Hartlauer Handelsgesellschaft*,[73] the Court, interpreting secondary legislation which did not conclusively cover the point, found that trade mark rights were not exhausted by consensual marketing outwith the EEA but added the comment that the scope of the principle of exhaustion could be extended to products put on the market in non-EEA countries by the conclusion of international agreements in that sphere, as had already occurred in the context of the EEA Agreement.

These are relatively cautious decisions, and it is not the concern of this paper to criticise them. Rather, their interest lies in the context in which the Court was called upon to make them. Some of the advances in the scope of Community law which the Court was invited to make were capable of being achieved via Treaty revision, today a realistic and increasingly frequent phenomenon. Others were capable of being achieved via legislative activity and today the Community enjoys a rather broad legislative competence, periodically supplemented by Treaty amendment, and the obstacle of unanimity in Council is no longer the norm. None of these observations on the institutional and constitutional context in which the Court today operates readily applies to its "heroic" period during the Community's early years. From this perspective, 1987, the entry into force of the Single European Act, was a hugely significant watershed. No longer was Treaty revision the forgotten engine for reform. No longer was all Community legislation adopted by unanimous vote and therefore controlled by a veto held by each State. The Community enjoyed a potentially more dynamic *modus vivendi* but with it arrived a new apprehension about what might be done in the Community's name by its institutions lest States in the minority should find the process uncontrollable and oppressive. The nature of the Community system was altered. For the Court, a new assessment of "lawmaking" in the EC was appropriate and, moreover, it could expect increasing scrutiny of its choices by national observers, especially national judges on whose fidelity the European Court is in practical terms wholly dependent for the effective penetration of its rulings into the fabric of national legal orders.

But this should be by no means a one-dimensional narrative of a Court on the retreat, whether or not such retreat might be reckoned justified. The Court deserves far more subtle appraisal. The ruling in *CIA Security International* reminds us that, at least in areas where enforcement of the laws of the internal market is concerned, the Court retains "law-making" boldness. A similar example is provided by the post-*Francovich* ruling in *Brasserie du Pêcheur SA* v.

72 Opinion 2/94 [1994] ECR I-1759.
73 Case C-355/96 [1998] ECR I-4799.

Germany and *R* v. *Secretary of State for Transport, ex parte Factortame Ltd and others*[74] in which the Court confirmed that a right to reparation in cases of loss caused to individuals as a result of breaches of Community law was "inherent in the system of the Treaty", reaching this decision in the face of the constitutional objections of the German government to alleged judicial usurpation of the function of the legislature, recorded at paragraph 24 of the judgment. This may be the Court's own version of the post-1992 emphasis on the improved enforcement of agreed laws, discussed in Part 4 above. It is in any event absolutely not the case that the Court has chosen wholly to abdicate its position as innovator in the light of recent institutional and constitutional change in the European Union. Nor should it.

VIII Conclusion

The European Court should not be underestimated. It has made a huge contribution to the shaping of integration in Europe. But nor should the Court be overestimated. Its ability to dictate its own agenda is constrained by the diet of cases it happens to be fed from time to time. Sometimes it has to bide its time, for it is no legislator. However, it is able to exploit "windows of opportunity", in the words of Daniel Wincott.[75] As Kenneth Armstrong and Simon Bulmer observe, it "explores" new techniques,[76] not necessarily fully in control of its environment nor able to foresee with certainty how its rulings will be digested, but rather shaping and testing the law, knowing that the fertile links it has established with the national courts via the preliminary reference procedure will allow it further bites at cherries polished by ingenious litigants. It provides room for the opening of the "jack-in-the-box" of which Thomas Wilhelmsson wrote,[77] injecting an internal dynamic into the fabric of EC law that is not readily controlled by the Member States and which may (for good or ill) shock observers and participants. The remarkable decision in *CIA Security International* offers a fine example of these features of the Court's activity. It was an exploratory leap in the direction of more effective enforcement of the rules of market management. The Court was aware of the interest of the Commission in achieving a ruling that non-notified measures should be regarded as unenforceable. In consequence, incentives for Member States to participate actively in the system of notification were sharpened, thereby tending to enhance the pursuit of effective, transparent market management. The ruling itself generated further case law in which the Court, confronted by cunning attempts to stretch its logic to breaking point, placed a limit on the depth to which the penalty of unenforceability should

74 Joined Cases C-46/93 and C-48/93 [1996] ECR I-1029.

75 Wincott, "The role of law or the rule of the Court of Justice? An institutional account of judicial politics in the European Community" 2 JEPP (1995) 583-602, 584.

76 In *The Governance of the Single European Market* (Manchester UP, 1998), p.273.

77 *Supra* note 64.

intrude into national legal orders (Part 6 of this paper), although in doing so it by no means robbed the issue of its fertility in future litigation, for example relating to the consequences of failure to adhere to other systems in other branches of Community law which are based on notification by national authorities to the Commission (Part 5). Effective and shrewdly developed judicial control remains of paramount importance in building a legal order fit for Europe.

32

SUBSIDIARITY AND JUDICIAL REVIEW

Derrick Wyatt

INTRODUCTION

Subsidiarity was the word, it is claimed, which saved the 1991 Maastricht Conference on the Political Union.[1] The importance of the word, or at any rate the ideas underlying the word, should certainly not be underestimated. At a joint hearing of the European Affairs Committees of the Bundesrat and the Bundestag on the subject of subsidiarity on 8 May 1996, the then Secretary General of the European Commission declared that the two most significant developments for Europe signalled by the Maastricht Treaty were European Monetary Union, and Subsidiarity.

Yet the words used to formulate the principle of subsidiarity in the text of the EC Treaty did not so much resolve the debate about the appropriate respective role of Community authorities on the one hand, and State authorities, on the other, as ensure that that debate could, and indeed would be placed on the agenda whenever the Commission initiated the legislative processes of the Community institutions on a matter which did not lie within the exclusive competence of the Community. That, perhaps, was the most important contribution made by writing subsidiarity into the Treaty; it legitimized the position, within the Community system, of those within the Council, or the Parliament, who might wish to argue that the Community should do less, should do what it does do better, and should always be mindful of the possibility, even the probability, that matters falling within national as well as Community competence, should be left to national, regional or local authorities to regulate, or to decide not to regulate, for that matter. It may of course be objected that that is a one-sided view of subsidiarity, since the latter principle also argues in favour of Community action where the Community is the appropriate level for such action to be taken. But such an objection is somewhat tendentious. The history of the twenty years prior to the adoption of the text of Article 3b of the EC Treaty (now Article 5) was a history of increasing Community legislative intervention, across a wide range of

1 Schilling, 'A New Dimension of Subsidiarity: Subsidiarity as a Rule and a Principle' 14 YEL 203 (1994), referring to Case, 'The Word that Saved Maastricht? The Principle of Subsidiarity and the Division of Powers within the European Community' 29 CML Rev 1107 (1992).

D. O'Keeffe (ed.), Liber Amicorum Slynn 505-519 (2000)

subject matter. The legislation in question was often adopted in truth for social, environmental, public health or consumer protection reasons, but on the jurisdictional pretext that continuing discrepancies between national rules in the field in question gave rise to distortions in the conditions of competition and thereby justified recourse to provisions of the Treaty primarily designed to facilitate the establishment and functioning of the single market. Subsidiarity was never needed to ensure that subject matter eligible for regulation at the Community level be so regulated;[2] it was sorely needed to temper what at least appeared to be the propensity to regulate at the Community level for its own sake, and for no more reason than the general conviction of the Commission and Council of the time that this or that legislation was politically desirable. Subsidiarity was in reality, and in very substantial part, a rallying point for "States' rights", within the framework of a Community system which continues to acknowledge, albeit grudgingly, that the nation State, with its regional and local democratic institutions, far from being a reprehensible throwback to a bygone era, is the vehicle by which most Europeans, most of the time, reflect their cultural traditions, and exercise direct control over those whose decisions regulate their daily lives.

SCOPE OF THE PRESENT ESSAY

All that said, important legal questions are posed by the nature of the principle of subsidiarity, by the terms in which it is incorporated into the legal system of the European Union, and by the terms of the related instruments which have been adopted to facilitate the application of the principle in practice. In this essay, which does not examine the scope of the exclusive competence of the Community, and is solely concerned with the application of the principle of subsidiarity in those cases where the Community does not enjoy exclusive competence, the present writer will address the following questions:

- Is subsidiarity a constitutional principle with a formal legal status the application of the substantive aspects of which is nevertheless *in practice* exclusively for Commission, Council and Parliament, acting within their respective allotted spheres of competence, and *in practice* so far

2 Thus even before any reference to the environment appeared in the EEC Treaty the Community institutions had adopted ambitious legislation for the protection of the environment on the basis of Article 100, either alone, or in conjunction with Article 235. See, notably, Directive 76/160, on the quality of bathing water, OJ 1976 L31/1 (Article 100 and 235); Directive 80/778 on the quality of drinking water, OJ 1980 L 229/11 (Article 100 and 235); Directive 84/538 approximating national laws relating to the permissible sound power level of lawnmowers OJ 1984 L 300/171 (based on Article 100 but the preamble stated that "the main objective of the provisions of this Directive is to ensure protection against nuisances due to noise by reducing the inconvenience caused by the noises emitted by lawnmowers").

immune from the judicial control of the European Courts, that its effect is akin to that of a constitutional convention in the United Kingdom constitutional system?

- Alternatively, is subsidiarity, as regards its substantive content, a justiciable principle of Community law, which, although it allows a wide margin of discretion to the Community institutions, has measurable limits which may lead to the European Courts questioning the validity of a Community act for manifest breach of its substantive scope?
- Whether or not application of the principle of subsidiarity by the Community institutions in the legislative process is justiciable as regards alleged breach of its substantive scope, are Community acts vulnerable to challenge on procedural grounds, either for failure of the institutions to address the criteria which determine whether Community action is justified or not, or for inadequate reasoning of a Community act as regards justification on subsidiarity grounds of the act in question?

SUBSIDIARITY AND THE MAASTRICHT TREATY

The principle of subsidiarity first appeared in the Union Treaty of 1991, and the EEC Treaty as then amended (and renamed as the EC Treaty). Article A TEU provided that "This Treaty marks a new state in the process of creating an ever closer union among the peoples of Europe, in which decisions are taken *as closely as possible to the citizen* (emphasis added)." Article B TEU provided that "The objectives of the Union shall be achieved... while respecting the principle of subsidiarity, as defined in Article 3b of the Treaty establishing the European Community." Article F(1) provided in the same vein that "The Union shall respect the national identities of its Member States, whose systems of government are founded on the principles of democracy." Most significantly, the new Article 3b of the renamed EC Treaty provided:

> "The Community shall act within the limits of the powers conferred upon it by this Treaty and of the objectives assigned to it therein.
>
> In areas which do not fall within its exclusive competence, the Community shall take action, in accordance with the principle of subsidiarity, only if and in so far as the objectives of the proposed action cannot be sufficiently achieved by the Member States and can therefore, by reason of the scale or effects of the proposed action, be better achieved by the Community.
>
> Any action by the Community shall not go beyond what is necessary to achieve the objectives of this Treaty."

It is to be noted that the first sub-paragraph of Article 3b was declaratory of the principle which was stated in the original text of Article 4 of the EEC Treaty, to the effect that "Each institution shall act within the limits of the powers conferred upon it by this Treaty." The third sub-paragraph of the Article is in part declaratory, and in part an innovation. It is declaratory in that the principle of proportionality has always been reflected in the text of the Treaty,[3] and has been developed as a general principle of law by the Court of Justice in an extensive case-law.[4] It is innovatory to the extent that in assessing the proportionality of the exercise of Community competence it appears both from the text and context that the Community would exceed its powers not only if it adopted a measure which went further than was necessary to achieve the objective contemplated by the Treaty base from which its competence is derived (e.g., in order, pursuant to Article 95 (ex 100a) to redress distortions in the conditions of competition and the free movement of goods and services), but also if the measures went further than was necessary to achieve the "comparative efficiency" gains contemplated by action at the Community level rather than the national level, and to this latter extent it complements and reinforces the words "only if and in so far as the objectives of the proposed action cannot be sufficiently achieved by the Member States".

THE GUIDELINES OF THE EDINBURGH SUMMIT AND THE 1993 INTER-INSTITUTIONAL AGREEMENT

The adoption of subsidiarity as a guiding constitutional principle of the Community system was followed by intense efforts by the Member States and the institutions to clarify what was understood to be the scope of the principle and its amenability to judicial review. The European Council met in Edinburgh on 11 and 12 December 1992 to discuss the central problems on the Community's agenda. *Inter alia* the European Council reached agreement on basic principles and guidelines to implement the subsidiarity principle.[5] As regards basic principles, the European Council considered that the principle of subsidiarity did not relate to and did not call into question the powers conferred on the European Community by the Treaty as interpreted by the Court. It provided a "guide" as to

3 See *e.g.*, Article 40(3) of the EEC Treaty, which refers to "all measures *required* to attain the objectives set out in Article 39...(emphasis added); Article 49 of the EEC Treaty, referring to "the measures *required* to being about... freedom of movement for workers.. (emphasis added)."

4 See *e.g.*, Case 181/84 *R.* v. *Intervention Board for Sugar ex parte Man (Sugar)* [1985] ECR 2889, para. 20; Case 21/85 *Maas* v. *Bundesanstalt fηr Landwirtschaftliche Marktordnung* [1986] ECR 3537, para. 15; Case C-265/88 *Messner* [1989] ECR 4209; Case C-193/94 *Criminal proceedings against Sofia Skanavi and Konstantin Chryssanthakopoulos.* [1996] ECR I – 929, paras 35-38; Case C-29/95 *Pastoors* [1997] ECR I – 285 (higher penalty for non-resident permissible in principle but must not be disproportionately higher); Case C-161/96 *Südzucker Mannheim/Ochsenfurt AG* v *Hauptzollamt Mannheim* [1998] ECR I – 281, para. 31.

5 Bull.EC 12-1992 pp. 9 *et seq.*

how those powers were to be exercised at the Community level, including in the application of Article 235 (now 308).[6] The Council further noted that subsidiarity was a "dynamic concept" which should be applied in the light of the objectives set out in the Treaty; it thus allowed Community action to be expanded when circumstances so required, and conversely, to be restricted or discontinued where it was no longer justified.[7] It might be argued that the foregoing features of subsidiarity – the reference to it as a "guide" as to how powers should be exercised, and the idea that subsidiarity, as a dynamic concept might preclude the exercise of a power in one year, but allow it the next – militated against its being treated as a binding rule of law capable of judicial application, but the Edinburgh Council intended no such inference. Indeed, while the Council did not consider that the principle of subsidiarity had direct effect, it stated that "interpretation of this principle, as well as review of compliance with it by the Community institutions are subject to control by the Court of Justice, as far as matters falling within the Treaty establishing the European Community are concerned." It is thus clear from the outset that the Member States believed that the principle which they had unanimously endorsed at Maastricht was capable of enforcement by the Court of Justice. While this is significant, it does not of itself suggest an answer to the question whether judicial review of the application of the principle of subsidiarity in a particular case may ever lead in practice to the conclusion that the Community institutions have exceeded the bounds of their discretion, as regards their determination of the comparative advantage of Community action, or whether such review would in practice be confined to an assessment of whether the Community institutions have taken into account those matters which they are obliged to take into account if the question of subsidiarity is to be properly addressed in the course of the law-making process.

Of considerable significance as regards the potential judicial review of Community acts based on the alleged failure to respect the principle of subsidiarity are the guidelines agreed by the Edinburgh Council. The guidelines drew a distinction between the requirements of the second paragraph of Article 3b (now 5), which covered the need for the Community to take the action in question at all, and the requirements of proportionality contained in the third paragraph of that Article, which governed the requisite nature and extent of Community action. As regards the former, the guidelines stated that for Community action to be justified the Council had to be satisfied that both aspects of the subsidiarity criterion were met: viz., that the objectives of the proposed action could not be sufficiently achieved by Member States' action and that they could therefore be better achieved by action on the part of the Community. The Council stated that the following guidelines should be used in examining whether the latter condition had been fulfilled.:

---

6 *Ibid.*, p. 13.
7 *Ibid.*, p. 13.

> "• the issue under consideration has transnational aspects which cannot be satisfactorily regulated by action by Member States; and/or
> • actions by Member States alone or lack of Community action would conflict with the requirements of the Treaty (such as the need to correct distortion of competition or avoid disguised restrictions on trade or strengthen economic or social cohesion) or would otherwise significantly damage Member States' interests; and/or
> • the Council must be satisfied that action at Community level would produce clear benefits by reason of its scale or effects compared with action at the level of the Member States."

The Council added that the reasons for concluding that a Community objective could not be sufficiently achieved by the Member States but could be better achieved by the Community must be substantiated by qualitative or, wherever possible, quantitative indicators.

As regards the third paragraph of Article 3b (now 5), regarding the question of proportionality, and possible resulting restraints on the nature and extent of Community action, the Council considered that Community measures should leave as much scope for national decision as possible. Care should be taken to respect well-established national arrangements and the organization and working of Member States' legal systems. Where appropriate, and subject to the need for proper enforcement, Community measures should provide Member States with alternative ways to achieve the objectives of the measures. Priority should be given to setting minimum standards, with freedom for Member States to set higher national standards. The form of action should be as simple as possible. Other things being equal, directives should be preferred to regulations and framework directives to detailed measures. Non-binding measures such as recommendations should be preferred where appropriate. Preference in choosing the type of Community action should be given to encouraging cooperation between Member States, coordinating national action or to complementing, supplementing or supporting such action. Finally, where difficulties are localized and only certain Member States are affected, any necessary Community action should not be extended to other Member States unless this is necessary to achieve an objective of the Treaty.

The Edinburgh guidelines also referred to the procedures and practices which would be applied for the purpose of complying with the obligation imposed by the Treaty to consider whether the provisions of Article 3b (now 5) EC have been observed.[8] The Commission indicated that it would consult more widely than previously before proposing legislation, and also made it clear that it would justify in a recital the relevance of its initiative with regard to the principle of subsidiarity, and, wherever necessary, the explanatory memorandum accompanying the proposal would give details on the consideration of the Commission in the context of Article 3b. The Council stated that the examination of the compliance of a measure with the provisions of Article 3b should be under-

---

8 Bull EC 12-1992, page 15.

taken on a regular basis; it should become an integral part of the overall examination of any Commission proposal and be based on the substance of the proposal. The latter examination would include the Council's own evaluation of whether the Commission proposal is totally or partially in conformity with the provisions of Article 3b (taking as a starting point for the examination the Commission's recital and explanatory memorandum) and of whether any change in the proposal envisaged by the Council was in conformity with those provisions. All the foregoing was stated to be without prejudice to "a future inter-institutional agreement". Such an agreement was indeed forthcoming and the Inter-Institutional Agreement of 25 October 1993 between the European Parliament, the Council and the Commission on procedures for implementing the principle of subsidiarity, which took effect upon the coming into force of the Treaty on European Union, emphasised the obligations of the various institutions as regards the importance of taking account of the principle of subsidiarity in carrying out their functions. The relevant procedures may be summarised as follows:

- In exercising its right of initiative, the Commission shall take into account the principle of subsidiarity and show that it has been observed.
- The explanatory memorandum for any Commission proposal shall include a justification of the proposal under the principle of subsidiarity.
- Any amendment which may be made to the Commission's text, whether by the European Parliament or the Council, must, if it entails more extensive or intensive intervention by the Community, be accompanied by a justification under the principle of subsidiarity and Article 3b.
- The three institutions shall, under their internal procedures, regularly check that any action envisaged complies with the provisions concerning subsidiarity as regards both the choice of legal instruments and the content of the proposal. Such checks must form an integral part of the substantive examination.

THE AMSTERDAM PROTOCOL

The Protocol on the application of the principles of subsidiarity and proportionality took account of the Inter-institutional agreement of 25 October 1993 and confirmed that "the overall approach to the application of the subsidiarity principle agreed by the European Council meeting in Edinburgh on 11-12 December 1992 will continue to guide the action of the Union's institutions as well as the development of the principle of subsdiarity....".[9] The text of the Protocol follows closely the conclusions of the Edinburgh Council. As regards the *basic*

9 Third and fourth recitals to the preamble.

principles referred to therein and explained above, the Protocol reiterates the propositions that subsidiarity does not call into question the powers conferred on the European Community, but comprises a guide as to how those powers are to be exercised,[10] and that subsidiarity is a dynamic concept.[11] The reference in the Edinburgh summit *basic principles* to review of compliance with the principle of subsidiarity by the Court of Justice is reflected in paragraph (13) of the Protocol, which states that compliance with the principle of subsidiarity "shall be reviewed in accordance with the rules laid down by the Treaty."

As regards the Edinburgh *guidelines* on the question whether the Community *should or should not* act, the Protocol repeats the considerations relating to transnational aspects, possible conflict with the requirements of the Treaty, and the need for action at Community level to produce clear benefits by reason of its scale or effects.[12] The proposition that the reasons for concluding that a Community objective cannot be sufficiently achieved by the Member States must be substantiated by qualitative or, wherever possible, quantitative indicators is also re-stated in the Protocol.[13]

As regards the *guidelines* on the *nature and extent* of Community action, the passages in the Edinburgh conclusions referred to above to the effect that Community measures should leave as much scope for national decision as possible, and to the effect that the form of action should be as simple as possible, are reproduced *verbatim* in the Protocol,[14] with the exception of the sentences in the latter passage to the effect that non-binding measures, such as recommendations, would be preferred where appropriate, and to the effect that consideration should also be given where appropriate to the use of voluntary codes of conduct. The failure to include these sentences may be explained by the fact that the principle of subsidiarity is regarded as a guide to how Community competence to adopt binding acts is exercised. A preference for non-binding measures such as recommendations, and recourse where appropriate to voluntary codes of conduct, might have been thought to *follow* from the conclusion that legislation was not necessary, rather than to comprise assistance in deciding whether legislation in a particular case is necessary or not. Another omission in the Protocol is the proposition endorsed at Edinburgh that where difficulties are localized and only certain Member States are affected, any necessary Community action should not be extended to other Member States unless this is necessary to achieve an objective of the Treaty. Nevertheless, the conclusion at Edinburgh that a general measure of harmonization might be disproportionate, at least in certain circumstances, if a measure addressed to one or more Member States could eliminate the basis for further Community action, seems in principle to be correct.

---

10 Protocol, para. (3).
11 Protocol, para. (3).
12 Protocol, para. (5).
13 Protocol, para. (4).
14 Protocol, paras. (7), and (6).

As regards *procedures and practices* the Protocol states that the Commission should, except in cases of particular urgency or confidentiality, consult widely before proposing legislation and, wherever appropriate, publish consultation documents.[15] The Commission should also justify the relevance of its proposals with regard to the principle of subsidiarity; wherever necessary, the explanatory memorandum accompanying a proposal will give details in this respect.[16] It is to be noted that the foregoing differs in minor detail from the reference in the Edinburgh conclusions to the Commission to the commitment to justify in a recital the relevance of its initiative with regard to the principle of subsidiarity. Finally, the Protocol's provisions on the role of the Council and the Parliament in the legislative process follows closely the terms of the Edinburgh conclusions. The Protocol provides that the European Parliament and the Council shall, as an integral part of the overall examination of Commission proposals, consider their consistency with Article 5 (ex 3b) EC. This concerns the original Commission proposal as well as amendments which the European Parliament and the Council envisage making to the proposal. In the course of the procedures referred to in Articles 251 (ex 189b) and 252 (ex 189c), the European Parliament shall be informed of the Council's position on the application of Article 5 EC, by way of a statement of the reasons which led the Council to adopt its common position. The Council shall inform the European Parliament of the reasons on the basis of which all or part of a Commission proposal is deemed to be inconsistent with Article 5 EC.

SUBSTANTIVE JUDICIAL REVIEW OF THE "COMPARATIVE EFFICIENCY" TEST BY REFERENCE TO THE TEXT OF THE SECOND PARAGRAPH OF ARTICLE 5 ALONE?

To what extent is it possible to contemplate a successful action for annulment of a Community act for an incorrect determination that the objectives of the proposed action could not be sufficiently achieved by the Member States and could therefore, by reason of the scale or effects of the proposed action, be better achieved by the Community. On any view this assessment leaves a discretion to the Community institutions, and the discretion is framed in a rather open-ended way, which suggests that it is a wide discretion. The standard for judicial review in such a case is well established, and was recently re-stated in *Upjohn Ltd* v. *The Licensing Authority established by the Medicines Act 1968 and Others*,[17] as follows:

> "According to the Court's case-law, where a Community authority is called upon, in the performance of its duties, to make complex assessments, it enjoys a wide measure of dis-

15 Protocol, para. (9).
16 *Ibid.*
17 Case C-120/97 [1999] ECR I – 223.

> cretion, the exercise of which is subject to a limited judicial review in the course of which the Community judicature may not substitute its assessment of the facts for the assessment made by the authority concerned. Thus, in such cases, the Community judicature must restrict itself to examining the accuracy of the findings of fact and law made by the authority concerned and to verifying, in particular, that the action taken by that authority is not vitiated by a manifest error or a misuse of powers and that it did not clearly exceed the bounds of its discretion..."[18]

In the first place, it is perhaps worth noting that the Court uses the word "discretion" in this context as meaning not so much as a choice of adopting different policy options (though this may be involved), as a measure of freedom to make the value-judgments necessary to take the decisions necessary to carry out the task allotted to the institutions in the context in question. In view of the applicable standard for review, it would appear that if the Court of Justice or the Court of First Instance (for convenience reference will be made hereafter solely to the Court of Justice) were called upon to review an act for compliance with the principle of subsidiarity, simply on the basis of the substantive text of the act in question, and the text of the second paragraph of Article 5 (ex 3b), it would be necessary for the applicant to establish that the institutions had manifestly exceeded the bounds of the discretion attributed to them by Article 5, read in conjunction with the Treaty base for the act in question. Yet on the face of it, the question whether or not the objectives of the act can be "sufficiently" achieved by the Member States, is so open-ended a test, that the Court would be hard put to find a basis for concluding that the test had *manifestly not* been satisfied, in circumstances where at the very least a qualified majority of the Member States expressed the conviction that the objectives of the act could not be sufficiently achieved by the Member States, and the Community institutions expressed the conviction that by reason of the scale or effects of the proposed action its objectives could be better achieved by the Community! It is also to be noted that the question of applying the test of subsidiarity only arises where the Community act in question falls *within the competence* of the Community, but it is said that it is manifestly contrary to the principle of subsidiarity to *exercise* that competence in the circumstances. Thus it does not necessarily advance the enquiry to devise outlandish hypothetical examples of Community acts which would patently infringe the principle of subsidiarity, where such acts might not in any event fall within the scope of the Treaty base in question.

Yet in truth it is somewhat artificial to contemplate a challenge to a Community act being made on the basis of the second paragraph of Article 5 EC

---

18 The Court referred to Joined Cases 56/64 and 58/64 *Consten and Grundig* v *Commission* [1966] ECR 299, Case 55/75 *Balkan-Import Export* v *Hauptzollamt Berlin-Packhof* [1976] ECR 19, paragraph 8, Case 9/82 *Øhrgaard and Delvaux* v *Commission* [1983] ECR 2379, paragraph 14, Case C-225/91 *Matra* v *Commission* [1993] ECR I-3203, paragraphs 24 and 25, and Case C-157/96 *National Farmers' Union and Others* [1998] ECR I-2211, paragraph 39.

without regard to the criteria adopted at the Edinburgh summit, and now contained in the Amsterdam Protocol and having the full force of law in consequence. It is by reference to Article 5 in the context of the Amsterdam Protocol that any realistic assessment of judicial review for breach of the principle of subsidiarity must be made.

SUBSTANTIVE JUDICIAL REVIEW OF THE "COMPARATIVE EFFICIENCY" TEST BY REFERENCE TO THE TEXT OF THE SECOND PARAGRAPH OF ARTICLE 5 IN CONJUNCTION WITH THE AMSTERDAM PROTOCOL

It must be said that the prospects in practice of judicial review of a Community act by reference to Article 5 become rather more feasible when that Article is read in conjunction with the conclusions of the Edinburgh summit and the Amsterdam Protocol. The reason for this is that the applicable standard of review, while according a wide margin of appreciation to the institutions, nevertheless contemplates review of the accuracy of findings of fact and law by the Community institutions, and it appears that, at least in certain cases, the application of the comparative efficiency test must involve findings of fact and law, which may in turn be reviewed by the Court of Justice. It will be recalled that the Amsterdam Protocol states that "the reason for concluding that a Community objective can be better achieved by the Community must be substantiated by qualitative or, wherever possible, quantitative indicators." This formulation is of some significance, since it is expressed in mandatory terms, and it suggests that, at least in certain cases, a factual analysis of some sort will be necessary in order to determine whether a Community objective can be better achieved by the Community. The explanation for this would seem to appear from the "guidelines" which the Protocol states should be used in examining whether the above-mentioned condition is fulfilled. The first guideline refers to the issue under consideration having transnational aspects which cannot be satisfactorily regulated by action by Member States. It is to be noted that assessing whether an issue has transnational aspects may, as a practical matter, involve qualitative and quantitative criteria. Thus, e.g., in considering the subsidiarity aspects of possible Community action in the field of water policy the Commission has noted the need to ensure the coordination of national measures to deal with international waters and transfrontier pollution.[19] In an assessment of a specific proposal for a Community measure having the aim of dealing with such waters and pollution it would seem to be necessary in principle, pursuant to the terms of the Protocol, to substantiate this assessment by reference to the nature and scale of the transnational aspects in question. Such assessment might in principle raise justiciable issues of fact which might be the subject matter of judicial enquiry in accor-

19 Communication on Water Policy, COM (96) 59 final, 5.12.

dance with the standard of review referred to in the *Upjohn* case and the case-law cited therein.

The second guideline in the Amsterdam Protocol refers to lack of Community action conflicting with the requirements of the Treaty, such as the need to correct distortion of competition or avoid disguised restrictions on trade or strengthen economic and social cohesion, or otherwise significantly damaging Member States' interests. It is to be noted that distortion of competition, restrictions on trade, and, indeed, more broadly the transnational aspects already referred to, are issues which may to a greater or lesser extent be relevant to the legal assessment of whether Community *competence* exists pursuant to various Articles of the Treaty, such as Articles 40, 47(1) and (2), and 55, and Articles 94 and 95. Thus, the preamble to European Parliament and Council Directive 98/5/EC to facilitate practice of the profession of lawyer on a permanent basis in a Member State other than that in which the qualification was obtained, states in the sixth recital to the preamble:

> "Whereas action is also *justified at Community level* [emphasis added] because only a few Member States already permit in their territory the pursuit of activities of lawyers, otherwise than by way of provision of services, by lawyers from other Member States practising under their home-country professional titles; whereas, however, in the Member States where this possibility exists, the practical details concerning, for example, the area of activity and the obligation to register with the competent authorities differ considerably; whereas such a diversity of situations leads to inequalities and distortions in competition between lawyers from the Member States and constitutes an obstacle to freedom of movement;.."

It might be objected that in the foregoing paragraph, the Community institutions are confusing subsidiarity and competence, but it is submitted that this is far from the truth. On the contrary, it might be said that one of the purposes of the adoption of the principle of subsidiarity was to equip the institutions with a principle which would, *inter alia,* compensate for the fact that Treaty bases which provide for the exercise of Community competence in cases in which disparities between national rules affect the free movement of goods, persons or services and/or distort the conditions of competition have been interpreted in such a way that *de minimis* or hypothetical effects on freedom of movement or the conditions of competition have in the past been deemed sufficient to justify the adoption of Community legislation. While experience has shown that it is not necessary, as a matter of *competence*, actually to establish substantial effects on freedom of movement, or the conditions of competition, the content of the Edinburgh and Amsterdam guidelines indicates that subsidiarity has made consideration of such factual questions part and parcel of the decision whether to *exercise* Community competence pursuant to Treaty articles such as those mentioned above. In such cases, it follows from paragraphs (4) and (5) of the Amsterdam Protocol, that where the reasons for concluding that action is justified at Community level are considered to follow from the need to correct distortion of competition or avoid restrictions on trade, those reasons "must be substantiated by qualitative or, wherever possible, quantitative indicators." It might well be said that the effects of the principle of subsidiarity and of the foregoing guidelines has been to render justiciable to a greater extent than hitherto the question whether the effects on trade and competition referred to in the preamble to a Community act to justify its legal base are capable of justifying the exercise of the competence in question. To put the matter another way, subsidiarity might bring about a position in practice similar to that which would have prevailed if the Community institutions and the Court of Justice had adopted a somewhat more rigorous and empirical approach to words in the Treaty such as those in Article 94 (ex 100) which authorize approximation of such laws of the Member States as "directly affect the establishment of functioning of the common market."

That is not to say that "substantive" review for alleged breach of subsidiarity is in all cases a practical justiciable option for the Court of Justice. Where the institutions conclude that lack of Community action would conflict with the need to strengthen economic and social cohesion, pursuant to the words referred to above in the guideline contained in paragraph (5) of the Amsterdam Protocol, and the proposed action is properly based on the social chapter of Title XI of the Treaty, this would appear *per se* to amount to compliance with the principle of subsidiarity. This is the explanation of the Court's rejection of the argument of the United Kingdom to the effect that the adoption of Council Directive 93/104/EC, concerning certain aspects of the organization of working time, contravened the principle of subsidiarity. The Court stated that once the Council has found that it is necessary to improve the existing level of protection as regards the health and safety of workers and to harmonize the conditions in this area while maintaining the improvements made, achievement of that objective through the imposition of minimum requirements necessarily presupposed Community-wide action.[20] The final words of the guideline referred to – "or would otherwise significantly damage Member States' interests," will no doubt take colour from their context. This formulation may in many if not most cases in which it is invoked leave to the Community institutions a wide margin of appreciation, but nevertheless an assessment that Community action is justified by reference to this criterion might in an appropriate case raise justiciable factual issues.

JUDICIAL REVIEW FOR FAILURE TO TAKE ACCOUNT OF THE AMSTERDAM GUIDELINES

A further ground upon which a Community act might in practice as well as in theory be amenable to judicial review would be a failure to take account of the

20 Case C-84/94 *United Kingdom of Great Britain and Northern Ireland* v *Council of the European Union*. [1996] ECR I – 5755, at paras. 47 and 55.

Amsterdam guidelines. Even in cases where the institutions enjoy the widest discretion, the failure to take account of matters which it is essential to take into account will itself amount to a ground for annulment.[21]

JUDICIAL REVIEW FOR BREACH OF THE PRINCIPLE OF PROPORTIONALITY

The principle of proportionality is too well established to justify repetitive exposition here.[22] But the principle is worthy of remark as regards two types of situation in which it might be said that Community acts might be particularly vulnerable to challenge for proportionality in this context. The first is as regards a consideration referred to in the Edinburgh guidelines to the effect that where difficulties are localized and only certain Member States are affected, any necessary Community action should not be extended to other Member States unless this is necessary to achieve an objective of the Treaty. This is omitted from the Amsterdam Protocol, yet it appears to represent a valid example of the principle of proportionality.

Proportionality might also be invoked in circumstances where disparities between national rules caused transnational effects and inhibited freedom of movement as regards certain distinct cross-frontier transactions. In such cases it might be considered to be disproportionate to harmonize national rules as they applied to all situations rather than simply harmonizing rules applicable to cross-frontier transactions. The point may be illustrated by reference to the unfair contract terms directive.[23] The directive is an internal market measure based on Article 95 (ex Article 100a). The directive harmonizes the laws of Member States as regards unfair terms in consumer contracts. The preamble indicates that one of the problems caused for the single market by the existence of different national rules on unfair consumer contracts is that consumers from one Member State may be deterred from purchasing goods and services in another Member State because they may be unaware of the rules of other Member States. If the foregoing – adverse effect on direct cross border purchases – were regarded as the *only* mischief identified as flowing from the disparities between national rules referred to it, it might be said that the directive was disproportionate in regulating *all* consumer transactions, and that the aim of the directive could be achieved by laying down harmonized rules for cross-border transactions. While such questions involve large elements of policy, and a wide measure of discretion, it is not impossible to envisage the Court of Justice intervening in a case

---

21 Case 191/82 *EEC Seed Crushers' and Oil Processors' Federation (FEDIOL)* v *Commission of the European Communities* [1983] ECR 2913, at para. 30; scrutiny to determine whether an institution has omitted to take into consideration any essential matters is part of the normal powers of review of the Court of Justice.

22 See above at page 510.

23 OJ 1993 L 95/29.

where there is a clear lack of proportion between the wide scope of Community legislation, and the relatively narrow ambit of the aim identified in the preamble of the measure in question.

JUDICIAL REVIEW ON PROCEDURAL GROUNDS INCLUDING WANT OF REASONING

Reference has been made above to the procedural requirements laid down in the Amsterdam Protocol. To greater or lesser extent these requirements may rank as essential procedural requirements for the purposes of judicial review. Non-compliance with these requirements, perhaps in conjunction with breach of the established duty of the institutions to provide adequate reasoning for binding acts could well provide the basis for judicial review. It is established, however, that if the reasoning of a Community act indicates in substance the grounds for the conclusion that objectives of the act in question could not be sufficiently achieved by the Member States, this is sufficient to satisfy the procedural requirements of Community law, and there is no requirement that specific reference be made to "subsidiarity".[24]

24 Case C-233/94 *Federal Republic of Germany* v *European Parliament and Council of the European Union*. [1997] ECR I – 2405, paras. 22-27. There is equally no need to make a specific reference to "proportionality", see Case C-150/94 *United Kingdom of Great Britain and Northern Ireland* v *Council of the European Union*. [1998] ECR I – 7325, para. 37.

PART 5

JUDICIAL REVIEW AND SUBSTANTIVE LAW

33

DRINKS IN LUXEMBOURG

ALCOHOLIC BEVERAGES AND THE CASE LAW OF THE EUROPEAN COURT OF JUSTICE

*Gil Carlos Rodríguez Iglesias**

Lord Chancellor, my Lords, Ladies and Gentlemen,

May I say that it is a great honour and a privilege to be here today to deliver the very first of the annual Lord Slynn of Hadley European Law Lectures.

This lecture has been organised by The Lord Slynn of Hadley European Law Foundation which, as I have understood, has been set up to advance studies in European, Comparative and Human Rights Law. I was particularly pleased to learn that it intends to be active throughout the whole of geographical Europe and especially in Central and Eastern Europe which to my mind is a particularly important objective. I am very sure that the efforts of the Foundation to encourage dialogue between lawyers from the east and the west will not only be greatly appreciated but will also lead to a better common understanding.

So may I thank the Foundation for inviting me here today and may I take this opportunity to wish the Foundation every success in its work.

* * *

I would now like to try to explain why I chose the topic of "Drinks in Luxembourg" for today's lecture. The title is, I admit, somewhat ambiguous and may conjure up ideas of parties in the Grand Duchy of Luxembourg. This however is not my intention, nor am I making a bid to promote the Luxembourg wine industry.

Instead I thought it was an appropriate topic with which to honour Gordon Slynn who, both as an Advocate General and as a Judge at the Court of Justice, made a substantial contribution to the Court's case law, including the case law where the subject matter alcoholic beverages was concerned.

---

* This is the text of the speech I delivered for the First Annual Lord Slynn of Hadley European Law Lecture organised by The Lord Slynn of Hadley European Law Foundation on Monday 22 March 1999. I am indebted to Elizabeth Willocks for her valuable assistance in its preparation.

D. O'Keeffe (ed.), Liber Amicorum Slynn 523-539 (2000)

He was for example, Advocate General in the famous German "beer purity case" which I will be mentioning later. And he was Judge rapporteur in a case I remember particularly well, perhaps not the most famous case of the Court, where we sat together in a chamber of three with our late colleague Judge Réné Joliet.[1] It concerned "alcohol free wine" and whether such wine could be considered to be "wine" under the Common Agricultural Policy regulations. If I can explain, it was a wine from which the alcohol had been removed. Well, after what I remember was a rather long discussion (and I cannot say anything further about that because I would risk breaching the secret of the *délibéré*) we decided that "alcohol-free wine" could not be defined as "wine". Indeed we decided that the presence of a certain degree of alcohol is an essential characteristic of any wine.

I can also vouch for the fact that Lord Slynn is quite an oenological expert. You may even have seen that he was reported in *The Times* wine column as being a "good judge of fine clarets". It will therefore not be a surprise to learn that during his time in Luxembourg he made quite a contribution, not only to the Court's case-law but also to its wine cellar.

I also had a personal reason for choosing the topic "Drinks in Luxembourg". This was because one of the first times I came into contact with the practice of Community law was in preparing the pleadings in the *Cinzano* case back in 1970 as an assistant to Professor Kaiser of Freiburg University.[2] It was a reference from the *Bundesfinanzhof* and concerned Cinzano's challenge of a German tax on ethyl alcohol. I went to the hearing of the case in Luxembourg in October of that year. Unfortunately we, the lawyers advising Cinzano, lost the case. That was perhaps the reason why I decided I would be better going back to the Court as a judge, rather than as an advocate, so as to be sure that I could not risk losing any more cases. (Of course, I was wrong, since as a judge it is still possible to find oneself in the minority).

The experience at any rate must have been decisive because the case was about the German alcohol monopoly and some time later I decided to write my PhD thesis on the subject of state monopolies of a commercial character.

And of course the final reason for choosing the topic of "Drinks in Luxembourg" today was because the Court's case law on alcoholic beverages is very rich and includes some of the leading cases of Community law. Indeed, there are some very good examples which can serve to show the decisive role the Court has taken in ensuring respect for the law and in developing the legal system of the European Community. So, by means of a special "cocktail of cases" which I have concocted for you today I will try to give you some interesting examples which show how the Court has contributed to the development of Community law.

I propose to focus on the area of law covered by the free movement of goods. As you know, this principle is one of the foundations of Community law

1 Case C-75/90, *Roger Guitard* [1991] ECR I-4205.
2 Case C-13/70, *Cinzano* [1970] ECR 1089.

and forms a core part of it and of the internal market. Moreover a significant number of the cases on free movement concern the free circulation of alcoholic beverages in the Community market.

I will deal first with those on Articles 30 (now Article 28) and 36 (now Article 30) of the Treaty.

Let me start with the seminal case of *Cassis de Dijon*.[3] As you all know it is an extremely important case but please bear with me as I recall the facts.

The case was referred to the Court by a German tax court, the *Hessisches Finanzgericht*. It concerned an action raised by a German company Rewe, against the German authorities for breach of Article 30 because they had refused to allow it to import "Cassis de Dijon" from France into Germany on account of the insufficient alcoholic strength of Cassis.

According to German legislation fruit liqueurs could only be marketed if they had a minimum alcohol content of 25 % whereas Cassis had an alcohol content of about 17%.

Rewe took the view that this legislative provision constituted a restriction on the free movement of goods since it meant that well known spirits, such as Cassis, in free circulation in other Member States could not be sold in Germany.

However there was no Community legislation harmonising the rules on the minimum alcohol content of fruit liqueurs and there was therefore an argument that for as long as there were no such rules, Article 30 could only apply where actual discrimination could be shown between the domestic and imported products.

The judgment made clear that Article 30 can indeed apply to national rules which do not discriminate against imported products as such, but inhibit trade nevertheless because they are different from the trade rules which apply in the country of origin.

In the leading paragraph of the judgment, which was drafted in very general terms, the Court stressed that,

> "obstacles to movement within the Community resulting from disparities between the national laws relating to the marketing of the products in question must be accepted in so far as these provisions may be recognised as being necessary in order to satisfy mandatory requirements relating in particular to the effectiveness of fiscal supervision, the protection of public health, the fairness of commercial transactions and the defence of the consumer."[4]

This judgment had the effect of introducing the principle of mutual recognition whereby Member States must accept in principle that if a product is lawfully produced in one country it is fit to be marketed in another. Exceptions to this principle can only be admitted if there are overriding reasons of general interest which justify the commercial or technical rules which give rise to the re-

---

3 Case C-120/78, *Rewe-Zentral AG* [1979] ECR 649.

4 Point 8 of the judgment.

strictions. That is to say that the purpose of the rules adopted in the general interest must be compelling enough to justify the exception.

The judgment was delivered in February 1979. About one year later the Commission issued an important Communication[5] about the consequences of the judgment. In that Communication it announced a new policy whereby it would monitor the application of the Treaty rules on the free movement of goods as interpreted by the Court more strictly. In particular, the Commission considered that, further to the judgment, its work of harmonisation should be more selective and directed mainly at those national laws which are admissible under the criteria set down by the Court and which have an impact on the functioning of the common market.

In other words, one could say that the *Cassis de Dijon* judgment implied a widening of the scope of Article 30 and thus of its direct effect. This led to a concomitant reduction of the need to harmonise the divergent commercial and technical rules of the Member States, since such harmonisation was not a prerequisite for the free movement of goods.

In a more recent judgment the Court has limited the scope of Article 30. I am sure you have guessed that I am referring to the case of *Keck and Mithouard,*[6] and the controversial judgment of 24 November 1993 concerning loss in leading sales of beer and coffee.

Some have gone so far as to claim that after *Keck*, *Cassis de Dijon* is no longer good law. I cannot share this view.

First the judgment in *Keck* quotes the leading paragraph of *Cassis de Dijon* verbatim.[7] It then goes on to say that,

> " contrary to what has previously been decided, the application to products from other Member States of national provisions restricting or prohibiting certain selling arrangements is not such as to hinder directly or indirectly, actually or potentially trade between Member States within the meaning of the *Dassonville* judgment, so long as those provisions apply to all relevant traders operating within the national territory and so long as they affect in the same manner, in law and in fact, the marketing of domestic products and of those from other Member States."[8]

So, where these conditions are fulfilled, such rules fall outside the scope of Article 30 of the Treaty.

In my view this judgment should be considered to be the correction of what can only be described as an erratic development of the case law in response to "Euro defences" which culminated in the Sunday Trading cases[9] whereby it was

---

5 Communication from the Commission concerning the consequences of the judgment given by the Court of Justice on 20 February 1979 in Case 120/78 ("Cassis de Dijon") O.J. 1980, C 256/2.

6 Joined Cases C-267/91 and C-268/91, *Keck and Mithouard* [1993] ECR I-6097.

7 Point 15 of the judgment.

8 Point 16 of the judgment.

9 See for example Case C-145/88, *Torfaen Borough Council* [1993] ECR 389.

possible to attack any national law on the grounds of incompatibility with Community law and Article 30 even where that legislation *per se* had nothing to do with the free movement of goods. This evolution thus obliged the Court to take a position on the possible justification of measures which could be politically controversial, such as the question of Sunday trading, but in fact had nothing to do with the free movement of goods.

I am pretty sure that if *Keck and Mithouard* were applied to cases decided prior to November 1993 there would be no significant change in their outcome. But the reasoning would have been much more straightforward. That said, I must admit that some cases like *INNO*[10] and *Yves Rocher*[11] are borderline and it is still not easy to say whether they have been overruled by *Keck*.

Let me now close the *Keck* parenthesis and come back to the aftermath of *Cassis de Dijon* in connection with alcohol.

About 8 years after *Cassis de Dijon* was decided came the case brought by the *Commission against Germany*[12] concerning its law on the purity of beer. You will recall that it concerned the fact that Germany would not allow any drink named "beer" to be marketed in Germany unless it conformed to the German rules on purity for beer, according to which the beer could only be made from barley, hops, malt, yeast and water. The Court was faced with different arguments justifying the German position.

The first main argument was based on the name "beer". The German government maintained that German consumers would be misled if drinks named beer were to contain ingredients other than those listed in the purity law. Indeed it was argued that German consumers expect when ordering a beer to receive a drink that has certain special characteristics.

The second main argument was founded on public health requirements and the fact that additives in beer could be bad for the public's health. *Inter alia* the German government had put forward that since average beer consumption in Germany was so high, one would have to be very cautious about allowing Germans to drink beer with additives.

Not surprisingly the Court rejected the argument. However Advocate General Sir Gordon Slynn, as he was then known, gave a much more graphic explanation. He said that

> "It seems to me disproportionate to seek to justify rules which exclude the whole of society from beer other than nationally produced beer because some additives may constitute a risk for a person who drinks in excess of 1000 litres of beer a year or for an alcoholic already suffering from cirrhosis of the liver. Accepting that such persons may need protection there are other ways of achieving it, medical advice as to quantum and self restraint to name only two."[13]

10 Case C-362/88, *GB Inno-BM* [1990] ECR I-667.
11 Case C-126/91, *Yves Rocher* [1993] ECR I-2361.
12 Case C-178/84, *Commission/Germany* [1987] ECR 1227.
13 Page 1257 of the Opinion as published.

I think this demonstrates the advantage of being an Advocate General in that you can say what you like. As a Judge you cannot and I hope I will bc forgiven if I now reveal one of the secrets of the *délibéré* in that case now that it is some years since it took place.

In the draft judgment my dear late colleague Judge Joliet, who I think you all must know was quite a character, had proposed to reply to the rather odd argument of the German government on the other point about the name "beer" by saying that it seemed that once Germans crossed the borders of their own country, which they do on a fairly regular basis, their attitude to beer changed since in foreign parts they had no difficulty in calling "beer" the whole variety of beers available to them, in rather large quantities.

Of course you will not find this in the judgment because when Judges have such brilliant ideas the collegiate body of Judges excludes them from the draft. This is perhaps why judgments do not make nearly as good reading as Advocate Generals' opinions. I am sure that Lord Slynn, who has been both Advocate General and Judge at the Court, would agree with me.

I would now like to mention two cases on the advertising of alcohol and the application of Articles 30 and 36.

The first is the judgment of the Court of 10 July 1980 in the case of *Commission v. France.*[14] In this case the situation was that under the French law on alcohol advertising there was a ban on advertising for some types of alcohol and for others there was a restriction on advertising. It so happened that under this law cognac was subjected to restricted advertising and whisky was subjected to a total ban.

The argument in defence of this differentiated law on advertising was made by the French government on grounds of public health. In particular, the French argued that one had to take account of French drinking habits. The habit in France is to drink cognac after lunch as a "digestif" whereas whisky is drunk before lunch as an "aperitif" and on an empty stomach and thus was far more dangerous to the health than cognac despite the relative similarity in strength of the two drinks concerned. The Court did not "swallow" the argument. It considered that the distinction between "digestives" and "aperitifs" was not an objective criterion of differentiation.

In the second case on advertising, *Aragonesa,*[15] a publicity company contested a regional law passed by the government of Catalonia whereby the advertising of beverages having an alcoholic strength of more than 23 degrees was banned. Aragonesa pointed out that the majority of Catalan-produced beverages have an alcohol content of less than 23 degrees and therefore the law was of a protective nature both in respect of products coming from other parts of Spain and from other parts of the Community.

---

14 Case C-152/78, *Commission/France* [1980] ECR 2299.

15 Joined Cases C-1/90 and C-176/90, *Aragonesa de Publicidad Exterior SA and Publivía SAE* [1991] ECR I-4151.

The Court held that such a legislative provision may constitute a hindrance to imports and, therefore should in principle be regarded as a measure having equivalent effect within the meaning of Article 30. However it considered that it could be justified on grounds of public health under Article 36 because it was neither disproportionate nor discriminatory. The Court acknowledged that a national measure which applies only to a part of the national territory cannot escape being characterised as discriminatory or protective on the ground that it affects both the sale of products from other parts of the national territory and the sale of products imported from other Member States. However it considered that the fact that Catalonia produces more beverages having less than 23 degrees than beverages with a higher alcohol content was not in itself sufficient to give rise to arbitrary discrimination or a disguised restriction of intra-Community trade.

It seems to me that the comparison of these two cases on alcohol advertising makes clear how important the assessment of the protective effect of a measure is in order to ascertain its compatibility with Articles 30 and 36.

It is interesting to note that the judgment in *Keck and Mithouard* is entirely consistent with this approach.

I would now like to turn to the application of Articles 30 and 36 to cases concerning the protection of trademarks.

The case of *Loendersloot*,[16] decided in November 1997, concerned the distribution of repackaged and relabelled Ballantine's whisky. Loendersloot, a transport and warehousing firm, had customers who were parallel traders. They bought products like Ballantine's whisky in countries where the prices where relatively low and resold them in countries where the prices were high. Ballantine's brought an action against Loendersloot alleging infringement of its trademark rights. They argued that, without informing Ballantine's, Loendersloot removed and then re-affixed or replaced the labels on the whisky bottles in order either to remove the identification numbers which were underneath the labels on the bottles or in order to remove the word "pure" and the name of the importer approved by Ballantine's from the original label. Loendersloot on the other hand argued that Ballantine's was simply trying to partition the market artificially.

The Court held that a trademark owner like Ballantine's could rely on its trademark rights even if this constitutes a barrier to free trade in the internal market *unless* four conditions could be satisfied. These were: 1) that it could be shown that in invoking its right, artificial partitioning of the market would occur; 2) that it could be shown that relabelling does not affect the original condition of the product; 3) that it could be shown that presentation of the relabelled product is not such as to be liable to damage the reputation of the trade mark; and 4) (and this was a new condition) that the person who relabels the products

16 Case C-349/95, *Loendersloot* [1997] ECR I-6227.

informs the trademark owner of the relabelling before the relabelled products are put on sale.

This case illustrates what I consider is now a well balanced approach to the protection of trademarks on the one hand and the requirements of free movement on the other.

The judgment is one of a line which has been adopted in a move towards more recognition for trademark rights and away from the older case law. The line started with the judgment in *HAG II*[17] (which concerned a different kind of beverage, namely decaffeinated coffee) where the Court, following the Opinion of Advocate General Francis Jacobs, expressly overturned its previous judgment in *HAG I*[18] and readjusted the relationship between intellectual property and the free movement of goods. The Court underlined that trade mark rights constitute an essential element in the system of undistorted competition in which undertakings must be able to attract and retain customers by the quality of their products or services. So whilst the judgment may have concerned the marketing of decaffeinated coffee, the judgment itself was not at all "decaffeinated". Indeed it is a landmark in the attitude of the Court towards intellectual property and in particular trademark rights.

And now I would like to move to the cases on Article 95 (now Article 90) and the taxation of alcohol.

I will deal first with two cases where the Court had to decide on arguments constructed on the similarities or differences between wine and beer – a very dangerous argument to attempt.

The first is that of *Commission v. United Kingdom*[19] from 1983 and the second is the case of *Commission v. Belgium*[20] from 1987.

In *Commission v. UK*, the Commission argued that an increase in excise duty levied in the UK on still, light wine favoured the domestic production of beer. The Commission claimed that still light wine and beer were in a competitive relationship. The UK on the other hand argued that in the UK beer is a popular drink consumed in pubs or in connection with work; domestic consumption and consumption with meals being negligible, whereas the consumption of wine was more unusual and special from the point of view of social custom.

The Court rejected the UK's argument and said that customer habits were irrelevant for an assessment of this kind and that instead one had to examine the tax structure and its development for the two products in question in order to assess whether it had a protective effect. The UK government argued that the tax system was not protective since it did not prevent an increase in imports of wine and moreover the increase in duty on wine had had no repercussions on con-

17 Case C-10/89, *HAG II* [1990] ECR I-3711.

18 Case 192/73, *Van Zuylen v. HAG* [1974] ECR 731.

19 Case C-170/78, *Commission/United Kingdom* [1980] ECR 417 and [1983] ECR 2265.

20 Case C-356/85, *Commission/Belgium* [1987] ECR 3299.

sumption. The Commission on the other hand argued that the consumption of wine would have been even greater if the UK had not increased the tax.

The Court was not satisfied with the facts available on the possible protective effect of the tax and therefore only delivered an interlocutory judgment pending more information to be supplied by the parties.[21]

In its later final judgment of 1983,[22] the Court found that the taxation of cheap, still, light wine (which it considered to be in a competitive relationship with beer), was on average five times higher, by reference to volume than the taxation of beer, and on the basis of alcoholic strength it bore a tax which was twice as heavy as that borne by beer. This tax burden, the Court concluded, afforded protection to domestic beer production since the effect of the tax was to stamp out competition from cheap, still, light wines and render wine sold in the UK as a luxury product.

In the infringement proceedings against Belgium,[23] the Commission alleged that Belgium had infringed Article 95 in having applied a higher rate of VAT to wine made of fresh grapes which was an imported product, than to beer which was a domestic product. But in this case, unlike the British case, the Court found that the Commission had failed to show that the lower tax on the beer had a protective effect. In particular the Court found that even if the tax rate on beer and wine had been the same, there would still have been a substantial difference in price between the two products and that a reduction in the tax on wine to the same rate as that imposed on beer was so insignificant that it would not have influenced the price. Therefore the higher tax on wine could not be considered as having the effect of protecting the domestic production of beer.

In two later cases of 26 June 1991,[24] which I consider to be very important perhaps because I was the Judge rapporteur, the Court decided on infringement actions brought against Belgium and Luxembourg which concerned differential taxes on domestically – and foreign – produced beer. These two cases raised substantially the same problem, which was rather complex, but I will try and explain it as simply as I can.

Domestically produced beer was taxed on the basis of the amount of hot wort used in the process of making beer. On transformation of the wort into beer there would be a certain amount of wastage, the amount depending on the efficiency of the brewery. Since the amount of tax was based on the amount of hot wort used and not on the amount of beer produced the method of calculating the tax could only be applied to domestically-produced beer since it is technically impossible to verify *ex post* the amount of hot wort actually used during the beer making process. For this reason, foreign imports of beer were instead subjected to a flat rate of tax.

---

21 Case C-170/78, *Commission/United Kingdom* [1980] ECR 417.
22 Case C-170/78, *Commission/United Kingdom* [1983] ECR 2265.
23 Case C-356/85, *Commission/Belgium* [1987] ECR 3299.
24 Case C-152/89, *Commission/Luxembourg* [1991] ECR I-3141 and Case C-153/89, *Commission/Belgium* [1991] ECR I-3171.

The Court considered that the tax system was completely lacking in transparency and therefore concluded that the onus, instead of being on the Commission to prove discrimination, was on the governments to prove that the beer tax systems in question were not discriminatory in any individual case.

This line of reasoning was confirmed last year in the case of *Outokumpu*[25] which had nothing to do with the taxation of alcohol but rather the taxation of electricity. In this case the Finnish customs authorities sued Outokumpu for payment of excise duties on the import of electricity from Sweden. In Finland there are various rates of duty levied on producers and importers of electricity. So far as Finnish-produced electricity is concerned, the rate of excise duty depends on the method of production of the electricity and on ecological considerations. There was, for example, a higher charge on coal-produced electricity than on water-produced electricity. However imported electricity was charged at a flat rate of duty no matter what method of production was used. This flat rate was calculated so as to correspond to the average rate levied on electricity produced in Finland. Finland argued that it was impossible to tax imported electricity in the same way as Finnish-produced electricity since they did not have the information necessary regarding its method of production.

In its judgment the Court first made quite clear that Article 95 did not preclude a differentiated tax on energy in so far as that differentiation is based on environmental considerations. But the Court found that Article 95 is infringed where the taxation on the imported product and that on the similar domestic product are calculated in a different manner on the basis of different criteria which lead in certain cases to higher taxation being imposed on the imported product. So in order to ascertain whether the system is compatible with Article 95, the tax levied on imported electricity must be compared with the lowest tax levied on domestic electricity rather than on the average tax levied on domestic electricity.

These cases on the taxation of beer and electricity are particularly striking examples of the interpretation of Article 95 which is, as far as fiscal matters are concerned, an essential complementary tool to ensure the free movement of goods. These cases are also representative of the case law on both Article 95 and on Articles 30 and 36 in that the protective effect of the measures concerned, which is assessed on the basis of the facts of each case, plays a decisive role.

The complementary character of these two sets of provisions is highlighted in the two French cases on alcoholic beverages.[26] These two cases, which were heard together, concerned on the one hand the application of Articles 30 and 36 to the French law on alcohol advertising, which I have already mentioned, and on the other Article 95 and the French manufacturing tax on alcohol. The Court used the same reasoning to reject the argument (apéritif, digestif) both where it was used as a justification under Article 36 and where it was used as an expla-

25 Case C-213/96, *Outokumpu Oy* [1998] ECR I-1777.

26 Case C-152/78, *Commission/France* [1980] ECR 2299 and Case 168/78, *Commission/France* [1980] ECR 347.

nation for the fact that the tax in question did not have a protective effect under Article 95. Thus we can see that Articles 30 and 36 on the one hand and Article 95 on the other, are two sides of the same coin.

I turn now to another Article of the treaty: Article 37 (now Article 31) on State monopolies of a Commercial Character.

Article 37 is, or at least was, a somewhat enigmatic provision (or rather a set of provisions) which tries to achieve something similar to the squaring of the circle: adjusting (rather than abolishing) state monopolies so as to ensure that there is no trade discrimination. In other words, it tries to integrate state monopolies into the functioning of the common market.

Now, one could ask (and indeed many have asked): is that possible?

That question is at the basis of all of the problems relating to the interpretation of Article 37. Nevertheless sometime in the early sixties, the *Conseil d'État* in France refrained from referring a case to the Court on Article 37 because its interpretation was "clear".[27] This curious application of the "acte clair" doctrine of course gave rise to criticism. I still remember an article written by Professor Colliard in 1964 with the very expressive title "L'obscure clarté de l'Article 37 du traité CEE".[28] But all this was a long time ago.

A certain number of old and new Member States have had alcohol monopolies which have given rise to a good deal of cases. As I said before, I happened to be involved in the *Cinzano* case and later, before I was a judge, I reviewed and sometimes criticised some of the cases decided by the Court.

Now, allow me to let you into another secret of deliberation which shows how dangerous it is for a Judge to have been a Professor. We were once discussing an Article 37 case in the Fifth Chamber of the Court and Judge Sir Gordon Slynn (as he then was) contradicted me and quoted extensively in support of his view an article published by a law professor ... I am sure you have guessed who that professor was!

But let us come to the case-law. I shall focus on a relatively recent case, *Franzén,*[29] which was about the Swedish alcohol monopoly. The Advocate General concluded that the monopoly was incompatible with Articles 30 and 37 of the Treaty and could not be justified on grounds of public health under Article 36.

The Court did not follow the Advocate General. It held that Article 37 does not preclude the existence and operation of a national monopoly on the retail of alcoholic beverages, but, at the same time, it considered that the provisions which extended the import prohibition to traders other than those holding a production licence or a wholesale licence were incompatible with Articles 30 and 36.

In my view, this judgment has advanced the case-law of the Court on state monopolies and, in particular, has introduced some clarification of the scope of

27 *Soc. des pétroles Shell Berre e.a.*, Conseil d'Etat (Act. jur. 1964 II 438), 19 June 1964.
28 *Recueil Dalloz* 1964 n° 40, *Chronique* – XXXVII, pp. 263-272.
29 Case C-189/95, *Franzén* [1997] ECR I-5909.

Article 37 and on the delimitation of its special rules with respect to Articles 30 and 36. The Court stressed that the rules relating to the existence and operation of the monopoly had to be examined with reference to Article 37, which is specifically applicable to the exercise, by a domestic commercial monopoly, of its exclusive rights. On the other hand, the effect on trade of the other provisions of the domestic legislation which were separable from the operation of the monopoly had to be examined with reference to Article 30. As far as the system of the monopoly was concerned, the Court considered that,

> "the purpose of Article 37 of the Treaty is to reconcile the possibility for Member States to maintain certain monopolies of a commercial character as instruments for the pursuit of public interest aims with the requirements of the establishment and functioning of the common market. It aims at the elimination of obstacles to the free movement of goods, save, however, for restrictions on trade which are inherent in the existence of the monopolies in question".[30]

This led the Court to consider that the existence and operation of the retail monopoly (ie. the central elements of the system) were conceived for the protection of public health and, on the evidence before the Court, did not appear to disadvantage imported products. Therefore (and now I depart from the wording of the judgment) they were compatible with Article 37, in spite of the fact that it is plain that the existence of the monopoly has *per se* a restrictive effect on trade. Restrictive, but not protective. That is, in my view, a decisive aspect.

On the same date (23 October 1997) the Court delivered four judgments dismissing the applications of the Commission against four Member States alleging infringements of the Treaty in connection with the electricity monopolies.[31] In three of these four judgments the Court found that the exclusive import and export rights at issue were contrary to Article 37, but they could be justified under Article 90 (now Article 86), paragraph 2 on grounds of public interest. Since the legal approach put forward by the Commission had neglected this aspect, the Court was not in a position to examine the proportionality of the monopoly systems at issue in the light of their public interest objectives and the applications therefore had to be dismissed.

Taken as a whole, all of these judgments of October 1997 have considerably developed the case law on state monopolies and have shown, in my view, a certain evolution in the balance between the requirements of free trade and the requirements of public interest, which, in this area, are expressly taken into consideration by the Treaty.

I would now like to turn to another aspect of the Court's case law which concerns the developments made in the field of effective judicial protection through cases which have concerned alcohol.

---

30 Point 39 of the judgment.

31 Case C-157/94, *Commission/Netherlands* [1997] ECR I-5699; Case C-158/94, *Commission/Italy* [1997] ECR I-5789; Case C-159/94, *Commission/France* [1997] ECR I-5815 and Case C-160/94, *Commission/Spain* [1997] ECR I-5851.

The first of these cases is, once again, the German beer purity case.[32] In this case the Court noted that there was no procedure whereby a beer importer could apply for a licence to import a particular beer which did not conform with the German purity law. Instead there was a blanket ban on all beers containing additives. The Court found that on grounds of the principle of proportionality there must be a procedure which is easily accessible and quick whereby traders are able to apply for an authorization to import beer which contains specific additives. The Court also found that it must be open to traders to challenge an unjustified refusal to grant an authorization before the courts and that the burden of proof was on the authorities (not the importer) to show that the refusal was justified on specific grounds relating to the protection of health.

The more recent case of *Lemmens*[33] concerned a driver who contested the breathalyser test effected by the police in the Netherlands on the grounds that the Dutch authorities had not notified the technical regulations on breathalysers to the Commission.

But before I analyze this case I should explain its background, which lies in the earlier landmark case of 1996, *CIA Security International*.[34]

The two cases concern the interpretation of Directive 83/189 which lays down a procedure for the provision of information on technical standards to the Commission and to other Member States.

In *CIA*, the Court, deciding on a reference from the Liege Commercial Court, was faced with the problem whereby CIA Security, a security firm, was not allowed, according to Dutch technical regulations on security systems, to use a particular type of alarm system.

CIA relied on the fact that the Belgian technical regulations had not been notified to the Commission in accordance with the Directive. In its assessment of the Directive the Court underlined that the Directive is designed to protect by means of preventative control the free of movement of goods which is one of the foundations of the Community. The Court underlined the useful purpose of this control in that technical regulations may constitute obstacles to trade in goods between Member States and that such obstacles are only permissible if they are necessary to satisfy compelling public interest requirements. The control is also effective in that all draft technical regulations covered by the Directive must be notified to the Commission and the other Member States so that they have an opportunity to examine whether the draft regulations create obstacles to trade contrary to EC law.

The Court then went on to interpret the Directive as meaning that a breach of the obligation imposed on national authorities to notify the Commission of any technical regulations renders these technical regulations inapplicable and thus unenforceable against individuals. The Court thus held that individuals could rely on the non-notification in proceedings brought against them on

32 Case C-178/94, *Commission/Germany* [1987] ECR 1227.
33 Case C-226/97, *Johannes Martinus Lemmens* [1998] ECR I-3711.
34 Case C-194/94, *CIA Security International SA* [1996] ECR I-2201.

grounds of non-respect of the technical regulations and that the national court must decline to apply the technical regulation in question.

The *Lemmens* case raised the question whether the same solution could be applied in a different context, actually a case about abuse of alcohol.

In criminal proceedings brought against him for drunk driving Mr Lemmens made the following statement:

> "I understand from the Press that there are difficulties regarding the breath sample apparatus. I refer to the fact that this apparatus has not been notified to Brussels and wonder what the consequences if any of this could be for my case."

The national court essentially asked whether the Directive was to be interpreted as meaning that if the obligation to notify the regulation regulating breath analysis apparatus had been infringed the effect would be that evidence obtained by means of such apparatus authorised in accordance with the regulation could not be relied upon against an individual charged with driving whilst under the influence of alcohol.

The Court rejected Mr Lemmens' argument and in so doing underlined the aim of the Directive which is to protect the free movement of goods. The Court drew a distinction between the use and marketing of a product which does not conform with the technical regulations and the use of a product which does conform with the regulations which have not been notified. Thus the use by the police of a breathalyser, which conformed to the Belgian technical regulations, was not liable to create an obstacle to trade which could have been avoided if the notification procedure had been followed. So, the Court did not go so far as to extend the protection of Community law to drunken drivers attempting to escape prosecution.

A summary of the case law on alcohol and effective judicial protection would not be complete without mentioning the case of *Codorníu*[35] which concerns in particular the question of access to justice.

The applicant, Codorniu, was a producer of quality sparkling wine in Spain for which he had a registered graphic trademark for the name "Gran crémant de Codorníu". The company had been using the mark since 1924 to designate one of its quality sparkling wines. In 1985 the Council passed a regulation which in essence limited the use of the word "crémant" to producers in Luxembourg and France. Codorníu therefore raised an action before the Court challenging the regulation.

As you know it is extremely difficult for an individual to attack a regulation since it is a measure of general application. Indeed it must be shown that the regulation affects them directly by reason of certain attributes which are peculiar to them or by reason of factual circumstances which differentiate them from all other persons and therefore distinguish them individually. However in this instance, the Court considered that Codorníu was able, by means of its registered

35 Case C-309/89, *Codorníu SA/Council* [1994] ECR I-1853.

trademark, to show that in being prevented from using its trademark it was directly and individually concerned.

The reasoning is not very explicit but the inspiring message is, in my view, that one of the fundamental principles of Community law is effective judicial protection, in other words access to justice.

This is a little bit more apparent although not yet explicit in the more recent case of *Greenpeace*[36] which concerned an action brought by that association in the interests of environmental protection regarding the Commission's decision to finance the construction of two power stations on the Canary Islands. Whilst the outcome of this case was not favourable to Greenpeace, the judgment seems to give importance to the fact that Greenpeace had a remedy before the national courts before which it could protect the same rights.

And now I come to one of the most significant cases on the rights of the citizen to have been decided by the Court in recent years, the case of *Brasserie du Pêcheur,*[37] better known to you as *Factortame*. I am sure that you are all very familiar with the aspects of the judgment relative to the *Factortame* case but in this context I would like to look at the aspects of the *Brasserie du Pêcheur* case which was joined with *Factortame* for the proceedings before the Court. While *Factortame* is about fisheries, *Brasserie du Pêcheur* – even though "pêcheur" means fisherman – was about beer.

This case results from the infringement action brought against Germany on its beer purity law and in which Sir Gordon delivered his famous opinion which I mentioned earlier. It concerned an action by the French company Brasserie du Pêcheur for damages because it was forced to discontinue exporting beer to Germany in late 1981 since the competent German authorities considered that the beer it produced did not comply with the German purity of beer requirement.

I shall tackle 3 aspects of the judgment:

The first of these concerns how the Court set about showing that it was entitled to develop a principle of state liability through its case law rather than waiting for legislation. The reasoning of the Court was in response to the German argument that a general right of reparation for individuals could be created only by legislation and that recognising such a right by judicial decision would be incompatible with the principle of conferral of powers between the Community institutions and between the Community and the Member States. The Court said that questions of the existence and extent of State liability for damage ensuing as a result of a breach of Community law are questions of Treaty interpretation. Since the Treaty contains no provision expressly and specifically governing the consequences of breaches of Community law by Member States, the Court had to rule on this question and had to do this by reference to the fundamental principles of the Community legal system and, where necessary, general principles common to the legal systems of the Member States. The Court thus

36 Case C-321/95 P, *Greenpeace Council/Commission* [1998] ECR I-1651.
37 Joined Cases C-46/93 and C-48/93, *Brasserie du Pêcheur SA and Factortame Ltd* [1996] ECR I-1029.

drew upon the principle of non-contractual liability of the Community as set out in Article 215 (now 288) of the Treaty which it found to be an expression of the general principle of the obligation to make good damage caused, and upon the law on State liability of the Member States.

The second aspect I would like mention to concerns the distinction which the Court drew when assessing the condition of a sufficiently serious breach. As regards this requirement the Court drew a distinction between on the one hand the fact that Germany had kept the legislation on what constitutes "beer" and had thus prohibited the marketing of other types of beer under the name beer in Germany and on the other hand that it had maintained the prohibition in the beer purity law on the import of beer with additives. As regards the first provision on the designation "beer", the Court found that the breach of Article 30 was such a serious breach since it had been clear since the judgment in *Cassis de Dijon* that such rules were incompatible with Article 30. In contrast the Court found that the prohibition on additives was excusable since the law on whether a prohibition of additives was compatible with Community law was not clear until the Court's judgment in *Commission v. Germany*, of 12 March 1987, holding the prohibition incompatible with Article 30. Thus it did not amount to a serious breach of Community law for the purpose of State liability.

The third aspect I would like to mention concerns the Court's answer to the German government's arguments on national procedural autonomy. In its reference the *Bundesgerichtshof* had told the Court that under the provisions of the German constitution the State is only liable for a breach of obligations conceived in favour of a third party and that since the task of the national legislature concerns only the public at large and is not directed towards any particular person or class of persons who could be regarded as "third parties" the State cannot be held liable. In other words breach by the legislature of its obligation to respect a higher ranking law would not incur liability. The Court held that while the imposition of such a restriction may be consistent with the requirement that the conditions laid down should not be less favourable than those relating to similar domestic claims, the restriction imposed in German law would in practice make it impossible or excessively difficult to obtain effective reparation for loss or damage resulting from a breach of Community law where the breach is attributable to the national legislature.

* * *

I think it is time to conclude or rather to finish since this very selective presentation of the case law of the Court on alcoholic beverages does not lead to a conclusion. I have just tried to show on the basis of a few examples how the Court exercises its task. A task to which Lord Slynn has made a very important contribution.

Since this lecture is a tribute to him I have also tried to provide you with some entertainment and I hope that it has not been too boring.

Perhaps I could have mixed my cocktail differently. There are, after all, many other cases on alcoholic beverages which I have not mentioned today and which have, in their own way, been important in the case law of the Court. I trust nevertheless that you have enjoyed your cocktail or at least appreciated some of the ingredients.

My Lords, Ladies and Gentlemen

Thank you for your attention.

34

FOUR FREEDOMS, ONE MARKET AND NATIONAL COMPETENCE: IN SEARCH OF A DIVIDING LINE

David O'Keeffe and Antonio F. Bavasso

I INTRODUCTION

> *"In an area where there are no common Community standards or rules, where a national measure is not specifically directed at imports, does not discriminate against imports, does not make it any more difficult for an importer to sell his products than it is for a domestic producer, and gives no protection to domestic producers, then in my view,* prima facie, *the measure does not fall within Article 30 even if it does in fact lead to a restriction or reduction of imports"*[1]

This statement in *Cinéthèque*, one of the most celebrated Opinions of Advocate General Sir Gordon Slynn, as he then was, deals with an issue that is still at the heart of the debate on the fundamental market freedoms guaranteed by the Treaty. It seems indisputable that his Opinion in *Cinéthèque* was a pre-cursor of the debate that eventually led to the adoption of the controversial *Keck* principle in the so called "November Revolution".[2] In *Keck,*[3] by excluding altogether the application of Article 28 [ex Article 30 EC] to certain types of national measures ("selling arrangement"), the Court of Justice, placed a limit on the extent of its case law on free movement of goods made all the more necessary by the so-called *Sunday Trading* saga.[4]

The *Sunday Trading* line of cases is one of the clearest examples of the "exploitative" use of Community law as recognised by the Court itself in *Keck.*[5] To a certain extent this process is physiological: provisions that were intended to

---

1 Joined Cases 60 and 61/84, *Cinéthèque* [1985] ECR 2605, per Advocate General Sir Gordon Slynn at 2611.

2 Reich, "The 'November Revolution' of the European Court of Justice: *Keck, Meng* and *Audi* revisited", 31CML Rev. (1994) 449

3 Joined Cases C-267/91 & C-268/91, *Keck and Mithouard* [1993] ECR I-6097, with annotation by Roth, 31 CML Rev. (1994) 845.

4 See Arnull, "What shall we do on Sunday?", (1991) ELR 112; and also White, "In Search of the Limits of article 30 of the EEC Treaty", 26 CML Rev. (1989) 235.

5 The Court referred to "the increasing tendency of traders to invoke Article 30 [now Article 28] of the Treaty as a means of challenging any rules whose effect is to limit their commercial freedom even where such rules are not aimed at products from other Member States", para. 14 of the judgment.

D. O'Keeffe (ed.), Liber Amicorum Slynn 541-556 (2000)

regulate the general economic interest for the common market were often pushed to their limits and applied situations that arguably were not foreseen by the Treaty makers. The exploitative use of Community law has positive effects, recognised since one of the "earliest leading" judgments in EC law[6] and has ultimately enabled a more rapid form of integration. However, in some instances, as in the *Sunday Trading* saga, this process has also left scope for abuse that risks upsetting the delicate relationship between national and Community competences. The danger is that of overloading the Community law competence above the limit of the original dividing line envisaged by the Treaty makers.

In this contribution in honour of Lord Slynn we intend to analyse how and to what extent the notion introduced in *Keck* is effective in limiting an exploitative use of these freedoms in the current mature phase of the internal market

II THE INTERNAL MARKET IN A WIDER PERSPECTIVE

In examining the functioning of the internal market, it is crucial to adopt a wider perspective having regard to the original structure of the entire system. However, the economic blueprint of the Community system should not be overlooked even as the Union sets new goals of integration which go far beyond the economic dimension.

In the multi-level Community legal order, one can detect a relationship between the principles of a quasi-constitutional nature such as non-discrimination and substantive provisions such as trade law (established in the internal context by the freedom of movement provisions). The very genesis of an internal Community trade law is firmly based on the principle of non-discrimination which is one of the cornerstones of the whole quasi-constitutional structure of the Union. The free movement of persons as set out in the Treaty provisions on workers (Article 39 EC), establishment (Article 43 EC) and services (Article 49),[7] have traditionally been regarded as expressions of the general principle of non-discrimination on grounds of nationality set out in Article 12 of the EC Treaty.[8] However, Article 49 and, even more clearly Article 28 on free movement of goods, arguably went beyond discrimination and banned restrictions on the free-

6 "Vigilance of the individual concerned to protect their rights amounts to an effective supervision in addition to the supervision entrusted by Article 169 and 170 to the diligence of the Commission and Member States", Case 26/62 *Van Gend en Loos* [1963] ECR1 at 25.

7 This is expressed most clearly in Case C 55-94, *Gebhard* [1995] ECR I-4165, para. 22 in which it was stated that the rules relating to the provision of services apply only if those relating to the right of establishment do not apply.

8 N. Bernard, "Discrimination and free movement in EC law", (1996) ICLQ 82 and in particular the Court found in *Reyners*, (Case 2/74 *Jean Reyners* v. *Belgian State* [1974] ECR 631) that the function of Article 52 (now article 43 EC) was to provide for the implementation of the general principle of non-discrimination on grounds of nationality contained in Article 12 of the Treaty.

dom to move within the Community in such a way that these provisions have acquired the true status of trade law provisions within the internal market.

In addition, the aim of creating an internal market constitutes a unifying thread or, at least, an interface between EC internal trade law and EC competition law.[9] Historically the link between these substantive provisions of the EC Treaty is that they were both aimed at establishing a common market by removing both restrictive measures imposed by national states and restrictions imposed by undertaking through collusion, or abusive exploitation of a dominant position. This system was complemented by provisions concerning state aid and the application of competition rules to public enterprises enjoying special or exclusive rights. By making a parallel between the free movement provisions and the competition law regime and by highlighting the different development of the two sets of rules, the proper role of the free movement provisions in the current stage of development of the Union becomes apparent.

However, another useful perspective can be derived from the quasi-constitutional dimension in the interrelation between Community law and national law. Given that in EC law there is a link between "constitutional" provisions and substantive rules, the dialogue between the Community legal system and the national legal systems can explain much of the case law concerning free movement.

The relationship between national and Community law is the special characteristic of the Community legal order which constitutes its strength and, potentially, its weakness. The primary interpretation of EC law by the Court can be divided into what we could call an endo-integrated approach and a hetero-integrated approach. The first category covers cases in which the rule applied by the Court is to be found directly in the Treaty provisions and there is no need for the ECJ to look at other sources, outside the Treaty system. The second category includes all doctrines which have been developed by the ECJ in its attempt to fill the lacunae of the Community system. These are wide ranging. They include the case law on protection of fundamental rights as well as the case law on damages for State liability. In most cases the ECJ looks at the legal traditions of the Member States or at specific legal doctrines that are assumed to be part of a common legal tradition.[10] In other cases the source has been found outside the Community system altogether by reference to international law.[11]

---

9 See E. Fox, "Toward World Antitrust and Market Access", 91 (1997) *American Journal of International Law*, 1 at 4.

10 See with regard to fundamental rights: K. Lenaerts, "Fundamental rights to be included in a Community catalogue", (1991), ELRev. 367; J.H.H. Weiler and N.J.S. Lockhart, "'Taking rights seriously' seriously: the European Court of Justice and its fundamental rights jurisprudence", 32 CML Rev. (1995) Part I, 51-94, Part II, 579-627; O'Keeffe and Bavasso, "Judicial protection of Fundamental rights and the European Citizen", in *Judicial Protection of Fundamental Rights*, (Brussels, 1997).

11 G. Schermers D. Waelbroek, *Judicial protection in the European Communities*, (Deventer) 5th ed., at p. 100; Case C-162/96, *A. Racke GmbH&Co.* v *Hauptzollampt Mainz* [1998] ECR 3655; and Case C-286/90, *Poulsen and Diva Navigation* [1992] ECR I-

Viewing the provisions concerning the internal market provisions, (in particular free movement provisions and competition law) through the prism of this perspective may assist us in identifying the dividing line between Community and national competences.[12] If it is true that the Treaty rules in both competition law and free movement aimed to achieve a common objective, the former provided for an endo-integrated and positive set of rules and principles whilst the second provided a negative rule, a prohibition of restrictions. As a result, EC competition rules developed as a self-standing body of law which, in some cases, existed in parallel with national rules and, in the majority of cases, filled a gap in the national legislation.

The common ancestry of competition and free movement can be traced to the fact that both sets of rules are subject, albeit in different forms, to an assessment of the effect on trade between Member States. This assessment is required expressly in the context of competition law and implicitly in free movement. However, the different interpretations given to this concept constitute one of the main differences between competition and free movement. Effect on trade between Member States in the context of the EC competition rules has gradually acquired the role of a jurisdictional test. It determines the competence of EC authorities and the applicability of EC rules as opposed to national rules.[13]

The system of EC competition law included a self standing set of rules and principles which were theoretically capable of being applied to individual behaviour or collusion regardless of whether they had a "Community dimension". It can be argued that, in the early stages of development of EC competition law, the jurisdictional test was interpreted "liberally" precisely because of the lack of substantial analogous safeguards at national level (with some obvious exemptions). Competition law is one of the areas where European law has created a real process of emulation, a virtuous circle one might say: the European rules have been followed at national level and in many cases have been taken as a model for national legislation. This has contributed to increasing even further the jurisdictional character of the effect on trade between Member States. As a result of the increasing uniformity at national level of competition law undoubtedly the test of effect on trade will be interpreted by the Commission and ECJ even more strictly to achieve decentralisation.[14]

6019, para. 9; Case T-115/94, *Opel Austria* v *Council* [1997] ECR II-39 paras. 90-91.

12 See also Martin, "Discriminations, Entraves et Raisons Impérieuses", (1998) CDE, 261, at 271 who notes that the provisions of Articles 81 and 82 go beyond the notion of equal treatment but recognises that the notion of discrimination is not absent from the system of EC competition rules.

13 For example, one of the restrictions that are in breach of EC competition law is market partitioning but this has to be evaluated in economic terms whilst the effect on trade between Member States is firmly considered as a rule of jurisdiction. See Bellamy & Child, *Common Market Law of Competition*, 4th ed. (Sweet & Maxwell, 1993), p. 107.

14 We believe that the ECJ judgment in Joined Cases C-215/96 and C-216/96, *Bagnasco* v. *Banca Popolare di Novara,* nyr judgment of 21 January 1999 and the subsequent Commission decision in Cases IV/34.010, IV/33.793, IV/34.234, IV/34.888, OJ 1999,

By contrast, a similar process is difficult to imagine with regard to free movement provisions which are negative in character and instrumental in nature: on the one hand they provide no "substantive" test of legality but prohibit restrictions caused by national rules; on the other, they are instrumental and vital for the achievement of the internal market. The Treaty rules on free movement taken in isolation from secondary legislation, ultimately, rely on national rules for their substantive content. In the context of freedom of movement the judicial effort to achieve the internal market has often led to a vicious circle of abuse and circumvention which risks jeopardising the legitimate aims of economic integration. The identification of a boundary between EC provisions on free movement and the national regulatory function is still unsettled.

III Non Discrimination and Free Movement in the Community Architecture

The existence of discrimination in national measures affecting free movement continues to have important consequences. This is due particularly to the "negative" nature of these provisions and their interface with national substantive rules.

The importance of discrimination is evidenced by the *Irish Souvenirs* case.[15] There, it was held that discriminatory measures with regards to goods can only be accepted if they fall within the justifications set out in Article 30 [ex Article 36] EC. Therefore this judgment implies that the admissibility of a measure which is contrary to a Treaty provision (in turn an expression of a general principle of the Treaty) can only be justified by reference to another Treaty provision. This judgment was the expression of an endo-determined interpretation of the relevant Treaty rules (i.e. the yardstick of legality of the provision was to be found within the Community legal system of rules).

In *Dassonville* it was declared that a national legislation has equivalent effect to a quantitative restriction prohibited under Article 28 of the EC Treaty, when it is capable of "*hindering, directly or indirectly, actually or potentially, intra-Community trade*".[16] The Court's ruling brought about an innovation which complicated the relationship between free movement of goods and discrimination. As a result of that ruling, Articles 28 EC et seq. seemed to apply to all restrictions of free movement of goods regardless of the discriminatory element. That is to say that whilst discrimination might be conclusive it was not the essential or exclusive element of an unlawful restriction (always subject to the justifications under Article 30 EC).

With regard to goods, even in the absence of discrimination, the emphasis of the analysis subsequently gradually shifted to the ability of the product to circu-

L 271/28 should be read in this perspective.

15 Case 113/80, *Commission* v. *Ireland*, [1981] ECR 1625.

16 Case 8/74, *Procureur du Roi* v. *Dassonville* [1974] ECR 837, para. 5.

late. Whilst the analysis of the national measure cannot ignore the element of discrimination which may exist, the *Dassonville* formula enabled an enlargement of the concept of free movement to a more economic approach based on the concept of access to the market. This approach upset the balance of the system in two ways: on the one hand the legislative justifications set out in Article 30 needed to be enlarged to allow further protection for certain requirements at national level which would otherwise be caught by too large an interpretation under the *Dassonville* formula (hence the mandatory requirements in *Cassis de Dijon*).[17] On the other hand, and as a consequence, the notion of mandatory requirements gives by definition a more prominent role to national laws and therefore introduces some elements of etero-integration in the EC rules on free movement.

With regard to services, in one Opinion of Advocate General Sir Gordon Slynn as he then was, we can find a forceful and clear endorsement of a similar process of enlargement of the concept of unlawful restrictions and a departure from reliance on the concept of discrimination. In *Webb*[18] Advocate General Sir Gordon Slynn, whilst recognising the importance of the principle of non-discrimination, stated that the scope of Article 49 EC [ex Article 59] "*is not to be so limited*". He stated that "*an examination of Articles 59 to 66 of the EEC Treaty discloses that while discrimination on grounds of nationality or place of establishment constitutes, in the absence of justification on such grounds such as public policy, conclusive evidence of "restriction" such as is envisaged by Article 59, it is not an essential or the exclusive element of such a restriction*".

Along the lines of *Irish Souvenirs* the Court has consistently held that "*national rules which are not applicable to services without discrimination as regards their origin are compatible with Community law only if they can be brought within the scope of an express exemption, such as that contained in Article 56 of the Treaty*"[19] (now Article 46 EC). Of course this also applies to the right of establishment and to the free movement of workers.

The cross-border element is more deeply rooted in the wording of the Treaty provisions on services which require that the services be provided by nationals of Member States who are established in a State of the Community other than the one of the person for whom the services are intended. This approach seems to be ultimately based on the traditional idea of a service provider who physically goes to a different Member State to provide services there. In turn the cross border element provides a stronger link with the notion of discrimination. As a consequence, an interpretation based on more economic and trade-oriented aims has struggled to find its way in the case law of the Court of Justice. We believe

17 Case 120/78, *Rewe-Zentral* v. *Bundesmonopolverwaltung für Branntwein* [1979] ECR 649.

18 Case 279/80, *John Webb* [1981] ECR 3305, per Advocate General Sir Gordon Slynn at 3331.

19 Case 353/89, *Commission* v. *The Netherlands, Mediawet*, [1991] ECR I-4069, para. 15; see also Case C-275/92, *Schindler* [1994] ECR I-1039.

that this is in the process of changing as a result of the influence of the case law on free movement of goods.

In the *Cabotage* case the Court held that a "*measure which has the effect of making the provision of services between Member States more difficult than the provision of services purely within one State*" is a breach of Article 49.[20] The French measure at stake imposed higher charges to boats engaged in intra-Community transport than those limited to internal cabotage. It was therefore indistinctly applicable despite bringing about a considerable restriction in the provision of cross border services. The decision seems here, more clearly than ever, to have been taken on the grounds of restriction of ability to provide services and hence access to the market in an economic sense rather than on the basis of discrimination.[21] There has been a shift of focus from access to the market in a physical sense to access to the market in an economic sense.

IV A CHANGING TEST IN A CONSTITUTIONAL PERSPECTIVE

It is submitted that, historically, despite appearances, *Dassonville* actually appeared to be less concerned with national discrimination and more with access to the market. In the constitutional balance of the Community legal system this required some form of counterbalancing to decentralise the centre of gravity in the evaluation of admissibility of a restrictive measure. This happened in *Cassis de Dijon*.

In fact in *Cassis de Dijon* the Court upheld *Dassonville* but clarified that, in the absence of harmonisation of legislation (which would rule out the influence of Member States), Article 28 EC prohibits obstacles to the free movement of goods lawfully manufactured and marketed in the Member States of origin which are derived from applying rules laying down requirements on content, presentation, labelling or packaging. This principle applies despite the fact that those rules are indistinctly applicable measures affecting both domestic and imported goods. However, the application of national measures can be justified on the basis of mandatory requirements pursuing public interest objectives. With *Dassonville* and *Cassis de Dijon*, discrimination changed its role: instead of recording the unlawfulness it confined the justifications available to national restrictive measures to the ones expressly stated in Article 30 whilst indistinctly applicable measures could be justified by reference to mandatory requirements. On the other hand *Cassis de Dijon* introduced an element of etero-integration in EC law which relies more heavily on the national mandatory requirements.

20 Case 381/93, *Commission* v. *France*, *cabotage*, [1994] ECR I-5145.

21 A similar approach with regard to obstacles created by the administrative requirements of insurance companies in Sweden lead the Court to declare unlawful a national measure affecting insurance companies, Case C-118/96, [1997] I-1897; Huglo, "Liberté d'établissement et libre prestationes de services", 34 RTD Eur. (1998), 573, at 577.

However, *Cassis de Dijon* was not entirely successful in avoiding exploitation of the EC rules. The potential for abusive exploitation of the *Dassonville* formula became blatantly clear with the so-called *Sunday Trading* saga.[22] Despite the introduction of the notion of mandatory requirements the case law on free movement of goods required a limitation given its broad, far reaching and ultimately undesirable effects. This prompted the adoption of a more radical or systematic approach. What was required was an independent or endo-integrated demarcation line which does not rely on the use of national mandatory requirements. Such an interpretation would exclude the application of free movement provisions altogether without resorting to national mandatory requirements. *Keck* should be seen against this background.

In *Keck* the Court primarily reaffirmed the *Cassis de Dijon* case law but went on to state that "*the application to products from other Member States of national provisions restricting or prohibiting* certain selling arrangements [emphasis added] *is not such as to hinder directly or indirectly, actually or potentially, trade between Member States within the meaning of the Dassonville formula [...], so long as those provisions apply to all relevant traders operating within the national territory and so long as they affect in the same manner, in law and in fact, the marketing of domestic products and of those from other Member States*".[23] The principle, although potentially debatable and effectively criticised,[24] has been reconfirmed by the Court in a series of decisions.[25]

V *KECK* AS ACCESS TO THE MARKET

The *Keck* ruling has effectively sanctioned the existence of an economic test which can be utilised regardless of discrimination. Undoubtedly the wording adopted by the court in *Keck* contains an element of excessive formalism by relying on the "unworkable distinction" based on the notion of selling arrange-

---

22 *Supra* note 4.

23 *Supra* note 3, para. 16 of the judgment.

24 For a comprehensive and lucid critique see Weatherill, "After *Keck*: Some Thoughts on How to Clarify the Clarification?", 33 CML Rev. (1996) 885; Cf for discussion Reich, "The 'November Revolution' of the European Court of Justice: *Keck*, *Meng* and *Audi* revisited", 31CML Rev. (1994) 449.

25 Joined Cases C-418/93, C-419/93, C-420/93, C-421/93, C-460/93, C-461/93, C-462/93, C-464/93, C-9/94, C-10/94, C-11/94, C-14/94, C-15/94, C-23/94, C-24/94, C-332/94, *Casa Uno and Others* [1996] ECR I-2975; C-189/95 *Franzén*, [1997] ECR I-5909; Case C-368/95, *Verteinigte Familiapress Zeitundsverlags und -vertriebs GmbH* v. *Heinrich Bauer Verlag*, ECR [1997] I-3689 annotated by Bavasso, 35 CML Rev. (1998) 1413; Joined Cases C-34/95, C-35/95 and 36/95 *De Agostini* [1997] ECR I-384309 annotated by Stuyck, 34 CML Rev. (1997) 1445; see Weatherill, "Recent case law concerning free movement of goods: mapping the frontiers of market deregulation", 36 CML Rev. (1999) 51.

ments.[26] In many cases this distinction may not work. In the *Mars* case,[27] the prohibition of a particular type of publicity on the packaging of the relevant product (arguably a selling arrangement), forced the importer to alter the presentation of his products. Nevertheless the Court excluded the application of the *Keck* principle.

According to Advocate General Tesauro in *Familiapress* the flexibility of the *Keck* principle lay in the word "certain."[28] This term is carefully linked to the formalistic notion of "selling arrangements" in order to exclude a rigid application of the formula to all those cases in which a prohibition on marketing actually affects access to the market. Advocate General Tesauro provided a comprehensive and explanatory list of measures which were considered by the Court to be within the category of selling arrangements[29] and remarked that the common denominator of all these cases is that they "*'affect directly the access to the market' of the relevant product*".[30]

It seems to us that if the key distinction is to be found in the impact on market access this should be spelt out in clear terms by the Court. To use the words of Advocate General Tesauro "*the only measures excluded from the scope of Article 30* [now Article 28] *are those which are absolutely general in nature, which apply – needless to say – without distinction, which do not impede imports and which might lead at most to a (hypothetical) reduction in the volume of imports only as a consequence of equally hypothetical reduction on the overall volume of sales*". A similar approach was also supported by Advocate General Jacobs who considers that the ECJ case law is consistent in its result even though some judgments "*appear to be based on different reasoning*".[31] Advocate General Jacobs seems to imply that the principle underlining Article 28 (and one

26 See *supra* note 24. Weatherill regards the formula as "disturbingly" formalistic in tone and proposes to refine the test in the following terms: "Measures introduced by authorities in a Member State which apply equally in law and in fact to all goods or services without reference to origin and which impose no direct or substantial hindrance to the access of imported goods or services to the market of that State escape the scope of application of Articles 30 and 59 [now 28 and 49]".

27 Case C-470/93, *Mars* [1995] ECR I-1923.

28 The same emphasis is also highlighted by Advocate General Léger in *Mars*, *supra* note 27, para. 29 of the Opinion.

29 Prohibition on selling at a very low profit margin, Case C-63/94, *Belgapom* [1995] ECR I-2467; rules governing the opening hours of shops and filling stations, respectively *Casa Uno supra* note 25 and Joined Cases C-401/92, and 402/92 *Tankstation* [1994] ECR I-2199; a prohibition on selling infant formula other than in pharmacies, Case C-391/92, *Commission* v. *Greece* [1995] ECR I-1621; a retailing system for manufactured tobacco products, Case C-387/93, *Banchero* [1995] ECR I-4663; a prohibition on pharmacists advertising quasi-pharmaceutical products outside pharmacies, Case C-292/92 *Hünermund* [1993] ECR I-6787; a prohibition on television advertising by distribution companies, Case C-412/93, *Leclerc-Siplec* [1995] ECR I-179.

30 Paragraph 9 of the Opinion.

31 Case C-412/93, *Leclerc-Siplec Supra* note 29, per Advocate General Jacobs para. 41 of the Opinion.

might add all free movement provisions) is that "*all undertakings should have unfettered access to the whole of the Community market.*"[32] The ambit of application of the Treaty provisions should be construed accordingly.

The *Keck* judgment does not operate this choice in clear terms and, in our opinion, further consolidation is required. However, it is in the area of free movement of goods that the case law of the Court of Justice has departed most clearly from the notion of discrimination. Yet this departure from a nationally based perspective (from discrimination to access to market) has been seen as a concession to national competence and indirectly influenced by the principle of subsidiarity.[33]

Deliberately or not, in the area of freedom of movement of goods, the Court has departed from the idea of nationality which is the basis of discrimination and has increasingly based its analysis on the idea of the market in economic rather than physical terms. This is to be seen as a positive aspect. The concept of the market has to be interpreted not in dismissive economic terms as a less sophisticated stage of the Union's development but rather as one of the facets and bases upon which the very idea of the Union reposes. Somehow paradoxically the concept of the market and freedom of movement is to be welcomed as another form of the abandonment of a national perspective in favour of a progressive vision which seeks a benchmark of legality within the Union in an endo-determined fashion.

Access to market for services and workers

The principle of access to market (interpreted as an evolution of the notion of selling arrangement) has been used in the context of services and workers. In *Alpine Investments*[34] the criteria to evaluate the prohibition on the provision of services in question was considered to be access to the relevant market. This approach was reiterated in *Bosman*[35] with regard to Article 39 and subsequently in *De Agostini*[36] involving both goods and services.

---

32 *Ibidem* para. 42.

33 See Roth, *supra* note 3.

34 Case C-384/93, [1995] I-1141 in particular para. 38, annotated by Hatzopoulos in 32 CML Rev., 1427.

35 Case C-415/93, *Bosman* [1995] I-4921; with annotation by Weatherill, 33 CML Rev. (1996) 991; in paragraph 103 of that judgment the Court held that rules on free movement of persons was infringed by rules concerning transfers between clubs which "directly affect players'" access to the employment market in other Member States; see O'Keeffe and Osborne, "L'affaire Bosman: un arrêt important pour le bon functionament du Marché unique européen", *Revue du Marché Unique Européen*, (1996), 17, at 35.

36 See *supra* note 25.

It has been argued[37] that the *Keck* principle is in contradiction to *Alpine* and *Bosman* or that *Alpine* ignored *Keck*.[38] We disagree. In *Alpine* the Court did not ignore *Keck*, it simply considered that the principle was inapplicable because, due to the very nature of the provision of services, the difference between content and selling arrangements is unworkable. Equally *Bosman* indicated that in the field of the free movement of workers a restriction on the activities of an individual cannot be seen otherwise than as a restriction on a component of that activity, thus impeding access to the market.[39]

It is submitted that, based on the idea of a single common market, there should be no distinction in the approach between goods and services or workers. *Alpine* and *Bosman* prove the inadequacy of a pure "selling arrangement" test and make a compelling case for a unitary approach modelled on a revised *Keck* test. If the distinction cannot be applied to the field of movement of workers or provision of services then the relevant test has necessarily to focus on access to the market and is subject to a rule of reason. In this scenario, maintaining the ambiguous notion of selling arrangement may in some cases lead the Court to adopt a double test. This occurred precisely in *De Agostini* where the Court considered legislation on cross border television advertising as a "selling arrangement"[40] subject to *Keck*, whilst advertising broadcasts for payment by a television broadcaster was held to be a service within the meaning of Article 49 and therefore outside *Keck* but subject to a "rule of reason" for protection of consumers.

On the one hand the notion of access to the market is the key to a unitary interpretation applicable to all *Keck*, *Bosman*, and *Alpine* situations on the other it simply shows the inappropriateness of *Keck*'s formalistic approach. The notion of access to market postulates an analysis which focuses on the unitary European perspective. We believe that a revised *Keck* test is sufficient to provide, in general terms, a clear demarcation between measures falling within or outside the scope of the Treaty. In this sense the Court has recently decided a case concerning free movement of goods expressly on the basis of an access to the market argument.[41] However, we appreciate that the Court's analysis might

37 Bernard, "La libre circulation des merchandises, des personnes et des services dans le Traité CE sous l'angle de la compétence", *Cahiers des Droit Européen*, [1998] p. 11, at 23.

38 *Contra* Stuyck cit. at 1466.

39 More generally with regard to the Court's approach in free movement of persons see, Daniele, "Non-Discriminatory Restriction to the Free Movement of Persons" 22 (1997) ELRev, 191; and Johnson and O'Keeffe, "From Discrimination to Free Movement: Recent Developments concerning Free Movement of Workers: 1989-1994" [1994] 31 CML Rev. 2323

40 See also Case C-412/93, *Leclerc-Siplec*, *supra* note 29.

41 Case C-254/98, *Schutzverband gegen unlauteren wettbewerb and TK-Heimdienst Sass Gmbh* nyr, judgment of 13th January 2000, para. 29. The case concerned free movement of goods but the Court interestingly referred to *Alpine* when formulating the access to the market argument.

have to be supplemented on a case by case basis by a factual scrutiny. Whilst national courts are best placed to perform the latter evaluation, there is some scope for guidance in the ECJ's approach.

One should explore further a supplemental means of demarcation between EC and national competence.

Advocate General Jacobs in *Lecrec-Siplec* sought to combine the principle of access to market with a *de minimis* test under Article 28 whereby the restriction should be substantial. This Opinion came after and despite the express rejection of a similar approach in *Van de Haar*.[42] However, Advocate General Jacobs' opinion was subsequent to *Keck* which, as we have seen, had introduced a new dimension to the analysis of free movement under EC law. Although the Court did not accept Advocate General Jacobs' suggestion, this approach has been indirectly reiterated by the Court more recently.[43] Whilst there are a number of arguments against the adoption of a *de minimis* test in the context of free movement,[44] the Court has never expressly given the reasons for its rejection. We believe that the strongest reservation does not lay in reasons of principle (it has been argued that fundamental provisions cannot tolerate a *de minimis* rule, but aren't competition rules in which the *de minimis* rule is successfully applied, also fundamental?)[45] but in practical reasons. It is true that *Keck* has introduced a notion of access to the market but coupling it with a *de minimis* rule may have been regarded as overstating the economic character of the test. It seems to us that this approach in the context of free movement may be difficult but not "downright impossible" (as Advocate General Tesauro put it[46]) and no more challenging than the application of a rule of reason to Article 81(1).

The criticisms of *Keck* expressed by Advocate General Jacobs in *Leclerc-Siplec* still remain valid. We subscribe to the view whereby "it is inappropriate to make distinctions between different categories of rules, and to apply different tests depending on the category to which the rules belong. The severity of the

---

42 Joined Cases C-177-8/82, [1984] ECR 1797; Advocate General Jacobs noted that the outcome of the judgment in which it was ruled that a price fixing regulation is contrary to Article 30 only if prices are fixed at such a level as to prevent imported goods from being marketed profitably or to cancel out a competitive advantage enjoyed by the manufacturer of imported goods, is in effect not very different from saying that Article 28 only comes into play if there is a substantial barrier to market access.

43 Case C-67/97, *Blume* [1998] ECR 1-8033; in that case one of the arguments of Denmark was that the measure in question fell outside Article 28 as is was *de minimis* since it covered only a minimal part of the national territory; the court did not specifically address the point which had been expressly rejected by A.G. Fennelly; see also Oliver, "Some further reflections on the scope of Articles 28-30 (ex 30-36)", 36 (1999) CML Rev, 783, p. 790.

44 See Oliver, *Ibidem*.

45 See most recently Case C-126/97, *Eco Swiss China Time Ltd* v. *Benetton*, nyr, judgment of 1st June, 1999, paras 36 and 37.

46 Case C-292/92, *Hünermund* v. *Landesapothekerkammer Baden-Württemberg*, [1993] ECR I-6787 at 6810-1; also Oliver, *supra*.

restriction imposed by different rules is indeed merely one of degree."[47] We believe that some of the cases referred to above support this view. It follows that it is possible that a marketing measure might well have the effect of an outright ban.

However, there may be a certain element of confusion in the terminology. By referring to a *de minimis* test it seems to us that Advocate General Jacobs intended to introduce an evaluation similar to that of the "rule of reason" in competition law. If the test adopted is that based on access to the market it would appear logical also to refer to the fact that a restriction must be substantial or appreciable. A "qualitative" evaluation of the measures that hamper the attainment of a single market is intrinsic to the notion of access to the market. The evaluation of the obstacle to access to the market is an unseverable part of this analysis.

The real problem lies in the need to give clear guidance to the national courts which have the primary responsibility to apply the Treaty provisions in the cases tried before them. Advocate General Jacobs recognises this need. In practice it is difficult to provide such guidance but all courts will have to exercise their discretion in the same way as they judge whether an agreement restricts competition under Article 81(1) or impedes trade between Member States.

A final word needs to be said about the role of discrimination within an access to market approach: whilst it is true that excluding from the scope of Article 28 measures which "affect in the same manner, in law and in fact, the marketing of domestic products and those from other Member States"[48] may amount to a step back towards a test based on discrimination, we believe that an "access to market" interpretation of *Keck* would not constitute a regression towards discrimination. It is submitted that discrimination has been overcome as a criterion for the legality of restricting measures, but its role is not over. If a measure is discriminatory then it is clearly within the ambit of Article 28 [43 and 49] and is subject to Article 30 [and 46]. It is only with regard to measures having equivalent effect that the *Cassis de Dijon* mandatory requirements or *Van Binsbergen*'s rule of reason apply. This further defence for a national measure is not allowed in cases that are openly discriminatory. Whilst it may be true that mandatory requirements have the same properties as the exceptions contained under Article 30, treating them as additions to the said expectations, as has been advocated,[49] would have undesirable consequences. On the one hand it would reduce the overall flexibility of the system,[50] on the other it would cancel the effect which the presence of discrimination still has: the exclusion of a wider range of justifications outside those expressly listed in Article 30.

47 Case C-412/93, *Leclerc-Siplec*, *supra* note 29 per Advocate General Jacobs para. 38.
48 *Ibidem* para. 39.
49 Oliver, *supra* note 42.
50 The list for mandatory requirements is not open-ended as confirmed by *Familiapress*. See also Weatherill *supra* note 25 at 64.

VI CONCLUSION: CROSS-BORDER ELEMENT TO LIMIT ABUSE?

In conclusion an interpretation of *Keck* which accepts a more market-oriented interpretation is to be welcomed and promoted. This would require looking beyond the infamous "unworkable" distinction between content and marketing. We also believe that it is appropriate that this test should be applied taking into consideration the magnitude of the effects of the measure. Such an interpretation should provide the national Courts with sufficient tools to determine whether the Treaty principles can be used in the circumstances of the case before them even if there is no discrimination.

Whilst this approach provides a fundamental substantive test to determine the scope of application of the Treaty provisions on free movement, possible distortions in their use can also be efficiently tackled by a "jurisdictional" analysis. The very idea of free movement depends on the cross-border nature of the activity or the circulation of products. Therefore there is a strong interrelation between the substantive analysis of the restriction and an evaluation of the cross-border element of the case. Unlike competition rules, in the free movement provisions, the circulation of the activity or of products is the value protected by the set of rules. It is true that both sets of rules ultimately relate to the attainment of a common market but in the case of the free movement provisions, the freedom of circulation is the very means to attain that objective.

Therefore the presence of a cross-border element is not merely a jurisdictional aspect but also a substantive requirement; it is the value which is protected by the rule.

The existence of a cross-border element is still a useful tool to determine if Community rules should come into play. This limb of the analysis may be as important as the one to be carried under a (revised) *Keck* test to see whether there has been any restriction. Advocate General Jacobs stressed this aspect in reaching his conclusions in *Pistre*.[51] He said unequivocally, "*the Court should decline to rule on the application of Article 30* [now 28] *to imports when it is clear from the facts that situation is wholly confined to a national territory*" in Para. 38 of the Opinion. This is a question of fact on which the national Court should decide. It seems to us that a clear signal should be given for a robust application of this rule which has both jurisdictional and substantive application. With regard to Article 81, in *Bagnasco*, the ECJ has summarised its case law in these terms: "*in order that an agreement between undertakings may affect trade between Member States, it must be possible to foresee* with a sufficient degree of probability *on the basis of a set of objective factors of law or fact that it may have an influence, direct or indirect, actual or potential, on the pattern of trade between Member States (Case 42/82 Remia and Others v Commission [1985] ECR 2545, paragraph 22). Accordingly the effect of intra-Community trade is normally the result of a combination of several factors which, taken separately,*

51 Joined Cases C-321/94, C-322/94, C-323/94 and C-323/94, *Criminal proceedings against Jacques Pistre and Other*, [1997] ECR I-2343, at 2345.

are not necessarily decisive (Case C-250/92 Gottrup-Klim v Dansk Landsbrugs Grovvareselskab [1994] ECR I-5641)."[52] We see no reasons why in principle this jurisdictional test cannot be applied in the interpretation of free movement provisions.

A number of cases can be dismissed purely on this basis. However, one should not overstate the benefits of this approach. One could easily imagine a transnational case with little impact on the common market and internal matter with a major effect on the common market. Perhaps the reference to the risk of undermining the unity of the Community contained in *Lancry*[53] is to be read in this perspective. However, there is no doubt that the case confuses an issue which has traditionally been clear. The potential for the use of a "jurisdictional" assessment as well as for flexibility in this respect varies depending on whether one refers to goods or services.

This safeguard might not be sufficient to determine at a preliminary stage a number of cases concerning the free movement of goods in which, as pointed out by Advocate General Elmer, a product is a compound of its components which may have come from different Member States.[54] Nevertheless, a rigorous cross-border test might contribute to limit the abuse in the use of the Treaty provisions. It would be in relation to services where the task could become more complex.

Whilst the wording of Article 49 contains inherently a stronger transnational element (by stating that the provision applies to services provided by nationals of Member States who are established in a State of the Community other than the one of the person for whom the services are intended) there is an increasing number of situations where this scenario is less clear. So far the case law has been as unequivocal as to exclude the application of Article 49 to activities whose relevant elements are confined within a single Member State.[55] However, in a modern economy based to a greater extent on communications technology an increasing number of services are provided by distance, trans-nationally and to an undefined group of people irrespective of their nationality.[56] In the future

---

52 Joined Cases C-215/96 and C-216/96 *Bagnasco v Banca Popolare di Novara*, *supra* note 14, para. 47 emphasis added.

53 Case C-363/93, *Lancry v Direction Générale des Douanes,* [1994] ECR I-3956

54 See Case C-194/94, *CIA Security International* v. *Signalson SA and Securitel SPRL* [1996] 1-2201, per Advocate General Elmer, para. 28.

55 Case C-97/98, *Peter Jägerskiöld v. Torolf Gustafsson*, nyr per AG Fennelly, para. 24; see also Case C-52/79 *Procurateur du Roi* v *Debauve* [1980] ECR 833, para. 9; Case C-35/94 *Aubertin and others* [1995] ECR I-301, para. 9; Case C-134/95, *USSL No 47 di Biella* v *INAIL* [1997] ECR I-195, para. 19.

56 An example may be broadcasting. This area can lead to various forms of abuse which were sought to be addressed by the Television Without Frontiers Directive, Directive 97/36/EC amending Directive 89/552/EEC; see *TV10 v. Commissariaat voor de Media* (Case C-23/93, [1994] ECR 4795) where a Dutch television company established itself in Luxembourg with the aim of broadcasting to the Netherlands without complying with certain provisions of Dutch law.

Article 49 will be less about the movement of persons and more about the provision of services. We see some differences between the situation in *Peter Jägerskiöld* where the dispute was between Finnish nationals (and the idea of a similar dispute involving non-Finnish nationals was regarded as merely theoretical) and the case in which a restriction on the provision of services is invoked in relation to activities addressed both to nationals of the same Member State and of other Member States. In *Peter Jägerskiöld* the application of Treaty rules was excluded on the basis of the fact that both parties were established in the same Member State. However, this does not address the case in which a restriction on the provision of a service to a recipient based in one Member State automatically prevents the service provider from supplying other customers based outside the national boundaries.

It seems to us that one could conceive of an interpretation enabling the application of the provision to services received "potentially" throughout the relevant market in the Community. Of course, as in the case of goods when the restrictive national measures are discriminatory in nature, this would make a stronger case not to justify an exception and to confine the possible defences to those expressly named in Article 46. However, undoubtedly an enlarged application of the services provisions would lead to more frequent recourse to rule of reason arguments. Maybe the dividing line is inevitably part of a variable geometry. One cannot always square the circle but we believe that something can still be done in the case law of the ECJ to refine the relevant tests.

35

MILK LAKES, SLOMS AND LEGITIMATE EXPECTATIONS – A PARADIGM IN JUDICIAL REVIEW

*Eleanor Sharpston**

In 1977, the market in milk was giving trouble. Products were (not for the first time) "substantially and increasingly in surplus";[1] and the Council decided "to encourage the trend noted amongst certain groups of holdings in the Community to cease milk production, or the marketing of milk and milk products".[2] To do so, it introduced a new system of premiums for the non-marketing of milk and milk products and for the conversion of dairy herds: Regulation 1078/78. Financed by the EAGGF, the scheme was simple and surely foolproof. To qualify for the non-marketing premium, a farmer currently engaged in milk production would give an undertaking not to market milk for five years.[3] In return, he would receive a "premium" that would provide ample compensation for refraining from flooding the Community market with milk.[4] When coupled with the new co-responsibility levy and the planned measures to expand the markets in milk and milk products,[5] these measures would bring equilibrium to the market in milk, albeit at a price.

Alas for central planning. By 1984, the market in milk was still "suffering from structural surpluses".[6] The Council frankly admitted that, despite application of the co-responsibility levy, "quantities of milk delivered are increasing at a rate such that the disposal of surpluses is imposing financial burdens and market difficulties which are jeopardising the very future of the common agricul-

---

* The author served as one of Sir Gordon Slynn's "référendaires" (legal secretaries) from 1988 to 1990.

1 Recital 1 of Council Regulation (EEC) No. 1078/77 (OJ 1977 L 131, p.1).

2 *Ibid.*

3 Article 2. Parallel provisions (Article 3) governed the four year conversion premium.

4 The premium, calculated as a percentage of the milk target price, was 95% for quantities up to and including 30,000 kg, tapering to 75% for quantities exceeding 50,000 kg up to and including 120,000 kg (Article 4(1)). The arrangements for the conversion premium were similarly generous (Article (2)).

5 Council Regulation (EEC) No. 1079/77 (OJ 1977, L 131, p.6), introduced simultaneously with Regulation 1078/77.

6 Recital 1 of Council Regulation (EEC) 856/84 (OJ 1984 L 90, p.10).

D. O'Keeffe (ed.), Liber Amicorum Slynn 557-567 (2000)

tural policy".[7] Undaunted, the Council hit on a new idea. "[A] careful examination of the different possible ways of re-establishing balance in the milk sector shows that, despite the administrative difficulties which its implementation may involve, the most effective method, and the one having the least drastic effect on the incomes of producers, is the introduction for an initial period of five years of an additional levy on quantities of milk delivered beyond a guarantee threshold".[8]

The "base regulation" governing the common organisation of the market in milk[9] was therefore amended by Regulation 856/84 so as to introduce a new Article 5c. With effect from 2 April 1984, this additional levy (soon to be immortalised under the acronym "SLOM": supplementary levy on milk) became payable on milk put onto the market which exceeded a reference quantity (to be determined).[10] Guaranteed total quantities were laid down for each Member State[11] and a Community reserve constituted in order to "supplement (...) the guaranteed quantities of the Member States in which implementation of the levy system raises particular difficulties liable to affect their supply or production structures".[12] In a separate regulation,[13] the SLOM was set at 75% of the target price for milk (fomula A or direct sales to consumption) or 100% of the target price (formula B). Thus, the SLOM was, and was intended to be, a swingeing levy that would surely dissuade farmers from producing and marketing milk beyond the reference quantities assigned to them. Provision was, naturally, made for "special situations";[14] and the system had sufficient flexibility to favour restructuring at national or regional level.[15] The Commission[16] and the Member States[17]

7 Recital 2. Significantly, no mention was made of the existence or effects of Regulation 1078/77, or of its effectiveness in curbing these surpluses.

8 Recital 4.

9 Regulation (EEC) No. 804/68 of the Council (OJ 1968 L 18, p. 13; English Special Edition 1968 p. 176).

10 Article 5c(1). Depending on the formula chosen by the Member State, the levy was payable by producer (formula A) or by purchaser (formula B).

11 Article 5c(3).

12 Article 5c(4).

13 Council Regulation (EEC) No. 857/84 (OJ 1984 L 90, p.13). It is perhaps an unfortunate gift to the uncharitable that Regulation 856/84 and Regulation 857/84 were both enacted on 1 April 1984.

14 Article 3 of Regulation 857/84.

15 Article 4.

16 Commission Regulation (EEC) No. 1371/84 (OJ 1984 L 132, p.11) – after frequent amendment, later consolidated in Commission Regulation (EEC) No. 1546/88 (OJ 1988 L 139, p.12).

17 E.g., in the Netherlands, by Order No J 1731 of 18 April 1984 (the "Beschikking superheffing" or "Super-levy Decree") (Staatscourant 79); in Germany, by the "Verordnung über die Abgaben im Rahmen von Garantiemengen im Bereich der Marktorganisation für Milch und Milcherzeugnisse" (Milch-Garantiemengen-Verordnung) ("the Milk Guaranteed Quantities Regulation") of 25 May 1984 (BGBl I, p. 720), as amended. In the UK, implementation was by statutory instrument (the Dairy Produce (Milk Quota) Regula-

duly put in place the necessary detailed rules and arrangements to administer the SLOM.

The difficulty about the new SLOM arrangements – one that apparently escaped the notice of the Community legislator throughout the process of examining and approving the new arrangements – was that there were a large number of milk farmers who had signed non-marketing undertakings in response to the previous Community measures, i.e., Regulation 1078/77. Inevitably, therefore, they had *no* milk production in the relevant reference years for their respective Member States. It was therefore impossible for them to obtain a reference quantity (other than "zero"). By the same token, however, they had never intended, by signing a non-marketing undertaking for five years, to place themselves in a position which would debar them from ever resuming milk production. They had merely meant to take up the offer of premiums in exchange for *temporary* non-marketing and *temporary* conversion.

At first sight, their position did not look particularly hopeful. It is well known that, in matters concerning the common agricultural policy, the Community legislature has a discretionary power which corresponds to the political responsibilities given to it by Articles 40 and 43 of the Treaty (now, Articles 34 and 37 EC); and that the Court's function in reviewing such measures is correspondingly limited. Thus, for example, when measured against the yardstick of proportionality, the legality of a measure adopted in the agricultural sphere can be affected only if the measure is manifestly inappropriate having regard to the objective which the competent institution is seeking to pursue.[18] Indeed, the Court had already confirmed the breadth of the Community institutions' discretion when operating in the milk sector in relation to the co-responsibility levy introduced by Regulation 1079/77.[19]

Two farmers in particular, Mr Mulder and Mr von Deetzen, who had signed undertakings and who found themselves shut out of the market for milk, brought actions before their respective national courts, challenging the national authorities' refusal to allocate them milk reference quantities. Mr Mulder had been delivering some 500,000 kg of milk prior to entering his non-marketing undertaking on 1 October 1979 and had made investments in August 1983 with a view to resuming dairy production at the end of the five-year non-marketing period.[20] Mr Von Deetzen had had a smaller production of 190,665 kg in 1980, when he entered his non-marketing undertaking; and sought that amount in 1985 as a reference quantity for the milk from his 40 cows so that, in due course, his youngest son could succeed him as a dairyman. The national courts duly made refer-

tions S.I. 1986 No 470).

18 See, e.g., Case C-331/88 *R. v. MAFF, ex parte FEDESA and others* [1990] ECR I-4023 at para. 14 and Case 265/87 *Schräder v. HZA Gronau* [1989] ECR 2237 at paras. 22-24.

19 See Case 138/78 *Stölting v. HZA Hamburg-Jonas* [1979] ECR 713 at para. 7 and Case 179/84 *Bozzetti v. Invernizzi SpA and Ministero del Tesoro* [1985] ECR 2301 at para. 30.

20 He had therefore sought a reference quantity of 726,000 kg (132 cows x 5,500 kg).

ences under Article 177 EC (now, Article 234).[21] The cases were retained before the full Court, Judge Everling acting as "juge rapporteur". Sir Gordon Slynn was the Advocate General.

The applicants put their cases in a number of ways, claiming that their exclusion from the milk markets violated the principle of legal certainty or "legitimate expectations", the principle of proportionality, their right to enjoy their property, the prohibition of discrimination laid down in Article 40(3) of the EEC Treaty (now Article 34(3) EC) and the prohibition on the misuse of powers. The core issue was, however, as straightforward as it was politically sensitive. The SLOM arrangements did not take into account persons who, in accordance with Regulation 1078/77, had delivered no milk in a reference year. Was that lawful?

In *Mulder I*, Sir Gordon began – as the first question referred requested – by looking at whether there was some way of construing the SLOM provisions for "special situations" so as to enable Mulder to be allocated a reference quantity under one of those headings. He reached the conclusion that the answer was, plainly, no: "I do not find it possible to read in such a power. To do so would in my view be to read in what is not there".[22] He therefore turned to the central question of whether the SLOM arrangements were, to that extent, void under general principles of Community law or contrary to the prohibition of discrimination found in Article 40(3) of the EEC Treaty. His analysis is a model of how to balance legislative discretion and respect for fundamental rights:

> "It is plain that when "quantities of milk delivered are increasing at a rate such that disposal of surpluses is imposing financial burdens and market difficulties which are jeopardizing the very future of the common agricultural policy" (third recital to Regulation No 856/84) stringent measures may have to be adopted and that some producers may be precluded from increasing or may be obliged to cut back production. Others may be precluded from entering the market. It is no less plain that the appreciation of the necessary measures is for the Council and the Commission but subject always to compliance with overriding rules of Community law such as those referred to in the second question. The starting point as I see it is whether those who have agreed not to market milk (in return for a premium) could be said to have accepted that they were leaving the market completely. Whatever the position of those who took the conversion premium, it does not seem to me that those who accepted the five-year non-marketing premium have done more than accept that they would not dispose of milk for a period of five years at a time when the Community wished to control milk production. They were suspending rather than terminating production. There was a mutual benefit – for the Community reduction in milk production, for the farmer an annual cash payment. There was nothing in the arrangement to insist, even to signal, that if the non-marketing premium was accepted, they would at the end of the period be out of business. This does not mean that they could assume that at the end of the period they could resume business as before. In the absence of

21 Case 120/86 *Mulder v. Minister van Landbouw en Visserij* ("*Mulder I*") [1988] ECR 2321 and Case 170/86 *Von Deetzen v. Hauptzollamt (HZA) Hamburg-Jonas* ("*Von Deetzen I*") [1988] ECR 2355. Since the arguments, and the reasoning of the Advocate General and of the Court, are very similar in the two cases, reference is here only made to *Mulder I*.

22 [1988] ECR at 2340.

an obligation entered into by the authorities they must accept restrictions as to the way their business is to be conducted which are subsequently adopted (Case 84/78 *Tomadini v Amministrazione delle Finanze dello Stato* ([1979]) ECR 1801 at 1815 (paragraph 21)). It seems to me, however, that they could reasonably expect at the end of the non-marketing period that the arrangements made for the control of the market would take into account the fact that they had given up production in the common interest and would not ignore them, nor, in business terms, exclude them totally from resuming production, which they had temporarily stopped, for a much longer period. To substitute a quota system (from which they were excluded because they had entered into a non-marketing arrangement limited to a five-year period) for such a non-marketing arrangement seems to me to be contrary to the legitimate business expectation of the farmers who took part in the non-marketing arrangements. It crosses the line between what is merely 'hard business luck' and what is unreasonable treatment."[23]

Sir Gordon went on to point out that such persons were in a different position from those who had never produced milk or who had given up production for reasons wholly unconnected with schemes adopted under the common organization of the market like the non-marketing premium scheme. It was therefore discriminatory to treat them all as if they were in the same position. Moreover, the system adopted did not treat with an even hand those in a similar position. Thus, a producer who signed a non-marketing undertaking in 1977, whose Member State adopted 1983 as the reference year, could have resumed production in 1983 so as to have a reference quantity. A producer who had signed the same undertaking in 1977 would fail if the Member State had taken 1981 as the reference year. If a producer had signed the same undertaking in 1979 or even late in 1978 he would not have been able to have a reference quantity whichever reference year was selected by the Member State.

Sir Gordon singled out one of the "special situations" which, under SLOM, gave entitlement to a special reference quantity for particular (and unfavourable) mention, as illustrative of the lack of clarity in the Council's approach.[24]

"(...) the fixing of 1 March 1984 (by a regulation published in the Official Journal on 1 April 1984) as the cut-off date for the lodging of a development plan or the making of investment without a plan (if there is such a temporal limitation as the institutions contend) is capable of discriminating between persons in a like position. To give prior warning "unless you invest by 'x' you are excluded" is quite different from saying that those who did not invest by 'x' (when the starting dates of the five-year period can be widely scattered) are post hoc excluded. In any event it seems to me that, even if there were power to give some reference quantities to persons who had accepted the non-marketing premium, these would have come out of the national reserve referred to in Article 5 of Regulation No 857/84. Assuming that there was something in such a reserve for such applicants, it seems probable that balancing out conflicting claims against vari-

23 [1988] ECR 2341.

24 This was the special situation potentially relevant to Mr Mulder, given his investments in the summer of 1983.

able available quantities could lead to very divergent grants in different Member States."[25]

Sir Gordon indicated that he did not consider that what had been done was to be categorized as misuse of powers or that there had been a violation of the right to enjoy property in the sense explained by the Court in *Hauer*,[26] in the absence of any discrimination or breach of legitimate expectations. Although the general scheme had not been shown to be more than was needed to achieve the objective sought to be achieved, he felt that it might be said that to leave out persons of the kind now being considered was itself disproportionate. "That, however, seems to me to be another way, and perhaps a more artificial way, of saying that what was done took away what such persons could reasonably have expected to receive on a non-discriminatory basis."[27]

Sir Gordon therefore concluded that the SLOM provisions were void in so far as they did not make any provision for the resumption of milk production by those who had contracted to give up production for a period of five years in return for a non-marketing premium and effectively excluded them from business, either on the ground that their legitimate expectations were not respected or that the scheme adopted was discriminatory.

To the Council's dismay, the Court followed the Advocate General. It was prepared to be slightly less absolute than he was (or, indeed, than the parties had been) about the possibility for Member States to allocate special reference quantities to farmers who had entered into non-marketing undertakings under the "special situations" provisions: they might do so, but "only in so far as each producer fulfils the specific conditions laid down in Regulation No. 857/84 and if the Member States have reference quantities available for that purpose".[28]

Turning to the central question, the Court followed Sir Gordon's analysis exactly:

> "It must be conceded (...) that a producer who has voluntarily ceased production for a certain period cannot legitimately expect to be able to resume production under the same conditions as those which previously applied and not to be subject to any rules of market or structural policy adopted in the meantime. The fact remains that where such a producer, as in the present case, has been encouraged by a Community measure to suspend marketing for a limited period in the general interest and against payment of a premium he may legitimately expect not to be subject, upon the expiry of his undertaking, to restrictions which specifically affect him precisely because he availed himself of the possibilities offered by the Community provisions. However, the regulations on the additional levy on milk give rise to such restrictions for producers who, pursuant to an undertaking entered into under Regulation No. 1078/77, did not deliver milk during the reference year (...) those producers may in fact be denied a reference quantity under the new system precisely because of that undertaking if they do not fulfil the specific conditions laid

25 *Supra* note 23, p. 2342.
26 Case 44/79 [1979] ECR 3727.
27 *Supra* note 23, p. 2343.
28 *Ibid.*, p. 2321, paragraph 20 of the judgment.

down in Regulation No. 857/84 or if the Member States have no reference quantities available. Contrary to the Commission's contention, total and continuous exclusion of that kind for the entire period of application of the regulations on the additional levy, preventing the producers concerned from resuming the marketing of milk at the end of the five-year period, was not an occurrence which those producers could have foreseen when they entered into an undertaking, for a limited period, not to deliver milk. There is nothing in the provisions of Regulation No. 1078/77 or in its preamble to show that the non-marketing undertaking entered into under that Regulation might, upon its expiry, entail a bar to resumption of the activity in question. Such an effect therefore frustrates those producers' legitimate expectation that the effects of the system to which they had rendered themselves subject would be limited. It follows that the regulations on the additional levy on milk were adopted in breach of the principle of protection of legitimate expectations. Those regulations must therefore be declared invalid on that ground, and it is unnecessary to consider the other arguments as to their invalidity put forward in the course of the proceedings".[29]

This was a triumph for individual rights. There *was* no way that the individual farmers could have foreseen the possibility of SLOM when they entered into non-marketing undertakings. Put more colloquially, it was as though they had bought open return tickets from London to Cambridge, only to have the return half of their ticket torn up at the ticket barrier in Cambridge when they tried to board the train back to London. Whether one approaches the case from English law principles of estoppel, or from the French administrative law concept of the "confiance légitime" which the "administré" is entitled to place in the administration, or from the analogous principle of "Vertrauensverschutz" in German administrative law, what had been done to those farmers stuck in the craw. It did indeed, as Sir Gordon rather more elegantly put it, "cross the line between what is merely 'hard business luck' and what is unreasonable treatment".

The Council was left with the question of how to comply with the Court's judgment without undermining the SLOM system. Unsurprisingly, it tried for minimum modification. The new arrangements it put in place[30] established a strict set of criteria with which farmers who had signed non-marketing or conversion undertakings had to comply before they could receive, provisionally, a special reference quantity. Even when those criteria were fulfilled, the special reference quantity was limited to 60% of the quantity of milk sold during the 12 calendar months before the start of the non-marketing or conversion period.[31] Producers whose period of non-marketing or conversion expired *before* 31 December 1983[32] were excluded from any entitlement.[33] The Community reserve

29 *Ibid.*, p. 2352-3, paragraphs 23 to 27 of the judgment.

30 Council Regulation (EEC) No. 764/89 (OJ 1989 L 84, p.2), inserting a new Article 3a into Regulation 857/84.

31 Article 3a(2). This limitation was "taking into account the overriding necessity of not jeopardising the fragile stability that currently obtains in the milk products sector" (recital 5).

32 Or before 30 September 1983 in Member States where the milk collection in the months April to September is at least twice that of the months October to the March of the following year.

was to be increased by 600,000 tonnes in order to create the necessary supplies to allow allocation of the special reference quantities.[34] The Commission duly made the necessary consequential amendments to the detailed rules for the application of the SLOM;[35] and the Community institutions must (understandably) have hoped that their difficulties were over.

The milk farmers were still not satisfied. Why were farmers whose period of non-marketing or conversion expired before a particular, magic, date excluded from obtaining a special reference quantity altogether? And why had those farmers who had managed to qualify only been given 60% of the reference quantity previously allocated to milk farmers who had been in continuous production?

Challenges to the new regime therefore came before the Court by way of two further references: *Spagl v. HZA Rosenheim*[36] and *Pastätter v. HZA Bad Reichenhall*.[37] The Court, unimpressed by the institutions' arguments,[38] held that both the specific limitations that the Council had chosen to apply were unlawful when viewed against the same principle of legitimate expectations that the Court had so firmly upheld in *Mulder I* and *Von Deetzen*.

Specifically, the Court held that the Community legislature was able validly to set a cut-off date by reference to the expiry of the non-marketing or conversion period, with a view to excluding from the benefit of the revised arrangements[39] those producers who had not delivered milk during the whole or part of the reference year for reasons unconnected with the undertaking as to non-marketing or conversion. What it could *not* do was to set the cut-off date in such a way that it had the effect of also excluding producers whose failure to deliver milk for the whole or part of the reference year derived from the fulfilment of a non-marketing undertaking.[40] Similarly, the Community legislature could validly apply to the volume of non-marketing producers' deliveries during a representative period preceding the non-marketing period or conversion period a reduction coefficient, designed to ensure that the category of producers con-

---

33 Article 3a(1) first indent.

34 Thus recital 5: interestingly, not mirrored by a substantive provision of the regulation itself.

35 Commission Regulation (EEC) No. 1033/89 (OJ 1989 L 110, p. 27), amending Regulation 1546/88.

36 Case C-189/89 [1990] ECR I-4539.

37 Case C-217/89 [1990] ECR I-4585.

38 These arguments were essentially pragmatic. For example, the Commission estimated that requests for the grant of special reference quantities made by producers who had given undertakings under Regulation 1078/77 would amount to approximately one million tonnes. It considered that an additional quantity of milk of 600,000 tonnes was the largest quantity compatible with the objective of the SLOM scheme. It had therefore increased the Community reserve by that quantity, kept the reference quantity of the other producers unchanged, and applied a 40% abatement rate.

39 I.e., Article 3a(1) of Regulation 857/84 as amended by Regulation 764/89.

40 At para. 13 of the judgment in *Spagl*.

cerned was not accorded an undue advantage by comparison with the producers who continued to deliver milk during the reference year.[41] However, where a reduction of that kind was applied, the principle of the protection of legitimate expectations precluded the rate of reduction from being fixed at such a high level, by comparison with those applicable to continuous producers, that its application amounted to a restriction which specifically affected the non-marketing producers by very reason of their non-marketing undertakings. The reduction of 40% provided for in Article 3a(2) of Regulation 857/84 as amended did not satisfy those requirements. A 40% abatement, far from being representative of the rates applicable to the continuous producers, was more than double the highest total of such rates (17.5%). It was to be regarded as a restriction which specifically affected the non-marketing producers by very reason of their undertakings. It was therefore impermissible.[42]

By now, the Council must have wished that it had never thought up the original non-marketing and conversion schemes. Again it went back to the drawing board. Deriving what comfort it could from hints dropped by the Court during the second rebuff, it re-amended[43] Regulation 857/84. As the Court has suggested, provision was made to increase national reserves. The abatement rate applied to non-marketing and conversion producers was now to be representative of all the abatements applied to *all* producers subject to the SLOM, including a basic reduction of 4.5% in reference quantities for deliveries. The qualifying dates were adjusted. Thus, the non-marketing and conversion producers were (finally) placed in a position neither better nor worse than if they had been in the market when reference quantities were introduced. The benefits of the new arrangements were limited to those whose reason for not delivering milk during the reference year was indeed their non-marketing or conversion undertaking.

Inevitably, of course, there were also damages claims by affected farmers against the Community institutions.[44] The Court first recalled the standard prin-

---

41 Para. 21 of *Spagl.*

42 Paras. 22-24 of *Spagl.* Mr Pastätter had entered into a conversion undertaking, rather than a non-marketing undertaking. The question referred in his case (C-217/89) concerned the application of the 40% abatement to his special reference quantity. The Court's conclusion and reasoning was as in *Spagl.* See also Case C-44/89 *Von Deetzen v. HZA Oldenburg* ("*Von Deetzen II*") [1991] ECR I-5119, in which the Court reiterated its rulings in *Spagl* and *Pastätter* in relation to the 40% abatement, but refused to rule that the special reference quantity should be transferable in the event of sale or lease of the holding.

43 Council Regulation (EEC) No. 1639/91 (OJ 1991 L 150, p.35). This regulation also dealt with the consequences of the Court's judgment in Case C-314/89 *Rauh v. HZA Nürnberg-Fürth* [1991] ECR I-1647, in which the Court had held – again, contrary to the Commission's urgings – that heirs and successors to a non-marketing producer likewise had rights of access to special reference quantities.

44 See Case C-104/89 *Mulder and others v. Council and Commission* ("*Mulder II*") [1992] ECR I-3061. Advocate General Van Gerven's Opinion contains a magisterial analysis of the chapter of SLOM disasters, and of the principles for the recovery of non-contractual damages from the Community institutions.

ciples that usually cause such claims to fail, precisely because of the high level of disregard for individual rights that the applicant must show:

> "The second paragraph of Article 215 of the Treaty provides that, in the case of non-contractual liability, the Community, in accordance with the general principles common to the laws of the Member States, is to make good any damage caused by its institutions in the performance of their duties. The scope of that provision has been specified in the sense that the Community does not incur liability on account of a legislative measure involving choices of economic policy unless a sufficiently serious breach of a superior rule of law for the protection of the individual has occurred (see, in particular, the judgment in Joined Cases 83 and 94/76, 4, 15 and 40/77 *HNL v Council and Commission* [1978] ECR 1209, paragraphs 4, 5 and 6). More specifically, in a legislative field such as the one in question, which is characterized by the exercise of a wide discretion essential for the implementation of the Common Agricultural Policy, the Community cannot incur liability unless the institution concerned has manifestly and gravely disregarded the limits on the exercise of its powers (see in particular the judgment in *HNL v Commission and Council*, paragraph 6).
>
> "The Court has also consistently held that, in order for the Community to incur non-contractual liability, the damage alleged must go beyond the bounds of the normal economic risks inherent in the activities in the sector concerned (see the judgments in Case 238/78 *Ireks-Arkady v Council and Commission* [1979] ECR 2955, paragraph 11, in Joined Cases 241, 242 and 245 to 250/78 *DGV v Council and Commission* [1979] ECR 3017, paragraph 11, in Joined Cases 261 and 262/78 *Interquell Stärke v Council and Commission* [1979] ECR 3045, paragraph 14, and in Joined Cases 64 and 113/76, 167 and 239/78, 27, 28 and 45/79 *Dumortier Frères v Council* [1979] ECR 3091, paragraph 11)."[45]

The Court went on to hold that those strict conditions were nevertheless fulfilled in the case of Regulation No. 857/84 as supplemented by Regulation No. 1371/84 (the original SLOM provisions). Those regulations were adopted in breach of the principle of the protection of legitimate expectations, which is a general and superior principle of Community law for the protection of the individual.[46] Insofar as it failed completely, without invoking any higher public interest, to take account of the specific situation of a clearly defined group of economic agents, that is to say, producers who, pursuant to an undertaking given under Regulation No 1078/77, delivered no milk during the reference year, the Community legislature had manifestly and gravely disregarded the limits of its discretionary power, thereby committing a sufficiently serious breach of a superior rule of law.[47] That breach was all the more obvious because the total and permanent exclusion of the producers concerned from the allocation of a reference quantity, which in fact prevented them from resuming the marketing of milk when their non-marketing or conversion undertaking expired, could not be regarded as being foreseeable or as falling within the bounds of the normal eco-

45 At paras. 12 and 13 of the judgment.
46 Para. 15.
47 Para. 16.

nomic risks inherent in the activities of a milk producer.[48] In contrast, the *second* error by the Council (the 60% rule applied when assigning special reference quantities to non-marketing farmers which the Court had declared unlawful in *Spagl* and *Pastätter*) was not capable of founding a claim in damages.[49]

As well as facing the political embarrassment and the considerable administrative inconvenience and difficulty generated by all the SLOM litigation, the Community institutions therefore also found themselves footing some of the bill for the damage flowing from the original SLOM measures.[50]

And all because Advocate General Slynn and the Court couldn't stomach a little basic injustice ...

48 Para. 17.

49 See paras. 18-21.

50 For the detailed analysis of what damage, how calculated, was deemed recoverable, see paras. 23-38 of the judgment.

36

FROM CO-OPERATION TO INTEGRATION: THE RELATIONSHIP BETWEEN NATIONAL AND EUROPEAN COMPETITION LAW THROUGH JUDICIAL REVIEW

Michael Reynolds

I INTRODUCTION

It is an enormous personal pleasure to be asked to contribute to this festschrift in honour of Lord Slynn. The contribution he has made to the development of European law has been colossal. He has tirelessly worked to teach and guide many lawyers in the United Kingdom, in Europe and around the world about our European legal system and as he nears seventy these efforts continue at an unflagging pace. I have been privileged to know and work with him for at least fifteen of these years and he has been a major inspiration and guide in my own work and practice.

The application of European Competition law at national level has traditionally been one of the areas of EC law in which the tension between the national systems and the supranational EC legal order has been most rich, prolific and creative, or to borrow a word from the modern lexicon, "interactive". Judge Bellamy has explained how, historically, the body of common law case law on illegality of price agreements and certain other restrictive agreements migrated across the Atlantic and was taken up in the US Sherman Act.[1] In a bizarre cycle of legal history those concepts, as subsequently developed by the American legislators, were reintroduced in Europe in the ECSC and EC Treaties. Over the recent years the circle has been completed with the introduction of national legislation modelled on the EC system. This occurred both in jurisdictions where there was no previous competition law tradition, for instance in Italy or Spain, and in jurisdictions where there was a strong tradition in this area of law such as in the UK where the new 1998 Competition Act is now designed to mirror the EC provisions. Judicial review and the body of case law developed by the European Court has given a decisive contribution towards this legislative process of uniformisation and decentralisation. As a result, the function performed by European judicial review has now entered into a new historic phase in which ef-

1 C. Bellamy, "The Europeanisation of UK Competition Law", in *The Europeanisation of UK Competition Law*, Green and Robertson (eds.), (1999, Hart Publishing).

D. O'Keeffe (ed.), Liber Amicorum Slynn 569-579 (2000)

fective decentralisation has to be guided and reconciled with a consistent approach at national level. Of course this need is even greater in the light of the reforms set out in the White Paper on Modernisation of the Rules Implementing Articles 81 and 82 of the EC Treaty.[2]

This article in honour of one of the most creative contributors to the case law of the ECJ will deal with two aspects of European judicial review. On the one hand we will look at how judicial review operates in the context of the decentralised application of EC competition rules. On the other hand we will see how EC judicial review has stimulated a process of legislative decentralisation and uniformation of national competition rules and in doing so created new functions for the courts in the European Union.

II DECENTRALISED APPLICATION OF ARTICLES 81 AND 82 (EX ARTICLES 85 AND 86)

The roots of decentralisation are based on direct effect of the EC Treaty competition law provisions. It has been clear for a long time that national courts and tribunals are competent to deal with Articles 81 and 82.[3] However, the Commission has remained the privileged forum for competition disputes. There have been a number of reasons for this.

Most importantly, up to now the Commission has retained exclusive jurisdiction to grant Article 81(3) exemptions by virtue of the centralised system set up by Article 9(1) of Regulation 17/62. At the heart of the European Competition law system the Commission retained the strongest monopoly of all, that of granting an exemption under Article 81(3). This limits the relief that a national court or authority can offer. Provided that the trans-national element required by the EC provision was satisfied (and the Commission has always taken a "liberal stance" in interpreting this criterion), this system contributed to make the European institution the natural forum for competition disputes. A number of practical considerations pushed the Commission towards its role as a privileged forum for competition disputes. A common argument has traditionally been that it is cheaper and more informal complaining to the Commission rather than litigating before national courts. Whilst it is true that complaining to the Commission can be done cheaply and informally, complaints are more likely to be acted on if they are well documented.[4] They are often preceded by meetings with Commission officials which require briefing papers; it is often necessary for a complainant to participate in the proceedings and, for example, comment on the Statement of Objections and appear at the oral hearing. Other significant advantages

---

2 Adopted by European Commission on 26 April, 1999.

3 Case 127/73 *BRT* v *Sabam*, [1974] ECR 51; see generally R. Whish, "The Enforcement of EC Competition Law, in Domestic Courts of Member States", (1994) 2 ECLR, 60.

4 House of Lords, Select Committee on the European Communities, "Enforcement of Community Competition Rules", Session 93-94, Memorandum by Mr. Reynolds p.12.

of proceedings before the Commission may include access to the considerable powers to obtain documents and information which would by-pass the procedural hurdles that may be encountered in proceeding before national courts and the availability of interim measures which can be used throughout the Union.[5] An equally important role has been played by another strategic aspect: the Commission is likely to be more "flexible and creative" than a national judge who will in most cases simply apply the law as he finds it without bearing in mind wider concerns of competition policy or Community objectives generally.

On the other hand the Commission, in an attempt to stimulate a decentralised application of Community competition law by national courts, has summarised what, in its opinion, are the advantages in applying to the national courts:

(a) the Commission cannot award compensation for loss suffered as a result of an infringement of Article 81 or 82; such claims may be brought only before the national courts; companies are more likely to avoid infringements of the Community competition rules if they risk having to pay damages or interest in such an event;
(b) national courts can usually adopt interim measures and order the ending of infringements more quickly than the Commission is able to do;
(c) before national courts it is possible to combine a claim under Community law with a claim under national law. This is not possible in a procedure before the Commission;
(d) in some Member States, the courts have the power to award legal costs to the successful applicant; this is never possible in the administrative procedure before the Commission.[6]

To a certain extent, the attractiveness of Brussels as the favoured forum for competition disputes (particularly those concerning costs) has been diluted by the availability of similar procedures before competition authorities at national level. However, in cases with a "European dimension" (i.e. when there was an effect on trade between Member States) Article 9(1) of Regulation 17 has, up to now, created an insurmountable barrier to full decentralisation. The Commission has decided to find a radical legislative solution to this problem. In April 1999, recognising the changes and development in competition law since the system was adopted in 1962 and acknowledging the more mature level of understanding of the issues at stake, the Commission proposed a new system of allocation of competencies.[7] The proposed system, based on a Council Regulation, would

5 It has been suggested that complainants have substantially greater procedural rights under Community law than in national systems; see XVIIIth FIDE Congress, Stockholm, 3-6 June 1998, National Application of Community Competition Law, general report by J. Temple Lang, p. 287.

6 See Notice on co-operation between national courts and the Commission in applying Articles 85 and 86 [now 81 and 82] of the EC Treaty, OJ 1993, C 39/6, para. 16.

7 See the "White Paper on Modernisation of the Rules Implementing Article 81 and 82 of

stipulate that all national authorities or courts before which the applicability of Article 81(1) was invoked would also consider the applicability of Article 81(3). To use the expression used by the Commission in its White Paper, "*Article [81] would then become a unitary norm comprising a rule establishing the principle of prohibition, unless certain conditions are met. The whole Article [81] would then become a directly applicable provision which individuals could invoke in court or before any authority empowered to deal with such matters.*"[8]

The Commission had already stressed in its Notice on co-operation between national courts and the Commission[9] that it intends to concentrate on cases that have a "particular political, economic or legal significance for the Community." In the Notice on co-operation with national competition authorities[10] the concept of cases of particular significance to the Community was expanded and clarified. The Notice stated that they include cases which raise a new point of law (that is to say which has not been subject of a Commission decision or a judgment of a European Court), cases where access to the relevant market by firms of other Member States is significantly impeded, or cases involving alleged anti-competitive behaviour by a public undertaking.

If the reforms envisaged by the White Paper go ahead, the Commission will strengthen these features even further. It intends to focus more on the legislative and competition policy-making roles by producing legislative texts and more notices and guidelines to explain its policy and provide guidance for the application of Community competition rules.[11] The White Paper envisages that in a directly applicable exemption system, the Commission would continue to take prohibition decisions in cases involving the most serious restrictions and "individual decisions that are not prohibition decisions."[12] Whilst it is not yet clear how the allocation of competence would work in practice,[13] a system such as this would give the Commission the role of guardian of legal consistency. This system would entrust the Commission with a guiding function directed particularly at decentralised enforcers (i.e. national competition authorities and national courts). Of course this function would still be subject to the ruling of the Court of Justice but the ultimate aim seems to be to pre-empt the need for a judicial review by setting clear guidelines in leading cases. The system of decentralised application of competition law postulates a number of adjustments to the current body of principles. Most importantly, national authorities would have to be al-

---

the EC Treaty", published 28th April, 1999.

8 See para. 69 of the White Paper.

9 Para. 14.

10 OJ 1997, C 313/3, paras. 33 and 34.

11 Para. 86 of the White Paper.

12 Para. 88 of the White Paper.

13 At least initially we understand that the system would be based on a pragmatic and informal system of cases allocation. This might cause a certain degree of confusion.

lowed to use evidence obtained by the Commission, thereby reversing the effects of the Spanish Banks judgment.[14]

The risk of a system such as this is that a policy-making function based on precedents develops unpredictably. It would be interesting to see whether the allocation of competence would allow the Commission to cream off the cases in which a combination policy-making and judicial role is required. In any event, the Commission clearly intends to give up a lot of its current quasi-judicial functions. The corollary of an enhanced role of national competition authorities and national courts, is a stronger need for some form of judicial review to ensure the unity of the system. To the extent that the Commission will not succeed through its "preventive" action by setting out policy and deciding most important cases, this will probably reflect on European courts through the complaints that are taken to court and may be subject to preliminary references under Article 234 EC (formerly Article 177 of the EC Treaty).

Furthermore we believe that the decentralised direct applicability of Article 81(3) could be an opportunity to promote a more mature approach in the analysis of the pro- and anti-competitive aspects of restrictive practices of Article 81(1). Regrettably, in the White Paper, the Commission states[15] that it has adopted this rule of reason approach to Article 81(1) only to "a limited extent". This is despite the fact that the European Court of Justice has endorsed this interpretation in a number of cases.[16] It is somewhat surprising that the Commission has used this analysis only "to a limited extent". The influence of the case law of the ECJ might have a stronger impact at national level. The risk is that there might be some confusion between the application of Article 81(1) and 81(3).

Some confusion has already emerged in the White Paper. The application of a rule of reason as interpreted by the Court does not affect the analysis under Article 81(3). Under Article 81(3) it is not necessary to consider whether an agreement or a practice has a material impact on competition but whether there are other benefits which counterbalance the restrictive effects of that agreement or practice. The Commission appears to be of the opinion that a more systematic use of a rule of reason approach would "cast aside" Article 81(3).[17] On the contrary, we believe that the Article 81(1) analysis should be kept clearly separate and the application of a rule of reason should be encouraged both at EC and national level. It is submitted that this would not be in contrast with a decentralised direct applicability of Article 81(3) as proposed in the White Paper.

14 Case C-67/91, *Asociación Espânola de Banca Privada* [1992] ECR I 4785.

15 Paragraph 57.

16 Case 258/78 *L.C. Nungesser and Kurt Eisele* v *Commission* [1982] ECR 2015 and Case 161/84 *Pronuptia de Paris GmbH* v *Pronuptia de Paris Irmgard Schillgalis* [1986] ECR 353.

17 Paragraph 57.

III Process of Legislative Decentralisation

We mentioned above that we believe that the process of judicial review and the direct effect of EC Treaty provisions of competition law stimulated a process of "legislative decentralisation" whereby Community rules have been reflected in national legislation. Whilst this statement might sound "dogmatic", it is indisputable that the majority of Member States now have legislation similar to Articles 81 and 82.[18] This development undoubtedly facilitates decentralisation. However, the application of EC provisions by the national courts may also create scope for inconsistency between national law and Community law.

The principle which has to inform this relationship between application of national law and Community law has been set out in *Ahmed Saeed.*[19] In that case the ECJ stated that national regulatory authorities should not approve under national law, agreements or practices which are contrary to Community competition law. The implication of this judgment, based on Article 10 EC (formerly Article 5 of the EC Treaty), is that national competition authorities should consult the Commission to ensure that they do not breach Community law. Furthermore this principle exposes the action of national authorities to attacks under judicial review in cases of infringement of EC competition law.[20] It can be argued that the principle of *Ahmed Saeed* applies *a fortiori* to competition authorities as well as to national regulatory authorities. The far reaching implications of this and other judgments of ECJ[21] is that "any national competition authority asked to approve an agreement or a merger under national competition law should always ask itself the question whether the agreement or merger is contrary to Community competition law even if it has no power under national legislation to apply Community competition law."[22] We will examine below more specifically the relationship between national law and Community law in cases of national provisions expressly requiring interpretation in accordance with Community law.

An uneven area in the harmonious application of national and Community competition law has already arisen with regard to exemptions to Article 81 and more restrictive national laws. Whilst it seems clear that national courts can apply the block exemption regulations, it is arguable that the principle of supremacy of EC law might be at odds with a stricter national law. Advocate General Tesauro (as he then was) raised the issue (that was subsequently not addressed by the Court) by stating that when a group or individual exemption is applicable to an agreement a stricter national law cannot be applied to it.[23] Whilst of course

---

18 *Supra* note 5.

19 Case 66/86 *Ahmed Saeed Flugreisen* [1989] ECR 803.

20 *Supra* note 5.

21 Case C-312/93 *Peterbroeck* [1995] ECR I 4599, Case 103/88 *Costanzo* [1989] ECR 1839.

22 *Supra* note 5.

23 Case C-70/93 *BMW* v *ALD Auto-Leasing*, [1995] ECR I 3439 per AG Tesauro para. 33

national law applies to agreements that do not affect trade between Member States the approach advocated by Tesauro reduces the scope for application of national law in a system where the Commission has the exclusive power to grant exemptions. The Commission seems to have expressed a similar view in the Notice on co-operation between national courts and the Commission by saying that an individual exemption given by the Commission must be respected by national courts[24] and, arguably precludes them from applying an inconsistent national law. The new approach taken by the Commission in its White Paper will to a certain extent remove those concerns.

In 1969 the ECJ recognised the parallel application of Community and national competition law subject to the condition that the application of national law must prejudice the full and uniform application of Community law or the effects of measures taken or to be taken to implement it.[25] The parallel application of two systems (the Community and the national) as envisaged at the early stages of the Community legal system[26] is now to be revised also in the light of decentralised application of Community law. The fact that the same courts and enforcers are increasingly responsible for applying the whole regime of Community law, including individual exemptions, might reduce the risk of inconsistencies between the two regimes. However, this will of course increase the risk of inconsistency within the Community system as a whole due to its decentralised application. It is submitted that this new structure will create a new pressure on European judicial review to ensure that these discrepancies are kept to a minimum.

However, Community competition law has influenced the national courts, not only in their general approach but also in a more radical way which varies from having an impact on interpretation of national legislation in the light of Community law to fully fledged legislative changes in the national regimes of competition law. Within these systems European judicial review and the system of preliminary references to the ECJ has and will play a substantial role.

in which he criticises recital 29 of Regulation 125/85 on the group exemption for car distribution which envisaged the application of a stricter national law; the point is reiterated in the same terms in Case C-266/93 *BKA* v *Volkswagen* [1995] ECR I 3477 per AG Tesauro, para. 46.

24 Notice on co-operation between national courts and the Commission in applying Articles 85 and 86 of the EC Treaty, OJ 1993, C 39/6, para. 25. See also Notice on co-operation between competition authorities and the Commission, para. 19.

25 Case 14/68 *Walt Wilhem* v. *Bundeskartellamt* [1969] ECR 1; see also Case 258/78 and 1-3/79 *Procurateur de la République iv. Giry and Guerlain* [1980] ECR 2327.

26 R. Walz, "Rethinking Walt Wilhem, or the supremacy of Community Competition Law over National Law", (1996) 21 ECLR, 449, see also B. Doherty, "Community Exemptions in National Law", (1994) 6 ECLR, 315.

IV NEW VARIETY OF PRELIMINARY REFERENCES AND CO-EXISTENCE OF EC AND NATIONAL LAW

A recent example of the influence of Community law in interpreting national competition rules has arisen in clear terms in *Oscar Bronner*.[27] The Austrian Court which made the preliminary reference argued that,[28] if the conduct of a market participant falls within the terms of Article 81 of the Treaty, then it must logically constitute an abuse within the meaning of Paragraph 35 of the *Kartellgesetz*, which has analogous content.[29] The Austrian Court made the preliminary reference not on the basis that Article 81 was applicable as such but that a ruling might assist the national court in applying its national law.

Advocate General Jacobs was doubtful as to whether it would be appropriate for the Court to rule on that basis. He seemed to accept the Commission's view which pointed out that the Austrian provisions on competition are not based directly on Community competition law and do not refer to it. He concluded that the case at issue was different from those where there is a direct link between national law and Community law such as, for example, where a national law consists of direct transposition of Community law.[30] Nevertheless, Advocate General Jacobs considered that the ruling was justified on the basis that "*the field of competition law has special features which should lead the Court to give a ruling, at least in cases where there is an effect on intra-Community trade.*"[31] On the basis that in the situation examined by the Court Article 86 applied, and, in the light of the uncertainty in the application of national law in cases falling within the scope of the Treaty provisions on competition law, the reference was found justifiable by the Advocate General. He stated "*against this background it is understandable that a national court even if it were competent solely to apply national law, should wish, especially where there is an effect on trade between Member States, to obtain guidance on the position under Community law with a view to achieving, where possible, an analogous result under its national rules.*"[32] To reinforce his reasoning which appears perfectly reasonable but possibly lacking legal rigour, the Advocate General stated that "*the above discus-*

---

27 Case C-7/97, *Oscar Bronner*, [1998] ECR I-7791.

28 See Case C-7/97, *Oscar Bronner*, [1998] ECR I-7791 per AG Jacobs para. 6.

29 Paragraph 35 of the *Kartellgesetz* provides that "The *Kartellgericht* shall, upon application, order the undertaking concerned to bring the abuse of a dominant position to an end. Such abuse may consist in particular, of: (1) directly or indirectly imposing unfair purchase or selling prices or other trading conditions; (2) limiting production, markets or technical development to the detriment of consumers; (3) placing other trading parties at a competitive disadvantage by applying dissimilar conditions to equivalent transactions; (4) making the conclusion of contracts subject to the acceptance by other trading parties of supplementary obligations which, by their own nature or according to commercial usage, have no connection with the subject matter of such contracts.

30 See above para. 20.

31 See above para. 21.

32 Para. 22.

sion is in my view hypothetical since, as already stated, it is clear that a national court hearing a claim such as that in the main proceedings must be able to apply Article 86 directly [and] the fact that Article 86 has not been invoked before the national court in the main proceedings does not call in question the Court's jurisdiction to provide the ruling sought."[33]

The ECJ took a more pragmatic and legalistic approach to the matter. It considered that it is for the national courts alone which are seized of the case and are responsible for the judgment to be delivered to determine both the need for a preliminary ruling in order to enable them to give their judgment and the relevance of the questions which they put to the Court.[34] The Court also noted that Article 177 of the Treaty, (now Article 234 EC) which is based on a clear separation of functions between national courts and the ECJ, does not allow the ECJ to review the reasons for which reference is made. Therefore a request from a national court may be rejected only if it is quite obvious that the interpretation of Community law or the validity of a rule of Community law sought by that court bears no relation to the actual facts of the case or to the subject matter of the main action.[35]

This statement potentially opens the way to a number of references by national courts in all those "purely internal" actions in which national legislation expressly refers to the Community law or case law. This issue has already been dealt with by the Court in another interesting case, *Leur-Bloem*.[36] In that case the question was whether the Court had jurisdiction under Article 177 (now Article 234 EC) of the Treaty to interpret Community law where Community law does not directly govern the situation in question but the national legislator has chosen, in transposing provisions of a directive into domestic law, to treat purely internal situations and those governed by a directive in the same way, thereby aligning its legislation to Community law. This question was answered by the Court in the affirmative. The Court noted that its case law had consistently held that "*it has jurisdiction to give preliminary rulings on questions concerning Community provisions in situations where the facts of the cases being considered by the national courts were outside the scope of Community law but where those provisions had been rendered applicable either by domestic law or merely by virtue of terms in a contract.*"[37] However, the Court has refused jurisdiction in cases in which the preliminary reference concerned a national law which took Community law (or, as in the specific case, the Brussels Convention) only as a

33 Para. 23.

34 Para. 16 of the judgment.

35 See paragraph 17 quoting Case C-446/93 *SEIM* v *Subdirector-Geral das Alfândegas* [1996] ECR I-73, para. 28.

36 Case C-28/95 *Leur-Bloem* v *Inspecteur der Belastingdienst/Ondernemingen Amsterdam 2* [1997] ECR I-4161.

37 Paragraph 27 which refers to Joined Cases C-297/88 and C-197/89 *Dzodi* [1990] ECR I3763; and Case C-231/89 *Gmurzyska-Bscher* [1990] ECR I-4003; Case 166/84 *Thomasdünger* [1985] ECR 3001; Case C-384/89 *Tomatis and fulchiron* [1991] ECR I-127.

model and only partially reproduced its terms without rendering Community law applicable as such.[38] The situation that has developed throughout the European Union over the last few years is that many countries have adopted national legislation based on Community law or which uses Community law as a model and follows with various degrees of resemblance. Some countries, including the United Kingdom, are now at the "Euro-friendly end" of this spectrum. Section 60 of the Competition Act 1998 contains in Section 60 a provision whereby "*so far as is possible (having regard to any relevant differences between the provisions concerned), questions arising under this Part in relation to competition within the United Kingdom are dealt with in a manner which is consistent with the treatment of corresponding questions arising in Community law in relation to competition within the Community*". English courts are under an obligation to act with a view to securing that there is no inconsistency between the principles applied, and decision reached, by the court in determining that question; and the principles laid down by the Treaty and the European Court, and any relevant decision of that Court, as applicable at that time in determining any corresponding question arising in Community law.

Clearly these provisions of the UK Competition Act encourage (or at least enable) the use of preliminary references in purely internal matters. In this sense (the case law of) the European Courts has potentially a new role. It contributes indirectly a form of integration between national and Community regimes. Furthermore this interrelation can be beneficial in another respect. Through an application of national law consistent with Community law one can, to a certain extent, aim at ensuring that national courts are familiar with the use of Community competition rules that they will be called to apply directly.

V CONCLUSIONS

It is clear that the Commission's policy of co-operation has now taken the route of decentralisation. This seems to be an irreversible and necessary direction. There is much to be decided as to the implementation of this structure. Many aspects will be refined with practice. However, it seems that the very idea of decentralised application of EC competition law is based on co-operation. At present the Commission seems to favour an informal approach and it seems that this is the most pragmatic solution. However, one has to bear in mind the need to provide legal certainty and the avoidance of forum shopping.

In this process we believe that the ECJ case law has provided an indirect support to the general process of decentralisation. The direct applicability of EC Treaty provisions on competition law has, over the years, enabled some national courts to familiarise themselves with these issues. Nevertheless the burden of case load and the pressure that national courts and authorities may face with the

38 See Case C-346/93 *Kleinwort Benson* [1995] ECR I-615, paragraph 16.

direct applicability of 81(3) EC is potentially substantial. The understanding of all the issues involved in a competition analysis will not be easy for a judge who is not familiar with these types of dispute. It has been argued that national courts might be supported by a law officer in each Member State, an *amicus curiae* with an economic and/or EC law expertise.[39] This solution struggles to reach the necessary consensus and bears the risk of creating an unnecessary procedural burden in national proceedings.

The EC case law has had another more important and subtle influence on the national systems of competition law. It has provided the bedrock for the greater harmonisation of national systems upon the model of the EC rules. In turn this facilitates a decentralised application of EC law by the national courts of authorities and enhances integration of the two systems. We believe that EC courts will have a major role in ensuring that uniformity and consistency is maintained in this historical process of transition.

39 See J. Temple Lang, "Decentralised enforcement of Community Competition Law, Paper delivered at a conference on "Modernisation & Decentralisation: the new relationship between Community and national competition law", Organised by UCL on 17th September 1999.

37

COLLECTIVE DOMINANCE

*Richard Whish**

I INTRODUCTION

One of the most complex and controversial issues in Community competition law has been the application – or non-application – of Article 82 (ex Article 86) EC and the EC Merger Regulation (hereafter the "ECMR") to so-called "collective dominance".[1] Discussion of this question in relation to Article 82 can be traced back at least to the early 1970s;[2] an enormous body of literature has developed on the same issue under the ECMR.[3] The law and decisional practice on collective dominance, under both legal instruments, developed considerably in 1999; of particular importance are the Court of First Instance's judgment in *Gencor v Commission*[4] and the Commission's decision under the ECMR in *Airtours/First Choice*.[5] These, and other, cases and decisions will be examined fur-

* I would like to thank Cristina Caffara of Lexecon and Professor Val Karah of University College London for helpful comments on an earlier draft; and also Christopher Brown, my research assistant at the Centre of European Law, King's College London, for his invaluable assistance during the writing of this essay.

1 The expressions "collective dominance", "joint dominance" and "oligopolistic dominance" tend to be used interchangeably. In Joined Cases C-395/96 P and C-396/96 P *Compagnie Maritime Belge NV v Commission* (judgment pending) Fennelly AG stated at paragraph 15 of his opinion of 29 October 1998 that he saw no meaningful distinction between these terms, but would himself use the expression "collective dominance" as this was the one that the Court itself usually employed. In Case IV/M. 1524 *Airtours/First Choice*, decision of 22 September 1999, the Commission said that it would use the terms "collective dominance" and "oligopolistic dominance" interchangeably (at paragraph 58). In this essay, the practice of the ECJ and Fennelly AG will be followed.

2 See footnote 14 below.

3 See for example Whish and Sufrin "Oligopolistic Markets and EC Competition Law" (1992) 12 *Oxford Yearbook of European Law* 59; Winkler and Hansen "Collective Dominance under the EC Merger Control Regulation" (1993) 30 CMLRev 787; Briones "Oligopolistic Dominance: is there a Common Approach in Different Jurisdictions?" (1995) 16 ECLR 334; Venit "Two Steps Forward and No Steps Back: Economic Analysis and Oligopolistic Dominance after Kali und Salz" (1998) 35 CMLRev 1101; Korah "Gencor v Commission: Collective Dominance" (1999) 20 ECLR 337.

4 Case T-102/96, [1999] 4 CMLR 971.

5 Case IV/M. 1524 *Airtours/First Choice* (decision of 22 September 1999); the case is on appeal to the CFI in *Airtours v Commission* (judgment pending).

D. O'Keeffe (ed.), Liber Amicorum Slynn 581-609 (2000)

ther in this essay. As we enter the new millennium, it can be stated with confidence that both Article 82 and the ECMR are capable of application, respectively, to the abuse of a collective dominant position and to concentrations that would create or strengthen a collective dominant position, and that the Commission is now paying closer attention to this issue than ever before. There is greater clarity, as a matter of economics, as to why collective dominance might be of concern to a competition authority. However, by no means all of the legal and economic problems associated with collective dominance are resolved, and it can be anticipated that this is a subject that will continue to attract close scrutiny and to be the subject of litigation for many years to come.

II THE LINGUISTIC BACKGROUND

There is a linguistic background to the matters discussed in this essay. Article 82 applies to "[a]ny abuse *by one or more undertakings* of a dominant position within the common market" (emphasis added). The same wording has been adopted in numerous domestic systems of competition law, both in the Member States themselves[6] and in third countries, particularly those in the "queue" for accession to the Union.[7] The fact that Article 82 is capable of application to dominance held on the part of more than one undertaking clearly envisages the possibility, though not the inevitability, of "collective" dominance being enjoyed by legally and economically separate undertakings; a narrow reading would be that the reference to more than one undertaking refers to different legal entities within the same corporate group.[8] In contradistinction to Article 82, Article 2(3) of the ECMR provides that a concentration that creates or strengthens a dominant position as a result of which competition would be significantly impeded in the common market or a substantial part of it may be declared incompatible with the common market; however this provision does not refer specifically to a dominant position *enjoyed by one or more undertakings*. Linguistically, therefore, it could be argued – as indeed it was by France, Société Commerciale des Potasses et de l'Azote (SCPA) and Entreprise Minière et Chemique (EMC) in the *Kali und Salz* case[9] – that the ECMR applies only to single firm dominance, even if Article 82 is capable of application to collective dominance. It has taken many years for the Community Courts to determine the proper scope of Article 82 and the ECMR: in each case in favour of the application of the measure in question to collective dominance.

6 See for example section 18 of the UK Competition Act 1998.

7 See for example section 9 of the Maltese Competition Act 1994.

8 See page 587 below.

9 Cases C-68/94 and 30/95 *France v Commission* [1998] ECR I-1375, [1998] 4 CMLR 829.

III THE ECONOMICS OF COLLECTIVE DOMINANCE[10]

Discussion of collective dominance as a legal concept is sterile in the absence of a consideration of why, as a matter of economics, a competition authority would be interested in the subject at all. There is a vast literature on the "problem" of oligopoly. Oligopoly is a phenomenon that exists somewhere on the continuum that begins at monopoly and ends at perfect competition, or "polypoly", where "mono" means one, "oligo" a few and the first "poly" in polypoly means many. The expression oligopoly is not entirely helpful in describing the situation of concern for competition authorities, since there are many markets in which there are only a few sellers and yet which are highly competitive; and there are others in which there may be many economic operators, and yet a failure of the competitive market mechanism. Some oligopolies are "benign" in terms of competition; others may be malign where they are particularly conducive to uncompetitive outcomes. For this reason, it is increasingly recognised that to address the problem of "oligopoly" is to miss the correct target. The expression oligopoly simply means "sale by a few sellers", but it is not the fact of "fewness", in itself, that is the problem. To depict the problem simply as a matter of numbers does not do full justice to economists' concept of "power over a market". It is market power (whether individual or collective) that confers the ability to suppress output and to raise price, to the detriment of consumers. It is no doubt true that the fewer the number of players in a market, the more likely it is that market power will exist; however the identification of market power cannot simply be a matter of counting heads. For this reason it is preferable to address the issue of "collective dominance" which, whilst not necessarily itself the perfect linguistic construct for the phenomenon in question, nevertheless connotes, through use of the expression "dominance", the power to behave independently of competitors, customers and ultimately consumers.

There is little doubt that there are markets in which it is possible for economic operators to coordinate their behaviour, without entering into an agreement or being party to a concerted practice in the sense of Article 81(1) (ex Article 85(1)) EC, and thereby to charge higher prices than they would be able to do without coordination; such behaviour will be to their own self-advantage and to the disadvantage of customers and ultimately consumers. This situation is often described by economists as "tacit collusion": enjoying the benefits of a particular market structure without actually entering into an agreement to do so; if the firms in question had achieved the same end through explicit collusion, economists would have the same objection – that prices would be higher than they would be in competitive market conditions. Economists have no particular

10 See Scherer and Ross, *Industrial Structure and Economic Performance* (3rd edition, 1990) chapters 6-8; Tirole, *The Theory of Industrial Organisation* (1988) chapter 6; Bishop and Walker, *The Economics of EC Competition Law* (1999) paragraphs 2.19-2.26; National Economic Research Associates, *Merger Appraisal in Oligopolistic Markets* (1999, OFT Research Paper 19).

interest in whether collusion is "tacit" or "explicit": it is the effects of the collusion that matter. Lawyers however are considerably less comfortable with the expression tacit collusion. "Collusion" is the evil at which Article 81 is directed ("any *agreement* ... or *concerted practice* ... which has as its object or effect the prevention, restriction or distortion of competition"); in the same way, section 1 of the US Sherman Act forbids "every *contract* in restraint of trade" where the notion of collusiveness is inherent in the idea of contract. For many lawyers, to ask whether tacit collusion could be caught by a theory of collective dominance under Article 82 appears to be a bizarre question, since any behaviour that could be called collusive in a legal sense would be caught by Article 81 anyway. If it is not collusive in the sense of Article 81, lawyers not unnaturally feel uncomfortable at characterising the same behaviour as collusive under Article 82. An alternative expression for the conduct in question, "conscious parallelism", may cause lawyers slightly less discomfort, the opprobrious word "collusive" being avoided; but even "consciousness" seems to move the enquiry back to a search for something sufficiently conspiratorial that it should really be investigated, if at all, under Article 81. In the interests of finding terminology which is meaningful and tolerable both to economists and to lawyers when considering the application of Article 82, it might be better to use the expression "tacit coordination", since this at least eliminates the pejorative word "collusion" while retaining the notion of parallel behaviour which is beneficial to the collectively dominant operators on the market and disadvantageous to customers and consumers.

For tacit coordination to occur, it is necessary for firms to indulge in a common form of behaviour. Typically this would involve the charging of similar prices; however it might also involve parallel decisions to reduce production or not to expand capacity: such decisions would, through the suppression of output, in themselves have an impact on prices in the industry in question. Tacit coordination also requires that each firm will be able to monitor quickly and easily how the others are behaving on the market: successful parallel behaviour requires that no one should cheat by deviating from the common conduct, so that transparency is vital to each economic operator to enable it to know what the others are doing, both in terms of their prices and the volume of their output. Finally it is important that discipline among the collectively dominant firms can be enforced. The benefits to the few of tacit coordination will be lost if one or more firms cheat by departing from the appropriate behavioural standard; in order to prevent such cheating, it is necessary that some retaliatory mechanism should be in place to impose sanctions on deviant firms. The most obvious sanction would be a sharp price war, harmful to everyone, but a severe warning that abandonment of tacit coordination will be to everyone's disadvantage.[11]

This summary is, of course, an enormously simplified account of what is a highly complex issue, but it should suffice to indicate that there does exist a

---

11 The question of whether an effective retaliatory mechanism is a legal requirement in a case of coordination arose, and was the subject of disagreement between the Commission and Airtours, in the *Airtours/First Choice* decision: see page 610 below.

phenomenon of tacit coordination; the task of the Community Courts and the Commission has been to determine the extent to which Article 82 and the ECMR can make a contribution to the alleviation of the problems posed by such coordination.

IV THE DEFINITION OF COLLECTIVE DOMINANCE UNDER ARTICLE 82 AND THE ECMR

It has taken the Community Courts a considerable time to develop a concept of collective dominance. As a result of recent judgments, it would seem clear that the abuse of a collective dominant position can be controlled under Article 82 and that the creation or strengthening of collective dominance can be prohibited under the ECMR; and that there is one concept of collective dominance which is common to each of these legal instruments. However it has taken a quarter of a century to reach this point, the landmark judgments having been the *Italian Flat Glass* case under Article 82, and *France v Commission* and *Gencor v Commission* under the ECMR. This essay will examine the evolution of the concept of collective dominance in the decisions of the Commission and the judgments of the Community Courts.

A "One or more undertakings": the narrow view of Article 82

Article 82 prohibits the abuse of a dominant position "by one or more undertakings". The "narrow" view of the reference to more than one undertaking is that it means that the market power and behaviour of undertakings within the same corporate group or economic unit can be aggregated and dealt with under Article 82. According to this view, parallel behaviour on the part of undertakings that are not within the same group falls to be dealt with, if at all, only under Article 81: "collusion" must be referable to an agreement or concerted practice, but is not to be controlled under Article 82. In several of the cases on Article 82 a dominant position was found to exist among the members of a group. For example, in *Continental Can,*[12] three different companies were involved in the Commission's analysis: Continental Can (a US company), SLW (its German subsidiary) which held a dominant position in Germany and Europemballage (also its subsidiary) which acquired a competitor, TDV. It was the overall effect of these companies' position and behaviour which led to a finding of abuse of dominance. Similarly in *Commercial Solvents v Commission,*[13] there were two legal undertakings within the same economic group, the US parent, Commercial

12 OJ [1972] L 7/25, [1972] CMLR D11; the decision was annulled on appeal to the ECJ because of the Commission's failure to define the relevant market: *Europemballage Corpn and Continental Can Co Inc v. Commission* [1973] ECR 215, CMLR 199.

13 Cases 6/73 etc [1974] ECR 223, [1974] 1 CMLR 309.

Solvents, and its Italian subsidiary, ICI. The controversial question in cases such as these is whether the companies are so closely related to one another that it is reasonable to consider them as essentially one economic unit. However, assuming that this issue is not in doubt, it is simple enough to see that the reference in Article 82 to an abuse by one or more undertakings might simply amount to separate legal entities within the same corporate group.

B "One or more undertakings": the wide view of Article 82

An alternative approach to the reference in Article 82 to one or more undertakings is that it has a wider meaning, so that legally and economically independent firms might be considered to hold a "collective dominant position". It would follow that abusive market behaviour on the part of the collectively dominant firms could be controlled under Article 82 (and, since the adoption of the ECMR, that the Commission would have control over a larger number of concentrations if the same approach could be taken in relation to that legal instrument). The Commission dabbled with the idea of collective dominance under Article 82 in the early 1970s,[14] but the ECJ appeared to have rejected it in *Hoffmann-La Roche v Commission.*[15] There the Court seemed to suggest at paragraph 39 that problems of tacit coordination could not be controlled under Article 82:

> "A dominant position must also be distinguished from parallel courses of conduct which are peculiar to oligopolies in that in an oligopoly the courses of conduct interact, while in the case of an undertaking occupying a dominant position the conduct of the undertaking which derives profits from that position is to a great extent determined unilaterally."[16]

This apparent rejection of Article 82 as a tool for controlling oligopolistic behaviour was understandable. Oligopolists who actively participate in agreements or concerted practices would be caught by Article 81 anyway. The Court may have taken the view that where oligopolists behave in an identical fashion because of the structure of the market on which they operate, rather than because of active participation in an agreement or concerted practice, they should not be condemned for abusing their position if their conduct is rational – even inevitable – behaviour. An approach to the "oligopoly problem" which is based on the concept of abuse in Article 82 seemed inappropriate: or to put it another way,

---

14 See for example the *Report on the Behaviour of the Oil Companies during the period from October 1973 to March 1974*: COM (75) 675 10.12.75; *Sugar Cartel* OJ [1973] L 140/17, [1973] CMLR D65 (where it held that the two Dutch producers held a joint dominant position: the ECJ on appeal said nothing about this because it considered there was no abuse by the companies anyway: Cases 40/73 etc *Suiker Unie v Commission* [1975] ECR 1663, [1976] 1 CMLR 295).

15 Case 85/76 *Hoffmann-La Roche v Commission* [1979] ECR 461, [1979] 3 CMLR 211.

16 *Ibid.*; similarly see Case 172/80 *Gerhard Züchner v Bayerische Vereinsbank* [1981] ECR 2021, [1982] 1 CMLR 313, paragraph 10.

where there was no explicit collusion contrary to Article 81, the Court was not prepared to characterise the economist's notion of tacit collusion as abusive under Article 82. After *Hoffmann-la Roche*, a period of relative inactivity followed. For example in *Alcatel v NOVASAM*[17] the Commission invited the ECJ to adopt a theory of collective dominance in an Article 234 case, but the Court declined to comment on the point in its judgment. In the *Magill* cases[18] the Commission took objection to the refusal of three television companies to grant licences of copyright in their TV schedules to a third party wishing to produce a TV listings magazine. The Commission could have tried a collective dominance approach to the case, holding that the companies had abused a collective dominant position in the TV schedules market. Instead the Commission found three individual dominances on the part of each company, and three individual abuses.

C Confirmation of the wide view

Any suggestion that the concept of collective dominance had been laid to rest was subsequently shown to be wrong. In *Italian Flat Glass*[19] the Commission held that three Italian producers of flat glass had a collective dominant position and that they had abused it. As participants in a tight oligopolistic market they enjoyed a degree of independence from competitive pressures that enabled them to impede the maintenance of effective competition, notably by not having to take into account the behaviour of other market participants. The conduct held to fall within Article 82 had already been condemned earlier in the decision as a concerted practice under Article 81. However the decision opened up the possibility that in other situations the conduct of oligopolists, *though not within Article 81*, might be attacked under Article 82. On appeal the CFI overturned the Commission's decision on collective dominance on the ground that the Commission had simply "recycled" the facts relied on as constituting an infringement of Article 81, instead of properly defining the relevant product and geographical markets in order to weigh up the undertakings' economic power, as is necessary in Article 82 cases. Nevertheless, the CFI confirmed the principle of collective dominance at paragraph 358 of its judgment:

> "There is nothing, in principle, to prevent two or more independent economic entities from being, on a specific market, united by such economic links that, by virtue of that fact, together they hold a dominant position vis-à-vis the other operators on the same market. This could be the case, for example, where two or more independent undertakings jointly have, through agreements or licences, a technological lead affording them the power to behave to an appreciable extent independently of their competitors, their cus-

---

17 Case 247/86 [1988] ECR 5987.

18 *Magill TV Guide* OJ [1989] L 78/43, [1989] 4 CMLR 757; upheld on appeal Cases T-69/89 *RTE v Commission*; T-70/89 *BBC v Commission*; T-76/89 *ITP v Commission* [1991] ECR II-485, [1991] 4 CMLR 586; and further, on appeal to the ECJ, Cases C-241/91P [1995] ECR I-743, [1995] 4 CMLR 718.

19 OJ [1989] L 33/44, [1990] 4 CMLR 535.

tomers and ultimately of their consumers (judgment of the Court in *Hoffmann-La Roche*, cited above, paragraphs 38 and 48)".[20]

The judgment in *Italian Flass Glass* was exciting and frustrating in equal measure. Collective dominance on the part of "two or more independent entities" did exist under Article 82, although the Commission had failed to demonstrate that it existed in this particular case. Clearly, the Court considered that infringements of Articles 81 and 82 were conceptually independent of one another: this is why the Commission was not permitted simply to "recycle the facts" used to find an infringement of Article 81 in order to determine an abuse of collective dominance. Each Article must be applied according to its own terms. Behaviour that amounts to a concerted practice is not automatically also abusive; and *vice versa*. However, what is frustrating about the judgment is that it does not really advance our understanding of what collective dominance consists of. Did the judgment *require* that collectively dominant entities must be economically linked, or did it simply say that links were an example of collective dominance?[21] If "links" were required, what exactly did this expression mean? Must the link consist of an agreement between the entities in question which the Court had given as examples "agreements or licences"? If so, would not such agreements be likely to infringe Article 81, in which case what was the purpose of the principle of collective dominance under Article 82? Could cross-shareholdings amount to an economic link? Or interlocking directorships?[22] Or the sharing of a common infrastructure such as an electricity grid or a gas pipeline? More radically, could firms be economically linked simply by being in a market in which the opportunity for tacit coordination existed? Quite apart from these questions, which concern the identification of the legal concept of collective dominance, the judgment did not ask the more fundamental one: what was the function of the doctrine of collective dominance? The judgment failed to provide adequate answers to any of these questions. Given that we now have the benefit of the judgments in *France v Commission* and *Gencor v Commission* it is perhaps now fruitless to take a divining rod to paragraph 358 of *Italian Flat Glass*. It is sufficient to say that an important landmark had been reached in this judgment, but that later case-law has shed much more light on the concept of collective dominance.

---

20 Cases T-68/89 *Società Italiano Vetro v Commission;* T-77/89 *Fabrica Pisana v Commission;* T-78/89 *PPG Vemante Pennitalia v Commission* [1992] ECR II-1403, [1992] 5 CMLR 302; note that the reference to *Hoffmann-La Roche* in this paragraph is a reference to the meaning of market power as defined in that judgment, *not* to the meaning of collective dominance which, as mentioned earlier, the Court appeared to reject.

21 Note the sentence in paragraph 358 that begins "This could be the case, *for example*, where two or more undertakings ..." (emphasis added).

22 AG Fennelly thought that each of these matters could give rise to collective dominance at paragraph 28 of his opinion in the *Compagnie Maritime Belge* case, footnote 1 above.

D Further judgments and decisions on collective dominance under Article 82

In the extreme south-west of England there is a creature known as the "beast of Bodmin Moor". It is known to be a member of the cat family; it is as large as, and may be, a puma.[23] This creature has never been positively identified, but it has caused a lot of damage, not least to the local sheep population. In the years after *Italian Flat Glass* there were several more sightings of collective dominance, and some partial descriptions; but not until *France v Commission* and, more particularly, *Gencor v Commission* did a true picture begin to emerge. In a series of judgments under Article 234, the ECJ delivered judgments dealing, *inter alia*, with collective dominance. For example in *Almelo*[24] it said that:

> "42 However, in order for such a collective dominant position to exist, the undertakings in the group must be linked in such a way that they adopt the same conduct on the market...
>
> 43 It is for the national court to consider whether there exist between the regional electricity distributors in the Netherlands links which are sufficiently strong for there to be a collective dominant position in a substantial part of the common market".

This formulation refers back to the concept of a link in *Italian Flat Glass*, without further elaborating on what this means. However it also introduces the idea that the significance of the link is that it enables the collectively dominant firms to adopt the same conduct on the market. The second part of the sentence therefore suggests that the Court is looking at what economists would look at: the adoption of the same conduct on the market or, in other words, tacit coordination. This was an improvement on *Italian Flat Glass*, in that it suggests an economic rationale for collective dominance, but it still left the mystery of "links" to be explained. In particular, *Almelo* appears to suggest that an economic link was an essential component of collective dominance, without shedding much more light on what the link should consist of.

In *Spediporto,*[25] *DIP*[26] and *Sodemare*[27] the ECJ repeated the *Almelo* formulation, but did not advance its notion of collective dominance. In the *Bosman* case[28] Lenz AG assumed that football clubs in a professional football league could be "united by such economic links" as to be regarded as collectively dominant. The ECJ did not address the issue. In the meantime the Commission began to reach findings of collective dominance in a number of decisions, both

23 Perhaps a non-economic lynx?

24 Case C-393/92 *Almelo v NV Energiebedrijf Ijsselmij* [1994] ECR I-1477.

25 Case C-96/94 *Centro Servizi Spediporto Srl v Spedizioni Marittime del Golfo Srl* [1995] ECR I-2883, at para. 33.

26 Cases C-140/94 etc. *DIP Spa v Commune di Bassano del Grappa* [1995] ECR I-3257, at para. 26.

27 Case C-70/95 *Sodemare SA, Anni Azzurri Holding SpA and Anni Azzurri Rezzato Srl v Regione Lombardia* [1997] ECR I-3395, at para 46.

28 Case C-415/93 *Union Royale Belge des Sociétés de Football Association v Bosman* [1995] ECR I-4921, [1996] 1 CMLR 645.

under Article 82 and under the ECMR. The decisions under Article 82 did not greatly add to the notion of collective dominance, since they involved collectively dominant undertakings which unmistakably were economically linked in some way. For example, in three decisions in the maritime transport sector the undertakings were members of liner conferences. In *French-West African Shipowners' Committees,*[29] the Commission concluded that members of the shipowners' committees had abused a collective dominant position by taking action designed to prevent other shipping lines establishing themselves as competitors on routes between France and 11 West African states.[30] This decision was adopted after the CFI's judgment in the *Italian Flat Glass* case, and the Commission specifically imposed a fine for the infringement of Article 82 as well as the agreements that were caught by Article 81. In its decision on *Cewal*[31] the Commission again found collective dominance between shipping lines that were members of a liner conference. The Commission's finding of collective dominance was upheld on appeal.[32] On this occasion, the CFI adopted the *Almelo* formula at paragraph 62 that "in order for such a collective dominant position to exist, the undertakings in question must be linked in such a way that they adopt the same conduct on the market". A judgment of the ECJ on appeal from the CFI's upholding of the decision of the Commission is awaited.[33] In *TACA*[34] the Commission imposed fines totalling 273 million ECU on the members of a liner conference for abuses of collective dominance, the largest fine to have been imposed in a single decision.

The Commission also reached findings of collective dominance in its decisions in *Port of Rødby*[35] and *Irish Sugar Plc.*[36] In the *Port of Rødby* decision, the Commission considered that two ferry undertakings that fixed common rates, coordinated timetables and marketed their services jointly were collectively dominant. In the *Irish Sugar* decision the Commission found "vertical" collective dominance between Irish Sugar and a distributor of sugar, Sugar Distributors Ltd (SDL). Without finding legal or *de facto* control of SDL, the Commission concluded that the combination of Irish Sugar's equity holding, the structure of policy-making of the two companies and the communication process established to facilitate it led to direct economic ties between them which created a clear parallelism of interest which amounted to collective dominance. On appeal, the CFI upheld this finding of "vertical" collective dominance.[37]

---

29 OJ [1992] L 134/1, [1993] 4 CMLR 446.
30 *Ibid.*, at paras 52-69.
31 OJ [1993] L 34/2, [1995] 5 CMLR 198.
32 Cases T-24/93 etc *Compagnie Maritime Belge Transports SA v Commission* [1996] ECR II-1201, [1997] 4 CMLR 273.
33 Cases C-395 and 396/96 P (judgment pending).
34 OJ [1999] L 95/1, [1999] 4 CMLR 1415, on appeal Cases T-191/98 etc. *Atlantic Container Line v Commission* (pending).
35 OJ [1994] L 55/52, [1994] 5 CMLR 457.
36 *Irish Sugar* OJ [1997] L 258/1, [1997] 5 CMLR 666, paragraphs 112 and 113.
37 Case T-228/97 *Irish Sugar v. Commission*, [1999] 5 CMLR 1300, paragraph 63; on verti-

These judgments and decisions under Article 82 after the CFI's judgment in *Italian Flat Glass* see the concept of collective dominance being quite regularly applied, and thereby becoming more familiar to officials, practitioners and courts. However, they do relatively little to answer any of the questions raised by that judgment, other than to introduce the idea of the adoption of common conduct on the market as a significant feature of collective dominance. An interesting glimpse of the way in which the Commission's view of collective dominance was developing was provided by its *Notice on Access Agreements in the Telecommunications Sector.*[38] At paragraph 79 it said that:

> "79 In addition, for two or more companies to be jointly dominant it is necessary, though not sufficient, for there to be no effective competition between the companies on the relevant market. This lack of competition may in practice be due to the fact that the companies have links such as agreements for cooperation, or interconnection agreements. *The Commission does not, however, consider that either economic theory or Community law implies that such links are legally necessary for a joint dominant position to exist.* It is a sufficient economic link if there is the kind of interdependence which often comes about in oligopolistic situations. *There does not seem to be any reason in law or in economic theory to require any other economic link between jointly dominant companies.* This having been said, in practice such links will often exist in the telecommunications sector where national [Telecomunications Operators] nearly inevitably have links of various kinds with one another" (emphasis added).

The passages emphasised are of interest when the judgment of the CFI in *Gencor v Commission* is considered below,[39] where the Court specifically said that the *Flat Glass* case did not require "links of a structural nature" in order for a finding of collective dominance to be made.

E The Commission and the ECMR

The Council of Ministers adopted the ECMR on 21 December 1989 and it entered into force on 21 September 1990. As mentioned, it enables the Commission to prohibit a concentration that will create or strengthen a dominant position as a result of which competition will be significantly impeded in the common market or a substantial part of it, but it does not expressly refer to a notion of collective dominance; nor does it refer to a dominant position on the part of one *or more* undertakings. The Merger Task Force (hereafter the "MTF") looked for problems of tacit coordination when investigating concentrations from the earliest days of the ECMR.[40] This was not surprising. A study carried out for the

---

cal collective dominance, see further below.

38 OJ [1998] C 265/2.

39 See page 599 below.

40 For analysis, see the articles cited in footnote 3 above.

Commission by Kantzebach and Kruse[41] as early as 1986 had been quite clear: "it should be the aim of competition policy to prevent situations arising which form a hotbed for tacit collusive behaviour". The very fact that Article 81 applies only to explicit collusion and that the scope of application of Article 82 had been unclear as a result, for example, of the judgment in *Hoffmann-La Roche*, made the case for preventing anti-competitive structures ripe for tacit coordination arising from concentrations all the more compelling. No doubt the fact that national officials were seconded to the MTF from Member States, such as the UK and Germany, where existing merger controls were already concerned with tacit coordination as well as single firm dominance, added to the pressures to apply the ECMR to collective dominance. Furthermore, experience in the US demonstrated that tacit coordination was a legitimate concern in merger analysis. Section 2 of the 1992 Horizontal Merger Guidelines of the Department of Justice and Federal Trade Commission,[42] which discusses the potential adverse competitive effects of mergers, begins with section 2.1 on the lessening of competition through coordinated interaction and then goes on in section 2.2 to discuss the lessening of competition through unilateral effects; to put this point another way, the US Guidelines suggest that collective dominance (coordinated interaction) is at least as important as, if not more important than, single firm dominance (unilateral effects): indeed earlier iterations of the Guidelines had been predominantly concerned with tacit coordination.[43] The first paragraph of section 2.1 of the 1992 US Guidelines sets the scene well for what follows in this essay:

> "A merger may diminish competition by enabling firms selling in the relevant market more likely, more successfully, or more completely to engage in coordinated interaction that harms consumers. Coordinated interaction is comprised of actions by a group of firms that are profitable for each of them only as a result of the accommodating reactions of the others. This behaviour includes tacit or express collusion, and may or may not be lawful in and of itself".

The possibility that concentrations could lead to market structures conducive to tacit coordination was considered in a very early case, *Varta Bosch,*[44] and again in *Alcatel/AEG Kabel,*[45] but on neither occasion did the Commission reach an adverse finding. The first occasion on which the Commission required commitments from the parties to a concentration as a condition for clearing, rather than prohibiting, a concentration that it considered would create or strengthen a

41 See the Commission's 16th *Annual Report on Competition Policy* (1986), page 285.

42 Note that the substantive test in a merger case in the US under section 7 of the Clayton Act 1914 is whether the merger "may be substantially to lessen competition": this phrase does not require an independent finding of collective dominance, as in the case of EC law.

43 See the 1984 Guidelines.

44 Case IV/M. 012, OJ [1991] L 302/26.

45 Case IV/M. 165, 18 December 1991.

collective dominant position occurred in *Nestlé/Perrier.*[46] The decision attracted enormous attention, since it demonstrated that the Commission was prepared to intervene on the basis of collective as well as single firm dominance under the ECMR: it would not have had power to demand the commitments in the absence of a finding of collective dominance. The parties to the concentration did not appeal against the finding of collective dominance, presumably since they were content with the outcome even though they had been required to divest themselves of certain brands.[47] Other decisions on collective dominance followed, including *Kali und Salz.*[48] In this case the Commission required commitments as a condition of clearing a concentration which, in its view, raised problems of collective dominance. France, SCPA and EMC appealed, contesting, *inter alia*, whether the ECMR was applicable to collective dominance at all. Since a Member State was among the appellants, the case came before the ECJ rather than the CFI. The first outright prohibition on the basis of collective dominance occurred in *Gencor/Lonrho*,[49] where the Commission found that the platinum and rhodium markets would have been collectively dominated by two firms, each with about 35% of the world market. Gencor appealed to the CFI. The ECJ's judgment in *France v Commission*[50] was handed down on 31 March 1998; the CFI's in *Gencor v Commission*[51] on 25 March 1999. Between them, these judgments on the substance of the Commission's decisions under the ECMR have advanced our understanding of collective dominance – under both the Regulation and Article 82 – considerably. The second outright prohibition under the ECMR on the basis of collective dominance, in *Airtours/First Choice*,[52] has also been appealed, and the judgment of the CFI in that case should shed important further light on the concept of collective dominance.[53]

F *France v Commission*[54]

This case concerned a concentration between two German undertakings, Kali und Salz AG and Mitteldeutsche Kali AG ("MdK"), in the potash sector. The Commission considered that the merged entity would have a dominant position in Germany but that there was no ground for opposition, since MdK was a fail-

46 See IV/M. 190, OJ [1992] L 356/1, [1993] 4 CMLR M17.

47 Appeals by two trades unions against the decision were found to be inadmissible: see Case T–96/92 *CCE v Commission* [1992] ECR II-2579 and Case T–12/93 *CCC de la Société Anonyme Vittel v Commission* [1995] ECR II-1247.

48 Case IV/M. 308, OJ [1994] L 186/38.

49 Case IV/M. 619, OJ [1997] L 11/30, [1999] 4 CMLR 1076.

50 Cases C-68/94 and 30/95 *France v Commission* [1998] ECR I-1375, [1998] 4 CMLR 829.

51 Case T-102/96 *Gencor v Commission* [1999] 4 CMLR 971.

52 Case IV/M. 1524 *Airtours/First Choice* (decision of 22 September 1999).

53 On the *Airtours* decision, see page 604 below.

54 See footnote 50 above; for comment on the ECJ's judgment in this case, see Ysenyn and Caffara *Two's Company, Three's a Crowd* (1998) ECLR 468

ing company; Kali und Salz would absorb its market share anyway, so that the concentration did not cause the creation or strengthening of the dominant position there. This application of the so-called "failing company defence" was upheld by the ECJ on appeal.[55] However, the Commission considered that the concentration would create a collective dominant position on the part of Kali und Salz and another undertaking, SCPA, in the rest of the Community, in particular because of structural links that already existed between Kali und Salz and SCPA in the form of a joint venture in Canada, an export cartel; and because of distribution arrangements that existed between them on the French market; in consequence it required various commitments on the part of Kali und Salz to terminate its links with SCPA as a condition of clearing the concentration. Kali und Salz gave the commitments required of it by the Commission, and the Commission cleared the transaction. France, SCPA and ECM, of which SCPA was a subsidiary, appealed. The ECJ was called upon to consider numerous points, ranging from the admissibility of SCPA's and ECM's application and the availability of the failing company defence to the application of the ECMR to collective dominance and the Commission's finding on this issue in the case in question. For the purpose of this essay, the importance of the judgment is that it concluded that the ECMR was capable of application to collective dominance;[56] however it concluded that the Commission had failed adequately to demonstrate that there would be collective dominance on the facts of the case. The Commission's decision was therefore annulled.[57]

On the first of these two points, the ECJ rejected the various arguments of the French Government and SCPA/ECM that the ECMR did not apply to collective dominance. Paragraphs 169-172 are of particular interest:

> "169 As may be seen from the first and second recitals in its preamble, the Regulation is founded on the premise that the objective of instituting a system to ensure that competition in the common market is not distorted is essential for the achievement of the internal market by 1992 and for its future development.

55 *Ibid.*, paragraphs 90-125; on the "failing company" defence under the ECMR, see Cook and Kerse, *EC Merger Control* (3rd edition, 2000), pages 178-179; Monti and Rousseau *Failing Firms in the Framework of the EC Merger Regulation* (1999) 24 ELRev 38.

56 In this respect, the ECJ declined to follow the opinion of Advocate General Tesauro, who considered that the ECMR did not apply to the creation or strengthening of collective dominance. In particular, he was concerned that a concentration between A and B could lead to the merged entity being collectively dominant with C, a separate entity not party to the concentration; and yet C was not afforded any specific procedural rights by the ECMR. The ECJ rejected this argument: whilst it was true that the ECMR did not confer any specific right on third parties in the position of C to be heard, there is a general principle of Community law that any party that could be adversely affected by a measure has a right to be heard: see paragraph 174 of the judgment.

57 Subsequently the Commission adopted a second decision clearing the concentration unconditionally: Commission's XXVIIIth *Annual Report on Competition Policy* (1998) paragraphs 175-179.

170 It follows from the sixth, seventh, tenth and eleventh recitals in the preamble that the Regulation, unlike Articles [81] and [82] of the Treaty, is intended to apply to all concentrations with a Community dimension in so far as they are likely, because of their effect on the structure of competition within the Community, to prove incompatible with the system of undistorted competition envisaged by the Treaty.

171 A concentration which creates or strengthens a dominant position on the part of the parties concerned with an entity not involved in the concentration is liable to prove incompatible with the system of undistorted competition which the Treaty seeks to secure. Consequently, if it were accepted that only concentrations creating or strengthening a dominant position on the part of the parties to the concentration were covered by the Regulation, its purpose as indicated in particular by the above-mentioned recitals would be partially frustrated. The Regulation would thus be deprived of a not insignificant aspect of its effectiveness, without that being necessary from the perspective of the general structure of the Community system of control of concentrations.

172 Neither the argument based on the lack of procedural safeguards nor the argument based on the 15th recital in the preamble to the Regulation can cast doubt on its applicability to cases where a collective dominant position is the result of a concentration".

Clearly this passage is of the greatest importance, since it establishes that the ECMR is capable of application to collective dominance. However, these paragraphs do nothing, in themselves, to advance our understanding of what the concept of collective dominance consists of; nor to answer any of the questions left unanswered by the earlier judgment of the CFI in *Italian Flat Glass*.[58] Some light is shed on the ECJ's notion of collective dominance in the context of its review of the Commission's actual decision. The appellants claimed that the Commission's finding of collective dominance was flawed and inadequate, not least in that it had based its findings on criteria not stated in the case-law on Article 82. The Commission said in reply that it did not accept that the criteria for determining collective dominance under the ECMR and the Article 82 were necessarily the same;[59] and that it had based its finding on a combination of the degree of concentration that there would be in the market after the transaction, structural factors relating to the nature of the market and the characteristics of the product and the structural links[60] that existed between Kali und Salz and SCPA. The Court looked at the various factors that the Commission had taken into account and rehearsed the arguments of the parties in relation to each of them. These factors were grouped under nine headings: the degree of concentration on the market; the characteristics of the eliminated competitor; the position of competitors; the market position of Kali und Salz/MdK and SCPA; the economic power of the customers; the barriers to entry for potash products in the

58 See page 590 above.

59 See paragraph 180 of the judgment.

60 It will be noted that the Commission uses the expression "structural" links; in *Italian Flat Glass* the CFI had spoken of "economic" links; see pages 601 and 602 below for a discussion of this terminology.

Community; the characteristics of the market and the product; the existence of parallel conduct; and the existence of structural links between the undertakings. Having reviewed the arguments of the parties in relation to each of these factors, at paragraphs 220 and 221 the ECJ set out its own view of collective dominance:

> "220 As stated above, under Article 2(3) of the Regulation, concentrations which create or strengthen a dominant position as a result of which effective competition would be significantly impeded in the common market or in a substantial part of it must be declared incompatible with the common market.
>
> 221 In the case of an alleged collective dominant position, the Commission is therefore obliged to assess, using a prospective analysis of the reference market, whether the concentration which has been referred to leads to a situation in which effective competition in the relevant market is significantly impeded by the undertakings involved in the concentration and one or more other undertakings which together, in particular because of factors giving rise to a connection between them,[61] are able to adopt a common policy on the market and act to a considerable extent independently of their competitors, their customers, and also of consumers".

The ECJ stated at paragraphs 223 and 224 that the Commission enjoyed a certain discretion in making its assessment in relation to matters of such an economic nature; however, it concluded that the Commission's decision on the facts of this case should be annulled. At paragraph 226, the ECJ noted that after the concentration, Kali und Salz and SCPA would have market shares of 23% and 37% respectively. It said that a market share of approximately 60%, subdivided in that way, cannot of itself point conclusively to the existence of a collective dominant position of those undertakings. Thus, the rule in *AKZO v. Commission*[62] that dominance can be presumed where there is a market share of 50% or more must be seen as applicable only to cases of a single firm, and not collective, dominance. The Court therefore analysed other features of the Commission's decision. In particular, since the Commission had placed so much emphasis on the structural links that existed between Kali und Salz and SCPA, the ECJ looked carefully to consider whether those links could contribute to any creation or strengthening of collective dominance on the part of Kali und Salz and SCPA. The ECJ considered that the Commission had failed to demonstrate this to the necessary legal standard.

The important issue arising from paragraph 221 of the ECJ's judgment and its actual annulment of the Commission's decision is the light that it sheds on the notion of collective dominance under the ECMR.[63] As for paragraph 221 it-

---

61 Note that this is the English translation in the official European Court Reports, and that it differs from the unofficial, and more opaque, translation in the Common Market Law Reports, "in particular because of correlative factors which exist between them".

62 Case C-62/86 [1991] ECR I-3359, [1993] 5 CMLR 215.

63 The ECJ did not comment on the Commission's suggestion that collective dominance might have different meanings under the ECMR and Article 82; this is dealt with in the *Gencor* judgment below.

self, the ECJ emphasised the issue of whether the firms would be able to adopt a common policy on the market: it will be recalled that this was the feature of collective dominance under Article 82 that the ECJ introduced in paragraph 42 of the *Almelo* judgment. In *France v Commission* the possibility of the adoption of a common policy is taken to be the key feature of collective dominance in the context of the ECMR. Such a common policy may arise "in particular because of factors giving rise to a connection between them": it is important to note that this clause is subordinate to the main thrust of the sentence. Instead of these "factors giving rise to a connection between them" constituting the essence of collective dominance, they are taken to be particularly relevant in determining whether firms will be able to adopt a common policy on the market. As to the factors themselves, the ECJ does not provide an exhaustive list of those that are to be taken into account, nor does it prioritise them; more specifically, it does not state that structural links between the collectively dominant firms are either the most important factor or even a requisite factor at all. Paragraph 222 of the judgment says that there must be a close examination of the particular circumstances of each case in order to consider the effects of a concentration in any particular market. The ECJ then went on to consider the impact of the structural links on the facts of the case, given that the Commission had placed so much emphasis on them, and disagreed with its assessment. It had failed to demonstrate that the structural links on which it had relied were capable of sustaining a finding of collective dominance. However it does not follow from this that the ECJ was saying that structural links were a pre-requisite for a finding of collective dominance; it was merely saying that, if the Commission adopted a decision on collective dominance on the basis of structural links, its reasoning on these links must be convincing. Thus it can be seen that the ECJ prepared the ground for the CFI to state in *Gencor v Commission* that structural links were not a pre-requisite to a finding of collective dominance at all.

G Gencor v Commission[64]

In *Gencor/Lonrho*[65] the Commission had prohibited a concentration that would have brought together the interests of those two undertakings in South Africa in platinum group metals: this group consists of platinum, palladium, rhodium, iridium, ruthenium and osmium. Gencor and Lonrho would jointly control these metals through a jointly-owned entity, Implats Ltd. As a result of the concentration, both Implats and Amplats (a separate South African undertaking) would have had about 35% of the world production of platinum and rhodium. In the view of the Commission, this would result in the creation or strengthening of a

---

64 Case T-102/96 [1999] 4 CMLR 971; see González-Díaz *Recent Developments in EC Merger Control Law* (1999) 22 World Competition 3; Caffarra and Kühn *Joint Dominance: The CFI judgment in Gencor/Lonrho* (1999) ECLR 355.

65 Case IV/M.619 OJ [1997] L 11/30, [1999] 4 CMLR 1076.

"dominant duopoly position"[66] as a result of which effective competition would be significantly impeded within the common market. The concentration was prohibited, the first occasion on which there had been an outright prohibition in the case of collective dominance. The Commission's decision was important in a number of respects: on the extraterritorial scope of the ECMR, on the meaning of control under Article 3(3) of the ECMR and on the nature of commitments that might be offered under the Regulation in return for a clearance. Each of these matters was dealt with in the judgment of the CFI on appeal. The decision was also of considerable interest on the concept of collective dominance.

At paragraph 140 of its decision, the Commission spelt out the "problem" of what it terms "oligopolistic dominance":

> "a mere adaptation by members of the oligopoly to market conditions causes anti-competitive parallel behaviour whereby the oligopoly becomes dominant. Active collusion would therefore not be required for the members of the oligopoly to become dominant and to behave to an appreciable extent independently of their remaining competitors and, ultimately, the consumers".

At paragraph 141, the Commission sets out those features of the platinum market that appeared to render it an uncompetitive oligopoly:

> "(a) on the demand side, there is moderate growth, inelastic demand and insignificant countervailing buyer power. Buyers are therefore highly vulnerable to a potential abuse;
> (b) the supply side is highly concentrated with high market transparency for a homogeneous product, mature production technology, high entry barriers (including high sunk costs) and suppliers with financial links and multi-market contacts. These supply side characteristics make it easy for suppliers to engage in parallel behaviour and provide them with incentives to do so, without any countervailing checks from the demand side".

In the succeeding paragraphs of the decision, the Commission considered each of these factors, concluding at paragraph 159 that "[t]he transparency of the market and the product homogeneity in combination with the other demand and supply characteristics have created a situation conducive to oligopolistic dominance". It then went on to look at the position of the platinum market historically (over the previous two decades), and found that the evidence was consistent with the suggestion that the industry is conducive to oligopolistic behaviour. The Commission concluded that the concentration would create oligopolistic dominance and, effectively, a duopoly for Implats and Amplats.

Gencor appealed on a number of grounds to the CFI. The Court upheld the Commission's decision.[67] On the issue of collective dominance, the CFI confirmed (as it was bound to do, given the judgment of the ECJ in *France v Com-*

---

66 *Ibid.*, paragraph 219; this term should be regarded as interchangeable with "collective dominant position".
67 See footnote 65 above.

mission[68]) that the ECMR was capable of being applied to collective dominance. Paragraphs 159-298 deal with the Commission's actual analysis of collective dominance in this decision. The CFI considered the Commission's analysis of each of the matters set out in paragraph 141 of its decision, concluding that there were no errors on its part. Of particular interest are the Court's comments on structural links. Gencor had argued that the Commission had failed to apply the test in *Italian Flat Glass* correctly which, it asserted, "requires for findings of collective dominance that there be structural links between the two undertakings ...".[69] The CFI answered this point clearly at paragraphs 273-275:

> "273 In its judgment in the Flat Glass case, the Court referred to links of a structural nature only by way of example and did not lay down that such links must exist in order for a finding of collective dominance to be made.
>
> 274 It merely stated (at paragraph 358 of the judgment) that there is nothing, in principle, to prevent two or more independent economic entities from being united by economic links in a specific market and, by virtue of that fact, from together holding a dominant position vis-à-vis the other operators on the same market. It added (in the same paragraph) that that could be the case, for example, where two or more independent undertakings jointly had, through agreements or licences, a technological lead affording them the power to behave to an appreciable extent independently of their competitors, their customers and, ultimately, of consumers.
>
> 275 Nor can it be deduced from the same judgment that the Court has restricted the notion of economic links to the notion of structural links referred to by the appellant" (emphasis added).

These paragraphs are of great interest. A number of points can be made. First, the CFI stresses that the *Italian Flat Glass* judgment did not require that there should be structural links in order for there to be a finding of collective dominance; rather such links were given as an example of when there might be a finding of collective dominance. Secondly, the *Italian Flat Glass* case concerned Article 82; the Court in *Gencor* does not distinguish Article 82 cases and ECMR cases in paragraph 273 of its judgment: in other words, it must be taken to be saying that structural links are not a pre-requisite under either legal instrument. Thirdly, the Court says that agreements or licences are simply examples of structural links, but that they are not the only economic links that might be found. Fourthly, the language of these paragraphs is confusing, since the CFI does not explain whether it considers that there is a difference between a structural and an economic link, and if so what that difference consists of. As was noted above, the CFI in *Italian Flat Glass* had used the expression "economic links", whereas the Commission in *Gencor* looked for "structural links". In *Gencor* it is not obvious from paragraphs 273 to 275 how the CFI considers that these two terms relate to one another.

Paragraphs 276 and 277 appear to provide an answer to this conundrum:

68 See footnote 50 above.
69 See paragraph 264 of the judgment.

> "276 Furthermore, there is no reason whatsoever in legal or economic terms to exclude from the notion of economic links the relationship of interdependence existing between the parties to a tight oligopoly within which, in a market with the appropriate characteristics, in particular in terms of market concentration, transparency and produce homogeneity, those parties are in a position to anticipate one another's behaviour and are therefore strongly encouraged to align their conduct on the market, in particular in such a way as to maximise their joint profits by restricting production with a view to increasing prices. In such a context, each trader is aware that highly competitive action on its part designed to increase its market share (for example a price cut) would provoke identical action by the others, so that it would derive no benefit from its initiative. All the traders would thus be affected by the reduction in price levels.
>
> 277 That conclusion is all the more pertinent with regard to the control of concentrations, whose objective is to prevent anti-competitive market structures from arising or being strengthened. Those structures may result from the existence of economic links in the strict sense argued by the applicant or from market structures of an oligopolistic kind where each undertaking may become aware of common interests and, in particular, cause prices to increase without having to enter into an agreement or resort to a concerted practice".

These paragraphs would appear to suggest that, where links are taken into account in establishing collective dominance, the controlling issue is whether links exist between firms which would facilitate tacit coordination. Such links could be "merely" economic, that is to say a consequence of the economic conditions of the market itself: this is what is envisaged in paragraph 276. However, they might also be structural, where for example the firms in question are bound to one another in some other way, through agreements, licences, cross-shareholdings or shared infrastructure.[70] According to this view, structural links would be a "sub-species" of economic links; the real issue being whether the links are conducive to tacit coordination. This is this author's attempt to explain a rather awkward passage in the judgment: further light may be shed on this in the *Airtours* appeal.

The *Gencor* judgment, while not entirely free from ambiguity, is clearly of immense importance. When read with *France v Commission* the meaning of collective dominance becomes a great deal clearer. A summary of the key points on this concept may be helpful:

- Economic theory suggests that there are some markets in which firms may be able to reap the benefits of "tacit coordination" by charging prices above the competitive level without expressly agreeing to do so.
- A concept of "collective dominance" may have a useful role to play in Community competition law in dealing with the problem of tacit coordination.
- Until the CFI's judgment in *Italian Flat Glass*, it was not clear whether Article 82 applied to collective dominance at all.

70 See the examples given at page 590 above.

- The CFI's judgment in *Italian Flat Glass* established that Article 82 is capable of applying to collective dominance; however, the judgment left many questions about the nature of collective dominance unanswered.
- After *Italian Flat Glass*, there were several further judgments of the Community Courts and decisions of the Commission on collective dominance under Article 82; the ECJ's judgment in *Almelo* stressed the adoption of the same conduct on the market as an essential feature of the concept.
- The Commission's own view of collective dominance, as expressed in the *Notice on Access Agreements in the Telecommunications Sector*, was that economic links were not an essential pre-requisite for collective dominance.
- When the ECMR came into effect, the Commission's view was that it was capable of application to collective dominance.
- The ECJ in *France v Commission* confirmed the application of the ECMR to collective dominance, although it annulled the Commission's finding on the facts of the case.
- The CFI in *Gencor v Commission* upheld the Commission's prohibition of the Gencor/Lonrho concentration on the basis of collective dominance.
- In *Gencor* the CFI confirmed that links were not a legal pre-requisite for collective dominance.
- In *Gencor* the CFI suggested that, where links are relied upon for a finding of collective dominance, they may be "economic" or "structural": the crucial question is whether the links are conducive to tacit coordination.
- In *Gencor* the CFI does not distinguish between the concept of collective dominance under Article 82 and the ECMR.

H Further decisions in collective dominance under the ECMR

The Commission has paid close attention to collective dominance in several subsequent decisions under the ECMR; it is noticeable that the factors set out in paragraph 141 of its *Gencor/Lonrho* decision form the starting point of its analysis.[71] Whilst it is reasonable and helpful to have such a checklist, it goes without saying that this should not be applied in too mechanistic a manner: as the ECJ said at paragraph 22 of its judgment in *France v Commission*, each case must turn on its particular facts. Different items on the checklist will have greater or lesser significance according to the industry in question. Two decisions on collective dominance are of particular interest.

---

71 See (apart from the two decisions in the text) Case IV/M.1225 *Enso/Stora* OJ [1999] L 254/9, paragraphs 66-68; Case IV/M.1532 *BP Amoco/Atlantic Richfield* (not yet published); Case IV/M.1383 *Exxon/Mobil* (not yet published).

(i) Price Waterhouse/Coopers & Lybrand[72]

In *Price Waterhouse/Coopers & Lybrand* the Commission investigated the proposed concentration between these two firms of accountants, in particular in relation to the market for auditing and accounting services for large clients. In its assessment of collective dominance, it looked at the factors set out in paragraph 141 of the *Gencor/Lonrho* decision. In considering whether collective dominance would be created, it did so on the basis of a "dual-merger scenario",[73] since two other major firms of accountants, KPMG and Ernst & Young, had also notified their own proposed concentration to it. The Commission's preliminary view had been that, if both of these transactions were to have been completed, the position "would be consistent with a hypothesis of collective dominance";[74] however, KPMG and Ernst & Young announced the termination of their own plans, so that the Commission did not have to reach a conclusion on this "scenario". What is intriguing is the possibility that the Commission might have been prepared to prohibit each of these concentrations because of a reduction in the "Big Six" firms of accountants to only four. As noted below, the *Airtours/First Choice* concentration was blocked where the transaction would have taken the industry from four to three players; but this decision might have been preceded by a prohibition on the basis of a reduction from six players to four. With the KPMG/Ernst & Young deal having collapsed, the Commission then had to consider whether there were grounds for prohibiting the Price Waterhouse transaction, and concluded that there were not. In the course of this decision, the Commission itself pointed out (at paragraphs 104-106) that a consequence of the ECJ's judgment in *France v Commission* is that there is a strong burden of proof on the Commission where it is considering whether it should adopt a finding of collective dominance. This evidential point should provide some assistance to firms contemplating concentrations in an industry which tends to oligopoly, although it proved to be of no avail to Airtours in its attempted hostile takeover of First Choice.[75]

(ii) Airtours/First Choice[76]

In *Airtours/First Choice* the Commission investigated a proposed hostile acquisition by Airtours of First Choice. The Commission concluded that the acquisition would create a collective dominant position in the market for short-haul package holidays in the United Kingdom on the part of the merged entity, Airtours/First Choice, and the two other leading tour operators, Thomson Travel Group and Thomas Cook. The Commission was not satisfied that commitments

72 Case IV/M. 938 OJ [1997] L 50/27, [1999] 4 CMLR 665.
73 See paragraphs 108 ff of the decision.
74 See paragraph 110 of the decision.
75 See below.
76 Case IV/M.1524 *Airtours/First Choice* (decision of 22 September 1999).

offered by Airtours could remedy the problems that it foresaw, and prohibited the concentration outright. This was the second outright prohibition under the ECMR on the basis of collective dominance. An obvious point of distinction from *Gencor/Lonrho* was that in that decision the collective dominance would be held by two entities, Implats and Amplats, whereas in *Airtours/First Choice* three firms would be collectively dominant. Without wishing to suggest that there is any magic in numbers, the first prohibition in a "four to three" case (*Airtours*) as opposed to a "three to two" case (*Gencor*) is of passing interest. However, this in itself should not be regarded as the key factor in the case. To suggest that the identification of collective dominance is a matter of numbers is jejune: the critical issue in each case is whether a concentration will make it easier for firms to achieve tacit coordination: as seen in *Price Waterhouse/ Coopers & Lybrand*, the Commission might have been prepared, in the context of the market under consideration there, to conclude that a reduction from six to four players should be prohibited under the "dual merger scenario". The *Airtours/First Choice* decision has been appealed to the CFI.[77]

The Commission analysed a number of market characteristics in *Airtours/First Choice* in order to determine whether the market was conducive to oligopolistic dominance: product homogeneity, low demand growth, low price sensitivity of demand, similar cost structures of the main suppliers, high market transparency, extensive commercial links between the major suppliers, substantial entry barriers and insignificant buyer power.[78] On the basis of this assessment, and of a review of the history of competition in the industry, the Commission concluded that the concentration would result in an oligopolistic market in which it would be rational for the three collectively dominant undertakings to restrict supply to the market, thereby increasing price.

There was fundamental disagreement between Airtours and the Commission on various aspects of this decision. In particular, in relation to collective dominance, Airtours disagreed with three features of the decision. First, the issue of tacit coordination itself. Prior to *Airtours*, the Commission's decisional practice and the Court's judgments in *France v Commission* and *Gencor v Commission* seemed to have established that the key issue in a case of collective dominance under the ECMR was whether the concentration enabled the undertakings "to adopt a common policy on the market" and to act to a considerable extent independently of competitors, customers and consumers.[79] However, in *Airtours* the Commission stated at paragraph 54:

> "54 Furthermore – contrary to the apparent view of Airtours – it is not a necessary condition of collective dominance for the oligopolists always to behave *as if* there were

---

77 *Airtours plc v Commission* (judgment pending).

78 See paragraph 87 of the decision, and footnote 63 pointing out that these are substantially the same characteristics that were considered in *Gencor/Lonrho* and *Price Waterhouse/ Coopers & Lybrand*.

79 See *France v Commission* (note 50 above), paragraph 221.

> one or more explicit agreements (e.g. to fix prices or capacity, or share the market) between them. *It is sufficient that the merger makes it rational for the oligopolists, in adapting themselves to market conditions, to act – individually* – in ways which will substantially reduce competition between them, and as a result of which they may act, to an appreciable extent, independently of competitors, customers and consumers" (emphasis added).

This language seems to suggest a departure by the Commission from the precedents. The adoption of a common policy, the test applied in earlier cases, does not appear to be the same as the rational, *individual* adaptation of policy, the test suggested in paragraph 54. To put the point another way, the Commission seems here to have lowered the threshold for a finding of collective dominance, by looking at the rational unilateral behaviour of individual entities rather than their tacit coordination. It is not entirely clear whether the Commission deliberately intended in this paragraph to extend the notion of collective dominance; this is a matter which will be dealt with in the appeal to the CFI.

A second disagreement between Airtours and the Commission concerned the application of the tacit coordination "checklist": in the view of Airtours the Commission failed to apply the factors in that list in a way that was convincing in the circumstances of the industry in question, which was, of course, very different from a "commodity" industry such as platinum and rhodium in *Gencor/Lonrho*. This will also be examined on appeal.

A third disagreement arose from the fact that, in the opinion of Airtours, tacit coordination could only be feasible where there is a plausible retaliatory mechanism in place that would deter the other firms from cheating; the retaliation could take the form, for example, of a price war or substantial increase in capacity.[80] The Commission's response to this was that (a) neither the Commission nor the CFI in *Gencor* had required that a specific punishment mechanism was necessary for a finding of collective dominance and (b) there were anyway significant possibilities for punishment.[81] As to (a), it is certainly the case that the literature on tacit coordination emphasises that the ability to punish firms that cheat is an essential requirement. For example *Scherer and Ross*[82] state that:

> "Detecting and deterring cheating has been termed *the* central cartel problem, and, because solving it is often difficult, many economists argue that price-fixing cartels are inherently unstable".

The US Horizontal Merger Guidelines make the same point:

> "Successful coordinated interaction entails reaching terms of coordination that are profitable to the firms involved and an ability to detect and punish deviations that would undermine the coordinated interaction. Detection and punishment of deviations ensure that

80 See paragraphs 52, 55 and 148-149 of the decision.
81 See paragraphs 151-152 of the decision.
82 See footnote 10 above, at page 245.

coordinating firms will find it more profitable to adhere to the terms of coordination than to pursue short-term profits from deviating, given the costs of reprisal" [83]

The Commission, however, concluded at paragraph 150 of Decision that:

"it is not necessary to show that there would be a strict punishment mechanism: what matters for collective dominance in the present case is whether the degree of interdependence between the oligopolists is such that it is rational for the oligopolists to restrict output, and in this sense reduce competition in such a way that a collective dominant position is created".

The CFI will be asked to examine this important issue in the *Airtours* appeal. It is arguable that it is implicit if not explicit in the existing decisional practice of the Commission and in the case-law of the Community Courts that a retaliatory system is a pre-requisite to a finding of collective dominance; or alternatively that, if it is not a pre-requisite, economic theory dictates that it should be.

V ABUSE OF A COLLECTIVE DOMINANT POSITION UNDER ARTICLE 82

We now know, as a result of the developments described in this essay, that Article 82 and the ECMR apply to collective as well as single-firm dominance; we have also seen that the Commission has prohibited concentrations that would create or strengthen a collective dominant position, or has required commitments from the parties as a condition for clearance. However, one further issue remains: what would constitute an abuse of a collective dominant position under Article 82? This is a topic that is still somewhat under-developed in the case-law. The economic theory around which the doctrine of collective dominance has developed is that in certain market conditions firms may be able to derive benefits from tacit coordination; and the very reason why the Commission might prohibit a concentration that would create or strengthen a collective dominant position is that it would make it easier for firms to benefit from this phenomenon. Does it follow from this that tacit coordination, when actually practised, should be condemned as an abuse of a collective dominant position under Article 82? To put the point another way, does symmetry require that, since predicted tacit coordination can be prevented through the prohibition of a concentration under the ECMR, actual coordination should be condemned under Article 82? If the answer to this question is no, what types of behaviour ought to be condemned under Article 82?

83 Guidelines at paragraph 2.1; paragraph 2.12 goes into greater detail on "conditions conducive to detecting and punishing deviations".

A Exploitative abuse of a collective dominant position

Textbooks on Article 82 habitually make a distinction between those abuses that are "exploitative" and those that are "anti-competitive", while recognising that this is not a watertight distinction.[84] A typical exploitative abuse would be the charging of excessively high prices, which is specifically given as an example of abuse in Article 82(2)(a). Cases on excessively high prices have been few and far between, not least because the Commission would not wish to establish itself as a *de facto* price regulator; as a general proposition where a dominant firm is able to charge very high prices, a competition authority's energies would be better devoted to an examination of why the market does not attract new entrants to share in any monopoly rent: for example, is the dominant firm guilty of anti-competitive abuses that are keeping other firms out of the market, or are there other barriers to entry that are impeding the proper functioning of competition? However, the Commission does sometimes investigate high prices under Article 82.[85] In the case of collectively dominant firms, one question is whether the Commission could characterise and condemn tacit coordination as abusive. It could be argued that this phenomenon is exploitative – prices are charged which are higher than they would be in a competitive market, but without the need to enter into an explicit agreement. However, the Commission has not attempted to condemn tacit coordination itself under Article 82, and it is submitted that, as a matter of law, it should not be able to do so. As explained at the beginning of this essay, tacit coordination is not caught by Article 81(1), precisely because it does not arise from an agreement or concerted practice in the sense of that provision. Tacit coordination comes about in certain market conditions, not because of a conspiracy between the collectively dominant firms in the legal sense of that term, but because they react rationally according to the conditions of the market in which they operate. To condemn their rational behaviour as abusive would be a nonsense: if Article 82 were to mandate that firms must behave *irrationally* in order to comply with the law, it would indeed be an odd provision. This explains the position taken by the ECJ as long ago as *Hoffmann-la Roche*: parallel behaviour should be condemned where it is attributable to an agreement or concerted practice contrary to Article 81(1); it is not, in itself, abusive under Article 82.[86] It might be suggested that this shows an inconsistency between the law under Article 82 and the ECMR: how can it be that the prospect of tacit coordination can be condemned under the Merger Regulation and yet the actuality of the same behaviour cannot be condemned under Article 82? The truth is that

84 See for example Whish, *Competition Law* (3rd edition, 1993) pages 271-280; Bellamy and Child, *Common Market Law of Competition* (4th edition, 1993) paragraphs 9-046 ff; the Commission itself made this distinction its decision on *P&I Clubs* OJ [1999] L 125/12 at paragraphs 127-136.

85 See for example *Mobile telephony pricing* Commission press release IP(98)707 and (98)1036.

86 See page 588 above.

the difference in treatment makes perfect sense: it is precisely because of the difficulty that Competition Law has in addressing the problem of tacit coordination when it does occur that competition authorities, through their merger controls, endeavour to prevent a market structure that will be conducive to this phenomenon from arising on the first place. This explains the emphasis that has been placed upon tacit coordination in the merger control system in the US.[87]

A distinct issue is whether collectively dominant firms could be held to have abused their position by charging excessively high prices: here the abuse would not lie in the parallelism of the prices, but their level. As mentioned, Article 82(2)(a) does condemn unfairly high prices, and it is not obvious that collectively dominant firms should enjoy an immunity from this offence which an individually dominant firm would not enjoy. In principle, therefore, it would seem that an action could be brought in these circumstances. Such actions are likely to be rare, however, since the Commission does not want to itself in the position of a price regulator; and they should be brought only because of the excessiveness of the prices, and not their parallelism. The Commission contemplated a finding of an exploitative abuse of a different nature in its *P&I* decision[88] on the basis that the P&I clubs that were members of the International Group, and which had been found to be collectively dominant, had limited the level of insurance cover available to customers, contrary to Article 82(2)(b); however an alteration in the rules of the Group meant that the Commission did not reach a formal finding to this effect.

B Anti-competitive abuse of a collective dominant position

Article 82 is applied much more often to so-called "anti-competitive" abuses than to exploitative ones. Exclusive purchasing, loyalty rebates, tie-ins and predatory pricing are examples of abuses where the concern of the Commission was that a dominant undertaking had resorted to commercial practices that somehow departed from competition "on the merits" and that should be condemned because they inhibited competition on the part of actual or potential competitors. Without going into the complexities here of what actually is meant by an anti-competitive abuse, it seems reasonable that Article 82 should be applicable to the anti-competitive behaviour not only of individually but also of collectively dominant undertakings. Indeed, given that tacit coordination arises where a few firms, without explicit collusion, are able to set prices above the competitive level, the "subversive" effect of new entrants into markets conducive to this phenomenon is likely to be welcomed by competition authorities: a good reason in itself for condemning attempts by the incumbent firms to impede such entry. In the Commission's practice, it has condemned anti-competitive

87 See page 594 above.
88 OJ [1999] L 125/12.

abuses by collectively dominant firms. For example, in *CEWAL*[89] the abuses consisted of various practices designed to eliminate competitors from the market, including selective price cutting and the grant of loyalty rebates. In *TACA*[90] the abuses consisted of a refusal by members of a liner conference to offer individual service contracts to customers, but only to supply certain transport services pursuant to terms collectively agreed by the members of the conference; and of abusively altering the competitive structure of the market by acting to eliminate potential competition: members of TACA had taken steps to induce any would-be entrants to the trans-Atlantic liner shipping market to do so within the TACA system. This smothered the emergence of new competition in the market. It can be anticipated that the Commission will investigate closely allegations of abusive behaviour by collectively dominant firms where actual or potential competitors which might be able to subvert tacit coordination on the market are the complainants.

C Individual abuse of a collective dominant position

The final question is whether a collective dominant position can be abused only by all of the undertakings which hold that position, or whether it is possible for one or some of them to commit an abuse. To put the matter another way, must there be "collective" abuse of collective dominance, or can there also be "individual" abuse? This has been clearly answered by the CFI in the *Irish Sugar* appeal:[91] "undertakings occupying a joint dominant position may engage in joint or individual abusive conduct".

VI CONCLUSION

Collective dominance is now firmly established in EC Competition Law; the judgments in *France v Commission* and *Gencor v Commission*, while not entirely free from difficulty, have considerably advanced our understanding of the subject. The Commission's decision under the ECMR in *Airtours/First Choice* has created some confusion, and the CFI's judgment in that case will be eagerly anticipated. What would be particularly helpful would be publication by the Commission of guidelines setting out its view of the law and economics of collective dominance: it is understood that this is under active consideration. One can anticipate that any such guidelines would quite closely reflect existing practice in the US: in the global market place of the new millennium, it is clearly de-

89 OJ [1993] L 34/2, [1995] 5 CMLR 198, upheld on appeal Cases T-24/93 etc *Compagnie Maritime Belge Transports SA v Commission* [1996] ECR II-1201, [1997] 4 CMLR 273; anti-competitive abuse was also found in the earlier *French-West African Shipowners' Committees* decision: OJ [1992] L 134/1, [1993] 4 CMLR 446.

90 OJ [1999] L 95/1, [1999] 4 CMLR 1415, appeal pending.

91 Case T-228/97 [1999] 5 CMLR 1300, paragraph 66.

sirable that antitrust authorities should as far as possible apply the same standards to economic phenomena such as tacit coordination.

38

COMPETITION APPEALS

James Flynn

INTRODUCTION

When I worked in Luxembourg for the dedicatee of this volume, a burning topic was the Court's proposal for the creation of a first instance court to hear appeals in competition and staff cases. Lord Slynn was a supporter of the project and seemed to face with equanimity the prospect of being relieved of the responsibility for assessing voluminous challenges to cartel decisions. (As regards staff cases, I rather fancy he enjoyed their human interest side, as befits a former President of the Employment Appeals Tribunal.) More recently, chairing a seminar with his usual charm and wit, he introduced a paper of mine on the legislation which has now become the Competition Act 1998 with the hope that he would have retired by the time any appeals from decisions of the Director General of Fair Trading (DGFT) reached the House of Lords.

This paper may not, then, be the one to which our honorand will most eagerly turn on reading this volume, although he recognised its importance in a generous foreword to my recent book on the new United Kingdom competition law regime.[1] But for me, thinking about the Competition Commission Appeal Tribunals irresistibly recalls the excitement and stimulation of working for Gordon back in the mid-eighties when the now almost venerable Court of First Instance was a hotly debated suggestion which might well not have come into being. The Competition Act 1998 is an interesting vignette of a Member State importing into its own "legal order" conceptual and practical problems which have been addressed earlier at the "European" level, bringing some comfort and a tinge of our glory days to those of us who toil at the coal face of domestic practice.

1 Flynn & Stratford, *Competition; Understanding the 1998 Act*, (Palladian Law Publishing 1998); foreword by Lord Slynn of Hadley.

D. O'Keeffe (ed.), Liber Amicorum Slynn 611-624 (2000)

THE COMPETITION ACT 1998

The Competition Act 1998 ("the Act"), due to enter fully into force on 1 March 2000, revolutionises United Kingdom competition law[2] by introducing effects-based prohibitions based on Articles 81 and 82 (ex articles 85 and 86) of the EC Treaty.[3]

However, this is a parallel and purely domestic system: the United Kingdom is one of the seven Member States which, contrary to the wishes of the Commission, have not empowered their competition authorities to apply Articles 81 and 82 directly. A stalemate was likely for as long as the Commission set its face against sharing the competence to grant exemptions under Article 81(3). The position may change now that the Commission has crossed the Rubicon and urged in its recent White Paper the conversion of Article 81(3) from a basis for centralised administrative exemption of notified agreements to a directly applicable legal standard.

Unless and until such a development occurs, it is intended that the United Kingdom prohibitions will be construed and applied in harmony with their supra-national role models. The principal device for securing such consistency is contained in Section 60 of the Act. Reading it indicates that the degree of consistency for which the section provides is less than completely slavish.

Section 60(1) describes the objective:

> "The purpose of this section is to ensure that so far as is possible (having regard to any relevant differences between the provisions concerned), questions arising under this Part in relation to competition within the United Kingdom are dealt with in a manner which is consistent with the treatment of corresponding questions arising in Community law in relation to competition within the Community."

Section 60(2) defines the scope of the obligation to secure consistency. It is imposed on courts, defined in terms which clearly embrace the Competition Commission Appeal Tribunals, and on the DGFT and the sectoral regulators by Section 60(4).

Section 60(2) and (3) reads as follows:

> "At any time when the court determines a question arising under this Part, it must act (so far as is compatible with the provisions of this Part and whether or not it would otherwise be required to do so) with a view to securing that there is no inconsistency between:
>
> (a) the principles applied, and decision reached, by the court in determining that question; and

---

2 Competition law is one of the very rare areas in which it is correct to speak of United Kingdom law. The Act applies throughout the United Kingdom, including Scotland.

3 Let it be said publicly in a volume which, by virtue of the distinction of its dedicatee, should be read widely across the Union: the Amsterdam Treaty's renumbering of the EC Treaty without a fundamental reordering of the provisions was a foolish and unnecessary step which causes and will continue to cause avoidable problems and is, so far as my experience goes, deeply resented by the professions and in academic circles.

(b) the principles laid down by the Treaty and the European Court, and any relevant decision of that Court, as applicable at that time in determining any corresponding question arising in Community law.

The court must, in addition, have regard to any relevant decision or statement of the Commission."

In Parliament, the government stated that, despite its referring only to questions relating to competition, Section 60 is intended to bring in the general principles of Community law as well as the principles used to construe Articles 81 and 82 themselves. Such general principles, deriving from the case-law of the Court of Justice but not explicit in the Treaty itself, include, for example, the principles of non-discrimination and proportionality and also fundamental rights of the kind protected by the European Convention on Human Rights.

It is accepted and intended, therefore, that there will be an overlay of EC principles which may substantially affect the interpretation of the UK prohibitions. However, the view has been taken that acceptance of the applicability of the general and fundamental principles of EC law (or "high-level" principles as they were called by the Minister) does not require the procedure followed by either the competition agency (that is, the DGFT) or the competition court (that is, the Appeal Tribunals) to be modelled on the Community prototypes. To the extent that they do follow the European model, and because a conscious decision has been taken to do so, this is voluntary.

Thus it was an option open to the United Kingdom legislator to entrust judicial review of decisions of the DGFT to the courts of ordinary jurisdiction (not an option for the founding fathers of the Community when setting up institutions to implement supra-national competition law). However, the solution adopted under the Act is inspired by the Court of First Instance.

A vital question raised by Section 60 is whether it will be possible to refer questions of interpretation of relevant EC law issues to the European Court of Justice under Article 234 (ex Article 177) EC. It has been made clear that, whatever may have been the views of the Conservative administration when previous reforms of competition law were under debate, the present government expects and wishes there to be references to Luxembourg as an integral part of securing consistency.

There are two aspects to the question. The first is whether the European Court would accept a reference at all, given that the Act has not been adopted in pursuance of any Community obligation. The second aspect is to consider from which domestic bodies it might accept a reference.

There have been some fluctuations in the European Court's enthusiasm for accepting references on questions of EC law to assist a national court in applying domestic law which does not implement a Community obligation. The key to the European Court's willingness to accept such references seems to be whether the national court is obliged to apply the ruling on EC law. *Kleinwort*

Benson[4] concerned the rules governing allocation of jurisdiction between England and Scotland, an internal matter governed by the Civil Jurisdiction and Judgments Act 1982. The Court refused to give an interpretation of the Brussels Convention because that Act only required the national court to "have regard" to the ECJ's case-law under the Convention. In later cases, despite a persuasive opinion from Advocate General Jacobs arguing that the Court should not accept references where the national court is not intending to apply Community law, the Court has said that in principle it is for national courts to decide when a reference on a point of Community law would be helpful to it and such cases may include situations where the national court is dealing with a purely internal situation to which the national legislator has decided to apply the same treatment.[5]

More recently, in *Bronner v Mediaprint,*[6] an Austrian court, specifically competent to apply national competition law, referred a question on Article 82. The test for dominance in the relevant provision of Austrian law was different from that in Article 82 as was the enforcement mechanism; however, the provision on abuse was closely modelled on Article 82. On this occasion, Advocate General Jacobs recommended to the Court that it should accept the reference on the basis that the referring body, being a court, was entitled and obliged to apply Article 82. The Court did not say explicitly on what basis it was prepared to answer the question, but stated that the national court might wish to avoid conflict between domestic and Community competition law. The Court also suggested that it would not accept a reference if it were clear that Community law could not apply to the facts of the case.

How might this case-law be applied to the Act? It is too simplistic to say that Section 60 is there to avoid inconsistency between the UK and EC systems: it expressly contemplates the existence of differences between them, and the section is full of quiet little escape routes. It is entirely conceivable that there are enough of them to deter the European Court from giving a ruling, at least unless the question is posed by a court which is able to apply Articles 81 and 82 directly.

If the Court would in principle accept a reference, despite the savings for inconsistency preserved in Section 60, the second issue arises, namely which bodies might refer. There is of course no doubt that the courts could do so. It seems most likely that the Appeal Tribunals could refer, although there might be a question under the *Bronner* rationale as to whether they were empowered to apply EC law directly. It is a nice question whether, as might be argued by reference to some of Advocate General Jacobs's statements in *Bronner*, the Appeals Tribunals are enough of a "court" to be obliged to apply EC competition

4 Case C-346/93 *Kleinwort Benson v City of Glasgow District Council* [1995] ECR I-615.

5 See Case C-28/95 *Leur-Bloem v Inspecteur der Belastingsdienst* [1997] ECR I-4161 and Case C-130/95 *Giloy v HzA Frankfurt am Main* [1997] ECR I-4291, in which Advocate General Jacobs delivered a single Opinion.

6 Case C-7/97 [1998] ECR I-7791.

law in appropriate cases, whatever their express statutory duties. Lastly, it is conceivable that the DGFT (and the sectoral regulators) could refer questions, especially given that recent case law of the European Court may indicate a relaxation of its attitude to references from administrative bodies.[7] However, in practice, it would seem more sensible for the DGFT to take his own view on the legal issues and have them corrected if necessary on appeal within the system set up by the Act. To refer the issue to Luxembourg before he makes his decision would put the European Court in a difficult position and also tie the hands of the Appeal Tribunals, almost to the point of precluding an appeal.

Appeals Under the Competition Act

The Competition Commission Appeal Tribunals forms one wing or "side" of the old Monopolies and Mergers Commission, now rebranded as the "Competition Commission".

A brief description of the Tribunal is followed by a summary of the decisions of the DGFT which may be appealed against and by whom. This is followed by a lengthier description of the procedural framework within which the Appeal Tribunals are to work. This is based on the first consultation draft of the procedural rules, recently released at the time of writing.

The Competition Commission is composed of individuals who are appointed to one or more of three "panels" which deal with the Commission's various functions: reporting on the competition implications of proposed mergers, assessing the existence and impact of monopoly situations, ruling on disputes between the utilities and their regulators and now hearing appeals under the Act. A member may be appointed to sit on more than one panel if he fulfils the necessary criteria.

One of the appeal panel members is designated by the Secretary of State to be the President of the Competition Commission Appeal Tribunals. The President must be a lawyer with "appropriate experience and knowledge of competition law and practice". The first president is Sir Christopher Bellamy, formerly a Judge of the Court of First instance (and a contributor to this volume).

Other members of the appeal panel will include legally-qualified individuals who are nominated as "panel chairmen". No specific qualifications are required for other appeal panel members.

When an appeal is lodged, the President must set up an appeal tribunal formed by three members of the appeal panel, including either the President himself or a panel chairman.

There may be at any time a number of tribunals hearing appeals, and hence the plural name. However, this gives rise to some clumsiness in usage and the

7 See Case C-54/96 *Dorch Consult* [1997] ECR I-4961 where the Court accepted a reference from the Federal Supervisory Board for Public Procurement, against the advice of Advocate General Tesauro.

tendency will be think of the Tribunal as a single body, composed of fluctuating sub-groups not unlike the "chambers" of the CFI.

Appealable decisions under the Act

The Act provides for two categories of appeals, those brought by addressees of a decision and those brought by third parties. It sets out (in section 46(3)) a list of the types of decision against which addressees may appeal, such as one determining whether there has been an infringement of the prohibitions, deciding whether to grant, extend or cancel an individual exemption and the terms on which it may be granted, or one imposing a fine, or "penalty" as the Act calls them (an appeal may also be brought as to the amount of any fine).

Third parties cannot appeal directly against such decisions, but may apply to the DGFT seeking the withdrawal or variation of any of the types of decision listed above (except those concerning fines). If the DGFT proposes to accede to the request, he must consult the addressee of the decision who may appeal against that new decision to withdraw or vary the original decision.

If the DGFT rejects the request, his rejection decision is itself an appealable act, addressed to the third party applicant. There are two grounds on which the DGFT may reject a request to withdraw or vary a decision. The first is that he may decide on the merits that no case has been made for the revocation or amendment of his original decision.

The second ground shows an interesting difference between the UK and EC systems. It is that the applicant does not have "sufficient interest", or does not represent persons having such interest. The notion of sufficient interest is not defined in the Act, although there is a clear parallel with the test of "direct and individual concern" in Article 230 (ex Article 173) of the EC Treaty where the test is essentially one of the impact of the decision on their legal interests. In contrast with the EC system, the Act puts the responsibility first for determining a third party applicant's interest in the decision in the hands of the DGFT rather than the Tribunal. However the test is defined, it is clearly more than a matter of administrative discretion in the hands of the DGFT and will add a different dynamic to judicial review

Neither the bringing of an appeal by an addressee, nor the making of an application for revocation or variation by a third party suspends the legal effect of the decision in question, except when the appeal is against a decision relating to a fine.

Procedure

The Act does not lay down more than the bare bones of the procedure for the hearing of appeals. It leaves that to rules to be made by the Secretary of State after consulting the President, as well as such other persons he considers appropriate. Draft rules were issued in October 1999,[8] with the intention that the rules should be in place with effect from the Act's full entry into force. The consultation document (discussed in more detail below) expressly identifies the Court of First Instance as the role model for the draft procedural rules. It also places great stress on the need for active case management by the Tribunal, in line with the significant and still fresh developments in English civil procedure overseen by Lord Woolf.

The Act itself makes some provision of a procedural nature. Thus it lays down that an appeal is launched by the sending of a notice of appeal to the Competition Commission setting out the grounds of appeal, including the errors of fact or law alleged and stating the extent to which the appellant is challenging an exercise of discretion by the DGFT.

The Act does not lay down the period within which appeals are to be brought. The equivalent under the EC Treaty is the two months allowed by Article 230 and it is that period which is suggested in the draft rules. That period can often seem extremely ungenerous when challenging an EC Commission decision, because of the requirement to lodge a fully argued application within that period. Although the Act authorises the Tribunal to give permission for the grounds in the notice of appeal to be amended (which could include supplementing them), the draft rules provide that the Tribunal may extend the period for lodging the notice only in exceptional circumstances. This seems an unnecessary and rather mean-spirited limitation on the Tribunal's powers. The fact that no upper time limit is set for the respondent (i.e. the competition agencies) to lodge a defence compounds the potential unfairness for applicants.

The Tribunal's task under the Act is to determine the appeal on the merits by reference to the grounds set out in the notice of appeal. In principle, therefore, the appellant determines the scope of the appeal and the Tribunal will not be required to consider of its own motion whether there are additional grounds on which the decision might be challenged. The draft rules are concerned more with the Tribunal's power to restrict the scope of appeals than to widen them.

The powers of the Tribunal on an appeal are extremely wide, and go beyond those which the EC Treaty confers upon the European Court. The Tribunal may substitute its own decision for that of the DGFT, which the CFI cannot. Even if it rejects the appeal and confirms the contested decision, it may nevertheless set aside any finding of fact by the DGFT. Alternatively, it may remit the decision in whole or part for reconsideration by the DGFT.

The Tribunals may impose a fine where none has been imposed by the DGFT. This is a corollary of the power to make its own decision, and of course exceeds the powers of the CFI which may only judicially review a fine which has been imposed. As to actual fines, the Tribunal's powers are essentially the same as those of the CFI in that it may cancel or vary the amount of a fine. That

8 Department of Trade and Industry reference number URN 99/1154.

includes the power to increase a fine as well as to reduce it. The CFI has the same power in the exercise of the "unlimited jurisdiction" conferred by Article 231 (ex Article 174) EC but has not so far taken the step of increasing a fine.

The Act provides for the possibility of majority decisions by the Tribunal, a matter still regarded as beyond the pale in Luxembourg.[9] In other words, two of the three members must agree, which gives rise to the possibility that the legally qualified chairman may be outvoted. It remains to be seen whether this will give a less legalistic flavour to the Tribunal's decisions than those of the Court of First Instance. The decision must be recorded in a document giving the Tribunal's reasons.

Procedural rules

As already noted, the Act does not lay down detailed rules of procedure, but it does list (in Part II of Schedule 8) some matters which may be provided for in the rules to be adopted, while leaving the Secretary of State a completely free hand to devise an entirely different scheme.

The list includes the following matters: the appointment of a Registrar; the form and contents of a notice of appeal and amendment of notices of appeal; rejecting a notice of appeal, either for disclosing no grounds or because the applicant is "vexatious"; the holding of pre-hearing reviews; the actual conduct of the hearing; the Tribunal's power to order interest to be paid, especially where an appeal against a penalty is dismissed; the charging of fees for the proceedings before the Tribunal; the Tribunal's powers in respect of withdrawal of appeals; its power to make interim orders; and joinder of parties and consolidation of appeals.

The draft rules elaborate on these themes and, as is natural when a period for reflection has been allowed, add one or topics of their own. These include provision in respect of leave to appeal and the making of references under Article 234.

The Department of Trade and Industry sets out the aim of the rules in an interesting note accompanying the consultation draft. The policy is that the Tribunal "should be primarily concerned with the correctness or otherwise of the conclusions contained in the appealed decision and not with how the decision was reached or the reasoning expressed in it." In the face of the apparent insouciance as to "how the decision was reached", matters are not made much clearer by the statement that "procedural irregularities will be taken into account if they are relevant to the merits of the case." As to the relegation of reasoning to the second division of considerations, one wonders whether the framers of the legislation are right to consider the principle enshrined in Article 253 EC (the duty to

9 But cautiously recommended by Lord Slynn: see the report of the EC Advisory Board of the British Institute of International and Comparative Law on *The Role and Future of the European Court of Justice* (1996) p.119 note 29.

give reasons; old Article 190) to be optional rather than a high-level principle brought in by Section 60 of the Act.

The Department will probably find readier concurrence where it states that the aims of entrusting appeals to a tribunal rather than to the courts are those of flexibility and informality, leading to speediness of result. It correctly states that the procedures provided for the Tribunal will be central in achieving those aims and sets the following objectives for those procedures:

- fairness and consistency
- thoroughness and rigour;
- transparency;
- timeliness.

These objectives are to be achieved by effective and active case-management in line with the parallel developments in the civil courts. "The essence of this approach is that the tribunal should seek to manage the focus and presentation of the appeal, as opposed to leaving these things largely to the parties to decide." The note goes on to indicate that there are limits to the writer's faith in the ability of parties to make a proper decision as to what needs to be presented to the Tribunal on appeal. It states that the objectives of case management should be to "narrow down the points under appeal so as to avoid peripheral points where possible", perhaps at pre-hearing reviews, and to "minimise irrelevant argument and evidence". There should be close controls on matters such as time limits on written and oral procedures "limiting the ability of parties to drag out proceedings."

There is a fine line between active case management of this kind and preventing parties from putting their case. Despite the tone of the parts of the DTI consultation quoted above, it can be expected that the Tribunal will be fully conscious of the need to guarantee a fair trial pursuant both to the high-level principles of EC law imported under Section 60 and to the European Convention on Human Rights to be given statutory force by the Human Rights Act 1998.

An examination of the draft rules shows that the structure is a fascinating blend of the procedure familiar from the way the Court of First Instance works and some "modern British" touches in relation to such matters as the handling of witness evidence and the powers of the Tribunal which closely resemble what may happen at case management conferences and pre-trial reviews in civil proceedings in England.

The consultation note expressly records that the procedures of the Court of First Instance are the model, with their emphasis on written pleadings and evidence and a limited role for the oral hearing.

Certainly, starting the proceedings will in many ways resemble the launching of an action before the CFI. The application (as it is called in the draft rules) is to be lodged at the Tribunal, and it is the Tribunal which, having verified that it is in due form, will serve it on the respondent. The normal English practice is of course that it is for the claimant to serve copies of pleadings[10] on the other parties.

This active role justifies the creation of a role of registrar, analogous to the synonymous office in Luxembourg where the registrars have responsibility for "judicial administration" and constitute the principal point of contact with the courts for parties. The draft rules envisage a registrar being responsible for the maintenance of a registry containing all pleadings and orders and decisions of the tribunal, and the acceptance, transmission, custody and service of documents. In line with Luxembourg, the power of deciding on requests for extension of time may be delegated to the Registrar.

The rules provide for parties to be represented by counsel or a solicitor, or by any other person whom the Tribunal may allow. The wording apparently precludes litigation in person, in that the party must be represented by someone, but what that means in the case of a corporate party (which all but a tiny proportion of the parties will be) remains to be seen. In-house lawyers will presumably be allowed to present the case, with or without assistance from counsel or independent solicitors, which is a form of self-representation.

As already noted, the notice of appeal must be sent within two months of notification of the contested decision, and the Tribunal may only extend that time limit if the circumstances are exceptional. It is to be hoped, therefore, that the DGFT does not follow the Commission's tradition of wrecking lawyers' Christmas and summer holidays by issuing major decisions just before starting off on their own vacations.

The rules of the European Courts do not permit amendment in the form of adding grounds of appeal which were available at the time the appeal was launched. The draft rules require the Tribunal's leave for amendment, and provide that wholly new grounds shall not be allowed unless they are based on subsequent matters of fact or law or, again, that the circumstances are exceptional.

The notice is required to summarise the "principal" grounds of appeal and give a succinct presentation of the arguments supporting them. This is a faithful transcription of the continental distinction between *moyens* and *arguments* which is so easy to state and so difficult to put into practice. It may be observed that, despite the reference to "principal" grounds, there will be no opportunity at a later stage for introducing and relying on "subsidiary" or "less important" grounds, for the reason already given: everything must appear in the notice of appeal unless the Tribunal invites subsequent argument on different points.

The applicant is required to annex to his application every document on which he relies including "as far as practicable" written statements of witnesses of fact and expert witnesses, if any. This is a tall order in two months, somewhat alleviated by the Tribunal's general discretion to admit further supporting documents at a later stage.

---

10 Or "statements of case" as they are called in the newspeak of British civil procedure.

Before serving the application on the respondent, the Tribunal is required to check that it complies with the formal requirements. It may also give it more careful attention and is empowered, if the application is "unduly prolix or lacking in clarity" to give directions that the application be put in order.

This may give pause for thought for those who have been in the habit of ensuring that every conceivable point has been taken and every conceivable document annexed and analysed in their pleadings before the Court of First Instance. Undoubtedly there have been parties whose case could have been put more concisely or clearly. However, it should not be forgotten that lawyers may have been tempted to throw everything they can dream of into the application because of the relative inflexibility of the Luxembourg proceedings as to amendment and the introduction of new heads of claim. The application is the first and perhaps only shot at getting it right. Allied to that is the fact that hearings are very short. Traditional English pleadings are short because hearings have been long and the rules on amendment relatively generous. While undoubtedly liberties have been taken by lawyers in Luxembourg pleadings, there is perhaps a basis for concern that a more important liberty could be removed if parties are squeezed at both ends and made to deliver short pleadings which they can neither amend nor expand to any significant degree in the proceedings before the Tribunal.

It is envisaged that the Tribunal may strike out applications in two situations. The first is that the notice "reveals no valid ground of appeal". The second is where the appellant is "vexatious", using similar wording as is to be found in Section 42 of the Supreme Court Act 1981 concerning the restriction of vexatious legal proceedings. This problem may be expected to be comparatively rare in competition litigation.

Once lodged, an appeal may be withdrawn only if the Tribunal consents and on such terms as it may impose (presumably, these will principally concern the costs of the respondent). It is provided that a fresh application cannot be made (implicitly, by the same applicant) in respect of the same decision. Most interestingly, and unusually, it is provided that the Tribunal may publish with notice of withdrawal details of the decision which it would have reached if the application had not been withdrawn. One imagines that this is something that would only be done if the proceedings had reached a fairly advanced stage, including in particular the filing of a defence by the competition agency whose decision was being challenged.

There are also detailed provisions concerning the settlement of proceedings by consent. The Tribunal is again given the last word: it has discretion as to whether to grant, refuse or amend the order. The parties are required to file their draft consent order with a statement (unattractively called a "consent order impact statement") explaining the impact on competition of entering into the consent order. If the Tribunal considers that there may be a significant effect on competition, it may publish a notice inviting comments, for which no admissibility threshold is set. This is an interesting example of the Tribunal's role straddling the division between the judicial and the administrative.

There are fairly straightforward provisions to cover the possibility of intervention by interested parties (most obviously, the addressee in the case of third party appeals and vice versa), subject to satisfaction of a "sufficient interest" test and an indication of the party whose position the would-be intervener wishes to support. The Tribunal is also given the power to order a party to be joined as an intervener. Applications may be consolidated when they concern the same subject matter or issues. Both of these are well known facets of litigation before the Court of First Instance. As to "joinder" of cases, this is frequent in the CFI when a number of applications are received in connection with the same decision of the Commission, most obviously in the case of a decision concerning a multi-party cartel.

A feature of the procedure is the choice of location: the Tribunal can decide to sit in any part of the United Kingdom having regard to such matters as the residence or place of business of the applicants or the parties.

A large section of the draft rules is taken up with a description of the Tribunal's powers to give directions as to the manner in which the proceedings are to be conducted in each case. The purpose of such directions is to secure the just, expeditious and economical conduct of the proceedings. Directions may be given at any time, including at a pre-hearing review. They may cover such matters as time limits for the oral hearing, requiring the parties to file additional pleadings, deciding what evidence is required and how it is to be presented, ordering the production of documents, enabling a disputed decision to be referred back to the maker (this is something that can also be done in a final order of the Tribunal, and will presumably not be done at the interlocutory stage in respect of the main aspects of a contested decision), ordering the appointment of experts either for the parties or for the Tribunal itself, and costs issues. The Tribunal may put questions to the parties, invite paper or oral submissions on specified aspects of the case, order the production of "documents or any papers relating to the case"[11] or summon the parties to meetings.

The purpose of pre-hearing reviews is said to be to ensure the efficient conduct of the proceedings, to determine points on which further argument or evidence is required, to clarify the "forms of order" sought by the parties (a direct echo of the Luxembourg procedure) or to clarify their pleas in law and arguments, to ensure that the parties agree as to what is in issue, and to facilitate settlement.

This catalogue can be seen as a full expression of the possibilities open to the Court of First Instance when ordering "measures of organisation of procedure". That Court has also instituted a practice of holding "informal meetings" attended by the judge-rapporteur, the Registrar and the parties and their advisers. They are used to discuss the conduct of the hearing, particularly in multi-party cases where it may be possible for overlaps in presentation to be avoided. The Court may indicate the issues on which it would like to hear argument and those

11 A thought-provoking distinction.

on which it considers itself sufficiently informed. Or they may be used to encourage settlement where that seems possible to the Court.

It seems likely that the greater proximity to its users that the Tribunal enjoys compared with the CFI may make the pre-hearing review a more frequent and perhaps less stiff occasion. Since the initiative and power lies with the Tribunal rather than the parties, no doubt the parties will have to be astute to ensure that the Tribunal is made aware, in correspondence perhaps, of their suggestions for the ongoing conduct of the procedure.

As to hearings themselves, while the Act does not make an oral hearing a compulsory feature of the appeal process, the rules seem to proceed on the basis that there will be a hearing.

They envisage the sending of a report for the hearing at the Tribunal's option. Such a report is of course entirely alien to English civil procedure. My own heretical view, having been both drafter and recipient of reports for the hearing, is that too much resource is devoted to them in Luxembourg for the benefits that can be obtained from them. If the Tribunal makes full use of its powers to control prolixity, the preparation of a hearing report is perhaps a chore it could spare itself.

The receipt of evidence is to be without limitation to the evidence available to the respondent at the time it took its decision and is to be unfettered by the general law on admissibility of evidence. Witnesses may be compelled, subject to the payment of their expenses.

Hearings are to be in public except where confidential information is to be considered at a hearing. They are to be conducted without formality and to proceed as the Tribunal considers most appropriate for the clarification of the issues before it.

The decision of the Tribunal is to be given in public, but notified to the parties in advance (and the time for appeal runs from such notification).

The Tribunal has full jurisdiction over costs, which it can assess summarily, or remit to a Supreme Court taxing officer. Although the Act refers to the possibility of the Tribunal charging fees for specified costs of the proceedings, the draft rules relate that only to the costs of witnesses or experts that the Tribunal has summoned or instructed on its behalf. Thus there would seem to be no filing fee for lodging appeals, unlike normal English civil proceedings but like Luxembourg where the proceedings are free, although the Registrar may order reimbursement on account of excessive translation costs incurred by the Court (a control on prolixity to which the Court has not, so far as I am aware, ever resorted).

The Act envisages a power in the Tribunal to order interest to be paid on fines, and in particular, compound interest if the fine is not reduced, or reduced by less than a specified percentage. No trace of this appears in the draft rules.

There are provisions for the obtaining of leave to appeal from the Tribunal and for the Tribunal at any time to make a reference to the Court of Justice under Article 234. There are also detailed provisions on the Tribunal's power to make interim orders, very closely modelled on those available to the CFI under

Articles 242 and 243 EC (old Articles 185 and 186). A significant difference is that it will be possible to apply for an interim order before the full application has been filed, which the Luxembourg rules do not permit. Since appeals do not suspend the operation of decisions, interim orders will be important.

FURTHER APPEALS

Appeals from the Tribunal require leave[12] either from the Tribunal or from the Court of Appeal. They lie on points of law only,[13] as in the EC system under Article 225 (ex Article 168A), except an appeal concerning the amount of a penalty.[14] Appeals to the Court of Justice from the CFI have become a speciality in their own right, with the Court exercising a rather frosty control through tight rules on admissibility to avoid appeals on points of fact being dressed up as appeals on points of law or against the reasoning of the CFI, and so on.

An important aspect of appeals will be the ensuring of consistency in the interpretation of the Act by the Appeal Tribunals and by the High Court in civil proceedings. The ultimate responsibility for that will lie with the House of Lords. Antitrust has always formed an important part of the jurisprudence of the US Supreme Court and, with the coming into force of the Act, competition law in this country will benefit from the wisdom and experience which judges such as Gordon Slynn are able to bring to appeals.

---

12 "Permission" is the post-Woolf buzzword, although the draft rules eschew it.
13 Section 49(1)(a).
14 Section 49(1)(b).

39

JUDICIAL REVIEW OF COMMISSION DECISIONS ON STATE AIDS TO AIRLINES

*Rosa Greaves**

INTRODUCTION

State aid to airlines normally requires authorisation from the European Commission to ensure that any financial assistance from the State is compatible with the EC rules on State aid which are to be found in Articles 87 to 89 (ex Articles 92 to 94) EC Treaty. Commission decisions granting or denying authorization can be challenged before the European Court of Justice ("ECJ"). Where judicial review of such decisions is sought by an undertaking (the proposed recipient or a competitor), the matter is decided by the Court of First Instance ("CFI" or "the Court").[1]

The aim of this paper is limited to making observations on some selected matters which have arisen in one or more of the following cases, *Air France*[2] ("Air France No.1"), *Cityflyer,*[3] *Air France*[4] ("Air France No.2"), *Ryanair*[5] and *Arbeitsgemeinschaft Deutscher Luftfahrt-Unternehmen (ADL).*[6] This paper is not intended to be a review of these judgments. The following matters will be considered within the context of the above cases: the scope of judicial review; the *locus standi* of "interested third party" to initiate proceedings; the scope of the Commission's obligation to re-open the procedure where a condition of the authorisation has not been met before a second tranche of the aid is due; the application of the concept of private investor to characterise the aid; and the failure

* The author would like to thank Mr. F. W. Pritchard for reading this paper.

1 As a State aid decision is addressed to the Member State concerned, it is common, where authorization has been denied, for the Member State in question also to seek judicial review of the decision. In these circumstances the case is lodged before the European Court of Justice (ECJ) and proceedings are normally stayed until the judgment of the Court of First Instance (CFI) is delivered. Once the judgment of the CFI has been delivered, the case before the ECJ is withdrawn.

2 Case T-358/94, *Air France* v *Commission,* [1996] ECR II-2109.

3 Case T-16/96, *Cityflyer Express Ltd* v *Commission,* [1998] ECR II-757.

4 Cases T-371/94 and T-394/94, *British Airways plc etc and British Midland* v *Commission,* [1998] ECR II-2405.

5 Case T-140/95, *Ryanair Ltd* v *Commission,* [1998] ECR II-3327.

6 Case T-86/96, *Arbeitsgemeinschaft Deutscher Luftfahrt-Unternehmen and Hapag Lloyd Fluggesellschaft* v *Commission;* [1999] ECR II-179.

D. O'Keeffe (ed.), Liber Amicorum Slynn 625-638 (2000)

to provide a statement of reasons in accordance with Article 253 EC Treaty (ex Article 190). A brief description of the State aid rules will be given by way of introduction.

STATE AID RULES[7]

Article 87 sets out the basic prohibition on State aids together with a number of mandatory and discretionary circumstances where such aids will be compatible with the common market. The Commission has exclusive competence to authorise a State aid where the aid can only be permitted under a discretionary condition (Article 87(3)). Article 88 is concerned with enforcement. The Article requires the Commission to monitor State aids (Article 88(1)), imposes a duty on Member States to notify State aids to the Commission before granting them (Article 88(3)) and provides for a Commission investigative procedure to be undertaken under Article 88(2). Until recently,[8] unlike the investigations carried out under the EC competition rules, no secondary measures had been adopted clarifying the powers of the Commission during the investigation procedure nor setting out the rights and obligations of the recipient and/or the complainant in State aid investigations.

As far as the air transport sector is concerned, State aid rules only become relevant in the nineties when the civil aviation market became liberalised . In 1987 the first civil aviation package of liberalising measures was adopted, followed by a second package in 1989 and a third one in 1992. Full liberalisation of air transport services became effective on 1 April 1997.

However, in the early nineties the industry was in economic crisis. The move towards liberalisation and a more competitive environment caused some inefficient, loss-making, State-owned airlines to seek financial assistance from their national governments in order to prepare themselves for operation in a fully competitive market. Thus in 1994 there was a flurry of State aid notifications seeking Commission authorisation for a number of State aid packages.[9] Consequently, the Commission adopted a Communication entitled "Guidelines on the application of the EC Treaty State Aid Rules to State aid in the aviation sector,"[10] with the objective of ensuring rigorous enforcement of the EC Treaty's

---

7 For a detailed explanation of the rules see, *inter alia*, D'Sa, *European Community Law on State Aid*, (Sweet & Maxwell, 1998).

8 Council Regulation 659/99, OJ 1999, L83/1.

9 Commission Decisions: 91/555, OJ 1991, L300/48 (Sabena); 94/118, OJ 1994, L54/30 (Aer Lingus); 94/653, OJ 1994, L254/73 annulled and replaced by 99/197, OJ 1999, L63/66 (Air France); 94/662, OJ 1994, L258/26 (Air France); 94/666 OJ 1994, L260/27 (TAP- Azores and Madeira); 94/696, OJ 1994, L273/22 (Olympic); 94/698, OJ 1994, L279/29 (TAP); 96/278, OJ 1996, L104/25 (Iberia); 96/369, OJ 1996, L146/42 (Lufthansa); 97/789, OJ 1997, L322/44 (Alitalia), and 98/337, OJ 1998, L148/36 (Air Belgium).

10 O.J. 1994, C350/5.

ban on State aids which distort competition. The Guidelines list the conditions which have to be met before the Commission will authorise the aid as compatible with the EC Treaty. First, the aid package must be part of a comprehensive restructuring programme enabling the airline to regain viability, normally without further aid. Secondly, the aid must be the last tranche ("one-time, last time" principle) granted to the recipient airline unless exceptional circumstances, which are both unforeseen and beyond the control of the recipient, justify it. Thirdly, the aid must not allow increases in capacity which are detrimental to other carriers and it may be conditional on capacity reductions. Fourthly, State interference in management for non-commercial reasons is forbidden. Fifthly, recipients of State funding must not acquire shareholdings in other carriers. Sixthly, the aid must neither be used for anti-competitive behaviour nor for purposes detrimental to the implementation of Community liberalisation rules. Seventhly, the aid must be transparent and the application of the funding controlled.

Nevertheless, some Commission decisions, either authorising or refusing to authorise specific aids to airlines, were challenged before the Court of First Instance. The Commission's decisions subjected to judicial review in all of the five cases referred to above were all adopted between 1994 and the first few months of 1996. The aid in each case, except in *ADL*, was granted in the form of capital injection. *ADL* concerned a fiscal aid. Some of the cases were brought by dissatisfied competitors (*Cityflyer, Air France No.2* and *Ryanair*), others by the recipient (*Air France No.1*) or by potential recipients (*ADL*). In some cases the aid had not been notified (*Citiflyer* and *Air France No.1*). The application for judicial review was dismissed in all cases except *Air France No.2* where the Commission's decision was annulled by the CFI.

SELECTED ISSUES

Scope of the Judicial Review

State aid rules permit the Commission to exercise wide discretion. The discretion involves carrying out complex economic and social appraisals of markets and reaching conclusions on the effect that such aid will have on the market. The CFI, when reviewing State aid decisions concerning airlines, applies general principles of judicial review and adopts the same approach that it takes for any other State aid case. Judicial review is confined to determining whether the Commission complied with the rules governing procedure and the statement of reasons, whether the facts on which the contested finding was based are accurate and whether there was any manifest error of assessment or misuse of powers.[11]

11 *Air France No.1*, above n. 2, para. 72; *Air France No.2*, above n. 4, para. 79, citing Case C-56/93, *Belgium* v *Commission*, [1996] ECR I-723, para. 14 and the case law cited therein.

In State aid cases the most common grounds are insufficient reasoning by the Commission in breach of Article 253 or failure to adhere to the procedural requirements.

The Court has also made it clear that it is not its role to substitute its own assessment for that of the Commission and it has confirmed that the legality of the decision is to be determined on the basis of facts and law existing at the time when the decision was adopted.[12] The complex assessments made by the Commission are examined solely on the basis of the information available to the Commission at the time when the assessment was made.

The scope of the review was a significant issue in *Ryanair*.[13] In 1993 the Irish Government notified the Commission of its intention to make a capital injection to Aer Lingus in the context of a restructuring plan. The injection was to be made in tranches to be paid in 1993, 1994 and 1995. The Commission authorised the injection of capital in tranches attaching conditions to be met before the second tranche could be paid out ("the 1993 Decision").[14] As one of the conditions had not been met by the time the second tranche was due, the Commission assessed the situation and decided to allow the second tranche to be paid out but added further conditions before the third tranche was paid out. Thus the Commission issued a further decision derogating from the earlier one.[15] A competitor, Ryanair, sought judicial review of the second decision on a number of grounds.

The Commission sought to limit the scope of the judicial review by submitting that the contested decision was a "hybrid" instrument consisting of a derogation from the 1993 Decision together with "comments" made pursuant to one aspect of the 1993 Decision.[16] The Commission, relying on earlier case law,[17] submitted that the "comments" did not constitute an actionable measure under Article 254 EC Treaty (ex Article 191) and therefore the decision was not open to review by the Court. The Commission submitted that the assessment of compatibility of the aid with the common market had been carried out before the 1993 Decision was adopted. Thus no further consideration of compatibility arose in respect of the subsequent tranches. The Commission did concede that if an expressed reservation to that effect had been included its initial approval of the aid, or if the Commission had concluded that the conditions laid down in its initial decision have not been fully complied with, then the situation would be different.

The CFI disagreed and ruled that the whole of the contested second decision was subject to judicial review. The Court did not accept that the thorough and detailed assessment the Commission had carried out before deciding to adopt the

12 *Air France No.2*, above n. 4, paras. 79 and 81.

13 Above n. 5.

14 Decision 94/118, OJ 1994, L54/30.

15 Decision 94/997, OJ 1994, C399 of 31 December 1994 but published in April 1995.

16 Above n. 5, para. 66.

17 Case 35/80, *Denkavit* v *Nederland*, [1981] ECR 45, para. 35.

second decision containing the derogation could be regarded as mere "comments" devoid of legal effect. The Court was satisfied that the "comments" were an integral part of the contested decision.[18]

The lesson for the Commission is clear. State aid decisions are binding acts which have legal effects not only on the addressee but also on the recipient and/or competitor. When asked to review a decision, the Court will wish to review all aspects of the decision.

Admissibility: are "interested third parties" sufficiently individually concerned to have locus standi?

The issue of admissibility was raised by the Commission in *Cityflyer, Ryanair* and *ADL*. The pleas of inadmissibility in *Cityflyer* and *Ryanair* where the applicants were competitors were rejected by the Court. In *Cityflyer* the plea was based on the specific facts of the case and therefore the Court's ruling is not of general concern. However in *Ryanair* the CFI, of its own motion, considered the question of admissibility as the Commission had withdrawn its objection. The Court decided to examine the plea that the action was out of time since such a finding would be an absolute bar to proceedings. The issue arose because the Commission's contested decision, although adopted in December 1994, was only published in the Official Journal in April 1995. In accordance with the fifth paragraph of Article 230 EC Treaty (ex Article 173) proceedings have to be started within two months of the publication of the measure, or of its notification to the applicant, or, in absence thereof, on the day in which it came to the knowledge of the latter. The applicant had been aware of the decision since December but only started proceedings after the publication of the decision. Had the applicant lost the right to seek judicial review of that decision? The Court ruled that the criterion of knowledge is subsidiary to that of publication or notification of the measure.[19]

In *ADL* the plea of inadmissibility was successful. The judicial review was sought by a potential recipient of an aid prohibited by the Commission. The aid was in the form of a German tax provision which allowed, under certain conditions, a special depreciation facility to be applied to aircraft. The scheme was of long standing and had been extended once. The German Government notified the Commission of their intention to extend the scheme until the end of 1999. The Commission, however, after opening the investigative procedure under Article 88(2), adopted a decision declaring that the aid was incompatible with the common market. The applicants, an association of German airlines (ADL) and a member undertaking of that association, Hapag-Lloyd Fluggesellschaft (HLF), sought judicial review of the decision.

---

18 Above n. 5, para. 82.
19 *Ibid.*, paras. 24 to 28.

The first matter the CFI considered was the Commission's plea of inadmissibility on the ground that the applicants were not individually concerned by the contested decision within the meaning of the fourth paragraph of Article 230. Article 230 provides that a non-addressee of a Commission decision has to establish *locus standi* by showing that he is individually and directly concerned by the decision.[20] The question facing the Court was to determine whether an "interested third party" for the purpose of the Commission's investigative procedure under Article 88(2) was automatically "individually concerned" for the purpose of establishing *locus standi* under Article 230.

The Court considered first whether the member undertaking, HLF, was individually concerned by the decision. Following established case law,[21] the CFI found that the contested decision affected the position of any natural or legal person purchasing a new aircraft registered in Germany and using it commercially for the international carriage of goods or persons. The contested decision prohibited the extension of tax provisions which had general application and covered situations which would be determined objectively and entailed legal effects for a class of persons identified in a general and abstract manner. Thus the decision was not individual in nature.[22]

The Court went on to explain that a person may be individually concerned, by reason of his status as an "interested third party" under Article 88(2), to challenge a Commission decision refusing to open the investigative stage. In these circumstances the procedural guarantees of the individual can only be guaranteed by recourse to the Court.[23] However the position is different where the interested third party has participated fully in the investigative procedure and now seeks annulment of the decision taken by the Commission at the end of its investigation. In this situation the applicant cannot rely on its participation in the investigative procedure to claim that it is individually concerned by the decision itself. The applicant has to establish, according to principles set out in established case law, that there are attributes which are particular to it or that there are special circumstances which distinguishes it from any other potential beneficiary of the aid. Thus HLF failed to show that it had *locus standi* to seek judicial review of this decision since it could not distinguish itself from any other potential beneficiary of the German tax provision.[24]

As far as the association of airlines, ADL, was concerned, the Court again followed established case law. The Court ruled that an association formed to further the collective interests of a category of persons cannot be considered to

---

20 There is a vast amount of literature on the meaning of "individual and direct concern." See for example: Albors-Llorens, *Private Parties in European Community Law – challenging Community measures*, (Clarendon, 1996), ch. 3; Brealey & Hoskins, *Remedies in EC Law*, (Longman, 1994), ch.12.

21 Above n. 6, para. 42.

22 *Ibid.*, paras. 43 to 46.

23 *Ibid.*, paras. 48 and 49.

24 *Ibid.*, para. 53.

be individually concerned for the purposes of the fourth paragraph of Article 230 by a measure affecting the general interests of that category. The association in these circumstances cannot bring an action for judicial review where its members may not do so individually.[25] The Court went on to consider whether ADL could justify its *locus standi* by virtue of special circumstances. The evidence was that the association intervened with the Commission in order to defend the interests of its members. Thus ADL had not established specific standing in its own right to seek judicial review of the contested decision.[26]

The ruling of the Court is perfectly acceptable in the context of a State aid in the form of a tax provision. However the Court considered the question of admissibility in a general context which may have implications for interested third parties wishing to challenge a decision concerned with other forms of aid. The manner in which the Court distinguished the status of "interested third party" from one of "individual concern" may be of wider application.

Essential procedural requirement: the extent of the Commission's duty to review authorised State aid where conditions imposed before subsequent tranches are paid have not been met

State aid to airlines combined with a restructuring plan often provides for payment of the aid in tranches. The Commission's decision authorising the aid sometimes includes conditions to be met before the State pays the next tranche. What is the appropriate administrative procedure for the Commission to follow in cases where it subsequently becomes apparent that one of the conditions imposed in the initial decision has not been met? The situation is even more complicated where an Article 88(2) procedure took place before the Commission declared the aid compatible with the common market under Article 87(3) since interested third parties may have participated in that procedure. Should the procedure be re-opened before the Commission decides what action to take? In *Ryanair* the Court was faced with this situation. Ryanair sought annulment of a decision claiming *inter alia* that the Commission was in breach of an essential procedural requirement, having failed to re-open the Article 88(2) procedure and thus give an opportunity to Ryanair to make submissions before the Commission adopted the contested decision.

The Court stated first that where a condition has not been met, a presumption arises that subsequent tranches are incompatible with the common market. Thus, a formal derogation from the condition in question is necessary before any further aid is granted. The Court, by way of analogy, cited earlier case law, and stated that, where the Commission, after examining all the facts, concludes that a subsequent tranche of the aid is no longer compatible, then a duty arises on the Commission to consult or, where appropriate, to re-open the procedure under

25 *Ibid.*, paras. 55 and 56.
26 *Ibid.*, para. 58 to 65.

Article 88(2). Furthermore, where the Commission adopts a decision authorising an aid subject to conditions after an Article 88(2) procedure, the Commission is not entitled to depart from its scope without re-opening that procedure.[27]

Thus, only in respect of relatively minor deviations from the initial condition will the Commission be able to adopt a decision derogating from its initial decision without re-opening the Article 88(2) procedure. The Court accepted that where the tranches are paid over a long period the Commission enjoys a power of monitoring the implementation and it may well be that in the light of changed circumstances the Commission will wish to vary the conditions governing the implementation of the restructuring plan or of its monitoring without re-opening the Article 88(2) procedure. This is naturally subject to the aid remaining compatible with the common market.[28]

Having examined the facts in *Ryanair* the Court dismissed the plea alleging breach of an essential procedure. The Court concluded that the Commission had not departed from the scope of the 1993 Decision. The Court must also have considered that the deviation was relatively minor since it stated that no specific factors arose which should have led the Commission to entertain doubts as to the compatibility of the second tranche of the aid with the common market. It is not clear from the judgment how important the Court considered the fact that additional stricter conditions had been imposed for the payment of the third and final tranche.[29] The Court however stressed its limitations in judicial review proceedings. It reiterated that its role is simply to determine whether the Commission has exceeded the limits of its discretion or committed a misuse or abuse of its powers.[30]

The ruling in *Ryanair* may well be a deterrent for the Commission to authorise State aid in tranches subject to conditions being met before the subsequent tranches are paid. Although this practice may have appeared attractive as a monitoring tool when State aid is combined with a restructuring plan, it may now be regarded by Commission officials as too risky. If the Commission had any intention of extending the practice beyond the airline industry it may well decide not to do so. The Court's ruling imposes a *prima facie* duty on the Commission to consult or reopen the investigative procedure before adopting a further decision derogating from the earlier one.

27 Above n. 5, paras. 86 to 88.
28 *Ibid.*, para. 89.
29 *Ibid.*, para. 106.
30 *Ibid.*, para. 90 where the Court applied, by analogy, Case C-225/91, *Matra* v *Commission*, [1993] ECR I-3203, para. 23 to 25.

Manifest error: the application of the private investor concept to determine the extent of the aid

An interesting issue that was examined by the CFI in two cases (*Air France No.1* and *Cityflyer*) was how to characterise interest-reduced or free loans. Is the loan as a whole a State aid and therefore, if found unlawful, to be recovered in full, or is it only the interest at normal market rates, or the difference between the interest actually paid and the normal market one which needs to be recovered in full? The CFI concluded that it depended on the application of the concept of private investor at the time when the decision was adopted. In both cases the applicants claimed the Commission had misapplied the test.

Both cases concerned aids which had not been notified. *Air France No.1* concerned a financial arrangement whereby a State-controlled enterprise, Caisse des Depots et Consignations-Participations ("CDC-P"), subscribed to almost all of the new securities issued by Air France. The Commission considered the injection of capital at a reduced rate of interest to be an operating aid and refused to authorise the aid. The Commission ordered full recovery of the aid after reduction of any interest which Air France had already paid to CDC-P. Full recovery of the aid ensured the elimination of all financial advantages from which Air France, the recipient of the illegal aid, had unduly benefited since the date of grant.

Cityflyer concerned an interest free loan granted by the Flemish Region to a regional airline, Vlaamse. The Commission found that the aid element of the loan was the reduced interest rate and so ordered recovery of the difference to date plus the imposition of a future rate of interest under normal market conditions.

The difference in treatment of the two capital injections reflected the fact that the Commission concluded in *Air France No.1* that a prudent private investor would not have been willing to subscribe to an important financial arrangement with Air France such as that entered into by the State-related agency. The Commission objected to the investment itself and not to the ways in which returns on the capital invested was provided. The Commission decided that, in the case of loss-making companies such as Air France, a long term investor would base his decision on a coherent restructuring plan, that is, when the details of the investment had been finally fixed. In considering the Commission's conclusion the CFI repeated established case law on the fact the Commission does enjoy a discretion on matters of complex economic appraisal and went on to acknowledge that the contested decision contained a detailed description of the economic situation of Air France, particularly the deterioration in its financial structure during a number of years prior to the investment in question.[31] The Court ruled that when exercising its discretion the Commission was not under a duty to mitigate the negative conclusion it had reached by taking into account

31 Above n. 2, para. 97.

the few signs and prospects of an improvement. The Commission was not obliged to isolate the element of the aid in each injection of capital with reference to the relevant normal conditions of the market. This follows settled law [32] supporting the proposition that the Commission is not required to weigh up meticulously all the negative and positive elements. The Commission was therefore entitled to review the investment in Air France in its entirety and to rely on a general conclusion that overall the risks involved were disproportionate to the advantages gained.

In *Cityflyer* the Commission decided that the aid element was the difference between the rate that the airline would have to pay under normal market conditions and that actually paid. The CFI stated that in respect of the loan "if the competitive advantage resides in the grant of a preferential interest rate and not in the actual value of the funds made available, the Commission, instead of requiring the principal sum simply to be repaid, is justified in requiring the interest rate which would have been charged under normal market conditions to be applied and the difference between the interest which would been paid under those conditions and the interest which was actually paid on the basis of the preferential rate to be paid."[33]

The competitive advantage is to be determined at the time the decision is adopted. Would a private investor have granted a loan having regard to the information available and the developments foreseeable at the time? The fact that the losses actually suffered were much higher than anticipated in the contested decision would only affect the legality of the decision if the private investor would have foreseen the losses to be higher than those estimated by the Commission. Since the contract provided for repayment of the principal sum and the Commission concluded that under normal market conditions Vlaamse would have obtained a loan at market rates, the loan cannot be regarded as a subsidy unless it is established that the last conclusion was wrong. Any other reasoning would undermine the purpose of the distinction made at point 32 of the Commission Guidelines on State aid to the Airline Industry[34] where it states that "the aid element will amount to the difference between the rate that the airline would pay under normal market conditions and that actually paid. In the extreme case where an unsecured loan is made to a company which under normal circumstances would be unable to obtain financing, the loan effectively equates to a grant and the Commission will evaluate it as such".

32 Case C-261/89, *Italy* v *Commission*, [1991] ECR I-4437, para. 14.
33 Above n. 3, para. 56.
34 Above n. 10.

Failure to provide a Statement of Reasons in accordance with Article 253 EC Treaty (ex Article 190)

In most of the cases the applicant pleaded the inadequacy of the statement of reasons. In each case the Court relied on established case law and reiterated that the Commission's duty under Article 253 is to provide sufficient information to enable the Court to exercise its power to review the legality of the decision and to allow those concerned to know the reasoning of the Commission in order to prepare a defence of their rights and to ascertain whether the decision is well founded.[35]

In *Air France No.1* the Court ruled the Commission was not obliged to quantify the economic advantage which Air France gained in relation to market conditions. A general conclusion was sufficient. The Court stated there was no duty on the Commission to pursue with the Member State concerned other arrangements by which Air France could be assisted lawfully.[36]

In *Cityflyer* the Court stated that in decisions where the State aid falls within the scope of Article 87(1) the reasons for such a conclusion must be stated.[37] Thus where the Commission decides that the element of aid incompatible with the Treaty rules is not the whole loan but the difference between the interest that the recipient would have paid under normal market conditions and the interest which it actually paid, it must explain sufficiently clearly its reasoning in reaching that conclusion.[38]

However in *Air France No2* the applicant was successful in establishing that the Commission was in breach of its obligations. The joined cases were brought by British Airways and British Midland who sought judicial review of a Commission decision authorising the French Government to inject FF 20 billion into the capital of Air France.

The notified aid was considered by the Commission to be compatible with the common market provided that Air France and the French Government complied with 16 commitments set out in the decision. The capital increase was to be paid in three tranches and payment of the second and third tranches were subject to the fulfillment of these commitments and to the actual implementation of the restructuring plan and the achievement of the planned results. The French Government was required to submit a report on the progress of the restructuring plan and on the economic and financial situation of Air France. The payment of the subsequent tranches were dependent on the report.

The Commission concluded that the aid was compatible with the EC Treaty as it found that a genuine restructure of Air France was in the common interest, that the amount to be granted was not excessive and that the aid would not affect conditions of trade to an extent contrary to the common market.

35 Joined Cases 43/82 and 63/82, *VBVB and BBB v Commission*, [1984] ECR 19, para.22.
36 Above n. 2, para. 166.
37 Above n. 3, para. 66.
38 Above n. 3, para. 67.

The applicants disagreed with the Commission's findings and sought judicial review of the decision authorising the capital injection. Several pleas were submitted to the Court of First Instance, including a plea that the decision should be annulled as it was in breach of Article 253. First, the applicants argued that insufficient reasons had been given for permitting Air France to buy 17 new aircraft. Secondly, it was submitted that there was a failure to assess the impact of the aid on a route-by-route basis and on the non-Community market.

As far as the first ground was concerned the issue was centred on established case law according to which investment intended to secure production capacity of an undertaking cannot be financed through State aid.[39] In addition the Commission's own policy and practice demonstrated its opposition in principle to all operating aid intended to finance normal modernisation of installations. The Commission consider that such investments cannot be treated as restructuring aid and must be financed out of the undertaking's own resources and not through State aid. However, in its decision the Commission impliedly authorised the purchase of the new aircraft as it considered that investment in fleet renewal was in itself a vital factor in restructuring the undertaking. The applicants claimed the purchase of new aircraft was a modernisation of Air France's fleet. Renovation of the fleet is part of the operational costs of an airline which must be achieved without State aid. The CFI agreed with the applicants and ruled that the Commission was in breach of Article 253 for failing to specify the rationale behind its decision to authorise the acquisition. It was not clear from the decision whether the Commission regarded existing case law as irrelevant in the circumstances of this specific case or whether the Commission intended to depart from the principle established in earlier case law.[40] The imaginative submissions of the Commission's agents were not upheld and the Court made it clear that only the Commission, as a collegiate body, could adopt any alteration to the statement of reasons.[41]

As far as the second ground was concerned the applicant claimed that the Commission was wrong to conclude that the aid did not adversely affect trading conditions to an extent contrary to the common interest. In the statement of reasons the Commission is not required to discuss all the issues of fact and law raised by the parties in the administrative procedure stage but it must nevertheless take account of all the circumstances and all the relevant factors of the case to enable the Court to exercise its supervision of the legality of the decision and to inform the Member States and the nationals concerned of the reasoning followed to reach its conclusion. The statement of reasons must disclose in a clear and unequivocal manner the reasoning followed by the Commission.[42]

39 Case 310/85, *Deufil v Commission*, [1987] ECR 901 and Joined Cases 62/87 and 72/87, *Executif Regional Wallon and SA Glaverbel v Commission*, [1988] ECR 1573.

40 Above n. 4, para. 112.

41 *Ibid.*, para. 116.

42 *Ibid.*, para.89 citing Case C-350/88, *Delacre and Others v Commission*, [1990] ECR I-395, para.15 and the case law there cited.

Although urged to do so by the applicant during the investigative procedure prior to the adoption of the decision, the Commission did not carry out an analysis of each geographical market affected by the aid, that is an examination of the competitive position on a route-by-route basis. The Commission chose instead to impose the 16 commitments on the French State. The Court was satisfied that the statement of reasons was adequate enabling the applicants to identify the Commission's reaction to their observations, to determine whether the approach adopted by the Commission was well-founded, and to defend their interests before the court by challenging the full and adequate nature of the choice of imposing 16 commitments to deal with any potential effect within the European Economic Area ("EEA").[43]

Nevertheless the court found that the statement of reasons completely ignored the competitive position outside the EEA. It was clear from Air France's restructuring plan that the development of long-haul flights was envisaged. The applicants had drawn the Commission's attention to the problems of defining the relevant market in air transport cases and the importance of identifying specific routes regarded by users as substitutable, for example attracting customers in The Netherlands for flights via Paris to non-EEA destinations. On routes with this destination Air France was in direct competition with other airlines within the EEA.

The Commission's agents and the interveners submitted explanations as to why the competition on non-EEA routes would not be affected by the grant of this aid. For example, it was submitted that traffic rights on non-EEA routes were governed by bilateral agreements and any restrictions imposed on Air France in respect of these routes would only have benefited non-EEA airlines. The Court held that in these circumstances the Commission should have set out its views on the competitive position of Air France on the network of its non-EEA routes with the associated feeder traffic.[44] It is recognized that information on the position of the recipient undertaking and of competing undertakings constitutes an essential element in the reasoning of a decision relating to the compatibility of a proposed aid with the common market within the meaning of Article 87 EC Treaty. Furthermore, the explanations given to the Court were not stated in the contested decision and were therefore not covered by the collegiate responsibility of the Commission. Such explanations, however justified, cannot remedy the defective reasoning of the contested decision.

Although the judgment was a victory for the applicants, the Commission quickly re-approved the aid incorporating the additional reasoning required by the Court. The latter decision[45] has not been challenged.

43 *Ibid.*, para. 269.
44 *Ibid.*, paras. 238 to 280.
45 Decision 99/197, OJ 1999, L63/66.

CONCLUDING REMARKS

Some issues have been highlighted from the judgments in these five cases which may be relevant to decisions other than those concerned with State aid to airlines. First, the authorisation of State aids in tranches, where subsequent payments are subject to conditions, may not be a trouble-free option. The Commission should perhaps find other means of monitoring authorised aids. Where it becomes necessary to adopt further decisions before subsequent tranches are paid out, the Court will review all aspects of that decision and not those merely related to conditions which have not been met (*Ryanair*). Furthermore where the conditions have not been met the presumption arises that subsequent tranches are incompatible with the EC Treaty and, therefore, the investigative procedure may have to be re-opened if the Commission intends nevertheless to authorise the subsequent payments (*Ryanair*).

Secondly, some of the cases provide further support for the view that State aid decisions are not treated by the Court in exactly the same manner as competition decisions. The mere fact that an applicant was an interested third party, and thus participated in the investigative procedure of Article 88(2) EC Treaty, does not mean that the applicant can show sufficient individual concern to satisfy the requirement of the fourth paragraph of Article 230 and seek judicial review of the decision resulting from that investigation (*ADL*). It is also clear that the Court accepts that in State aid cases "relevant markets" are defined more generally by the Commission than those covered by its analysis in competition cases. The geographical market to be taken into consideration to limit the effect of the aid on competition may be either the EEA market in its entirety or a specific regional market particularly subject to competition, whereas the Commission undertakes a route-by-route analysis when applying Articles 81 and 82 of the EC Treaty to civil aviation markets (*Air France No.2*).

Thirdly, arguments or explanations advanced by Commission agents and interveners before the Court, if not featured in the contested decision itself, cannot be accepted (*Air France No.2*)

Finally, the application of the private investor market principle in order to determine whether the financial assistance is a loan or a capital injection has been clarified.

40

THE PRINCIPLES OF SUBSIDIARITY AND PROPORTIONALITY IN COMMUNITY SOCIAL AND EMPLOYMENT LAW

Bob Hepple

The application of the principles of subsidiarity and proportionality to EC employment and social measures raises particularly sensitive issues. Although a former President of the European Court of Justice has suggested that "far too much has been made of [the] principle [of subsidiarity],"[1] the current President predicts that "it will just be a matter of time" before the Court will have to give proper consideration to this principle.[2] The subject has already been touched upon in a few judgments,[3] and academic attention now tends to be focussed not on whether the principles (or some aspects of them) are a proper basis for judicial review of Community acts, but rather on the intensity and nature of that review.[4]

I have chosen to examine the principles in the context of employment and social measures because, I shall argue, the principle of subsidiarity is inconsistent with the new direction of social policy since the Treaties of Maastricht and Amsterdam. This makes the task of the Court in this field an extremely difficult one.

1 Lord Mackenzie-Stuart, "Subsidiarity – A Busted Flush" in *Constitutional Adjudication in European Community and National Law; Essays for T.F.O'Higgins,* D.Curtin and D O'Keeffe (eds.), (Dublin, Round Hall, 1992), p.19.

2 Gil Carlos Rodriguez Iglesias, "Reflections on General Principles of Community Law" in *Cambridge Yearbook of European Legal Studies,* vol. 1, 1998, p.15

3 Case C-415/93, *Bosman* [1995] ECR I-4921, para.80; Case C-84/94, *United Kingdom v Council (working time directive)* [1996] EC R I-5755, para.55; Case C-233/94, *Germany v European Parliament and Council* [1997] ECR I-2405,paras. 26-8.

4 See e.g. J.H.H. Weiler, *The Constitution of Europe* (Cambridge, Cambridge University Press, 1999), p.211; P. Craig and G. de Burca, *EU Law: Text, Cases and Materials* 2nd ed. (Oxford, Oxford University Press,1998), pp.128-9.

D. O'Keeffe (ed.), Liber Amicorum Slynn 639-650 (2000)

THE PRINCIPLES OF SUBSIDIARITY AND PROPORTIONALITY[5]

Article 5 of the EC Treaty (inserted by the Maastricht Treaty as Art.3b) provides:

> " [1] The Community shall act within the limits of the powers conferred upon it by the Treaty and of the objectives assigned to it therein. ·
> [2] In areas which do not fall within its exclusive competence, the Community shall take action, in accordance with the principle of subsidiarity, only if and insofar as the objectives of the proposed action cannot be sufficiently achieved by the Member States and can, therefore, by reason of the scale or effects of the proposed action, be better achieved by the Community.
> [3] Any action by the Community shall not go beyond what is necessary to achieve the objectives of this Treaty" [paragraph numbers inserted].

The first paragraph of Art.5 simply restates the long-established principle that the Community must act within the limits of its powers. The importance of this in the social field is reduced by the ever-growing list of Community objectives and competences. So while Art.117 (now Art.136) of the Treaty of Rome set out the limited objectives of improved working conditions and standard of living, Art.1 of the Maastricht Social Policy Agreement added the objectives of "the promotion of employment... proper social protection, dialogue between management and labour, the development of human resources with a view to lasting high employment and the combating of exclusion."

The original Article 118 only required the Commission to promote co-operation in respect of a limited list of matters. After the Single European Act, Article 118A allowed measures to be adopted by qualified majority voting to encourage improvements "especially in the working environment, as regards the health and safety of workers". Art.2 of the Social Policy Agreement (now art. 137 (1)) makes qualified majority voting sufficient as well for measures on working conditions, information and consultation of workers, integration of persons excluded from the labour market, equality between men and women with regard to labour market opportunities and treatment at work.[6] Art.137(2) envisages measures to encourage co-operation between Member States in respect of a variety of measures to combat social exclusion.

Art.137(3) allows measures to be adopted unanimously in respect of social security and social protection of workers, protection of workers where their employment contract is terminated, conditions of employment for third country na-

5 See generally, N.Emiliou in D.O'Keeffe and P.M.Twomey (eds.) *Legal Issues of the Maastricht Treaty*, (London, 1994) chap.5, and in (1992) 17 EL Rev.383.

6 Thus overlapping with Art. 141(3) which permits unanimous Council measures to ensure equal opportunities and equal treatment of men and women in matters of employment and occupation. It is to be noted that Art. 137(1), contains no provision, analogous to that in Art.141(4), for "measures providing for specific advantages in order to make it easier for the underrepresented sex to pursue a vocational activity or to prevent or compensate for disadvantages in professional careers."

tionals legally residing in Community territory, and financial contributions for promotion of employment and job creation.

The same Article allows measures for the representation and collective defence of the interests of workers and employers including co-determination.[7] However, the Maastricht Treaty applied the principle of subsidiarity to most aspects of collective labour law. Article 136(6) EC excludes from the competence of the Community measures relating to "the right of association, the right to strike or the right to impose lock-outs." Moreover pay – the most common subject of collective bargaining – is also excluded from the list of competences in Article 137. (Equal pay for men and women is covered by Art.141 (ex.Art.119).) There is, of course, nothing in Community law to stop European-wide collective agreements on pay, the right of association or the rights to strike or lock-out, but agreements on these topics could not become legally enforceable "decisions" under Art.139(2) (on which see below). There is no European-wide right to organise, nor to bargain collectively, nor to strike or lock-out, despite the fact that these are mentioned as "fundamental rights" in the 1989 Community Charter of Fundamental Social Rights of Workers.

The second paragraph of Article 5 (ex Article 3b) makes it clear that the principle of subsidiarity is relevant only in areas where the Community does not have exclusive competence.[8] There is much controversy as to what is meant by "exclusive competence,"[9] but it is generally agreed that the area of social policy is one in which the Community's powers are not exclusive. This means that Community measures in the social field must satisfy the criteria prescribed by the second paragraph: (1) the Community can act only if the objectives of that action cannot be sufficiently achieved by the Member States, and (2) the action can be better achieved by the Community because of the scale or effects of the proposed measure. This is what the Commission has termed a test of "comparative efficiency".[10]

While the first two paragraphs of Article 5 are concerned with subsidiarity, the third paragraph involves the well-established test of proportionality. The Community action must not go beyond what is "necessary" to achieve the stated objectives.

---

7 See e.g. the European Works Councils Directive 94/45/EC.

8 This is confirmed by the Protocol on the Application of the Principles of Subsidiarity and Proportionality attached to the Treaty of Amsterdam, para.3.

9 Compare A.G.Toth, "A Legal Analysis of Subsidiarity" in *Legal Issues of the Maastricht Treaty*, *op.cit.*, chap.3, with J.Steiner, "Subsidiarity under the Maastricht Treaty", *op.cit.*, chap.4.

10 Commission Communication to the Council and European Parliament, Bull EC 10-1992, p.116.

THE LIMITS OF JUDICIAL REVIEW

To date, the Court has taken a non-interventionist approach, limiting review to situations of manifest error, misuse of powers, or manifest excess of discretion. The Council has been allowed a wide discretion in an area which involves the legislature in making social policy choices and requires it to carry out complex assessments. In the *Working Time* case,[11] the United Kingdom did not expressly invoke disregard of the principle of subsidiarity as one of its grounds for seeking annulment of the Working Time directive, but argued that Article 118A should be interpreted in the light of this principle. On this basis it was said that the Community legislature had not established that the aims of the directive would be better served at Community level than at national level. The Advocate-General argued that the principle of proportionality must be carefully distinguished from that of subsidiarity, since they operate in turn at different levels of Community action. "The principle of subsidiarity comes into play before the Community takes action, whilst the principle of proportionality comes into play after such action has been taken."[12] The Court seems to have agreed with this analysis for it rejected the argument of non-compliance with the principle of subsidiarity,[13] stating

> "Once the Council has found that it is necessary to improve the existing level of protection as regards the health and safety of workers and to harmonise the conditions in this area while maintaining the improvements made, achievement of that objective through the imposition of minimum requirements presupposes Community-wide action, which otherwise, as in this case, leaves the enactment of the detailed implementing provisions required largely to the Member States."[14]

The Court did, however, go on to consider whether there had been a breach of the separate principle of proportionality, that is whether "the means which it employs are suitable for achieving the desired objective and whether they do not go beyond what is necessary to achieve it."[15] The U.K. had argued that although reductions in working time might have certain beneficial effects on health and safety, they did not constitute "minimum requirements", as required by Article 118A; that the Commission and the directive failed to explain why the desired protection could not have been achieved by less restrictive measures, such as risk assessments (as prescribed in principle by the framework health and safety directive 89/391/EC) if working hours exceeded certain norms; and that it had not been shown, in the present state of scientific research, that there were reasonable grounds on which to expect the envisaged measures to improve health and safety.

---

11 Case C-84/94 *United Kingdom v Council* [1996] ECR I-5755.
12 AG, at para.126.
13 Judgment at para.55.
14 Judgment at para.47.
15 See e.g. Case C-426/93, *Germany v Council* [1995] ECR I-3723, para.42.

The first argument put forward by the U.K., relating to minimum requirements, was rejected because Article 118A "does not limit Community action to the lowest common denominator, or even to the lowest level of protection established by the Member States."[16] In relation to the second argument, the Court was persuaded by the detailed provisions of the directive that they allowed a high degree of flexibility of application, and that the framework health and safety directive simply laid down general principles and was not apt to regulate working-time.[17] As regards the third argument, instead of examining the controversial scientific evidence of a link between long working hours and health and safety in order to weigh its sufficiency, the Court simply said that the evolution of social legislation at national and international level confirmed this link.[18]

Judicial review based on a breach of Article 5 failed in the *Working Time* case on substantive grounds. In *Germany v European Parliament and Council,*[19] a procedural objection failed. It was held that Article 190 EC (now Art.253) did not require Community measures to contain an express reference to the subsidiarity principle, provided that the recitals made it clear why the Community institutions believed that the aims of the measure could best be achieved by Community action. One may note, in this context, that the Protocol on the Application of the Principles of Subsidiarity and Proportionality attached to the Treaty of Amsterdam also requires the Commission, in its explanatory memorandum, to provide a justification for the measure in terms of the subsidiarity principle.[20] So, too, any amendments by the Council and Parliament extending Community intervention must be accompanied by a justification.[21] Provided that these requirements are observed, there is little basis for judicial review.

FUNDAMENTAL RIGHTS AND SUBSIDIARITY

The development of the notion of "fundamental rights" as a judicially-imposed constraint on Community and Member State action is well-known.[22] The more problematic issue is whether fundamental rights are a source of Community competence?

In the *Bosman* case,[23] dealing with Article 48 EC (now Art.39), the Court said that,

16 Judgment at para.56; see too AG at para.134.
17 Judgment at paras.61-64; see too, AG at paras 135-42.
18 Judgment at para.38.
19 Case C-233/94, [1997] ECR I-2405 at paras.26-28.
20 Paras.4,5 and 9 of the Protocol.
21 Para.11.
22 See e.g. Paul Craig and Grainne de Burca, *EU Law: Text, Cases and Materials,* 2nd ed. (Oxford, OUP,1998) chap.7; and J.H.H.Weiler, *The Constitution of Europe,* (Cambridge, CUP,1999), chap.3.
23 Case C-415/93, [1995] ECR I-4921, para.81.

> "the principle of subsidiarity, as interpreted by the German Government, to the effect that intervention by public authorities, and particularly Community authorities, in the area in question [professional football], must be confined to what is strictly necessary, cannot lead to a situation in which the freedom of private associations to adopt sporting rules restricts the exercise of rights conferred on individuals by the Treaty."

This suggests that a challenge to a Community act, on grounds of a breach of the subsidiarity principle, will fail if that act is simply ensuring observance of a fundamental right conferred on individuals by the Treaty. The question then is, which rights will trump subsidiarity?

The Preamble to the Single European Act 1986 gave the first express recognition to human rights, as embodied in the European Convention on Human Rights (ECHR), and also to social rights, set out in the European Social Charter of 1961 (ESC), as a basis of Community action. Respect for human rights was referred to in the Preamble and various articles of the Maastricht Treaty of European Union. The major changes introduced by the Treaty of Amsterdam are the amendment of Article F (now Article 6) of the Treaty of European Union, and the addition of a new Article F.1 (now Article 7). The EU is now said to be "founded upon" the principles of liberty, democracy and respect for human rights. This provision has been made justiciable,[24] and some or all of the rights of Member States may be suspended by the Council for "serious and persistent breach" of these principles.[25]

The status of social rights was at one time problematic. However, the Preamble to the Treaty of European Union confirms the attachment to "fundamental social rights" as defined in the 1961 ESC and also in the 1989 Community Charter of Fundamental Social Rights of Workers. Although these two instruments are not referred to in Article 6 TEU, "fundamental social rights" such as those set out in these instruments are recalled in the Social Chapter (Art.136 EC). The most important feature of the *Working Time* judgment was the legal recognition of social policy as a free-standing Community activity under Article 118A of the pre-Amsterdam Treaty. The integration of the Maastricht Social Policy Agreement into the EC Treaty and the express reference to fundamental social rights in both the Preamble to the TEU and in Article 136 EC serves to confirm the competence of the Community to act in order to implement these rights. The recitals in employment and social directives now routinely refer to these fundamental social rights as a basis of action, and the Court itself has referred to them in passing on several occasions. The new provisions no longer lay the emphasis on harmonisation (as in the original Article 117) but on "minimum requirements" which means a level acceptable either to a majority of Member States, or in some cases to all Member States. There is to be a "high level of social protection", and a compulsory minimum beyond which Member States can adopt rules for greater protection.

24 Art.46 TEU, as amended.
25 Art.7 TEU.

Moreover, the Treaty of Amsterdam added a specific new competence in Article 6A (now Art.13) allowing the Council, acting unanimously and after consulting the European Parliament, to take "appropriate action to combat discrimination based on sex, racial or ethnic origin, religion or belief, disability, age or sexual orientation". The existence of this new power was one of the reasons given by the Court in *Grant v Southwest Trains*[26] for its refusal to extend the protection given by Article 119 and the Equal Treatment Directive 76/207/EC beyond discrimination on grounds of sex (including transvestism)[27] to sexual orientation. Any such extension is now a matter for the Council under Article 13. Two draft directives have been prepared. It seems obvious that any challenge based on subsidiarity would fail, given the Community legislature's express power to enact vertically or horizontally effective rights on the topics in question. There is still a limit of proportionality because the Council may only take "appropriate action". So it is open to argument that some forms of discrimination, such as age where there is a wide variation in the legal and social practices of the Member States, are more appropriately dealt with by "soft" law, in the form of recommendations, than directives. This is not a question of subsidiarity but of proportionality.

The more difficult question is whether the Community's legislature can invoke the general references to fundamental social rights as a basis for action, where the subject is neither specifically permitted nor disallowed. This could arise because both the ESC and the Community Charter contain social rights which do not specifically feature in the Social Chapter. The Court's Opinion 2/94 on Accession by the Community to the ECHR[28] indicates the limits of human rights as a legislative foundation for Community action, and similar limits would exist in the case of social rights. However, the Opinion does not rule out "soft" law which does not have the effect of purporting to amend the Treaty or to go beyond the Community's defined objectives and activities.

FALSE "SUBSIDIARITY": THE SOCIAL DIALOGUE

It has been suggested[29] that the social dialogue, now constitutionalised in Articles 138 and 139 EC, is a means of curtailing the legislative powers of the Community, and so represents a form of subsidiarity. This is doubtful because, as Gerard Lyon-Caen argues, the effect of Article 138 (formerly 118A) is to extend "Community-level competence, in the broad sense of the term (including that of the social partners), to the detriment of competence at the national level."[30]

---

26 Case C-249/96, [1998] ECR I-621.

27 Case C-13/94, *P v S and Cornwall County Council* [1996] ECR I-2143.

28 [1996] ECR I-1759.

29 E.g. by P.Langlois, " Europe soçiale et subsidiarite", [1993] *Droit Social* 201.

30 G.Lyon-Caen, "Subsidiarity" in *European Community Labour Law: Principles and Per-*

Article 138 requires the Commission to promote the consultation of management and labour at European level, and to ensure balanced support for the parties. Before submitting social policy proposals the Commission must consult both sides on the possible direction of Community action (the "first stage").[31] If, after such consultation the Commission considers Community action advisable, it must consult management and labour on the content of the envisaged proposal (the "second stage").[32] Management and labour must then forward an opinion or recommendation to the Commission, and may inform the Commission that they wish to reach an agreement (the "third stage").[33] They then have nine months to do so, but with the agreement of the Commission this period may be extended. The Community-level dialogue may lead to "contractual relations, including agreements".[34] These agreements may be implemented in one of two ways: either "in accordance with the procedures and practices specific to management and labour and the Member States" (route A, the articulation procedure), or in matters covered by Art.137, at the joint request of the signatory parties, by a Council "decision" on a proposal from the Commission (route B, the Community action procedure).[35] This procedure has led to a number of Council directives implementing agreements of management and labour, such as on parental leave, part-time work, and the burden of proof in discrimination cases.

An analysis of these provisions makes it clear that the Commission and Council retain control of the process of social dialogue law-making. In respect of any of the matters specified in Article 137, it is the Commission which is in the driving seat. The Commission initiates the first and second stages. Although management and labour may then decide, at the third stage, to reach an agreement and may decide to implement it by route A, their agreement is unlikely to gain Community-wide legal effect without following route B. In practice, management and labour have opted for route B, no doubt because in only a minority of Member States does there exist any kind of national framework for legally-effective collective bargaining or for the extension of collective agreements.[36] Route B therefore overcomes a crucial weakness of articulation procedures. There does, however, remain a role for national collective bargaining, because once the Community has legislated under route B, Member States may allow management and labour to implement a directive subject to the duty of the Member State to guarantee the results imposed by the directive.[37]

---

spectives P.Davies *et al.* (eds.) (Oxford, Clarendon Press, 1996), p.59.

31 Art.138(2).

32 Art.138(3).

33 Art.138(4).

34 Art.139(1).

35 Art.139(2). This "decision" (a term not used in the usual technical sense of Art. 249 (ex Art. 189)) may be adopted by qualified majority voting, except in respect of the matters specified in Art.137(3) where unanimity is required.

36 See B.Hepple, *European Social Dialogue: Alibi or Opportunity?* (London, Institute of Employment Rights, 1993), pp.27-30.

37 Art.137(4), which codifies decisions such as Case 235/84, *Commission v Italy* [1986]

The overall effect of the social dialogue provisions is to authorise collective bargaining on a wide range of matters at the European level, and to implement the resulting agreements through Community action, rather than leaving these matters of social policy to the national level. As Lyon-Caen says, "what we have here is a new application of contractual freedom".[38] But this is not the same as subsidiarity.

The Court of First Instance (CFI), in *UEAPME v Council,*[39] has recognised that the social dialogue is part of the Community legislative process and has asserted its right to review the representativity of the social partners, their dialogue, their agreements, and any resulting directives. Had the social dialogue simply been an extension of national collective bargaining regimes (subsidiarity), there would have been no real scope for review by the Court .

UEAPME, an organisation representing small and medium undertakings, brought an action under Article.173 (now Art.230) EC for annulment of the Parental Leave Directive 96/34 which gave effect to a framework agreement of the social partners under the Maastricht Social Agreement (now Arts.138 and 139 EC). UEAPME had been consulted by the Commission at the first and second stages of the social dialogue procedure. However, it was excluded by the other social partners from the third stage, that of collective bargaining to reach an agreement. UEAPME's argument was that because it had a right to be consulted, it had a right to negotiate. The Council, supported by the Commission intervening, argued that the application was inadmissible. It claimed that since the Directive is a legislative measure addressed to Member States, it was of neither direct not individual concern to UEAPME. Therefore it had no standing to bring the application. Alternatively, the Council argued that the application should be dismissed as unfounded.

Although the CFI held that in this case UEAPME had no general right to negotiate merely because it had been consulted, the CFI laid down the important principle that the Commission and Council must verify that the parties to a social dialogue agreement are "sufficiently representative" having regard to the content of the agreement in question. Where that degree of representativity is lacking, consultees whose participation is necessary in order to raise the collective representativity of the signatories to the required level, have the right to bring an action for annulment. The CFI went on to review the evidence which was available to the Council and concluded on these facts that the Council could not be criticised for having taken the view that the three signatories were sufficiently representative of small and medium undertakings without the participa-

---

ECR 2291; Case 91/81, *Commission v Italy* [1982] ECR 2133; Case 143/83, *Commission v Denmark* [1985] ECR 428. In the U.K. it would be impossible to use this procedure not only because of the absence of an "extension" procedure, but also because collective agreements are not usually legally enforceable between the collective parties: see generally, Lord Wedderburn, "Inderogobality", (1992) 21 *Industrial LJ* at 251-8.

38 *Loc.cit.*

39 Case T-135/96, [1998] ECR II-2335.

tion of UEAPME.[40] The important principle laid down by the CFI is based on the notion of democratic legitimacy. The social dialogue procedures did not envisage the participation of the European Parliament. In the absence of such participation, the Commission and the Council were under a duty to verify that management and labour were sufficiently representative.

This reasoning from the notion of democratic legitimacy is not significantly weakened by the Treaty of Amsterdam, which came into force after the *UEAPME* judgment. The European Parliament's role has been enhanced, but it can still be side-stepped or its role minimised. The Parliament can still be ignored if route A (above) is followed (but in practice the Commission informs and consults the Parliament.) If route B, leading to a Council decision, is followed, the Article 251 (ex Art. 189B) co-decision procedure applies in respect of the adoption of a directive on matters where qualified majority voting is permissible (Art.137(1)). In those cases where unanimity is required (Art.137(3)), the only obligation on the Council is to consult the Parliament (Art.137(3)). It seems that the principle enunciated by the CFI will continue to apply post-Amsterdam.

It has been argued,[41] that the CFI's equation of the social dialogue with the EC's legislative process, based on democratic legitimacy, is defective because it ignores the autonomy afforded to the social partners by national systems of labour law. This argument, however, seems to presuppose an element of subsidiarity which limits the obligations of the Commission and Council and limits review by the Court. In other areas of EC law, the Court of Justice has not been willing to allow autonomous collective bargaining to undermine fundamental principles, such as the right to equality.[42] It would be curious if the process of European-level bargaining could avoid either substantive or procedural judicial review.

SUBSIDIARITY AND THE NEW SOCIAL MODEL

The Court and other institutions cannot avoid the question of subsidiarity, simply because the concept is ambiguous and intensely "political". Much of the argument about the Community's intervention in the social sphere – including the United Kingdom's notorious opt-out of the Maastricht Social Chapter – has revolved around this concept. The new post-Amsterdam European social model seeks to find a "third way" between so-called doomsday thinking (the EU is the enemy of social progress and power must be returned to national governments)

40 UEAPME did not appeal against this decision but instead entered into a co-operation agreement with UNICE (one of the signatories of the Framework Directive) dated 12 November 1998.

41 B.Bercusson, "Democratic Legitimacy and European Labour Law", (1999) 28 *Industrial LJ* 153.

42 E.g. Case 127/92, *Enderby v Frenchay Health Authority* [1993] ECR 5535.

and wishful-thinking (the EU will automatically promote social democratic ideals).

This new model requires all the Community institutions to find a balance between efficient markets and social justice. Three fundamental values underlie the model.[43] The first is that there should be no rights without responsibilities. The Community has to protect fundamental individual rights but recognise that these rest upon mutual obligations – what Ulrich Beck calls "institutionalised individualism".[44] This is strongly reflected in the new Employment Chapter (Title VIII EC) which constitutionalises co-ordinated employment strategies and the creation of a "skilled, trained and adaptable workforce and labour markets responsive to economic change". The Member States remain the principal actors, and the role of the Community is to support and complement their actions. The Community can adopt labour market policies, but these are in the form of "soft" law, including guidelines for employment and annual reports by Member States.[45] Significantly, however, the Employment Chapter does not envisage deregulation or a weakening of individual employment rights as a means of realising high levels of employment. There is to be a "high level of employment and social protection".[46] The 1999 Guidelines envisage active labour market policies including reform of the tax and benefit systems to make it more attractive for unemployed people to take up work or training, increased lifelong learning, special attention to disabled persons and persons from ethnic minorities suffering from disadvantage, more accessible and affordable child care and flexible working conditions to enable women and men to reconcile work and family life.

The second value is that there can be no authority without democratic legitimacy. Traditional authority in the state, the family and the workplace is losing its legitimacy. The new social model depends upon participatory democracy. This is reflected in the *UEAPME* judgment in regard to the social dialogue, and in the swathe of measures emanating from the Council on workers' participation, such as the European Works Councils Directive 94/45/EC, and the proposal for a Council directive establishing a general framework for informing and consulting employees.[47]

The third value is that of equality of opportunities. The operation of free markets results in growing inequalities which can threaten social cohesion, cause high crime rates, and strengthen the far right political parties to undermine European unity. The Court has developed a fundamental individual Community right to equality between men and women. However, legal intervention against other forms of arbitrary discrimination remains patchy at national level, and virtually non-existent at Community level.[48] The Council has now been given

43 See A.Giddens, *The Third Way* (London, Polity Press,1998) pp.64-68.
44 U.Beck, *The Risk Society* (London, Sage,1992).
45 Art.128(2) EC (ex 109g).
46 Art.2 EC.
47 COM (98) 612.
48 See B.Hepple, "Equality and Discrimination", in *European Community Labour Law,*

the explicit power to take Community-level action against discrimination based on racial or ethnic origin, religion or belief, disability, age or sexual orientation; a clear move away from subsidiarity.

The recognition, first in the *Working Time* judgment, and now in the Amsterdam Social Chapter, that social policy has an independent legal basis, aiming to achieve minimum requirements based on fundamental social rights, rather than the pie-in-the sky of a level playing-field (*sub.nom.* harmonisation), is welcome, but at present suffers from the curious limitation that questions of pay and the rights of association and to strike and lock-out remain outside Community legislative competence. There is a contradiction between the importance attached to collective bargaining (*sub.nom.* social dialogue) at the Community level, and the principle of treating collective bargaining (and pay which is the main subject of collective agreements) as a matter for national regulation under the subsidiarity principle. There is also a continuing democratic deficit in the social dialogue, although the CFI's judgment in the *UEAPME* case provides a basis for developing the legitimacy of this process as a Community-wide principle. But perhaps the most important role for the Court will continue to lie in the development of the fundamental Community principle of equality of treatment.

---

op.cit., chap.11.

41

JUDICIAL REVIEW IN THE AGE OF GLOBALIZATION: CHINESE TOYS IN THE EUROPEAN COURT OF JUSTICE

Francis Snyder

INTRODUCTION

What is the role of courts and judicial review in the age of globalization? This paper pays tribute to Gordon Slynn, in particular his contribution to EU external relations and international trade law, by presenting a case study of EC trade law in action.[1] It focuses on the international toy industry, imports of Chinese toys into the EU, and the relationship between multinational firms, the EC legislator, and the European Court of Justice (ECJ) in determining the social and economic meaning of EC law.

Globalization refers to an aggregate of multifaceted, uneven, often contradictory economic, political, social and cultural processes which are characteristic of our time. An especially salient feature, driven by multinational firms, is the development of international production networks. The international toy industry is a prime example of a global commodity chain driven by the buyers. At the top of the hierarchy are large buyers from the US and Japan as well as one EU company, which control design, brands, and marketing. The EU toy market is supplied mainly through importer-wholesalers. Further down the hierarchy come the Hong Kong firms which act as intermediaries between these multina-

1 This paper stems from a research project on the settlement of trade disputes between the EU and China. For related publications, see Snyder, *International Trade and Customs Law of the European Union* (Butterworths, 1998); Snyder, 'Governing Economic Globalization: Global Legal Pluralism and European Union Law', 5 ELJ (1999) 334 (hereafter 'Governing Economic Globalization'), on which this paper is partly based; Snyder, 'Legal Aspects of Trade between the European Union and China: Preliminary Reflections', in N. Emiliou and D. O'Keeffe (eds), *The European Union and World Trade Law after the GATT Uruguay Round* (John Wiley & Sons 1996), 363-377; Snyder, 'Global Economic Networks and Global Legal Pluralism', in G. Bermann, M. Hedeger, and P. Lindseth (eds), *Transatlantic Regulatory Cooperation*, (Oxford University Press, 2000); 'Europeanisation and Globalization as Friends and Rivals: European Union Law and Global Economic Networks', in F. Snyder (ed), *The Europeanisation of Law,* (Hart Publishing, in press) [hereafter 'Friends and Rivals']; 'Legal Issues in EU-China Trade Relations', *Wuhan University Law Review*, forthcoming 2000 [in Chinese]; and (with Song Ying), *Introduction to European Union Law*, 2nd edition (Peking University P, forthcoming 2000 [in Chinese]).

D. O'Keeffe (ed.), Liber Amicorum Slynn 651-664 (2000)

tionals and the factories. At the bottom of the hierarchy are the factories, mostly in China. Today China and Hong Kong account for nearly 60% of world's toy trade.[2]

Such economic globalization is governed a new form of global legal pluralism: the totality of strategically determined, situationally specific, and often episodic conjunctions of a multiplicity of sites throughout the world.[3] Concentrating on the EU site, this paper explores briefly the way EU law and institutions have dealt with trade in toys from China. It considers first the evolution of EC legislation and then a recent ECJ decision, including the Advocate-General's Opinion and the ECJ judgment. The conclusion sets the discussion in a broader context.

EC Legislation

In 1985 the EC and China concluded an Agreement on Trade and Economic Cooperation.[4] The pre-existing Council Regulation 3420/83 provided for quotas on imports of toys from China into Germany, France, and Greece.[5] When Spain joined the Community, its previously existing restrictions were added to the list.[6] In 1992, with the 31 December 1992 internal market deadline in mind, the European Commission proposed to replace national quotas with Community quotas. The Council enacted the proposal into law.[7] Contrary to past practice, existing national quotas were not automatically renewed,[8] and new quotas were fixed only for Germany and Spain.[9] Community quotas were not fixed, however, for 1993. Instead, the Commission authorized national quotas, including those of Spain, for toy imports from China.

In March 1994 the Council of the European Union adopted two major, complementary legislative reforms. Council Regulation 519/94 on common rules for imports from certain third countries governed imports from non-market economy countries, except for textile products.[10] Council Regulation 520/94 established a new way of administering quotas, based on a system of licenses issued by the

---

2 'Chinese Toy Making: Where the Furbies come from', *The Economist*, December 19, 1998, p. 95-99 at 95.

3 See my 'Governing Economic Globalization'.

4 OJ 1985 L250/1.

5 Council Regulation (EEC) 3420/83 on import arrangements for products originating in State-trading countries, not liberalized at Community level, OJ 1983 L346/6.

6 Council Regulation (EEC) 3784/85 amending, on account of the accession of Spain and Portugal, Annexes I and III to Regulation (EEC) 3420, OJ 1985 L364/1.

7 Council Regulation (EEC) 2456/92 fixing the import quotas to be opened by Member States in respect of State-trading countries (OJ 1992 L252/1), which thus amended Regulation 3420/83.

8 *Ibid.*, art. 5.

9 *Ibid.*, Annex VIII.

10 OJ 1994 L67/89.

Member States according to quantitative criteria established at Community level.[11] These reforms were part of a package deal, which included acceptance of the results of the Uruguay Round (UR), reinforcement of EC trade policy instruments, and completion of the EC's common commercial policy (CCP). In essence, they communitarized the existing quotas on toys from China

Having opposed Council Regulation 519/94 in the Council of Ministers, the United Kingdom brought an Article 173 action in the European Court of Justice to annul the Chinese toys quota.[12] It argued that the new Regulation introduced quotas on imports into the UK market that was previously free from quotas. Governmental litigation and trade association lobbying were two facets of the same political strategy.[13]

This paid off in a series of continual legislative reforms, six in total during a brief four-year period. The first occurred when, five weeks after the UK brought its case, the Commission proposed an increase in the quota,[14] and when the Member States did not agree, the Council adopted a compromise solution.[15] It raised the quota for certain toys from China by almost 30% for the period from 15 March to 31 December 1994.[16] This compromise itself, however, provoked further litigation by Spain[17] and the European subsidiary of Tyco Toys, Inc..[18] The second legislative reform occurred in March 1995, when the Council agreed to raise the toy quota for the year starting 1 January 1995.[19] This was part of a more general revision of quotas on imports from China. Third, in April 1996 the Council fused the three existing quotas into one, to take effect as of 1 January 1996.[20] Fusion of the three quotas into one also created a greater space for restructuring of the toy sector. Small EU firms were faced from international

11 Council Regulation 520/94 establishing a Community procedure for administering quantitative quotas, O.J. 1994, L66/1.

12 Case C-150/94, *United Kingdom of Great Britain and Northern Ireland v Council of the European Union*, [1998] ECR I-7235.

13 See Snyder, 'Governing Economic Globalization'.

14 *Agence Europe* no. 6272, Wednesday 13 July 1994, at 9. J. Newton and L. Tse, '"Kids' Stuff:" The Organisation and Politica of China-EU Trade in Toys', in R. Strange, J. Slater and L. Wang (eds.), *Trade and Investment in China: The European Experience* (Routledge 1998), 147-165, at 159.

15 Council Regulation 1921/94 amending Council Regulation 519/94 on common rules for imports from certain third countries, O.J. 1994 L198/1. See also *Agence Europe*, no. 6277, Wednesday 20 July 1994, p. 13.

16 *Ibid.*, art. 1. The toys in question were those falling within Code HS/CN 9503 41 (stuffed toys representing animals or non-human creatures), such as Furbies.

17 Case C-284/94, *Kingdom of Spain v Council of the European Union* [1998], ECR I-7309. The Council was supported by the Commission.

18 Case T-268/94, *Tyco Toys (UK) Ltd and Others v Commission and Council*, O.J. 1994, C254/14, subsequently withdrawn.

19 Council Regulation 538/95 amending Regulation 519/94 on common rules for imports from certain third countries, article 1, Annex II, O.J. 11.3.95 L55/1.

20 Council Regulation 752/96 amending Annexes II and III of Regulation 519/94 on common rules for imports from certain third countries, article 1, O.J. 26.4.96 L103/1.

competition from other producers, as well as being squeezed by the dominant international buyers. They were gradually regrouping and restructuring. Fusion of the quotas was intended partly to encourage these economic and social processes. Fourth, in May 1996 the Commission took a further step towards an open market by revising the procedures for allocating quota amounts.[21] This revision, as the previous reforms, moved EC law closer to meeting the interests of multinational toy buyers and manufacturers, thus gradually undoing the 1994 compromise.

At this point, in September 1996 the Advocate-General gave his Opinion jointly in the two cases brought separately by the UK and Spain. He proposed that the ECJ should uphold the policy-making and legislative discretion of the Council. This was taken by many in the toy sector as a clear signal that the actions brought by the two governments against the Community legislator would ultimately be rejected. At least some academic commentators shared this view.[22] While not legally correct, this perception captured nicely the real political and symbolic significance of the Opinions of the Advocate-General.

Despite its lack of legal force, the Advocate-General's Opinion encouraged, if not stimulated, the Member States to adjust further the basic 1994 legislation. A subsequent reform in mid-1997[23] excluded toy parts and accessories from the quota, placing them instead, as well as certain other categories of toys,[24] under Community surveillance, first for the period from publication of the measure on 14 May 1997 until 31 December 1997,[25] and then for the period from 1 January 1998.[26] These changes followed the main conclusions of the Commission's 1996 annual report.[27] The latter, in turn, presented a somewhat simplified version of the recommendations of what were then the two main trade associations.[28] They testified to the close coordination between firms, trade associations, Member States and EC institutions. This coordination, in turn, ensured that the adjustments in the law were in step with the changing dominant interests in the EU toy sector, which was

---

21 Commission Regulation 899/96 establishing the quantities to be allocated to importers from the Community quantitative quotas redistributed by Regulation 612/96, O.J. 21.5.96 L121/8.

22 Newton and Tse, *op.cit.* n 14, at 161. Doubtless the plaintiff governments and the large trade associations were more aware of the legal status of such an opinion and its relation to the eventual judgment by the European Court of Justice. Small businesses, however, are often much less aware of these crucial legal and institutional distinctions.

23 Council Regulation 847/97 amending Annexes II and III to Regulation 519/94 on common rules for imports from certain third countries, O.J. 14.5.97 L122/1

24 HS/CN code 9503 30 (Other construction sets and construction toys of wood, plastic or other materials).

25 *Ibid.*, art. 1, Annexes I and II.

26 *Ibid.*, art. 2, Annexes III and IV.

27 Commission of the European Communities, '2nd Report from the Commission to the Council on the surveillance measures and quantitative quotas applicable to certain non-textile products originating in the People's Republic of China', COM(97)11 final, Brussels, 29.1.97, at 45.

28 *Ibid.*, at 38.

then in the process of restructuring within the EU market and of adapting to the new challenges posed by the international market.

A sixth reform followed soon afterwards. Less than a month after the 1997 reform took effect,[29] the Council abolished entirely, with effect as of 1 January 1998, the quotas of toys falling within HS/CN codes 9503 41, 9503 49, and 9503 90.[30] It subjected these products (and continued to subject toys of HS/CN code 9503 30) to prior Community surveillance to ensure adequate monitoring of the volume and prices of imports.[31] This occurred in the context of – and contributed to – the transformation of the EU toy industry. The EU's restructured toy enterprises imported items that were no longer produced in Europe.[32] EU producers also were able to compete in foreign markets.[33] Restructuring of the global commodity chain and EC legislative changes, as well as the transformation of interest representation with the EU, went hand-in-hand.

The abolition of quotas was, according to the preamble of the 1998 Regulation, neither inconsistent with the objective of taking account of the various interests in play nor liable to disrupt the Community market.[34] In fact, it was the culmination of more than a decade of conflict between Member States and between competing firms. It also represented the temporary conclusion of diverse attempts by EU institutions to manage conflicting interests. These conflicts were inherent in the process of market building and market management, partly because of the changes in the way in which the EU market was integrated into the international toy commodity chain. They began with the Chinese opening-up in 1979, the subsequent restructuring of the international toy industry, and the creation of new economic networks and the thin globalization[35] of this sector of the Chinese economy. Changes occurred in the domestic and international interests in the sector, and the lines between the domestic and the international were not merely blurred but actually reconfigured. In turn, these changes were to a large extent encapsulated in legislative form. Just as the 1994 compromise legislation expressed the balance of interests at the time, changes in the structure of interests led to demands for re-negotiation of the law. The legal reforms not only represented these new, changing configurations of interests; they also helped to

29 It took effect on the date of publication, 14 May 1997: *ibid.*, article 3.

30 Council Regulation 1138/98 amending Annexes II and III of Regulation 519/94 on common rules for imports from certain third countries, O.J. 3.6.98 L159/1, article 1 and Annex I.

31 *Ibid.*, article 1 and Annex II.

32 See Commission of the European Communities, '3rd Report from the Commission on the quantitative quotas and surveillance measures applicable to certain non-textile products originating in the People's Republic of China, COM(1998)128 final, Brussels, 9.3.1998, especially 26-29, 35.

33 *Ibid.*, at 26.

34 Cf, preamble, second and third recitals of Council Regulation 1138/98 amending Annexes II and III of Regulation 519/94 on common rules for imports from certain third countries, O.J. 3.6.98 L159/1.

35 I am grateful to David Trubek for the expression 'thin globalization'.

crystallise and perhaps even to create new interests, especially with regard to the number and nature of units of production.

THE OPINION OF THE ADVOCATE-GENERAL

During this saga, the Advocate-General, the distinguished French judge Philippe Léger, delivered his Opinion in the cases brought separately in 1994 by the UK[36] and Spain.[37] Here I focus mainly on the UK case.[38] Viewed from the ground up, strategic actors such as companies, trade associations, national governments, the Commission, the Council and the ECJ were playing to establish the rules of the globalization game. Viewed from the top down, the issue concerned the operation in practice of the EU as a site of global legal pluralism, in particular inter-institutional relations between legislator and judiciary and the relations of these EC institutions to market forces and their political representatives.

The UK's basic argument, supported by Germany, was that the EU toy industry was concentrated in only one country, namely Spain, and that an existing national restriction to protect only one country's producers should not have been translated into an EC restriction. The UK argued that there was no threat to Community industry as a whole, and a regional safeguard measure would have sufficed to protect Spanish producers. This argument was articulated in terms of failure to give adequate reasons, failure to carry out any appreciation of the facts or manifest error of appreciation, arbitrary nature of the quotas, breach of the principle of proportionality, and breach of the principle of equal treatment.

The Advocate-General's Opinion dealt with three important issues: the function of quotas, the scope of judicial review of legislation, and the difference between national and EU levels of governance. Here, for reasons of space, it is possible to consider only some aspects of this analysis, its assumptions, and the conclusions proposed to the ECJ. Even a brief discussion, however, should illustrate the dynamics of the EU judicial process and help us to understand better the connection between globalization and judicial review.

First, the function of a quota. According to the Advocate-General, a quota has a specific function. It is a protective measure, designed to protect economic operators against harmful competition due to imports. The adoption of a quota, in itself, shows that, in the view of the legislator, EC interests require protection.[39] It demonstrates that the third country product enjoys a favorable competitive situation vis-à-vis similar Community products, such that imports could jeopardize the markets, or even the existence, of Community producers of similar products.

---

36 Case C-150/94 *United Kingdom v Council* [1998] ECR I-7235

37 Case C-284/94 *Spain v Council* [1998] ECR I-7309.

38 Case C-150/94, *United Kingdom v Council*, [1998] ECR I-7235.

39 Case C-150/94 *United Kingdom v Council* [1998] ECR I-7235, per A.G. Léger, para. 47.

This view makes several assumptions. First, a quota is a purely defensive instrument, which comes into play when imports cause, or may cause, harm to Community economic operators. Second, the circumstances for imposing a quota are to be determined according to a competition policy analysis, in particular regarding price competition.[40] Third, the determination of market share should consider the share on the EC market of the targeted third country supplier not only relative to Community producers but also relative to other third country suppliers. A fourth assumption concerns economic evidence.

With due respect, each of these assumptions is however open to question. To give an example, the notion of the quota as a protective instrument is consistent with the idea of a global market based on relations among states or trading blocs. Each unit imposes quotas, in appropriate circumstances, to protect its own economic operators. But we can also consider a quota as an interface instrument. It is a buffer, not only to manage relations among different (types of) economies, but also to permit the mutual adjustment, adaptation and change of different parts of global economic networks.[41] The Advocate-General's Opinion may potentially be open to such a view: by putting together various parts of the Opinion, it is possible to draw out the general point that quotas regulate the level of competition between Community producers and third-country producers,[42] and at the same time balance the interests of different economic categories within the Community.[43] But this dual conception of quotas is not really developed in the Opinion, which is premised on a sovereign-state conception of international trade. More importantly, third-country interests are not included in the balancing at all. The traditional view of quotas may be inappropriate, however, if there is little coincidence between polity, territory, and legal system, on the one hand, and economic organisations and networks, on the other hand. Globalization requires that we revise our conceptions of trade policy instruments. According to such a revised view, a quota is not merely defensive. It has also a positive, proactive function, in that it is oriented towards structural adjustment or longer term market management, including markets in an interdependent global economy.

Second, the scope of judicial review. According to the UK, the challenged Regulation breached the requirement of the duty to state reasons. In the UK view the Council was required in this case to give especially detailed reasons. This was because, first, a Community measure of significant impact replaced a national measure of limited impact; second, the volume of the quotas was quasi-penal in nature; and, third, the introduction of new quotas was an exception to the basic principle of freedom of imports, which was reiterated in the Regulation itself. The Advocate-General rejected all of these arguments.

---

40 *Ibid.*, para. 106.

41 See also 'Ideologies of Competiton: Two Perspectives on the Competition of the Internal Market', in my *New Directions in European Community Law* (1990), pp.63-99.

42 See Case C-150/94 *United Kingdom v Council* [1998] ECR I-7235, per A.G. Léger, paras. 47, 193, 201.

43 *Ibid.*, paras. 164, 192.

The starting point of the Advocate-General's analysis was the distinction between acts of general application and specific measures. Regulation 519/94 as an act of general application, not a specific measure.[44] As part of the Regulation, the adoption of quotas did not require a detailed statement of reasons. For one thing, according to the Advocate-General, the very adoption of a quota expressed the reasons for its adoption. For another, the Member States, and in particular the United Kingdom, already knew before the Regulation was adopted that quotas on toys from China were going to be introduced. The Member States had participated in the deliberative political process of elaborating the Regulation. They were aware of the Commission's view that restrictions should be placed on Chinese products because of their low price and recent increase in volume.

Finally, in the Advocate-General's view and contrary to the UK argument, the principle that an exception to a rule must be interpreted strictly served to determine the substance of the limits of an exception, not the degree of detail of the reasons required to be given for its adoption.[45] A general act could include an exception without destroying the systematic nature of the act.[46] The legislator could therefore satisfy the giving reasons requirement by giving reasons that referred only to the general systematic framework.

This reasoning, it may be suggested with respect, is both formalistic and startling. For example, the claim that a legislative text speaks for itself, so that a legislator is not required to give reasons independently of the text, negates the distinction between politics and law. The same is true of the proposition that the giving-reasons requirement can be satisfied by participation in the legislative process. Can political participation and knowledge of deliberation, bargaining, and compromise fulfill the basic functions of Article 253 (ex Article 190)? Since the First Hormones case,[47] if not before, the ECJ has drawn a line between political process and legal procedure; political agreements cannot replace legal obligations under EC law. Indeed, there is a strong argument that current trends such as widespread use of 'package meetings' and the growing power of committees requires more respect, not less, for the giving-reasons requirement. Procedural requirements imposed on the legislator by the Treaty, such as the duty to state reasons, should be respected and enforced independently of the process of political deliberation itself.

The third major issue raised in the Advocate-General's Opinion concerns the difference between levels of governance. What is the difference between the Member States and the EC in the EU system of multi-level governance? In the Advocate-General's view, Council Regulation 519/94 entailed a change in the level of governance but not in the nature of policy.[48] Both the previously authorized national quotas and the new EC quotas formed part of a systematic

---

44 *Ibid.*, para. 42.
45 *Ibid.*, para. 65.
46 *Ibid.*, para. 65.
47 Case 68/96 *United Kingdom v Council* [1988] ECR 855.
48 Case C-150/94 *United Kingdom v Council* [1998] ECR I-7235, per A.G. Léger, para. 59.

whole, which was an evolving EC legal instrument designed to complete gradually the common commercial policy.[49] As part of this process, 'the power of assessment had to be concentrated at the level of the institutions at the same time as the perspective for assessing Community interests in the internal market as a whole had to be widened. The previous existence of one or more national restrictions ... was merely one factor among others which had to be taken into account, the most important being the economic data relating to the entire Community....[50] The EC legislator was therefore not required to give specific reasons for its choice of specific protective measures, import restriction rather than liberalization, or the level of duties imposed.[51]

It is extremely salutory that such careful attention is given to the problem of the level of analysis problem in EC law.[52] EC decision-making, as the Opinion emphasizes, is different in nature from decision-making by an individual Member State. Nor is it simply the sum of the interests of the individual Member States. Instead, it starts from a different objective and point of departure, which is the general Community interest. On this view, the EC decision-making process examines problems in a broader context, and may seek solutions for them based on compromise dictated by the general interest.[53] The EC institutions thus can decide, for example, to introduce a Community-wide quota, even though previously only a few Member States had quotas. This is a political compromise, framed and legitimated in terms of the Community interest.

The treatment of this issue in the Advocate-General's Opinion is not, however, wholly convincing. It is legally correct to say that the previous national restrictions were derogations from but nonetheless part of an EC commercial policy, in the sense that they were permissible only if specifically authorised by the Community.[54] But this simply raises the well-known issue of the extent to which the EC's common commercial policy was really 'common'. There also remains a certain ambiguity about the comparator of the new Regulation, the baseline against which it is being measured. In addition, in the adoption of the new Regulation the previous restrictions were only one factor among others to be

49 *Ibid.*, para. 61.

50 *Ibid.*, para. 58.

51 *Ibid.*, para. 62.

52 See R. Dehousse, 'Comparing National and EC Law: The Problem of the Level of Analysis', (1994) 42 Am J Comp L 761-781; see also Snyder, 'EMU Revisited: Are We Making a Constitution? What Constitution Are We Making?, in Craig and de Burca (eds); *The Evolution of EU Law* (Oxford University Press, 1999), pp 417-479 at 470-471. See generally Singer, 'The Level-of-Analysis Problem in International Relations', in K. Norr and S. Verba (eds), *The International System: Theoretical Essays* (1961); Buzan, 'The Level of Analysis Problem in International Relations Reconsidered', in K. Booth and S.. Smith (eds), *International Relations Theory Today* (Pennsylvania State University Press, 1995), pp 198-216.

53 See Case C-150/94 *United Kingdom v Council* [1998] ECR I-7235, per A.G. Léger, para. 128.

54 *Ibid.*, 56, 57.

taken into account. However, the weight they were given in the choice of detailed policies, or to put it differently, in the necessary balancing of interests, is not at all clear.[55] The extreme sensitivity of this question is evident from the litigation itself. and from the legislative changes that occurred after the Regulation was enacted and before the Advocate-General's Opinion, as well as later. More fundamentally, it is doubtful whether it is possible in practice to change the level of governance without changing the nature of the policy. Indeed, the very statement that there was in fact a change in the level of governance would appear to be inconsistent with claim of continuity regarding the common commercial policy. Unfortunately, on this point the Opinion is ambiguous.

The Advocate-General's Opinion concluded, therefore, that the Court of Justice should substitute its decision for that of the Council only when the adopted measures were manifestly inappropriate.[56] I agree with this general conclusion here, though not entirely with the reasoning or the assumptions which lay behind it. The conclusion followed the Council's argument in respecting the integrity of and leaving space for political compromise. It also was consistent with the ECJ's earlier case law. As summarised by the Advocate-General, the ECJ has consistently held that, in evaluating complex economic situations, the EC legislator enjoys wide discretion. Consequently, judicial review is limited to ascertainment of manifest error, abuse of power, or manifest going beyond limits of power of evaluation.[57] With regard to future events, the legislator's evaluation can only be criticised if it appears to be manifestly wrong in the light of the elements (knowledge) which the legislator had at the time the measure was adopted.[58] This applies not only with respect to the choice of the nature and type of measure to be adopted, but also with regard to the evaluation of the facts, in the sense that it is permissible for the institution to base the measure on a general assessment.[59]

JUDICIAL REVIEW

In 1998, four years after the litigation started and two years after the Advocate-General's Opinion, the ECJ decided the cases brought by the UK and Spain. The point of departure for its analysis was the principle of liberalization of trade; the in-

---

55 In examining the Article 173 EC action brought by Spain, Case C-284/94 *Spain v Council* [1998] ECR I-7309, the Advocate-General's Opinion pointed out that the intention of the Council was to make progress in completing the internal market, while also balancing the interests of various national governments and groups of enterprises, in particular importers, distributors, and processors of imported toys: see Case C-150/94 *United Kingdom v Council* [1998] ECR I-7235, per A.G. Léger, para. 186.

56 Case C-150/94 *United Kingdom v Council* [1998] ECR I-7235, per A.G. Léger, para. 165.

57 *Ibid.*, para. 89.

58 *Ibid.*, para. 90.

59 *Ibid.*, para. 91.

troduction of quotas was an exception. This starting point differed from that of the Council, which had proposed that the main aim of the 1994 Regulation to create a uniform, or at least harmonized, EC law. The ECJ noted, however, that the abolition of quotas on imports was 'not a rule of law which the Council is required in principle to observe, but rather the result of a decision made by that institution in the exercise of its discretion'.[60] In its view, the role of the Council in making economic policy choices required a substantial measure of institutional discretion.[61]

The ECJ remarked that more than 98% of the imports in question were liberalized before the contested Regulation was adopted,[62] and that the quotas introduced by the Regulation reduced the level of Community trade by almost 50% for some of the toys in question.[63] It followed its previous case law, however, in concluding that when assessing complex economic situations the Council enjoyed substantial discretion, including making findings of fact,[64] and that the exercise of this discretion was subject only to limited judicial review.[65] Similarly, in adopting new Community rules the Council was required to take account only of the general interests of the Community as a whole.[66] The Court further held, following its Advocate-General on this point also, that the Council was entitled to do so by basing its evaluation on 'the mere risk of disturbance', and this could be deduced from the increase in Chinese toy imports.[67] In other words, the judiciary will not substitute its evaluation of the facts for that of the legislator unless the legislator's assessment appears manifestly incorrect in the light of the information available to it at the time of the adoption of the rules.[68] The ECJ therefore dismissed the United Kingdom's application for annulment. In this case, as in the Spanish case,[69] the ECJ thus insulated the Council from a legal challenge in court by a Member State that was dissatisfied with EU foreign trade legislation. Litigation could not be used in this way by governments, even at the behest of powerful firms or trade associations, to revise or upset a complex political compromise.

The ECJ judgment was unanimous, as required by the ECJ decision rules, but the fact that four years passed between registration of the case and the judgment suggests that formal unanimity masked deep disagreement. If this interpretation is accepted, we can consider the judgment, just as the Council Regulation that pro-

---

60 *Ibid.*, para. 34.

61 The Court's analysis starts at *ibid.*, paras. 25-26 by emphasizing, with regard to the legal duty to state reasons, the scope of the Council's discretion when it enacts measures of general application, as distinguished from measures which apply to a limited number of parties.

62 *Ibid.*, para. 44.

63 *Ibid.*, para. 40.

64 *Ibid.*, para. 55.

65 *Ibid.*, para. 54.

66 *Ibid.*, para. 62.

67 *Ibid.*, para. 65.

68 *Ibid.*, para. 87.

69 Case C-284/94 *Spain v Council* [1998] ECR I-7309.

voked the litigation, to be a very delicate compromise. It was a compromise, however, in two different senses.

First, within the ECJ itself. The starting point of the judgment was the principle of trade liberalization. This also represented the position of the plaintiff UK government, the importers of toys from China, and the dominant buyers in the international commodity chain. It may, or may not, reflect the majority of views within the ECJ. Nevertheless, it provided the point of departure and general framework for the Court's analysis. This ultimate judicial accord was reflected in the drafting of the judgment. Within the judgment itself, however, it was balanced by other principles. Read as a whole, the ECJ judgment stands primarily for the principles of legislative discretion and limited judicial review. In matters regarding quotas, the EC legislator is not usually required to give detailed reasons when adopting legislation, and the exercise of its discretion is subject only to very limited judicial review. The Member States, acting together as the Council, thus are the joint masters of EC trade policy The political compromises they reach and then enact in legal form remain (usually) the law.

Second, the judgment represented a compromise between EU institutions. More precisely, it represented a judicial compromise, articulated in the form of a unanimous judgment, that protected the integrity of a prior legislative compromise expressed in the form of a complex regulation. This second-order compromise, achieved by judicial deliberation, served to insulate the EC political process to some extent from the judicial process (and judges) and hence ensure its discreteness and integrity. The frequent revision of the toy quota legislation within a short period of time, after the litigation began but before judgment was rendered, simply underscored the fragility of the legislative bargain, as well as the openness of the legislator to economic interests and processes. It also rendered the judicial compromise all the more crucial and delicate, as a matter both of inter-institutional relations within the EU and also of relations between firms within as well as outside the EU and a non-majoritarian judicial institution.

This double-order compromise formed part of the continuing revision of the EU toys quota legislation and occurred within this political context. In both the UK and the Spanish cases, the complainant Member State lost, and the Council won. The main point was legislative discretion with limited judicial review. Seen in terms of inter-institutional relations, this legal principle gave primacy to the EC legislator. Seen in political terms, it protected the integrity of the EC political process, the results of which reflected the economic changes that were occurring alongside but outside the judicial process.

CONCLUSION

Globalization is governed by the totality of strategically determined, situationally specific, and often episodic conjunctions of a multiplicity of institutional, normative, and processual sites throughout the world. The totality of such sites represents a new global form of legal pluralism. This paper focused on a single site: EU institutions, norms and dispute settlement processes. It aimed to illustrate some aspects of the relationship between globalization and courts.

Some years ago I pointed to the very important role that the ECJ played in EC policy-making and both micro- and macro-politics. I suggested that, "[a]t the same time and in the same social practices in which it seeks to operate as a check on other European Community institutions, it is also making economic policy." Its decisions thus should be seen as an element in a continuing political process.[70] The present paper develops this argument in a different setting.

What is the role of courts and judicial review in the age of globalization? The ECJ judgment helped define the EU rules for the globalization game. These rules concerned relations among market actors, relations between market actors and structures of governance, and relations among different governance structures. We can imagine the resulting configuration as a political market, with a supply of and demand for regulatory law. This political market was structured by and interwoven with the global toy commodity chain, including the EU economic market for toys. It was characterised by what Weber called the factual 'autonomy' of the propertied classes,[71] that is, an asymmetry of property, information, power, and influence upon the Member States and the EC legislator.

The ECJ addressed these issues indirectly, by implication, or, more precisely, by emphasizing the importance of judicial restraint in the face of politically sensitive Council legislation. Its judgment insulated the EU political process to some extent from collateral attack by means of judicial review. It maintained a political space, structured to some extent by objective interests, populated by conflicts among subjective interests, and involving Member States, firms, trade associations, and EU institutions. The double-order compromise tended to insulate and enhance the integrity of this political space and strengthen its market-oriented normative order.

The ECJ judgments in the UK and Spanish cases thus occurred in a highly political context, and were in fact highly political. Their main importance lay not in short-term economic impact but rather in consolidating and establishing principles for the future. These principles concerned four basic elements. The first element was inter-institutional relations involving the ECJ and the Council. The second was the role of the EC legislator in dealing with foreign trade. The third referred to the impact that the international commodity chain could have in influencing EC legislation, both by means of its structural position and by direct and indirect pressure on national governments, the Commission and the Council. Fourth, the ECJ helped to structure the institutions, norms, and dispute settlement processes of EU law as one site among the multiplicity of sites which comprise global legal pluralism.

---

70 Snyder, *New Directions in European Community Law* (Weidenfeld & Nicolson, 1990), 25-26; the quotation is from p. 25.

71 *Max Weber on Law in Economy and Society*, Max Rheinstein, (ed) (trans. by Edward Shils) (Harvard University Press, Cambridge MA, 1966), at 146.

By sanctioning the integrity of the EU political process, the ECJ judgment confirmed the political and legal salience of market structure. This included the way in which the international commodity chain in toys participated objectively and subjectively in the EU political and legislative process. It thus imported into the EU political and legal processes the results of the institutions, norms, and processes of other global sites, for example US intellectual property law or multinational company soft law concerning toy production in southern China. The latter were of course among the costs of doing business for international and sometimes even local firms in the EU toy sector. In addition, they were among the numerous elements that helped to create, consolidate or structure these economic, political, and legal relations and thus are an integral part of them. Conversely, the norms produced by the Council and the ECJ in EU legislative and judicial processes became part of the structure of the global commodity chain in toys. They conditioned, shaped and became integral to the decision-making calculus of strategic actors, including governments and firms, in this specific global economic network.

This case study also indicates that, at least in some instances, the role of courts confronting the economic and political consequences of globalization is limited in two senses. First, the judiciary may recognize the primacy of the legislator. In this instance law-makers, not courts, are primarily responsible for dealing with the consequences of globalization. This is consistent with the view, which I accept, that majoritarian institutions are usually best-equipped to make decisions about the redistribution of resources. Second, the judiciary can nonetheless have a significant impact by articulating broad principles. These principles, as demonstrated by Gordon Slynn's great contribution to EU law, help to shape and condition the emerging economic, political, and legal order. In addition to providing a framework for social action, they will be integrated in the decision-making calculus of the new strategic actors which are emerging in the age of globalization.

ESSAI TYPOLOGIQUE

42

SONS, AND HATERS...!

Joseph Weiler

I "*FEW AND EVIL HAVE THE DAYS OF THE YEARS OF MY LIFE BEEN*"[1]

One of the defining characteristics of Scripture as literary narrative is its unflinching and brutally frank depiction of its principal protagonists. The flawed personalities of Adam and Eve, Cain, the daughters of Noah[2] are famous examples at the genesis of Genesis. But these persons are, after all, minor figures – mere "extras" and a prelude to the main narrative, the unfolding saga of the House of Abraham. And yet, the same moral and psychological candor is employed also in the treatment of the Patriarchs themselves and their spouses, frequently to the great discomfort of the classical commentators.[3] Abraham is revealed in a less than glowing light when, for example, he twice sacrifices his wife's dignity, feelings and honour by making her pretend she is his sister rather than his wife and thus allowing her to be taken into concubinage.[4] Sarah's treatment of Hagar is far from noble[5] and earns the chagrin of Abraham himself. Of

1 The Patriarch Jacob to Pharaoh. Gen. 47:9.

2 Noah, too, is an ambivalent character. His failure to protest against the pending slaughter contrasts negatively with Abraham who challenges the Almighty for a planned act of destruction, that of Sodom and Gomorrah, of a far lesser magnitude. It is not surprising that a famous homiletic exegesis suggests that Noah's alleged righteousness was only relative to the iniquity of his generation.

3 In this, as in all my other essays on the Bible, I confine my secondary sources to the generation of *Rishonim*, the "Early Ones" – the Jewish medieval commentators of whom I am a lifelong student and for whose erudition, insight, creativity and modern sensibility my admiration has no bounds. See, e.g., Weiler, *The Patriarch Abraham, Law and Violence in the Modern Era in Festschrift for Maihoffer* (1988); "Jethro and the Gift of Judging" in, *Divenire Sociale e Adeguamento del Diritto: Studi in Onore di Francesco Capotorti* (A. Giuffrè, Milano, 1999); *The First Human Transgression: Fall and Ascent in Mélanges en hommage à Michel Waelbroeck* (Bruylant, Brussels, 1999).

4 This judgment should not be taken as an imposition of latter day moral sensibility on an earlier narrative – a common and tiresome feature of much current literary analysis. The exegetical pyrotechnics employed throughout centuries of biblical commentary to justify or explain Abraham's conduct and that of other Biblical heroes are testament to the deontological discomfort and implicit moral condemnation of that which has to be explained away about these episodes.

5 Though here it truly may be justified. The *King James* uses the term Mock to describe Ishmael's behavior towards Isaac. Gen 21:9. The Hebrew text is Metzachek which has a

D. O'Keeffe (ed.), Liber Amicorum Slynn 667-674 (2000)

Isaac we know very little. His principal narrative role is as object rather than subject, mainly the object in the fearsome tale of the Binding. Reconstructing Isaac as subject will be one central element of this essay. But even this "pale" figure, all the more pale when set against his formidable wife, Rebecca, is far less than perfect when for example, he, too, takes a leaf out of his father's book, and risks his wife's dignity, feeling and honor for his self-preservation.[6]

It is, however, in relation to Jacob, arguably the principal protagonist of Genesis, that Scriptural narration challenges the believing reader to the utmost. For it is by Jacob, renamed by word of God Israel, father of Dinah and her twelve brothers from whom the twelve tribes will issue, who is true begetter of Israel the nation, a people Chosen to carry the heavy yoke of Sinaitic Nomos, through whom God's covenant is to play out throughout history. It is as if Scripture mocks us. Consider the character of Jacob: Here is a man who already at birth attempted to precede his twin brother by grabbing at his heel. His very name, Yaakov, shares the Hebrew root for heel and for 'crooked.' And a streak of crookedness undoubtedly he possesses. What he did not achieve at birth he successfully achieves later by tricking Esau out of his birthright for a pottage of lentiles. When the admirable Rebecca, working under divine guidance, albeit unknown to Jacob, prompts him to trick his ailing and blind father and receive the patriarchal Blessing intended for Esau, Jacob displays no moral hesitation and his only concern is the fear of being discovered.[7] When he leaves Laban, himself a crook of considerable distinction, Jacob employs his superior intelligence and understanding of genetic breeding to enrich himself at the expense of his employer, cunningly pretending that this is thanks to some supernatural force beyond his control.[8] Scripture is not indifferent to these and other failings. The

---

distinctly sexual connotation. Cf. Gen. 26.8 where the same verb is used to describe Isaacs amorous attentions to Rebecca. Here King James more accurately, though less elegantly, uses the term 'Sporting'.

6 *Ibid.*

7 Gen. 27:6-12 "*And Rebekah spake unto Jacob her son, saying, Behold, I heard thy father speak unto Esau thy brother, saying, Bring me venison, and make me savoury meat, that I may eat, and bless thee before the Lord before my death. Now therefore, my son, obey my voice according to that which I command thee. Go now to the flock, and fetch me from thence two good kids of the goats; and I will make them savoury meat for thy father, such as he loveth: And thou shalt bring it to thy father, that he may eat, and that he may bless thee before his death. And Jacob said to Rebekah his mother, Behold, Esau my brother is a hairy man, and I am a smooth man: My father peradventure will feel me, and I shall seem to him as a deceiver; and I shall bring a curse upon me, and not a blessing.*"

8 Gen. 30:27-43 Lest the shadow obscure the light, an important parenthesis is now in order. The true greatness of Jacob emerges when one considers the totality of his life which is of truly epic dimensions, in which he overcomes adversity, trials and travails, sadness and tragedy which would defeat normal mortals. As he ages and matures the covenantal responsibility increasingly shapes his personality, the most visible turning point being his return with wives and family to Canaan, his struggle with the Angel and his assumption of the name of Israel: "*...Thy name shall be called no more Jacob, but Israel: for as a prince hast thou power with God and with men, and hast prevailed.*" Nowhere is the

laconic description of his death speaks volumes: "...*[H]e gathered up his feet into the bed, and yielded up the ghost, and was gathered unto his people*."[9] Compare the description of Isaac's death: *And Isaac gave up the ghost, and died, and was gathered unto his people, being old and full of days*[10] and of that of Abraham: *Then Abraham gave up the ghost, and died in a good old age, an old man, and full of years; and was gathered to his people*.[11] Jacob himself has no illusions of his life and responding to Pharaoh does not mince words: *And Jacob said unto Pharaoh, The days of the years of my pilgrimage are an hundred and thirty years: few and evil have the days of the years of my life been, and have not attained unto the days of the years of the life of my fathers in the days of their pilgrimage*.[12]

II "*IT IS MY SON'S COAT; AN EVIL BEAST HATH DEVOURED HIM .... I WILL GO DOWN INTO THE GRAVE UNTO MY SON MOURNING*"[13]

There can be little doubt that the worst calamity to afflict Jacob was the loss of his son Joseph whom he believed to have been devoured by an evil beast. It is the moving lament of King David over his son Absalom in which Scripture captures the depth of pain felt by a parent losing a beloved son. "*And the king was much moved, and went up to the chamber over the gate, and wept: and as he went, thus he said, O my son Absalom, my son, my son Absalom! would God I had died for thee, O Absalom, my son, my son!*"[14] There is every reason to believe that Jacob's pain was as deep, for it was said that "...*Israel loved Joseph more than all his children*...."[15] Why was it that Jacob loved Joseph more than all his children? The text gives us one answer: "*[B]ecause he was the son of his old age*."[16] But that, after all, is not strictly true: Benjamin, more than Joseph, was the son of Old age. The most ready answer, though I shall presently also explore another possibility, is that he loved Joseph most since he was the first born of his beloved wife Rachel. We should not belittle this reason, even if the text itself does not mention it. One of the most striking, and defining, features of Biblical narrative is the marginality of the theme of human erotic love so central in other great literatures of antiquity. In the Pentateuch, the striking exception is

combination of Jacob the Statesman and moral leader more evident than in the story of the rape of Dinah. He is appalled by the wanton slaughter committed by his sons Simon and Levy and objects both on utilitarian and moral grounds – and does not shy from expressing his moral indignation in the very blessings he bestows on both sons.

9 Gen.49:33.

10 Gen. 35:29.

11 Gen. 25:8.

12 Gen. 47:9.

13 Gen. 37:33, 35.

14 Sam II. 18:33.

15 Gen. 37:3.

16 *Ibid*.

Jacob's love for Rachel. The text leaves to our imagination the passion and commitment involved in a betrothal that lasted fourteen years before its consummation. We cannot thus blame Jacob for the special passion he felt for Joseph and maybe even a preference for him over Benjamin who was, perhaps, in the eyes of his father, responsible for the death of Rachel.

What is far less excusable is the fact that Jacob did not hide the fact that he loved Joseph more than all his children, indeed he made an exhibition of it by giving Joseph the Coat of Many Colours – a sign of regal significance. Couple that abject preferential treatment with the precociousness of the young Joseph and we cannot be surprised that "...*when his brethren saw that their father loved him more than all his brethren, they hated him, and could not speak peaceably unto him*."[17] The rest is history: The conspiracy to kill, the eventual sale of Joseph, the cruel deception of Jacob and the beginning of the saga of Israel in Egypt.

We have seen the moral flaws in the young Jacob. But how can we explain the psychological obtuseness of the mature Israel, making such a display of his preferential love and courting the calamity which was to afflict him? When Jacob laments to Pharaoh that evil were the days of the years of his life, he himself, individually and directly, can take responsibility for the worst episode in his life. That in some way this was all the design of God, as Joseph, years later, consoles his brothers, is only satisfactory as a reductionist explanation. It is foundational of Biblical discourse that divine determinism does not negate the free choice of humans and that explanation for individual action must be sought in the realm of the here-and-now. (We can leave it to the philosophers to spend their days sorting out this scriptural premise.)

One of the most obvious answers to Jacob's psychological obtuseness in this respect must be his own childhood experience – indeed an affliction that runs through the House of Abraham. For Jacob, too, grew up in a household in which his father preferred, and demonstrated that preference, one son to another, except that Jacob was the rejected son: "*And Isaac loved Esau, because he did eat of his venison: but Rebekah loved Jacob*."[18] Much of Jacob's behavior must be read in the light of this signal fact. It may not excuse his behavior towards Esau and Isaac, but it certainly explains the sensibilities (or lack of them) that he must have harbored towards a father who preferred his brother and towards a brother who must have been the object of his jealousy and resentment. One last detail: Consider the description of the young twins: Gen. 25:27 *And the boys grew: and Esau was a cunning hunter, a man of the field; and Jacob was a plain man, dwelling in tents.*[19] Note how the description of the young Jacob has more than a fleeting resemblance to Joseph the young dreamer.

Two issues now find some possible new resolution: First, Jacob's love of Joseph was not only the love of a father for the son of his beloved deceased

17 Gen. 37:4.
18 Gen. 25:28.
19 Gen. 25:27.

wife. I would like to suggest that Jacob's special love of Joseph was an act of compensation: He was bestowing on him the love that he did not receive from his father. Second, he grew up in a household in which parental preferential treatment among siblings was the norm – with disastrous and lasting consequences to the relationship between the sons, and between the sons and their parents with an inevitable concomitant effect on the fortunes of the entire dynasty. Divine determinism there may have been in the overall scheme of things as there may be in all affairs of man. But in the here-and-now it was psychological determinism which was at play. It is said that the Deeds of the Fathers are a Sign for the Sons.[20] Jacob was the son of his father – in this case with dire consequences.

III *"And Isaac loved Esau..."*

The fact that Isaac loved Esau, the "wrong" son, gives great discomfort to the commentators and they are at their exegetic best to explain this away. Here are a few of these attempts: Esau the cunning hunter "cunned" Isaac into loving him; Isaac loved Esau (past tense) whereas Rebecca loves Jacob (present tense in the original Hebrew); Isaac's love for Esau was a dependent love – dependent on him bringing him venison, and not a profound love et cetera. Let us however take his love for Esau as genuine paternal preference. Why would Isaac have preferred the cunning hunter, the man of the field, to Jacob the plain man (meaning, in the original Hebrew, pure and innocent), dweller of the tents? And why would *he* demonstrate that preference so blatantly?

Let us follow the same route: The Deeds of the Fathers are a Sign for the Sons. First we note another intergenerational similarity: Clearly Esau, Isaac's son, the cunning hunter and the man of the field bears a resemblance to Ishmael, Isaacs elder brother. Of Ishmael it was said: "*And God was with the lad; and he grew, and dwelt in the wilderness, and became an archer.*"[21] Whereas Jacob, the dweller of tents bears a resemblance to his father, the placid Isaac. And another intergenerational similarity: also in the Abrahamic household blatant filial preference was practiced – with a vengeance: Ishmael is actually banished from the house. But in this case, can there be any doubt as to Abraham's love for Isaac? After all, in this case was not Isaac the son of his beloved wife, Sarah? Was not Isaac the son from whom, according to the covenant, the House of Abraham would be built? Scripture is explicit. When God commands Abraham to make a sacrifice of his son he leaves Abraham with no doubt: "*Take now thy son, thine only son Isaac, whom thou lovest*".[22] Here Isaac is conceived as Abraham's only son, and explicitly the one he loves. I do not think we can be in reasonable doubt about Abraham's love for Isaac.

20 See, e.g., Nachamanides to Gen.12:6 and sources therein.
21 Gen. 21:20.
22 Gen. 22:2.

But the narration, and indeed the whole story, of the Binding of Isaac is "Abraham-centric." It is a story about Abraham, Kierkegaard's "knight of faith," who was willing, with fear and trembling perhaps, in a terrifying demonstration of faith which we were then commanded never to repeat again, to sacrifice that which was dearer to him than his own life, his beloved son Isaac. This is not the place to reflect on the significance of this story. Few if any Old Testament narrations have been the object of more reflection and even artistic expression than the story of the Binding. But rarely is the Binding examined from an Isaac-centric perspective. Abraham may have demonstrated that his love of God transcends any human love, but the effect of his deed on his near and dear ones could be devastating. The narration of Sarah's death comes immediately after the Binding – and the commentators do not flinch from suggesting that she died when she heard of the trial through which her son was put through.[23] Of Isaac the typical commentary is that by offering himself without resistance to his father's knife, he too was a knight of faith. But there is another possible view of the text. That the trusting child suddenly found himself tricked by his father who deceived him all along their three day trip in the desert and now bound him on the altar. And there he was, terrifyingly above him, knife in hand ready to slaughter him and stopped at the last minute by God. Once you take the Isaac-centric view of the binding, one does not need much of an imagination to speculate on the possible devastating effect it could have had on Isaac. All prior events in his life would now be interpreted in the light of this emotional trauma. The sending away of Ishmael, his elder brother could, for example, now be interpreted as his father's way to keep his truly beloved son out of harm's way. We can only guess at what would have gone through the lad's mind. But one thing is excluded from this perspective: an uncomplicated father-son loving relationship.

So we must now speculate on the possible effect of the Binding Trauma on Isaac's relationship to *his* sons. There are, I think, two basic possibilities, though many possible permutations between them.

At one pole we could speculate that Isaac did not experience his father's love to him, but quite the opposite. He experienced any previous paternal affection as duplicitous, a ploy to get him to the altar. He felt rejected by his father in the most extreme way. He tries to understand how and why this would have come about. He feels that somehow he let his father down, that he was not the son his father hoped he would be, that Ishmael, who dwelt in the wilderness and was an archer, was what his father would have liked him to be. He feels that he failed to give his father that which he lost when his brother, the truly beloved son was banished by Sarah. So when, Isaac, looks at his twins, at Esau and Jacob, he sees in Esau the son that he Isaac would have wanted to have been to his father so as to gain his love and not to end on the altar. In this intergenerational episode we find another commonality: Isaac does not prefer the son that resem-

23 See, e.g., Rashi to Gen. 23:2.

bles him, but the son that resembles that which he would have liked to have been. And true to the tradition in the House of Abraham, he makes no bones of this preference.

There is another startling yet exquisite possibility.[24] Isaac is, of course, aware of Abraham's deep love for him. He knows that he is the preferred one. But he also knows that it is this fact which was crucial for God's selection of the intended sacrifice. That God demands that from him who is loved most. His heart goes to Jacob in whom he sees his heir and a suitable custodian of the Covenant. And thus, thwarted and twisted as he must have been by the experience of the Binding, he decides to love Esau so that if God turns to him, as he did to his father, Jacob would be spared.

Affective preference in the House of Abraham and the norm of demonstrated differential love towards Isaac and Ishmael, wreaks havoc on Isaac and his relationship towards Esau and Jacob, which in turn wreaks havoc on the relationship of Jacob to Joseph and his brothers. Where does the cycle end? And whence its source? It does not end with Joseph. Let the reader peruse carefully the relationship between Joseph and *his* sons and the sad lesson about the Deeds of the Father will be apparent again. But what of Abraham?

Originality in scholarship – especially in the humanities (and law) – is almost invariably just a mask for ignorance. Research a bit further and you will find that your bright idea was already thought of and written about before. But of the following tiny and rather trivial little insight I have not yet found that earlier discovery.

Consider the following passage from the early life of Abraham in Gen.11:26-32.

And Terah lived seventy years, and begat Abram, Nahor, and Haran.

Now these are the generations of Terah: Terah begat Abram, Nahor, and Haran; and Haran begat Lot. And Haran died before his father Terah in the land of his nativity, in Ur of the Chaldees. And Abram and Nahor took them wives: the name of Abram's wife was Sarai; and the name of Nahor's wife, Milcah, the daughter of Haran, the father of Milcah, and the father of Iscah.

But Sarai was barren; she had no child. And Terah took Abram his son, and Lot the son of Haran his son's son, and Sarai his daughter in law, his son Abram's wife; and they went forth with them from Ur of the Chaldees, to go into the land of Canaan; and they came unto Haran, and dwelt there.

And the days of Terah were two hundred and five years: and Terah died in Haran.

24 I am indebted for this and many other insights to the discussions in the Bible Class I hold at Harvard Law School. The class meets weekly to study the Pentateuch so that over one year all five books are covered. The class brings together Americans and non-Americans, men and women, Jews and Gentiles, believers, agnostics and atheists et cetera. The only common denominator is love of and respect for Scripture.

There is something odd in this story. We read that Haran, son of Terah and brother of Abram (as he was then called) dies. So now the family has two sons, Abram and Nahor. Then we read that Terah, the father, leaves with his family to go to Canaan except that they are delayed on route and stop in Haran (the place). What is odd is that it appears that Nahor, brother of Abram, is left behind. He is not banished from the family. Eventually, it will be from his issue that Rebecca will emerge as consort of Isaac. But why would the text include Abram and Lot in the story of the voyage and exclude Nahor? Are we faced again with yet another instance of the same Deed of the Fathers which becomes a Sign for the Sons?

The precocious reader will now ask whence Terah learnt his lesson of affective preference and demonstrated differentiated love. There is no originality here – was it not possibly a human misunderstanding of our Father in Heaven and His treatment of Cain and Abel? But reflecting on the significance of that story will await another occasion.